THE NUREMBURG TRIAL

Ann Tusa and John Tusa
New Foreword by Ann Tusa and John Tusa

SKYHORSE PUBLISHING

Skyhorse Publishing books may be purchased in bulk at special discounts for sales promotion, corporate gifts, fund-raising, or educational purposes. Special editions can also be created to specifications. For details, contact the Special Sales Department, Skyhorse Publishing, 307 West 36th Street, 11th Floor, New York, NY 10018 or info@skyhorsepublishing.com.

Skyhorse® and Skyhorse Publishing® are registered trademarks of Skyhorse Publishing, Inc.®, a Delaware corporation.

Visit our website at www.skyhorsepublishing.com.

10 9 8 7 6

Library of Congress Cataloging-in-Publication Data

Tusa, Ann.
 The Nuremburg Trial / Ann Tusa and John Tusa ; new foreword by Ann Tusa and John Tusa.
    p. cm.
 Includes bibliographical references and index.
 ISBN 978-1-61608-021-1 (history)
 1. Nuremberg Trial of Major German War Criminals, Nuremberg, Germany, 1945-1946. I. Tusa, John. II. Title.
 KZ1176.5.T87 2010
 341.6'90268--dc22

                                                                    2010010524

Printed in the United States of America

Acknowledgements

It was John Eidinow who first drew our attention to the Nuremberg Tribunal and suggested that it would repay scrutiny. At his suggestion we all wrote a series of radio programmes about Nuremberg which were transmitted in 1975. These confirmed his opinion that the subject was fascinating and showed us areas and questions which published sources did not cover. In a review of the programmes in *The Listener* Derek Parker considered that a history of the Tribunal would be of interest to the general reader. We are grateful to both of them for setting us on the road and to John for the interviews he then conducted for us with many of those who had been at Nuremberg.

Macmillans have given us valued support. Caroline Hobhouse took the risk of commissioning the book from untried authors – hers was a much appreciated act of trust. Alan Samson first allowed us a long leash then, at the right moment, tugged it to discipline our gambolling in research and guide us to complete a manuscript. His patience and encouragement have soothed, reassured and cheered us. So too have Deborah Rogers' wisdom and calm. We are glad to acknowledge our debt of gratitude to them.

We have a further great debt – to all those who have been so generous with their time and observations and who allowed us to pick their brains and memories. We record their names in our list of interviews. All spoke with the priceless gift of having been present at an occasion we were struggling to reconstruct; they gave us insights and understanding, the whiff of reality, and an injection of their continued concern for the Tribunal. We thank them all. Some were especially generous. Above all we owe a lot to Kenneth Duke. He not only entrusted to us many papers made available for an earlier and aborted projected history by Sir John Wheeler-Bennett, but he also provided much valuable information about the collection of documents before the trial and the workings of the British prosecution team. Anthony Marreco has regularly broadened the perspectives with which we approached the subject and gently nudged us along fruitful lines. Thilo Bode has given us painstaking and expert help over the naval case. Where we have ignored their advice we acted from stubbornness not lack of appreciation; where we took it, we gained.

Finally we would like to thank our sons, Alexander and Francis, who cheerfully endured for so long lack of the attention which was their due and who never showed boredom when the subject of Nuremberg was raised yet again. In this, as so often, they have shown a tolerance which parents are fortunate to receive but have no right to expect. We hope the book will interest them in what was done in the past and provoke them to consider what should happen in the future.

Foreword

The trial of the 22 major Nazi war criminals at Nuremberg lasted for ten months from November 1945 to September 1946. The Nuremberg Trial was first published in 1983. Since then, no new evidence has emerged to cast serious doubt on the verdicts of the judges or to change the views of the authors.

Our opinions and those of the judges were based on documents. The book relies heavily on the 22 published volumes of the transcript of the proceedings, the verbatim record of everything said and read out at the trial. The court hearings and final judgement were mainly based on Nazi records; those read in evidence and another published twenty or so volumes of documents submitted for further consideration. Virtually all of these documents were written or at least signed by the defendants themselves. They remain incontrovertible proof of crime. Any new evidence which has been produced since 1946 (such as the Wannsee Protocol, setting out the decision to exterminate the Jews) has only hardened the case—if it was needed—against the Nazi regime.

From the day the intention of setting up a tribunal at Nuremberg was announced, some have carped at the justice of holding proceedings at all. People still sneer "victors' justice"—without knowing—or caring—that they are quoting the view of the chief defendant, Hermann Goering. The judges were, indeed, appointed by the four major powers who had defeated Nazi Germany in the Second World War. But this was no "show" trial: nine months of evidence was heard in court; much more time was given to the defence case than to that of the prosecutors; three of the 22 accused were acquitted, only twelve were hanged.

Other questions were raised about whether the right men were in the dock, whether other egregious criminals should have been there side by side. Well, better known Nazis such as Adolf Hitler and Heinrich Himmler had already taken their own lives, or had taken the boat to South America. No one can plausibly argue that no alleged murderer should be tried unless or until all likely murderers have been arrested. There were complaints, too, that high Nazi leaders sat in the dock with comparatively lowly placemen or mere regime dogsbodies. Yet the verdicts showed that the judges were well aware of the ranges of guilt facing them – rather, it could have been claimed that the lesser defendants received lighter sentences than they deserved because their crimes were so completely overshadowed by those of their superiors sitting by their sides.

There are other more serious matters to debate. Did an international court have the right to examine a state's treatment of its own citizens, however vile? The judges dodged a decision and instead rested their verdicts on crimes committed by Nazi forces in occupied territories. Was the charge of aggressive war based on retrospective law, even newly-minted for the occasion? Was the charge of conspiracy acceptable in international law or was it an American import and convenient "catch-all"? The members of the Tribunal were aware of these pitfalls and were duly nervous of acting without precedent. They stated that aggressive war had been long outlawed by international treaty; they listened carefully to the prosecution case on conspiracy by the Nazi regime. But their sentences were based on the age-old crime of murder; their verdicts were based on what one prosecution counsel called the defendants' "nearness to the corpses".

Whatever the legal arguments, many of the Tribunal's decisions on the law were adopted by the United Nations and absorbed into international criminal law. But has the Tribunal's impact been as great as was hoped? Aggressive war was denounced yet it continues; genocide seems endemic;, kidnapping was condemned—but has been re-named "extraordinary rendition;" torture has re-emerged as "enhanced interrogation;" civilians continue to be the victims of battle but are explained away as "collateral damage." The demands for justice, punishment, collective judicial action and legal restraints remain powerful but often go unheard.

And the proponents of trial in 1945 certainly had ambitious dreams. They laid down a corpus of international criminal law and hoped for a permanent international court of criminal justice. Instead of a jurisdiction over all nations, we hear individual states calling for others to be punished but declining to back a court before which they themselves risk appearing, some of the loudest refusals coming from states which actually created the Nuremberg Tribunal. Ad hoc courts hear cases against camp guards, ethnic cleansers but no state willingly offers its own leaders to such scrutiny. Present behaviours offer few grounds for optimism about the creation of a universal criminal jurisdiction.

In part, this is because the practical lessons of Nuremberg's success have not been understood or put into practice. Subsequent courts have forgotten that justice should be speedy; it took the Tribunal just 9 months to hear cases against 22 defendants and to review the evidence of twelve years of Nazi criminal activity across the continent of Europe. Long trials lose public concentration, yet trials must be held in the public interest. The Nuremberg judges also understood that they would lose respect for the judicial process if they allowed proceedings to lapse into chaos. Discipline in the Nuremberg courtroom was strict; no repetition of any point already made by defence or prosecution; no piling up of redundant evidence; no rambling tirades; no emotional outbursts, neurotic self-exculpation or the microphones would be switched off. These lessons are still there to be learned and to be put into practice.

The trial was heavily document based. Eye witnesses played a part—some spoke in support of the defendants, others expressed the outrage and grief of those who had suffered Nazi cruelty. All spoke with events fresh in their minds, unlike some current instances of arraigned perpetrators of decades old crimes. But ultimately, the Nazi regime was judged—and largely found guilty—on the basis of its own obsessively well kept records. It is doubtful if such overwhelming evidence will ever again be assembled in the years of the email and the shredder.

These questions, doubts, problems do not mean that Nuremberg did not deliver justice or that international criminal courts can never succeed—scrupulous consideration of them is the requirement. Humanity's most profound hopes and aspirations were thoroughly and painstakingly played out in the courtroom at Nuremberg between 1945 and 1946. They explain why the Nuremberg Tribunal is constantly invoked, continues to fascinate and inspire and remains of current applicability. They are driven by the eternal hope of justice. The Nuremberg Trial keeps that hope alive.

—ANN TUSA AND JOHN TUSA, 2010

Contents

Contents

Chapter One

Monday, 30 September 1946 was a bright and sunny but cool day in Nuremberg. At first light, armoured cars carrying steel-helmeted American military policemen slid into position round the Palace of Justice. It was a drab, dark pink sandstone building about a kilometre outside the old town; it was pockmarked with bullets and shell holes. The armoured cars were its inner ring of defence. The whole city was in fact surrounded by US Army vehicles; every road into it was barricaded, every form of transport and every pedestrian trying to enter was being stopped and searched.

By seven o'clock in the morning crowds were arriving at the entrance to the courtroom of the Palace. Some of the visitors wore uniform and were high-ranking officers; many of the civilians were distinguished, their faces familiar from newsreels and newspaper photographs. Even so, they were stopped outside the building and scrutinized by MPs and US Intelligence officers. They were asked to present passes; if the passes were out of date, their bearers were turned away. Today, everyone entering the courtroom had to have a special pass. Even inside the building the security checks continued – passes had to be shown again, women who had ignored the ban on handbags were sent to deposit them in a guarded cloakroom.

By eight o'clock the corridors were jammed. In one room a group of about three dozen men was assembling. They wore a variety of academic gowns, nearly all black, one bright purple. They were German lawyers. At nine o'clock security officers came and checked their passes, gave them a body search and rifled through their files of papers. Then at nine thirty the doors of the courtroom were opened. In flooded spectators who went upstairs to their gallery, journalists who moved to seats at the back of the room, defence and prosecution counsel who made their way to tables in the well of the court. The room was dazzlingly bright. Banks of lights had been turned on while newsreel cameras whirred and press photographers darted around spotting eminent faces for their shots. After a few minutes of chatter and bustle, the courtroom fell silent. All eyes turned to a panel in the wall which had slid to one side. Through it, at intervals of a few seconds, came groups of men in twos and threes whose names and faces had been famous for years, escorted by American guards in immaculate white helmets and webbing. These men were defendants in a trial which had begun ten months before. Today their judges would deliver the judgement of the International Military Tribunal at Nuremberg. (1)

The prisoners took their seats on a double row of benches in the defendants' dock. The photographers swarmed round them. Smiling, and greeting the audience, was Field Marshal Hermann Goering, once Commander-in-Chief of the German Luftwaffe and Lord High Nearly Everything Else. At one time Hitler had named Goering as his eventual successor as ruler of the Third Reich. There were other former military commanders in the dock too: Grand Admirals Doenitz and Raeder, Field Marshal Keitel, who had been the Chief of the High Command of the Armed Forces, and General Jodl, his Chief of the Operations Staff. There were diplomats and politicians: Constantin von Neurath, Franz von Papen, Ribbentrop, who had been Hitler's Foreign Minister, Frick, once his Minister of the Interior, Sauckel, who had been responsible for Labour Mobilization, and Speer, Hitler's architect and his Minister for Armaments and War Production. In the front row, next to Goering, sat Rudolf Hess, once the Deputy Leader of the Nazi Party. He seemed to have a headache and kept striking his forehead with his right hand. Further along the row sat Alfred Rosenberg, the Nazi party's ideologist; Streicher its publicist, who had called for the extermination of the Jews; and Kaltenbrunner who had controlled the Gestapo and the concentration camp system through which the extermination was to be carried out. Sitting with them were two financial experts – Walther Funk and Hjalmar Schacht, both of whom had been Minister of Economics and President of the Reichsbank. There were two men who had administered countries conquered by Germany – Arthur Seyss-Inquart, the Reich Commissioner of the Netherlands and Hans Frank, the Governor-General of Poland. Towards one end of the back row, Baldur von Schirach, the leader and educator of German Youth, had taken his place.

Stuck at the farthest corner of the back row was the lowliest of the defendants, the man least known to the general public – Hans Fritzsche, a journalist and broadcaster. Even after so many months of the trial most people wondered why he was here. But there was no doubt about why the rest of them were in the dock. They were the surviving leaders of the former Nazi Reich and for the last ten months they had been on trial for the crimes that regime was alleged to have committed in Germany and all over Europe.

Their judges, whose findings and sentences were now about to be delivered, constituted an International Military Tribunal – 'international' because there was now no German state and the victorious Allies in the war had decided to establish this tribunal to try Germany's former leaders; 'military' because there was no civil authority in Germany. The country was run by the occupying forces of the four major Powers who had defeated it. They had appointed eight judges – American, British, Russian and French. They could mount this trial of Germany's former leaders because they had insisted on, and since May 1945 acquired, total power over Germany. After the defeat of her armed forces Germany had not been allowed to negotiate terms with her invaders. The Allies recalled the myth after the First World War that the German Army had been stabbed in the back by politicians and deprived of victory; they remembered the interminable negotiations at Versailles and the failure of the Treaty they produced to prevent renewed German aggression. They had abhorred the savagery of the Second World War and the appalling atrocities which had besmirched it. This time, they had said, Germany's enemies will not treat. President Roosevelt had been the first Allied leader to call for 'unconditional surrender' at Casablanca in 1943; the other three major Powers had affirmed the demand at Yalta. In the First World War, it was felt, the German population had escaped unscathed by experience of the realities of war; this time the lessons of aggression had been brought home to them, literally. They were bombed by the Allies and invaded; their state had collapsed, their armies had been defeated. By May 1945 no German institutions survived. Germany was completely taken over by the Allies and lay at the mercy of her enemies.

In May 1945 Jodl had to sign a document of unconditional surrender. With his signature German sovereignty passed to the Allied forces. As he wrote his name, Jodl said: 'With this signature the German people and the German Armed Forces are, for better or worse, delivered into the hands of the victors ... In this hour I can only express the hope that the victors will treat them with generosity.' That was a lot to ask. Thanks to the War, the cities of Europe were in ruins. No one yet knew how many had died in the bombing and the fighting, but they could see around them the millions of maimed, orphaned, homeless and starving. As the Allied forces advanced they encountered hordes of foreign slave workers who had been held captive in German labour camps; they had opened the gates of concentration camps, seen the gas chambers and ovens, looked in horror at the huddled masses of skeletal inmates clad in lice-infested rags and riddled with typhus. The Nazis had once disposed of the bodies of those they murdered in the camps. As their government collapsed so too did the organization for disposing of its victims; Allied bulldozers now had to shovel mounds of corpses into mass graves. After fighting a war for five years and seeing the results of Nazi rule in Europe, few people felt generosity towards the Germans. Surely, they said, they have caused all this, their leaders especially. They should pay for it, suffer as they have made others suffer. In May 1945 an instinct for revenge and punishment was stronger than that of generosity.

The men who sat in the dock at Nuremberg on 30 September 1946 awaiting the judges' verdict had not expected anything other than revenge and punishment when they were first brought into court, ten months before. Goering had said then: 'As far as the trial is concerned, it's just a cut-and-dried political affair and I'm prepared for the consequences. The victors are the judges ... I know what's in store for me.' (2) Yet four days before the

International Military Tribunal gave its judgement, Rebecca West, who had observed parts of the trial, wrote: 'The judgement that is now about to be delivered has to answer a challenge which has been thrown down not only by Germans but by many critics among the Allies. It has to prove that victors can so rise above the ordinary limitations of human nature as to be able to try fairly the foes they vanquished, by submitting themselves to the restraints of law ... The meeting of the challenge will also warn all future war-mongers that law can at last pursue them into peace and thus give humanity a new defence against them. Hence the judgement of the Nuremberg Tribunal may be one of the most important events in the history of civilization.' (3)

There was a noticeable disparity in the view of the Nuremberg Trial between the early expectation of Goering and the final aspiration of Rebecca West. Both had deep roots in a debate which had gone on for hundreds of years – did might make right or should there be a higher law to govern the relationships of nations and control their behaviour? The debate had become more intense and had been accompanied by practical steps in the last fifty years. Was it possible to get international agreement to establish laws and punish those who broke them, above all those who committed the ultimate brutality – aggressive war? The nations had tried. They had passed resolutions condemning violence by states and individuals; after the First World War they had formulated a Treaty which it was hoped would punish the aggressors and deter any future resort to arms; they had founded a League of Nations and hoped that it would govern the world peacefully through negotiations and co-operation. The Second World War had not destroyed all hope of this. Instead it had fuelled the will to find a better way with an extra determination. Faced with destruction, death and atrocity on a scale the world had never seen, people cried: 'This must never happen again.'

The trial of the Nazi leaders at Nuremberg was not held just to establish their guilt and decide whether to punish them for committing crimes. It was part of the search for a better way to control strong human impulses, aggression and revenge. It was an attempt to replace violence with acceptable and effective rules for human behaviour.

While the trial lasted many people saw it as the essence of courtroom drama, some as a graphic display of the history of a regime or the psychology of its leaders, others as a vital experiment in international co-operation and the application of law. The trial was much more than a hearing of cases against twenty-odd men accused of crimes against the law of war and against humanity and of the crime of launching aggressive war. It was the focus of strong emotions, troubling questions and profound longings. The very events which led up to the trial and shaped it were in themselves dramatic, a nexus of history and a study in the clash of personalities and principles. Those events involved political, legal and moral conflict.

When the eight judges of the Military Tribunal entered the courtroom in Nuremberg at ten o'clock on 30 September, more was expected of them than a judgement on twenty-two individuals. In bringing those Nazi leaders to judgement some hoped for vengeance, some for a just basis for the post-war settlement of Europe. Others hoped for a solution to problems which had plagued the civilized nations for centuries.

References* for Chapter One

1   The scene and the security surrounding the court are described in various newspaper accounts of the day
2   Gilbert
3   *Daily Telegraph*, 26 September 1946

* A list of abbreviations used in the References will be found in the Sources, p. 505

Chapter Two

For centuries war had been the standard method for settling disputes between nations and satisfying their ambitions. Once a war was over the motto was the old Roman one: *'vae victis'* – woe to the conquered, because the victors could treat them as they saw fit. There were no universally accepted limits to the right of the victors to punish those who had fought against them, nor definitions of war crimes, though there was some sense of the 'laws and customs of war' and a shifting view of what was acceptable practice. The defeated might hope for leniency or even a gentlemanly acknowledgement that nasty things happen in war, but often they feared retribution for having fought at all, let alone for fighting with ferocity or means outside whatever happened to be the contemporary norm.

In the 17th century, Hugo Grotius collected and examined the various laws and customs of war, and considered what principles governed or should govern the behaviour of nations towards each other in a book called *De Jure Belli ac Pacis (Concerning the Laws of War and Peace)*. In the view of some, Grotius is the father of International Law. He wrote his book during the Thirty Years War – as savage and destructive a conflict as had ever lacerated Europe. Then, as in 1918 or 1945, actual experience of cruelty and suffering jerked people into thinking how their violence and brutality could be controlled.

Grotius was a scholar and a theorist. From the second half of the 19th century, international opinion began to demand practical action to get agreed limits on methods of fighting and to establish rules of behaviour towards those at the mercy of either side in a war. The Red Cross was founded and its right to look after the wounded was gradually recognized, then extended to such matters as the inspection of prisoner-of-war camps and bringing solace to prisoners in the form of food parcels or extra blankets. A series of Geneva Conventions was widely ratified – beginning in 1864 and developing to that of 1925 on gas and bacteriological warfare, and that of 1929 on wounded and sick prisoners-of-war. Most nations signed the 1899 and 1907 Hague Conventions laying down the rules of war on land and sea, limiting the weapons which belligerents might use, governing the opening of hostilities, and defining the rights of neutrals. By 1914, the international community had decided on definitions of crimes and certain limits on methods of fighting and the treatment of the helpless. But their decisions could not be said to have the full force of law – there were no agreed sanctions to be applied to those who broke the rules, no international courts had been established to try those accused of crimes.

In practice it was accepted that a country where war crimes had been committed could summon, try, and if need be punish those accused of them – whether they were nationals or aliens. Alternatively, the country whose subjects were accused could be left, or put under pressure, to try cases of alleged criminal behaviour.

It became clear to many, however, that these methods for dealing with war criminals were unsatisfactory. They were only applied to little men – individual brutes or subordinates ordered to commit atrocities; the leaders who condoned or encouraged the crimes tended to go scot-free. Furthermore, nations could try the war criminals they caught, but there was no way to compel other states to try their own. The inadequacy of this existing machinery was demonstrated after the First World War, and the experience of its failure and of the attempts to replace it were to influence the thinking of many during the Second World War and to shape the International Military Tribunal at Nuremberg.

From the early days of the First World War the public was fed stories of 'Hunnish atrocities'. A few of these stories contained an element of truth. Most of those about raped Belgian nuns and impaled babies did not. They had sprung from the lurid imaginations of the pressroom. They were believed partly because people wanted to believe them: they wanted a comprehensible reason for hating the Germans and fighting them. But as a result of their acceptance of the tales the public increasingly demanded more than military victory. They called not just for the punishment of German war criminals but the punishment of those in high places whom they considered guilty of formulating criminal plans and issuing criminal orders. To disentangle the facts and to try to determine whether war crimes were directed by German civil and military leaders, the Bryce Committee was set up in France. In December 1914, J.H. Morgan of the Home Office was sent to join it. This committee was dissolved in 1915. But largely on Morgan's insistence, a replacement was organized in October 1918 under Birkenhead to enquire into outrages committed by the German forces and in particular to establish the guilt of the General Staff and 'other highly-placed individuals'.

The British government was undecided about what to do once the facts were gathered, but thought the exercise might have immediate practical benefits. As Lord Milner, the Secretary for War put it, it was doubtful whether a trial should be held but meanwhile 'it would not at all be a bad thing that the offenders should think that we intended to punish them'. The committee had not intended to include the Kaiser in its brief. They regarded him as a mere figurehead and feared that to accuse him of crimes would obscure the responsibility of the real criminals. (1) The politicians, however, thought otherwise. Lloyd George raised the cry of 'Hang the Kaiser'. It was taken up and amplified by the public – hang the Kaiser, hang the generals, hang the politicians; they caused the war, now let them suffer for it.

It was, however, characteristic of those who were trying to frame an international peace settlement at Versailles and hoping to achieve a measure of international government through a League of Nations, that rather than allow public vengeance, they preferred due legal process and international decisions. They set up a multinational committee of lawyers to draw up charges against German leaders accused of war crimes and of crimes against humanity. This committee considered adding a further charge – that of causing the war itself – but they could not agree whether causing war was actually a crime in international law. Nor could they feel certain that evidence to establish Germany's sole responsibility for the hostilities was conclusive – indeed they feared that a thorough investigation might well implicate the victors to some extent. So the lawyers dropped the idea.

The politicians promptly picked it up. They had no inhibitions about the legal niceties or the historical problems. They confidently wrote German war guilt into the Versailles Treaty and in Article 227 they accused the Kaiser himself of 'a supreme offence against international morality and the sanctity of treaties'.

The politicians ignored the lawyers' advice on another matter too. The legal committee had recommended the establishment of an international court to try the accused. This idea first fell foul of the French and Italians who would not countenance the presence of Germans or neutrals on such a tribunal. It then met dogged opposition from Lansing, the American Secretary of State and chairman of the Versailles political committee considering war crimes. Lansing felt that any trial of Germans would hamper his own pet scheme of restoring good relations with Germany as quickly as possible. After much argument among and between politicians and lawyers it was decided that a special tribunal with judges from Britain, the United States, France, Italy and Japan should be set up to try the Kaiser. In addition Article 228 of the Versailles Treaty called for a series of military tribunals to deal with those German leaders deemed to have ordered and committed acts in violation of the laws and customs of war. The accused were to be given the right to name counsel for their defence.

But even this compromise between lawyers and politicians broke down in practice. For a start it proved impossible to try the Kaiser. He refused to leave Holland where he had fled after revolution in Germany. The Dutch saw international demands to hand him over as bullying and an attempted infringement of their right as a sovereign nation to chose their own guests. In 1920, the Kaiser toyed with the idea of surrendering himself in the hope of winning better peace terms for his people. But he quickly thought better of it and decided that his conscience would not allow a divinely appointed ruler to submit to any mortal judge. He stayed in Holland until his death in 1941.

More seriously, the Allied attempt to try other Germans before military tribunals nearly caused the collapse of the peace settlement. In 1920 the German government, presented with a list of over 900 names ranging from the Crown Prince through civil and especially military chiefs, simply refused to hand them over for trial. They claimed that many in the Reichswehr preferred a renewal of war to such a capitulation. The Allies believed them and were convinced that German public opinion would back the Army. Morgan, now working with the Disarmament Commission in Berlin, was assured by one of its military members that not only was the Commission's work threatened, but so too were the lives of its members, given the ugliness of the public mood. The German press had launched a campaign of intimidation and the appeals of the Defence Minister 'not to do violence to the members of the Commission' seemed more like fanning the flames. (2) In an attempt to salvage something from the mess the Allies finally persuaded the Germans to hold their own trials of those on the Black List and to accept observers appointed by the international community.

These trials eventually opened in Leipzig late in 1922. They were a fiasco. It proved difficult to find the accused or witnesses; it was almost impossible to force them to appear. Eight hundred and eighty eight out of the 901 finally charged were acquitted or summarily dismissed. For the rest derisorily low sentences were passed. When several of the convicted escaped from prison, public congratulations were offered to the warders. (3)

At least the First World War had introduced new thinking about the problem of dealing with war criminals, however ineffective its outcome. The idea had developed that leaders should be punished for policies which resulted in criminal acts. Lawyers had separated two strands in illegal behaviour and drawn a distinction between war crimes against and by the military and crimes against civilian populations; they had even considered the possibility that war itself might be a crime. The politicians had sensed a need for nations to co-operate in deciding what were crimes and who were criminals; some wanted to substitute an international court for the trial of a major criminal rather than leave him to the retribution of the aggrieved. But the fruit of this thinking had been bitter. In 1918 existing law, especially on whether war itself was criminal, had seemed vague and contentious. International co-operation had been invoked but not obtained. The impotence of the international community to compel a nation to try its own leaders had been exposed – even had German courts existed in 1945, it is doubtful whether anyone would have trusted them to try prominent Nazis, not after what had happened at Leipzig. The attempt to find a better way of dealing with war crimes had foundered on legal and political rocks. Hopes of preventing aggression by the punitive clauses of the Treaty of Versailles and the establishment of the League of Nations failed too. But the inability to introduce international sanctions to give force to international rules after 1918 did not extinguish the desire to establish them; lawyers and politicians from time to time gnawed at the theoretical and practical possibilities. And the renewal of war in 1939 gave impetus and urgency to their discussions.

For, undeterred by previous failure and the lack of existing machinery, every Allied nation between 1939 and 1945 demanded punishment for those who committed war crimes. Criminals of all nations were denounced. During the War both German and Allied military authorities held courts martial of their own nationals. From 1942 an Extraordinary State Commission in the USSR was investigating German war crimes in Russia; in 1943, three German officers were tried in Kharkov and shot. Inevitably once the War finished there would be many more trials and executions of individuals who had committed atrocities. Yet, even more strongly than in the First World War, there was the conviction that the enemy's leaders constituted a criminal regime, that the incidents of atrocity were part of a deliberate policy of crime and that those who were most responsible and deserving of severest punishment were the Nazi leaders themselves. There may have been uncertainty in the Great War about who had caused it; in this one there was no doubt in Allied minds that the Nazis had planned it, then attacked every country in Europe without ultimatum and in spite of treaties and assurances. In the First World War the German General Staff and government may or may not have condoned war crimes; in the Second it was believed that the wholesale nature of such crimes could only be explained by deliberate intention and use of resources – they were way beyond the nature and number to be expected simply from the vicious behaviour of criminal individuals and groups. Furthermore there had been crimes against humanity in Germany itself and in occupied Europe which exceeded anything suffered previously and which again could only be explained as Nazi policy. In the Great War the atrocity stories had been exaggerated; during this war the scale of atrocity was, if anything, underestimated.

Even so, it was shocking enough. No matter if the full horror of the concentration camps was only understood when they were liberated, there was always at the very least an awareness that such camps held people without charge, trial or right of appeal and treated them cruelly. No one might be able yet to calculate the figures for murders, enslavement and pillage by the Nazis but partizans and Resistance workers had given enough indication of the bestial nature of Nazi rule. The Nazis themselves had publicized such outrages as the destruction of the Czech village of Lidice, the murder of its menfolk and deportation to concentration camps of its women and children – all in reprisal for the assassination of Heydrich, the Protector of Bohemia. As a French government memorandum to the European Advisory Commission on War Crimes put it: crimes were taking place on such a scale 'by an enemy who has sought to annihilate whole nations, who has elevated murder to a political system, that we no longer have the duty of punishing merely those who commit but also those who plan the crime'. (4)

As awareness of these crimes grew throughout the War and public disgust increased, the Allied governments issued threats of punishment, both to express the general sense of revulsion and in the hope of deterring Nazis from criminal acts in the future. For the first time, the punishment of war crimes became not just the automatic result of a war but a declared official policy in fighting it. Even so, the wording of that policy remained vague for several years. There was to be much procrastination, confused thinking, tortuous negotiation, and haphazard decision before it was clarified. It was a long road between the determination to punish and the establishment of an International Military Tribunal to decide who should be punished.

In October 1941, while the United States was still neutral, President Roosevelt drew attention to the wholesale execution by the Germans of hostages in France and he warned that 'one day a frightful retribution' would be exacted. Later in the month Churchill joined Roosevelt in a public declaration: 'The massacres of the French are an example of what Hitler's Nazis are doing in many other countries under their yoke. The atrocities committed in Poland, Yugoslavia, Norway, Holland, Belgium, and particularly behind the German front in Russia, exceed anything that has been known since the darkest and most bestial ages of humanity. The punishment of these crimes should now be counted among the major goals of the war.' (5) The governments in exile of the occupied countries of Europe joined in the outcry and threats. Warnings of punishment were also issued in response to specific incidents. The British government, for example, threatened retribution for the killing after recapture of fifty British airmen who had escaped from the prisoner-of-war camp Stalag Luft III at Sagan. During the 1944 Rising in Warsaw, they also warned the Nazis that captured Polish soldiers must be treated as lawful combatants (so entitled to protection under the Geneva convention) or justice would be exacted from them.

But who was to exact justice? Under what conditions? Was it enough after this war to fall back once again on leaving each country to try its own criminals and as many of the enemy's as could be caught? How scrupulous would these countries be when trying those who had conquered and occupied them? As after 1918, many felt that mere revenge was not enough; that the impulse must be channelled and controlled by international action. In January 1942 the representatives of nine occupied countries in Europe held a conference at St James's in London to discuss such questions. They issued a declaration on 13 January that: 'international solidarity is necessary to avoid the repression of these acts of violence simply by acts of vengeance on the part of the general public and in order to satisfy the sense of justice of the civilized world.' (6) The declaration announced that punishment for war crimes, whoever committed them, was now a principal war aim of the governments at the conference. It also made clear an additional intention: to bring to justice not only those who themselves perpetrated crimes, but

– more ambitiously – those who ordered them. After this war at least it seemed that the leaders would not escape punishment. The St James's Declaration was approved by Britain, the United States and the USSR.

It had expressed disgust not only at atrocity but at the idea of mere vengeance. It implied a desire for some form of judicial proceeding to determine guilt and satisfy a sense of justice. It was an unmistakable warning to the Germans that international action was intended against war criminals and that Nazi leaders would bear their full share of responsibility. The declaration, however, was expressed in general terms. It did not come down to the nuts and bolts – no names of alleged criminals were given, no machinery for trial was outlined. The St James's Conference was followed by only one practical step. The United Nations War Crimes Commission was set up in London in 1943 to collect and collate information on war crimes and criminals. It was made up of representatives of seventeen nations – but had no Russian member. Stalin would only join if every Soviet Republic were given separate representation. This was refused.

It was a bad start to an experiment in international co-operation. From then on, things only got worse. A memorandum from Sir Cecil Hurst, the British Chairman of the Commission, sent to the Lord Chancellor's office in March 1944, said that the body was incapable of doing the job it was designed for – collecting evidence. They relied on the assistance of the governments represented and their help was not forthcoming. Hurst complained that after four months of work the Commission had only received seventy cases; half of them were so incomplete as to be useless and most were trivial.

The governments had made a lot of noise about war crimes but did not seem to be making a lot of effort to substantiate their allegations. Hurst was clearly irritated by what he regarded as laziness or incompetence. Perhaps he did not recognize the major problem of the governments he criticized: they were in exile, cut off from the scenes of the alleged crimes and without access to witnesses or documentary evidence. What worried him even more than the paucity and flimsiness of the cases presented to the Commission was the members' sense of frustration that the UNWCC was 'limited by its present terms of reference'. It was limited to investigating war crimes pure and simple. These, he said, were not the incidents which had most outraged public opinion and distressed the governments in exile. The biggest demand was for punishment of those who murdered and terrorized civilian populations (what the legal committee at Versailles had called crimes against humanity) and Hurst himself felt that it was a major priority to investigate charges of acts against Jews.

Many people too had come to believe that Nazi institutions as well as individuals were guilty of crimes. The organization most often accused of crimes against humanity was the Gestapo, and Hurst put forward a radical UNWCC proposal that not only should individuals be arrested and held for trial but that 'all members of a body like the Gestapo should be responsible for the acts of the individual members' and interned until proceedings could be instituted. (7)

Hurst's searching comments fell on deaf ears in the British government – which as host to the governments represented on the Commission could have done most to influence their attitude and its work. No steps were taken to introduce changes in the UNWCC's brief; little was done to encourage allied governments to speed up the flow of information. By the end of the year, Hurst was writing to Lord Simon, the Lord Chancellor, that he was conscious of 'a feeling of doubt in some quarters as to whether HMG really means business in connection with the policy proclaimed by the Allies of bringing war criminals to justice.' He pointed to 'the lack of effective contact between HMG and the Commission'. He blamed one body in particular for the difficulties the UNWCC was experiencing: 'In general the Foreign Office makes no response to the Commission's recommendations.' (8) Schuster, too, was critical of the attitude of the Foreign Office. He wrote to Lord Simon on 24 November 1944: 'I cannot conceal from myself the idea that the Foreign Office are not deeply interested in the subject.' He conceded that they were no doubt busy men who thought other matters more important, 'but the general impression left in my mind is that they regard the whole thing as a nuisance, but perhaps a necessary nuisance.' (9)

The murmurs of discontent at last reached the Foreign Secretary himself. Anthony Eden wrote a long letter to Hurst in December 1944 flatly denying all charges of Foreign Office neglect. He poured out soothing assurances that everything would speed up and ease as Europe was liberated. He even offered the ultimate official balm – the possibility of finding extra staff for the Commission. (10) Eden's letter did not prevent the resignation of Sir Cecil Hurst from the UNWCC in the following month. 'I have had a bit of a breakdown,' he wrote, 'and the doctors have told me that I must give it up.' (11)

The UNWCC continued to collect evidence and names of suspected criminals. It had never been asked to define crimes, consider whether distinction should be made between major and minor criminals, or to decide what form judicial proceedings against them should take.

A significant move to clarify some of these issues had been taken at the Moscow Conference of Foreign Ministers in November 1943. Here, Britain, the United States and the Soviet Union had issued a joint declaration condemning Nazi atrocities in occupied Europe. This stated that 'at the time of the granting of any armistice to any government which may be set up in Germany, those German officers and men and members of the Nazi Party who have been responsible for or who have taken part in the above atrocities, massacres and executions, will be sent back to the countries in which their abominable deeds were done in order that they may be judged and punished according to the laws of those liberated countries and of the Free Governments which will be erected therein.'

The Moscow Declaration broke no new ground thus far; the return of criminals to the scenes of their crimes was a standard procedure. But the foreign ministers then tackled the harder questions raised at the St James's conference – how to deal with those Nazi leaders who had condoned or ordered crimes all over Europe and the need for international solidarity in seeking their punishment. In so doing they began to categorize the war criminals and create a class of criminal leader. They stated that 'the above declaration is without prejudice to the case of major criminals whose offences have no particular geographical location and who will be punished by a joint declaration of the Governments of the Allies'. (12) So the foreign ministers had created two groups of war criminals and proposed two forms of treatment: national action for localized offences, and international action for those whose criminal orders had applied in several countries. But there was one important omission in the Moscow Declaration – there was no mention of trial before punishment for the major criminals. Indeed talk of punishment by 'joint declaration' seems to preclude trial. Why was there no mention of judicial proceedings? Was it the memory of the practical difficulties and the final farce of the Versailles discussions and the Leipzig trials? Or was it that the foreign ministers reckoned that justice was too good for such men?

There is no record that Leipzig was mentioned at the Moscow Conference. There is however evidence that those present did not think the fate of leading Nazi criminals merited much time or trouble. At Moscow the US Secretary of State, Cordell Hull, actually said: 'If I had my way I would take Hitler and Mussolini and Tojo and their accomplices and bring them before a drumhead court martial, and at sunrise the following morning there would occur an historic incident.' (13)

At the Tehran Conference at the end of 1943 Roosevelt's son, Elliott, gained the impression that Stalin was prepared to go even further. In the boozy atmosphere of a banquet the Russian leader gave to the other Allied statesmen, Stalin proposed a toast: 'to the quickest possible justice for all German war criminals ... I drink to the justice of the firing squad.' He estimated that the firing squad should rid the world of about 50,000 leading Germans, mainly military. Churchill expressed shock. Roosevelt tried to cool the atmosphere with a jocular suggestion that perhaps the number could be cut to 49,000. Stalin and Molotov then claimed that the whole idea had only been a joke. (14) Perhaps indeed it was. When discussing policy on official occasions Stalin always recommended that war criminals be given a judicial hearing before (inevitably) being shot. Churchill, on the other hand, can only have been shocked by Stalin's proposal because of the huge number of executions suggested, not the method. For a long time his government would argue against any form of trial and would favour some kind of dressed-up summary execution.

By the end of the war many people would have been content with summary execution, naked and unashamed. The public would have found it easy to draw up lists of ogres who had haunted the imagination in recent years; their deaths would have occasioned little soul-searching. The shock expressed when Mussolini and his mistress, Clara Petacci, were shot by Italian partizans in 1945 came less from the fact that they had been summarily executed than because their bodies was first hung upside down from lamp-posts, then left to lie in the gutter. There are, it seems, a few decencies which ought to be observed even in a lynching. And 'summary execution' is really a euphemism for lynching. When in March 1945 Anthony Eden, the British Foreign Secretary, was asked in the House of Commons whether when a British soldier met Hitler it would be his duty to shoot him or take him alive Eden replied: 'I am quite satisfied to leave the decision to the British soldier concerned.' (15) This was veiled encouragement to lynch. Eden had implied that he did not mind what the soldier did. Yet the law is categorical – it is any soldier's duty to take and keep a prisoner-of-war alive, however notorious he may be.

Cordell Hull's idea of a drumhead court martial only applied a little cosmetic to the procedure of shooting out of hand. This roughest form of justice would allow several minutes to be spent establishing that the prisoner really was *the* Adolf Hitler or whoever, and the charges to be read to him to explain why he was about to be shot; and would provide the court with the authority to give orders to a firing squad. When the British Foreign Office was considering this method with some enthusiasm in 1944, it reckoned that the whole process from the moment of arrest would be over and done within six hours. (16)

Others considering what to do with major war criminals rejected the solution of short, sharp military action. Eden changed his mind about it from time to time. On one occasion he might suggest lynching Hitler, but he told a meeting of the Prime Ministers of Belgium, Czechoslovakia and Poland, and the Foreign Ministers of Greece, Luxembourg, the Netherlands, Norway, Yugoslavia and France in 1942 that the disposal of Hitler and other principals should 'be settled as a matter of high policy'. (17) This indicated that at this moment he saw the responsibility for dealing with top criminals as a political rather than a military or indeed legal matter. Those who shared his views argued that since the charge against Hitler and his colleagues was not based on a series of isolated incidents but on the totality of their acts, since the aim in punishing them was to give expression to international condemnation of their entire policy and to cleanse the moral atmosphere of their polluting presence, then what was involved was a political indictment and what was appropriate was political, executive action by the international community. Underlying this argument was the belief that no kind of hearing was required to establish guilt – as the Lord Chancellor put it: 'Fancy "trying" Hitler!' (18) Many felt his guilt and that of his leading associates did not need proving. What was left to the international community was to settle punishment. In Lord Simon's view that was not a question to be left to 'a posse of jurists'; it was a responsibility for world leaders, and they could look to history for an example of successful international action.

For there was a precedent for executive action by allies against a former enemy whose acts seemed abhorrent: that of Napoleon. His case offered interesting parallels with the problems faced after the Second World War and persuasive arguments for those who favoured joint political decision on the fate of major war criminals.

When Napoleon escaped from Elba, broke the terms of the 1814 Treaty of Fontainebleau, and marched again on Europe, he was declared '*hors la loi*' by the representatives of all the European states attending the peace negotiations at Vienna (significantly France herself was one). A unanimous condemnation having been passed, the states then had to decide what to do about the man they had outlawed. The Prussian military leader, Blücher, said he would shoot the Emperor if he fell into Prussian hands (lynch him). The Russians pressed for summary execution (drumhead court martial perhaps). Finally, however, the Powers agreed to exile Napoleon permanently on St Helena. Here he would be out of harm's way and kept at British expense without incurring the embarrassment of executing a sovereign. (All European rulers had condemned the execution of Louis XVI and did not want their subjects to imagine that killing rulers was an acceptable way of expressing their opinion of them.) This was a decision reached by the entire European community (including France) – and it was a purely political decision. No one had seriously considered a trial for Napoleon; it was not deemed necessary since his crimes seemed self-evident, condemnation was universal, and the European statesmen had no qualms about punishing him for them.

However, the idea of a form of trial for major Nazi war criminals was attractive to many even though the form they favoured might seem repugnant to others. There were recognized advantages in more recent precedents than that of Napoleon – show trials. Stalin had punished his opponents and frightened others by the trials he had mounted in the 1930s; Hitler had made a public spectacle out of the trial of those who had plotted against his life in July 1944. Should the nations now decide on a show trial for Nazi war criminals, they could present massive evidence of their guilt to convince any wavering public opinion, to put on record their abhorrence of the crimes and to justify the inevitable punishment. In a show trial it is even possible to allow a little defence – just enough to demonstrate how feeble it is.

There was one final option open for those who were shocked by the roughness of military justice, convinced that executive action is no justice at all, and worried by the practical problems, political repercussions and moral implications of punishing war criminals. It was to do nothing at all. For those whose consciences were too tender to throw the first stone, it was appealing to tell the targets of international loathing to go away and sin no more. Doing nothing could become a high moral stance. Refusal to assess guilt, degrees of responsibility or mitigating circumstances not only spared effort, it could be seen as a sign of greater moral sensitivity than that displayed by people demanding punishment. The chances were, of course, that alleged criminals whose guilt it was apparently immoral to determine would simply be lynched by those who had suffered as a result of their crimes. But then the blood would be on the hands of the lynchers, not on the hands of those who claimed moral courage in avoiding decision lest it prove painful to themselves.

Before the end of the war, each of these different possible ways of dealing with top Nazi war criminals had some vocal support. But what sort of basis did any of them offer for the new and better world which many believed they had been fighting for? How could they be reconciled with the indignation expressed during the War at Nazi ruthlessness and disregard for existing laws and civilized standards? How could those who expressed concern for the rule of law or claimed superior moral sensitivity stomach mob rule and lynching? For lynching is what virtually everyone expected would be the mass instinct once the War finished. It was to stop the people as well as nations taking the law into their own hands that the St James's Conference had called for international action to avoid mere vengeance and to satisfy a sense of justice. People's grievance and bitterness were recognized, but lynching is revolting and uncontrollable. If it is accepted as the natural and indeed the justifiable expression of the people's anger, where should the lines be drawn? Is it justified for a week, a month, a year? Who deserves lynching and for what? Is law and order to be restored after the lynchers have murdered 50,000, or only after every public and private grudge has been settled?

There are objections too against all the other canvassed solutions to the problem of top war criminals. Can military action either by a soldier with a captive in a ditch, or by a drumhead court martial, be seen as much more than institutionalized lynching? Military action certainly carries worrying implications. To kill out of hand German prisoners-of-war for killing Allied prisoners-of-war can be seen as breaking the very Geneva Convention being invoked. Should the military be asked to accept the responsibility for mistaken identity or the possibility that the rumour of a man's guilt is unfounded?

The politicians might be willing to take the responsibility from the soldiers, but they had had problems enough reaching a common decision on the fate of Napoleon – agreement over a long list of Nazis would multiply the problems. And executive action might create martyrs – arguably the reputations of Napoleon, Louis XVI or Charles I were glamourized by their politically ordained punishment and no one wanted to create myths round the leading Nazis. Carefully worded official briefs explaining and justifying executive punishment might well be dismissed as propaganda, hiding the victors' spleen against their former opponents. There are better ways of showing the strength of indignation at crimes and the determination of nations to punish those who transgress the rules of the international community than by issuing press handouts after a firing squad.

Show trials are no better. They may provide a more dramatic display of the evidence and an opportunity to the victors to justify their fight and bring home to the vanquished the nature of their leaders. But they are, at best, only a more sophisticated form of propaganda, not a true legal process in which, according to the civilized standards which the Allies had claimed they wished to reintroduce to Europe, evidence is presented by both sides, allowing full argument and ample opportunity for rebuttal by the defence. It may be tempting to give your enemies a dose of their own medicine, but conducting the kind of trial Hitler gave the Bomb Plotters in 1944 merely suggests that you are no better than him, and ultimately suggests that the high-sounding aims expressed in the War were no more than battle cries. It leaves the German people, whose future attitudes and behaviour it is hoped to influence, with the impression that for the moment – and perhaps only temporarily – the Allies, not the Nazis, have the power to terrorize and kill.

Torn between the conflicting alternatives for dealing with major war criminals, aware of the demand to find some way to meet public aspirations for some better way to run the world, the Allied leaders had made little progress by 1944 beyond the St James's and Moscow Declarations. They had defined a distinction between war criminals and the leaders who promoted their crimes; they had agreed on punishment of the minor criminals by national courts and of the major criminals by international action. But they had not decided what that action should be. The matter was delegated by Heads of State to their Foreign Ministers. It slipped down the agenda of meetings and little was done. J.H. Morgan had written to the Lord Chancellor as long ago as March 1940 to explain the attitude of governments to war crimes in the First World War and to draw attention to the failure of the Leipzig trials. He had emphasized then the need to start gathering evidence of war crimes and lists of criminals, and the urgency of deciding well in advance what action would be taken so as to be ready to announce proceedings as part of the terms of armistice. The lesson he drew from 1918 was that everything had been left too late. But the reply he eventually received from the Lord Chancellor's office was inevitable: 'At the present time we are more fully occupied in beating the Germans on the field rather than in hanging them afterwards.' (19) That was also the view of the Allied statesmen. Despite occasional stabs of conscience and flashes of rhetoric, war crimes had a low priority; the politicians had an alliance to keep together, a war to win, all the complexity of the post-war settlement of Europe to consider.

With the Allied invasion of Europe though, the need for an agreed policy on the principal war criminals became more pressing. Lord Wright, the new chairman of the UNWCC, pointed out to Churchill in September 1944 that many criminals would escape unless machinery were introduced immediately to catch, hold and try them. (20) He suggested that a 'great number' of military courts be set up. Churchill was pricked by Wright's criticisms of government sluggishness so far; he confessed to Eden that they caused him 'great uneasiness' and wondered about, rather than decided upon, any action. Eden, who had become a proponent of political action in theory but of no action in practice, suddenly woke up to the immediacy of the problem. He wrote to the UNWCC insisting that as the Allied armies took prisoners they must be equipped with lists of wanted men and evidence of their crimes so that the suspected criminals could be segregated. The Foreign Office, having balked the work of the UNWCC since its inception, now demanded an immediate report on criminals and their crimes. 'We do not want,' Eden said, 'to fall into the First World War trap where we did not extract the wanted as a condition of the armistice.' (21) J.H. Morgan's letter to the Lord Chancellor had finally been vindicated after four years.

But Eden and the British government were merely aware of a problem; they took little action themselves to solve it. By April 1945, the British military authorities were exasperated by government failure to give clear directives on the handling of suspected war criminals. There was a flood of telegrams to the War Office from the theatre commanders. Alexander, the Supreme Allied Commander, Mediterranean Theatre, cabled on 21 April asking whether the Army was to apprehend those on UNWCC lists; 'guidance required urgently for future planning' he pleaded. (22) A note on this telegram by a War Office official pointed out that American Chiefs of Staff had agreed to order their theatre commanders to apprehend those named by the Commission, but the War Office could not make up its mind what to do. They still could not reach a decision when they got another telegram from Alexander on 30 April saying that the capture of Mussolini and Clara Petacci made instructions 'imperative'. Only on 11 May did the Combined Chiefs of Staff promise their commanders that a list of suspects was being 'prepared'; once received, those named should be apprehended and detained as normal prisoners-of-war. (23) Quite what was to be done with them thereafter, no one said.

Official American response to the problem had not been much quicker. For a long time in the United States there had been scepticism in some circles about the amount of atrocity committed on the Continent and a suspicion that pre-war refugees and exiled governments' stories were to be taken with large pinches of salt. The attitude of George Ball, later to achieve distinction as the right-hand man of Dean Rusk, was typical. He wrote: 'Of course I had heard dark stories of the treatment of the Slavs, Jews, Gypsies and others who did not meet the Wagnerian standards of the Master Race. But I believe ... that I had tended to think those rumours exaggerated ... Nor do I think I was less well-informed than most other Americans, including those like myself who had served in the government. Perhaps we were so preoccupied with the squalid menace of the war we did not focus on this unspeakable ghastliness. It may also be that the idea of mass extermination was so far outside the traditional comprehension of most Americans that we instinctively refused to believe in its existence.' (24) (A European might like to add that the idea of mass extermination was way beyond the comprehension of anyone; it is still difficult to grasp.)

America, thanks to geography, had been insulated against the horrors of the War. Only in December 1944 did the American public have its first direct experience of Nazi brutality. Seventy American prisoners-of-war were shot by the First SS Panzer Regiment at Malmédy in Belgium. Before Malmédy such crimes had been committed against other people, not Americans. The question of war crimes could be seen as remote and rather abstract; now it was painfully real. And as the Allied armies advanced through Europe and into Germany the concept of crimes against humanity took on meaning as well. Newsreels showed the squalor and degradation of the slave labour camps and the horror of the gas chambers; newspapers were filled with stories of the conditions suffered by prisoners-of-war, eyewitness accounts of extermination squads, the piles of corpses discovered by the liberating armies in the concentration camps. A telegram from the British ambassador in Washington, Lord Halifax, told the Foreign Office in April that the American Press had been full of such reports for weeks; there had been a call in the House of Representatives to speed up the work of the UNWCC. (25) The public put more pressure on the politicians after a visit to Buchenwald and Dachau concentration camps by sixteen newspaper editors and publishers in May and similar tours by Senators and Congressmen at the same time. The British Embassy reported that their stories had received 'wide and sustained publicity', unequalled by any other coverage. Those visitors had all reached the same conclusion – that the Nazis had had 'a master plan ... based on a policy of calculated and organized brutality'. They all called for speedy action by the United Nations. (26)

So too did the general public. The National Opinion Research Centre of the University of Denver had carried out a small poll at the end of 1944 and in January 1945 to discover how Americans viewed Germans. They found then that a large section of the population had friendly feelings towards them (though the more educated tended to be harsher); most people spoke of a need for 're-education', approved of sending relief to the Germans, objected to the country's dismemberment and hoped the Allies would help to rebuild German peacetime industry. (27) But by the middle of the year many of those friendly feelings had evaporated. In the view of the British Embassy in Washington the newspaper reports and the newsreels had made the American public think again. They were thinking of punishment.

There had been clamour for a clearly defined policy from other quarters too. Once Europe was invaded by the Allies governments in exile feared, rightly, that Hitler would inflict a final programme of death and destruction in their countries as he was forced to withdraw his troops. They called for specific declarations by all the Powers on how such action would be punished. Jewish organizations hoped to save some of the Jews still in Nazi hands. They lobbied governments to issue threats of retribution for any future murders.

The governments of the major powers resisted public outcry and military requests for a long time. Until the invasion of Europe it had been possible to haver and to defer any concrete decisions on the treatment of major war criminals. Indeed, it could be seen as desirable to postpone a decision. They expected German maltreatment of Allied prisoners-of-war if they emphasized at this stage the intention of punishing Nazi war criminals. This was the reason for stopping the war crimes trials in Sicily in 1943 and the Anglo-American decision in 1944 not to segregate suspects in their prisoner-of-war camps.

However, as public opinion grew more bitter, and once the Allied armies crossed into Germany itself and top Nazis began to fall captive, the statesmen could delay no longer. They were faced with the realities of an occupation of Germany and the reconstruction of Europe. They must decide now what to do with the high-ranking Nazis who had led their country into war, decimated and destroyed much of Europe, and who in consequence were thought of as criminal by most of the rest of the world.

References for Chapter Two

1 Letter and memorandum to the Lord Chancellor's Office from J.H. Morgan, 19 March 1940. LCO 2. 2972
2 Ibid
3 Much of this section on Versailles and the Leipzig Trials is based on the two draft chapters which Sir John Wheeler-Bennett wrote for a projected history of the Nuremberg Trial and which is now in the library of St Antony's College, Oxford. Details have been added from the memorandum of J.H. Morgan and from the report of the International Commission for Penal Reconstruction and Development, July 1943. LCO 2. 2973
4 French memorandum to European Advisory Commission on War Crimes, 21 February 1945. LCO 2. 2978
5 Both quotations appear in the transcript of the Nuremberg Trial. IMT Vol. V
6 Quoted by Telford Taylor in an article in *International Conciliation* No. 450. April 1949 and elsewhere
7 Memorandum from Sir Cecil Hurst, 30 March 1944. LCO 2. 2976
8 Letter from Hurst to Simon, 22 November 1944. LCO 2. 2976
9 Letter from Schuster to Simon, 24 November 1944. LCO 2. 2976
10 Letter from Eden to Hurst, December 1944. LCO 2. 2976
11 Letter from Hurst to Simon, 3 January 1945. LCO 2. 2976
12 Telford Taylor article op. cit.
13 Minutes by Bohlen, quoted by the then Sir Hartley Shawcross in *Tribute to Jackson*, address to the New York Bar Association 1969
14 Quoted by Heydecker
15 Ibid

16   From the draft chapters prepared by Patrick Dean for Sir John Wheeler-Bennett's proposed history

17   Minutes of meeting at the Foreign Office, 6 August 1942. LCO 2. 2974

18   Simon to Eden commenting on a Cabinet Paper, May 1944. LCO 2. 2976

19   Schuster to Morgan, 27 November 1941. LCO 2. 2972

20   Wright to Churchill, 12 September 1944. LCO 2. 2976

21   Eden to Hurst, 18 October 1944. LCO 2. 2976

22   FO 371. 51019

23   FO 371. 51023

24   George Ball, *The Past has Another Pattern*

25   FO 371. 51018

26   FO 371. 51023

27   Forwarded to the Foreign Office from the British Embassy in Washington, 8 June 1945. FO 371. 51026

Chapter Three

The problem of what to do with the leader of all the Nazis, the Führer, had been solved for the Allies by Hitler himself. He was dead. Not that the Allies could be certain – no identifiable body was found. A British Intelligence officer and historian, Hugh Trevor-Roper, was detailed to investigate the story of Hitler's last days and to cross-examine witnesses before there could be any confidence that Hitler had not escaped and gone into hiding. His report deducing that Hitler was indeed dead was submitted on 1 November 1945. What was known meanwhile was that on 1 May, Hamburg Radio interrupted a performance of Bruckner's Seventh Symphony. There was a role of drums, followed by a solemn announcement: Hitler 'fighting to the last breath against Bolshevism, fell for Germany this afternoon in his operational headquarters in the Reich Chancellery'.

Not surprisingly in a radio service controlled by Dr Goebbels, this brief announcement was a tissue of lies and evasions. Hitler had in fact died the previous afternoon; he had not been killed in his last fight, he had committed suicide. Bolshevism had not been his only enemy; the Russians had indeed reached Berlin, but their allies were in occupation of much of the rest of the country. Nor did he die for Germany, or at least not for the German people. He had come to hate them and blame them for military defeat. In revenge for what Hitler regarded as their betrayal he had given orders in March for the total destruction of all military, industrial and communications installations, all means of transport. When Albert Speer protested that this order would destroy the basis of existence for the nation, the Führer told him: 'If the war is lost the nation will also perish ... Besides those who remain after the battle are only the inferior ones, for the good have been killed.' It is doubtful that Hitler had proved himself to be either superior or good by shooting himself through the mouth in his bunker in the Reich Chancellery.

Those who had been closest to him in the final weeks and shared his delusions of victory while Germany outside the bunker was bombed and shelled to ruins would have come top on anyone's list of criminal Nazi leaders in 1945. Dr Goebbels, however, was certainly dead. He had marketed Hitler as the saviour of Germany, used his oratory and theatrical flair to foist Nazism on Germany, deployed the media and his own venom to incite the people to hatred of Jews, Slavs, Marxists and Christians, then screamed at them his fantasy that the Allies would split and be defeated. On the day after Hitler's death, Goebbels poisoned his own six children, then he and his wife were shot, on his instructions, by an SS orderly. Some time before his death he had commented: 'We shall go down in history as the greatest statesmen of all time, or as the greatest criminals.' History has put Goebbels in the latter class.

By the time Berlin fell it was probable that Heinrich Müller, the former head of the Gestapo, and director of the extermination of the Jews, was dead. He had shared the final madness in the Führer's bunker and was last seen there on 28 April. Thereafter he disappeared. His burial was recorded on 17 May, but when the body was finally exhumed it could not be identified. Given the lack of certainty, rumours flew about Müller. Some said he had defected to the East, others that he had been seen in South America. The public imagination was to be titillated for years by similar unsubstantiated reports of the reappearance of Martin Bormann. Bormann had been Hitler's private secretary and Head of the Party Chancellery. His posts had given him unparalleled knowledge and power: control over Party finances and appointments, control over what documents Hitler saw and who had access to him. Bormann had the Führer's total trust; by 1942 he was virtually his Deputy. He was hated and feared by everyone else.

When the Allied authorities started looking for Bormann in May 1945, most reports suggested he was dead. But how he died remained a mystery. He had left the bunker on 30 April. One witness swore he had then committed suicide and that his body had been seen in Berlin; another, Hitler's chauffeur, claimed to have seen him killed by a Russian anti-tank shell as both men sheltered either side of a German tank trying to break through the Russian lines.

There were no such doubts about the fate of Heinrich Himmler, the man who had developed the SS from a bodyguard for Hitler of 200 men into a state within the state, controlling all police, concentration camps, and the Waffen-SS to rival the Wehrmacht. Himmler had died before many witnesses. He alone of Hitler's inner circle had admitted the reality of defeat. His only hope was to save his skin. He abandoned Hitler and Berlin, tried to start peace negotiations with the Allies, hoped to curry favour by calling off the slaughter of the Jews. Hitler had denounced him in his last will and testament and stripped him of all offices. Once Germany surrendered, Himmler made pathetically feeble attempts to go to ground – he shaved off his moustache, wore a patch over one eye. But while he was trying to work through Allied lines into Bavaria on 3 May he was captured at a British control point. He remained at a British interrogation centre for several weeks without being recognized until he seemed to lose patience with his captors and decided to announce his identity. Soon afterwards Himmler bit on the cyanide capsule in his mouth and died.

The disappearance from the scene of the major figures still left a long list of Nazi leaders whom the Allies wished to capture and treat as war criminals. Few of them were found in Berlin; most had fled the city long since, while it was still possible to escape from the Russians.

Walther Funk, the president of the Reichsbank from 1939 and former Minister of Economics, was found there, though. An early interrogation report described him as 'a tubby homosexual suffering from diabetes, and afflicted at the moment with bladder pains.' (1) When he was moved to internment in Baden-Baden, Funk lived up to his name – sweating furiously and scared to death of his interrogator. (2) In Berlin too was Admiral Raeder, the commander-in-chief of the German Navy until 1943. He was captured by the Russians and kept under close house arrest. They moved to Moscow however, Hans Fritzsche – a subordinate of Goebbels at the Propaganda Ministry. His broadcasts during the War had earned him the title of 'His Master's Voice'. Since the Russians could not take Goebbels prisoner, they had to rest content with his dog. They put Fritzsche in the Lubianka prison and for the next few months gave him the customary Russian treatment for prisoners: deprivation of sleep, intensive interrogation, and standardized confessions to sign. (3)

There was no difficulty in finding one group of suspects on the Allied lists. They were known to have formed a new government under Admiral Doenitz at Flensburg in Schleswig-Holstein, near the Danish border. Hitler had named Doenitz as his successor in his will. This cabinet had no illusions about escaping military defeat; they defined their main task as staving off surrender while they pulled back as much as possible of the Germany Army and the civilian population in the East to save them from the Russians. They had sent Admiral Hans von Friedeburg and General Jodl to General Eisenhower's headquarters in Rheims to stall, but within a week of taking office Doenitz had been obliged to accept unconditional surrender.

Even so, visitors to Flensburg then witnessed a ludicrous example of the muddle of Allied policy at the end of the War. Though the Allies occupied the city, though German sovereignty had been signed away, for a further fortnight Doenitz's skeleton government still gave the impression of functioning. Every morning its members held cabinet meetings and solemnly discussed and voted on plans they had no power to implement. When J.K. Galbraith, the American economist, arrived there on 19 May as part of the American team investigating the effects of Allied heavy bombing of Germany, he boggled at the sight of the Allied officers scrupulously saluting German officers who were milling about the streets supervising the massive influx of their troops returning from Denmark and the east. When Galbraith's survey team drove out of the town, they had to stop twice at German military control posts before reaching the moated schloss where Albert Speer was in residence and at leisure after cabinet meetings to help them with their investigations. The schloss and the minister were guarded by an SS detachment. The Americans reached the conclusion that the

Allied authorities simply could not work out the correct protocol for taking the surrender of a government that had ceased to exist in consequence of its unconditional surrender. So for the moment they were leaving it some trappings while acting elsewhere as if it did not exist. Speer wished it did not. He suggested to Galbraith and his colleagues that they 'arrest him and so spare him this *opéra bouffe*' which with some pride in his mastery of the American idiom he called 'Grade B Warner Brothers.' (4)

The last act of the *opéra bouffe* was finally performed on the morning of 23 May. Galbraith stood on the upper deck of the Hamburg-America line vessel the *Patria* and watched Admirals Doenitz and Friedeburg as they 'came smartly along the quay, saluted the ship and flag and marched up the gangplank' to surrender the final tattered remnant of the Third Reich.

The capitulation of the Doenitz government resulted in the arrest of all its members; among them several of those who were to end in the dock at Nuremberg: Doenitz himself, Jodl, Speer, and Keitel who had previously escaped arrest by the Russians when he refused their pressing invitation to stay in Berlin when he took them a draft surrender.

Lurking in Flensburg was someone who had been refused a post in the Doenitz cabinet – Alfred Rosenberg, the Nazi ideologue, Party member before Hitler, once the supreme authority in the Eastern Occupied Territories captured from the Russians, and Goering's greatest rival as an art looter. His books had been the bibles of the doctrine of Aryan racial superiority. He would only allow them to be translated into the suitably 'Aryan' Scandinavian and Baltic languages (the Baltic states had to be Aryan – that was where Rosenberg himself was born). An interrogation report said that Rosenberg's books had 'assured him a place among the more unintelligible prophets' but the interrogator complained: 'It would take time and patience for an ordinary mortal to get a footing in the world of Alfred Rosenberg.' (5) He had been found by British soldiers, who were actually searching for Himmler, in a hospital where he was recovering from a sprained ankle – the result of a drinking bout in which he had been drowning his sorrows, or his panic.

As panic had gripped so many of the Nazi leaders in the final weeks of the War, they had scattered – hoping to lie low, hoping above all to escape the Russians from whom they expected short shrift or a lingering death in a prisoner-of-war camp in the coming winter. It was a daunting task to track down those listed as major war criminals. For a start the Allied forces had so many other problems to tackle. Their military duties did not cease with Germany's formal surrender: they were still on alert in case fanatics tried to continue the fight and they had to bring in and install the equipment needed for military occupation. Furthermore, the forces were now responsible for the entire administration of the country. That was a frightening challenge. The country was divided into Four Zones under each of the four major Powers. In the British zone alone there were something like a million wounded Germans, a million and a half prisoners-of-war, up to a million foreign workers who were unwilling or unable to go home. The occupying forces had to keep law and order, decide whether to shelter and feed the population which, thanks to the fighting, was now huddled in the ruins of cities and, thanks to the destruction of transport, virtually unable to obtain food unless the Allies provided it. They had to repair or construct from scratch basic services – water, electricity, sewage. They had to establish institutions for running their own Zones and co-ordinating with the others. Given the plight of Germany and the complexity of the problems the Allies faced, war criminals might well seem a secondary priority.

The physical problems of going out to find them were acute. Ivone Kirkpatrick, the newly-appointed British Political Adviser to General Eisenhower, witnessed some of them when he struggled to drive from British headquarters at Bad Oeynhausen to Frankfurt. 'Everything which modern man considers necessary to the maintenance of life in a civilized society had disappeared,' he wrote. 'There was no government authority, no police. No trains, trams or cars; no factories working, no postal service, no telephones, no newspapers, no banks. No shop was open and it would have been impossible to buy a loaf of bread, a glass of beer or an aspirin. Every bridge was blown and the available rolling stock could be seen marooned between the ruins ... In the countryside the sudden departure of the foreign labourers had halted agricultural work ... The only sign of life was provided by hundreds of thousands of Germans on foot, trekking in all directions.' (6)

Somewhere among those miserable crowds on the roads might be the leading Nazi war criminals. Where should anyone start looking for them when half the population seemed to be constantly on the move? The UNWCC lists gave the last known addresses of suspects – sometimes it was that of the official residence in Berlin, now deserted; sometimes it was that of the old home, not lived in for years, thanks to the exigencies of official life and the war. The military went to the addresses they had been given – time and again all they found was a pile of rubble. They looked too in their prisoner-of-war and internment camps. Sometimes they found they already held wanted men; sometimes prisoners gave them information on likely whereabouts. Given the vast number of such camps, not just in the Four Zones of Germany but in Austria and the liberated countries, all of which were constantly receiving new inmates, checking them was time consuming and frustrating. There was too little communication between the searchers and with the authorities who might hold their prey; up-to-date intelligence circulated haphazardly if at all. Under these circumstances it is hardly surprising that the roundup of many leading Nazi war criminals took months. It is amazing that they were found at all. Tip-offs, folly and fluke were as important as skill and determination in running them to ground.

One of those who evaded capture longest was Joachim von Ribbentrop, Hitler's Foreign Minister. He was arrested by the British on 14 June in Hamburg where he had been denounced by an acquaintance from his former days as a champagne salesman. He was discovered in bed in pink and white pyjamas. A medical examination revealed a small tin of poison taped to 'the lower part of his body'. (7) Clearly he did not expect to have to use it for when he was escorted from his flat he was carefully carrying a letter addressed to 'Montgommery' and asking for an interview with 'Mr Vincent Churchill' (sic). No doubt he hoped to show the British Prime Minister the paper he had been working on dealing with Hitler's purported last wishes relating to German friendship with Britain. Churchill seems to have been anxious to prevent Russian suspicion of Western collusion with the last remnants of the dying Hitler regime. He immediately forwarded a copy of the Ribbentrop paper to Stalin, adding characteristically: 'I thought you might be interested in some of its contents, though it is extremely lengthy and dull.' (8)

The man Ribbentrop had succeeded as Ambassador to London and as Foreign Minister, Baron Constantin Neurath, was captured by the French. The Canadians caught Arthur Seyss-Inquart, who for four days had once been the Chancellor of Austria, but more recently had been Reichsprotektor of Holland.

Fritz Sauckel, who had run the Nazi forced labour schemes and been Governor of Thuringia, was unmasked by a young Austrian improbably called Rudolf Ripper. When Edgar Snow, the American journalist, snatched a brief interview with Sauckel in an internment camp he found him at first 'a dark little man, sullen and suspicious'. Sauckel soon became a little more relaxed and assured Snow that Hitler had understood the problems of unemployment, Jewish profiteering and the Red menace, and that Nazism had been supported by the entire nation – 'only a few troublemakers opposed us'. He strenuously maintained that few people had been murdered by the regime, though 'some enemies of the State had to be eliminated, of course', and that all his foreign workers had been volunteers – they were so much better off in Germany than at home. Concentration camps? Sauckel himself had inspected them; he could promise Snow that they were models of hygiene and health. Having reviewed with some pride the achievements of the regime he had served, Sauckel suddenly broke into lachrymose bewilderment. 'For two days now I have been kept here, and again and again I have asked myself why? Why? I swear by God that I am an innocent man who wronged no one. My only crime is that I loved Germany.' Here Snow noted that Sauckel's eyes filled with tears. 'I love the German working people. Do you understand? I married a working woman, a good woman. She served me well. She gave me ten children – a good German wife.' (9)

Others carried off arrest and detention with rather more aplomb and style than Sauckel. Franz von Papen, Reich Chancellor in 1932, who had negotiated the appointment of Hitler as Chancellor of Germany in 1933, and then served as his Deputy Chancellor before going as ambassador to Vienna at the time of the Anschluss, was run to ground by an American platoon in Westphalia. Papen had been constantly on the run since leaving his embassy in Turkey in August 1944, fearing arrest first by the Gestapo, then by the Allies. As he told the story, the Americans found him eating stew with his grandchildren in a lodge in the woods where he was living with his daughter. Papen asked them to sit and wait while he packed a few things in a rucksack. (10) A few Nazis had the forethought to pack sensibly at the moment of arrest, and they were to be grateful for it in the coming months. Many did not – according to temperament they either expected instant execution or immediate release. Changes of underwear, a spare shirt, warm woollens for the winter did not seem a major priority.

Papen's arrest caused consternation at the Foreign Office. It raised in far more acute form than Ribbentrop's the danger of Soviet misinterpretation of his presence behind Western lines. 'I cannot imagine a more unwelcome prisoner,' wrote a Foreign Office official. 'More peace feelers have been associated with his name than almost any other prominent German.' (11) The Foreign Office moved fast to head off any possible Allied misunderstandings. Within six days of his detention, Papen found himself at Eisenhower's headquarters facing the senior British and American military intelligence chiefs in Europe – and two Soviet generals. He told them little of any military or political significance, but demonstrated an amazing self-confidence. 'He was extremely well-dressed, beautiful silk suit etc., and it was clear that he had intended to fall into the hands of the Americans and had dressed up for the occasion,' said the Foreign Office report on the meeting. He indicated his belief that he still had a role to play liaising between the Germans and the Allies. When Major General Strong, the British Head of Military Intelligence at SHAEF, asked the Foreign Office if he should seek a further, private, interview with Papen, he was put sharply in his place: 'Such an interview must under no circumstances take place – Papen is as dangerous as a hamadryad snake – he could do us no good.' (12) So he was moved to a chateau near Spa, where he found 'comfortable accommodation' and a 'normal civilized life' (13) chatting to old acquaintances like Admiral Horthy, the ex-Regent of Hungary.

The richest haul of prospective defendants of the Nazi regime fell to the Americans in the South. In Austria they found Dr Ernst Kaltenbrunner – with the death of Himmler and Müller, and the disappearance of Eichmann, the nearest who could be found as a Gestapo chief. Baldur von Schirach, the former Gauleiter of Vienna and leader of the Hitler Youth movement, was there too. For a long time he had been thought to be dead; indeed he heard a report of his own death on the BBC. It was assumed that either he had fallen in the last fight for Vienna or had been shot by Austrian patriots. In fact he was living in the Tyrol, posing as 'Richard Falk the novelist' and writing a detective story called *The Secrets of Myrna Loy* – it is not clear whether the title indicated an infatuation with the Hollywood filmstar. Perhaps he might have escaped detection, but on 4 June he heard on the radio about the arrests of Hitler Youth leaders and decided to give himself up and accept his responsibility for the movement. He tried writing to local American headquarters to announce his whereabouts and desire to surrender, but his letter was treated as a bad joke. Finally he came to the headquarters in Schwaz, announced in English 'I am Schirach', and was duly arrested. He wrote to his wife from prison: 'I want to speak before a court of law and take the blame on myself. Through me the young have learned to believe in Hitler. I taught them to have faith in him, now I must free them from this error. Once I have had the opportunity to say this before an international court of law, then let them hang me.' (14)

Much less co-operative was Wilhelm Frick, caught in Munich. He was the lawyer who had drawn up Hitler's application for German citizenship, the Enabling Act which gave the Nazi Party its grip on Germany, and so much of the Anti-Jewish legislation. His pet scheme had been the euthanasia programme – the State-ordained killing of 'useless eaters'. Up to 1943 Frick had been Minister of the Interior; he then went to Bohemia and Moravia as Protector. His interrogator sourly noted that: 'the attempt to combine the character of an ardent Party member with that of an orthodox minister has resulted in Frick in a rather negative and defensive witness, with something of the expression of a cornered rat when he is pressed.' (15) Frick was not to change in the coming months.

As the war ended, the Berchtesgaden area became a great magnet for leading Nazis. Here they were near their Führer's favourite retreat, the Berghof. There may never have been a plan for a final stand in the mountain redoubt as the popular press believed, but at least they felt happy in the mountains, finding reassurance among the scenes of their former glory when in the early days of the War they had relaxed on Hitler's terrace, eating chocolate cake, bullying foreign visitors and posing for Eva Braun's home movies, their every wish catered for by particularly fine specimens of Aryan manhood in immaculate SS uniform.

Whatever their precise motives, Hans Frank, the lawyer and civil administrator of Poland was picked up there in the course of a routine American round-up. He handed over to his captors the diary of his administration of Poland – 11,367 typed pages of it. Then he tried to sever his arteries, cutting his throat and both wrists, but only succeeded in paralysing his left hand and arm. When Edgar Snow visited him in 193 Evac Hospital near Munich, he reported that Frank's neck and wrists were ringed with jagged festering sores where he scratched his wounds. Frank protested that he was a man of culture, not a gangster. After all, he had opened the first Chopin museum Cracow ever had. He added that the extermination camps at Maidanek and Auschwitz were Himmler's work not his. 'All Poles know that I loved their country,' he claimed to Snow. 'They are a fine people.' (16) It was a praise that squared oddly with a reference in his diary: 'If we win the war then as far as I am concerned the Poles and the Ukrainians and the rest can be turned into minced meat.'

Near Berchtesgaden, the Americans also found Dr Robert Ley – in a mountain hut, shaking from top to toe and dressed in blue pyjamas, a Tyrolese hat and climbing boots. Ley's Labour Front had replaced the independent German trades union and been a mere instrument of the Nazi party: fixing wages, hours and working conditions. He had created the 'Strength through Joy' movement to control the workers' leisure activities. Ley had once told the workers: 'The Führer is always right. Obey the Führer.' He now offered himself to the Americans as a brilliant leader of the working classes who could help them solve all their social problems. But they were far from impressed by this quivering alcoholic. An early interrogation report noted Ley's speech impediment which appeared when he got excited, 'as he is apt to do when, for example, he thinks of the attempt on the Führer's life on 20 July 1944', and the tears when he thought of his failure to get Anglo-German understanding or the implementation of all the social reforms he had planned. (17)

In the same area an American patrol stumbled on Julius Streicher, the Jew-baiter, the editor of the anti-Semitic paper *Der Stürmer*, a journal so obscene and repulsive that even many devoted Nazis could not bear to read it. He was sitting painting on the verandah of a farmhouse when the patrol's commander, Major Blitt, came to ask for a glass of milk. Streicher explained that he was not the farmer but 'Mr Seiler, an artist'. They began to talk; Blitt wanted to know why people had joined the Nazi party. They talked in Yiddish. But Streicher could not keep up his act for long. When Blitt commented on his resemblance to Julius Streicher he blurted out: 'How did you recognize me?' Off went Streicher in the jeep. (18)

Rather further from Berchtesgaden, 35 miles from Salzburg, was the biggest catch of all, Hermann Goering, a man who had held innumerable posts and for a long time had been second only to Hitler in military, economic, and diplomatic matters, a man who had looted Europe for his private art collection, but who by May 1945 had been sacked by the Führer for offering to take over the leadership of the Reich. He was refused any office in the successor government by Doenitz and was under SS house arrest at Mauterndorf. Always ready with the grand gesture, Goering had sent Field Marshal Brauchitsch to Eisenhower and the local American commander asking for protection from the Gestapo and the SS. Concerned too to be suitably dressed for the occasion, Goering had ordered a new uniform in the colour of his captors rather than of the Luftwaffe. When the Americans failed to provide the required assistance and welcome, Goering drove off to surrender, graciously waving from side to side and acknowledging German soldiers trudging to their prisoner-of-war camps.

The following day came closer to measuring up to his expectations. He was given a press conference at Army headquarters at Kitzbühel, with popping champagne corks and flashing cameras. It was just what he was used to and just what he had expected. But Goering's little pleasures proved shortlived. He was moved from Kitzbühel to Augsburg the following day, where he lived with two aides in a working-class suburb. He was under house arrest again but this time in a dingy flat with no bath and no lavatory.

Perhaps the only man with any reason to welcome arrest was Hjalmar Schacht, once President of the Reichsbank, Minister for the Economy and

Plenipotentiary for the War Economy. Since being accused of complicity in the 1944 Bomb Plot against Hitler, Dr Schacht had been in prison and concentration camps; guards at the Flossenburg camp had instructions to shoot him should the Americans arrive. Instead, he was moved to Dachau, to a special enclosure for distinguished prisoners called a 'prominenten laager'. There Schacht joined an extraordinary collection of some of the more remarkable people to fall foul of the Führer, including Pastor Martin Niemoeller, the distinguished Lutheran theologian, Fritz Thyssen, the industrialist, Leon Blum, and the former Austrian Chancellor, Kurt Schuschnigg.

Finally Schacht did indeed fall into American hands and was interned in Kransberg Castle in the Taunus Mountains. He was taken off on one occasion for interrogation – against a receipt for 'the live body of Dr Schacht'. His interrogator recorded that Schacht 'appeared to be in excellent health if somewhat too querulous and disconcerted for a coherent discussion'. Schacht was in fact fizzing with rage. He could not understand why a man imprisoned by the Nazis should now be held captive by their enemies; he kept telling his interrogator that he had plotted against Hitler. He was most indignant that his captors had taken his watch and that he had too few clothes. When asked if he had ever tried to inform himself about conditions and policies under the Nazis by considering Allied versions of the facts – listening to the BBC for example – he dismissed the idea with characteristic contempt: 'The BBC dealt only in rotten propaganda – Jewish if not in diction in style, of the kind no decent German would listen to.' (19)

Then he was sent back to Kransberg. The castle had once been renovated and decorated by Albert Speer as a Luftwaffe headquarters for Goering. Appropriately enough, the architect himself arrived in August to join Schacht and the other civilian leaders interned there. Soon after Speer learned that he was to be tried as a war criminal he was visited by George Ball, another member of the American bombing survey still anxious to pick Speer's brains. Speer was more interested in his trial than in bombs. 'Will you be my lawyer, Mr Ball?' Mr Ball thought not. 'Well, you're making a mistake,' chided Speer. 'Many young lawyers have made their reputations by representing notorious personalities and you'll never get a better chance.' (20) But Ball still refused the offer. Having missed this chance he had to make his reputation the hard way, as a politician and diplomat.

Men like Speer and Schacht had been classified by the Allies as 'technicians'; Kransberg was known irreverently to the jailors as 'Dustbin'. The leading politicians, diplomats and military figures were concentrated in another camp, equally sardonically called 'Ashcan'. 'How these creatures must loathe each other.' commented a Foreign Office official as he mused on the list of the inmates of 'Ashcan'. (21)

Fifty-two eminent Nazis, from whom fifteen would eventually be chosen as defendants before the Military Tribunal, were collected between May and August in Bad Mondorf – or Mondorf-les-Bains – in Luxemburg. Mondorf stands on a plateau about six kilometres from the dramatic gorge of the Mosel and the border with Germany. A tiny stream trickles along one side of the town and marks the frontier with France. The rolling countryside can be seen from almost every part of the town – mainly vineyards, but scattered with patches of light mixed woodland. It was a convenient place to keep such prominent prisoners. It was small (in 1982 its population was only 2,000) and stood at the T-junction of two roads going nowhere in particular, so the American military would have no problem in surrounding and guarding the area and suspicious visitors would be easy to spot. The town offered reasonable housing for a garrison in substantial, comfortable, mainly late-19th-century villas or in three or four small hotels. It also provided ideal accommodation for the prisoners – the Grand Hotel. Mondorf was a spa, promising that its two thermal springs would do wonders for rheumatism or complaints of the liver. The Grand Hotel had been its leading hotel and the centre for the cure. It was rather a graceless building – shaped like a boomerang, the entrance on the north side, a broad terrace facing the sun on the south. It was six stories high, with two additional tiers of attics, and its plain stucco façade was hardly cheered by crude art deco panels. It can never have been a delightful hotel; it made a reasonably suitable prison. Access to it along the only road could easily be barricaded. The hotel's garden and park, with some fine old trees, were overlooked by slopes on three sides which gave a clear view of any activity in the grounds, and sight of all approaches from the countryside beyond.

Before the first prisoners arrived, the US Army stripped the Grand Hotel of any of its fading splendour and comfort. Out went the furniture and carpets to be replaced with camp beds and straw mattresses. Windows too were replaced, first with wire netting, then, as soon as available, with shatterproof glass and bars. A stockade with four watchtowers went up round the garden.

None of this was good enough for 'Ashcan's' new commandant, who was to figure prominently in the months of the trial itself. Colonel Burton C. Andrus was once described in a *Time* profile as a 'pompous, unimaginative and thoroughly likeable officer', 'a plump little figure looking like an inflated pouter pigeon ... impeccably garbed in his uniform and highly shellacked helmet.' (22) In his *Memoirs*, Andrus leapt to defend himself against the charge which hurt most: 'My weight was 160 lb, height 5 feet 10 inches, chest 44 inches, waist 36 inches – kept trim by fresh campaigns in combat and active water polo matches against subordinates. A *plump* pouter pigeon?' (23) Colonel Andrus had been a cavalry officer in the First World War; he had spent much of the Second in England as an observer, and then moved to Europe with the US Army at the time of the invasion. His qualification for the new job seems to have been the months in 1917 he spent as a military prison officer at Fort Ogelthorpe, Georgia.

Andrus looked at the Grand Hotel, sized up his prisoners, and evidently saw the position in a flash. 'Mondorf,' he wrote, 'no one had to tell me, was a powder keg.' (24) Did nobody realize these Nazis would try to commit suicide? (Goering had arrived carrying two cyanide capsules.) The fountain in the garden had to be drained – not much harm could be self-inflicted on a sundial. Braces, shoelaces, razors, watches, all had to be removed – they could all be used for suicide, for savage attacks on fellow prisoners, as weapons in a mass break-out. And the tables in the prisoners' rooms had to go; only tables which collapsed at a touch would do – there was no limit to what a crazed Nazi could do with a table. And this was not all. Who had stopped to think of the hordes of SS fanatics, the Werewolf suicide squads? Any minute now they could storm the perimeter fence, hail down on the hotel roof in parachutes, rescue their heroes and charge off to restore the Reich. To prevent this possibility, everything had to be floodlit, machine gun posts put at every angle, and camouflage nets draped to fool daredevil Luftwaffe pilots. Had no one heard of Skorzeny, swooping down to rescue Mussolini from internment in 1943?

And Andrus spotted another threat wantonly ignored by others – lynching. Who would not want to lynch these evil Nazis? In Luxemburg alone, 160 people had just returned from Dachau. Europe was filled with hundreds of thousands of Nazi victims itching to tear Andrus' prisoners limb from limb. And look at those trees in the park – gifts to snipers. Even by July, Andrus could not rest secure in the formidable defences he had created: day or night he had to be ready to 'knock our allies back with guns' to prevent lynching.

All too soon, Andrus lost a valuable element in his security arrangements – secrecy. The authorities did not want the whereabouts of the Nazi leaders known, but rumours spread. The newspapers began to print stories about top Nazis and their 'life of luxury and ease'. By 14 July, the *Chicago Daily News* had identified the location as 'The Palace Hotel, Mondorf'. For Moscow Radio a few days later, this was easily translated into 'a Luxemburg palace' where Nazi War leaders were 'getting even fatter and more insolent ... These notorious war criminals rest in Luxemburg after their sanguinary carnage ... Nothing but the finest vintages and finest foods will do for them. Servants noiselessly bring delicious wines on silver trays ... and the latest model automobiles are theirs to drive around the grounds.' (25) Given the general Press picture, it was little comfort to Colonel Andrus that a very few newspapers had already christened him 'The Mondorf Monster'. He had to get the record straight.

On 16 July, representatives of the world's Press were invited to visit Mondorf. They were followed in later weeks by many more – public curiosity about the Grand Hotel's inmates was insatiable. Andrus made the situation clear to his visitors: (26) 'We stand for no mollycoddling here. These men are in jail. We have certain rules and these rules are obeyed.' He scotched the rumours about luxury. The reporters were given a briefing on the prisoners' diet: breakfast at 7.30 a.m. – cereal, soup and coffee; lunch at midday – pea soup, beef hash and spinach; supper at 6.30 p.m. – powdered eggs, potatoes and tea. All standard prisoner-of-war rations, all eaten off glazed earthenware with one spoon. And – 'they roll their own cigarettes.' The reporters peered at the rooms, noted the sparse furniture, were duly impressed by the stockade, the floodlights, the machine guns. The *Daily Telegraph* expressed some surprise that Admiral Doenitz's cupboard contained pink underwear (27) and the *New York Herald Tribune* recorded with interest that Ribbentrop's room was said to be often untidy. An American captain had complained: 'He is often lackadaisical in this respect and I have had him on the carpet several times.' (28) There was no such problem with Keitel. His room was always spotless, his blankets perfectly boxed, everything constantly ready for kit inspection. Andrus approved of Keitel – he would have made an excellent First Sergeant, he would obey anything his commander ordered. He was a perfect prisoner – until the day that he wrote to General Eisenhower to complain that his Field Marshal's baton had been taken from him by the prison authorities.

As Andrus' charges arrived at 'Ashcan' he worried about how to lick them into shape. So many of them were obviously unhealthy. Frank in particular was deep in melancholia and needed constant attention. According to an American doctor who examined him on arrival: 'his left elbow and wrist were severely cut, his right wrist was cut. The wounds have practically healed now but he will have a permanently crippled left hand.' More luridly, the *New York Times* confided to its readers that on his arrival Frank was wearing 'only lace panties'. (29)

There were several doctors at hand, including Dr Pfluecker, a fellow prisoner. But they needed watching, thought Andrus. Prisoners asked for sleeping pills, then hid them and started a collection. Andrus knew what that was for. Too many of these Nazis, he thought, did not yet seem to understand that the good old days were over. Ley had told a prison officer that he could do without food and drink but he must have female company. Perhaps he could provide the authorities with some really interesting statements, if only he could dictate them to a golden haired secretary. (30) When Streicher arrived, no one wanted to sit near him; no one ever did, especially at meals. 'I fixed that,' Andrus told the *New York Herald Tribune*. 'I told them the Wehrmacht and Navy no longer existed, that even their state no longer existed and that they would eat with anybody I choose to place at the table.' (31)

Andrus's biggest problem, however, was Goering. (32) The Field Marshal had arrived at the Grand Hotel suitably equipped for his stay in a spa, with sixteen monogrammed suitcases, a red hatbox, a dazzling collection of rings, watches, medals, cufflinks, and his valet, Robert Krupp. Andrus looked at the luggage; during the medical examination, he surveyed the Field Marshal. Goering without clothes was surely more awful than with them. He had red finger nails – and red toe nails. And as if that was not bad enough, Goering had brought with him 20,000 paracodeine tablets, his substitute for his morphine addiction – he took twenty every morning and twenty every evening. Andrus was not going to have an addict in his prison. He contacted the Director of the FBI, the legendary J. Edgar Hoover, who replied with instructions from the Narcotics Bureau. Goering's dose must be cut by one tablet at a time. It was a painful process. Goering whimpered, and complained of headaches and sleeplessness. But he was weaned by 12 August. In the opinion of Dr Kelley, an American psychiatrist who worked with the prisoners at Mondorf and later in Nuremberg, Goering's pill taking was more of a habit than an addiction by now – he munched handfuls of what were in fact specially made paracodeine tablets of a very low dosage as others might munch sweets. Prison life proved to be good for his figure too. When he came to Mondorf, he weighed 270 lb. By the end of July, he was down to 240 lb and a doctor proudly told an Associated Press reporter: 'We had to take a six inch tuck in his pants to keep him from losing them.' (33)

As his health improved, so did Goering's personality. At first he was frightened, saying accusingly to the guards: 'You are going to kill me tomorrow.' He was so nervous that Andrus appointed Field Marshal Kesselring to look after him. Even so, one night during a thunderstorm, Goering had a heart attack. 'I was all by myself when the storm came. It worried me.' (34) But soon the old Goering resilience, the vitality, the magnetism came back. He began to attract a circle of prisoners around himself – dominating them, cheering them up, giving them doses of his courage and determination to fight. Not all the prisoners were attracted. The old Flensburg group clung to Doenitz and retained their dislike for flashy Hermann. As the two rival social groups coalesced, only two men were left out – no one wanted anything to do with Ley or Streicher.

Colonel Andrus had tackled his security difficulties, solved his prisoners' health problems, and tried to impose some good order and military discipline on men used to command. Yet Andrus was never satisfied; he worried incessantly. Others, however, noticed that his regime was beginning to have an effect. When Ivone Kirkpatrick came to the Grand Hotel, he found Ribbentrop, Rosenberg, Streicher, Doenitz, Neurath, Raeder and Funk sunning themselves in basket chairs on the terrace. There was a quickening of interest as they saw a visitor. A corporal called them to attention. All stood except Doenitz, who sat huddled and sulking in his chair. 'Get up, that man,' roared the corporal, and Grand Admiral Doenitz shuffled to his feet. (35)

Kirkpatrick like many others came to the Grand Hotel to interview the prisoners. He was glad to leave – he compared the place to a 'criminal lunatic asylum'. When Galbraith came he, too, was far from impressed by the inmates. He shared the reaction of a man who escorted him: 'Who'd have thought that we were fighting this war against a bunch of jerks?' (36) 'Ashcan' was not just an internment camp; it became increasingly an interrogation centre where some of the preliminary spadework for the future trial was carried out. Sixteen booths were built; interrogations were carried out in them every day, often lasting several hours at a time. The prisoners encountered the usual tricks of the trade: the harmless questions to throw them off their guard, the constant harping back to check consistency in accounts, the alternating rough and friendly approaches. Everything was taken down in shorthand. It was an experience most of them looked forward to. When some Russian interrogators appeared on 24 July, Goering shouted: 'I won't see them. I won't talk to them.' (37) But he did – for two days. Interrogations were enjoyed. They offered a chance to relish former power and conquest, to fight old battles and produce the old political arguments – perhaps more effectively than last time. Sometimes the interrogations fed a sense of superiority. When Papen was interrogated by Thomas Dodd, ultimately a prosecutor at Nuremberg, at the beginning of September he noted that Dodd was 'polite, correct, even kind' but 'in the course of our discussion it became clear that he had only a very superficial knowledge of events and internal developments in Germany.' (38) No doubt – but Dodd and the others were learning fast, thanks to interrogating the very men who had controlled events and developments. So were the prisoners. Though they might not know it, the interrogations gave them a chance to rehearse their stories and excuses for later use in the trial.

In the case of Ribbentrop, he began as he was to continue – emphasizing his own 'lack of importance and responsibility'. Before his American and British military interrogators, Ribbentrop's once renowned public pose of cold austerity and aloofness was replaced by a rather desperate and unconvincing jocularity and affability. What struck the interrogators was Ribbentrop's general vagueness – genuine, they assumed, not feigned – and what they could only describe as a 'rather obvious lack of mental fibre'. On these grounds they cautioned that Ribbentrop's interrogation report should be treated 'with reservation'. What was clear was that Ribbentrop was already desperately anxious about the future. As the interrogation ended, he ventured the opinion that 'he had not thought that the war would come to such proportions that governments were placed under arrest'. When his interrogators sat in stony silence, ignoring what was in effect a plea for reassurance, they noted that 'Ribbentrop's expression was one of nervous consternation and his exit less assured than his entrance.' (39)

Yet, in general, interrogations made a welcome break in what became a dull routine: talking, walking under escort, playing chess, drafts, or Monopoly. The prisoners were cut off entirely from the outside world; they had no radio, no newspapers, they received no letters. Andrus made some attempt to relieve their boredom. General Warlimont and Vice Admiral Buerkner were persuaded to give English lessons every day. Other prisoners were timetabled to give lectures three afternoons a week – Count Schwerin von Krosigk, the former Finance Minister and later Prime Minister under Doenitz, treated them to his views on Shakespeare; Funk enlightened them as to the benefits of paper currency; and Ley staggered them with his plans to reconstruct Germany using prefabricated units and *private* enterprise. How his views had changed! They were given occasional film shows – but only Allied films of the concentration camps.

The prisoners at Mondorf took time to adjust to their confinement, and they remained puzzled as to exactly why they were there. No one told them about the fast-maturing plans for a trial. Some of them had shared Ribbentrop's expectation on arrest: 'I know that we are all on the list of war criminals and I can see that in the present state of world opinion only one verdict can be expected – sentence of death.' (40) They had expected instant execution. Others, however, could hardly believe that persons of their eminence could conceivably be tried. At his post-surrender Press conference in Kitzbühel, Goering had been surprised at the question: 'Do you know that you are on the list of war criminals?' 'No,' he replied, 'that question surprises me very much for I cannot imagine why I should be.' (41) By July, he was still complaining about his imprisonment: 'I don't understand it at all. I have lots of affairs to settle in Germany.' (42)

Doenitz too was all injured innocence and self-importance. 'They cannot condemn me just because I assumed power in a country where everyone wanted me to take over. The Allies will end by regretting the passing of the old regime.' (43) Most prisoners accepted that some of their colleagues were war criminals. Papen moved from an annexe into the Grand Hotel at the beginning of August. 'To my horror,' he wrote, 'I found myself in the company of Goering, Ribbentrop, Rosenberg and their satellites.' (44)

Unknown to all of them, this was to be the company in which they were to stand trial for their part in the Third Reich. Unknown to them, the plans for the trial were – despite difficulties – drawing to fruition. Typically, it was the canny Speer who first heard of the trial and his involvement in it. Radios were not allowed in 'Ashcan' but were permitted in the less strict 'Dustbin'. A fellow prisoner rushed in at six in the morning to tell Speer that he had been named as a defendant in the planned war crimes trial. Speer was shocked: 'I had never expected to be a defendant ... I was dumbfounded. In the camp there was a chemist who was said to possess several capsules of poison such as Himmler had used for his suicide. I cautiously hinted to him that I was looking for such a capsule, but he refused me in evasive language.' (45)

His co-defendants were to know soon enough. On Sunday 12 August, Colonel Andrus rounded up fifteen of his 'Ashcan' charges into two ambulances. They drove under escort to Luxemburg airport, then flew in two C-47s to Nuremberg. During the flight, Goering demonstrated a vigorous brand of gallows humour, continually pointing out to Ribbentrop geographical features such as the Rhine and urging him to take a look at them as he was unlikely to have another opportunity to do so. (46) Streicher was sick.

References for Chapter Three

1 Jackson Papers, Box 210
2 Conversation with his interrogator, later a prosecutor, Dan Margolies
3 Fritzsche

4   Galbraith
5   Jackson Papers, Box 210
6   Kirkpatrick
7   FO 371. 48478
8   FO 371. 46780
9   *Saturday Evening Post*, 28 July
10 Papen
11 FO 371. 46780
12 Ibid
13 Papen
14 Heydecker
15 Jackson Papers, Box 210
16 *Saturday Evening Post*, 28 July
17 Jackson Papers, Box 210
18 Heydecker
19 Jackson Papers, Box 210
20 George Ball
21 FO 371. 46777
22 *Time*, 28 October 1946
23 Andrus
24 This and many subsequent details of life in Mondorf from Andrus
25 Moscow Radio broadcast, 24 July forwarded by British Embassy to Foreign Office
26 *New York Herald Tribune*, 22 July
27 *Daily Telegraph*, 2 August
28 *New York Herald Tribune*, 22 July
29 *New York Times*, 25 July
30 *Daily Telegraph*, 2 August
31 *New York Herald Tribune*, 22 July
32 Details from Andrus' memoirs
33 AP 28 July
34 Ibid
35 Kirkpatrick
36 Galbraith
37 *New York Times*, 25 July
38 Papen
39 FO 371. 46786
40 Heydecker
41 Ibid
42 *Daily Express*, 18 July
43 Ibid
44 Papen
45 Speer *Spandau Diary*
46 FO 371. 51035

Chapter Four

The impetus to establish an international tribunal to try these major Nazi war criminals had come from America. It was accelerated by the outcry over the Malmedy massacre and direct experience of other atrocities once American forces invaded Europe, but it had begun and was sustained by the debate over the post-war settlement of Germany and Europe. Indeed it can almost be said that the Nuremberg Tribunal originated in an inter-departmental row in Washington over plans for the future of conquered Germany. (1)

Tentative thinking about what should ultimately be done with Germany had started in March 1943 when the American President, Franklin Roosevelt, asked his Secretary for War, Henry Stimson, and his Secretary of State, Cordell Hull, to outline their views. Both men had agreed that the Allies should insist on Germany's unconditional surrender, full Allied military occupation, de-Nazification, disarmament, and the dismantling of war industries. Neither wished to destroy German industry as a whole – they saw a tolerable standard of living as an essential condition for a flourishing future German democracy – and the only slight difference between them was that Hull thought subsistence adequate whereas Stimson preferred to allow for something slightly more comfortable.

These suggestions were not taken up by the President. While Allied victory remained a distant prospect, he preferred to devote his time and energy to winning the War rather than considering the peace. Thereafter, once Europe was invaded, he became increasingly sensitive to the argument that this time Germany must be taught more thoroughly than in 1918 the lesson of what happened to those who started and lost wars; he also became alert to public demands for punitive action against war criminals.

In this mood Roosevelt rejected two occupation policy guides which had been drawn up by the War Department in the autumn of 1944 for the use of the military, on the grounds that they were too lenient towards the Germans. He was prepared to lend a ready ear to strongly contrasting proposals from another member of his government.

In the United States Treasury, the Secretary, Henry Morgenthau, con-ceived and nurtured from August 1944 a dreadful retribution to be visited on Germany. The country which had waged war on Europe, exploited its peoples and resources, committed atrocities and exterminated millions, was to be torn to shreds. Germany must suffer – and must never again be capable of causing suffering to others. Under Morgenthau's plan, Germany must be demilitarized: the stern limitations on her armed services and armaments imposed by the Versailles Settlement in 1919 had not been enough – Germany had insisted on the right to defend herself, broken her Treaty obligations, and used her restored military might to subjugate and destroy Europe. This time demilitarization must be total and permanent. The Nazi Party had imposed a totalitarian regime on Germany, then used its country's strength to extend its evil doctrines over Europe. The Nazi Party must be destroyed: Germany must be de-Nazified, its officials at all levels of government and administration must be removed from their posts and interned. In view of their treatment of others it seemed fitting that they should in their turn be exploited – let them now be directed to forced labour, repairing some of the damage they had caused in Europe. Above all, Morgenthau saw German industry as the source of that country's seeming capacity for evil. German industrialists had backed Hitler, enthusiastically joined the Nazi Party in its schemes and finally and fatally provided the materiel for a second war. So German industry must be destroyed. For ever. Germany must be pastoralized: the country stripped of its industrial plant and reduced to a nation of farmers. Within this ruthless and bleak conception, where Morgenthau saw an entire nation as criminal, dealing with war criminals became a simple matter. Minor offenders could be sent back to the countries where their crimes had been committed. The names of major criminals should be issued to the Allied Forces. As the men were captured, they would be identified and shot.

The Morgenthau plan was repulsive to Henry Stimson, the Secretary for War. Stimson too wanted to achieve a permanent peace, but he did not believe, like Morgenthau, that this could be bred from vengeance and castration. Stimson saw lasting peace as the fruit of two strains: international co-operation and international legality. In principle, therefore, he could not accept a plan for the future of Europe which was based on Allied destruction of Germany – because Germany too must become a collaborator in the settlement. Neither could he accept a plan which countenanced Allied diktat and summary executions – from the beginning the new Europe must found its relations on legal processes and justice. In Stimson's eyes, Morgenthau's very principles were wrong. Furthermore, when it came to the details, Morgenthau's plan was both simplistic and self-defeating. As Stimson saw it, the destruction of German industry would seriously damage the economy of the whole of Europe. This could be no basis for reconstruction; it certainly made no sense to punish the whole of Europe for the alleged sins of German industrialists. In addition, by reducing Germany to starvation, the Allies would be creating all the conditions needed for dictatorship and war to breed again; the marginally more lenient treatment of the Versailles Settlement had provided ample scabs for the war-mongers to pick and infect, and Germans could not be secured as valuable contributors to the new European order if they were treated as criminals.

Stimson's criticisms of Morgenthau's plan for the Germans did not, however, involve any softness towards war criminals. He wanted to substitute more discriminating methods; to shift the approach from one based purely on punishment to one aimed at some degree of rehabilitation. He was unwilling to criminalize the entire German nation, but saw a therapeutic value in punishing internationally recognized war criminals: cleanse the German body politic to obtain a healthy partner for the future.

On 5 September 1944, Secretary Stimson sent a memorandum to the President and to Morgenthau: 'It is primarily by the thorough apprehension, investigation and trial of all the Nazi leaders and instruments of the Nazi system of terrorism such as the Gestapo, with punishment delivered as promptly, swiftly and severely as possible, that we can demonstrate the abhorrence which the world has for such a system and bring home to the German people our determination to extirpate it and its fruits forever.' Given Stimson's views on establishing international legality, there could only be one way in which this lesson could be delivered to the Germans and in which other nations could share in the educative process. Stimson wrote to Roosevelt on 9 September: '... the very punishment of these men in a dignified manner consistent with the advance of civilization will have the greater effect on posterity ... I am disposed to believe that, at least as to the chief Nazi officials, we should participate in an international tribunal constituted to try them.' (2) In taking this stand, Stimson had not only revived the scheme devised by the lawyers at Versailles, he had added his voice to those who had called for international action in the St James's Declaration.

It was apparent, then, that though the aim of Morgenthau and Stimson was the same – lasting peace – the methods they wanted to use and the principles behind their thinking were as far apart as they could be. There was little chance they could be persuaded to co-operate and reach a compromise. Stimson was seldom troubled by spasms of doubt. He regarded the voice of his conscience as the most reliable guide and on this issue he had heard it loud and clear. Morgenthau was a more flexible character and in nearly all his dealings a man of warmth and generosity. But he was prepared to dig in his heels over this issue and argue passionately for rigorous punishment for Germany. The two men had one thing in common – both had viewed aspects of German life with some dislike for many years. Stimson had hated Prussianism in the Great War and had thoroughly enjoyed fighting it for seven months in France. Morgenthau had been deeply shocked at the same time by what he saw as a tendency to resort to brutality among the German officials he met while staying at his father's embassy in Turkey.

From then, however, their views had diverged. Stimson might have opposed the Covenant of the League of Nations in 1919, but he had been influenced strongly by the views of Elihu Root, head of the law firm he had joined as a young man, and championed instead a World Court and the increased effectiveness of international law to control relations between states. For Stimson, the defeat of Germany in 1945 seemed to offer the chance of advancing this cause. Morgenthau, on the other hand, was more influenced by memories of the 1930s when he had been appalled by what he saw as the timorousness of American policy towards Japanese militarism and European fascism. He had urged a strong line then: from the time of the Sudetenland crisis he had called for positive aid to France and Britain; after Munich he had demanded readiness for war. He felt the result of ignoring his advice had been disastrous. Soft words and conciliatory action had not secured the peace in 1939; Morgenthau was certain they would not be adequate bases for lasting peace in 1945.

As if character and beliefs were not enough to keep Stimson and Morgenthau apart, they also had conflicting ambitions for their departments. Stimson already felt that the War Department had only received half-hearted support for its policies during the War. It had played little part in military strategy; he now wanted it to play a fuller part in the strategy for peace. After all, he could argue, if part of Germany was to be run by American military authorities, then their activities were primarily the responsibility of his department. Morgenthau, however, saw American involvement in the government of Germany more as a foreign policy matter. This view did not mean he was prepared to leave it to Cordell Hull and the State Department. He had often seen aspects of foreign policy as coming within the Treasury brief and he and Hull had clashed over such overlaps for years. Before the War Morgenthau had been exasperated by what he considered Hull's obsession with Free Trade as the cure for all the world's problems and the State Department's hesitant diplomacy in tackling the Nazi regime; he did not trust them to get matters right now. He was taking a risk in sticking the Treasury's nose yet again into what would be seen as a foreign policy matter. Cordell Hull might give a mild-mannered impression, but this concealed strong personal ambition and jealousy of his prerogatives. He would not brook interference from the Treasury and had not enjoyed criticism from its Secretary and Roosevelt of his joint memorandum with Stimson on the future of Germany.

Given the similarity of their views, it was inevitable that Hull would fight with Stimson and against Morgenthau. Morgenthau, however, even if resisted by two such formidable rivals, could count on several doughty weapons: the respect and trust of the President built up over years of political co-operation since they first met in 1915, a close friendship between the Roosevelt and Morgenthau families, and the instinct he shared with the President that any policy towards Germany must be tough.

If Stimson wanted to dish the Treasury and see the triumph of his own principles over those of Morgenthau, he needed an ingenious instrument to lever the President away from a position where his political and personal inclinations tended to keep him. A possible tool to achieve this purpose might be an attractive solution to the niggling problem of what to do with the major war criminals. Quite obviously Morgenthau's plan to dispose of them by firing squad had the instant appeals of simplicity and cheapness.

Stimson's proposal of an international tribunal would probably involve the President in lengthy and intricate diplomatic wrangling, then risk incurring public irritation at incomprehensible legal procedures and the time and trouble involved. Was it possible to package a scheme which at one and the same time would embody Stimson's demand for legality, yet seize the imagination of the President and public?

On 9 September, Stimson sent a memorandum to his Assistant Secretary, John McCloy, which condemned Morgenthau's plan for summary execution of Nazi leaders. He insisted that: 'the method of dealing with these and other criminals requires careful thought and a well-defined procedure. Such procedure must embody, in my judgement, at least the rudimentary aspects of the Bill of Rights, namely notification to the accused of the charge, the right to be heard and, within reasonable limits, to call witnesses in his defence.' (3) Obviously then, Stimson did not see a show trial as an adequate tool for eradicating the criminal elements in Germany, nor as a fit beginning for an era of international relations governed by law. He wished the Nazi leaders to be tried by an international tribunal which applied the rules and safeguards normally used in a court of law.

Having laid down the principles, Stimson left the details to be filled in by McCloy, and he speedily passed the buck down to a lowly section in the War Department, the Special Projects Branch – and to the office which up to then had spent much of its time considering how to prevent German reprisals against Allied prisoners-of-war. The head of the Branch was Colonel Murray C. Bernays, in civilian life a not very distinguished New York lawyer. Like so many Americans, Bernays had passed the War relatively insulated from the current horrors of Europe. He seems to have framed his picture of Nazi brutality mainly from the accounts of refugees who came to the States before the War. (Indeed, he learnt little later. In 1949 he could still say that most anti-Jewish atrocities had been committed before the War.)

By 15 September Bernays had produced a six-page scheme for a trial. In it he criticized Morgenthau's proposal for military executions on the grounds that it did not accord with American views of justice. He admitted that a trial of Nazi leaders would be difficult: it would have to cope with unwieldy numbers of defendants and to reconcile the demand of the victims for punishment of their tormentors with the demand for justice. Even so, he loyally opted for the establishment of an international tribunal, and being a man of tidy mind with a penchant for order and system, he drew up a concise, logical plan by which not only all the individual defendants but also all the Nazi institutions whose policies had been denounced by the Allies could be tried at once. As if all this were not enough, in a plan covering a mere six pages Bernays stretched the concept of Nazi criminality to cover not just occupied Europe but Germany itself and extended it back in time to the very beginning of the Nazi regime.

In doing so, according to Bernays, the Nazi regime would implicitly be on trial. The defendants would be tried not just as individuals accused of specific crimes but as representatives of the organizations in the Nazi state to which they had belonged and which were allegedly criminal. As leaders and organizations were tried at the same time, evidence against an individual could be held against his organization and vice versa. Finally Bernays wove a net to hold them all and enmesh them with Nazi crimes at any period. All would be charged as criminal conspirators. The Nazi regime, its leaders and its institutions would be seen as plotting from the very beginning all the crimes of which they were now accused. They would be indicted for a series of acts which must all be seen as part of the same criminal intention – plotted for many years, begun at home and then gradually extended all over Europe to fulfil the intention to dominate, to establish Aryan supremacy, and to subject all human and physical resources to German needs.

At first glance a proposal which only covers six pages can seem simple. Indeed, the Bernays proposal had the supreme bureaucratic attraction of brevity. It had considerable virtues besides. In a few days, Bernays had met Stimson's demand for international judicial proceeding and the avoidance of ruthless vengeance. He had also formulated a plan which would obviously appeal to politicians and public opinion. A single trial with leaders and organizations lumped together could be comparatively quick and cheap. It would make a dramatic impact, exposing graphically to the German people the criminal nature of the Nazi regime and demonstrating that the Allies meant to put into effect their declared war aims on punishment and justice. Out of the jumble of abhorrent acts, evil men and the complexities of law incomprehensible to the layman, Bernays had composed a single theme to explain it all and capture the imagination – one huge criminal plot carried out by a group of criminal conspirators. And more than this – after the trial was over, what a contribution the plan could make to the speedy de-Nazification of Germany; how quickly lesser officials and military men could be rounded up and tried. Thanks to the evidence against the Nazi organizations on which the Tribunal would be asked to make declarations of criminality, the subsequent proceedings would not get bogged down in defence claims that their defendants were innocent cogs in the State machine or patriots performing a duty to their country. Once these declarations were on record, later courts would know that the accused were members of criminal organizations; the defence would be limited to trying to show that their clients had not committed criminal acts or to finding mitigating circumstances. The plan was gratifyingly coherent and seductively comprehensive. So much so that many of its elements were to shape the Nuremberg Tribunal – for good and bad.

Whatever its immediate attractions, however, Bernays' plan showed all the signs of having been written in a few weeks to a departmental brief, and by a not very distinguished lawyer. It hinged on the idea of conspiracy. Conspiracy is a fairly familiar charge in American and British law. It is a useful one to bring against a gang leader who does not himself blow the safe, kill the bank guard or drive the getaway car; who cannot therefore be charged with the actual crimes, but who has played the vital part in planning them and in hiring and directing those who committed them. The charge of conspiracy had been much used in the United States; it is a catch-all which was often the only effective way of dealing with large-scale, organized crime. Even so, conspiracy is always difficult to define and the charge can cause problems in court. Judges have to decide exactly what makes a man a conspirator – planning a crime but not actually carrying it out? Being a plotter at an early stage but leaving the conspiracy before the crimes are committed? Implied in the conspiracy charge can be the idea that all members of a gang share guilt for all its acts. In Anglo-American law, defendants can be accused of conspiracy to commit all its acts whatever their length of stay in a gang and regardless of whether they even met most of its members. These are concepts found dangerous by many judges and ludicrous by many juries. If such a wide definition of the charge could be difficult to prove in cases involving relatively small numbers, how much more difficult it would be to pin it on an entire regime whose acts were allegedly criminal for twelve years. Bernays had recommended a wide definition of conspiracy when experience showed that many judges tended to narrow it: and to endeavour to impose limits of time during which they would accept that the conspiracy was active and to look for incontrovertible evidence to prove criminal purpose and criminal action on the part of individual defendants.

Worse still, the charge of conspiracy is viewed with even greater suspicion on the Continent, even though there it is not as widely defined as in Anglo-American law. Yet Bernays was suggesting that the charge be heard by an international tribunal, in which Continental judges would expect charges of criminal acts rather than of criminal intentions. Furthermore, he was recommending trying German defendants on a charge relatively unfamiliar in German law and unknown in international law. Even more disturbing, the potential defendants had received no prior warning that the charge would be brought against them. Most of the charges relating to war crimes were already well-established in international law (any German murdering a prisoner-of-war, for example, knew that he was committing a war crime). There had been plenty of warnings from the Allies that men committing these categories of crime would be punished. But there had been no specific warnings that men would be accused and punished for conspiring to commit them. All legal systems condemn the idea of *ex post facto* law – law which retrospectively makes criminal acts which were not illegal at the time they were committed. It is a fundamental principle of justice that a man can only be accused of committing a crime if he knew in advance, or should have known, that his acts would be crimes.

Bernays was on equally weak legal ground in extending the conspiracy charge to include the pre-war period in his anxiety to cover such policies as the persecution of German Jews, the Trades Unions, the Christian Churches, the establishment of concentration camps and the euthanasia programme. Before the War, most of these allegedly criminal acts had been committed by the sovereign German state against its own German nationals. International law recognized the right of a nation to try foreigners who committed crimes in war against its subjects; it accepted that once Germany had surrendered unconditionally, the occupying Powers were sovereign and could establish tribunals to try German nationals for war crimes against others. But there was no precedent in international law for other nations to try defendants on charges relating to domestic acts by a sovereign state. International law dealt only with the relations between nations and the acts committed by one nation against another.

Similarly without precedent not just in international but in every national legal system was Bernays' idea of trying organizations as well as individual defendants. It carried with it a dangerous possibility – that mere membership of a group might automatically make a man criminal; that there was no need to show the nature of his membership (whether it was voluntary, active, and based on full information about all the aims and activities of the group). Like conspiracy at its widest definition, the idea of asking a court to declare whole organizations criminal could be seen as creating a 'catch-all' charge. This, unless severely limited by the most scrupulous safeguards, can easily become an instrument of injustice.

To be fair to Bernays, he had done his best to cobble together some working suggestions. It was now up to better lawyers to turn them into something more viable and in conformity with accepted legal principles and procedures.

Better lawyers abounded in the US War Department, the Judge Advocate General's office, the Legal Division of the State Department and in the Justice Department. From the second half of September they began to sink their teeth into Bernays' plan. Not surprisingly the Justice Department, though in favour of a trial in principle, was extremely critical of what was seen as Bernays' sloppy thinking. On 29 December, Assistant Attorney General Herbert Wechsler, in a memorandum to his superior Francis Biddle, urged dropping the charges concerned with pre-war acts and acts against German nationals on the grounds that they were *ex post facto*. He objected to the idea of trying organizations since it was without precedent and involved too great a risk of injustice. He considered the charge of conspiracy to be purely Anglo-American and therefore inapplicable in an international court, and against German defendants.* Biddle was in full

*It is indeed true that the conspiracy charge as broadly defined as in the American and British systems does not exist elsewhere. Other legal systems do have similar, more tightly defined charges which give a superficial appearance of similarity: the French have the concept of an *association criminel*; the Germans talk of criminal associates; the Russians have sweeping charges to deal with banditry. On the Continent, however, the law stresses the need to prove a clear connection between the plotting and the criminal acts; to show complicity in the crimes which the conspirators actually carry out. In Britain and America the mere act of conspiracy can be treated as a crime. It is odd indeed that when lawyers were planning a trial of men they were certain were criminals, and when ample evidence was available to prove it, they should have stuck to a vague and contentious charge of conspiracy when complicity could have been demonstrated and all participants been satisfied.

agreement. So were many others – not just in America, but even more so later when the trial was under discussion in Europe and the charge came under heavy criticism from Continental lawyers. Even so, though the Bernays plan drew heavy fire from all sides, though much of it was damaged and even wiped out, the essentials were to remain. Their seductions were irresistible.

Yet personal experience as much as legal judgement shaped reactions. Biddle may have viewed the conspiracy charge with a particularly jaundiced air since as Attorney General he had an uncomfortable recent failure with it in court when prosecuting Nazi sympathizers. Conversely, Stimson could associate the charge with success – in the 1920s he had effectively prosecuted big business in trust-busting cases by alleging conspiracy. In fact his immediate reaction to Bernays' suggestion of the charge was to tell lawyers in the War Department that 'in many ways the task which we have to cope with now in the development of the Nazi scheme of terrorism is much like the development of business' in the United States. (4) Others, with slightly different legal experience might have substituted for 'business' 'organized crime' – the conspiracy charge had been equally damaging against big gangs.

At least the conspiracy charge had often been used by American lawyers. Stimson now threw into their discussions an idea totally unfamiliar which was viewed by many with deep distaste. During the War, several of the leaders of the smaller Allied states had revived the possibility once discussed by the legal committee at Versailles that launching aggressive war was in itself a crime. They suggested that one day Nazi leaders should be punished for it. Stimson had found this proposal most attractive at the time; it would now fit neatly into Bernays' wide concept of a trial. If this element were added, it could be argued that the war crimes and crimes against humanity with which the Nazi leaders were charged had inevitably and intentionally resulted from the aim and act of waging war to dominate Europe. To obtain that domination the conspirators had committed all their crimes – those against German nationals to strengthen their grip on Germany, the war crimes to ensure victory, the crimes against humanity to terrorize and enslave captured populations. The central crime, to and from which all the others flowed, was war.

The intellectual neatness of this idea and its acceptability to several nations might in themselves have been enough to win Stimson's support. But there was an even deeper appeal. As a constant and vocal proponent of the development of international law, Stimson had hailed as a crucial step the signing by sixty-three nations (including Germany) of the Pact of Paris (or the Kellogg-Briand Pact) in 1928. The signatories of that Pact had renounced war as an instrument of national policy for the solution of disputes. Some people regarded this as little more than yet another expression of pious hope. They pointed to the considerable number of similar agreements since the end of the First World War, to the constant vows not to resort to violence, then to the constant failure of the nations to make them binding. Stimson, and others, however, believed that the Pact was not mere aspiration but the expression of a legal commitment on the part of its signatories. Previous international agreements, starting with the Covenant of the League of Nations, had expressed the nations' belief that aggressive war should be seen as a crime; this Pact had made it so. Stimson had acted on his belief. Convinced that Germany was an aggressor, he justified escalating action against her while America remained neutral: economic pressure, embargo, naval threat. As he told a congressional hearing in 1941, he interpreted the Kellogg-Briand Pact as having changed international law so as to free nonbelligerents from any obligation to withhold aid when given against an aggressor.

But though Stimson and many others might think that war was now illegal, some did not. They argued that the Pact did not have the character or force of true law. It failed on two counts. Firstly, like innumerable scholars and politicians from Grotius to the drafters of the Covenant of the League of Nations, it had not succeeded in giving a clear, unambiguous definition of aggression. Next, critics of the Pact pointed out, it neither specified punishments for those who committed aggression nor proposed courts to try those accused of it. Real laws, they said, need sanctions and recognized institutions to apply them. Stimson was never impressed by any of these arguments. He believed that not only had the sixty-three nations made war illegal by their denunciation, they had also implied their preparedness to impose sanctions. They may not have done so this far but, as he put it in 1947, 'a legal right is not lost because it is not used.' (5)

Morgenthau's plan for the treatment of Germany had stirred up one hornet's nest; Stimson's plan for a trial had stirred up another. It had provoked bitter disputes over the international acceptability of the conspiracy charge, the legality of indicting organizations, the status of aggression in law, the extent to which many of the charges might be seen as *ex post facto*. It was Stimson's contention that in a properly constituted tribunal of the kind he had in mind, these disputed points would be subject to the test of evidence, the attacks of the defence, and to the practised scrutiny of the judges. Many maintained that the international community must clarify its wishes in adequately drafted law before such a trial could take place. The reply of Stimson and his supporters was that the wishes of the nations and their condemnation of crimes had been adequately expressed in dozens of declarations and agreements in the inter-war years; in the Common Law tradition, at least, law develops through court decision as well as by statute. The law was not being pushed into a dangerously extended leap as the opponents of this trial alleged; it was being encouraged to take a natural step along the line indicated by the international community.

Lawyers thrive on precedent. Critics of Stimson's proposals were not only hostile to the charges to be heard in the trial, they condemned the idea of trying a country's leaders as being without precedent. The Stimson camp could reply that there always has to be a first time; at some moment there had been the first trial for murder, so why not now the first trial of criminal leaders of a state? Indeed, they would urge, this was the perfect time. Sufficient international agreement and law had been established; there was a strong demand for punishment of war criminals, a need to prevent blind vengeance, an intense desire to deter future criminals and aggressors and a cry for a just and permanent peace in Europe. What better justifications could there be for holding such a trial? What better moment for edging forward the rule of law than after a period of such lawlessness and resultant suffering? The detractors of the proposed trial would counter: are such responsibilities appropriate tasks for an *ad hoc* court, hearing disputed law in the atmosphere of hatred and recrimination following such a war?

Lawyers still wrangle over all these arguments. The proposal to set up an international tribunal to try Nazi war criminals had raised some of the most fundamental questions lawyers must ask about the law itself and the nature of judicial proceedings. Those who discuss these matters now, however, have the luxury of untroubled quiet for reflection and freedom from the responsibility for making effective and immediate decisions for a shattered continent. Statesmen in 1944 did not. The collapse of Germany was imminent; they had no time to hum and ha. They had to decide how to settle Europe and treat a defeated Germany; the policies put forward by Stimson and Morgenthau came near the extremes of the spectrum of choice available. It was now up to the politicians to make that choice.

For a brief moment it looked as if Morgenthau's policies would prevail. Roosevelt went to a meeting with Churchill in Quebec from 11 to 19 September 1944. Roosevelt was concerned to assist British post-war recovery and Churchill had come to Quebec with the intention of asking for American financial assistance. It was logical, therefore, that Morgenthau, as Secretary of the Treasury, should be brought into the talks, and inevitable that he should take the opportunity of presenting his Plan for Germany. He found the British leader receptive. Whether or not Churchill suspected that support for the Plan was a *quid pro quo* for American financial aid, he was certainly in favour of one of its elements – summary execution for major Nazi war criminals. Before he and Roosevelt left Quebec they initialled the entire Plan. Morgenthau seemed to have scored a decisive victory.

He had not. His Plan had only been initialled, not signed. The two heads of government had kept their options open, and had decided to consult Stalin before reaching a decision even on the punishment of major war criminals. By sticking his head above the parapet at Quebec, Morgenthau had become an easy target. Details of his Plan were leaked to the Press, and all hell broke loose. The American public may have demanded punishment for war criminals, may have wanted all Germans taught a sharp lesson, but they had never envisaged anything as ruthless and vicious as this; Morgenthau's measures went far beyond anything they could find acceptable.

Public indignation was kept boiling by a Press campaign denouncing Morgenthau himself. Meanwhile he came under bureaucratic assault from the formidable alliance of the War, State and Justice Departments. These allies might still not agree over details, but their principles were the same, and they were united by a departmental ambition – to stop Morgenthau. It was a daunting combination for Roosevelt to face, while at the same time his economic advisers were warning him that the dismantling of German industry would destroy the economy of Europe. He was faced too with criticism of the Morgenthau proposals from a man for whom he felt as much trust and affection as he did for Morgenthau – Judge Sam Rosenman. Rosenman was Roosevelt's favourite speech writer and his special legal adviser. He was in favour of a trial. So too was one of the most respected figures in Washington, Justice Felix Frankfurter of the Supreme Court.

Roosevelt could not possibly withstand such a tide for long. A final wave hit him at the end of September. The Allied advance in Europe was stopped dead by German resistance. Once details of the Morgenthau Plan reached Goebbels, he had had a field day: 'I myself am Number One on the list of war criminals,' he boasted. The Nazi media cried for a fight to the last – why not, since the Allies demanded not only unconditional surrender but threatened to be merciless in victory? However unfairly, everyone in America blamed Morgenthau for the military setback; the Press campaign against him reached a new pitch of antagonism. With Roosevelt now a tired and sick man, there was no longer any possibility of standing up for Morgenthau.

So it was that Roosevelt was swept into the opposite camp. On 22 January 1945 he received a memorandum from Stimson, Hull and Biddle. In it they proposed setting up an Allied court to try Nazi leaders and organizations for 'atrocious crimes' and for their part in a 'broad criminal enterprise' to commit them. They recommended that the charges to be heard should include those concerned with acts committed before the outbreak of war against German citizens and suggested that a military tribunal was preferable to a civil body, since it would be 'less likely to give undue weight to technical contentions and legalistic arguments.' Having taken Morgenthau and his Plan to Quebec, Roosevelt took this altogether different memorandum to his meeting with Churchill and Stalin at Yalta in February 1945. Stimson, Hull and Biddle had decisively won the battle in Washington. They now had to see if Roosevelt would win a campaign with the European leaders.

Until now the odds had been heavily against winning British support for an international tribunal. In London, the views of politicians and officials had been perfectly clear at least since 1942. None of them wanted a trial of major war criminals. When Eden had told European Prime Ministers and Foreign Ministers on 6 August that the disposal of such men should 'be settled as a matter of high policy' and that it was 'undesirable' that anyone should commit themselves to 'a policy of bringing them to trial,' (6) he was giving a précis of a paper drafted for him the previous month by the Foreign Office. This had argued that no international court should be set up to try arch-criminals such as Himmler since 'the guilt of such individuals is so black that they fall outside and go beyond the scope of any judicial process.' (7) Lord Simon, the Lord Chancellor, had felt his lawyer's conscience slightly bruised by this declaration. He commented that he did not think 'that this programme will either satisfy public opinion or achieve a measure of substantial justice', and he drew attention to the wishes expressed in the St James's Declaration. Lord Simon's legal conscience was not so very tender, however. He expressed the hope that 'the principal criminals will be disposed of by their fellow countrymen before peace comes' – presumably meaning that he hoped the Allies would be relieved of the problem by prior German resort to the lamp-post or firing squad rather than judicial process. If not then the Allies must dispose of them; he disapproved of the notion that men like Himmler be considered 'too black to be dealt with as war criminals while their subordinates may be hanged'. (8) He appears to have believed that 'public opinion', the criteria of 'substantial justice' and the aspirations of the St James's Declaration could be satisfied with rather quicker and rougher methods than those to be expected from an international tribunal.

The consensus between British government ministers and civil servants was not shaken from 1942. Nor was their policy of postponing any further decision for as long as possible. They closed ranks against those who asked for specific details about the proposed 'high policy' action; indeed they tried to prevent anyone raising the question of war criminals at all. When a debate in the House of Lords on the matter was threatened in September 1942, a Foreign Office official spoke with the authentic voice of servants of the British democratic system; he preferred to discourage 'untimely public discussion.' (9) Their Lordships were persuaded to postpone their debate, then in October distracted from a thorough analysis of the whole question by the announcement of the establishment of the UNWCC (which gave the impression of government concern without guaranteeing any action) and finally soothed in December by Lord Simon's promise that major war criminals would receive 'exemplary punishment.' (10) He did not actually tell them what form it would take.

Thereafter British official opinion simply hardened – a process assisted by finding plenty of justifications for sticking to their policy. Most of these were summarized in a brief prepared by Sir William Malkin of the Foreign Office for Eden in February 1944. It was uncompromisingly entitled *Against the Establishment of an International Court*. In Malkin's opinion such a court would take too long to establish, it would look no more impartial than a national body, its proceedings would be intolerably slow thanks to language and procedural problems, it might very well not be recognized by those being tried and they would be given plausible grounds for contesting its legality. Send the minor criminals to be tried in whatever country seemed appropriate, said Malkin, and reserve the arch-criminals for the Four Powers. (11) Lord Simon noted his approval of every word. He agreed too with a Cabinet paper from Eden in May which proposed drawing up a list of less than fifty top criminals 'whose position or reputation is such public opinion will not object to their guilt being taken for granted without being established by any form of legal proceedings'. Once the world was convinced that action against these men was 'justified on the highest moral and political grounds' they could be punished by summary action. (12)

Thus far, the British had always taken for granted American approval of their views. They had been somewhat startled back in November 1942 when the Soviet Foreign Minister, Maisky, had written to Eden suggesting setting up a tribunal for major criminals. Eden had replied firmly that the United Kingdom wanted a 'political decision of the United Nations at the end of the war' (13) and everyone thought the Russians had been put back in their place when a note was received from them in January 1943 saying that any difference of opinion between the British and Soviet governments could 'be considered as eliminated'. (14) In fact, it was not. Whatever Stalin might say *sub rosa* at Tehran, his official line was constant. By late 1944 the Foreign Office had to admit with some bewilderment that Stalin wanted leading Nazis to be put to death – but only after a trial. There was some relief at the realization that Stalin did not necessarily require such complicated preliminaries for imprisonment for life. (15)

So by the time the Big Three met at Yalta no one could be surprised when Stalin demanded that 'the grand criminals should be tried before being shot' (16) and there had been a complete reversal of the American position – Roosevelt had brought the Stimson-Hull-Biddle proposals and not the Morgenthau Plan. The British were isolated. The question of war criminals was discussed only briefly, but in that short time a major step was taken. The Big Three reaffirmed the decision of the Moscow Conference to send minor criminals back to the scene of their crime, but they adjusted the Moscow intention to punish the major criminals by joint 'declaration' into a specific commitment to a trial. The British had been routed.

They preferred to believe that they lived to fight another day. They issued an invitation in March for an American delegation to come to London to discuss the entire problem of how to deal with major war criminals. It was their undoubted intention to talk the Americans out of the idea of a trial. But when the delegation arrived in the first week in April, it was made up of three convinced proponents of the idea who had come to London with the aim of inspiring the British to buy the entire American package, give or take some minor adjustments to suit British taste. Judge Sam Rosenman was accompanied by Colonel Cutter (assistant executive officer to McCloy in the War Department) and Major General Weir (the Deputy Judge Advocate General). They had not yet reached a final decision on the details of their plan and its charges but they were committed to the outline of the Bernays paper.

Their first official meeting took place in the Foreign Office on 4 April. As Sir William Malkin put it: 'It soon became apparent that we and the

Americans had totally different ideas as regards the scope of the discussions.' (17) He behaved throughout the meeting as if he had not noticed. The Americans laid out their wares: they tried to discuss the composition of an international tribunal, the nature of the charges they proposed, the legal difficulties of dealing with crimes against German nationals and the criminal liability of superiors who issued orders but did not actually commit the crimes. The British ignored them and all the issues; Malkin continued to talk about minor practicalities such as who should figure on a list of arch-criminals. He had however been alarmed by the American commitment to such a broad concept and by their declaration that they had full powers from Washington to sign an immediate agreement. The Foreign Office did not want to go in their direction, let alone move anywhere quickly.

The next day the British tried to douse American enthusiasm with some cold legal water. Rosenman, Cutter and Weir went to the Lord Chancellor's room in the House of Lords and were presented with a very full memorandum by Simon forcefully setting out British objections to holding any trial of major Nazi war criminals. (18) In it he agreed that Hitler and others should suffer death for their actions, but he then argued that a trial would be 'exceedingly long and elaborate' and would undoubtedly give rise to the comment that 'the whole thing is a put-up job designed by the Allies to justify a punishment they have already resolved on.' Besides, he said, such a trial would have to allow a proper hearing to the defence and full consideration of evidence and in so doing it would give the Nazi leaders a chance to turn the tables on the prosecution and score points. He hinted darkly that they might raise in their defence topics of Allied foreign policy and aggression which could prove 'embarrassing' and he expressed the doubt that many unprovoked German attacks after the beginning of the War could 'properly be described as crimes under international law'. He was most scathing of the suggestion that Hitler himself might be tried, repeating the long-held British view that the totality of Hitler's acts made him 'the scoundrel he is' but that they could never be adequately examined in a judicial proceeding however long and complex. The attempt to do so, said Simon, would be seen by the public as a farce; they would declare 'the man should be shot out of hand.'

Though by this stage it was hardly necessary to say so, Simon pointed out in the discussion which followed the presentation of his memorandum that he was strongly in favour of the summary execution of the leading Nazi criminals arising from 'joint executive action' by the Allies. He invoked the precedent of Napoleon and suggested that there was no need to depart from it. However, he then revealed a minute softening of the British hard line. He put forward the suggestion, as if it were a compromise, of dealing with the arch-criminals by means of an Instrument of Arraignment. Under its terms they would be charged as common criminals on counts which could include plotting to dominate Europe, breaches of the laws of war, and maltreatment of the Jews. Those accused would be allowed to defend themselves before a tribunal (which need not be composed of lawyers) who would report their findings to the Allies. The Allies would then determine judgement and sentence. (19)

'Instrument of Arraignment' is a most impressive title. Under it Lord Simon had put charges which the Americans wanted to pursue and included provision for a form of hearing. Even so it could hardly be seen as much more than a proposal for an elaborately decorated show trial; it was certainly not the kind of full judicial proceeding the Americans were calling for, not one where final decisions rested with judges rather than politicians. Even so, Rosenman's instant response was that the idea was 'novel, ingenious and sound in principle'. Not that he was considering abandoning his plan in favour of Simon's. He was merely wondering if it was possible to arrange a marriage between them by offering acceptance of Arraignment as a dowry.

This meeting had uncovered a hitherto unsuspected piece of common ground. Rosenman explained American thinking behind their wish to put on trial representatives of such organizations as the Gestapo and the SS. Simon found it attractive and commented that there was 'a strong feeling in this country that the members of these organizations must be punished'. That said, the discussion for the remainder of the week only served to prove how very different were British and American forms of hearing and charges and how impractical it was to try to join the Arraignment procedure with the plan for a fully-fledged trial. It was a grotesque understatement by a British official at the end of the talks to suggest that there was merely 'some divergence of opinion on the nature of the trial of the arch-criminals'. (20) The divergence was almost total. The British noted that the Americans 'clearly felt themselves very bound to defer to Mr Stimson's desire for a 100 per cent judicial process'. They themselves did not really want much more than a fraction. Simon announced on 10 April that his Arraignment procedure would not actually allow for witnesses to be introduced for the prosecution or defence. That was not a trial in any normally accepted definition and the Americans inevitably retorted that they could not possibly countenance such a denial of an elementary right for the accused.

By the time Rosenman left London, the only concession he had wrung from the British was their agreement to sound out the feelings of the French and Russians. To make matters worse, Churchill had leapt at Simon's idea of Arraignment, passed it through his historian's mind and brought it forth transformed into a Bill of Attainder: get Parliament to pass one, he urged.* He and his Cabinet colleagues were unanimous on 12 April: 'for the principal Nazi leaders a full trial under judicial procedure was out of the question.' By all means publish a formal statement of the case against them, but on no account give them much of a chance to answer it. (21)

Whatever gloom the American delegates might have experienced at their failure to budge the British, it paled into insignificance on that very day

*Such an Act would have violated Article I, Section 9(3) of the American Constitution which prohibits any Bill of Attainder.

when the news reached them that President Roosevelt had died. Their sadness was natural faced with the death of a great leader and a man who had been a close personal friend of Rosenman. To be callous, however, Roosevelt's death can be seen as a positive advantage. He had never been more than a reluctant supporter of the plan for a trial; though he had been forced to accept the idea in theory, he had delayed giving approval to any specific proposals for the form it should take. His successor, Harry S. Truman, on the other hand, was a wholehearted supporter. He had a profound belief in the beneficent power of law and the wisdom of judges, an abhorrence of summary execution, sensitive antennae to the balance of political forces in Washington and greater drive and disposition to make decisions than his ailing predecessor. Truman wanted a trial and he wanted agreement of its details quickly – preferably in time for the next great international meeting scheduled to take place in San Francisco from April.

John McCloy was also determined to get the trial plan implemented. He was in Europe when Roosevelt died. He asked De Gaulle for his views; the General favoured a trial. As at Yalta, so now, the British could be out-gunned. McCloy could use a combined American, French and Russian barrage. Thus equipped, and staunchly backed by Truman, McCloy arrived in London with strong forces (Rosenman, Cutter and Wechsler among them) in mid-April. He brought a new vigour and passion to the joint talks. While the British niggled about the 'political and practical dangers' of a trial, McCloy issued a clarion call to take the chance history was offering to show that 'Hitler and his gang had offended against the laws of humanity.' The British might be beset with anxieties; McCloy was 'prepared to take any risks or embarrassments which might theoretically ensue' if a trial were instituted. He dismissed the suggestion of summary execution with contempt; it was 'contrary to the fundamental conception of justice.' He swatted away the Napoleonic precedent; it was a 'retrogressive step' when a 'great opportunity now presents itself to move forward'. (22)

The British continued to worry about the administrative problems of mounting a trial; McCloy confronted them with a memorandum in which he accused them not of arguing against a trial as such but against 'the ability of Allied brains to produce a fair, expeditious, reasonable procedure to meet the novel situation which is present'. He swept aside the British plaint that it was impossible to deal with the totality of acts over twelve years of the Nazi regime: 'the very breadth of the offence is not in itself an argument against judicial action.' He scoffed at British fears that the Nazis would use the trial for propaganda and counter charges: 'the advantages of the trial method over political action are so fundamental that we should not allow the bug-a-boo of possible embarrassment to hinder us from establishing the principle' of bringing international law into action against the whole 'vicious broad Nazi enterprise'. (23)

Such certainty, such energy, so roundly expressed would have been hard to resist. The British were in no position to do so. McCloy had also brought to the talks the weight of Truman's commitment (emphasized by a telegram the President sent to the Cabinet on 24 April) (24) and the support of the French and Russians for an international court and full legal hearing. The only wonder is that the British held out for so long. They struggled until 30 May. Then the Cabinet, sweetening capitulation with such humbug as 'the United States has gone a long way to answer Cabinet objections', and calling the proposed procedure 'carefully designed to prevent the accused from using the court as a platform' for propaganda, gave its approval to the draft American proposals. (25)

It would hardly have mattered if they had not – though an international tribunal would have looked less international without them. Without waiting for their decision, Truman had gone ahead. At the end of April he had appointed a man to lead a prosecution team and prepare a case. His choice for the post was a decisive one with immense repercussions on the future trial. He appointed Robert H. Jackson.

References for Chapter Four

1   Full details of the genesis of the plan for a trial in America are given by Bradley Smith in *Reaching Judgement at Nuremberg* and *The Road to Nuremberg*
2   Both quotations taken from Bradley Smith, *The Road to Nuremberg*
3   Quoted by Hartley Shawcross *Tribute to Jackson*
4   Quoted by Richard Current *Secretary Stimson*
5   Ibid
6   Minutes of meeting at Foreign Office, 6 August 1942. LCO 2. 2974
7   Foreign Office paper, 18 July 1942. LCO 2. 2974
8   Simon to Prime Minister, second half of July 1942. LCO 2. 2974
9   Beckett to Simon, 3 September 1942. LCO 2. 2975
10 Simon in House of Lords, 15 December 1942. LCO 2. 2974
11 Brief by Sir William Malkin, February 1944. LCO 2. 2976
12 Cabinet Paper *Treatment of Major War Criminals*, May 1944. LCO 2. 2976
13 Maisky to Eden, 12 November 1942 and memo for reply. LCO 2. 2974
14 24 January 1943. LCO 2. 2974
15 Malkin to Simon, 18 November 1944. LCO 2. 2976
16 FO 371. 50977
17 FO 371. 51016
18 Jackson Papers, Box 202
19 Quotations from the discussion from FO 371. 51016 and LCO 2. 2980
20 Minutes of meeting, 10 April. LCO 2. 2980
21 Minutes of War Cabinet meeting, 12 April. LCO 2. 2981
22 Minutes of meeting, 16 April. LCO 2. 2980
23 Memo from McCloy, 30 April, LCO 2. 2980
24 Telegram from Truman to War Cabinet, 24 April. LCO 2. 2980
25 War Cabinet minutes, 30 May. LCO 2. 2980

Chapter Five

Robert Jackson was a thick-set, round-faced man of medium height, frequently dapper in appearance – a gold watch-chain across the waistcoat with an inner white facing, black jacket, striped trousers and gleaming spats. He had had a distinguished legal and public career. Born in 1892 in Spring Creek, Penn., the son of a horse breeder, he had qualified as a lawyer without ever attending law school. He began in an attorney's office, and then built up a law practice in New York State before moving into public service, becoming Solicitor General in 1938, and Attorney General in 1940. In 1941, Jackson became an Associate Justice of the Supreme Court. A Foreign Office briefing pointed out that Roosevelt was said to believe that one day Jackson would make a great liberal President. 'Opinions differ as to the depth and breadth of his intelligence but he is undoubtedly highly respected as a jurist.' (1)

More vital for the development of the trial than his previous record and experience were Jackson's character and the vision he had of the law and the part it should play in society. His British counterpart in the trial, Sir David Maxwell-Fyfe, wrote of him later: 'In the truest sense of the word, he was a romantic of the law. For him, the vocation of the lawyer left dull huckstering and pettifogging things. It caught the full wind of the traditions of natural justice, reason and human rights.' (2) Jackson was a crusader for the rule of law. He brought immense energy and a total commitment to the idea of a trial of major war criminals – and to the plans recently put forward as to the form it should take. For many years Jackson had had a passionate conviction of the need to transform international law from a mere collection of hopes into an effective binding set of rules to govern the behaviour of nations. He believed that international law was the only means for realizing man's wish for peace.

Jackson had no doubts that aggressive war was a crime, no doubts either that courts should be established to try those who waged wars. Back in 1941, he had written a paper for a meeting of the Inter-American Bar Association in Havana, a meeting he could not attend because of bad weather. In this paper, he made a series of typically forthright statements. 'It does not appear necessary to treat all wars as legal and just simply because we have no court to try the accused.' (3) He urged that great international agreements, such as the Covenant of the League of Nations and the Kellogg-Briand Pact, should not be allowed to become dead letters;

they must be given life through sanctions. 'A system of international law which can impose no penalty on a law breaker and also forbids other states to aid the victim would be self-defeating and would not help ... to realize man's hope for enduring peace.' Later that year, in a speech at Indianapolis to the American Bar Association, he again appealed for international action to put muscle into international law – above all to prevent war. He admitted that the machinery had not yet been created, and he well knew lawyers' reluctance to take the first step. But Jackson was clear in his own mind: 'We may be certain that we do less injustice by the worst processes of the law than would be done by the best use of violence. We cannot await a perfect international tribunal or legislature before prosecuting resort to violence, even in the case of legitimate grievance. We did not await the perfect court before stopping men from settling their differences with brass knuckles.' (4)

This is not to say that Judge Jackson would settle easily for second best; he certainly would not accept anything that smacked of a show trial. On the day of Roosevelt's death, he told the American Society of International Law in Washington that it was better to shoot Nazi criminals out of hand after a military or political decision than to destroy belief in judicial process by conducting farcical trials. True trials must be based on the clear traditions of justice, must follow the principles and methods universally adopted by those with respect for the law. 'You must put no man on trial before anything that is called a court ... under forms of judicial proceeding, if you are not willing to see him freed if not proved guilty. If you are determined to execute a man in any case, there is no occasion for a trial; the world yields no respect to courts that are merely organized to convict.' (5)

This accidentally well-timed Washington speech seems to have been shown to the new incumbent at the White House, President Truman. Jackson, obviously, was the man for the job. The President asked Judge Rosenman to approach him to lead the American prosecution team. Jackson hesitated before accepting the position. He had to consider that his appointment would be criticized by many on the Supreme Court bench – a member might be expected to remain aloof from political affairs, indeed to take no part in any trial. Jackson did not consult any of his colleagues; Chief Justice Stone would have advised against the job – he had firm views on the need for exclusive devotion to the Supreme Court and a distaste for the projected trial which led him later to call it 'Jackson's lynching expedition'. (6) Jackson hesitated only for a few days, however. The job was irresistible. He was not easy at the Supreme Court; his relations with colleagues were scratchy and the Court at the moment did not have the glamour and excitement of its pre-war role. Leadership in a great international trial, on the other hand, would give him freedom of action and tremendous powers. He would be in a position to give substance to international law, to lay the foundations of a new world order under law. It was his moral and legal crusade.

On 29 April, Robert Jackson agreed to become the United States Chief of Counsel. In his letter to President Truman accepting the appointment he stressed that 'Time is of the essence' in getting an international agreement to mount the trial and in preparing the case. He feared that delay would only encourage men to take the law into their own hands. For this reason he was prepared, to some extent, 'to sacrifice perfection to expedition'. In addition, although he hoped for international co-operation, he wanted to start work on the prosecution case even before it was obtained – not least so as to take and keep control over the case. 'The best way to gain confidence and leadership in the matter, in my opinion, is not to ask for it but to be best prepared.' (7)

His appointment was announced on 2 May. Immediately Jackson threw his vitality, his fervour and his impressive eloquence into his task. The German surrender took place on 7 May and within days he had to fight off a challenge to his trial. The Treasury proposed that members of organizations which might be declared criminal should meanwhile be allocated to penal labour – mopping up some of their mess. Jackson was resolute: there must be no decision, no punishment until a proper trial had been held. He was rapidly preparing for it. His chief associates were chosen: Robert G. Storey, a Texan law professor in civilian life, and Thomas J. Dodd were to be the executive trial counsel. Working with them were John Amen, now in the Marines but formerly a New York lawyer and special assistant to the US Attorney General investigating violations of the anti-trust laws, official corruption and gambling; Sidney Alderman, the General Solicitor to the Southern Railway Company; Francis Shea, once Dean and Professor of Law at the Buffalo Law School but from 1939 to 1945 the US Assistant Attorney General; and William Donovan, also with experience in the Attorney General's office, but from 1941 the head of OSS (the Office of Strategic Services, the predecessor of the CIA). The Foreign Office was relatively pleased by this particular appointment. In a briefing they prepared on Jackson's team they commented that 'Despite the tendencies of so many of the foreign-born employees of OSS, he himself, so far as we know, has been consistently pro-British ... He is a man of great personal charm and considerable ability; more of a fighter than an administrator, with an Irishman's wit and mercurial temperament.' (8)

These men would form the inner circle around Jackson from now on and would in their turn recruit junior counsel to the prosecution team. They worked with representatives from the State, War, and Justice Departments on a draft agreement for a trial to be presented to the Powers at San Francisco. They could call on experts from any department for help in preparing their case, but they were not responsible to any department. They answered to Jackson and he, on the instructions of Truman, was totally independent on a special assignment and answerable only to the President himself.

On 28 May, Jackson and Donovan left for Europe, intending to confer with the United Nations War Crimes Commission in London and to galvanize the Allies. During the San Francisco Conference the British had finally given the impression that they would consider the idea of a trial 'in principle' though somewhat reluctantly. Jackson now hoped to secure their agreement to recently drafted outline proposals for the proceedings. Jackson had full powers from the President to draw up and sign an agreement and was rearing to go. The British, on the other hand, were an *ad hoc* collection from the various departments who had been passing the war crimes parcel – the Lord Chancellor's office, the Attorney General and Solicitor General's offices, the Foreign Office and the War Office. They had set up an interdepartmental committee in February to consider war criminals in general but had applied little energy to the task and failed to coordinate efforts. Every department had grumbled that they lacked the staff for the job, then left the work to others. (9) Until 30 May they had no final government approval for a trial. Thereafter the imminence of a General Election tied their hands, since it was not certain whether a new government would wish to share the commitment of its predecessor.

However, Jackson's meetings in London were not a waste of time. He was pleased by the approval the British seemed to give his draft, and he was given the impression they would only wish to make a few amendments. The British wanted to get down to brass tacks and draw up lists of defendants; Jackson preferred to wait for more evidence to come in before making decisions. He made a good impression on the Foreign Office. Donovan came in for a little criticism for his 'somewhat cavalier notions of dealing with the minor Allies' (i.e. not consulting them) but on the whole confirmed his standing in Foreign Office eyes because he 'appeared very anxious to help', and rather surprisingly they also approved his desire to 'get a move on'. (10) It was agreed that the British would issue invitations to the French and Russians to join America and Britain at a conference in London in June to draw up an agreement on the whole project of a trial.

The new Attorney General of the caretaker government, Sir David Maxwell-Fyfe, was appointed on 29 May to lead the future British negotiating team. He was also to lead a prosecution team to be known as the British War Crimes Executive (BWCE). This was to replace the previous random dabblings of the interested government departments. It had a nucleus of members whose concern was primarily with the practical matters of the trial and the prosecution case.* Grudging though the Foreign Office had

*Working under Maxwell-Fyfe were G.D. ('Khaki') Roberts KC · Senior Treasury Counsel at the Central Criminal Court; Mervyn Griffith-Jones a barrister who had spent the War in the Coldstream Guards (and who from 1950 would be Crown Counsel at the Central Criminal Court); Elwyn Jones Deputy Judge Advocate from 1943 to 1945 (and one day Lord Chancellor); John Barrington a barrister who had been in the Royal Artillery since 1939; and Harry Phillimore who had been called to the Bar in 1934 and was now Secretary of the BWCE. Watching briefs were held by the Treasury Solicitor and representatives from the Lord Chancellor's department and the Foreign Office.

been about a trial, they insisted on being kept in the picture ('unwelcome though it is') (11) because the planning involved negotiations with the Allies which they would not entrust to mere lawyers. In fact, the Foreign Office turned out to be invaluable to the prosecution case because of its access to the intelligence of their specialized sections such as the German Department and the Political Intelligence Department and the knowledge of the treaties and diplomacy of the inter-war years. It contributed the services of Jim Passant, a man capable of preparing at minimal notice comprehensive and lucid briefs. (He had recently been working with the Naval Intelligence Division at the Admiralty. He would soon become Deputy Director of the Foreign Office's Research Department and Head of the German Section.) Representatives from the Judge Advocate General's Staff and the Services were also called upon when their expertise was required or their weight could be useful – military assistance comes quicker in response to military orders.

From 5 June the BWCE met regularly and it was soon established in temporary headquarters at Church House in Great Smith Street. As they started to examine a possible case against the Nazi leaders, they began to get cold feet about Jackson's draft proposals for the charges to be brought against them. They felt his case was abstract and high faluting, too complicated to be effective in court. They would have preferred a trial with fewer defendants, limited charges and simple procedure, not what Maxwell-Fyfe called Jackson's concept: 'an exordium of International Law in civilized countries'. As Sir Thomas Barnes, the Treasury Solicitor put it: 'we ought to get Mr Justice Jackson to look at it from a practical point of view of the attempt to dominate Europe.' (12)

Elsewhere strong opposition was being expressed to the idea of having a tribunal of the four Powers at all. Mr Troutbeck of the German Department of the Foreign Office finally boiled over: 'Surely to have a Russian sitting in a case of this kind will one day be regarded as almost a high point in international hypocrisy.' Surely the Russians had 'entered into a common plan or enterprise aimed at domination over other nations' which involved 'atrocities, persecutions and deportations' on a colossal scale. 'Is not the Soviet Government employed today in that very same thing in Poland, the Baltic States, the Balkan States, Turkey and Persia?' (Someone added in the margin: 'And what about Finland?') 'All this,' seethed Troutbeck, 'cannot be excused on the principle of the housemaid's baby. There have been two criminal enterprises this century – by Germans and Russians. To set up one lot of conspirators as judges of the other ... robs the whole procedure of the basis of morality.' (13) A note later added to this outpouring said the Lord Chancellor had exactly the same view. Lawyers might reply that judges do not have to be without sin to assess guilt and apply the law to others. Politicians could only add that, like it or not, they were stuck with the Russians as allies, fellow victors, captors of some potential defendants and witnesses and perhaps the most bitter sufferers from Nazi brutality. The Russians could not be excluded now. The only way to make the best of a bad job was to keep a very wary eye on how they intended to prosecute and to try the Nazis.

All these doubts were raised behind closed doors. They did not seep through to the Americans. Jackson assumed from the end of May that he would get full co-operation and approval from the British. But by 6 June when he wrote a progress report to the President, the French had not yet appointed a negotiating team and the Russians, though still interested, had not yet fully committed themselves to this trial. Jackson was irked by the delays. In his report he made it clear that he thought it preferable to hold a trial in association with the others but he was quite prepared to act alone if necessary. He rejected any thought of freeing captured war criminals without trial: 'it has cost immeasurable thousands of American lives to beat and bind these men. To free them without trial would mock the dead and make cynics of the living.' He would not countenance any suggestion of punishment without trial; this 'would violate pledges repeatedly given and would not sit easily on the American conscience or be remembered by our children with pride'. (14)

Many of the basic issues in the trial were already clear in Jackson's mind. The 'crime which comprehends all lesser crimes is the crime of making unjustifiable war'. International law had thrown 'a mantle of protection around acts which otherwise would be crimes, when committed in pursuit of legitimate warfare': killings, destruction, oppression. He was not worried about a lack of precedents or the absence of legislation: international law must grow 'as did the Common Law, through decisions reached from time to time and adapting settled principles to new situations'. Nor had he any doubts that pre-war treaties and agreements had made aggressive war a crime; and 'it is high time we act on the judicial principle that aggressive war-making is illegal and criminal.' There could be no accepting claims that heads of state are immune from legal liability: American citizens could bring their officials before courts; this right should be available in the international sphere. Nor should leading officials and military men be allowed the defence that they bear no guilt for carrying out orders from their superiors. Let them show the facts about those orders, then leave judges to decide whether they were illegal and to what extent they might constitute extenuating circumstance. 'We do not accept the paradox that legal responsibility should be least where the power is the greatest,' said Jackson and he quoted Lord Chief Justice Coke's rebuke to James I: 'A King is still under God and the law.' Jackson's views on responsibility would be readily appreciated by Truman whose desk bore the notice: 'The buck stops here'.

Jackson had intellectual certainty. He had a sense of urgency that the legal crusade must be launched immediately. He had great resources of energy which needed to find an outlet in action. It is not surprising that when he and his team returned to London on 20 June with proposals for a trial based on the main features of the Bernays scheme, they were filled with confidence and impatient to get the signatures of the others to their plans. Committed and convinced, they could not conceive that others would need convincing. Impatient and inexperienced in international negotiation, they were not ideally suited to overcome the inertia, the philosophical doubts or the practical criticisms of their prospective colleagues. Jackson expected that the London Conference would reach agreement within a week, and that it would fully agree to all the American proposals. In fact he was to face six weeks of wearing negotiations and to be alternately puzzled and appalled by the argument and the rejection of many of his views by the others.

The first few days in London gave him some false reassurance. Jackson found the British as co-operative as in May; news came that the French had accepted the invitation to the conference and although there was as yet no firm commitment from the Russians, the British Embassy in Moscow thought a Russian representative would leave for London on the 23 June. Some differences did emerge in discussion. The British talked more of practicalities than the cause of establishing the rule of international law. They were anxious to name the defendants, limit the scope of the trial, whereas Jackson talked of general aims and charges and in a memo stressed the need to authenticate the whole history of Nazism and show its criminal design. (15) All this, however, did not seem significant enough to ruffle Jackson's confidence. The British War Crimes Executive was keen on the principle of a trial and he was certain his draft proposals would only require minor modifications to ensure their full agreement.

Jackson's troubles began with the arrival of the French negotiators on 24 June and the Russians on the 25th. Both groups must have suspected that the Americans and the British had been ganging up on them in their absence. The French would react with the prickliness of a delegation from a small, weak nation, the Russians with the assertiveness of a powerful one – and with traditional Russian suspicion of Western intentions.

The French team was led by Robert Falco of the Cour de Cassation. Patrick Dean of the Foreign Office, who was an observer at the conference, found him 'rather a nonentity. He is pleasant and speaks English, but is over-legalistic in his approach.' (16) All these characteristics must have appeared in discussions behind the scenes. M. Falco hardly spoke at all during the conference – his very occasional comments in the transcripts of the session come as a startling reminder that he was there at all. French views were on the whole put forward by their representative at the UNWCC, Professor André Gros, a man with a sharp mind, an easy manner and with a wide experience of the problems of war crimes.

The Russians were led by General Nikitchenko, Vice-Chairman of the Soviet Supreme Court and one-time lecturer in criminal law at the Academy of Military Jurisprudence in Moscow who had started his working life as a coal miner at the age of 13. Nikitchenko's steadfast refusal to admit he understood any English, his carefully preserved poker face over which only an occasional wintry smile would pass, his frequent stalling as he referred matters back to Moscow for instructions, all gave a misleading impression of a mere Party hack. In fact it was all a mask which could only temporarily disguise his warmth, his decency, and his genuine concern for the law. Those who cherished a stereotype of Russian law as kangaroo courts and politically controlled hanging judges were to be shaken by finding in Nikitchenko a shrewd legal mind and a devotion to the basic principles of justice. They were further surprised by his colleague at the Conference, Professor Trainin – a legal scholar whose writing Maxwell-Fyfe was later to recommend to his team as authoritative on several legal issues in the trial, and an agreeable man to do business with.

The French and the Russians were not men to be steam rollered; Jackson could not expect them to sit quietly and accept every American suggestion with a nod. They had views of their own, and convictions as strong as his, but sometimes different. What was disturbing for him, too, was that they represented the Continental legal tradition based on the Roman Law which he seems to have encountered in London for the first time. With the British, Jackson had colleagues whose reactions stemmed from the same Common Law assumptions, whose procedures and principles were very similar to those of American lawyers. With the French and Russians, however, he faced a different mentality, not conditioned by the Common Law and indeed potentially critical or even hostile to some of its bases. The proceedings at the London Conference were to reveal an appalling ignorance by both groups of the principles and methods of their counterparts – a preliminary crash course on the Roman and Common Law systems would have speeded up the discussions, not least because after interminable wrangling they were often to find that their laws and systems had more in common than they thought.

The London Conference opened on 26 June in Church House. The delegates sat around a square table, one side for each. Their deliberations were recorded in full by Mrs Elsie Douglas, Judge Jackson's secretary. (17) The meetings were held in private and they were informal – gruelling though the full day sessions often became, at least they spared the delegates endless prepared official speeches. Perhaps, in fact, the meetings were too informal to be efficient. There seems to have been no agenda; if there was, it was ignored and the delegates rambled, interrupted and wandered off the point. The discussions were repetitious and frequently at cross-purposes. On the whole the meetings were chaired by Sir David Maxwell-Fyfe – except when he was obliged to go to defend his parliamentary seat in Liverpool in the General Election. Maxwell-Fyfe on other occasions was to show a remarkable aptitude for the quick despatch of business. Here he made little attempt to rein in the speakers or direct their thoughts. His major contribution was to apply praise with a trowel when some accord was established and to end meetings abruptly if tempers were fraying. At the main sessions the delegations submitted draft proposals and argued over them and the principles they raised. As time went on a drafting sub-committee was established to draw up final proposals on which agreement had been reached. There were fourteen full sessions in all, but plenty of informal meetings behind the scenes (alas, unrecorded). In the evenings White Ladies at Claridges and generous dinners at the Savoy restored relations strained at the conference table.

A high proportion of the time at the Conference was spent on procedural matters – working out how the trial should be run, what should happen when, who should have what powers. All were agreed that a military rather than a civil tribunal would free them to pool the best elements from all their national systems. Since they were embarking on a totally new enterprise they need not be hidebound by previously established procedures. For instance, they could ignore the rules of evidence which normally applied in trials with juries and allow the Tribunal to admit any evidence which seemed to have probative value – provided it was clearly relevant to the point it was substantiating and was not repetitious. All were agreed they could create a new court procedure for the occasion which must be efficient and fair. The trouble was they could not then agree on how to do it. All tended to cling to the conviction that their own national way of doing things was best. This was illustrated most clearly in the recurring argument over the nature of the indictment.

In Anglo-American trials, the indictment is a brief statement by the prosecution of who is accused and on what charges. The prosecution presents it to a court which fixes the time of trial. Once the trial opens, the full prosecution evidence for the charges is produced in open session. The court hears it, weighs it against that of the Defence and then determines guilt. In Continental Law, however, preliminary work on a case is not carried out by the prosecution; it is the responsibility in France of a *juge d'instruction*, in Russia of a commission of enquiry. They prepare an indictment which not only states the charges but is accompanied by the full evidence on which they are based and the law which applies. The prosecution only takes over once the case comes to trial. Though a judge may later call for more evidence or witnesses to clarify points and allow the prosecution and defence to apply for more, the bulk of the prosecution evidence has been presented with the indictment and is available for the defence to study from the moment the accused have been served with the indictment.

And this, said the French and Russian delegates to the London Conference, is the best system: it is more efficient, because the case has been thoroughly examined to check its soundness before a court is asked to spend time on it; it is quicker, because only effective evidence and witnesses are called in court; and it is infinitely fairer to the defendants who will be spared a hearing if the case against them is poor, and who will have had ample opportunity to prepare a defence against the prosecution evidence should they be brought to trial. The French and Russians were deeply shocked that in the Anglo-American system, as Professor Gros put it: 'the prosecutor could come out of the blue with evidences which were completely unknown until the moment of the trial'. (18) Falco was so shocked he was actually stung to speech and complained that if the indictment did not present the full prosecution evidence, the defence would be faced during the trial with the 'opening of a Pandora's box of unhappy surprises'. (19) Maxwell-Fyfe continued to assure them that he had worked with the short indictment for twenty years and had not found the system unfair in practice – the court could always give the defence time to prepare answers to unexpected evidence. He was willing to compromise and suggest a fuller indictment on Continental lines plus greater latitude to introduce new evidence in court than Europeans were used to. Jackson was not. Day after day he argued for 'a longer trial but a shorter indictment'. (20) In spite of constant reassurance, he continued to believe that the Continental system prevented the calling of new evidence and witnesses. Even after umpteen explanations, Jackson still seemed to think, wrongly, that if the evidence was in the indictment it would not be heard in court. He complained that the American public would not believe it was 'a real trial' (21) if the evidence was not produced in court. (The French and Russians forebore to reply that they were arguing for a system which was fairer to the defendants, not one which satisfied an ill-informed American public.) Jackson was never reconciled to the unfamiliar Continental system and remained blind to its virtues. He was rather pleased with Gros' description of Anglo-American procedure as 'perhaps the more combative and sporting system'. (22) He spoke with the emotion of the Common Law courtroom lawyer when he finally complained that if all the evidence went into the indictment there 'wouldn't be anything left for a trial'.

There were arguments too over the role of the judges. The French and Russians wanted their familiar system where judges intervene frequently to direct the course of the trial and examine defendants and witnesses. The British and Americans were more accustomed to the adversary process of challenge and cross-examination by opposing counsel.* The Continental delegates also wanted to insist on the right of defendants to speak when not under oath and to make a final speech in their own defence.

It was certainly arguable that the Continental court procedure would be acceptable to half the judges in an international tribunal and undoubtedly more familiar to German defendants. It proved difficult, however, to combine elements of it with those aspects of common law procedure on which the Americans and British insisted. Would a compromise be a triumph of selective breeding or a dog's dinner?

On all procedural matters the French and Russians were the more prepared to compromise. Jackson was less willing to meet half way. He was the first to confess he was stubborn. He admitted that these procedural matters were 'so deeply ingrained in the thought of the American people'

---

*In an aside recorded in Foreign Office minutes but not printed in the official record of the conference, Maxwell-Fyfe commented that British barristers tend to find judges interrupt rather too often anyway.

that alternatives were unacceptable. (23) But it was not just that he was so stuck on the 'American Way' as to have tunnel vision. He had been given ample reason to be wary of Continental attitudes. At the second session of the conference, Nikitchenko had thrown a bombshell by suddenly announcing: 'We are dealing here with the chief war criminals who have already been condemned and whose conviction has already been announced by both the Moscow and Crimea Declarations by the heads of government.' The Tribunal's job was simply to announce 'just punishment for the offences which have been committed'. (24) So presumably Nikitchenko did not want a trial, merely formal confirmation of political decision; saw no need for a careful examination of the evidence; thought the rights of defendants to be nothing more than an impediment to speedy punishment.

That is certainly what Jackson assumed. He leapt to defend his belief in a true trial. Amazingly calm and coherent under such provocation he insisted that the political declarations had been an accusation, not a conviction; 'if we are going to have a trial then it must be an actual trial.' He laid it firmly on the line that the Americans 'would not be parties to setting up a mere formal judicial body to ratify a political decision to convict' – the judges must 'inquire into the evidence and reach an independent decision'. He was prepared to agree with Nikitchenko that 'there could be but one decision in this case' – the Nazi leaders were beyond all doubt criminal. But 'the reason is the evidence and not the statements made by the leaders of state'. (25)

Nikitchenko's statement had undoubtedly shattered Jackson's assumption that Russian presence at the Conference implied acceptance of the basic principles of his scheme for a trial. It had also suggested a willingness to ride roughshod over the normal standards of justice. It must have created a deep suspicion in Jackson's mind that the Russians lacked any commitment to true legality. (The suspicion deepened towards the end of the Conference when Nikitchenko again said: 'The fact that the Nazi leaders are criminals has already been established. The task of the Tribunal is only to determine the measure of guilt ... and meet out the necessary punishment.' (26)) And yet these two flashes from Nikitchenko seem totally untypical in the general context of Russian attitudes. On all other occasions, Nikitchenko and Trainin were great sticklers for legal rectitude. They were firmer than anyone on the rights of the defence to have early and full access to prosecution evidence. They maintained a particularly hard line in opposition to the American suggestion that Masters be appointed to take evidence on commission from witnesses it would be difficult to bring to court. They insisted this scheme would lessen the Tribunal's authority; all evidence must be presented and challenged fully in open court. They were also anxious that the judges should have maximum independence to determine the law and run the trial fairly and efficiently. So untypical are Nikitchenko's remarks one wonders if he had been ordered by Moscow to trail a coat. Alternatively he could have been speaking without due care and only wanting to say what all the other delegates believed: the Declarations had said what everyone knew – that the Nazi leaders were criminals; that this was an open and shut case with incontrovertible prosecution evidence and the Tribunal would hardly need much time to reach their decision on the guilt of the defendants.

Whatever the reason, Nikitchenko's words caused a lot of damage to the negotiations in London. Jackson was constantly prepared to place the worst construction on any Russian suggestion. When they proposed a scheme for replacing judges during the trial, he instantly assumed they were suggesting replacing them for 'unsatisfactory decisions', (27) though the Russian draft had made it clear they were worried about judges becoming ill or being recalled for other work. Patrick Dean, the Foreign Office's observer at the conference, had decided by the end that Jackson was 'afraid of the Russians, particularly of their methods of trial'. (28) Dean was worried during the negotiations that the Americans were trying 'to magnify the differences between their own views on the one hand and the Russian views on the other'. The British thought the Russians were being 'very reasonable' and were 'keen to have a fair trial and adopt the best features of all procedures'. Dean blamed Donovan rather than Jackson for American intransigence towards the Russians: he 'clearly does not like the Russians much' and 'would happily do without them in the trial'. (29)

Suspicion and differences in legal thinking widened the rifts between the delegations when they began to discuss the American wish to indict the Nazi organizations. Nikitchenko's very first comment at the opening session was: 'I am not quite clear on the point of including the organization.' (30) Jackson had hoped it was self-evident. From the days of the Bernays plan the declaration of criminality against the main organizations had been a fundamental part of trying the whole regime through its leaders. As the Americans saw it, these Nazi institutions had been the instrument through which the conspirators had carried out their evil plans. A legal pronouncement would confirm the criminality and speed up subsequent proceedings against members who would not be able to argue the matter all over again.

Nikitchenko tried to argue that no declaration was needed – the Moscow and Crimea Declarations had said that the Nazi Party and its organizations and institutions would be wiped out and they had been. All had been disbanded by the occupying forces; criminal proceedings and de-Nazification courts would deal with their members. But Gros quickly pointed out that the statesmen had made declarations of intention, not legal pronouncements. The French and Russians were in total agreement with Jackson that the Nazi organizations were criminal groups. They were, however, very dubious about the legality of a court pronouncement on their criminality. They worried about blanket condemnation, guilt by association. Jackson had to make clear that he envisaged safeguards: the need to prove voluntary membership, knowledge of criminal aims and so on. Even so, as Nikitchenko put it: 'trying an organization to reach all its members – I do not think it would be right and I do not think it is practicable.' (31)

French and Russian difficulties in understanding Jackson's plan were not the result of the lack of a concept of criminal groups in their own legal systems.* In both, members of criminal bands could be held responsible for the collective acts of their colleagues as well as for their own. But guilt had to be established by trying individuals; thereafter, from the proof of individual crime, the picture of group criminality could be built up, but an organization could not be tried. As Nikitchenko put it: 'Soviet law does not provide for the trial of anybody who is not a physical person.' (32) Jackson tried to argue that in American law corporations can be seen as judicial persons. So too in Russian civil law, replied Trainin; but not in criminal law, let alone international law (to which there was no reply).

All were agreed that the main Nazi organizations were criminal. In the course of discussion all began to be persuaded that they wished this view to be established in court. Nikitchenko finally admitted (33) that before the London Conference, the Soviet Government had objected to the trial of organizations; they had now come round to respect the American view. What they could not do was to agree on the correct way to prove guilt. And the argument really intensified when Jackson insisted that members of all organizations charged must be given notice of the trial and a chance to defend their group. In American law a judgement against someone is only effective if he has been, in some manner, party to the proceeding. Gros objected that this would turn the hearing into a complexity of trials of minor offenders. Nikitchenko envisaged hundreds or thousands of members turning up and the court grinding to a halt faced with sheer numbers. Jackson thought that no one would dare to come forward to defend the indefensible – unless he was desperate enough for prison food. (Nikitchenko was to be proved right, Jackson wrong).

Trainin thought the whole idea merely muddled. Were those who came forward witnesses, accused or experts? Unless they fitted into one of those categories, they could have no status in court. Jackson was adamant – there must be notice, there must be a hearing, otherwise the American sense of justice would be outraged. The Continentals were appalled. They were equally worried about injustice, but over the very idea of trying organizations; and Jackson's method seemed to be a morass of practical problems. Jackson tried to sway them with some of the horrors he had recently read in Nazi documents: 'These organizations are criminal beyond anything I can dream.' (34) The Russians and French did not need to read Nazi documents; they had lived under, suffered from these organizations too long. But that did not mean they would accept just any scheme for ensuring the punishment of their members. It had to suit their sense of justice too.

*Professor Gros had written a memo for the UNWCC in March pointing out that crimes by groups such as the Gestapo had raised the 'entirely new phenomenon of mass crime' and the need to hold groups responsible before the law. He quoted those articles of French Penal Code and the Code of Military Justice in which the criminality of groups is defined.

This unshakeable determination that a trial of major Nazi leaders must be based on the norms of justice and on sound legal practice lay at the heart of the crucial confrontation of the London delegates over the fundamental issue of whether the defendants should be charged with launching wars of aggression. Jackson saw the charge of aggressive war as the cornerstone of the case against the Nazi regime, the 'central point of the show' as his son described it. (35) From this crime stemmed the others. The French too believed that the charge was 'morally and politically desirable'. (36) The trouble was they did not think it was legal. They believed the Americans were trying to invent a crime which, however unfortunately, did not exist in international law. And Gros quoted with approval Professor Trainin's opinion: 'The effort to make war of aggression a crime is still tentative.' To leap ahead of international decision and claim aggressive war as criminal was 'shocking' to the French. They thought it would be better simply to declare the intention to punish those who had launched wars. This might be arbitrary but it was less of an outrage against justice because it made no claim to be legal.

Nikitchenko agreed – he thought the United Nations must reach a decision on the criminality of aggression and that until they had defined it others must not pre-empt them. He and the French were only prepared to charge the defendants with specific acts of breaking treaties and invasions, 'deemed criminal', and leave it to the judges to decide the law which covered them. Jackson, on the other hand, like Stimson, was certain that the crime existed in law and wanted it clearly defined – he feared a trial becoming a platform for Nazi propaganda about 'self-defence' and 'fears of encirclement'. He could not stomach Russian draft proposals covering the question of aggression. They limited the definition to aggression committed 'by the Axis Powers'. This was because of their belief that all aggression was not yet criminal in international law.

But Jackson found the implications intolerable. 'If certain acts in violation of treaties are crimes, they are crimes whether the United States does them or whether Germany does them, and we are not prepared to lay down a rule of criminal conduct against others which we would not be willing to have invoked against us.' (37) Jackson may well have considered that a nation which had invaded Finland, which was based on an ideology that preached a distinction between imperialist wars and people's wars, had every reason to dodge the embarrassment of a general condemnation of war. He did not make allowances for the genuine Russian reluctance to move ahead of the law; nor did he take into account that a nation which had suffered so much more than his own from the War might well think it enough on this occasion to deal with Nazi aggression and leave the general question of aggression to more settled times. It took gentle prodding from Maxwell-Fyfe to elicit from Trainin the admission that the law should apply equally to all – but that, in his belief, in the case in hand they must limit their charges to the actual defendants in the trial.

Jackson had shown fervour for the cause of international law. He had taken care to consult such eminent jurists as Hersch Lauterpacht to confirm his belief that aggression was a crime. He was gifted with persuasiveness in arguing the need to outlaw war for the future. It is a great pity that so little of this appeared during the London Conference. Jackson, in fact, very much lowered the tone of the debate on aggression by constantly harping on one theme: that American policy before she entered the War, her help to neutrals, her lend-lease programme had all been based on the conviction that the War was illegal. In one heated moment he went so far as to mention that he would rather do without an agreement on an international tribunal than 'stultify the position which the United States has taken throughout'. (38) This might seem a theoretical matter to others, 'but it was not too theoretical a basis for our help in action'. (The others were too polite, or shocked, to reply that they were there to organize a trial, not an *ex post facto* justification of American policy – or, indeed, to get Mr Justice Jackson off the hook of what they considered the ill-founded advice he had given his government as Attorney General on the illegality of the War).

Robert Jackson's talents were not those of a diplomat. It had probably not occurred to him that it would require diplomacy to get international agreement to his plan for a trial. His convictions were so strong he could not believe they were not shared by everyone. He became hurt, bewildered or angry when he discovered they were not – and then lost his capacity for superbly phrased argument and well-directed passion. A man whom close colleagues found reasonable and patient all too easily blew his top in public argument. And the six weeks of the London Conference placed an increasing strain on him. As the arguments and frustrations mounted he toyed with the idea of calling the whole thing off. 'I am really getting very discouraged about this, I must say ... I am getting very discouraged about the possibility of conducting an international trial with the different viewpoints ... I think the United States might well withdraw from the matter.' (39) Maxwell-Fyfe, who described himself as 'a born optimist and also a working politician', assured him that there were bound to be difficulties. What was remarkable was the wide area of agreement. (40) As Falco said of his approach in negotiation: 'I find Judge Jackson is always optimistic (before he starts) but I find him pessimistic towards the end.' (41)

Jackson was soothed by his fellow delegates' repeated assurances. He found some relief from the strains of the conference table by flying to Potsdam to discuss his problems with Secretary of State Byrnes. A visit to the American prosecution document collection centre in Paris reassured him that some progress was being made somewhere and that there could be no doubt of the criminality of the Nazi regime. However the delay in establishing a court to hear that evidence was intolerable. Not that he was the only one to feel impatient. Nikitchenko snapped one day when yet another row began over the definition of aggression: 'If we start discussion on that again I am afraid the war criminals would die of old age.' (42)

The only American plan which was not discussed exhaustively day after day at the Conference was the intention to charge the Nazi leaders with conspiracy, the essential bond of the Bernays plan. The conspiracy charge, as Jackson argued at London, was to deal only with 'those who deliberately entered a plan aimed at forbidden acts' not with the millions of soldiers, or the farmers who occasionally employed slave labour at harvest time. He wanted to reach 'the planners, the zealots who put this thing across'. These were the people the British, French and Russians wanted to reach too. They just did not think that the American concept of conspiracy was the way to do it. The charge was little discussed at their main sessions – while it endured death by a thousand cuts in the drafting sub-committee. In draft and redraft, conspiracy was either omitted altogether, or it was whittled away to an accusation of 'planning' or 'organizing' specific crimes.

The British might take the American concept for granted, but their pragmatism suggested its use was too vague, too grandiose to be effective in court. The Russians and French were accustomed to the idea that conspiring to commit crimes is illegal, but in their law the concentration must be on the criminal act itself. Given their experience of invasion and occupation in recent years, it seemed only too obvious that the Nazis had committed crimes and that these crimes had been planned and supervised by their leaders. Why, then, bother to make planning, for which conspiracy only seemed a fancy word, a separate charge? There was evidence in plenty to prove the top Nazis committed actual crimes.

Jackson had to face much more argument over what might have seemed a straightforward question – where the international tribunal should be established. Jackson wanted an early decision so that work could start on preparing a prison for the defendants and many of the witnesses, a courtroom, accommodation for the judges, barristers and their staffs as well as for the numerous journalists and visitors who could be expected. A multitude of facilities would be needed for feeding those present, giving them communications with the outside world, for storage, duplication and circulation of the thousands of sheets of record and printed documentary evidence. It would be a major logistical task at any period. In the rubble of a starving Germany – where everyone was agreed the trial must take place – it was a herculean one. The US Army had advised Jackson that Berlin was already overcrowded and its resources overstretched. He visited Munich whose ruins offered little possibility for staging a trial. General Clay, however, recommended Nuremberg. Although Allied bombing had reduced the city to the point where 90 per cent of it was officially termed 'dead', by a miracle certain essentials had escaped destruction. Jackson went to look. He reported to the Conference that the courtroom in the Palace of Justice at Nuremberg 'is not as large as it ought to be, perhaps, but it is larger than any other courtroom standing' (43), and 'the jail facilities are very adequate' (1,200 prisoners could be accommodated) and linked directly to the court. There was enough office space in the Palace of

Justice and possible billetting in the suburbs – all in need of repair, but at least reparable in a country virtually bereft of building materials.

Added to these advantages were other attractions. Nuremberg had symbolic significance. It was the scene of the huge Nazi Rallies, the promulgation of the infamous Laws against the Jews. Not least – it was in the American zone. American rations were notoriously better than anyone else's in 1945; the Americans had the money, the access to equipment, the 'can do' for the construction work and the provision of adequate comforts for a major international event. The British and French were delighted with the offer. The Russians were not. Nikitchenko insisted that the trial must be held in Berlin. So keen was he on Berlin he even described it as 'central'. (44) His best argument was that it was jointly run by the Four Powers, which made it fitting for an international tribunal; he thought the Allied Control Commission could provide the necessary back-up personnel (the ACC was less certain). It was clear to the others, though, that Berlin was an island in the Russian sector. The trial would be dependent on the Russians for rations and communications – and Russians were not famous for comfortable living or efficiency. Jackson must have raised their hearts talking about installing central heating; their hearts must have sunk again as Nikitchenko disputed the need for heating in the early months of the winter – even in the mornings, as Jackson recommended. Jackson offered everyone a trip in his plane to see Nuremberg. At the last moment, the Russians refused to go.

Everyone else went and was impressed. Gradually they wore the Russians down into accepting Nuremberg as the site of the trial on condition that Berlin was named the 'permanent seat of the Tribunal' and that the judges met there first. The compromise was eased by Maxwell-Fyfe who had delighted Nikitchenko with the analogy of a business firm with registered offices in one place and actual activities in another. The old Communist gleefully began to refer to the Tribunal as 'this new firm of ours'.

Agreement on the site of the trial was not reached until 2 August. It took quite as long to agree on the nature of the charge of aggressive war. The Russians had stuck to their guns for weeks. When they finally compromised it was probably because of outside political pressure. The Potsdam Conference had opened on 15 July. The British had persuaded the other Powers to include the question of war criminals on their agenda (though Jackson had been worried that this would look like political interference in what he wanted to keep a purely legal matter). Once the question of the trial was discussed at Postdam, British and American enthusiasm for a trial finally won Stalin over to approval of the plans under discussion in London. In a communiqué from the heads of state, the hope was expressed that 'the negotiations in London (would) ... result in speedy agreement' and that the trial would 'begin at the earliest possible date'. The Powers called for the publication of a list of defendants early in September.

Given Stalin's backing, the Russian representatives in London could drop their final objections, and everything now fell rapidly into place. Agreements were ready for signature by 2 August. Jackson was empowered to sign; the others, however, had to wait a few days for the approval of their governments. Trainin had been anxious that their decisions should take the form of an international treaty – in his view treaties were the source of international law and this form would give binding force to their agreements. Others were not certain about imposing law in this way, and Jackson pointed out that any treaty would have to be ratified by the US Senate which might cause renewed argument and would certainly cause delays. So, finally, on 8 August the heads of delegation in London signed two documents which they had been working on at the suggestion of the Russians from the earliest stages of the Conference. The first was a statement of the general intention to fulfil the wishes of the United Nations and the signatories of the Moscow Declaration. This London Agreement announced the intention to establish an International Military Tribunal 'for the trial of war criminals whose offences have no particular geographical location, whether they be accused individually or in their capacity as members of organizations or groups or in both capacities'. Nineteen other nations later expressed their adherence to this London Agreement.*

Attached to it was a fuller document setting out the composition, jurisdiction, powers and procedure of the Tribunal. The name for this document had caused a certain amount of bother to the drafting sub-committee. Sidney Alderman thought 'Annex' was adequate; Trainin wanted it to be called a 'Statute' – to imply its legal binding force. Sir Thomas Barnes, the Treasury Solicitor, finally suggested the name which stuck – the Charter. (45)

The Charter expressed the eventual happy union between the Common Law and Continental systems of procedure. As everyone had wished, the accused were given the right to counsel, and to an indictment and trial in their own language. As a compromise between the two systems the defendants would be served in advance of the trial with an indictment which gave a full summary of the evidence against them and which was accompanied with as many of the relevant documents as possible; others could then be produced in court and time given to the defence to study them. The Tribunal might decide to have evidence taken by Masters on commission, but, thanks to Russian insistence, these Masters were only to take statements, they could not make recommendations to the court, as Jackson had wished. Defendants would have the right to take the stand and testify under oath, subject to cross-examination (which is not usual on the Continent); and to make a final statement without prosecution challenge and not under oath (a right unfamiliar in Anglo-American courts). The result of the blend of two systems was, in Jackson's view, to give rather more rights to the defendants than might have been available in either system separately. (46)

*Greece, Denmark, Yugoslavia, The Netherlands, Czechoslovakia, Poland, Belgium, Ethiopia, Australia, Honduras, Norway, Panama, Luxemburg, Haiti, New Zealand, India, Venezuela, Uruguay, and Paraguay.

When it came to the definition of the charges, however, the London Conference had found compromise more difficult. Some of the contentious issues had not been settled by the Charter. Nor had the French and Russian delegates been prepared to set out the law on which the charges were based – given the unprecedented nature of the trial and the uncertain state of international law, they insisted on leaving it to the judges. The conspiracy charge had virtually disappeared – into a phrase attached to the first count and a hazy sentence added to the other three. And the Charter was no clearer about asking the Tribunal to declare indicted organizations criminal. Thanks to delegates' doubts about the legality and practicality of the matter, Article 9 did not say the Tribunal 'must' decide the guilt or innocence of the groups; it merely said 'the Tribunal may'. Some sort of compromise between the warring viewpoints had been reached in the provision that the criminality of organizations must be connected with the criminal acts of individual defendants, together with the entitlement of members to be heard in their organization's defence.

Individual defendants and organizations were to be heard on three counts. The first was the crime of planning and waging aggressive war. It had been given a new name – previously coined by Professor Trainin – Crimes against Peace. In view of the doubts of the French and Russians as to the status of aggressive war in international law, it was not given a general definition, and the introduction to the charge made it clear that the Tribunal was empowered only to try and punish those who acted in the interests of 'the European Axis Powers'. This was an undoubted defeat for Jackson who had so longed for the chance to show that any war was criminal. But he put the best face he could on the situation in a Press release which stated: 'If we can cultivate in the world the idea that aggressive war-making is the way to the prisoner's dock rather than to honours, we will have accomplished something to make the peace more secure.' (47) The Charter had created a minor problem for him as the leader of a prosecution team, however. In defining a crime against peace as the waging of war, it had probably ruled out reference by the prosecution to the takeover of Austria in the Anschluss or the invasion of Czechoslovakia, since in those cases no actual fighting had occurred. Law Ten of the Allied Control Council cleared this up for subsequent proceedings by talking of wars *and* invasions.

In the deliberately created murk of the wording on conspiracy it seemed the Nazi leaders would be held to account for planning Crimes against Peace. However, it was far from clear that they would have to answer for planning the other two forms of criminal activity in the Charter, as Jackson had wished. Count Two dealt with War Crimes. At first glance this charge was less novel than Crimes against Peace. The Charter's definition of War Crimes followed that of firmly established international agreements; war criminals had frequently been prosecuted and punished for these crimes. It was however an innovation to suggest that responsibility for these criminal activities ultimately rested with those who governed or commanded those who engaged them. Jackson may not have convinced the

86

London Conference that war crimes were an intended result of the War rather than an unhappy by-product, nor had the wording of the Charter made clear his belief that the Nazi leaders had conspired from the beginning to commit them. But he had found ready ears for his argument that those at the top must bear the brunt of responsibility for the acts of their underlings. Article Seven of the Charter emphasized their view that those at the top could not shelter behind their official positions – holding high office was to be an implication of greater guilt, not a mitigating factor.

The final Count in the Charter – that of Crimes against Humanity – was a totally new charge. The name first coined at Versailles was recommended to the Conference by Professor Hersch Lauterpacht to cover the persecution of racial and religious groups and the wholesale exploitation of European people and resources. Perhaps many of the acts covered by this charge could have been included in the list of war crimes. But existing laws did not always envisage the nature and scale of the atrocities which had been committed. Nor could the charge of War Crimes be stretched to deal with, for example, the attempted extermination of German Jews. The charge of Crimes against Humanity expressed the revulsion against Nazi attitudes and methods which had been so strongly felt by those who drew up the Charter. As lawyers, however, some of them had felt scruples about the right of an international court to interfere in the domestic policy of a sovereign state. Strong though the temptation had been to prosecute German leaders for persecuting the Jews, the Christian churches, and political opponents in the 1930s, the Charter resisted it. Persecutions had to be examined 'in connection with any crimes within the jurisdiction of the Tribunal'. This strongly suggested that they must be directly connected with the War and probably had to be committed after 1939. Jackson would have a hard job to convince the Tribunal of his belief that they were all deliberately part of the entire Nazi design right from the beginning of the regime.

No such problems of limitations hedged Article Eight of the Charter which made clear that no defendant could claim the protection of having obeyed orders from a superior, though superior orders might be considered by the Tribunal as a mitigating factor in sentencing. The denial of the defence of superior orders has often been called the 'Nuremberg Principle'. It was not, however, new at the trial. It was perfectly familiar in national legal systems – and, indeed, it was probably even more familiar to the German military than to anyone. Every German soldier's paybook contained 'Ten Commandments' one of which stated that no soldier should obey an illegal order.* (Only in 1944 did the Americans and British clarify their military legal manuals to emphasize that any soldier is personally responsible for the acts he commits.) As Maxwell-Fyfe had pointed out at

*Article Forty-seven of the German Military Code provided that: 'If the execution of a military order in the course of duty violates the criminal law, then the superior officer giving the order will bear the sole responsibility therefore. However, the obeying subordinate will share the punishment of the participant (1) if he has exceeded the order given to him, or (2) if it was within his knowledge that the order of his superior officer concerned an act by which it was intended to commit a civil or military crime or transgression. (Quoted by Jackson 21 November Vol. II IMT. Code in Reichgesetzblatt 1926).

the London Conference, (48) the defence of superior orders had not been allowed by German judges in at least one of the Leipzig trials after the First World War; and in recent editions of Oppenheimer – the Bible of international lawyers – superior orders were likewise inadmissible in international law.

Clear though the Charter might be on questions such as this, it was in fact riddled with unanswered questions; not least, what was the law on aggressive war? Had the Nazis planned to commit crimes other than launching war; if so, from what date? What makes a man a conspirator? Can declarations of criminality against organizations be made and then be binding on subsequent courts? Nor had the framers of the Charter chosen to impose many rules on the Tribunal for handling the case in court.

It might have been expected that the signatories of the London Agreement would have invented the game, evolved rules for playing it which gave the advantage to one side only, then gone out to play certain of victory. Instead, thanks to lawyers' rectitude and national differences, the rule book was vague, the options available to the players ill-defined but not limited to one side, and even the size of the pitch was not specified. In this situation the referee can start to create much of the game. The Charter had established the outline for a trial of the Nazi leaders, but it left many of the important details to be settled by their judges. Through their analysis of the law and the interpretation of the sketch they had been given for the trial, by the way they chose to use the powers given to them and by the rules they evolved for controlling the process, they could shape it and largely determine its outcome. This was going to be very much a trial held by the judges, not one staged by the prosecution. The negotiators at the London Conference had all been agreed on one thing – that the case against the Nazi leaders was open and shut; they would all be found guilty and punished. Whether they now realized it or not, though, the Charter had taken the initiative from the prosecution and given it to the judges. A walkover victory for the prosecution was no longer guaranteed.

It might well be argued that this very failure to build in a guarantee of prosecution success was one of the great strengths of the Charter – even if it was not one of its intended virtues. It had other virtues too. Given the extent of the doubts and the intensity of the differences between the delegations it is perhaps surprising they could have agreed to so much. It is easy to accuse them of slack drafting in places – but this was necessary to avoid snapping national tolerance and in some cases an honest admission of uncertainty which they wished to leave to others to consider. The Charter certainly demonstrated the intention to hold a fair hearing according to commonly accepted principles of justice. Basic issues as well as prosecution and defence cases remained to be heard fully in court. The delegates in London had had to engage in negotiation and co-operation of a kind that seasoned diplomats would have found testing. As lawyers they were faced with the added nightmare of legal innovation. Under the circumstances the London Agreement and Charter were remarkable achievements.

Few of the questions they raised, philosophical or practical, troubled the public at large in August 1945. Some of them were highly technical and only appreciated by lawyers. Some of them would only become apparent during the trial itself. The Agreement and Charter were universally welcomed by the Press. The *New York Herald Tribune* acclaimed the Charter as 'a great and historic document, an essential companion piece to the Charter of the United Nations'. (49) All papers spotted – as the *Glasgow Herald* put it – that 'the court is new and so are the charges'.(50) All of them too, like the *New York Times*, welcomed 'a new code of international morals' in the Charter. (51) Lawyers might wince at acting without precedent. Press and public alike in 1945 were delighted by innovation. In the post-war mood men were looking for a new and better world; new, they thought, would undoubtedly be better than the old. As the *New York Times* put it, 'these are not days in which the people of the world are inclined to quibble over precedents. There must sometimes be a beginning.' (52)

No one questioned the desirability of a trial. Like *The Times* they called on the 'Grand Assize' at Nuremberg 'to record the solemn abjuration by the general conscience of the supreme offences against humanity (by the Nazis), to vindicate the effective reality of the law of nations and to leave to posterity a supreme warning of the fate of the guilty'. (53) Least of all did any newspaper question the right of the victorious powers to conduct it. The Press had already condemned the Nazi regime. They might welcome a full judicial procedure and the right of the accused to defend themselves, but everyone would agree with the *New York Times* that: 'Most of the people of the world would judge it poor justice if the men who brought about this war were to escape their punishment.' (54)

In his statement to the Press on the signing of the London Agreement, Jackson tried to preempt any criticism of the victors trying the defeated Germans. He feared the trial would be seen as the victor wreaking vengeance on the vanquished. But 'however unfortunate it may be, there seems no way of doing anything about the crimes against peace and against humanity except that the victors judge the vanquished.' The questions of victory or defeat were in fact irrelevant. 'We must make it clear to the Germans that the wrong for which their fallen leaders are on trial is not that they lost the War, but that they started it.' (55)

An interview for home consumption with the *New York Times* showed something of the spirit with which Jackson had negotiated in London – and something of the lessons he had learned there. He said he feared yet another European war, and found Europeans fatalistic, resigned to *plus ça change*. 'They are less obsessed than Americans with the ambition to reform the world and have less confidence in their ability to do so. Hence there is more disposition to accept future wars as natural.' Even within this philosophy, Jackson thought there was much to be said for a serious attempt 'to make the conduct of wars as humane as possible'. But Jackson denounced this European defeatism and passivity. He wanted the trial to show that war was a crime and outlaw it for the future. His visits to Europe in the last few months had shown him cities in ruins; people 'hungry, feverish and sullen', homeless and without fuel. Something of his former exuberant confidence had gone. He admitted it would be hard to restore a sense of law and order. He even toyed with the idea that perhaps Americans needed a dose of pessimism to 'shatter their illusions'. (56)

Deep down, however, Robert Jackson only believed in minute homeopathic doses of pessimism. His vitality, optimism and crusading spirit were now to be launched in full measure into the preparations for the trial. The four prosecuting nations must choose their evidence for the final attack on the Nazi regime.

References for Chapter Five

1   FO 371. 51022
2   Obituary in *Stanford Law Review*, December 1955. Quoted by Maxwell-Fyfe (Kilmuir) in his memoirs
3   Quoted by Telford Taylor in *Columbia Law Review*. Vol. 55 1955
4   Ibid
5   Ibid
6   Quoted by Biddle in *In Brief Authority*
7   Jackson Papers, Box 201. National Archives, Washington
8   FO 371. 51022
9   FO 371. 51019
10 FO 371. 51024
11 FO 371. 51019
12 FO 371. 51026
13 FO 371. 51029
14 Jackson Papers, Box 200
15 Printed in *International Conference on Military Tribunals, London 1945* (Division of Publications. Office of Public Affairs. Department of State. Publication 3080. 1949)
16 FO 371. 51033
17 Transcript printed in *International Conference on Military Tribunals*
18 Ibid 3 July
19 Ibid 20 July
20 Ibid 26 June
21 Ibid 20 July
22 Ibid 3 July
23 Ibid 29 June
24 Ibid 29 June
25 Ibid 29 June
26 Ibid 19 July
27 Ibid 3 July
28 FO 371. 51033
29 FO 371. 51029
30 Transcript printed in *International Conference on Military Tribunals*, 26 June
31 Ibid 29 June
32 Ibid 13 July
33 Ibid 13 July

34   Ibid 13 July
35   Conversation with William Jackson
36   Transcript printed in *International Conference on Military Tribunals*, 19 July
37   Ibid 23 July
38   Ibid 25 July
39   Ibid 23 July
40   Ibid 23 July
41   Ibid 2 August
42   Ibid 25 July
43   Ibid 17 July
44   Ibid 17 July and passim
45   Report 11 July from Sidney Alderman to Jackson. Printed with transcripts
46   Jackson's introduction to *International Conference on Military Tribunals*
47   Jackson Papers, Box 213
48   Transcript, 24 July
49   Leader *New York Herald Tribune*, 10 August
50   *Glasgow Herald*, 9 August
51   Leader *New York Times*, 9 August
52   Ibid
53   Leader *The Times*, 9 August
54   *New York Times*, 9 August
55   Ibid
56   Interview *New York Times*, 9 September

Chapter Six

The least difficult question the prosecutors faced was who to put in the dock. In a sense most of the defendants chose themselves; they were the most notorious of the Nazi leaders. The man-in-the-street would have known of them and labelled them as criminals long since. The British had always wanted the list of defendants to be short to ensure a quick trial and to achieve a clear and dramatic impact. In June and July they circulated lists of ten – Goering, Hess, Ribbentrop, Ley, Keitel, Streicher, Kaltenbrunner, Rosenberg, Frank and Frick – though there were doubts that Hess was fit to stand trial. (1) Ever since he had landed in Scotland in May 1941, asking to see the Duke of Hamilton and claiming German preparedness to discuss peace with Britain, he had been in the care of psychiatrists. Doubts about his sanity had increased with his two suicide attempts and increasing accusations that his jailors were trying to poison him. For the last three years the periods when he claimed amnesia had grown. However, Stalin at Potsdam had been most insistent that Hess must be brought to trial; the Russians continued to believe that Hess had been trying to buy the British out of the war so that Germany could free its hands to attack Russia. Rather than encourage the impression that the British government had considered colluding with Hess, it was decided to offer him as a possible defendant. The British also considered adding Schacht, the banker, and Krupp, the industrialist, to their list – both of them were on UNWCC lists. Bormann was also a strong possibility. Jackson opposed the idea since Bormann had not been found but Maxwell-Fyfe thought there were so many rumours that the man was alive that the public would expect him to be charged. Anyway, it was a pleasing professional point that 'there must be a very big case against him.' (2)

The British practical approach – choose a few obvious candidates and try them quickly – did not appeal to the Americans. Given their concept of putting the whole Nazi regime from 1933 on trial their lists had to be more complicated and comprehensive; they needed representatives of all its policies, and all its allegedly criminal institutions. An early attempt by Bernays to name them in June produced forty-six potential defendants. His list included Hitler, but not Raeder or Fritzsche – because it was not known that the Russians had captured them – nor Papen, Schirach and Neurath – because they were associated only with the earlier years of the regime and the Americans had not yet decided exactly how they wished to handle this part of the case. (3) American lists always included Doenitz. This worried the British. The British Admiralty took the view that the German Navy had fought a pretty clean war (some people got a very strong impression that the Admiralty simply did not like the idea of trying admirals at all). As the evidence against the German Navy was examined it was judged to be very weak. But the Americans could not conceive of a rounded case without Doenitz – the man who had fought the submarine war, commanded the Navy and finally been named as Hitler's successor.

By the time the Chief Prosecutors met in London on 23 August, they had decided that Hitler was dead, even though Trevor-Roper's findings were not yet known. It seemed worth indicting Bormann, on the off-chance that he was alive, and twenty-one others. Many extra names were canvassed – military commanders such as Rundstedt, Milch, Wolff, and Brauchitsch and Hitler's Food and Agriculture Minister, Darré – but although it was felt that good cases could be made against them they in fact duplicated other, even stronger, candidates for inclusion. On 28 August, the Russians seem to have discovered that they held Raeder and Fritzsche and insisted on adding them. (4) Was this because they believed that both men really were major criminals or because they wanted to make a national contribution to the list? The other prosecutors accepted Raeder and Fritzsche but rejected five other Russian suggestions.

At the request of the French and Russians these names and others were added to a separate list for consideration for a second trial. The idea of a second trial had originally been raised at the London Conference; the French and Russians were always keen that the Nuremberg Tribunal should be the first in a series – they argued that while the prosecutors worked on a case for a first trial they could easily start a preliminary sifting of evidence for a second. They were anxious to indict many more generals and to hold a fuller inquiry into the attitudes and acts of German financiers and industrialists. Some Americans, too, wanted to develop a broader economic case. (5) Jackson, however, was dead set against planning for a second trial. He undoubtedly thought that one trial would be enough if planned on a sufficiently wide scale, and he argued – plausibly – that they must first wait and see how successfully they could handle the first. He only succeeded in stunning the idea; it was to be constantly revived by the French and Russians.

The list of individual defendants was published on 29 August 1945: Goering, Ribbentrop, Hess, Kaltenbrunner, Rosenberg, Frank, Bormann, Frick, Ley, Sauckel, Speer, Funk, Schacht, Papen, Krupp, Neurath, Schirach, Seyss-Inquart, Streicher, Keitel, Jodl, Raeder, Doenitz and Fritzsche. The Press approved of the list, on the whole. It welcomed confirmation that individuals would be held responsible for the crimes of their state. As the *Manchester Guardian* put it: 'Grave precedents are being set. For the first time the leaders of a state are being tried for starting a war and breaking treaties. We may expect after this that at the end of any future war the victors – whether they have justice on their side or not, as this time we firmly believe we have – will try the vanquished.' (6) The *Glasgow Herald* made a point missed by others: 'Scanning this list, one cannot but be struck by the completeness of the Nazi catastrophe. Of all these men, who but a year ago enjoyed wide influence or supreme power, not one could find a refuge in a continent united in hate against them.' (7) *The Times,* looking at the list more critically than most, thought there was no doubt that the Nazi Party leaders – Goering, Hess, Ribbentrop – should be tried but wondered whether the generals would be proved to have been war criminals or 'merely stooges in the hands of their political masters.' (8) It welcomed the presence on the list of Papen, as a member of the school of 'ruthless German imperialists', and of Schacht – a man of the same school who 'undoubtedly personifies the worst type of political irresponsibility'. But it raised doubts about Neurath, who was said to have always been a 'nonentity' and thought other industrialists were probably more culpable than Krupp.

How right *The Times* was to question the inclusion of Krupp – because the list named the wrong Krupp: Gustav. He was only a Krupp by marriage to 'Big' Bertha, the owner of the shares in the family business. Contrary to usual practice he had taken her surname. From 1940 when he was already suffering from arteriosclerosis, Gustav had been removed from control of the firm and put into the purely titular position of chairman. The management of the massive munitions combine had been taken over by his son, Alfried, and from 1943, by agreement with the Nazi government, Alfried had become sole owner of the firm. So it was Alfried who had provided the weapons for the war, Alfried against whom there was so much evidence regarding the use of slave labour and prisoners-of-war in Krupp factories. Yet the list named his father. It was undoubtedly a slip of the pen – early lists of defendants had used Alfried's name, not Gustav's – and had not been noticed. It was an acutely embarrassing slip. They soon discovered the case against Gustav was very weak and that they had missed their intended culprit. The situation would get worse, however, as information was gathered on the health of Gustav. He was seventy-five and seriously ill. Was he fit to stand trial?

Once the list of defendants was prepared and published, the national teams, formed first to negotiate the London Agreement and Charter, began to disintegrate. As always intended, Jackson remained in charge of the American prosecutors. As a result of the British general election, Maxwell-Fyfe was out of office; the new Labour government appointed Sir Hartley Shawcross as its Attorney General. Logically, therefore, Shawcross might have been expected to take charge of the British prosecution team. However, the new government proposed an enormous programme of sweeping reforms; it needed all its legal skills to draft and steer this programme through Parliament, and it could not spare the Attorney General (not even

for the few weeks it was optimistically imagined the whole trial would last).
(9)

In consequence, although Shawcross was named to head the British team, day-to-day direction remained in Maxwell-Fyfe's hands. A Foreign Office minute grumbled that Maxwell-Fyfe was 'not an ideal appointment' and doubted he was strong enough to 'hold the thing together'. (10) Their objections seemed to be based purely on the complaint that he had not pushed strongly enough at the London Conference for two points (unspecified) that had seemed of importance to the Foreign Office. Time and his legal colleagues would tell a less grudging story. Nikitchenko and Falco were withdrawn by their respective governments. After an interval the Russians appointed Roman Rudenko – the Procurator of the Ukraine. Though very little seemed to be known about him, the British Embassy in Moscow reported that in recent trials 'in cross-examination he tended to adopt a bullying manner' – a judgement which would be borne out during the Nuremberg proceedings. (11) Rudenko later became Soviet Procurator General. He returned to the headlines in the West in 1960 as the prosecutor of Francis Powers, the U2 pilot shot down on a reconnaisance flight over the USSR. His French counterpart was to be François de Menthon, who had served as Minister of Justice in the Provisional Government of France in Algeria.

Nikitchenko and Falco did not disappear altogether. Both were to become judges at Nuremberg – Nikitchenko as the Russian member of the Tribunal, Falco as the French alternate member. These appointments and others raised a question of propriety. Both these men had negotiated the terms of the Charter. They had helped to draw up the rules for the trial. Should they then have been responsible for applying them? Equally, Jackson and Maxwell-Fyfe had contributed to the Charter – was it correct that they should lead prosecution teams? Furthermore, Francis Biddle, as US Attorney General, had been involved in American planning for a trial. Was it suitable that he should then be made an American judge? These questions have been raised since and there has been some criticism in legal circles of the appointments. At the time, few people worried. The matter did not even seem to have occurred to the British. Biddle actually thought that his previous involvement and consideration of the legal problems would enhance his capacity to make a decent job as a judge. (12) Jackson thought that some might carp but dismissed their scruples. In the United States it is a familiar problem – Senators can be promoted to the Supreme Court where in their new judicial capacity they handle questions they previously dealt with as legislators. This does not seem improper – withdrawal is only considered necessary where private interest or conflict of interest is involved. In the case of the Nuremberg Trial no such problems seemed present.

The revised prosecution teams settled into Church House, Westminster, to draw up an indictment specifying the charges against the defendants and to prepare their cases for court. There was a mountain of evidence to sift. London seemed a convenient place to do it.

Communications with the rest of the world were relatively good, and there was much expertise available. British military intelligence during the War had been of a high standard and the British had received reports from agents commuting to Resistance groups on the Continent. The Foreign Office had up-to-date records on the Nazi leaders and their powers and on their military and occupation authorities. The intelligence from British sources was not impeccable, but it was less patchy and usually more recent than that available from the OSS which had gaps and had relied too much on pre-war refugee sources. To supplement British government information there was the headquarters in London of the UNWCC. After its initial years of frustration the organization had now come into its own. By June it was issuing thick bulletins at least once a fortnight giving names, last known addresses and charges against suspects. London, too, was still the base for many of the European governments in exile who had struggled to compile lists of alleged crimes and criminals during the war and were now amassing much fuller intelligence as communications with their countries improved and they received reports from citizens who had suffered German occupation or were returning home from camps and forced labour.

To add to these resources, the prosecutors began to receive information from the Allied military teams who were interrogating German prisoners-of-war and civilian internees as their armies overran Europe. Something of the confusion of innumerable military sources was at last tidied up by the establishment in Paris in March of CROWCASS – the Central Registry of War Criminals and Security Suspects. It was an off-shoot of Allied headquarters, SHAEF (Supreme Headquarters Allied Expeditionary Forces) and co-ordinated lists of those wanted with information on their actual whereabouts. It added a registry of fingerprints and eventually had to solve its problems of coping with complex information and innumerable requests for help by installing a computer – an object of great wonder to those who contacted the agency in 1945.

All the agencies which the prosecution teams could consult were valuable for compiling background information or for finding witnesses. But the case against the defendants was to be based on a much harder, much more damning form of evidence – that of captured German documents.

As the Allied armies closed in on Germany, orders had gone out from Berlin to destroy German archives; military, Party, administrative documents were not to fall into enemy hands. Their archivists were faced with a dilemma – how, as the historian Sir John Wheeler-Bennett put it, 'to strike a nice balance between the dominant conscience of the archivist and the inborn obedience of the German bureaucrat'. The men proved to be bureaucrats only by employment. The vast bulk of the archives remained undamaged – largely due 'to the lack of understanding on the part of those who issued the orders of the professional psychology of archivists, who would rather eviscerate their own children than destroy the material entrusted to their charge.' (13)

So it was that much of the documentary record of the Nazi regime could fall into Allied hands. The British and Americans had drawn up lists of archives they wished to secure. These were issued to their armies once the invasion of Europe began and military units were ordered to report any relevant discoveries as they advanced. Anglo-American teams of experts were then called to identify them and in turn brought in similar bi-partizan groups to safeguard and exploit the archives. These were massive. As the American prosecutor was to tell the Tribunal at Nuremberg: 'The Germans kept accurate and voluminous records. They were found in Army headquarters, Government buildings and elsewhere. During the later stages of the War, particularly, such documents were found in salt mines, buried behind false walls ... for example the personal correspondence and diaries of Rosenberg ... were found behind a false wall in an old castle in eastern Bavaria. The records of the OKL of the Luftwaffe – equivalent to the records of the Headquarters of the Air Staff of the US Army Air Forces – were found in various places in the Bavarian Alps.' (14) These were taken to Berchtesgaden and finally moved to England where the official Luftwaffe historian was employed by the Allies to continue his work until his death. In May the Americans had found the complete records of the concentration camps of Buchenwald and Nordhausen, giving details of prisoners and their guards. Prudently, someone had destroyed the records of Belsen.

A signal from units of the 1st US Army alerted the attention of Ivor Pink of the British Element of the Control Commission and his American counterpart B.H. Morris to the existence of a remarkable hoard. They went to a lonely house in the Harz Mountains where they were given a warm welcome by the chief archivist of the German Foreign Ministry. He was anxious to show them the several sites in the mountains where much of his archive had been hidden, and delighted to give them his expert guidance in packing the documents in proper order and transporting them as quickly as possible to safekeeping. A great fear of all archivists, Allied or German, was that documents would be found first by the Russians and simply disappear. Indeed it was a fortunate chance that this area of the Harz had been overrun by the Americans; it had been earmarked for Russian occupation. Many of the Foreign Ministry papers had been here since 1943, when fears of bombing raids on Berlin had become acute; others had arrived more recently having first been sent East to Silesia then moved again when the Russians began to advance.

Now the collection, weighing 485 tons, went to Schloss Marburg in the American Zone where an Anglo-American team under Colonel 'Tommy' Thomson, the Assistant Librarian and senior translator of the Foreign Office, and Dr W.R. Perkins of the State Department, the editor of *Foreign Relations of the United States*, processed and scrutinized it. Checking had to be expert and thorough. There was a strong risk that 'plants' might lurk in the files. The team could call on the help of several German archivists who were all too pleased to be with their files and able to ensure proper treatment. Thereafter, Italian prisoners-of-war carted the files down to the courtyard where an RAF micro-filming unit copied them, using machines which could only cope with about 1,000 pages a day. The lists and summaries of documents prepared at Schloss Marburg would finally be used by the prosecutors in London as they began to choose evidence to be used against diplomats and ministers; those relating to foreign policy were to be valuable when assembling the case on the planning of aggressive war.

Schloss Marburg soon became an Aladdin's cave of documents. Thanks to a tip-off from Karl Loesch, an assistant to Hitler's chief interpreter Paul Schmidt, Thomson was led to a spot in the Thuringia Wald where Loesch and Schmidt had buried microfilms of Foreign Ministry files in a tin box wrapped in a torn mackintosh. A month later Thomson dug up in the same area a large wooden box containing Schmidt's personal collection of papers. Between them these two treasure troves provided an almost complete record of all Hitler's conversations and correspondence with foreign statesmen. Historians owe a great debt of gratitude to Schmidt and Loesch. (15)

Given the extraordinary contents of Schloss Marburg and the cloak-and-dagger way in which some of them had been found, it is not surprising that the place began to attract stories. A popular one, as told by Sir John Wheeler-Bennett, concerns the GI who parked a lorry in the castle courtyard one day, saying that he had found it abandoned by the side of the road and thought it might interest the Schloss Marburg staff since it contained three packing cases. He took a receipt for his load and drove off in the lorry. The packing cases were opened. Inside were three coffins. In the coffins were the bodies of Hindenburg, Frau von Hindenburg and Frederick the Great.*

Less exotic than the bodies of the great, but of much more value to historians, was the capture of the German Naval archives. Like those of the Foreign Ministry they had been moved from Berlin following the 1943 Hamburg raid, which had alerted the authorities to the dangers of aerial attack. It was a fortunate move – the next night the building which had housed them was gutted by the first major incendiary raid on Berlin. The archive was taken to Schloss Tambach near Coburg, where the archivists and historians continued to tend and work on them. By 1944 the staff had orders to keep the dried-out swimming pool in the grounds at the ready; logs and petrol were provided – should the enemy approach, the archives must be burned. The orders went against nature. Not only could the guardians not bear to harm their precious charges, but in the winter months elderly gentlemen found the logs irresistible in a damp and freezing building, the petrol invaluable for supplementing their meagre ration. To everyone's relief, at the last moment the orders were countermanded. Admiral

*Some readers may prefer the Ivone Kirkpatrick version which adds the body of Kaiser Wilhelm I. Those with no romance in their souls, however, might question whether the Kaiser's body ever left Berlin and whether the bodies of the Hindenburgs and Frederick II were likely to meet in the same lorry.

Doenitz himself insisted that the Naval archives be handed over to the Allies intact.

So this unique collection, 60,000 files with signals, logs, diaries and memoranda of the Navy, some of them dating back to 1868, and all impeccably maintained up to April 1945, was kept in its original order, escorted by its archivists and shipped to London. There it was kept safe underground in Churchill's bunker on the parade ground at Whitehall, until eventually a team under Major Kenneth Duke went to work on it and began to develop the case against the German Navy.

The German Naval archives fared better than those of the Army. Many of these were shipped piecemeal to the United States; though some were concentrated in Alexandria, Virginia, others were scattered and they all suffered the depredations of competing military and civil intelligence agencies. More fortunate was a collection weighing two and a half tons of still photographs taken by Hitler's photographer, Heinrich Hoffmann. These were delivered to Nuremberg, where an advance party of the American prosecution team was frustrated by the absence of a catalogue or even labels. All was well, however, when they discovered that Hoffmann himself was in jail in Mannheim. He was released and came to more comfortable confinement in a villa in Nuremberg where he sorted and explained his picture history of the Reich. (16)

In view of the sheer volume of captured German documents and the chaotic conditions under which the collecting teams were working in Germany, some muddle was inevitable. Literally tons of documents, for example, were stuck for the whole of August on Antwerp docks; no one was certain what the consignment contained, just that it might perhaps prove useful to the prosecution in London if only they had access to it. (17) (The consignment was finally opened; it contained German Army documents.) It was an appalling task to sift the tonnage of documents and determine their value. When in September the card index of Nazi Party members was found near Munich, it had simply been thrown on to a tip. There were nine million cards, scattered in heaps. It was reckoned they would take months to sort. (18) Would they contain anything useful to the prosecution? Would it be discovered too late? It is surprising that many more documents did not get lost.

One document, vital to the prosecution case, actually did. It was known as the Hossbach memorandum, the notes made by Hitler's adjutant Colonel Hossbach, of a conference held in the Reich Chancellery in Berlin on 5 November 1937. This conference was a crucial element in the prosecution argument that Nazi leaders had conspired to wage aggressive war. Present at the meeting were the Minister for War (Blomberg), the commanders of the Army, Navy and Air Force (Fritsch, Raeder and Goering) and the Minister for Foreign Affairs (Neurath). From 4.15 p.m. to 8.30 p.m. they were harangued by Hitler with his views on foreign policy – a statement which he said should be viewed as his last will and testament. According to Colonel Hossbach's notes Hitler defined the main problem of Germany, a nation of 85 million people, as one of 'living space' or *'lebensraum'*. To prevent 'sterility', 'tension' and above all to gain enough food, Germany must secure a 'greater living space'. 'It is not a case of conquering people, but of conquering agriculturally useful space' – and in Europe. The conquest of Czechoslovakia and Austria would 'constitute the conquest of food for five to six million, upon the basis that a compulsory emigration of two million from Czechoslovakia and one million from Austria could be carried out'. The Führer thought that England and France, Germany's 'two hateful enemies', must be reckoned with but that they had probably already written off Czechoslovakia; Poland would be disinclined to risk a war with Germany with Russia at her rear. 'The German question can be solved only by way of force,' he said. The force should be available by 1943–45 when rearmament would be practically complete.

The Hossbach memorandum may not have predicted exactly what was to happen in Europe, but it was obviously major evidence of Hitler's aggressive intentions and his subordinates' early knowledge of them. Though a microfilm of it was sent to the State Department in Washington on 25 May, a summary of its contents reached Jackson in London only on 25 June. A covering note pointed out that the memorandum was not verbatim minutes of the conference that had taken place on 5 November, for Hossbach seemed to have written up his notes only on the 10th. However, 'neither content nor style of the document should justify any doubt as to its authenticity.' (19) The prosecution at last got a photostat of the microfilm of the memorandum towards the end of September. But the original – a most important document for historians as well as the Nuremberg prosecution – disappeared. There is no record of it after May.*

Coping with the sheer quantity of evidence in German documents posed an immense problem for the prosecutors. Jackson pointed out in his June report to the President: 'Up to now the task of military intelligence services was to gather military information, not to prepare a case for a trial ... we must now sift and compress within a workable scope voluminous evidence relating to a multitude of crimes committed in several countries and participated in by thousands of actors over a decade of time.' (20) All that, and the evidence was in several languages but mainly German and needed translation into English, French and Russian before its value could be assessed.

Three American prosecution collecting centres had been set up by June – in Washington, in Paris under Colonel Storey and in London under Colonel Bernays. Their staffs could hardly cope with the flood of relevant – and irrelevant – evidence which came in. As Colonel Amen complained

---

*Bradley Smith, the author of *Judgement at Nuremberg*, thinks the original was quietly entombed in the security restrictions which apply to SHAEF records. But SHAEF was perfectly willing to allow the early copies to be made and to release many other original documents for use in court. It is equally likely it simply got lost in the plethora of documents they were trying to catalogue and file. The defence at Nuremberg made strong attacks on the authenticity of the Hossbach memorandum; the failure of the prosecution to produce the original gave rise to rumours that it had been faked.

to a reporter: 'These Nazis had a mania for writing things down. It is an amazing psychological phenomenon that not one of these men could have a minor political conversation without recording it ... So now we are swamped with more documents than can possibly be gone through thoroughly in the time allotted to us and new batches are being uncovered each day.' (21) It was one thing for the prosecutors to look for evidence of the murder of Jews, the ill-treatment of prisoners-of-war. It was quite another when 240 tons of such evidence turned up in one haul alone. (22) Later in court an American prosecutor was to echo the cry of Job: 'Oh that mine enemy would write a book.' (23) The Nazis had written whole libraries.

There was debate in the American team as to the emphasis which should be given to documentary evidence in the case. Colonel Storey, a law professor surrounded by racks of documents in Paris, was convinced the whole case should be based on them. Some of them might be technical, not the sort of material which would excite a jury in a normal criminal trial, but they were 'The Truth'. They were what the defendants themselves had thought, written, ordered. Anything the prosecution might want to accuse them of was here, in their own words, with their own signatures. Many people wanted the trial to establish a record, an unchallengeable history of the Third Reich. It was here – in German documents. Besides, calm presentation of documents in court suited Storey's personality. He was an academic whom colleagues found pedantic; courtroom drama would strike him as flamboyant, even meretricious. Colonel Amen, on the other hand, was a different personality, from a different background. He was a trial lawyer who, as his colleagues were only too aware, had got himself much publicity recently in a big 'rackets' case. Amen believed in witnesses, preferably colourful ones. So did Thomas Dodd, who feared that a purely documentary case would be dull and argued that drama and excitement were needed – of the kind that witnesses and sparkling cross-examination would provide.

The proponents of the documentary case won. Jackson himself felt strongly the need to establish a record. He saw it would be beyond question if based on German records. There was a practical point as well. The trial itself would be shorter – it can take hours to extract evidence from witnesses. Jackson had enough courtroom experience to know there can be little argument with a document, and it cannot be cross-examined. Witnesses are unreliable, they have fallible memories and all too often collapse under cross-examination; there are some things no amount of skill can persuade them to admit. A document cannot cover up. So the American case, and indeed that of the other three teams, was to be based largely on documents. Jackson was to make occasional concessions later to those who craved excitement. A few witnesses were to be introduced to add colour. (24)

Evidence for the prosecution was available in abundance. The flow to London where it was needed was far from steady. National governments were on the whole slow to prepare reports on Nazi crimes committed in their countries under occupation. The Polish government was relatively quick to prepare a report – but slow in sending it to London. They had no copying machines; everything had to be typed out, and the Polish government simply did not have enough typewriters to make sufficient copies. The governments of the Four Powers might have decided to co-operate in an International Military Tribunal, but they were less enthusiastic about supplying their prosecution teams with records – either German or national. The Russians continually failed to provide any evidence. Everyone blamed the failure less on a desire to avoid sharing documents than on incompetence: either the Russians had failed to capture German documents, failed to assess their importance, or simply lost them.

By contrast, the British government departments were fully aware of what they held and of how important it was, but they were damned if they wanted anyone else to get access to it. In August, the British prosecutors had to bring very heavy pressure to bear on the Foreign Office to unfreeze its German material. The Foreign Office had been prepared to let the British team look at its documents – but only to look. Not to take copies. Passing anything to the Americans, let alone the French or Russians, was totally forbidden. This obstructiveness infuriated Bill Donovan who had violently protested to Patrick Dean, the Foreign Office man on the BWCE, about the hold-ups and called him 'several sorts of liar' when Dean tried to pretend the State Department had somehow caused the delay or that the FO needed time to sort out 'mixed up' documents. (25) (Dean was prepared to admit in an internal memo that he himself had only recently heard of the existence of some of the documents. The FO kept its cards very close to its chest indeed – even out of range of its employees.) The Admiralty was equally cagey about the German documents it held. They requested the US Naval liaison officer with Jackson's team 'to hold as confidential the fact that the archives are presently held in joint possession of both navies and in the actual custody of the Admiralty'. (26) They were persuaded that these documents might eventually be used at the trial – but meanwhile insisted that 'the non-Anglo-American members' of the prosecution should not see copies, let alone learn their source. The War was over, a shaky alliance need not be propped up; it was, blessedly, every man for himself and bureaucratic secrecy again.

As the evidence reached London, it was divided up among the four prosecution teams. On 13 August the Russians had suggested dividing the case into four – one count for each national team. This was to give each a stake in the case and avoid duplication of effort. It was decided that the British would deal with Crimes against Peace. War Crimes and Crimes against Humanity were to be shared by the French and Russians on the criterion of whether they had occurred in East or West Europe. The

Americans were left to tackle the alleged criminality of the organizations and the question of conspiracy. The undiminished American enthusiasm over a case against the organizations began to worry the British. Clyde, the secretary to BWCE, pointed out that during the London Conference Jackson had agreed just to ask for a declaration of criminality against them; but it was becoming clear from the work the Americans were doing that they intended to mount a very full case involving a long and contentious hearing. (27)

The British should have reserved more anxiety for the fact that the Americans were dealing with conspiracy. It had, after all, been only an implied charge in the Charter, and the actual wording there seemed to attach it to one charge only – that of waging aggressive war. But as Jackson developed the conspiracy case he was obviously intending it as the intellectual key to the whole prosecution, extending it to become a vital part in all the charges. That was not just because he had always believed there had been a criminal conspiracy from 1933 deliberately planning to commit all the crimes. He had a strong practical motive too. Jackson revealed it in a memo on 17 September to Colonel Storey: 'Candidly, I think we must use Committee Four (i.e. the US team dealing with conspiracy) as the basis for keeping the bulk of the case in American hands. To this end, I think we must regard the work of Committees One, Two and Three (Britain, France and Russia) as primarily to assemble the evidence on what was done in their respective spheres and only incidentally the evidence on who did it and who was responsible, and that Committee Four will have to take primary responsibility for the development of this case in all its aspects on the question of a common plan, conspiracy and individual and organizational responsibilities.' (28) To put it more crudely – the Americans would run the show and the others would be the dogs-bodies. That was certainly Jackson's intention – could he manage it?

Whatever potential rows were brewing over the division of power and glory between the prosecuting teams, there was to be a more united front on one matter. From mid-September the Poles began to request the right of a Polish prosecutor to appear at Nuremberg. (29) They were especially anxious to be involved in the case against Frank, the former Governor General of Poland. The Polish request was soon followed by others from the Czechs and Yugoslavs. Rudenko offered to include them on his Russian team – since he would be dealing with war crimes and crimes against humanity in Eastern Europe, their interests were involved, and their languages and experience might be useful. The British Ambassador in Warsaw too pressed for the inclusion of the Poles – arguing plaintively that this was practically the only reasonable thing the Polish government had asked for in recent months. (30) But the prosecutors opposed the requests on the grounds that they would 'hopelessly overcrowd the Prosecution'. (31) There were problems enough already in trying to run a case in four languages without adding at least three more; let the Poles, Czechs and Yugoslavs in and goodness knows who else would apply. It was strongly felt too that since the whole idea of an International Tribunal had been to try those whose crimes had no particular geographical location, there was no point in mounting a prosecution based on a multitude of individual national accusations.

As the prosecutors prepared their cases and analysed the evidence, their lawyers' minds not only weighed up the strengths and weaknesses of the prosecution, they also began to anticipate the line the defence would take. Jackson had always worried that the Germans would accuse the Allies of aggressive intentions so as to argue that they themselves had acted in self-defence. That is one reason he had pressed for a very careful definition of aggression in the Charter. It was a reasonable expectation that the Tribunal would forbid defence pleas of *tu quoque* – you were doing it too. This had never been an acceptable defence in any law court, any more than it is acceptable from small children in playgrounds – never mind who else was doing it, never mind who started it – it was wrong, is the reply. Even so, the prosecutors wondered how many skeletons would be produced in open court before the judges ordered them back into their cupboards. There was particular anxiety that Nazi defendants would launch attacks on Russian foreign policy. These fears were raised in acute form in August when the prosecutors discussed using the Nazi-Soviet (Molotov-Ribbentrop) Pact of 1939 and its secret Protocol. There was no anxiety over the Pact itself – it was a non-aggression agreement between the two powers and could be seen as yet another treaty the Germans had cynically signed intending to break it as soon as convenient. The Protocol, however, was a different matter. It agreed that Germany and Russia would carve up Poland between them and that Russia would be allowed to take over the Baltic States. Clearly, if published the secret Protocol was highly damaging to one of the prosecuting nations – Russia. (32)

The timid in the Foreign Office advised against using the Pact at all. Others thought that it could not be concealed – and that an attempt to hide it would be counter-productive. As someone in the German Department pointed out: 'the Germans on trial are bound to bring out as much Russian dirty linen as they can to mix with their own, and I rather suspect that this document will be quoted by the Germans anyhow. Our hope is that the trials will prove conclusively to the German people that they, almost exclusively, were responsible for the War and it will not help if we try to suppress important items of evidence. It seems to me that the present document is no more than an official record of what the world knows already.' Another official added: 'We do not want to show unnecessary zeal in embarrassing the Soviet representatives in the prosecuting agency and it is not our aim to discredit our ally; but we do want to bring the war criminals to book and we should not squeamishly suppress valuable evidence against them.' (33)

This attitude on the whole prevailed. Embarrassing documents were usually supplied and it was left to the prosecutors to decide whether to use them. It was quite another matter whether the Defence would be allowed to use them. The Nazi-Soviet Pact became a running theme in defence applications and prosecution counter-argument at Nuremberg. Given the number of skeletons in everyone's cupboard, the prosecutors urged each other to draw up lists of them and to prepare their replies to potential defence attacks well in advance – and to confess their embarrassments to their colleagues. (34) The British prosecutors soon requested Foreign Office and Admiralty help in preparing an answer to any accusation that the Germans invaded Norway merely to pre-empt a British attack.

Though the prosecution teams were having some success in outlining their cases for court by mid-August, progress on the actual Indictment was slow. A subcommittee was set up to draft it at the end of the month, divided into four sections under national heads to deal with each count, the evidence on which it was based and the relation of each defendant to the charge. Undoubtedly the drafting was hindered by logistical problems. Vital evidence was only trickling through as late as September or even October – for example the *Nacht und Nebel* Decree (Night and Fog), which initiated a policy of spreading terror by kidnapping hostages and denying all information to their relatives; or the Commando Order instructing that captured commandos, whether uniformed or not, must be killed rather than taken prisoner. Only on 20 September did London receive the Führer Order that Moscow and Leningrad must be 'wiped from the face of the earth'.

Even when the documents turned up there was an appalling shortage of copiers and translators, so the prosecutors often remained unaware of the material available. There was also an irritating lack of liaison between those working on documents – in Paris and London – and those interrogating defendants and witnesses – mainly in Nuremberg. Each waited for prompting from the other before ploughing on. Jackson's answer to this particular problem was to urge that the whole operation should move to Nuremberg. The French, Russians and British were convinced they must stay in London where communications with the rest of the world were relatively good and they were protected from the hurly-burly of the physical preparations for the trial. Jackson was irked by their refusal to see his point – and simply spent as much time as he could in Nuremberg (in between flights to Paris and Washington), with the inevitable result that his absence from London delayed progress even more.

The British blamed attitudes rather than organizational problems for the delays. Shawcross reported to Bevin, the Foreign Secretary, on 10 September that: 'The French so far have apparently done little in that part of the case for which they are responsible.' (35) He was, however, able to record that the Russians had just started to put in a few documents. Not before time – on 22 August, the Russians, who had suffered perhaps twenty million deaths and certainly the most appalling atrocities under Nazi occupation, were so frantic for any concrete evidence that they asked the British for an official report on the mistreatment of Russian prisoners-of-war in the Channel Islands. (36) Thanks to what Shawcross modestly called 'not unsatisfactory progress' on the British section of the indictment, his team had been helping the Russians and French with their sections. The major delays, as Shawcross saw it, were caused by the Americans. Their subcommittee 'has met once only, and although the Americans have apparently amassed an enormous collection of documentary evidence we have had no opportunity of seeing it or assessing its relevance and cogency'. He did not see this as a matter of the Americans holding on to all the best bits. 'My impression is that they are over-organized and that little effective gets done,' especially since 'Justice Jackson, who alone seems to possess any real authority, has been away in the States for the last ten days and is now going to Nuremberg.' (37)

It was certainly a fact that the American team was huge – bigger than the other three put together – and it contained rather more would-be chiefs than Indians. Still preserved in Jackson's files in Washington is a four-inch-thick sheaf of memos from over a dozen sources each suggesting ways other people could speed things up. (38) There must have been some sighs of relief when Colonel Bernays resigned in August – he had been given responsibility for co-ordinating American efforts, but to judge by the welter of paper he distributed, he concentrated only on trivia and irrelevancies.

Jackson's energy might inspire others when he was present, but that was not often. And he was no organizer – and knew it. He had admitted at the London Conference when the question of co-ordinating all the teams was raised that he always found it difficult enough to keep control of his own team. But muddle apart, American slowness was also a reflection of their attitude to the case. They were thinking on the broadest scale and as Sidney Alderman had told the indictment drafting committee, they were unwilling to make any decisions until they had seen all the evidence. (39) Jackson constantly repeated his view that a quick start to the trial was less important than preparing a good case – and that must be soundly based on documents. (40)

Which was all very well, but, as the British grumbled, a sense of urgency and some rough and ready headings under which documents could be arranged as they arrived would help in seeing the wood for the trees. They wanted a target date – preferably 1 November – for the presentation of the indictment to the Tribunal. Then it could be served on the defendants, the defence could start work on their cases, and the trial could begin within the month. This scenario suited the British way of work and their desire to retain public interest. It expressed their instinct that an early starting date would concentrate the minds of the prosecutors. For the British feared that American wallowing in documents was reinforcing their urge to explore 'the whole Nazi philosophy in fields which it is not really necessary to traverse' as Shawcross said. (41) As the British saw it, the case was getting overblown and too far from the concrete evidence of crimes. They wanted a quick trial, clear evidence to convict the defendants and a dramatic impact on the public. Leave it to others to write the history and analyse the ethics of the Nazis. A lawyer's job is to win cases.

Yet these particular lawyers were, like it or not, having to work as historians in writing an indictment based on German documents dealing with every aspect of the Nazi regime over twelve years. Quarrying from raw sources is difficult enough. An academic historian with background knowledge of Germany and the Nazi system, with time for reflection and the benefit of hindsight, might well have blenched at the task. The prosecutors lacked these advantages. They were faced with instant history of the most complex kind and with their own inevitable ignorance. It is understandable that they groped uncertainly, and frequently committed blunders. Something of their problem showed when they had to decide which organizations to indict.

On 29 August only the names of the individual defendants had been announced, not the organizations. From the beginning, however, there had been agreement on at least three which must be indicted: the Gestapo – the Secret State Police; the SS – with its own police, intelligence and military units; and the SA – the private army of the Nazi Party, which had been used before they came to power to create disorder and terrorize opponents and thereafter for physical and ideological training. There seemed to be no doubt that the Gestapo and SS had been handpicked brutes and the instruments for the most appalling crimes. The prosecutors assumed that the SA had been similarly foul and disgustingly active. Only much later when the evidence was finally assessed did it slowly dawn that the SA was a group of much less importance. It was then seen to have been too large an organization, with too many involuntary members and too diffuse a set of activities, to be considered a cohesive, dedicated Nazi institution. Its role had dramatically diminished after the Roehm Purge in 1934. For the moment the prosecution realized none of this. The SA was confidently indicted.

After brief discussion they were also confident about indicting the Reich Cabinet. Inclusion seemed self-evident. Since the Nazi regime was on trial, what could be more logical than to indict its most central institution, the government itself. It was a clearly defined group; and small – only forty-eight people had ever held Cabinet office. Surely they must all have known what criminal decisions were being made; surely they all condoned the criminal acts that were authorized? But the prosecutors were misled by the term 'Cabinet'; they thought it implied 'Cabinet government', and that was not the way Nazi Germany had been run. Experts told them so: Hitler decided policy without consulting his Cabinet, then simply gave orders to whichever departmental head was needed to carry them out. (42) The prosecution picture of a Cabinet was to be fatally damaged when they at last discovered that the Nazi Cabinet met for the last time in 1937. But by then they had ignored expert advice and indicted it. The very fact that seventeen of the individual defendants were former members surely proved the Cabinet had been a criminal group, they argued. And they added to the Cabinet itself members of the Council of Ministers for the Defence of the Reich and those of the Secret Cabinet Council. These were grand titles, so it was assumed that the groups must have been important. All the prosecutors were happy with the decision to indict the Reichsregierung. They were to be less happy when they had to present this part of the case in court.

Pat assumptions again clashed with expert knowledge when it was proposed to indict the General Staff. The Americans above all seem to have had an image of the top Nazi military leaders in conclave with Hitler, standing round the map table and conspiring to wage war on Europe, directing attacks, issuing orders which resulted in war crimes on such a massive scale. Well, perhaps they must admit that the German General Staff had been abolished in 1918. But surely, they argued, the commanders-in-chief of the three armed services and their Chiefs of Staff together with the field commanders – the OKW and the High Command of the German Armed Forces – were still the same thing really, just with different names. There must have been an élite organization which acted like the old General Staff – why not call it 'General Staff *and* High Command'. At most the group had only involved about 130 officers over the whole period; several of them were defendants, others would soon stand trial for war crimes. These were the men who had planned the war and fought it so brutally. This was the group which summed up the worst aspects of militarism. As Jackson argued to Maxwell-Fyfe: 'Everybody is agreed it is a menace to the peace of Europe, that it is as guilty as any organization of the aggressive warfare, and it seems a little peculiar to convict others of aggressive warfare if they are innocent.' (43) The French and Russians were not entirely convinced by the American picture of a General Staff, but they were prepared to accept any formula which gave an opportunity to condemn the German military. The British were far from convinced that this formula would stand up in court. They took seriously the warnings of experts: Hitler had allowed no cohesive group to form and to direct military policy; even more than in the case of the civil government he alone had devised strategy, then given his orders to the relevant sections. It was with the most severe misgivings that at the very last moment the British prosecution team gave way to American insistence and accepted the indictment of the General Staff and High Command.

The Americans did not press their argument for indicting Ley's Labour Front for long. It was too large and vague a group and too many of its members had been involuntary and clearly non-criminal. Nor did they insist on indicting the Einstab Rosenberg – his institution for the wholesale looting of European works of art. It was a thoroughly nasty organization, but Jackson was ready to agree that it had 'a somewhat secondary status'. (44) For a time, too, he was prepared to drop his idea of indicting the Leadership Corps of the Nazi Party – the organization through which the Nazi leadership disseminated propaganda, distributed orders and kept check on the political attitudes of the people. It was feared that the Leadership Corps was too big – even when minor officials were excluded, there were at least 600,000 members involved – and that it would be difficult to show who had determined policy. Given the Corps' varied activities, many of which were non-criminal, it was doubted that an effective case could be mounted. But it was finally decided to indict it, asking for a declaration of criminality to be limited to the higher officials only.

Much of the discussion about the organizations had taken place with Jackson over the phone or by letter. He was spending more and more of his time in Nuremberg where he had a responsibility from which the other prosecutors were spared. Jackson was concerned with the physical arrangements for the trial. The US Army was working in a ruined Nuremberg where 'utilities, communications, transport and housing had been destroyed'. (45) He had to create a courtroom, a secure jail, and accommodation for up to 600 lawyers and staff, interpreters, clerical assistants and the Press and visitors. Ensuring adequate air and rail transport, setting up a motor pool, installing telephones and other forms of communication with the outside world was a nightmare. The military installed 124 miles of telephone wire in the courthouse alone; (46) 250 Pressmen were expected to file 180,000 words a day and needed signals equipment. (47) A hospital and dispensary had to be provided; messing and shopping laid on. Colonel Gill directed teams of US Army units and German POWs, including numbers of SS men in the building operations.

In midsummer the courthouse had been a shambles – one wing had been smashed in the bombing and further damage inflicted in the course of a last stand by SS units. Over everything hung a pink powdery dust which rose each time the wind blew over the devastated centre of the building. The courtroom itself was then being used as a recreation centre for a US anti-aircraft unit – the future judges' bench was the bar with pin-ups behind it, there was debris in all the corners, and spent shells, rags and rusty cans littered the floor. (48) The room only seated 200, so a wall had to be ripped out and a gallery constructed to make room for 500. Just as construction work was making some impact in August, the floor suddenly collapsed and faced the engineers with yet another problem. Yet when representatives of the prosecution teams flew out for a two day visit on 17–18 August they were reassured by the progress which had been made. They visited the jail where Andrus reported that Goering was in 'a filthy temper' and Ribbentrop had 'let himself go' and had not shaved for four days. They went to choose their future billets. The Russians found an ideal home – a house on the outskirts of the city which was large enough to accommodate almost the entire legal team and which had 'a large wall round it'. (49)

A major decision had been taken which solved the problem of how to run a trial in German, Russian, French and English. The Chief Interpreter at the US State Department had suggested using the new simultaneous translation method. (50) Robert Jackson's son, William, got in touch with

IBM in New York who could provide immediately their International Translator System. Its control panel provided up to five language channels for translators; these were then fed to headsets to be worn by participants in court, allowing them to switch to any language they chose. IBM were willing to provide this equipment free of charge, together with 200 headsets and the necessary boxes and cable, on condition someone else paid for the transport and installation. (This was an outstanding example of a 'loss leader'. Thanks to the great success of the system at Nuremberg, IBM were later able to sell it to the United Nations in New York.) This simultaneous translation system had actually been used recently, for instance at the International Labour Organization office in Geneva, but it was still relatively unknown. The initial reaction of the prosecutors in London to the idea of simultaneous translation was highly sceptical – it was hardly credible that one system could provide access to five languages, and beyond imagining that translations would ever be able to keep up with the proceedings. They could only believe that it would work for prepared speeches and previously translated documents. (51) However, under Jackson's persuasion, they agreed to a trial run.

Since the system was so new, it was obvious that translators would be difficult to find. Approaches were made to the State Department who recommended an outstanding man to run the system and hire the staff – Leon Dostert, at present a Lt. Colonel, but with wide experience in teaching languages and translating. He set to work to audition staff, finding that the job required 'mental concentration, fluency, composure, alertness and clear enunciation'. (52) The young were better than the old, he said, men were better than women, bilingual speakers better than those who spoke several languages. More headsets would be needed. The Army was scoured for a further 400. In addition it was decided to record the entire proceeding on wire – to give a check on the actual words used and the accuracy of their translations into the four languages. Did the US Signals Corps have enough wire recorders? Court reporters would also be needed to provide a daily transcript of proceedings. All the staff had to be hired and transported, then fed and billeted. All their equipment had to be found. How many typewriters, filing cabinets, desks, copying machines would be needed? How would they find enough paper in a continent so bereft?

Having sold the idea of a simultaneous translation system to his colleagues, Jackson went to the States at the beginning of September to persuade his government to speed up its decision on which American judges would be appointed to the Tribunal. Their choice finally fell on Francis Biddle – a Philadelphia Biddle, so an East Coast aristocrat. Biddle had always told Roosevelt that he did not enjoy being a judge and when Jackson was promoted from Solicitor General to Attorney General in 1940 Biddle got his heart's desire and became Solicitor General. Not for long, however. From 1941 to 1945 he again replaced Jackson, this time as Attorney General. In this post he won the respect of Truman – because of, rather than in spite of, Biddle's stern attitude to Truman's somewhat unsavoury political dealings in Missouri. Though Truman removed Biddle from office when he became President, he seems to have welcomed the chance to show his respect and to give Biddle a prestigious post on the International Tribunal. For most of his career Biddle had been one step behind Jackson; now he was in charge. It was an ironic situation which Biddle was to relish very much more than Jackson. Biddle's alternate – at this stage merely seen to be an understudy with no voting rights or active role in discussion – was to be Judge John Parker, a Southern Republican from North Carolina. Parker had become a circuit judge of the US Court in 1925. In 1926 he had been nominated an Associate Justice of the Supreme Court, but then failed to get Senate confirmation by one vote.

Robert Falco reappeared as the French alternate to a man even more silent – Henri Donnedieu de Vabres. Donnedieu de Vabres was professor at the Law Schools of Paris and Montpellier and an associate of the Institute of International Law at the Hague. He seemed a strangely scholarly choice at first – academic and impractical – but was eventually to prove incisive and tough in legal argument with the other judges. The Russian judge was already familiar to the prosecutors – Nikitchenko. His alternate was a complete unknown – Volchkov – and he remained unknown. He was said to be a member of the Soviet District Court; there was rumour that he had taught international law. But nothing he ever said or did suggested any particular legal interest or experience. Given his appearance and manner, it was universally assumed that he was Nikitchenko's 'keeper' – he smacked much more of the KGB than the Bench. (The head of the Soviet Secretariat at Nuremberg, A.I. Poltorak, has said in his book *The Nuremberg Epilogue* that Volchkov worked pre-war in the Soviet Foreign Ministry; at one stage he was sent to the Soviet Embassy in London. During the War he worked in the Army legal department.)

The British for their part made a complete meal of the appointment of their judges. Shawcross had insisted to the Prime Minister that the judges should be 'persons of high legal standing and experience'; the Foreign Office emphasized that they must be as senior as their American counterparts and that first-class men were needed given the international importance of the trial and its probable impact on international law. (53) The Lord Chancellor's office preferred to believe that imminent appointments to the International Court at the Hague were of greater importance, and they were reluctant to spare a Lord of Appeal on the grounds that without him legal business in the House of Lords would grind to a halt (though someone in the Foreign Office commented tartly that business there 'is surely often rather leisurely'). Finally, at the end of August the Lord Chancellor approached Norman Birkett, a judge of the King's Bench Division of the High Court since 1941. The letter he sent certainly gave Birkett the impression that he was to be chief British judge. He was delighted, but then shattered a few days later when Jowett told him that the Foreign Office wanted a Law Lord for the post. 'I cannot record the secret anguish this has been to me,' he noted in his diary; 'to have been elected as Member and then asked to become Alternate merely because of the absurd snobbishness of the Foreign Office.' (54)

Everyone continued to dither about who should be the British judge, and many names were canvassed until on 25 September the Lord Chancellor wrote to Sir Geoffrey Lawrence, from 1932 Judge of the High Court King's Bench Division and from 1944 Lord Justice of Appeal. Lawrence was surprised by the invitation but keenly aware that it was a duty to accept. Birkett was mortified – to be pushed to Number Two by a man who was not a Law Lord and for whose legal mind he had not the slightest respect. The Lord Chancellor's office had been much luckier than they deserved – they had hit on Lawrence by blundering, but though they did not realize it they had acquired a gem. Great legal mind he might not be but there were several adequate minds already on the Bench and his was far from inadequate. Lawrence's unique attribute was his ability to express the high standards he attached to his role. For many people at Nuremberg – including all the defendants – he would come to personify Justice.

So, with the judges chosen, the site of the trial being prepared and the prosecution cases well under way, it should have been possible to fix a date for the trial. But what was glaringly lacking from mid-September was an indictment. By about 18 September, the prosecutors in London had reached rough agreement on their proposals. Jackson in Nuremberg had not. He rejected their draft and began to rewrite it. The British sensed that his dissatisfaction was a symptom of the American 'wish to indict and obtain a conviction of the whole Nazi system as such'. (55) They were convinced that if the prosecution could obtain convictions of the majority of the individual defendants, then the world could be safely left to draw conclusions about the regime as a whole. In London Maxwell-Fyfe persuaded the drafters to speed up their work by treating only the four counts in documented detail. They should then attach a brief annexe on the individual responsibility of the defendants – the evidence with which they were charged could be produced in court as was Anglo-American practice; the documents attached to the charges should be sufficient indication to defence counsel of the line the prosecution would take.

Maxwell-Fyfe and de Menthon then flew to Nuremberg for two days to chivvy Jackson and coax him to accept the latest London draft. They found him stubborn; deaf and blind to their appeals that the case must begin and finish before the year was out (a wildly optimistic timetable, even given their view of the case). Their firm impression, however, was that he was relatively pleased with the draft they had taken. It was literally as Maxwell-Fyfe left that Jackson thrust into his hands an alternative indictment which bore little relation to their draft. (56) Maxwell-Fyfe was in despair. Perhaps this was a job for diplomats. Patrick Dean of the BWCE and Foreign Office was sent to Nuremberg on 25 September with yet another version. His reports were quite cheerful. Jackson had yet again rewritten the conspiracy charge – this version was 'an improvement'; Jackson and Alderman had been most co-operative. (57) Maybe. But the British were still resisting American determination to claim that every Nazi act from 1933 was somehow part of the intention to dominate Europe, by foul means if necessary. The British argued the idea was unprovable – and unnecessary since there was a perfectly good case from 1937 onwards. Nor could they accept the American insistence that every defendant must be charged with conspiracy. The case against some of them seemed too weak – Doenitz and Fritzsche in particular – and not being able to fit them all in was 'the penalty we have to pay for having rather too many defendants'. (58) Maxwell-Fyfe returned to Nuremberg on 27 September to urge these views. Slowly, agreement was pieced together. On 2 October, Jackson at last got the vote to indict the General Staff and High Command. On 3 October, he suffered a minor defeat when the other prosecutors refused to add two or three more industrialists to the indictment.

As if there had not been problems enough in drawing up an indictment, the Russians at the last moment demanded that the massacre of 925 Polish officers at Katyn be added. It was breathtaking. They had never mentioned it before. Everyone else was pretty certain that the Russians themselves had murdered the Poles. All those anxieties about protecting the Russians in particular against embarrassing evidence, all that concern about avoiding accusations of *tu quoque*, and here were the Russians wanting to deliver as large a collection of skeletons as could have been found. The others tried to argue the Russians out of their folly. They pointed out that there were not witnesses to the Katyn murders who 'would meet the high standards of credibility required in a criminal trial'; they pleaded that all the other prosecution evidence was from German sources whereas this charge was backed only by a Soviet government report. (59) The Russians were adamant. So on their heads be it. The charge went into the indictment; the other prosecutors made it quite clear they would play no part at all in this section of the case. In a final twist, which only made matters worse, twelve days after the indictment was signed the Russians insisted on changing the number of Polish officers killed to 11,000.

The indictment was finally agreed by the prosecutors on 6 October. An early British draft in July had covered two and a half pages; the final version occupies sixty-five pages in print. For the moment it was a secret: it had to await formal presentation to the judges at their first meeting in Berlin. That could not take place until it was translated into four languages and enough copies were available. It was reckoned that up to 1,000 copies would be needed for prosecution, defence and the Press among others, and there simply was not enough printing capacity available – possibly not even enough copying machines. (60) According to the Continental practice agreed to in the London Conference, as much evidence as possible had been attached to the indictment though full prosecution proof had still not been collected and chosen. Within that general framework national differences of approach showed. The French and Russian sections on War Crimes and

Crimes against Humanity (Counts Three and Four) were very detailed; those sections on aggressive war which had been drafted mainly by Jackson's staff were instantly recognizable to an American lawyer as in the narrative style of anti-trust indictment. American views had prevailed. In London the Americans had failed to convince the others of the importance of a conspiracy charge – the Charter had named three counts. Now Count One was concerned with the Common Plan or Conspiracy – and it covered all the crimes. Crimes against Peace had slipped down to Count Two; being drafted by the British it occupies three quarters of a page, and an annexe of broken treaties. The indictment introduced a new word to the English language – 'genocide'. It had been coined for a lamentable need by Professor Rafael Lemkin, a Pole by birth who was an adviser at the War Department in Washington. Given the differences of national approach, the scale of the case and the sheer tonnage of documents on which it was based, the indictment was no mean achievement. It remained to be seen how it would stand up in court.

References for Chapter Six

1 FO 371. 51025
2 Minutes of British Prosecution team, 29 June
3 Bradley Smith
4 BWCE N/10
5 See, for example, the Francis Shea memo to Jackson, 23 July. Jackson Papers, Box 197
6 *Manchester Guardian*, 29 August
7 *Glasgow Herald*, editorial, 30 August
8 *The Times*, 29 August
9 FO 371. 51033
10 Ibid
11 FO 371. 51038
12 Information kindly supplied by Professor Herbert Wechsler who discussed the problem with Biddle and Jackson
13 Sir John Wheeler-Bennett in his autobiography
14 IMT Vol. II
15 Much of the information on the discovery of the documents was provided by Kenneth Duke.
16 Jackson Papers, Box 213
17 Jackson Papers, Box 205
18 Telegram from US Army to Jackson. Jackson Papers, Box 193
19 Jackson Papers, Box 222
20 6 June Report to the President from Jackson
21 Interview with the *New York Herald Tribune*, 6 September
22 James Reston, *New York Times*, 9 September
23 Sidney Alderman. IMT Vol. II
24 This version of the debate is largely based on conversations with Dan and Harriet Margolies and William Jackson
25 FO 371. 51034

26 Lt. Commander Bracken to Jackson 30 August. Jackson Papers, Box 225
27 FO 371. 51034
28 A copy of this memo was kindly lent to the authors by Drexel Sprecher
29 BWCE N/10
30 BWCE N/30
31 BWCE N/10
32 Memo from Dean to Shawcross, 19 August. FO 371. 51034
33 FO 371. 51034
34 BWCE N/9
35 FO 371. 50988 Shawcross memo to Bevin
36 BWCE N/10
37 FO 371. 50988. Shawcross memo to Bevin
38 Jackson Papers, Box 205
39 FO 371. 51037
40 For example chief prosecutors' meeting, 13 September. FO 371. 51038
41 Shawcross memo to Bevin. FO 371. 50988
42 Passant at BWCE meeting 26 September. BWCE N/10
43 Jackson to Maxwell-Fyfe 22 September. BWCE N/10
44 Jackson. Indictments committee meeting. BWCE N/10
45 Jackson report to the President, 15 October.
46 Cooper
47 *New York Herald Tribune*, 18 August
48 Bernstein
49 British report on the visit. FO 371. 51035
50 Jackson Papers, Box 231
51 Prosecutors' meeting, 31 August. FO 371. 51036
52 Biddle Papers, Box 15
53 FO 371. 51037
54 Montgomery Hyde
55 19 September. FO 371. 50988
56 BWCE N/10
57 FO 371. 50988
58 Ibid
59 Jackson quoted by Kilmuir
60 BWCE N/10

Chapter Seven

Until the indictment was drawn up, the prosecutors had the principal responsibility for advancing the trial of the major Nazi war criminals. Now authority passed to the members of the Tribunal – the judges. Thanks to the insistence of the Russians at the London Conference, the judges were to meet for the first time in Berlin. Here they would formally receive the indictment and announce the date of the trial. The action would move to Germany at last; from this point the judges would control it.

They were faced with a series of worrying problems. They had to draw up Rules of Procedure to govern all aspects of the trial left undefined by the Charter; this meant reaching compromises between four national systems of conducting a trial. They had to supervise and approve the physical arrangements for the proceedings: the layout of the courtroom, the security arrangements for the defendants, witnesses and visitors, the translation equipment. They had to provide adequately for the defence, to decide on the appointment and payment of counsel, determine their access to documents in prosecution hands and facilitate ways of obtaining their own evidence and witnesses. Questions of recording and reporting the trial were still open: should there be sound recording of all proceedings for archive purposes; should filming be permitted; could a daily transcript be copied and circulated in time for all who needed it; what rights should the press be given? None of these problems usually disturb judges – all arrangements and procedures are well-established, with experienced staff available to carry them out. For the Nuremberg Trial everything had to be invented from scratch. Perhaps even the law itself? Certainly Judge Biddle had worried about the *ex post facto* elements in the trial as he travelled to Europe on the *Queen Elizabeth*. He discussed his worries with two aides, Quincey Wright and Herbert Wechsler – was the law being invented to fit the case? Wright assured him that although the procedure and sentencing would be *ex post facto*, the law they would apply had been firmly in existence before 1939. Biddle was satisfied: 'Our opinion must at least have its roots in the past even if its fruits are to open in the future.' (1) As far as procedure was concerned, and the rights of the court, he would accept the Charter as mandatory. On one question, however, Biddle remained uneasy. He was not convinced that it was right to try organizations. This was a doubt that would trouble his colleagues too in the coming year.

The Americans arrived in Berlin on 8 October, having lost a day when they were mistakenly flown to Paris. The British judges and their staff had arrived the previous day and were installed in a house requisitioned for the British Element in the Allied Control Council. As they waited for their fellow judges, there was time to go sightseeing, and men accustomed to the effects of the blitz on London were shocked by the condition of Berlin. John Phipps, once Lawrence's Marshal and now his Personal Assistant, described the 'unbelievable destruction on every side – street upon street, nothing but gaunt shells and rubble'. (2) They were struck by the contrast between the comfort of their own accommodation and the 'obvious poverty and distress of the Germans'. (3) Once the Russians arrived on 9 October, the judges could settle to a routine of daily meetings in the Allied Control Council building, which had once performed the function of a German Old Bailey. On most evenings they gave each other dinner. It was useful to talk shop under less formal circumstances and to establish friendly relations. After strenuous effort on the *Queen Elizabeth*, Judge Biddle had at last persuaded his American colleague, Judge Parker, to use his Christian name; but this was a familiarity Parker was most reluctant to extend to others. They also saw the prosecutors. Given the range of practical decisions to be made, it was essential to consult those who had been concerned with drawing up the Charter, who could estimate how long their cases might last and explain how they would be divided – nuts and bolts of organization rather than discussion of the case itself. Had defence lawyers been appointed, they too, no doubt, would have been approached. But it was an uncomfortable necessity for judges who are used to maintaining a certain distance from the prosecution. However, there seemed no alternative if sound decisions were to be reached quickly.

The first problem to be settled by the judges in Berlin was the delicate question of the presidency of the Tribunal. It was standard practice in international cases to rotate the presidency. The practice had the obvious disadvantage of introducing lack of continuity; and the British and Americans were determined to avoid it for this trial – they did not want to see the Russians in the President's chair. The British Foreign Office were keen to see Lawrence as President. They even lightheartedly promised a case of champagne to George Coldstream and John Phipps if Lawrence were chosen. At the first meeting, Geoffrey Lawrence, whose personal ambitions were not those of the Foreign Office, launched straight in to business. Biddle's sensitive nose was put out of joint. Lawrence had 'shoved in front of our noses a short and wholly inadequate agenda', he complained. 'I think the British are peculiarly inept.' (4) Biddle himself would have loved the role of President, but he was forced to accept that 'my own delegation think I should not preside as Jackson has taken such a leading part in the prosecution, and I have reluctantly agreed'. In private correspondence, the British were scathing about Biddle's estimate of his own abilities, and believed they were not alone in their views. (5) He therefore tactfully approached Lawrence behind the scenes and Lawrence agreed to take the position.

Next Biddle squared Donnedieu de Vabres. (6) Everything seemed set for a neat coup. What consternation there must have been, therefore, when at the Tribunal meeting on 13 October, General Nikitchenko, mistakenly omitted from the stratagem, proposed the nomination of Biddle as permanent president. (7) However many ashes Biddle found in his mouth, with typical charm and aplomb he managed to make a gracious little speech turning down the offer in favour of Lawrence and paying tribute to his experience and personification of the Common Law tradition. Infected by this spirit of international good will and good manners, the others promptly accepted Lawrence as their permanent president (they had been rather more impressed by his chairmanship thus far than had Biddle), but called on Nikitchenko to preside over the Berlin proceedings. Francis Biddle could only comfort himself by confiding to his notes: 'Lawrence depends on me for everything and I'll run the show.' (8) Experience would prove otherwise.

While still concerned with precedence and formalities, the judges next had to define the status of their alternates. Their decision was precipitated by Judge Parker. At their first meeting his eye had fallen balefully on their chairs: high-backed and carved for the judges, low and plain for the alternates. An observer noted that Judge Parker 'nearly split a gut'. (9) With enthusiastic support from Birkett – not at all a man to welcome a subordinate position – he pushed the judges to define a worthy role for the alternates. By the time the trial opened, it had been decided they would play a full part in it: they could ask questions in court, vote in judges' conferences, and be fully consulted before decisions were made on verdicts and sentences. They were promoted from understudies to major actors in the cast. Their chairs at Nuremberg were identical to those of the judges.

There only remained one pleasurable decision to be made before the essentials had to be tackled. What should the judges wear? The topic of clothing had enlivened many a prosecutors' meeting. Since the Tribunal was to be military as well as international, should everyone be given suitable rank and uniform? Back in August, Nikitchenko had always been confident that the Russian Army had a plentiful supply of distinguished judges and lawyers; the French were less certain about the legal talents of their military, and doubtful about the correctness of instant elevation of civilians to high military title. (10) By September the prosecutors had decided to remain civilians and had elected to wear their own national robes in court. (11) On 10 October, Nikitchenko suggested the Tribunal, however, should wear suits. His fellow judges wanted robes; Donnedieu de Vabres thought robes would 'conform to our intelligence and dignity' and anyway he was used to them. Nikitchenko protested that gowns reminded him of the Middle Ages. He was tickled by Lawrence's offer of a gown to try, but emphatic that nothing would ever induce him to try a wig. (12) In the end, the judges settled for wearing whatever they liked – and their own hair. Moscow's sartorial views obviously conflicted with Nikitchenko's. Both Russian judges appeared at Nuremberg in uniform; the rest in gowns.

And now the judges could address the problems of the trial itself. They began to hammer out their Rules of Procedure. They organized a secretariat and appointed Harold Willey (once secretary to the Supreme Court) as the General Secretary. From their Zones in Germany they obtained lists of German counsel from which defendants might choose if they had no lawyers of their own. By 15 October, sixty-four names had been collected but there was no background information on them. They might very well be Nazis, many of them could be members of the indicted organizations. However, it was decided that the Tribunal could not interfere with the rights of the defendants to choose counsel and that the list must be shown without any recommendations or prohibitions. It was agreed to adopt Lawrence's suggestions to appoint a fluent German-speaker as a clerk to deal with the defendants and explain their rights. They chose Airey Neave – a man whose pre-war competent German had been polished by residence in and escape from prisoner-of-war camps since. After consultation with the prosecutors it was decided to leave Martin Bormann on the indictment; there was still a possibility he was alive and the Charter permitted trial *in absentia* if he could not be found. (13) Meanwhile, notices were issued to inform him of the right to a hearing should he come to court. In the coming weeks 200,000 copies were distributed throughout Germany, the notice was broadcast once a week for four weeks on radio stations in the four Zones and published in newspapers in Berlin and other cities where Bormann had lived. The Tribunal issued another set of notices informing members of indicted organizations of their right to speak for them. These, too, were distributed, published and broadcast, and were sent to prisoner-of-war camps. One hundred and ninety thousand posters were sent round for display. (14)

Unfortunately the judges had all too much time for these decisions – because the indictment was not ready for them. When the Tribunal first met in Berlin it was still awaiting the formal signature of the French and Russians. Then Rudenko arrived late – according to Nikitchenko because he had not been told of the meeting – and the indictment had to wait again. (15) Finally, on 14 October, Rudenko requested postponement of the formal presentation on the grounds that the indictment contained 'inaccuracies in facts which require verification' and inaccuracies in the Russian translation. (16) The Tribunal was far from pleased at the delay. Biddle noted that: 'We all had the impression that he was taking orders directly from Moscow and perhaps that he had been severely criticized for silly mistakes in statements of facts.' (17) But it was just as likely to have been a delaying tactic while the Russians scrambled to pull their case together. The request for postponement confirmed John Phipps' view that the Russians had been 'dilatory and obstinate throughout', not least because they had to work on such a tight rein held in Moscow. (18) After asking the Russians to leave the room, the other judges decided to postpone the meeting for the presentation of the indictment and to issue a Press statement to save Russian faces. (19)

So the first formal session of the Tribunal was finally held in the morning of 18 October. It was a short, dignified ceremony. The members of the Tribunal swore on oath to exercise their powers and duties 'honourably, impartially, and conscientiously'; a representative from each prosecution team then made a brief speech and presented a copy of the indictment in his own language; the rights of the defendants were read out. Publication of the indictment was forbidden until 8.00 p.m. GMT that evening so that it could take place simultaneously in the capitals of the four Powers. (But several newspapers jumped the gun.) At last the starting date for the trial was announced – 20 November.

The text of the indictment was received with approval by the Press, and instantly generated a sense of horror. For the first time it was possible to see the range and nature of the charges against the defendants. The *Daily Telegraph* admitted that the sheer size of the document was enough to make anyone realize it had been unreasonable to criticize delays in publishing it. (20) The *Evening Standard* pinpointed the reaction of all the Press: 'In its concise, factual phrases it catalogues crimes so vast, so nightmarish, that it would seem at first impossible to convey the sense of them to the imagination.' (21) Many noticed its innovatory nature. *The Times*, however, believed that 'new evils require new remedies ... new sanctions to defend and vindicate the eternal principles of right and wrong'. (22) And the *Observer* was certain that men in the street would applaud the indictment for the very reason that 'it establishes a precedent, because it does not shrink from calling a crime what they know to be a crime.' (23) Both *The Times* and *Observer* pointed out that the creation of a tribunal was a political act. *The Times* argued this was unavoidable where existing procedures were inadequate; it presented no danger as long as it was 'honestly acknowledged and that no attempt be made to disguise the trial as a purely judicial process'. The *Observer* drew attention to the unhappy irony of current events in eastern Europe – Germans being deported from the Sudetenland and east of the Oder-Neisse Line. The *Daily Express* was surprised at the indictment of the General Staff which it rightly attributed to the insistence of Jackson, even though he admitted that the General Staff was not a body and had no definite organization or fixed membership. (24)

The German reaction to the indictment is more difficult to calculate. After all, the Press and radio in the four Zones were controlled by the occupying powers. The *Berliner Zeitung* was reported as saying that the punishment of Nazi leaders would be a big step towards Germany's atonement, (25) but perhaps a more accurate guide to the opinion of the Germans comes from the comments they made to interviewers. At the end of August, Robert Kempner, a German-born lawyer on the American prosecution team, had taken a straw poll as he travelled through several German cities. At that time, of the hundred Germans he spoke to, seventy-nine knew nothing about any trial of the Nazi leaders – though the London Agreement and Charter had recently been published. Kempner had urged Jackson to try to secure more publicity for the trial and its issues. (26) Once the indictment was published, Drew Middleton of the *New York Times* interviewed thirty Germans. (27) Many of them expressed dislike of retrospective elements in the trial (though his report does not specify which), and still felt that Hitler had been right to struggle against the so-called '*Diktat*' of the Versailles Treaty. Opponents of Nazism and those who had become disillusioned with it said they looked forward to the punishment of some, rather than all, of the accused, but many people feared that the trial would unleash anti-German feeling. Indeed several hoped that no details of prosecution evidence would be published. All too many Germans, however, would have agreed with the man who later spoke to the *Stars and Stripes*, the American services newspaper: 'We are too hungry to think about legalistics. Death is too good for the swine, but we are not interested.' (28)

The defendants were served with the indictment in Nuremberg jail on 19 October. Airey Neave had been approached the night before by Biddle in the foyer of the Grand Hotel and asked to distribute it. (29) Next morning, in his best service dress, Neave went the rounds of the cells, escorted by Willey, Andrus, Douglas Kelley, the prison psychiatrist, Pastor Gerecke, the Lutheran chaplain, an interpreter, a posse of military policemen and two soldiers carrying piles of the weighty document. Each defendant was given a copy and a list of lawyers. Frank burst into tears; Rosenberg and Ribbentrop trembled and moaned that they knew no lawyers. Keitel drew himself to attention and tried to click his heels – an attempt doomed by his thick felt slippers. (30) Jodl worried whether he should choose a criminal or an international lawyer; Neave suggested both. Goering, on the other hand, believed that no German lawyer would dare appear before the Tribunal. (31) Only Doenitz was prepared. He wrote on a slip of paper the name of his chosen counsel – Otto Kranzbuehler, a brilliant young naval lawyer from the German Judge Advocate's office. If he was not allowed to have Kranzbuehler, Doenitz said he was prepared to settle for a British or American U-Boat Admiral. Streicher had as yet made no choice, but his general principles were clear: he must have an anti-Semitic lawyer, for he had gathered that several of the judges were Jews. (32)

The next day Neave and Willey were carpeted by Biddle and Parker. The judges were shocked that remarks made by the defendants as they received the indictment had appeared in *Stars and Stripes*. Investigation proved that the leaks had come from members of Andrus' staff. The judges were infinitely more shocked, however, when they realized that the defendants had not yet got lawyers: these men had been in jail for three months without legal representation. If that had happened in America it would have constituted grounds for a mis-trial. (33) It was no excuse to argue that machinery for providing defence simply did not exist in Nuremberg. The machinery must be established. Adrian Fisher, one of their aides, and Airey Neave were ordered by the Tribunal to go back to the jail and make sure the defendants understood their rights. Every day for a month they were to be available in the jail and offer any help required in finding counsel. (34)

By 27 October only eleven defendants had found counsel. Some of them had discussed their choice with Frank who had once been president of the Academy of German Law. (35) Others asked their family lawyers for advice. Confusion occurred. Three defendants applied for the same lawyer; (36) Dr Dix, whom Schacht's wife had been advised to contact as a good criminal lawyer, took so long in deciding to accept the post that meanwhile Schacht had hired Professor Kraus, an international lawyer. (37) He kept them both – and so deprived Papen of his first choice, Dix. Instead Papen took the recommendation of a friend and obtained the services of Dr Kubuschok. Papen was delighted with him and his 'keen intelligence'. (38) Others were to regret the choice. Norman Birkett found him intolerable and jotted in his trial notes: 'he is not exactly to be described as a windbag, because that implies some powers of rhetoric and possible eloquence. Of these qualities this man is strikingly bereft.' (39) There was mutual satisfaction in Goering's choice of Dr Stahmer, a High Court judge from Kiel. Goering was delighted with him, and a newspaper interviewer found that Stahmer 'likes the job, enjoys the sessions with his client and is fully conscious that his name will go down in legal history as the defender of the chief defendant at Nuremberg'. As well as a pleasure he saw it as a duty to defend the former Speaker of the Reichstag and was 'not finding it difficult to persuade himself of Goering's innocence'. (40) No wonder Goering was delighted.

Inevitably the defendants were suspicious that the Tribunal would try to prevent a free choice of counsel. These suspicions seemed to be confirmed when for several weeks Keitel had no reply from a lawyer he had contacted. This looked like an official block. In fact it was one of the many hold-ups caused by sheer inefficiency. All the prisoners' mail was read by the prison authorities, as the defendants well knew. At this time only one soldier was available to do the job. He was plodding through mounds of letters, helped only by a smattering of school German and frequent consultations with a dictionary. Keitel's application was simply stuck in the pipeline. (41) The only occasion when the Tribunal did actually prohibit a choice of counsel was when Rosenberg applied for Frank to represent him. (42) The judges were not prepared to see one of the accused weaving from the defendants' box to the defence lawyers' lectern and then to the witness stand.

The application for counsel which caused most to-do was that of the Krupp family for an English lawyer, Andrew Clark KC, a Chancery Barrister. It produced much fluttering in British dovecotes. The Foreign Office was patently more concerned with personality than principle. It blamed Clark rather than the Krupps for the situation. 'It is consistent with our experience of Mr Clark that he should place us in this embarrassing position.' He had been Chief Designate of the Legal Division of the British Element of the Control Commission where his 'aggressive behaviour, hectoring manner and inconsiderate attitude' had 'irritated every official'. (43) The Foreign Office felt it would be difficult to stop him accepting the post, but were determined to make his job as difficult as possible and plotted to refuse any help in getting fees or finding accommodation. They were extricated from their 'embarrassment' – and Mr Clark was spared a potentially most uncomfortable stay in Nuremberg – by the legal establishment. On 22 October the Bar met and expressed a strong opinion that he should not go. The General Council of the Bar then issued a brief categorical statement, ignoring any principle involved and offering no explanation of their view, to the blunt effect that: 'It is undesirable that a member of the English Bar should appear for the defence.' (This was blinkering themselves to the fact that a Major Winwood was already appearing as a defence counsel at the Belsen trial. Or perhaps responding to the Press criticism of his appearance.) The Krupp family had to look elsewhere for a lawyer.

The Tribunal was constantly worried by the issues raised in the defendants' choice of counsel. They were concerned at the slowness of counsel in coming to Nuremberg – valuable time for preparing the defence was being lost. (44) They rejected Neave's suggestion that counsel might be compelled to appear; they preferred encouragement. Biddle suggested making repeated assurances that the Tribunal had confidence in German lawyers and that defence of Nazis would in no way reflect badly on them; Parker urged they be told that the Tribunal 'regard it as a duty' for lawyers to provide defence. This approach proved successful in the case of Dr Servatius who came to Nuremberg to offer his services: the reward for his conscientiousness was to be given the unenviable duty of defending Sauckel. (45) The judges found it distasteful that several defendants asked them not to appoint Jews as counsel but they felt that although the accused had no right to insist on such an unpleasant demand, the Tribunal was bound to take their tastes into account. (46) Similarly, they accepted Parker's view that 'it is all right to let a member of the Nazi Party appear, but it is probably not wise for the Court itself to select one to represent the defendants.' (47) In the event they accepted the appointment of a few former Nazis.* Sir Hartley Shawcross said of the final list that most of the German counsel 'although not brilliant were quite adequate and that we were anxious that this should be so'. (49)

The German lawyers had accepted their posts from mixed motives. Some undoubtedly had their hearts in the job: they were pleased to defend

*Bernstein suggests that 'nearly a score' of the defence counsel were acknowledged Nazis. A much lower figure was produced for the information of the British prosecutions by their German adviser, Dr Braun, who suggested six. (48)

their client, or the Nazi Party or the German people. Others regarded it as a lawyer's duty to defend, however difficult or obnoxious the client.

Kranzbuehler was surprised to be asked to defend Doenitz – he had not even realized that the Admiral had been charged. As a naval officer himself, as well as a lawyer, he was convinced his former commander had done his duty by trying to win the war and had done so without resort to criminal means. When the call to Nuremberg came, Kranzbuehler was a serving naval officer, part of a German team lifting mines from the port of Hamburg. With the approval of his immediate superior and a British Admiral, he became a naval officer on leave; as a Captain in uniform he felt entitled to a car and a driver to take him to Nuremberg. He got them, and a British officer to navigate. (50) He set off in relatively good heart to defend not just Doenitz but the German Navy. This was a very different mood from that of Dr Merkel who was horrified when a military policeman delivered a message to his office in Nuremberg to say the Tribunal had appointed him to defend the Gestapo. He had no desire to appear for 'these hangmen'; he was certain that the job would blight his career and probably involve some punishment in the near future. But he was persuaded by his brother-in-law that a lawyer must be impartial and decided to risk the consequences. (51) Dr Sauter was at first reluctant to accept approaches from several defendants but then impressed by his wife's view that he should take part in what promised to be the biggest trial in world history. Dr Seidl, a junior in Sauter's chambers, went to see some of the possible clients on Sauter's behalf and was himself snapped up by Frank. (52)

Underlying all their motives, however, there was one irresistible attraction which lured them to Nuremberg. It was not money. They would be paid 3,500 marks per month for one client, 5,200 for two. But occupation marks meant little in a ruined country with no resources. Much more important was food. The citizens of Nuremberg were living on an official ration of 1,365 calories a day, but the ration did not always provide meat and never included milk, fresh eggs or cooking fat. (Much had to be exported to Berlin where conditions were even worse.) (53) Those working for the Tribunal, however, would certainly get lunch provided by the Americans. Even better, they would be allocated PX supplies: every Friday a ration was issued of soap, chocolate, cigarettes, possibly even razor blades. These were goods more precious than rubies. They were unobtainable elsewhere, and were the most valuable currency in the barter economy. Twenty cigarettes might be worth £5 of marks, but marks were useless; what people wanted was cooking fat, sugar, light bulbs, soles for their shoes, fuel for their fires. With American rations and supplies a lawyer's family could live well above the standard of the average German. And a lawyer could attract some staff. All this, and anyone nominated by a defendant or requested by a counsel might well be released from prison or prisoner-of-war camp – Papen's son was given his liberty for the duration of the trial and came to assist Dr Kubuschok.

The lawyers' clients were now settled into Nuremberg jail. What a contrast with the way they used to stay in Nuremberg, at the Guest House as stars of the Nazi Party Rallies. Then they were escorted through the streets like Roman generals in triumph, they received flowers from shy blonde maidens, gazed down from the podium as the rally opened to the overture from 'Rienzi', soaking in the 'Sieg Heil' and the adoration. How the city had suffered since. When Albert Speer arrived from detention in 'Ashcan' he 'could only guess where the streets had once been. Amid the piles of rubble I now and then saw burned out or bomb-blasted houses still standing by themselves. As we moved farther into the centre of the city, I grew increasingly confused, for I could no longer get my bearings in this gigantic rubble heap, though I have known Nuremberg well since the planning of the buildings for the Party Rallies ... There in the midst of this destruction, as though spared by a miracle stood the Palace of Justice. How often I had driven past it in Hitler's car.' (54) This time, however, he was in a bus under heavy guard, and he stopped round the corner at the jail. Streicher had actually stayed there before – a brief imprisonment after he had whipped a boy prisoner for sexual gratification during an official visit to the cells as local Gauleiter.

Life in Nuremberg jail was different from the defendants' former imprisonment in 'Ashcan' or 'Dustbin'. Until now they had been allowed to mix, to talk, to attend lectures or sit on a terrace. Now they were largely confined to their cells, alone. They could write letters at last but only once a week and the length was restricted. Goering wrote 'the best and the longest'; Streicher could only manage three or four lines. (55) Parcels were forbidden. When the defendants arrived, Andrus promised them humane treatment; anything less, he said, was unbecoming to the United States. (56) But their former rank would gain them no privileges. Everyone was equal in the eyes of Andrus. When Hess was added to his clutch on 8 October it took time for the Colonel to find he was 'a good boy. When he arrived here he had some notions. But I pulled him up with a sharp "stand to attention when you speak to me" and he does as he is told now.' (57)

Many of the defendants were infuriated by Andrus' lack of respect; they could not forget their former status and the consideration due to it. Others were irritated by his pomposity and niggling attention to rules. But the more observant spotted the fundamental decency in the man – he was no sadist, and his peremptory manner did not always hide his rough kindness. When Fritzsche was brought to Nuremberg with Raeder from Russian detention, he was in a state of bewilderment. The Russians had told him he would be kept by them in solitary confinement. He had expected another Lubianka. Instead he was welcomed by Andrus, solicitously enquiring if he had been given drugs or beaten up in recent weeks and apologizing that there was no hot food because the kitchens were closed in the evening. Seeing his new prisoner tired and hungry after a non-stop journey by lorry from Berlin, Andrus sent a lump of cake to his cell. (58)

Nuremberg jail was connected to the courthouse by a wooden covered walkway. The building was made up of five wings radiating from a central rotunda, each with three tiers of cells. Two of the wings were reserved for civilian prisoners. In the others, Colonel Andrus was responsible for defendants and witnesses expected to appear before military tribunals. One of the wings held women like Ilse Koch from Buchenwald, allegedly pregnant by a guard; Margarete Blank, Ribbentrop's former secretary, Frau Himmler who had originally been lodged in the Grand Hotel because, she said, that was where she always stayed. Andrus was short of guards and grumbled that he was only sent 'cast-offs' (59) because the lowest grade of soldier was deputed to prison work. But with such men he had to keep check not just on an average of 250 prisoners but on the German prisoners of war who were repairing the building and performing the menial tasks. Many of his charges had been the leaders of Nazi Germany; Andrus was not alone in fearing there would be attempts to rescue them. There was another way Andrus could lose his prisoners, too. Between the tiers of cells he hung heavy wire mesh. As he explained: 'This is just a routine anti-suicide precaution ... When we take these men out for exercise we don't want any of them diving to their death.' (60) One day before the mesh was installed Goering was being taken to the Palace of Justice. From about eight feet above him an SS combat knife was thrown and landed at his feet. A guard grabbed it. The man who threw it disappeared. (61)

The defendants for the main trial were concentrated in one wing, on the ground floor. They were spread along a wide corridor with some twenty cells on either side. All the cells were roughly similar. Fritzsche carefully measured his; it was about thirteen feet by six and a half. They all had uneven stone-flagged floors, rough plaster peeling from brick walls, damp patches. In the wall facing the door was a high window; standing on a chair to look out was forbidden. At first the window was barred, later wire mesh was fitted, but as the weather got colder opaque glass was put in – the prisoners could no longer see the sky but the older ones were glad to be protected from the draught. Each cell was furnished with an iron bedstead with a straw mattress and grey American Army blankets. There was a wooden chair which could be made more comfortable by folding blankets as a cushion, and a table – deliberately rickety and anguishing to write at, let alone type. In a corner by the door was the only spot which could not be surveyed through the hatch in the door – the flush lavatory. Some of the prisoners contrived to obtain a box in which to store their possessions. They had few: most had not packed for a long stay and when they arrived at Nuremberg, ties, shoe laces, belts and nail files were all taken away. Some of them found a shelf where they kept their library books. Andrus was keen on them reading 'because I don't want them to become stir bugs [prison crazy]. A guy could go nuts sitting in a little cell with what some of these boys have got on their minds.' (62)

The prisoners were under constant surveillance. When they first moved to Nuremberg there was a guard to every four cells, with instructions to look in through the door hatch every thirty seconds, day and night. They were irked by the lack of privacy; some of them were maddened by their guards' attempts at conversation. But the checks did provide one never-failing entertainment. No guard could for long resist the temptation to prop his elbows on the ledge under the hatch on the corridor side. Time after time the ledge snapped off. It was one of the few laughs the prisoners had. For the rest surveillance became unendurable. The only escape was the lavatory. Surveillance was worst at night when a spotlight was beamed from the corridor on to each bed. It was forbidden to turn away and face the wall; anyone turning in his sleep would be shouted at by a guard or even prodded with a pole. Sleep was difficult enough anyway, with guards whistling and talking and stamping their feet as they changed shifts every two hours.

The prisoners' lives were governed by routine. They were woken in the morning as the spotlight was turned off and the guard changed yet again. Washing water was passed through the hatch by prisoner-of-war workers, followed by breakfast at about 7.00 a.m. – cereal and biscuits in an Army metal meatcan, coffee in a handleless canteen. Sometimes there might be scrambled dried eggs – 'a sensation', thought Fritzsche. (63) The utensils were then exchanged for mops and brooms. Cleaning out the cells was a task resented by some, never done properly by the sloppy Ribbentrop. But Keitel was, as ever, immaculate; he was back in Andrus' good graces as a model prisoner. And for Seyss-Inquart the job could actually be comforting. He wrote to his wife: 'it's strange to imagine a Reichsmarschall – usually with good humour – Field Marshal, Reichsminister, etc. single handedly cleaning their cells, but who otherwise would do it? . . I have sorted myself out an old washrag and every day I wash the floor. This beastly task always reminds me of the time after the war in 1919–20, when I had to do such chores in the confined space of my wife's household and these memories make me happy. A blanket over the table as a cover, the night clothes folded . . . the rest of my things in a large box that I begged. Isn't it really cosy, this cell 14?' (64)

Before the trial opened a barber came to shave the prisoners every other day. Later, for their public appearances, Andrus made sure his charges were spruced daily. Twice a week they were taken down to the basement where there were baths and showers in separate cubicles. When a new shower was put in on the ground floor the boiler was only lit on Fridays and even then the plumbing could only provide a thin trickle of water. (65) So, in compensation, daily cold showers were allowed; Frank, Sauckel, Fritzsche and Seyss-Inquart availed themselves of the privilege. (66) At mid-morning, drinking water came through the hatch, or even hot coffee if the weather was particularly chill. Then there were thirty minutes of exercise in the prison yard – 137 feet by 97½ with high prison walls on two sides, the walkway on the third and a wall with wire on the fourth.

The prisoners trudged along beaten paths between stunted trees. They were supposed to keep ten yards apart, but they invariably fell into groups

– it was the only chance in the day to chat to each other. They were a motley collection: Goering in a pair of beautiful yellow top boots for which he got constant offers ranging from cigarettes to regular payments to his family; Rosenberg in an overall like a member of the Tank Corps; Schirach in thin black American canvas breeches with baggy pockets and a German camouflage jacket; Frank in a tattered taxi driver's waterproof. Ribbentrop invented every possible excuse to avoid exercise but Papen was a keen believer in it and walked purposefully from one side of the yard to the other. So did Doenitz, who still strode with keen awareness of his own importance. Not everyone welcomed a chance to talk. Jodl 'displayed a formidable reserve', according to the gregarious Fritzsche. Schacht seemed 'cold, aloof, nearly always alone' but 'seething with rage inside'. Keitel found it difficult to break from his 'bewildered taciturnity' but he was always courteous. As was Neurath, who could on occasion show consideration and kindness to the prisoners he approved of. As the others chatted, Kaltenbrunner wandered from group to group, but found acceptance nowhere. Streicher was shunned. Frank treated everyone to 'yards of tragic verse'; Sauckel confided his fears for his family whom he dreaded falling into Russian hands. Schirach was often a focus – he sometimes managed to get American newspapers from his relatives and everyone clustered round to hear news of the outside world and details of the trial. But the life and soul of the exercise yard was Goering: affable, always trying to keep up everyone's spirits and inspire them to a good performance at the trial. (67) Their only crime had been to lose the War, he assured them. If all else failed he would try bracing, on one occasion promising them all marble sarcophogi from a grateful nation, on another guaranteed places in Valhalla, where he himself was expecting a hero's welcome as 'Treue Hermann', staunch defender of Leader, Party, Country. (68)

Then, after half an hour of fresh air, they went back up the eight steps and to their cells. There was lunch to look forward to – usually soup, meat and vegetables, bread. Supper, at 6.00 p.m. was a repeat of breakfast.

A Foreign Office official who visited the jail the following summer reported that a stipendiary magistrate who had been with him found the conditions similar to those experienced by a prisoner in a British jail at the start of a sentence. This opinion raised the question of whether the inmates at Nuremberg should not be living rather more comfortably and treated as innocent until proved guilty. The official was reluctant to cause embarrassment by putting the matter to the American authorities – anyway, by summer 1946, it seemed too late. (69) It was Andrus' view that though his prisoners were not molly-coddled, they were not in Dachau either.

With luck the afternoon might be enlivened by a call from a prison officer to hear complaints or from Dr Pfluecker to check on their health. He was a man of remarkable tact and discretion. Through all the long months he kept the trust and respect of prisoners and Andrus alike. He was a most welcome visitor – a German, so easy to talk to, and he might slip a sweet or a piece of chocolate to anyone who seemed in low spirits. On most visits he would be greeted by Ribbentrop with a new ill: a headache, a toothache and the complaint that he was 'a sick old man who should not be in prison'. (70) Or by Hess complaining of stomach cramps or hinting darkly that the guards were trying to poison him. Pfluecker thought that all Hess's pains were pyschological in origin; there could be no effective treatment while he was in prison.

Dr Pfluecker and his American assistants were doing a good job. He had a surgery on the floor above the defendants' cells, draped with blankets to make it warm and more cheerful. Nearby was the dentist's surgery and Dr Hansbach's physiotherapy room. By mid-November, Goering's hands were no longer shaking in reaction to deprivation of paracodeine and he no longer experienced acute stabs of pain. Ribbentrop's neuralgia was responding to heat treatment and Jodl's lumbago had abated. (71) Thanks to medical attention, Keitel's flat feet began to respond to exercise, Seyss-Inquart's stiff knee showed improvement and Frank's hand, paralysed since his suicide attempt, began to recover some use. (72) All this was due to good professional care. But Andrus, as usual, had a more earthy explanation for the general improvement in health of all the defendants, their lower blood pressure and firmer pulses: 'laying off caviar and champagne has done these boys a lot of good.' (73)

The prisoners' mental health was equally tenderly looked after, mainly by the psychiatrist, Dr Kelley, and the psychologist, Dr Gilbert. Those who disliked one usually responded warmly to the other. Goering was particularly devoted to Kelley. (74) Gilbert made a point of almost daily visits to the prisoners, chatting about whatever concerned them, questioning them about their attitudes to the past, the trial, each other, and making very detailed records of their conversations in his diary. Some enjoyed his visits – Speer thought 'he helped all of us, including Streicher, though Gilbert is Jewish. After he has left us I feel something akin to gratitude.' (75) Schacht found his talks 'were in parts exhilarating'. (76) Papen, on the other hand, complained about visits 'by gentlemen who called themselves psychiatrists; ... few of them gave the impression of having any genuine scientific qualifications'. (77)

Papen was particularly irritated when asked by Gilbert to do some intelligence tests – indeed only Goering, Schacht, Speer, Ribbentrop, Rosenberg, Sauckel, Hess and Fritzsche seem to have enjoyed them. (78) They began with ink blot tests. Schacht thoroughly enjoyed these because he could find 'an astonishing number of pictures and shapes'. (79) Then followed the Wechsler-Bellevue test, lasting for an hour, in which Gilbert tested memory, power to think in words and figures and to solve practical problems, speed of co-ordination and powers of observation.* Goering

*The test Gilbert used made allowances for the deterioration of I.Q. with age. In it a score of 100 was to be seen as average; university graduates would be expected to come in the 120–140 range. Gilbert recorded the following results for the defendants: Schacht 143; Seyss-Inquart 141; Goering 138; Doenitz 138; Papen 134; Raeder 134; Frank 130; Fritzsche 130; Schirach 130; Ribbentrop 129; Keitel 129; Speer 128; Jodl 127; Rosenberg 127; Neurath 125; Funk 124; Frick 124; Hess (tested later) 120; Sauckel 118; Kaltenbrunner 113; Streicher 106.

loved it. He behaved 'like a bright egotistical schoolboy, anxious to show off before the teacher'. (80) When told he was doing well he praised American methods; 'much better than the stuff our psychologists were fooling around with'. But he was furious to discover that Schacht had beaten him – as had Seyss-Inquart. Papen was not surprised by Schacht's high score. Nor by Streicher's bottom place – it was 'a position that could have been occupied by almost any of the other Gauleiters' he thought. (81) Gilbert had to abandon a test in which prisoners were asked to arrange a series of cards to make a comic strip – none of them could make any sense of it. He had waited patiently while Streicher struggled to work out how much change he would get from half a mark if he bought seven two-pfennig stamps. Streicher was sure the answer was twenty-six pfennigs; given a second try he stuck to his belief. Gilbert had been more amazed at Schacht's inability to do mental arithmetic; he had expected great things from a financial wizard. Schacht was not prepared to admit to any inadequacy: 'Any financial wizard who is good at arithmetic is probably a swindler.' From the tests, Gilbert drew the conclusions that all the defendants were 'intelligent enough to have known better'. (82) Andrus was not impressed by the results. 'From what I've seen of them as intellects and characters I wouldn't let one of these supermen be a buck sergeant in my outfit.' (83)

The only other relief from dull prison routine which the prisoners had been offered recently was interrogation. The number of interrogations had increased enormously in the first two weeks in October; Colonel Gill had pointed out that once the indictment was served the defendants would be more reluctant to speak. (84) After it was served, a notice was sent round telling the defendants that they would no longer be interrogated if they felt their interests were best served by refusing. (85) The interrogations had been conducted almost entirely by the Americans. The British preferred not to interrogate on the grounds that, however skilfully it was done, it would reveal the lines along which the prosecutors were thinking. (86) The Russians and French simply did not have enough staff or interpreters; they had to work through the Americans. American methods were far from ideal. The early arguments between Amen and Storey over the relative importance of witnesses and documents had intensified to the point where the two men were hardly on speaking terms and their sections deliberately co-operated as little as possible. Amen would only allow a member of his group to interrogate. As a result, when, for instance, prosecutors wanted to ask Ley about the relationship between the Nazi state and the Reich government, every question had to be fed first to one of Amen's staff – who knew nothing about the subject and needed explanations before he could frame the question, then to an interpreter – because few interrogators spoke German – and only then to Ley. The process took all day. Even Ley became so frustrated that he began to speak directly to the prosecutors in broken English. (87) The chronic lack of German speakers could cheer interrogations for those with a sense of humour. One day Russians were feeding questions to Jodl through an American interpreter and intermediary. They were trying to pin responsibility on him for one particular criminal order. Jodl denied ever seeing it. The Russians tried a sideways approach: 'If this order had been put before you, would you have approved of it?' Jodl batted the question back with contempt: 'If my grandmother had wheels, would she have been a bicycle?' The Russians were fascinated: 'Your grandmother was there? Why was she concerned in the matter?' (88)

The man most absolutely resistant to interrogation was Hess. Since his arrival in Nuremberg his amnesia had seemed almost total. He made no response when old friends or members of his staff were brought to the jail. After being shown a film of great moments in Nazi history with Jackson, Donovan, and three psychiatrists observing his reactions, Hess said: 'I recognized Hitler and Goering. I recognized the others, but only because I heard their names mentioned . . . I must have been there, because obviously I was there. But I don't remember.' (89) Gilbert observed him closely, but remained uncertain whether the amnesia was total, and whether it was all genuine. 'Occasionally he would seem to be deliberately suppressing a recollection that flitted through his clouded mind.' (90) Given the impenetrability of that mind, the prosecutors finally agreed to take up Goering's offer to interrogate Hess himself. Goering and Hess were put into a room alone – but the room was bugged. Those listening were delighted with the result. Goering produced a wonderful performance, a beautifully observed parody of an American interrogation. It was great entertainment, but no more successful than any of the attempts it was based on. Hess yielded nothing. Only Goering profited. He had won a little applause and a few hours escape from the torture of solitary confinement. (91)

The excitements of intelligence testing and interrogation were few and far between. Day after day the prisoners endured the dull routine of prison life, the long hours alone in their cells. The latter part of the day was the worst. After supper there were no breaks, nothing to look forward to, except perhaps the offer of a sleeping pill from Dr Pfluecker, until cell lights went out at 9.30 and the hated spotlight came on. Many noticed that they were lapsing into a 'kind of chronic drowsiness' – the disease of the institutionalized. (92) So the serving of the indictment came as a shot of adrenalin. The prisoners began to study the charges, write memos to their counsel, prepare their defences. They could now ask to see their lawyers – and a visit meant escape from the cell. They were escorted to Room 57 in the Palace of Justice. At the door they were frisked by guards as were their counsel. Then they were taken through the outer office and into the Defendants' Visiting Room. As yet it was not divided into separate cubicles. The defendants sat on one side of a row of tables, the counsel at the other. Guards stood behind them.

The prisoners' reaction to the indictment had varied according to their characters. Gilbert had given each of them his copy and asked for an autograph and a comment on it. (93) Not surprisingly Hess just wrote: 'I can't remember.' Goering provided his stock response: 'The victor will always be the judge and the vanquished the accused.' Seyss-Inquart hoped the trial would be 'the last act of the tragedy of the Second World War'.

A few such as Speer recognized some truth in the indictment. He wrote: 'The trial is necessary. There is a common responsibility for such horrible crimes even in an authoritarian system.' Fritzsche saw it as 'the most terrible indictment of all times' and added: 'Only one thing is more terrible: the indictment of the German people will make for the abuse of their idealism.' Sauckel took it more personally: 'The abyss between the ideal of a social community which I imagined and advocated as a former seaman and worker and the terrible happenings in the concentration camps, has shaken me deeply.' Jodl was prepared to accept that the indictment contained some truth, but he added that he regretted 'the mixture of justified accusations and political propaganda'. Later he told Gilbert he had had no idea of 90 per cent of the accusations. 'The crimes are horrible beyond belief, if they are true.' Jodl was most bewildered by being held responsible for his acts as a soldier. 'I don't see how they can fail to recognize a soldier's obligation to obey orders. That's the code I've lived by all my life.' Obviously he had not recently read the commandment in his army paybook which forbade any soldier to obey illegal orders. Nor had Keitel who commented on Gilbert's indictment: 'For a soldier, orders are orders.'

A common reaction was to disclaim all involvement. Doenitz: 'None of these indictments concerns me in the least. Typical American humour.' Schacht: 'I do not understand at all why I have been accused.' Funk: 'If I have been made guilty of the acts ... through error or ignorance, then my guilt is a human tragedy and not a crime.' Kaltenbrunner felt no guilt: 'I have only done my duty as an intelligence organ and I refuse to serve as an *ersatz* for Himmler.' Ribbentrop, too, thought others should be on trial, not himself. He wrote: 'The indictment is directed against the wrong people,' but decided not to add 'We were all under Hitler's shadow.' Frank had no such scruples about mentioning his Führer: 'I regard this trial as a God-willed world court, destined to examine and put an end to the terrible era of suffering under Adolf Hitler.' And Papen was prepared to attribute blame. He wrote that he was horrified by the irresponsibility with which Germany had been thrown into the War and the world-wide catastrophe; and by the 'accumulation of crimes which some of my people have committed, the latter is psychologically inexplicable. I believe that paganism and the years of totalitarianism bear the main guilt. Through both of these Hitler became a pathological liar in the course of the years.' Schirach, on the other hand, thought: 'The whole misfortune comes from racial politics.'

A few of the defendants were more concerned with their immediate legal position. Neurath commented, 'I was always against punishment without the possibility of a defence.' Frick complained: 'The whole indictment rests on the assumption of a fictitious conspiracy.' Rosenberg too rejected 'an indictment for conspiracy' and added, 'The anti-Semitic movement was only protective.' Streicher no doubt thought such protection was still needed: 'This trial is a triumph of World Jewry.'

Only two of the accused did not record their comments on the indictment for Gilbert. Raeder refused to; Gilbert believed this was partly the result of his recent treatment by the Russians and that Raeder was not prepared to commit himself to anything. The other was Robert Ley. By the time Gilbert circulated his copy for comment, Dr Ley was dead.

In recent weeks, Ley had stopped writing to Henry Ford to ask for a job when the trial was over. (He had emphasized his admiration for Ford's technical abilities and the way he had learned from him when planning Volkswagen.) (94) He had been complaining of sleeplessness and often wept. When Gilbert and Kelley visited Ley in his cell on 23 October he was pacing up and down and clearly agitated. He said he could not prepare a defence, that he knew nothing about any of the crimes alleged. He stood against the wall, arms raised as if in crucifixion, and asked why the victors did not shoot their prisoners if they wanted more sacrifices. 'But why should I be brought before a Tribunal like a c ... c ... c ...', Gilbert supplied the word 'criminal'. (95)

On the evening of 25 October, Ley stuffed his mouth with strips of his underpants, attached the zip from his field jacket to the water tank of the lavatory, then tied it to a noose of wetted towel around his neck. He strangled himself. A guard on a routine check found the body still warm, but Pfluecker's attempt to give injections and artificial respiration could not revive him. In the cell a series of notes was found saying he could stand the shame no longer and that 'I was with Hitler in the good days and ... I want to be with him in the black days.' He condemned anti-Semitism, and said it had distorted the Nazi outlook. 'We have to declare to youth that it was a mistake.' (96) No one mourned Ley. Not even Streicher, though Ley had forced workers to buy *Der Stürmer* and had been the only prisoner prepared to associate with him. Streicher thought suicide a coward's act and the condemnation of anti-Semitism a 'big mistake'. (97) Goering thought it was just as well Ley was dead. 'I had my doubts about how he would behave at the trial ... I'm sure he would have made a spectacle of himself. Well, I'm not surprised he is dead, because he has been drinking himself to death anyway.'

The defendants only heard of Ley's death on 29 October; Andrus had wanted the news to be kept secret in case suicide became contagious. He had already lost one prisoner that way – Dr Leonardo Conti, the so-called 'Head of National Hygiene' who had set about his task of cleansing the nation through medical experiments and 'mercy killings'. Conti had hanged himself on 5 October with a towel tied to the bars of his window. After Conti's death, Andrus had replaced the bars with wire mesh. After Ley's death he quadrupled the guard – a man to every cell.

As the accused worked on their defence, the prosecutors too were struggling to pull their case together. For a long time the teams had been split. The American advance party went to Nuremberg on 7 September, most of the other Americans flew out on the 15th. The other teams stayed in London – the British presence in Nuremberg was only complete by 28 October. Progress on the documentary evidence was painfully slow. When Maxwell-Fyfe had seen Jackson in Nuremberg on 21 and 22 September, the Americans had chosen 1900 documents for their case but had only thoroughly analysed 500 of them; the rest had merely been given a rough card-index description. (98) A memo from Gill to Jackson admitted that only 600 of the 1900 had even been translated. (99) Gill pleaded for more staff: secretaries could keep up with copying, though they had no photostat machines by 13 September, but he was desparately short of screeners and translators. (100) Maxwell-Fyfe blamed the delays not on shortage of staff but on lack of selectivity. He decided to by-pass the American system and despatched Barrington to choose documents and send them back to London for analysis. The rate of American document processing did not improve. By 1 November they had to introduce a night shift in the translators' pool; by 4 November they had had to enrol 40 extra typists. (101) But by 5 November they had still lodged only 40 per cent of their documents. Maxwell-Fyfe saw this as a sign that American material had 'outgrown the power to handle it' and offered British help in selection. (102)

The arrival of the other prosecution teams in Nuremberg merely increased the strain on American resources. The Russians arrived without any translators. Jackson rightly complained when they tried to borrow his. (103) The French were lagging too; few of their documents were ready to be lodged. Jackson threatened to complain to their governments in Paris and Moscow about the failure to provide adequate staff and equipment. But thanks to British help, by 27 October the situation had improved: three quarters of the French documents were translated, so were the Russian official reports. Dubost could now graciously offer the other teams the use of the French photostat machine – when it arrived. (104)

The duplication problem was so acute because copies of documents had to be provided not just for prosecution use but for the defence. On the Tribunal's instruction six copies at least had to be deposited in the Defendants' Information Centre in the Palace (ideally there should have been more, but six tended to be the limit given the shortage of typists and copying machines). The room was ready by the beginning of November. But since the prosecution material was not, at first only lists of documents to be used could be deposited; a deadline of 15 November was set for the provision of the copies. (105) The Centre also had to be supplied with documents requested for the defence case, relevant published material and any extracts from interrogations of defendants the prosecution intended to use (though not even non-American prosecutors could get copies of interrogations by the end of October). (106) The Tribunal had expressed the hope that the prosecution would help the defence to obtain material for their case. (107) Jackson was furious – it did not seem to him the job of prosecutors to work for the defence and he pointed out he had needed 700 people to assemble prosecution evidence. He insisted on very careful assessment of the value of evidence requested by the defence before any effort was made to obtain it. Eventually day-to-day consideration of defence applications was handled by a Court Contact Committee and major disputes were settled by the Tribunal. Meanwhile the defence's practical problems were alleviated by the appointment on 6 November of a new General Secretary to the Tribunal – Mitchell. He was more efficient than Willey and able to pull his rank as a Brigadier General to enrol Army help in finding evidence and witnesses for the defendants.

Given the way the Americans were developing Count One on conspiracy, clashes over the division of the prosecution case were inevitable. They first occurred with the British who accused the Americans of having 'poached considerably' on the British count dealing with Crimes against Peace. Patrick Dean was charitable enough to believe that the overlap had arisen 'not so much from American ill will as out of the fact that their mechanical arrangements for presenting evidence are not very satisfactory, and having prepared briefs for the whole of Count One, the Americans find it difficult not to stray over into matters which more properly belong to Count Two' and the British. (108) Maxwell-Fyfe was not convinced. He blamed the problem on the American belief, 'which is legally quite wrong', that the conspiracy charge must show the aggression which resulted and indeed the atrocities which followed. (109) He was determined that the American case must stop with the takeover of Czechoslovakia; he wanted the British to deal with Poland – not least because they had good documentary evidence to cover it. And certainly he insisted on presenting the case on the invasion of Russia – a clear crime against peace, and one for which the British held the essential evidence, the Barbarossa File which contained all the invasion plans and which Maxwell-Fyfe reckoned was 'one of the few interesting documents which the British Delegation can produce'. To clarify the division of the case, and to try to pre-empt any further American poaching, Maxwell-Fyfe presented a memo to the chief prosecutors on the demarcation of areas of responsibility. It was finally accepted on 7 November – the French and Russians were obviously pleased to guard their own cases against American encroachment. The Americans had been forced to limit their count to general background on Russia and to allow the British to intervene during the presentation of the conspiracy case to deal with Poland.

As if processing evidence, legal arguments and jockeying for position were not enough, the chief prosecutors had practical demands to satisfy. As Maxwell-Fyfe put it in a letter to his wife, he had three roles: 'Running a seemingly unending international conference, partly running a small department, and lastly getting up a case for trial'. The department was not so small. In November there were 168 British personnel in Nuremberg, if drivers, cooks and bottlewashers were included, and Maxwell-Fyfe was directly responsible for over a hundred of them. Colonel Turrall might officially be administrative officer but, given problems great or small, the British staff went to the top, to Maxwell-Fyfe. He had to help with their billetting, their transport, their feeding arrangements. He had to soothe ruffled feathers and try to establish a reasonable working atmosphere. It was a complex task; '. . . if the military counsel of the delegation are billetted separately from the civilian counsel, the delegation will fall into two camps; if they remain mixed Colonel Turrall will get on Mr Elwyn Jones' sensitive socialist nerves. Miss Kentish's billet's bathroom has no curtains and none of the female staff can have a bath for fear of being overlooked; there are no driers for the photostat machine; 'Khaki' Roberts has failed to remember to bring a towel and has pinched mine just as I was going to have a bath; the Russians wish to add twenty-eight new documents at the last moment, the French have no translators . . .' (110) He thought these were teething problems and he was right. The British team soon had a pleasant working relationship and could rely on Maxwell-Fyfe to combine the parts they had cast him in: capable lawyer, efficient administrator and concerned housemaster.

The judges, too, had troubles before they could settle into Nuremberg. When Judge Biddle and Judge Parker first arrived they were entirely dissatisfied with their accommodation. The two men, with little or nothing in common, had been squashed into the same house with several of their staff. Biddle blamed their discomfort on the then General Secretary: 'Willey is utterly incompetent.' (111) The basic furniture only arrived after they did. It was a particular shock to Americans to realize that eggs and fresh milk were unobtainable. One thing might cheer them. As Biddle's secretary wrote to Mrs Biddle: 'All we would like to have is a light so that we are able to read or write.' (112) The house had few electrical fixtures and seemingly no bulbs over forty watts. The judges' complaints to the Army got neither an immediate nor a sympathetic response. Army resources were stretched to the limit and as one GI put it to Biddle, he could not see the point of bringing over 600 men (Jackson's) to kill twenty-four. (113) The Tribunal might be thought lucky to have roofs over their heads; some GI's had been moved into tents because of shortage of housing and in the centre of the city many of Nuremberg's remaining 175,000 inhabitants were living in cellars which were all that remained of the buildings; whisps of smoke from their fires came eerily through the rubble on the ground.

Physical arrangements had not improved by the time the British judges arrived on 27 October. 'We have been faced with what amounts to an American administrative breakdown' their staff reported. (114) The judges and their staffs were crammed into one small house. They found 'one sheet each and straw-filled pillows'. There were no cooking utensils, no running water, no electricity. Their offices were not yet ready and they had no photostat machines. Colonel Turrall was made Quarter Master Sergeant and within two days had found more sheets and within a week a house for Birkett; pillows, cutlery and glasses took longer. Fortunately this was only a temporary stay for the judges. They went home and only returned to Nuremberg on 13 November. On this occasion fog saved them from the nasty business of landing at the airfield near Nuremberg – it was an experience to turn the stomach of all but hardened combat pilots. Instead they had driven from Brussels – two judges, several of their staff, and three doctors going to examine Hess – through rain, sleet and fog in two cars with no windscreen wipers, (115) driven by Phipps and Shawcross because their army drivers had already had twenty hours at the wheel. But at least they arrived to find that administrative problems were 'greatly eased' (116) partly thanks to the appointment of General Mitchell. And a vital creature comfort had been provided. On their previous stay they had been acutely embarrassed by the need to apply to the Americans for drink. After a lengthy correspondence conducted by the British prosecutors which went as high as the Foreign Secretary, the Chancellor of the Duchy of Lancaster had arranged to send three cases of gin and whisky weekly to Nuremberg to satisfy British needs. (117) Things were looking up.

The judges settled to work; hard work which Biddle thought might be eased if only they could find an electric kettle. They sat 'often until 6.30 ... tea would be nice'. (118) He wrote to his wife on 18 November: 'We have had a hard week with the Russians who have taken to opposing everything,' but it might be better now that Nikitchenko, after a week's delay, had turned up. They published the Rules of Procedure, making it clear that they might be adjusted in the interests of a 'fair and expeditious trial'. They tackled the physical aspects of the trial: ordered a dress rehearsal for the interpreters, approved security arrangements for the courtroom and escort of prisoners, set up the procedure for the transfer of documents to the defence and agreed to the installations for photographing and filming in court. They pushed constantly for the speedy provision of counsel for the defendants and set up channels for finding witnesses and transporting them to Nuremberg. They met the defence counsel to brief them on the arrangements and to assure them there would be a fair hearing.

The judges were faced with pressing problems concerning the defendants. Repeated medical examinations had still not clarified the extent of Hess' amnesia. Was he fit for trial? Was Streicher sane? His counsel, Dr Marx, believed that the virulence of his anti-Semitism proved he was not. The Tribunal directed French, Russian and American doctors to examine him to decide whether he was fit to appear and present his defence; and whether, if insane, he was capable of understanding his acts during the period covered by the indictment. (119) The three doctors reported on 19 November. After being harangued by Streicher on how he had studied the Jewish problem for twenty-five years they had decided he had a neurotic obsession but was legally sane.

The judges' knottiest problem was that of Gustav Krupp. They were aware that he might be too ill to stand trial. Therefore they had given instructions to the court officer who served him with the indictment on 19 October to report back on his state of health. James Rowe, an aide to the American judges, had found Krupp virtually comatose. He sent three medical reports to the Tribunal, all telling the same story: that Gustav Krupp was suffering from progressive arteriosclerosis, the symptoms of senility and the after-effects of strokes. He was totally bed-ridden, required intensive nursing and for over a year had had no bladder or sphincter control. He was almost incapable of speech; he just managed the occasional 'Ach Gott' or 'Donnerwetter' when he was irritated by being moved, or a few sounds which his wife could interpret. For the rest only sporadic bouts of weeping stirred him. (120) To confirm these reports, the Tribunal sent a high-ranking medical commission of British, American, French and Russian doctors to examine Krupp. Their report could add nothing to those of previous experts. Although Gustav Krupp had gasped 'Gutten Tag' as they went into his room, he had been incapable of understanding them or co-operating in any way. He could not possibly take part in court proceedings, indeed any attempt to move him would endanger his life. There seemed no hope that he would ever recover sufficiently to stand trial in the future. (121) On 4 November Krupp's counsel, Dr Klefisch, filed a motion requesting the Tribunal to suspend proceedings against his client.

Dawning awareness of Gustav Krupp's condition had thrown the prosecution into disarray. Their different solutions to the problem were already clear by 26 October. Jackson wanted to add the name of Alfried Krupp to the indictment – it was essential that the family be represented at the trial and that it should be made the scapegoat for German industry. Dubost actually suggested that Bertha, Gustav's wife, should be indicted, but the idea was totally unacceptable to the Americans and Russians (and indeed implies that the French thought the name 'Krupp' enough, regardless of who bore it). Faced with this rejection the French fell back on their treasured solution to all problems: the immediate announcement of a second trial, one in which Alfried and many other industrialists and financiers could be tried and a full examination of the economic case against Germany carried out. As ever, the others opposed announcing a second trial; they wanted to see how successfully they could cope with the first. (122) Maxwell-Fyfe continued to argue that the loss of Gustav Krupp did not mean the loss of the industrial element in the case as a whole; this could be adequately dealt with in the conspiracy count. (123) The British fear was that any attempt to amend the indictment would delay the start of the trial (a new defendant would have to be allowed at least three weeks to prepare a defence before the proceedings began). For the British the desire for a prompt start always overcame any other consideration.

British fears increased in November when Jackson began to press determinedly for the trial of Gustav *in absentia* or for the addition of Alfried to the indictment, possibly with two other industrialists. (124) The British temporarily kept the support of the French and the Russians and Jackson's plan to amend the indictment was twice out-voted. (125) But it was clear that the French were wavering – if the Tribunal showed willingness to add the name of Alfried Krupp they would swing to support Jackson. The British totally failed to appreciate the importance in American and French eyes of having a representative of German industry in the dock. They saw all arguments as a cover. As Maxwell-Fyfe wrote to Shawcross on 9 November, he believed that Jackson was looking for excuses to postpone the trial because his case was not ready; 'this is yet another move in that direction.' (126) And when Jackson finally won French and Russian support, the British reported to London that 'neither delegation was ready to begin'. (127) The three teams, but not, significantly, the British, filed a request to the Tribunal that either Gustav Krupp should be tried *in absentia* or his son Alfried should be added to the indictment.

The Tribunal was horrified by the request. They were particularly outraged by the idea which had occasioned little debate among the prosecutors, that Alfried should be indicted only if Gustav was not tried. This was no longer a matter of adding a name. It was actually asking for a name to be substituted, and substitution is a practice unacceptable in any court. The Tribunal minutes, always carefully composed to conceal argument or opinion, record that several members found the suggestion 'shocking'. (128) Judge Parker paced up and down in a park with his aide, Adrian Fisher, and gnawed over the issue. 'Cap'n, if we were to grant this motion, there wouldn't be a lawyer in North Carolina that didn't think we had permitted substitution in a criminal trial.' (129) The North Carolina Bar was always for Parker the most trusty yardstick against which principles and procedures would be measured. Jackson's proposal fell far short of the standards of that estimable body.

The whole matter was thrashed out in an open session of the Tribunal on 14 November. (130) Dr Klefisch presented the facts on his client's health and argued effectively against his trial *in absentia* on the grounds that it would be contrary to the provisions for defence in the Charter and contrary to recognized procedure in all civilized countries. He hit hard at the idea of adding the name of Alfried: 'It seems to me to be a bit strange, to say the least, if Alfried Krupp were to be put on the list as a principal criminal now, not because he was marked as one from the beginning, but because his father cannot be tried.' In reply, Jackson pleaded the need for a representative of the German armaments industry, vagueness in the Charter over trial *in absentia*, and the fact that the Krupp family was wealthy enough to employ unparalleled facilities for defence. He suggested that should Alfried be indicted the subsequent delay in starting the trial would be minuscule considering that eight months previously 'the German Army was in possession of this room, and in possession of the evidence that we now have'. His argument was not impressive. Much of the ground had been cut from under his feet by the British refusal to sign the motion. It was hacked away further when Sir Hartley Shawcross told the Tribunal:

'This is a court of justice, not a game in which you can play a substitute if one member of the team falls sick.'

That was very much the Tribunal's view. Although they wrangled until 17 November over the exact wording for their rejection of the motion to add Alfried, reject it they did. They also refused to try Gustav *in absentia*. The Tribunal had accepted the need for such a procedure in the case of Bormann, but in their opinion 'where nature rather than flight or contumacy has rendered a trial impossible, it is not in accordance with justice that the case should proceed in the absence of a defendant'. But Gustav's name was left on the indictment just in case he should recover during the proceedings.

What a prelude to the trial! Prosecution disagreements had been aired in open court, a defence motion had been accepted by the Tribunal when two linked prosecution requests had been refused. Whatever the defence had feared on this occasion, at least the promises of the Charter and the Tribunal that they would be given a fair hearing had been kept. A small public opinion poll conducted for the *Stars and Stripes* on the eve of the trial showed that most Germans assumed that the defendants would all be executed after a brief hearing. A girl had told the interviewers: 'It is all cut and dried. We are sick of propaganda.' (131) But after this first hearing such doubters might have picked up the hint that 'victors' justice' would not turn out to be a sham. Perhaps there was going to be a real trial.

References for Chapter Seven

1   Biddle Papers, Box I. Notes on Conference
2   Letter to his wife kindly lent by John Phipps
3   11 October entry in his diary kindly lent by John Phipps
4   Biddle Papers, Box I. Notes on Conference
5   LCO 2. 2982
6   Conversation with John Phipps
7   Tribunal minutes, 13 October
8   Biddle Papers, Box I. Notes on Conference
9   Conversation with Herbert Wechsler
10 FO 371. 51036
11 Minutes of prosecution meeting, 26 September. BWCE N/10
12 Biddle minutes of session. Biddle Papers, Box II
13 Tribunal minutes, 17 October
14 IMT Transcripts. Vol. I
15 LCO 2. 2982. Minutes of Tribunal meeting 10 October
16 Tribunal minutes, 14 October
17 Biddle Papers, Box I. Notes on Conference
18 John Phipps letter, 15 October
19 Tribunal minutes
20 *Daily Telegraph*, 19 October
21 *Evening Standard*, 19 October
22 *The Times*, 19 October
23 *Observer*, 21 October

24 *Daily Express*, 19 October
25 Quoted in *Manchester Guardian*, 19 October
26 31 August. Letter from Robert Kempner to Jackson. Jackson Papers, Box 216
27 *New York Times*, 31 October
28 *Stars and Stripes*. Germany Edition, Frankfurt. 21 November
29 Airey Neave *Nuremberg*
30 Airey Neave *They Have Their Exits*
31 Neave *Nuremberg*
32 Neave *They Have Their Exits*
33 Conversation with Adrian Fisher
34 BWCE N/9
35 BWCE N/9
36 Tribunal minutes, 30 October
37 Schacht *My First 76 Years*
38 Papen *Memoirs*
39 Quoted by Montgomery Hyde
40 *Daily Mail*. Rhona Churchill, 19 November
41 Conversation with Adrian Fisher
42 Tribunal minutes, 31 October
43 Dean Minute. FO 371. 8619
44 Biddle Papers, Box 2
45 Conversation with Dr Servatius
46 Tribunal minutes, 30 October
47 Biddle Papers, Box 2
48 Notes by Dr Braun for BWCE. Bernstein
49 Minutes of British prosecution meeting, 15 November
50 Conversation with Dr Kranzbuehler
51 Conversation with Dr Merkel
52 Conversation with Dr Seidl
53 Information booklet for the Press. Jackson Papers, Box 213
54 Albert Speer *Spandau Diary*
55 *New York Herald Tribune* Marguerite Higgins, 7 September
56 Ibid
57 *Daily Star*, 3 January
58 Fritzsche *The Sword in the Scales*
59 Andrus
60 *Sunday Express*, 19 August
61 Andrus
62 *The Star*, 3 January
63 Fritzsche
64 Letter from Seyss-Inquart to his wife, kindly lent to the authors by Thilo Bode
65 Fritzsche
66 Letter from Seyss-Inquart
67 This paragraph based on Fritzsche
68 Gilbert *Nuremberg Diary*
69 FO 371. 57549
70 *New York Herald Tribune*, 6 September
71 Ibid, 19 November

72 *Daily Worker*
73 *New York Herald Tribune*. 6 September
74 Fritzsche
75 Speer *Spandau Diary*
76 Schacht
77 Papen
78 Fritzsche
79 Schacht
80 Gilbert
81 Papen
82 *Manchester Guardian*, 12 December
83 *New York Herald Tribune*
84 Memo from Gill to Jackson, 29 September, Jackson Papers, Box 211
85 Jackson Papers, Box 211
86 Chief prosecutors' minutes, 27 October
87 Conversation with Seymour Peyser
88 Conversation with Dan Margolies
89 *New York Times*, 9 November
90 Gilbert
91 Conversation with Dan Margolies
92 Fritzsche
93 All comments on the Indictment taken from Gilbert
94 *New York Herald Tribune*
95 Gilbert
96 Andrus
97 Gilbert
98 BWCE N/10
99 Jackson Papers, Box 205
100 Jackson Papers, Box 201
101 Jackson Papers, Box 211
102 British prosecution minutes, 5 November
103 BWCE N/10
104 BWCE N/10
105 BWCE N/40
106 BWCE N/10
107 Tribunal minutes, 31 October
108 Telegram to FO. BWCE N/33
109 British prosecution minutes, 8 November
110 Kilmuir
111 Biddle Papers, Box I. Notes on Conference
112 Ibid
113 Ibid
114 BWCE N/40
115 John Phipps
116 BWCE N/4
117 FO 371. (File 16 U9200)
118 18 November letter to Mrs Biddle. Biddle Papers, Box 1
119 Tribunal minutes. 16 November
120 IMT Transcripts Vol. I
121 IMT Transcripts Vol. I

122 BWCE N/10
123 For example, British prosecution minutes, 30 October
124 BWCE N/40. 3 November
125 BWCE N/40. 9 and 12 October
126 BWCE N/30. 9 November
127 BWCE N/40
128 Tribunal minutes, 14 November
129 Conversation with Adrian Fisher
130 IMT Vol. II
131 *Stars and Stripes*, 21 November

Chapter Eight

The date fixed for the opening of the Nuremberg Tribunal was Tuesday 20 November. It was not certain, however, until the very last moment that it could open on time. All the prosecution teams had been working frantically to get their cases ready but there was no guarantee they would succeed. The British had the further problem that Sir Hartley Shawcross, the leader of their team, could not be spared by the Labour Government in London because of the weight of their new legislative programme; he only reached Nuremberg on 14 November. Meanwhile his opening speech had to be mapped out for him by Jim Passant of the Foreign Office and Mervyn Griffith-Jones under Maxwell-Fyfe's direction. Shawcross had then to convert the raw material they had provided into a speech worthy of the occasion. The American team for its part was scrambling to prepare and copy the trial briefs which, according to national practice, summarized their case and laid out the evidence for the Tribunal. By 19 November they had still not got enough copies to show their versions of Counts Three and Four to the British. (1) But regardless of their own difficulties, the British and Americans were determined to stick to the opening date.

The French and Russians, however, wanted a delay. On 19 November they applied jointly to the Tribunal for a postponement of the start of the trial. The Russians asked for a twelve day delay, their avowed reason being that their chief prosecutor, Rudenko, had malaria. As a Foreign Office official saw it, it was 'malaria of the diplomatic variety' – the plain truth was that the Russian case was not ready. (2) Their main problem lay in the translation and copying of documents. The British found them an extra Russian typewriter and lent them some translators. (3) The French stratagem for delay was to revive the old canard of inserting Alfried Krupp into the indictment. From the first week in November they were leaking stories to the Press that there would be a postponement. They too were trying to conceal the fact that they were not ready – though they admitted it privately. (4) The British and Americans chivvied and coaxed. Once the formal request for delay was made to the Tribunal, the French and Russians met pressure from every quarter. Shawcross argued vehemently against any delay. The British Ambassador in Moscow urged the Soviet government to insist that the opening date be kept and reminded them that Stalin himself at Potsdam had wanted an early start. He pointed out that their prosecutors had plenty of leeway since Russian material would not be needed in court for at least three weeks. (5) But the decisive pressure came from the Tribunal – none of the judges wanted a delay. The British and French judges threatened that if there was to be a postponement they would publicly announce who had pressed for it. (6) The French and Russian prosecutors gave way.

They had been hoping merely for postponement; the defence now made a last ditch stand to stop the trial opening at all. On 19 November, defence counsel filed a joint motion to the Tribunal claiming that although the international community might have shown a desire to outlaw war, it had not as yet provided any valid international law to do it. They asserted that the Tribunal was acting *ex post facto*, that much of the Charter contravened the basic legal principle of *nulla poena* or *nullum crimen sine lege* – there can be no punishment or indeed crime without previously declared law. They also criticized the departure from what they defined as commonly recognized principles of jurisprudence in allowing one side only to create the Tribunal, its statute and rules of procedure, and to appoint the judges and prosecutors. The defence counsel requested the Tribunal to confine itself to an examination of allegedly criminal acts on which states might later choose to legislate, and meanwhile to call for opinions from recognized authorities on international law as to the legal bases of the trial. The Tribunal rejected the motion on 21 November. They pointed out that Article Three of the Charter ruled out any challenge to the authority of the Tribunal itself, but promised that arguments on the law involved could and would be heard at a later date. (7) This was a degree of victory for the defence – questions of *ex post facto* law and the issue of *nulla poena* would not be brushed under the carpet. The prosecutors would have to convince the judges of the legal soundness of their case.

The Tribunal might have been able to fend off lawyers' attempts to postpone or prevent the trial. There was a far greater threat which they could not counter. Disease. On 18 November Kaltenbrunner was rushed to an Army hospital with all the symptoms of contagious spinal meningitis. For several hours quarantine for all the prisoners was threatened. So was the beginning of the trial. However, further investigation proved that he had had a cranial haemorrhage and that blood had seeped into his spinal column. There was no risk of an epidemic. If Kaltenbrunner could survive the next seventy-two hours, he would be fit for trial within three weeks. He came back to court on 10 December but soon had another haemorrhage; doctors attributed his condition partly to strain and anxiety and noted that for many weeks he had had fits of hysteria and bouts of weeping.

Most menacing of all to the prospect of a trial, however, was the possibility that attempts would be made to rescue the defendants or destroy the court and all in it. Christine Rommel, the nineteen-year-old niece of the Field Marshal, who was employed in the courtroom library, had told reporters that she believed Bavarian Nazis would attempt to blow up the defendants and all the evidence against them: 'There is so much that they do not want exposed and they are so bitter.' (8) There were very many similar rumours and the authorities had to take them seriously. Before the trial began, five M24 tanks armed with 75 mm guns surrounded the courtroom wing, the corridors and roof were packed with troops and MPs searched everyone who entered the building. Anyone entering or leaving, even the judges, might have to show an official pass between three and six times; the defendants were the only people not required to have official documents. Once in the courtroom itself, only Andrus was to carry a weapon – he had a shoulder holster under his jacket. His men had to rely on white painted 'billies' improvised from lengths of mop handle. (9)

After all the alarms, all the doubts, all the attempts at obstruction, the International Military Tribunal's first session did begin, as arranged, on the morning of 20 November. It opened with a brief statement read by the President, Sir Geoffrey Lawrence, reminding the public of the need for order and decorum and calling on all involved in the trial 'unique in the history of jurisprudence ... and of supreme importance to millions of people all over the globe ... to discharge their duties without fear or favour, in accordance with the sacred principles of law and justice.'

The courtroom was packed. It still smelt noticeably of new wood and fresh paint. Everyone had arrived early to make sure of seats. There was an atmosphere of intense excitement and anticipation – many people thought it resembled a theatrical first night. (10) Some spectators in the public gallery had actually brought binoculars. Before the proceedings opened, Press photographers snapped in the well of the court and film cameras whirred. Once the trial began, the filming was less obtrusive: filming was restricted to cameras permanently installed in sound-proof booths. But the room always retained its theatrical air, with curtains perpetually drawn to exclude daylight and the harsh glare of the lights needed for the cameras. As the day wore on, the room became unbearably hot, thanks to the lights; Judge Parker especially suffered but all the judges were relieved when it was decided to take a mid-morning break to escape the heat. (11)

The room itself on the second floor of the Palace of Justice's annexe was not innately impressive: dark wood-panelled walls almost the full height of the room, a heavy coffered wooden ceiling, thick dark green curtains, ponderous dark green marble surrounds to the doors. The trial took place under the lights at the south end of the long room. The judges sat on a dais under the windows at the far end of the west wall; the Russians were in uniform, the others in black robes, only the French brightened by their white jabots. Behind them were their national flags, and interpreters for their Bench discussions. Immediately in front of the judges sat two rows of court reporters. To their right, on the shorter south side, was a platform with the door by which the judges entered, then the witness box, and above it a stretch of the wall against which charts could be unrolled and films projected. In the far corner on the south side stretched the glass-fronted booths in which the translators sat – twelve of them on each shift. Facing the judges across the narrow room sat the defendants in two rows of a box abutting on to the interpreters' booths. The box was surrounded by white-helmeted GI guards, the 'Snowdrops', arms behind their backs, sometimes wearily wilting against the back wall or flopping against the box. The defence counsel were ranged in front of their clients. Some gave a sudden decorative note to the room. Kranzbuehler wore his German naval uniform, but most of them wore legal gowns, many of which bore academic colours. Several counsel sported their academic caps: one, Dr Exner, the counsel for Jodl, was all in purple. (12) At the end of the defendants' box was the main door. Then, parallel with the Bench and the box, four rows of tables for the prosecuting counsel where they sat sideways, propping their elbows, to face the well of the court. Ahead of them was the lectern from which both defence and prosecution counsel spoke. The effect of this entire arrangement was to concentrate the trial in a small area. All its participants were crammed close; increasingly this constriction would create a sense of intimacy.

Onlookers were confined at the north end of the room, in the new space opened up by ripping out a wall. The Press sat behind the prosecutors. They perhaps enjoyed greater comfort than anyone – 250 upholstered, sprung, tip-up seats in rows spaced widely so that no one need stand to allow a colleague to pass. The gallery for visitors was above them; all of its 150 seats were taken on the opening day. Except for the guards everyone in the room wore headphones to receive the simultaneous translation. One reporter thought the room looked like a telephone exchange. (13) Each headset had four switches to allow a choice of language. The microphones on the defendants' box, witness stand, lectern and Bench carried a yellow light to warn if a speaker went too quickly for the translators, and a red light to stop him. It had proved impossible to recess all the cables needed to connect the system. Wires ran across the floor and even after nine months people would still trip over them so that sections of the system were disconnected or wires became crossed and produced the wrong translation.

The procedure on the first morning was to be followed at all the sessions. The defendants were the first to enter. A panel in the back wall of their box slid to one side and three or four came in at a time. They had been brought up in batches in a lift from the end of the wooden walkway which led to the prison. The lift had a closed section for the prisoners at the back and room for their escort at the front. Andrus had carefully rehearsed their first public appearance in court. Like a headmistress before speech day, he had lectured them on the need to behave properly and make a good impression. He had taken great care over the seating plan and the arrangements for bringing the defendants into court. On the first morning Jodl, Papen and Seyss-Inquart were erroneously brought up before Fritzsche and he had to push past them to get to his place. Andrus was not the sort of man lightly to undertake any adjustment to any arrangement. For the next 403 sessions Fritzsche had to step over his three fellow prisoners to reach his seat at the end of the row. (14) To make sure his charges created a good impression in court, Andrus had carefully checked their clothing: 'My object is to have these prisoners look reasonably respectable when they enter the courtroom,' he said. 'We do not want them to be in a condition where they might inspire pity.' (15) Those who had good suits had them pressed; those without were measured by a tailor and provided with new suits which Schacht complained were made of 'very inferior material.' (16) Belts, shoe laces and ties were returned to them, but had to be handed back every evening. Raeder had requested a red tie and Andrus took care to find him one. (17)

In spite of the care with which they had been dressed, in spite of the morning visit of the barber to shave them, the defendants' appearance in court came as a great anticlimax to the spectators. The image everyone had of them was as the central characters of the Nazi newsreels, the heroes of the Leni Riefenstahl films; they had been given stature by the flattering camera angle, glamour from the skilfully placed lights. They now appeared as two rows of elderly, sallow men. They were all so much smaller than anyone had imagined. 'They are so insignificant you wouldn't notice them on the tube,' was the reaction. There sat Jodl and Keitel – in uniform with brass buttons but stripped of insignia; Goering in pale blue Luftwaffe tunic but bereft of all his decorations. For the rest they were all in dull suits, many of them saggy since their owners had lost weight on prison food. The only interest came from the sight of Frick in a loud brown check jacket; he looked like a bookie. They chatted (a great delight after recent solitary confinement); some of them read copies of *Stars and Stripes* handed round by a defence counsel. (18) Meanwhile defence and prosecution counsel squeezed past the end of their box and edged to their tables.

Finally the judges entered. Falco first, scurrying to his seat at the far end of the bench, gown flowing behind him. He always moved so quickly that in the coming months onlookers would lay bets as to whether he could reach his place before the other judges even got through the door. (19) The judges were seated, Lawrence raised the gavel and promptly at 10 o'clock the International Military Tribunal opened.

Anyone who had come expecting courtroom drama was to be sadly disappointed. The whole day was taken up with the reading of the indictment. Sidney Alderman, Sir David Maxwell-Fyfe, Pierre Mounier, Lt Colonel Ozol and Captain Kuchin delivered their respective national counts. Early in November there had been worries when the Americans pointed out that if the full indictment with all its documentary backing had to be read, even at fifty words a minute, the process would take eleven hours. The prosecutors finally agreed only to refer to the supporting documents not to read them – the defence and tribunal already had them. (20) The reading was a formality: the defendants had had copies of the indictment since 19 October and full details had already been published in the Press. It must have come as something of a relief therefore when in mid-afternoon the Russians became confused several times and began to read sections already dealt with by the French. The President soon set them back on the right track. On the whole, the reading was competently done. Birkett commented on the day that: 'everything went well ... Everybody agreed the whole thing was most dignified.' (21)

Many onlookers had enlivened the day by observing the defendants. Streicher had only reacted to the reading when his own crimes were mentioned; then he sat forward, chin jutting belligerently; for the rest of the time he chatted incessantly with Frick. Frank too tried to distract his neighbours with talk; when he failed he smirked or scowled. (22) Hess remained absorbed in his light reading – *Der Loisl, The Story of a Girl* – except when Hitler's name was first mentioned. Then he sat up and smiled broadly. Late in the day he had a fit of cramp and had to leave the courtroom for a few minutes. (23) Ribbentrop, on the other hand, began alert and interested, but as the day wore on the strain began to show on his face; at 4 o'clock he suddenly collapsed. Guards took him out and gave him a sedative. He returned twenty minutes later wearing dark glasses. (24) 'The room was too close: I had been sitting too long,' he explained. (25) Schacht ignored his headphones and Funk's constant fidgeting, rib-scratching and attempts at conversation. He tried to maintain an attitude of detached interest, occasionally referring to his own copy of the indictment. When the conspiracy charge was read he uttered a sharp, disdainful laugh. (26) The military men sat rigid and impassive – though several observers guessed that Keitel was struggling to keep his temper under control. Only Fritzsche and Seyss-Inquart were thought to show signs of fear. Throughout the day, Goering made every effort to draw attention to himself with exaggerated nods or shakes of the head at the charges and comments to his neighbours and counsel. But he hid his face during passages describing the concentration camps and his plundering, only cheering up and gazing round the room hoping for a laugh when there was mention of the eighty-seven million bottles of champagne he had stolen from France.

At lunch time most people were glad to leave the hot courtroom. Only the defendants remained; for the one and only time their lunch was brought up to them. They stretched, let off steam, joked. Goering handed round cigarettes and Andrus gave permission for them to be smoked in the lift. (27) There was little talk of the charges they had heard but several remarks about the improved quality of the food: 'I suppose we'll get steak the day you hang us,' said Schirach. (28) But by the end of the day all their ebullience had gone; they were tired. The judges went off to a dinner party at the American judges' house; it was in honour of Judge Parker's birthday. But many of the defendants were asleep by seven o'clock. Before going to bed Streicher asked for a different shirt to wear next day – one with a bigger collar. (29) It had been too dark for exercise in the yard after the session. A few of the prisoners took the opportunity of a walk in the gymnasium, (30) a gloomy building which had been largely stripped of its equipment and was covered with a thick layer of dust. Andrus' men used it to play basketball games. One day several of the defendants would be hanged there.

On the second day of the trial the defendants had to plead to the indictment, guilty or not guilty. The defence counsel complained that, thanks to the zealous security arrangements, they had been prevented from consulting their clients about their pleas either the previous night or that morning. The Tribunal allowed them fifteen minutes for discussion. Goering was the first to stand at the microphone in the dock. He held a typewritten speech in his hand. 'Before I answer the question of the Tribunal whether or not I am guilty . . .' Lawrence cut him off; defendants could only plead guilty or not guilty, speeches were forbidden.* Baulked of his hopes of challenging the court and assuming the heroic role, Goering had to rest content with a brief statement: 'I declare myself in the sense of the indictment not guilty.' Ribbentrop, Rosenberg, Schirach and Fritzsche adopted the same formula. Sauckel, red-faced and with clenched fists, declared himself not guilty 'in the sense of the indictment, before God and the world and particularly before my people'. Jodl added to his plea of not guilty: 'for what I have done or had to do I have a pure conscience before God, before History and my people'.

The others gave the formal reply, Schacht emphasizing he was not guilty 'in any respect', Papen 'in no way.' Hess shouted 'Nein' which Lawrence said would be entered as a plea of not guilty. There was laughter in the room and he restored silence by threatening that anyone who caused a disturbance would have to leave.

All formalities over, the atmosphere in the courtroom became more tense, the defendants leant forward on their benches, the spectators craned in their seats as Judge Robert Jackson stepped up to the lectern to begin his speech opening the prosecution case.

He had prepared the speech alone, and meticulously. He probably began work on it in the spring. (32) Since then it had been redrafted and polished innumerable times. Many versions still exist in his archives, the earlier ones covered with notes and corrections, the later ones scored with underlinings for stress and broken with oblique lines between phrases. By nature Jackson spoke quickly. In the coming months the interpreters would often have to flash the yellow light to make him slow down; sometimes they had to

---

*The speech Goering had tried to read was handed to the Press.
'As Reichsmarschall of the Greater German Reich I accept the political responsibility for all my own acts or for acts carried out on my orders. These acts were exclusively carried out for the welfare of the German people and because of my oath to the Führer. Although I am responsible for these acts only to the German people and can be tried only before a German court, I am at the same time prepared to give all the necessary information demanded of me by this court and to tell the whole truth without recognizing the jurisdiction of this court. I must, however, most strongly reject the accusation that my acts for which I accept full responsibility should be described as criminal. I must also reject the acceptance by me of responsibility for acts of other persons which were not known to me; of which, had I known them, I would have disapproved and which could not have been prevented by me anyway.'(31)

stop him altogether. He kept a note they once sent him on a torn scrap of tissue paper: 'Will you please tell the Justice that we will break down if he does not slow down.' (33) Today, however, Jackson had pinned to the first page of his speech a slip of paper; on it the word 'slowly' was written in large letters, underlined four times. (34) Every phrase was delivered with measured weight; his voice rang in the courtroom.

The core of his speech, constituting its central two-thirds, was the outline of the conspiracy charge which the Americans were responsible for proving in court. Given their interpretation of the charge Jackson could range freely over the entire case against the Nazi leaders; he encapsulated all the crimes of which they were accused. His theme to link them was one of premeditated, organized criminality which, he argued, flowed intentionally into and from the greatest of all crimes – aggressive war.

First, Jackson established the history of the Nazi party which Hitler had led from 1921. He outlined its programme: at home a range of social measures which Jackson said 'would commend themselves to many good citizens', abroad the destruction of the Versailles settlement, the union of all Germans, the acquisition of new territory. These were all legitimate aims in foreign policy, he said, but only if attained by peaceful means. Yet the Nazis had always used violence, disregarded law, unashamedly contemplated war. Once Hitler became Chancellor in 1933, he had used the pretext of the Reichstag Fire to persuade President von Hindenberg to suspend civil liberties; then he declared 'ruthless war upon those whose activities are injurious to the common interests' – the trade unions, the Churches and the Jews. Jackson aimed to establish that the methods which the Nazis used against their targets at home – legislation, imprisonment in concentration camps, vandalism and physical violence – were being rehearsed for later use against opponents in occupied Europe. They were one strand in the Nazi policy of domination; the other was war. Briefly he described the state organized persecution of the German Jews: at first disenfranchisement, discrimination, obstacles to economic activity; then the 1935 Nuremberg Decrees which ensured their exclusion from professions and any cultural life or education, their segregation, and the confiscation of their property. Such persecution by the law had been accompanied by an intensifying campaign of bullying and vicious physical attack culminating in 'Kristallnacht', the Night of Broken Glass, 9–10 November 1938, when Heydrich organized a 'spontaneous uprising' against the Jews; hundreds were beaten up or killed, their property was smashed, their synagogues burned. Within a few days the Nazi government had the effrontery to fine the Jews a billion Reichsmarks for the destruction they had suffered. Jackson put this hideous narrative, which was to end in the gas chambers, into the context of Nazi ideology and the concept of the Master Race. He quoted Frank: 'The Jews are a race which has to be eliminated'; but as Jackson unwound the story of the Nazi occupation of Europe, not just 60 per cent of all Jews would die to establish Aryan supremacy but Gypsies, Slavs, Greeks, Frenchmen would experience the same fate for the same reasons.

In Jackson's analysis, once Germany had been terrorized into submission, the Nazis were free to turn outward against Europe. In preparation they had militarized the Party, secretly trained and equipped the armed forces, won over financiers and industrialists, and directed German production to the needs of war. Hitler had not disguised from his leaders and commanders his ambition to regain territory lost in the Great War, to acquire fertile lands in the East and weaken his neighbours to gain domination. 'The German question can be solved only by way of force,' he had said on 5 November 1937 at the conference recorded by Hossbach.

Jackson established the practical consequences of that policy. First what he called 'experiments in aggression': probing for weakness in intended victims, testing the reactions of potential opponents; always prepared to withdraw if challenged because Germany was not yet ready for all-out war. This was the period in which the Rhineland was occupied, then fortified in violation of the Versailles Treaty and the Locarno Pact; when Austria was annexed to Germany in the Anschluss; when, thanks to agreement with the French and British at Munich, Hitler could first take the Sudetenland from Czechoslovakia, then break his agreement and seize Bohemia and Moravia in March 1939.

Thus far, as the American chief prosecutor pointed out, Hitler had encountered no armed resistance. He had given assurances and ignored them, signed agreements and broken them. He had achieved his aims without war, but plans for it had been minutely prepared should war prove necessary. Details for armed attack on Austria – code-named 'Case Otto' – were in prosecution hands; so was 'Case Green', which prepared for war with Czechoslovakia should trickery and bullying fail. But Hitler had not as yet achieved all his ambitions. He intended to take over Poland. Jackson quoted him telling his commanders on 23 May 1939: 'We cannot expect a repetition of the Czech affair. There will be war.' It came in September. Next, with Poland and Czechoslovakia subdued and Russia secured by the Non-Aggression Pact, Hitler could move West – against Denmark and Norway (April 1940); then the Low Countries and France (May 1940). He invaded Greece and Yugoslavia in April 1941, and finally turned on Russia in June. Jackson drew attention to the fact that Hitler never declared war; he attacked without warning. Every country he attacked was first given assurances of his peaceful intentions, but as he told his military commanders on 23 November 1939: 'Agreements are to be kept only as long as they serve a certain purpose.'

Such cynicism, Jackson argued, had been the attitude towards the international conventions and agreements which Germany had signed on methods of fighting and treatment of occupied territories. The Nazis deliberately broke all of them. As Jackson saw it, their policy was summed up in a naval memorandum of October 1939: 'if decisive successes are to be expected from any measure considered as a war necessity, it must be carried through even if it is not in agreement with international law'. Such an outlook, said Jackson, had entirely predictable consequences – the officially sanctioned wholesale commission of war crimes. Whole categories of Allied captives lost the protection of prisoner-of-war status. Civilians were incited to lynch captured airmen. In 1943 the Nazi government directed that the police must not 'interfere in clashes between Germans and English and American fliers who have bailed out'. The Commando Order of 1942 decreed that all captured commandos were 'to be slaughtered to the last man'. Nazi treatment of prisoners-of-war transgressed every convention, every decency. Men too weak from hunger or exhaustion to march to their prison camps were shot at the road side; Russian prisoners-of-war were shackled and branded.

Jackson revealed that contrary to every international agreement, Sauckel had insisted that 'all prisoners-of-war ... must be incorporated into the German armament and munition industries. All the men must be fed, sheltered and treated in such a way as to exploit them to the highest possible extent at the lowest conceivable degrees of expenditure.' At least Sauckel recommended feeding them. Rosenberg on the other hand told Keitel in 1942 that of 3,600,000 Russian prisoners-of-war in Germany, only a few thousand were fit to work: 'A large part of them have starved or died because of the hazards of the weather, thousands also died from spotted fever.' Camp commanders had forbidden civilians to feed the prisoners, 'they have rather let them starve.'

Callous brutality and disregard of established law were also the themes of Jackson's description of Nazi treatment of civilians in the countries they occupied. What became known as the *Nacht und Nebel* (Night and Fog) policy was intended to spread fear – people were arrested and any information as to their whereabouts or condition was deliberately kept from friends and relatives. Where opposition was encountered, hostages were taken and killed; entire villages – people, cattle, buildings – were burnt. The Nazis systematically plundered, a sordid as well as illegal depradation. They took money, industrial plant, art treasures, food. That Germany might be well nourished, whole populations were left to die. Jackson quoted the report of the Reich Ministry for the Eastern Territories: 'Food rations allowed the Russian population are so low that they fail to secure their existence. The population does not know if they will still live tomorrow ... The roads are clogged by hundreds of thousands of people ... who wander around in search of nourishment.'

The Nazis stripped Europe of its human beings too. Five million foreign workers were brought to Germany; 'not even 200,000 came voluntarily', Sauckel had cheerfully admitted to a ministerial meeting. Children between ten and fourteen years old formed part of the slave labour force. The pillage of the occupied territories had more than one purpose alleged Jackson. The Nazis were not just concerned to increase production and support the war effort. One aim of the policy of stripping resources and deporting populations was, according to Rosenberg, 'to ensure a desired weakening of the biological force' of the conquered peoples. Himmler saw Slav children as future enemy soldiers; the policy towards them must be to Germanize or destroy. 'Either we win over any good blood that we can use for ourselves and give it a place in our own people, or, gentlemen – you may call this cruel, but nature is cruel – we destroy this blood.'

Jackson then offered the evidence to show what Himmler's depraved rhetoric had inspired. Those destined for destruction might go to the concentration camps. Those unsuited to work were sent to the gas chambers. Many of those who remained died of starvation, torture, disease or obscene experiments. Sometimes they were forced to execute each other; sometimes they were deliberately worked to death. Others in the East were victims of incited local pogrom or were rounded up by the Einsatzgruppen, special action squads who followed the Army and trapped peasants, political commissars, Jews. They shot, burned their captives alive, or forced them into gas vans. The preferred procedure was to drive the vans off the roads to secluded sites; but, according to an SS officer quoted by Jackson, this was only possible in dry weather 'since those to be executed become frantic ... such vans become immobilized in wet weather.' The officer had appealed for his men to be relieved of the task of unloading the corpses – the work had such 'an atrocious spiritual and physical effect on them'.

Jackson's considerable achievement in presenting the American case was twofold. He had demonstrated the thorough documentation on which it was based and by quotations from the Nazis themselves he had converted what could have been an arid catalogue of crimes into palpable evil. He evoked for his listeners the misery, the pain, the stench to which the Nazis had reduced Europe. By using the Nazis' own words he graphically displayed their callousness, brutality, greed and arrogance. The defendants in the box no longer seemed the puny, insignificant individuals of their first appearance in court; they had taken on a stature of wickedness. Through the conviction with which he argued, these men became the planners of atrocity on a scarcely graspable scale. Jackson's outline of the case against them had been deft. In thirty-eight pages he had given a masterly resumé of the main charges, the key evidence and the nature of the responsibility of the accused. His argument that their crimes had been premeditated and systematically carried out had been persuasive. His speech was a superb introduction to the matter of the trial.

But it was more even than this. Jackson was not content with advocacy, however skilful. He would not rest content if the trial were seen merely as a judicial proceeding against a handful of alleged criminals. Jackson had always wanted it to be more: a major step in the development of international law, a significant move to prevent war, an opportunity to control human behaviour and institutions with morality as part of the law. So into his speech he poured everything he had thought and cared most about in the law. His heart as well as his mind was there.

From his opening words Jackson exposed with a fine eloquence what he believed to be the importance of the trial. 'The privilege of being the first trial in history for crimes against the peace of the World imposes a grave responsibility,' he said. 'The wrongs which we seek to condemn and punish have been so calculated, so malignant and so devastating that civilization cannot survive their being repeated. That four great nations, flushed with victory and stung with injury, stay the hand of vengeance and voluntarily submit their captive enemies to the judgement of the law is one of the most significant tributes that Power has ever paid to Reason.' He reminded the Tribunal of the gravity and immensity of its responsibility in imposing the law. 'The common sense of mankind demands that the law shall not stop with the punishment of petty crimes by little people. It must also reach men who possess themselves of great power and make deliberate and concerted use of it to set in motion evils which leave no home in the world untouched.'

Jackson stressed the responsibilities of the prosecutors, the responsibilities of the judges and he analysed the very different responsibility of the accused. For Jackson the foundation of the law must be morality and the fundamental question of the trial was that of individual moral responsibility. He contemptuously dismissed the theory that only states could be held responsible before international law – in that case the only effective sanction against states who broke it would always be war. The very idea that states commit crimes, he said, 'is a fiction. Crimes are always committed only by persons.' Men who exercise great power cannot be allowed to shift their responsibility on to the fictional being, the State, 'which cannot be produced for trial, cannot testify, and cannot be sentenced.' He berated those who had sworn an oath of inviolable fidelity and absolute obedience to Hitler; he called it 'an abdication of personal intelligence and moral responsibility'. He spoke of the sacrifice of millions of Allied lives in the fight to reassert the rule of law against men who acted with savagery and accepted no restraints, legal or moral. Then came the cry from Jackson's heart, as characteristically honest as it was passionate: 'I cannot subscribe to the perverted reasoning that society may advance and strengthen the rule of law by the expenditure of morally innocent lives but that progress in law may never be made at the price of morally guilty lives.'

The morally guilty, the men responsible for the crimes committed in the name of their state, according to Jackson were represented by the men in the dock; 'men of a station and rank which does not soil its own hands with blood ... men who know how to use lesser folk as tools'. These were the planners and designers, the inciters and leaders, 'without whose evil architecture the world would not have been so long scourged with the violence and lawlessness and wracked with the agonies and convulsions of this terrible war.' They were not alone in guilt, Jackson said. Nor would they be alone in punishment – lesser men would appear before other tribunals. Men of the Allied nations had committed crimes too, their states must deal with them. The men in the dock had duped and terrorized and exploited the German people who now lived in the ruins of their aggression. 'The German, no less than the non-German world, has accounts to settle with these defendants.' The accused might be viewed as 'twenty-odd broken men. Reproached by the humiliation of those they have led almost as bitterly as by the desolation of those they have attacked, their personal capacity for evil is forever past.' But they still symbolized hatreds, greeds and the arrogance and cruelty of power; 'any tenderness to them is a victory and an encouragement to all the evils which are attached to their names' and which might still be revived in the world.

Jackson then addressed himself to undoubtedly the most sensitive issue of the trial – the question of whether what Goering called 'victor's justice' could be true justice. Jackson admitted that there was 'a dramatic disparity between the circumstances of the accusers and the accused.' The war had left few neutrals to act as judges. 'Either the victors must judge the vanquished or we must leave the defeated to judge themselves', and the futility of the latter course had been all too clear after 1918. However: 'these defendants may be hard-pressed, but they are not ill-used'. Many nations had made strenuous efforts to give them a fair and dispassionate hearing, and the chance to defend themselves was 'a favour which these men when in power rarely extended to their fellow countrymen'. Then Jackson drove his attack home. 'They might be the first national leaders of a defeated nation to be prosecuted, but they are also the first to be given the chance to plead in the name of the law.' Public opinion had condemned them already, but the Charter guaranteed a presumption of their innocence until they were proved guilty and obliged the prosecution to provide conclusive evidence of their crimes and individual responsibility.

Jackson was passionate, he was persuasive. More impressive than the eloquence of his speech, however, was its honesty and the courage with which he admitted to the problems which faced all connected with the trial. To some of these problems he had found an answer. As an American he was the first to admit that everywhere there were examples of 'the arrogances and pretensions which frequently accompany the intermingling of different peoples' and which could result in crimes against those of other races. But he made this vital distinction: prosecution charges were limited to those of 'an official plan rather than ... a capricious policy' of individuals or groups. Similarly Jackson acknowledged that all armies loot; their pilfering tended to increase as their discipline weakened. But other governments did not direct the looting as the Nazis had done. He was candid in confessing that the Germans were not alone responsible for reducing European cities to rubble: 'the ruin that lies from the Rhine to the Danube shows that we have not been dull pupils' but he claimed that the Allies had never destroyed, as had the Nazis, with relish and for the sake of vandalism rather than military need. He insisted that Allied destruction was a forseeable result of the initial Nazi aggression and a justifiable means to defeat it. Above all, he maintained that the prosecution did not call criminal any ambition or conduct that was 'natural and human, if illegal'; nor did it denounce the 'cutting of corners such as many of us might well have committed had we been in the defendants' position'. The Nazi defendants were called criminal because they had planned their abnormal and inhuman acts. However justified many of Germany's needs and grievances might have been, they could never justify aggressive war, still less the scale of crimes committed to prepare and conduct it.

Jackson did not boast that he had found solutions to other problems the trial faced. His honesty would only allow him to identify them and insist they must be faced. He expressed a regret that the Charter had not provided an adequate definition of aggression, but in spite of the arguments at the London Conference and criticism since, he remained convinced that the crimes listed in the Charter were well established in international law, above all that war had been outlawed by international agreements. Jackson confessed that the attempt to apply this body of law was 'novel and experimental'. He warned that the Tribunal would be called to consider, for the first time ever, cases against leaders held responsible for the crimes of the state they had led, and that the Tribunal would be working in a context and be obliged to hear revolting evidence which would place severe strains on their detachment and integrity. They must face the daunting task of distinguishing between 'the demand for a just and measured retribution and the unthinking cry for vengeance which arises from the anguish of war'. Even if this could be achieved, there would be no easy rewards. The Tribunal's judgement alone could not prevent wars; their establishment of a procedure to try aggressors would not stop aggression – 'judicial action always comes after the event'. Their work would only form part of a wider effort and would only be effective if that effort were made. The United Nations, too, must evolve political and if necessary military methods at least to ensure that any nation which started a war lost it and that those who began a war would pay for it personally.

Jackson had not just opened the trial with a succinct exposition of a uniquely complicated case. He had confronted all concerned with the immensity of their difficulties and responsibilities. He had challenged the lawyers, the judges and all who followed the proceedings to consider the implications of what they were doing. And he had set rigorous standards against which he suggested they measure their work.

Jackson had spoken nearly all day. Everyone in the room listened intently. There were no smirks, no pretences of boredom in the defendants' box. Even Goering was still and tense; even Hess stopped reading and followed the speech, only leaving the box for ten minutes when he had another attack of cramp. As Jackson finished, colleagues clustered round to praise him. The Press reacted unanimously – 'magnificent' was the word they all used to describe his achievement. They commented on the deep effect he had made with the examples and quotations he had used. Jackson had admitted in his speech that he himself had frequently not believed many of the atrocity stories which had percolated from Nazi Europe. But his listing of villages annihilated, the account of the 'cold' experiments at Dachau, the way in which he had read SS General Stroop's account of the destruction of the Warsaw Ghetto from a commemorative volume lavishly illustrated, beautifully bound, all this had cut through any scepticism in his listeners and deprived them of the comfort of thinking in abstract terms and bald figures. There was little doubt in the minds of Jackson's listeners that the responsibility for such miseries lay with the defendants.

The defendants themselves went back to their cells that night and blamed others. Even Goering, in spite of the grandiloquent gesture he had tried to make with his speech, told Funk that he would take full responsibility for the Four Year Plan for the economy, but he told Gilbert that all atrocities had been carried out in secret by Himmler and 'his chosen psychopaths'. (35) No defendant that night gave a hint of awareness of that sense of personal responsibility for which Jackson had called.

After the tensions of the opening day and the passions of Jackson's speech, the trial now lapsed into several days of humdrum prosecution business. Jackson took a back seat and left it to his team to present the American charge of conspiracy. It was necessary to explain the hierarchy of the Nazi Party and its control over the state machinery; to build up their picture of criminal aims and methods evolving from the very establishment of the Party. It was important to show the Nazis' aims, their education and propaganda techniques, how they had suppressed opposition, and to present the evidence on the preparations for war. But none of this, however carefully illustrated with charts and diagrams, was the stuff of courtroom drama. The visitors and the Press became restive and bored. More importantly, the vital points the Americans were trying to establish were too often blunted by their inept presentation and bumbling approach. Sydney Alderman in particular made a poor impression, introducing documents with comments like: 'it is headed with a number of initials the meaning of which I do not know' and prefacing the presentation of Jodl's diary by saying it was 'in German script which I cannot read'. Much of their documentary evidence would have been of interest, but the American prosecutors relied on making assertions, quoting the reference numbers of the documents that supported them and 'handing over the whole bundle' – all at a pace that no one could follow. (36)

The general picture of muddle was intensified by the disclosure that the Americans had only provided six copies of their documents to the defence counsel, and these were in English. (The British could have told the defence that they themselves had received no copies at all.) Understandably, the defence registered indignant complaints to the Tribunal. Colonel Storey might offer translators to go through the documents with the counsel, he might complain of the 'tremendous physical burden' imposed by the request to supply every defence counsel with copies of documents. But the defence expected prior access so that they could challenge evidence, and Storey's explanations of the physical burdens involved seemed a little weak when it was disclosed one day that the defence had only been given five copies of a document whereas the Press had received 250. The Tribunal was far from pleased when it had to rule that relevant sections of evidence would have to be read in court and passed through the translation system since they were unavailable in print. The impact of the evidence might be greater, but it was a ponderous procedure and a profligate use of time.

Public interest in the trial began to revive on 26 November when the Americans began the section of their case dealing with Nazi plans for aggressive war. This interest was largely a response to the nature of the evidence quoted and the shameless brutality of its language. The Hossbach memorandum of the 5 November 1937 conference especially horrified listeners by its callousness, and their horror increased with the reading of Hitler's speech to his commanders at Obersalzburg on 22 August 1939. No matter that the defence pointed out that two versions of this meeting existed, that both were unsigned and took the form of summary rather than verbatim transcript. Both of them made clear Hitler's intention to wage war on Poland *and* the West. Both recorded his determination to fight: 'I am only afraid that at the last minute some *Schweinhund* will make a proposal for mediation.' He declared he would use any excuse to start the war. 'The victor shall not be asked later on whether we told the truth or not. In starting and making a war not the Right is what matters but Victory.' (sic)

Whatever the doubts about these two accounts and the accuracy of the Hossbach memorandum there could be no challenge to the validity of the minutes of the conference on 23 May 1939 when Hitler harangued fourteen of his military leaders. The same aims, the same attitudes were expressed, as Hitler talked about his views of the intended war with Poland. 'Danzig is not the subject of the dispute at all. It is a question of expanding our living space in the East and of securing our food supplies, of the settlement of the Baltic problem. Food supplies can only be expected from thinly-populated areas. Over and above the natural fertility, thoroughgoing German exploitation will enormously increase the surplus.' The provision of food would become even more vital 'if Fate brings us into conflict with the West'. Full details from the Barbarossa file were read in court. The plans to invade Russia had been perfected six months before the attack actually came and while the Non-Aggression Pact was repeatedly invoked. Hitler's words to his state secretaries on 2 May 1941 soared to new heights of callousness: 'The war can only be continued if all the Armed Forces are fed by Russia in the third year of the War ... There is no doubt that as a result, many millions of people will be starved to death if we take out of the country the things necessary for us.'

Even the defendants were shocked by some of this evidence. Schirach called the Hossbach speech 'concentrated political madness' (whatever doubts others might cast, he at least recognized the authentic Hitlerian note). Seyss-Inquart insisted he would never have joined Hitler if he had known about the speech. Goering tried to rally them: 'What about the grabbing of California and Texas by the Americans? That was plain aggressive warfare for territorial expansion too.' (37) The Press quoted the evidence fully. As the *New York Herald Tribune* put it they had been appalled by this first introduction to the inside story of ruthless planning for war; these documents 'should decisively undermine propaganda myths which hundreds of thousands of Germans and even people of other nations still believe' – that Germany was forced into a war of self-defence. (38)

There was to be an even stronger reaction, a sickened revulsion, that afternoon when the prosecution showed a film to the court of the concentration camps as they had been found by the advancing Allies. The defence counsel had been offered the opportunity of seeing the film the previous night. Only eight of them turned up. No one who saw it in court ever forgot it. A viewer recorded: 'The impression we get is an endless river of white bodies flowing across the screen, bodies with ribs sticking out through the chests, with pipe-stem legs and battered skulls and eyeless faces and grotesque thin arms reaching for the sky ... On the screen there is no end to the bodies, tumbling bodies and bodies in mounds and single bodies with holes between the eyes and bodies being shoved over cliffs into common graves and bodies pushed like dirt by giant bulldozers, and bodies that are not bodies at all but charred bits of bone and flesh lying upon a crematory grate made of bits of steel rail laid upon blackened wood ties.' (39) While the film was shown, a spotlight was left on the defendants' box for security reasons. Many people in court preferred to watch their reaction rather than the film. Few of the defendants could bear to watch it for long. Only Streicher leant forward throughout, looking avidly, nodding his head. Goering seemed the most calm but at the end he was wiping and wiping his sweaty palms. Schacht turned his face away throughout; Ribbentrop tried to cover his with his hands but often fell to the temptation to look at the screen. Doenitz seemed alternately shocked and fascinated, glancing and turning away, putting on dark glasses then removing them to watch more carefully. Keitel mopped his face and finally wiped his reddened eyes with his handkerchief. (40)

As the film ended the courtroom remained in stunned silence. At last the judges left. Lawrence had not even managed to speak the usual formal words of adjournment. A journalist murmured, 'Why can't we shoot the swine now'; a soldier said, 'God, this makes me feel like killing the first German I meet.' The defendants sat on. At last Hess began to speak: 'I don't believe it,' but Goering silenced him. Frank did not move for ten minutes. He sat huddled until a guard touched him on the arm and he was led to the lift. (41)

That evening Gilbert visited the prisoners in their cells. Goering was trying to pull himself together. He had relished a moment of glory that morning when all attention turned to him as the prosecution read transcripts of the telephone conversations by which he had directed the German march into Austria. 'Everyone was laughing with me and then they showed that awful film and it just spoiled everything' he grumbled. Fritzsche was in tears: 'No power in heaven or earth will erase this shame from my country.' Funk sobbed 'Horrible, horrible'. Sauckel, Neurath, Jodl, Doenitz all denied that they had known such things happened, but Frank said 'Don't let everyone tell you that they had no idea. Everyone sensed there was something horribly wrong ... even if we did not know all the details. They didn't want to know.' As ever, the impulse was to shift the blame elsewhere. 'I'd choke myself with these hands,' promised Sauckel, 'if I thought I had the slightest thing to do with these murders.' 'It was those dirty SS swine,' said Keitel; he would never have allowed his son to join them if he had known. 'I'll never be able to look people in the face again.' But unlike most people that evening he was able to eat a hearty supper. (42)

The American prosecutors had been slowly overcoming their initial technical clumsiness and the tendency to fire documents at random. With this film, the reality of their accusations hit target. But before they could ram their attack home, there was a hiatus, even knockabout comedy.

The proceedings had to be interrupted on the afternoon of 30 November for the Tribunal to hear defence and prosecution arguments on the fitness of Hess to stand trial. The judges had expressed their anxiety at Hess's condition to the chief prosecutors at a private meeting on 6 November. Jackson and Maxwell-Fyfe, however, had seemed confident that he could cope with the proceedings and that an imperfect memory was merely a hindrance to his defence rather than an insuperable obstacle. (43) The judges were still uneasy and they lent sympathetic ears to the request on 8 November from Hess's counsel, Rohrscheidt, for a thorough medical investigation. They rejected his suggestion that Swiss doctors should be consulted; they had already asked medical experts from the four Allies to stand by. (44) The doctors (three Russian, three American, three British – including Churchill's physician Lord Moran – and a Frenchman) saw Hess on 14 and 15 November and wrote four national reports presenting their conclusions. All told roughly the same story. The doctors believed he was legally sane but that he was suffering from hysterical amnesia, a form of escape from uncomfortable realities which they said was frequently employed by those with Hess's unstable personality. It had been triggered first by the failure of his mission to England and captivity there and had been developed since as a protective measure against the stress and the problems he was now facing. All the teams believed that his amnesia was temporary and would vary in intensity. The Americans thought it would disappear if Hess was relieved of the threat of punishment; the Russians on the contrary thought that it would go if he had to face the unavoidable necessity of confronting the situation. (45)

At the hearing on 30 November, Rohrscheidt pleaded that these reports showed that Hess could not adequately defend himself because there was no certainty he could remember names or incidents vital to his case. He said that conversations with his client showed Hess was incapable of grasping the charges against him. He argued that trial in absentia would be a grave injustice since it would deny Hess the right to give evidence and to challenge witnesses personally. Rohrscheidt therefore requested that proceedings against him should be suspended, as in the case of Krupp, only to be resumed should Hess's condition improve.

In reply Maxwell-Fyfe gave a rococo display of legal erudition and British case law in arguing the differences between insanity and amnesia, emphasized the Russian view that the need to defend himself might cure Hess's complaint, and said that since he could follow proceedings he was fit to stand trial. ('Damned lawyer's bull at first blush,' thought Biddle.) (46) Jackson's angle was more matter of fact: Hess had already opted for loss of memory in England and had then admitted that his condition was simulated; he was playing the same game again, malingering to escape trial. What really riled Jackson (and he was clearly sincere and avoiding any lawyer's bull) was that Hess had consistently refused any of the treatment prescribed by the Allied doctors. He could not be forced to accept treatment; 'if he should be struck by lightning a month afterward, it would still be charged that something we had done had caused his death.' Jackson summed up his annoyance with Hess in the vernacular which was his alternative to the high oratorical style: 'he is in the volunteer class with his amnesia'.

Throughout these arguments Hess had sat alone in the defendants' box. During Rohrscheidt's opening statement he had tried to attract his counsel's attention, waving his arms, sending notes. He had followed the discussion without headphones, clearly understanding the English, and grinning at the quotations from the medical reports. (47) Once the lawyers' views had been heard, the Tribunal, with scrupulous concern, asked if Hess wanted to speak. He did. He stood at the microphone in the defendants' box and in a clear, calm voice read a coherent, unambiguous and clearly premeditated statement. 'Henceforth my memory will again respond to the outside world. The reasons for simulating loss of memory were of a tactical nature. Only my ability to concentrate is, in fact, somewhat reduced. But my capacity to follow the trial, to defend myself, to put questions to witnesses, or to answer questions myself is not affected thereby ... I also simulated loss of memory in consultations with my officially appointed defence counsel. He has therefore represented in good faith.' Then he sat down.

For a moment everyone was thunderstruck. Then Rohrscheidt laughed and several people followed suit. Reporters rushed from their section; everyone else began to talk at once. (48) The President closed the session. It was impossible to follow such bathos.

Later when they had got their breath back, people tried to analyse Hess's motives and state of mind. Dr Kelley's view was that Hess had shown 'the return of the typical hysterical personality he has constantly shown'. He suggested that Hess might have been acting from his 'conscious malignity towards Jackson'. (49) The *Daily Worker*, endorsing the Moscow view that Hess was totally untrustworthy (his mission to England was still seen as an attempt to neutralize Britain while Germany attacked Russia) thought Hess's statement a cynical confession that his loss of memory was quite bogus. (50) But other papers recorded the view that it was uncertain whether he had genuinely recovered or was completely mad. Rohrscheidt had put it to reporters that 'any man who acts as Hess had acted today seems ... to be in a very curious mental state indeed'. (51) Such a curious state indeed that the *Stars and Stripes* could later flaunt across its front page the resounding headline: 'Hess Nuts. Fake Story Fake, says Nuremberg Psychologist'. Gilbert had told them that Hess's confession had been a hysterical reaction to the possibility that he might be removed from the limelight of the courtroom. (52)

The judges had to weigh all these possibilities. It did not take them long. They went into private session immediately after the hearing. They do not seem to have been influenced by Hess's attempt to talk himself into the trial, nor indeed to have seen it as a sign of insanity. They had, however, been impressed by the unanimity of medical opinion (Jackson had suggested that such accord was historically unique). Parker at least was persuaded that amnesia was not a legal impediment to an adequate defence. They all agreed to try Hess. 'We think he is simulating,' said Biddle. (53)

After such an afternoon of almost light relief, the American prosecutors had to regain the initiative and remount their attack on the defendants. Fortunately they had a new weapon, one certain to seize the imagination of the court and the public – their first witness. He was Major General Erwin Lahousen who as an Austrian military intelligence officer had been transferred to the German Abwehr – military intelligence – after the Anschluss. There, as an assistant to Admiral Canaris, the head of military intelligence, he had recorded meetings attended by his superior and personally been present at several conferences with Hitler, Keitel, military commanders and Cabinet ministers. He had brought with him notes made at the time. The Abwehr had insinuated its tentacles everywhere. Lahousen's value as a witness was that he had sat at the centre of things; he had seen how decisions were made and by whom, he knew the chain of command and to what level orders were sent, he had personal proof of orders and policies which had not been committed to paper even by those most obsessive and shameless of record keepers, the Nazis. (54)

Lahousen told a squalid tale: the tricks by which Hitler had hoped to excuse his attacks on Poland (dressing Germans in Polish uniforms, giving them Polish equipment and papers, then sending them to attack German installations hoping they would be killed); plots to assassinate the French Generals Weygand and Giraud lest they lead a military resistance; proposals to provoke an uprising in the Ukraine as an excuse to launch a wholesale slaughter of Jews and peasants. Lahousen could directly implicate Keitel, Ribbentrop, various officers in the General Staff and High Command in the drawing up of official policies such as the Commando Order, the instructions to Einsatzkommando and for the treatment of Russian prisoners-of-war. He had been present at the conference in the summer of 1941 when General Reinecke, the Head of the General Wehrmacht Department (a part of the OKW), put forward the official view that the Russian campaign was a war between ideologies; in consequence all political commissars must be exterminated, all prisoners identified by the SD as bolshevized must be executed, all other prisoners deprived of the protections of international law. Lahousen had visited the Eastern Front several times with Canaris and seen the results of this policy. He explained in court that 'enormous crowds of prisoners-of-war remained in the theatre of operations, without proper care ... with regard to housing, food, medical care; and many of them died on the bare floor. Epidemics broke out, and cannibalism – human beings, driven by hunger, devouring each other ...' What was most damning in his evidence was his personal experience that such policies were not the secrets of a tight circle of leaders. Their intentions and the likely results were widely known. '... the Wehrmacht was involved in all matters which referred to prisoners-of-war, except the executions which were the commandos of the SD; they were entirely responsible for the camps.' Lahousen insisted: '... these orders were discussed a great deal, in casino clubs and elsewhere, because all these matters ... had a most undesirable effect on the troops.' He concluded that not all soldiers condoned such policies. Many 'either did not transmit these orders or sought to evade them in some way, and this was discussed a great deal.' Evasion, discussion, but who had protested?

Lahousen himself claimed to have protested to Army leaders and others about contraventions of international conventions and soldierly decencies. Perhaps the most revealing moment in his testimony came during his cross-examination when he was asked why he did not go directly to Hitler to protest. His reply sounded rather limp: he had been too junior to be admitted to Hitler, and he was only an Austrian officer. What was significant, however, was the roar of laughter from the defendants' box at the idea of such an approach to the Führer. It was Lahousen's claim that his protests were approved and encouraged by Admiral Canaris, who himself had frequently blocked orders and sabotaged policies. His view of Canaris was of 'a pure intellect, an interesting, highly individual and complicated personality, who hated violence as such and therefore hated and abominated war, Hitler, his system, and particularly his methods'. Historians now would probably modify that view by describing the Admiral as an enigmatic personality and a labyrinthine mind, and being devious to the point where none of his motives were untarnished. But Lahousen spoke of him with devotion and of his intimate circle with passion, pointing out how many of them had died for their involvement in the July Bomb Plot against Hitler.

This was undoubtedly a motive for his appearance as a witness for the prosecution. He told Gilbert that afternoon: 'I have to speak for those whom they murdered, I'm the only one left.' Unlike so many of the witnesses at Nuremberg he had no need to plead personal innocence or speak literally for his life. There were no charges against Lahousen; he was in protective custody in one of the houses kept in the city for those whose lives might be at risk. Something of the consequences of speaking for the prosecution were shown in a letter he wrote to Jackson on 28 December to draw his attention to a broadcast that day on Radio Munich in which his testimony had been abused and dismissed as biased. He warned that such attacks might deter other potential witnesses. Jackson pencilled a note that the matter should be taken up with the military government. There is no record of any action taken. (55)

Lahousen's testimony had come as a shock to the defendants. They had squirmed in their seats as he implicated first one and then another. They had been appalled at the idea that sabotage and plotting against the Führer was said to have taken place in military intelligence headquarters. While in the courtroom, they had tried to conceal their discomfort – smirking derisively, passing sneering comments along the rows. At lunchtime, however, their feelings boiled over. Keitel and Jodl expressed anger at the 'treacherous statements' of a serving officer. Goering exploded: 'that traitor. That's one we forgot on 20 July.' Ribbentrop had been hardest hit by the accusations against him that morning. He quavered: 'What shall I do?' (56)

The defence counsel had been shocked by Lahousen's very appearance in court. They had received no notification that he would be produced as a witness, though journalists had told them that morning that the Press had been informed the evening before. The defence counsel made a strong protest through Dr Nelte that they did not have an opportunity to prepare a cross-examination. Jackson was clearly angry at an attack on a prosecuting lawyer's right to produce rabbits from hats; he was going to fight hard to defend the use of surprise. He denied the suggestion that there was an agreement with the defence to disclose names of witnesses as well as documents (the suggestion was withdrawn) and argued that by issuing advance copies of evidence the prosecution was already doing much more for the defence than would be considered normal or even proper in an American court. Jackson stressed security reasons for concealing the names of witnesses. And when hard-pressed, he played it dirty: 'we are trying this case in the very hotbed of the Nazi organization with which some of the defence counsel were identified.' Lawrence cut him short. Dr Dix, very typically, poured oil on the troubled waters and promised that 'mutual understanding and goodwill' would gradually iron out such difficulties. For the moment though the Tribunal smoothed the defence by reassuring them that they would always be allowed time to consult their clients on questions to be put in cross-examination and they postponed the cross-examination of Lahousen until the next morning.

That cross-examination was an interesting indication of the style of the defence counsel and the cases they would try to present. Their questions were very long and often took the form of assertions to which it hoped the witness would agree. The technique was that of the bludgeon. As was to be shown time after time during the prosecution case, the defence had really no challenge to offer to the evidence itself. All they could try to do was to lessen its damage to their individual client. Thus Kubuschok did not claim that Papen had been unaware of aspects of Hitler's policies: he only suggested to Lahousen that Papen had tried to exercise a mitigating influence on them (Lahousen agreed he had received that impression). Nelte made no attempt to disprove allegations that Keitel had planned the bombardment of Warsaw, the assassination of the two French generals, had passed on the Commando Order, or been fully involved in the inhumane treatment of Russian prisoners. Instead he fell back on claims that Keitel had regularly told OKW officers to inform him of any orders against their consciences (Lahousen had no recollection of this); that he had tried to lessen the effect of orders; that the Gestapo and SD had behaved contrary to the intentions of his orders; that he had actually forbidden the circulation of the order to brand Russian prisoners but that a few copies had slipped through because of 'a regrettable, a terrible misunderstanding'. To all such claims Lahousen replied with confidence and ease. The constant theme of his replies was that of the prosecution as a whole – even if the defence claims were true, they could not alter the fact that the orders *were* given, they *were* carried out; protests and attempts to mitigate them may have been made, but the policies continued without modification and those who claimed to have protested remained in office and administered them.

The American prosecutors now turned to those charges within the conspiracy count which dealt with Crimes against Humanity. Their evidence was gruesome. Even Jackson's terrible outline had not prepared listeners for the appalling details. Thomas Dodd dealt with the forced labour programme. He quoted Sauckel's letter to Rosenberg (20 April 1942): 'The aim of this new gigantic labour mobilization is to use all the rich and tremendous sources conquered and secured for us ... for the armament of the Armed Forces and also for the nutrition of the homeland. The raw materials as well as the fertility of the conquered territories and their human labour power are to be used completely and conscientiously to the profit of Germany and her allies.' He read the speech of Erich Koch, the loathsome Commissar of the Ukraine, to a party meeting in 1943: 'I will draw the very last out of this country. I did not come to spread bliss. I have come to help the Führer. The population must work, work and work again ... We are a master race, which must remember that the lowliest German worker is racially and biologically a thousand times more valuable than the population here.' Dodd produced evidence to show that the population of the conquered countries was set to work at home or was removed to Germany – 4,795,000 people. Labourers in the West were obtained by trickery: Sauckel openly told the Central Planning Board in March 1944 that he had trained French and Italian men and women and paid them to go hunting for workers, 'just as it was done in olden times for shanghaiing', duping them, plying them with liquor. In the East the methods of 'labour mobilization' were even less subtle. Frank, as Governor General of Poland, wrote in his diary that he had 'no objections at all to the rubbish, capable of work yet often loitering about, being snatched from the streets' but he preferred organized raids to *ad hoc* kidnapping. A Ukrainian Nazi had complained in 1943 that 'Every man is exposed to the danger of being seized suddenly and unexpectedly anywhere and at any time by the police and brought to an assembly camp; thereafter his family are lucky if they ever received news of his whereabouts.'

Dodd also submitted evidence to show how the foreign labour was used. Some workers were sent to factories. An affidavit by a doctor at one of the Krupp labour camps in Essen had described them being fed on 1,000 calories a day less than the minimum prescribed for any German, and receiving condemned meat. They were infested with lice and fleas, riddled with tuberculosis. When they were sick, there were few medical supplies to treat them; they were forced to work on. Other forced labourers were sent to concentration camps where Himmler hoped to produce goods exclusively for the SS. Here death from starvation and disease was more frequent and discipline more brutally maintained than in the labour camps. Himmler decreed in September 1942 that some categories of prisoner such as Jews, gypsies, Russians, Ukrainians and Poles must suffer 'extermination through work'. Not all slave labourers were engaged in industrial production, however. Dodd had evidence of Field Marshal Milch telling Sauckel at a meeting of the Central Planning Board that he intended to take 50,000 Russians into the anti-aircraft artillery; 30,000 were already employed as gunners. 'It is amusing to think that Russians must work the guns.' Nazi policy in the East was that expressed by Himmler to his SS generals: 'Whether the other nations live in prosperity or starve to death interests me only in so far as we need them as slaves for our culture ... Whether 10,000 Russian females fall down from exhaustion while digging an anti-tank ditch or not interests me only in so far as the anti-tank ditch for Germany is finished.'

The evidence then produced by Dodd on the concentration camps and Walsh on the persecution of the Jews was, if it is possible to make such a distinction, even worse. The anguish of the tales of the mass executions, the gas vans and gas chambers was followed by the bleak report of Eichmann announcing briefly the death of four million Jews in the concentration camps and a further two million at the hands of the police in the East. An unequalled depth of cynicism was touched by the authorities at Mauthausen in their official report for one day in March 1945 which noted that 203 people had died, at regular intervals, all of heart attacks and in alphabetical order.

Unbelievably, much of the effect of this dreadful evidence was dissipated by the American presentation. Faced with the mounds of documents, they had failed to discriminate in their choice. They just dumped them on the judges' bench. They had failed to weave their evidence into a clear argument, forgotten to mention the international laws broken by Nazi policies, lost track of the conspiracy charge, and made little attempt to link evidence with individual defendants. The Tribunal became restive. Dodd and Walsh were frequently interrupted by demands from the Bench to show the relevance of their documents and by complaints at the cumulative nature of so much of their material. To no avail. One morning, as yet another repetitious document was produced, Lawrence expressed the irritation of his colleagues: 'Mr Dodd, don't you think that we have really got this sufficiently now?' 'Yes but . . .' and Dodd read on regardless.

Such evidence was so repellent, so difficult for the mind to take in, that the Americans should have been extremely selective. Instead, by inundating the court with it they blunted the sensitivity of all their listeners, saturated them with horror until they could absorb no more. But on 13 December, the prosecution produced in court concrete evidence which quickened the senses and restored the responses. First they showed an SS film, lasting only ninety seconds. Jerky, amateur shots of girls running naked and terrified through the streets, old women dragged along by their hair, five men being beaten senseless while SS men stood apathetically by. Then they held up the head of a Polish officer with luxuriant wavy hair, neat beard and full moustache – shrunken to the size of a fist to make a paperweight. Finally they produced strips of tatooed skin, flayed from the bodies of prisoners, which, according to the affidavit they submitted, Karl Koch, the commandant of Buchenwald, and his wife Ilse had used as lampshades.

The defence was stung into angry challenge. Kauffmann (Kaltenbrunner's counsel) leapt to his feet to protest that the Kochs had been sentenced to death by the SS for their inhumanity. He demanded that the defence be given immediate opportunity to rebut such evidence before it was reported in the Press and became generally accepted as fact. He insisted that allegations could not be made by affidavit alone; those who made such accusations, such as the man who described the use of the skin in lampshades, must be produced in court for cross-examination. Bergold (for Bormann) further maintained that German practice should be followed and exculpatory as well as incriminating evidence be provided by the prosecution. This was a red rag to Jackson. 'I do not in any instance serve two masters.' But he pointed out that the Charter gave the defence the right to call witnesses either for their case or for cross-examination – a right confirmed by the Tribunal at the end of the argument.*

Except for reassurance on this procedural point, the defence had had a bad week. The prosecution may have handled its evidence clumsily but that evidence had been weighty and it had told on the defendants. Word leaked to the Press (undoubtedly through Gilbert and members of Andrus's staff) that the defendants had been 'alarmed at the failure of their counsel to shake the evidence' and by Friday 14 December they were 'dazed by the impact of yet another day of horror stories . . . a bunch of scowling and worried

*The defence never used its right to cross-examine over the matter of the skin lampshades. Proof was offered by the prosecution on 14 January that Koch had been tried and executed for the embezzlement of SS funds and for the murder of someone with whom Koch had 'had some personal difficulties'. (Vol. V)

men left the dock' that night. (57) Back in their cells they were reported to be having 'their worst weekend since the trial began'; all except for Schacht were said to be resigned to death. (58) Even so, they still told Gilbert they had known nothing that was happening; they still blamed others for it.

The only fleeting brightness in their week had come on Tuesday 11 December. With peculiar timing, since it did not seem relevant to the plans for aggressive war they had been discussing nor a fitting introduction to the Crimes against Humanity, the Americans had shown a film called 'The Nazi Plan'. It was a compilation of German footage showing the History of the Nazi Party, its rule in Germany and the War up to 1944. It lasted for four hours, so it is hardly surprising that the American President sent a message to the team in Nuremberg in February to say that he had not found time to see it. (59) The defendants adored every moment of it. They gazed entranced at the newsreels of the Nazi Rallies in Nuremberg, tapped their feet to the marching songs, revelled in the sight of the flags and the sound of the 'Sieg Heils' and Hess crying 'The Party is the Führer and the Führer is Germany'. (60) Schirach became increasingly excited as he watched his Hitler Youth parade past the reviewing stand. Goering relished his every appearance on the screen and dug Hess in the ribs in case he had not noticed. He and Doenitz exchanged jocular taunts as airmen or sailors were shown, each claiming his own men as the best of the lot, Goering shouting out the type of each plane and the name of any pilot he recognized. (61) He did not laugh, as some did, at the scene showing him slapping his thighs and rubbing his hands as Chamberlain signed the Munich Pact. (62) Schacht was clearly moved by the sequence on the German pre-War industrial programme. 'Can you see anything wrong in that?' he asked his neighbours. (63) When they got back to the prison several of the defendants were in tears – of pride and nostalgia this time. (64)

Not one of them commented on a sequence in the film that had particularly impressed others. It showed the trial before the People's Court in Berlin of the 1944 Bomb plotters. They had seen abject men, clutching at their trousers from which the belts had been taken, deprived of the dignity of their false teeth and the aid of their spectacles. There had been no defending counsel and the accused had been literally dragged by SS guards before Judge Freisler. As soon as they tried to speak he screeched at them a torrent of abuse. The contrast between Nazi justice and the tone of the Nuremberg trial and its Charter was vivid and telling – to those sensitive enough to see it.

After a week of modified success, the American prosecution now staged a week of scarcely alleviated shambles. Their case on the Germanization and spoliation of occupied territories had been conscientiously prepared, and effective use had been made of the documentary evidence to back it. But Captain Sam Harris, who was responsible for it, aborted its impact by prefacing his presentation with the words: 'My knees haven't knocked so much since I asked my wonderful little wife to marry me.' Birkett was aghast: 'The shocking bad taste is really almost unbelievable.' (65) Biddle's note was more succinct: 'Jesus.' What had touched him on the raw was the feeling that an American lawyer had let down his profession in front of the infinitely correct British. (66) Others might have thought them decorous to the point of being mannered. Poor Harris was given a dressing down by the Judge in private. Significantly his opening remarks do not appear in the official transcript. His shame was covered with a discreet veil. The transcript only records his undoubted competence.

Alas, there was no veil big enough to cover the disaster of Colonel Storey's presentation of the case against the Leadership Corps, the Cabinet and the SA. (67) The hundreds of thousands of documents that Storey had collected and sifted in Paris had obviously inebriated him. He could no longer walk a logical line or focus on facts of importance. For most of three embarrassing days he lurched around his case in court and blundered blindly against the Bench. Storey produced police reports on some befuddled assumption that they were evidence against the Leadership Corps; tried to contort totally irrelevant documents into something approximately apposite by giving anyone named a title from the Leadership Corps. Lawrence and Biddle came down on him in wrath. 'What exactly does this document prove?' they enquired icily. 'Relevance, relevance,' they demanded. During the case against the Cabinet, Lawrence pulled him up at least fifteen times: 'Colonel Storey, it would help me if you explained what conclusions you are asking us to draw from these documents.' His evidence became increasingly repetitious – even to the extent of trying to read documents twice. Lawrence and Biddle snapped as yet more cumulative material was submitted, until even Storey began to spot that a document 'might be considered strictly cumulative'. 'Well, if it's cumulative, we don't really want to hear it.' Doenitz went to sleep. (68) The other defendants were in transports of delight. They nudged each other and giggled; they roared with laughter every time Storey was reprimanded. They had not had such fun since the showing of 'The Nazi Plan'.

Farr, dealing with the SS, was not the man to save the day. He had a kind of logic but it was scarcely discernible in the morass of his ponderous thought processes. The Bench was irritated; their tempers snapped when he could give no figures on how many SS men worked in what sections and ranks of the hierarchy. The return of Storey to deal with the Gestapo was simply the last straw in the load of tedious repetition. The adjournment on 20 December for the Christmas break must have come as a vast relief to everyone.

This section of the American case had been humiliating in personal terms. Much more importantly, though, it had been a failure they could ill afford. The case against the organizations was both a vital element in their aims for the trial, and at the same time legally contentious and technically difficult to prove, and they had muffed it. They were saved from complete disaster by a superb presentation by Telford Taylor of a masterly case

Justice Robert H. Jackson's failure to control Goering caused scandal and alarm, a permanent breach in his relations with the judges and much personal bitterness. (Fox Photos)

The cross-examination of Goering. (John Topham Picture Library)

Maxwell-Fyfe re-established the prosecution's grip over Goering. (BBC Hulton Picture Library)

This pile of transcripts of the daily proceedings represents only one-fifth of the total. The files contain just a small proportion of the documents processed by the Translation Division. (Associated Press)

Captain Otto Kranzbuehler. As counsel for Doenitz, Kranzbuehler was reckoned to be the most brilliant of the defence lawyers. As a serving officer in the German Navy he appeared for much of the trial in uniform. This so infuriated the Russians that he was finally obliged to strip off his braid and buttons to appear as a civilian. (Keystone Press)

Lord Justice Lawrence reads the tribunal's verdicts on the accused. Birkett is on the left, and Biddle is beyond Lawrence. (John Topham Picture Library)

The defendants immediately after hearing the verdicts. Note Schacht, who has just been acquitted, eating a sandwich. (Keystone Press)

The three acquitted hold a press conference. From the left, Papen, Schacht and Fritzsche. (Keystone Press)

Colonel Burton C. Andrus, the defendants' jailer at Mondorf and Nuremberg, announcing Goering's suicide. He himself designed the coat of arms on his flash and helmet with, as he described it, a key for security and scales for Justice on a field of azure for Truth; a base gules for the Pit of Wrath in which appeared an eagle to represent Germany, fallen and destroyed. The brodure was to be sable for Solemnity. (Keystone Press)

The site of the execution. The condemned men were led down the steps from the jail, across the yard and into the gymnasium on the right. (Associated Press)

John C. Woods, the hangman, and those condemned to death. Clockwise from top left: Goering, Frank, Frick, Streicher, Ribbentrop, Seyss-Inquart, Keitel, Kaltenbrunner, Rosenberg, Jodl and Sauckel. (Associated Press)

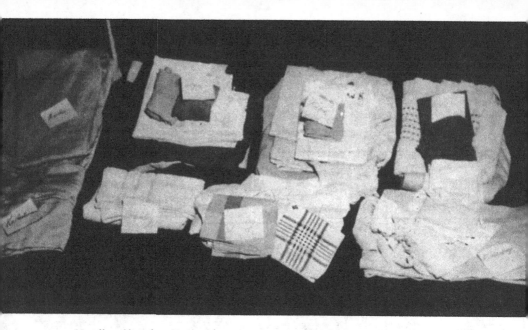

Uncollected laundry of some of the executed war criminals laid out in the prison laundry room.
(Popperfoto)

Germans protest against the acquittals. Demonstrations took place mainly in the Russian Zone. This one, in Berlin, attracted an estimated 50,000 people. (Associated Press)

against the General Staff on 4 January.* But given the overall mess they had made, they were now dangerously dependent on an equivalent degree of failure by the defence and a painstaking review by the Tribunal of the evidence they had misused if the case against the organizations was to succeed at all.

The end of the American case re-established their grip – thanks largely to the witnesses produced. Three of them were not objective, innocent observers of the crimes of the defendants. They might well have been in the defendants' box themselves; they would in fact be tried elsewhere. Their role was that of living documents on the criminality of the Nazi leaders. Otto Ohlendorff had been Number Three in the Gestapo, the chief of Amt III in the RSHA (Reich Security Main Office).** He was a lean, mousey man, dressed in a crumpled grey suit. He spoke in a matter-of-fact manner about his work, occasionally displaying a little pride in his professional prowess. What he said chilled the court. From 1941 to 1942 he had led the Einsatzgruppen D, working in the Ukraine and then Russia. In that time, Ohlendorff had organized and directed the killing of 90,000 people. In his professional opinion shooting parties were less of an emotional strain on his men than the unloading of bodies from gas vans. Yes, he had had scruples about his work, but 'to me it is inconceivable that a subordinate leader should not carry out orders given by the leader of the state'. How often the court was to hear that view in the coming months. As so often the defence could not challenge the evidence; they could just search for mitigating factors for their clients.

Dieter Wisliceny showed a similar professional calm and total unawareness of the horror with which his testimony was received. He was a friend and colleague of Eichmann; they both came from Linz and called each other 'du'. He knew everything about the 'Jewish Question' and the 'Final Solution'. He had seen Eichmann's order from Hitler to carry it out and could quote the subsidiary orders by which the policy was administered. He could also repeat the comment that Eichmann had made to him that if Germany lost the War he would leap laughing into his grave because the five million dead Jews were a source of such extraordinary satisfaction to him. Wisliceny could retail his knowledge without a qualm, without an apology, without even the usual attempts to claim personal innocence. His evidence was so bald that neither prosecutors nor defence counsel could find any questions to ask.***

General Bach-Zelewski, called as a witness in the General Staff case, was an alternative specimen of Nazi pathology. He was spare, bespectacled; to Biddle he looked like 'a mild and rather serious accountant'. (69) He described the savage reprisals and mass executions of the Anti-Partizan

*Dealt with in separate chapter on the organizations.
**Ohlendorff was sentenced to death in 1948 by a subsequent Nuremberg Tribunal. He was hanged with three other Einsatzgruppen commanders in 1951.
***Wisliceny was tried in Czechoslovakia and hanged in February 1948.

Partizan Units which he had commanded in Russia. But he would not admit any responsibility for their actions. He distributed it among the whole Wehrmacht – everyone had taken part. He claimed to have tried to modify policies, but complained that he was not given authority or that publication of his orders was delayed. He produced the earliest example of what was to become a standard plea of so many Nazis at Nuremberg: he could not resign because 'if someone else had been in my position the disaster would have been greater'.* In a final dose of humbug, Bach-Zelewski expressed disapproval of Himmler's call to exterminate thirty million Slavs. He condemned it as 'the logical consequence of our ideology' and added, 'It is difficult for a German to fight through to this conviction. It took me a long time.' Did he really imagine that anyone would respect his tardy victory in his moral fight? Certainly Goering did not. As Bach-Zelewski passed him to leave by the main door, Goering spat out: '*Schweinhund*. You damned traitor.' Strengthened by his new-found moral purity Bach-Zelewski simply returned a pitying smile. (70) As a punishment for his outburst, Goering was deprived of tobacco and exercise for a week. Andrus gave the defendants one of his Headmistress's speeches on the need for quiet and dignified behaviour – and from this time, all witnesses were taken out through the interpreters' door. (71)

In the two remaining witnesses for the American prosecution case, there was tragic illustration of how such men had used others and what they had reduced them to. Alois Hollriegel was a simple peasant with a thick Austrian accent. Before the Anschluss he had been unemployed for many years; 'consequently I thought I would join the civilian SS and there I would get work in order to marry my wife'. He described watching men worked to death in the stone quarries at Mauthausen, dropped 100 feet over the cliffs as punishment and as warning to others. He could only laugh when asked why he had not reported such incidents – who cared? Franz Blaha was a Czech doctor. (72) He too had been drafted to a concentration camp, to Dachau, but as a prisoner. Here he was subjected to typhoid experiments. When he refused to perform operations on twenty healthy prisoners, he was sent to the autopsy room; by 1945 Blaha had performed 12,000 post-mortems. He told of filthy experiments, sadistic executions, squalor, the substitution for formal execution in 1943 of death from exhaustion and hunger. 'Absolutely horrible. I omit details,' wrote Biddle in his notes. (73) Everyone in the neighbourhood knew about the conditions in Dachau, Blaha said, many prisoners were sent every day to work in Munich. Most damningly he described visits to the camp by Bormann, Frick, Rosenberg, Funk, Sauckel, Kaltenbrunner. There was consternation in the defendants' box and then 'the liveliest cross-examination yet seen in

*Bach-Zelewski escaped threatened extradition to the USSR. In 1951 a Munich de-Nazification court sentenced him to ten years' 'special labour', but he remained under house arrest. In 1961 he was sentenced to four and a half years' imprisonment for his part in the Roehm purge. In 1962 a Nuremberg jury sentenced him to life imprisonment for murdering six communists in 1933. He died in prison in 1972.

the courtroom'. (74) Defence counsel tried to trip up Blaha over precise dates – he had a remarkably accurate memory. Over names – he knew them all. Frick's counsel tried to imply that Blaha had not seen his client at Dachau but had been briefed to recognize him in court – not true, he had asked a friend in the camp to point out Frick, who was 'a well-known person in Bohemia and Moravia' (he had been their 'Protector'). Others tried to trick Blaha: Rosenberg came to the camp in his black uniform? No, the SS wore field grey once the War started. How could he know about the brutal treatment of prisoners since he claimed to have been so constantly busy? 'I performed the autopsies on those beaten to death or shot.'

With evidence like this it hardly mattered that the American case had been a curate's egg. The good parts had been in a majority and they had made a decisive impact. The sheer volume of evidence, however badly presented at times, had smashed their points home. Nearly all that evidence had come from the mouths or pens of the defendants themselves. The conspiracy charge had covered the entire range of the charges against them; their counsel had challenged minor details, fretted at minutiae, but they had not as yet found a single answer to any of them.

References for Chapter Eight

1 British prosecutors' minutes, 19 November 1945
2 FO. File 16 U9934
3 British prosecutors' minutes, 16 November
4 Dean cable, 21 November. FO. File 16 U9198
5 FO. File 16 U9154
6 John Phipps' diary, 19 November
7 IMT Volume II – as all other quotations from proceedings until noted
8 *Daily Mail*, 23 November
9 Andrus
10 *Christian Science Monitor* J Emlyn Williams, 20 November
11 Biddle Notes on Evidence Vol. I Box 3
12 Biddle Notes on Evidence Vol. I Box 3
13 *Stars and Stripes*, 20 November
14 Fritzsche
15 *New York Herald Tribune*, 19 November
16 Schacht
17 *New York Herald Tribune*, 19 November
18 *Stars and Stripes*
19 Cooper
20 British prosecutors' minutes, 12 November
21 Montgomery Hyde
22 *New York Herald Tribune*, 20 November
23 *Daily Express*, 20 November
24 *Daily Telegraph*, 20 November
25 Ibid
26 *New York Times*, 20 November
27 Fritzsche

28 Gilbert
29 *New York Times*, 20 November
30 Fritzsche
31 *Daily Express*, 21 November
32 Conversation with William Jackson
33 Jackson Papers, Box 198
34 Jackson Papers, Box 197
35 Gilbert
36 British War Crimes Executive Report 3, 25 November. N/40
37 Gilbert
38 *New York Herald Tribune*, 23 November
39 Bernstein
40 Several Press reports, chiefly those of *Daily Telegraph* and *Daily Mail*
41 *New York Times*, 23 November
42 Gilbert
43 Tribunal minutes, 6 November
44 Tribunal minutes, 8 November
45 All reports printed in IMT Vol. I
46 Biddle Notes on Evidence Vol. I Box 3
47 *New York Times*, 30 November
48 *News Chronicle*, 30 November
49 *New York Times*, 30 November
50 *Daily Worker*, 1 December
51 *New York Herald Tribune*, 30 November
52 *Stars and Stripes*, 4 December
53 Biddle Notes on Evidence Vol. I Box 3
54 IMT Vol. III as all subsequent quotations until noted
55 Jackson Papers, Box 213
56 *New York Times*, 30 November – clearly based on information from Gilbert
   whose diary contains much the same comments
57 *Daily Herald*, 14 December
58 *New York Times*, 16 December
59 Jackson Papers, Box 213
60 *The Times*, 11 December
61 *Evening Standard*, 11 December
62 Cooper
63 *New York Times*, 11 December
64 Gilbert
65 Montgomery Hyde
66 Conversation with Jim Rowe
67 IMT Vol. IV as subsequent quotations until noted
68 *Daily Herald*, 18 December
69 Biddle Notes on Evidence Vol. I
70 *Daily Herald* and Gilbert
71 Fritzsche
72 IMT Vol. V
73 Biddle Notes on Evidence Vol. I
74 *New York Times*, 11 January 1946

Chapter Nine

The scope and presentation of the American case created certain difficulties for the prosecutors who now had to follow with the British, French and Russian cases. From the days when the indictment was being compiled, Robert Jackson intended to use Count One on conspiracy as a means of 'keeping the bulk of the case in American hands'.* His intended sleight of hand did not go unnoticed. The British were the first to spot that his broad interpretation of the conspiracy charge would allow him to poach aspects of the case which other national teams would wish legitimately to develop as part of their own counts. Maxwell-Fyfe's memo to other prosecutors in November trying to create clear areas of responsibility and to limit the breadth of the American case was the expression of their anxiety.** Others were slower to realize that the American interpretation of conspiracy and their decision to present evidence not just on Nazi intentions but on the acts which resulted from them would take the wind from their own sails. It was only on 12 December during a meeting of the chief prosecutors, that Rudenko, with the backing of Edgar Faure of the French team, asked the Americans to leave the actual reading of many of the documents they were submitting in court to other teams as support for their cases. Jackson dug in his heels. He insisted that every document the Americans intended to use was relevant to conspiracy. When Storey suggested some give and take and pointed out that the Russians and the French had been co-operative in giving the Americans material to back their charges on slave labour, Jackson merely promised to do his best to leave some evidence and charges to his Allied colleagues. (1)

Despite Jackson's minimal concession, the American approach does not seem to have changed at all. In fact, by this stage it was too late to protest. The Americans had already scooped the other prosecuting teams; all the charges had been covered, many of the best documents to prove them had been read in court and made their impact. As a result of this the English, French and Russians faced real problems. Their cases would seem lacklustre and repetitious, and they would risk running foul of the Bench – the Charter had stipulated an expeditious trial and forbidden the use of cumulative evidence. Though the danger was clear, the other teams did not decide to prune their cases. Too much work had been put into them to wish

*Chapter Six p. 103 Quote 28.
**Chapter Seven p. 135.

175

to sacrifice it now; too much national pride was involved. No one wished to appear as a mere appendage to the American case. All wanted to present their own cases in the manner and at the length they saw fit. The French and the Russians in addition wanted to speak for those who had suffered Nazi occupation and felt they could do it more knowledgeably than the Americans.

As a result, it was inevitable that the trial would be infinitely longer than anyone had originally prophesied. At the end of November word leaked out to the Press that the prosecutors were now suggesting it would go on until June. The trial would undoubtedly lose public interest, even arouse public impatience. Faced with the knowledge that the judges would not tolerate cumulative material, as they had shown during the American case, and faced with the technical problem of trying to present convincing cases with stale evidence, the other three prosecuting teams could only seek consolation in the belief that the American case had been too complicated and too inefficiently handled to make its points adequately.

Thanks to Maxwell-Fyfe's determination that the British would not be squeezed out of the account of Nazi aggression, their case on Crimes against Peace had been interleaved with the American case on conspiracy to launch aggressive war. So once the Americans had dealt with Nazi rearmament, the documents illustrating aggressive intentions and the story of the Rhineland and the Anschluss, they had stood down briefly on 12 December while Sir Hartley Shawcross outlined the British view of the crime of aggression.

Shawcross was in an unenviable position. He had to follow Jackson whose speech had been a superb, moving piece of oratory. Furthermore Jackson had already devoted much attention to aggression since war was, for him, the greatest of Nazi crimes and the fount of all others. But Shawcross rose to the occasion. His speech was beautifully composed. It made a great impression, not least because it was in no way a pale reflection of Jackson's. Shawcross's style, his manner of delivery and above all his intellectual approach were entirely different. Unlike Jackson he was no crusader. He was a first-class practising barrister, whose primary instinct was to win cases. Shawcross was aware of the potential importance of the trial in developing international law, and of the possibility that it might go some way to fulfilling the contemporary aspiration for peace. But his method was to concentrate on expounding the law which he believed already existed, not to stress, as Jackson had done, how it could develop. He avoided the broad sweep which had been appropriate to Jackson's conspiracy charge and to his role as the first prosecutor to speak. Instead he disciplined himself to the British case in hand and to showing how the relevant law covered the crimes and the defendants. Sometimes he just nudged his listeners to consider the implications of the trial, but he issued no ringing challenges to rise to the opportunities it presented. In contrast to Jackson, Shawcross's manner of delivery was on the whole dispassionate; a manner suitable to the forensic style of his speech. One newspaper described it as a lecture to a learned society in London. (2) Only occasionally did he allow a trace of scorn to enter his voice as he made specific references to the defendants. (3) Rhetorical language and tone were eschewed until the final moments.

In his opening Sir Hartley gave short shrift to any arguments over the desirability or legality of the trial. He defined the British desire to establish a Tribunal as being a recognition 'that victory is not enough, that might is not necessarily right, that lasting peace and the rule of law is not to be secured by the strong arm alone.' (4) He suggested that one task of the Tribunal was to 'provide an authoritative and impartial record to which future historians might turn for truth and future politicians for warning'. Future generations must be made aware that 'the waging of war is not only a dangerous venture but a criminal one.' Cries of *'vae victis'*, and resort to summary executions could do none of this. What was needed was a judicial hearing based on law.

Shawcross argued throughout his speech that the law which the Tribunal was being asked to apply already existed; the only novel element in the Charter was the introduction of machinery to carry it out. Aggressive war, as he put it, was a crime not because the victors in the recent war said so, but because international law since 1918 had defined it as such. The Charter did not embody the law of the victors but the accepted principles of international usage; it did not create law, it only created 'a jurisdiction in respect of what was already the law of nations'. That law had been expressed in a series of international agreements and treaties, starting with the Covenant of the League of Nations and culminating in the Kellogg-Briand Pact. In addition it had been channelled into a range of particular agreements between individual nations. Shawcross calculated there had been ninety-nine of them. Germany had been a party to many of them. Since he claimed that treaty is the accepted source of international law, he dismissed as 'superficial learning or culpable sentimentality' all suggestions that there was any element of retroactivity in the Charter as regarding wars of aggression. The treaties of the inter-war years had conclusively established the corpus of law on which Count Two was based. By signing so many of the agreements, Germany had knowingly limited her sovereignty and accepted international obligations; logically, therefore, she must accept international judgement and punishment as a consequence of breaking them.

Shawcross now focused his attack on the men in the defendants' box. The defendants could not shelter behind claims that only states commit crimes in international law, he said. Contrary to Jackson's definition, Shawcross maintained the state is not an abstract entity: 'its rights and duties are the rights and duties of men'. But starting from a different definition, he reached the same conclusion: like Jackson he supported the view that 'it is a salutary principle that politicians should not seek immunity behind the intangible personality of the state; it is a salutary legal rule that persons who, in violation of the law, plunge their own and other countries into aggressive war should do so with a halter round their necks.' Though hitherto individuals might not have been held responsible in courts of law for crimes against peace, the principle of individual responsibility had always applied to war crimes. By introducing it to the crime of aggressive war the Charter was not retroactive but simply filling 'a gap in criminal procedure'. Nor could the defendants shelter behind claims of obeying orders – common soldiers were not given that protection when orders were patently illegal. These defendants were far from common soldiers, they were 'no mere willing tools'; they had had power and responsibility. 'Political loyalty, military obedience are excellent things, but they neither require nor do they justify the commission of patently wicked acts. There comes a point where a man must refuse to answer to his leader if he is also to answer to his conscience.'

Shawcross's neat analysis of the law took only a third of his speech. The rest was devoted to a detailed and skilful account of Nazi aggression. He suggested that there was no point in trying to find a single, exact, all-embracing definition of aggression – any definition at all would 'cover and cover abundantly and irresistibly in every detail the premeditated onslaught by Germany on the territorial integrity and political independence of so many sovereign states'. But as he had already argued that treaty is the basis of international law, he concentrated on the breaking of treaties as the key to Nazi criminality under Count Two. As Shawcross examined in turn the invasion of Poland, Norway and Denmark, the Low Countries, Greece, Yugoslavia and Russia, his method was the same. First he laid out Germany's treaty obligations towards each country – both the broad obligations such as those imposed by the Locarno Pact and the Peace of Paris (Kellogg-Briand Pact), by which Germany had renounced aggression in disputes; and the specific treaties of non-aggression with each state. Then he quoted the assurances Germany had given to each country, pointing out that Hitler had shown that he meant what he had said: 'agreements are to be kept only as long as they serve a certain purpose.' It could be said, observed Shawcross, that an invitation from Ribbentrop to enter a non-aggression pact with Germany had been a sign that Germany intended to attack; the nearer Germany came to invasion, the more numerous and fervent were her avowals of peaceful intent. Finally Shawcross quoted the plans which had long existed for each invasion, drawing attention to the careful preparation, the deliberate intent, and the role of individual defendants who had been privy to Hitler's ambitions and who had willingly used their positions to further them. Throughout, Shawcross established his points with a cold clarity. His case was effective because it did not rely merely on his frequent eloquence but on the use of incontrovertible facts – treaties, military orders, the words of the defendants and their acts. It was all on record.

Only in his peroration did Shawcross allow some fire into his voice. He had already conceded that the story of Nazi diplomacy 'founded upon cunning, hypocrisy, and bad faith' might seem less gruesome than that of their robberies, degradations, murders. But he warned that their conduct of diplomacy was 'no less evil and deliberate' than their other crimes and 'should it be taken as a precedent of behaviour in international relations, its consequences to mankind will no less certainly lead to the end of civilized society.' Shawcross called for punishment of the defendants as a step 'to restore sanity and with it the sanctity of our obligations towards each other'.

For the rest the speech had been deliberately low-key. It was no less effective for that. Indeed Birkett often told Airey Neave that 'for lucid presentation and effectivenes this was the best speech in the whole trial.' (5) Onlookers noticed the increased tension among the accused as point after point was calculatedly launched and pushed home with meticulous attention to detail. The defendants followed his every word – Ribbentrop in particular, since so much of what was said concerned his work as ambassador and Foreign Minister. Even Hess stopped reading his novel for a time and took notes. (6) When the speech was over all the defendants seemed visibly shaken. As the *Sunday Times* pointed out, Shawcross had not resorted to calling them names. Instead he had undermined one of their main hopes of defence – that what they had done was not an actual crime in law. (7) He had pinpointed each man's responsibility under the law and outlined all too clearly the nature of his acts. The case on aggressive war was going to be much harder to answer than might have been expected.

The speech was on the whole warmly received by Shawcross's professional colleagues. They more than most could appreciate its skill and its contribution to the prosecution case. Oddly, however, it came under fire from the Russians. Patrick Dean reported to the Foreign Office that they had pressed strongly for the deletion from the printed text of a number of passages which gave the impression that the Soviet Government might have been misled by the Nazi-Soviet Pact and the subsequent protestations of German friendship for the Soviet Union. They stoutly maintained that Moscow was fully aware of German intentions from the first and was prepared to go to war at any time with Germany. They also objected to the statement that after the collapse of France and the Low Countries, Great Britain was left alone to face Germany. Dean added: 'The motive of these rather naive arguments is difficult to see.' (8) Indeed. The second of their complaints was to a historical fact: Shawcross had in no way implied that Britain remained alone to fight Germany to the end of the War. The first of their complaints was even odder. They did not protest at all, as they might well have done, at reference to the Nazi-Soviet Pact; it would have been understandable if they had wished to avoid any hint of its Protocol with the proof of their greed and ruthlessness. Instead the Russian prosecutors were taking umbrage at a historical judgement – that they had been misled. In so doing they risked giving the impression that the Soviet Union had signed the Pact with as much cynicism as had the Germans; and it was the Germans who were now on trial charged with using treaties as a convenience. National pride is all very understandable; no nation likes to admit that it was gulled. But the Russians could have swallowed their pride in the interests of the prosecution case; much better to show the Germans as duplicitous.

Perhaps most breathtaking of all was their assumption that the official records of the proceedings could be doctored to suit the self-esteem of a prosecuting nation. (Their demand was different in kind from the decision to hide the shame of Sam Harris; his remarks had not been in any way part of the case.) Usually it is possible to guess that the Russian prosecutors were driven into complaints by instructions from Moscow. On this occasion their complaint was delivered so rapidly that it seems to have been the conditioned reflex of the men on the spot.

Once Shawcross had laid the foundations so firmly, the rest of the case on Crimes against Peace could be built quickly. Alderman dealt with the American evidence on the takeover against Czechoslovakia making it part of the conspiracy charge (in this way the problem of whether it was technically aggression was avoided). The British came back to present their evidence on other Nazi aggressions up to the invasion of Russia. They took less than three days. Sir David Maxwell-Fyfe dealt in detail with the fifteen main treaties which Germany signed then broke, and dealt a damaging pre-emptive strike against a possible defence by pointing out that in German jurisprudence the publication of a treaty in the official *Reichsgesetzblatt* automatically made it part of the statute law of Germany. Then his junior colleagues, Griffith-Jones, Elwyn Jones, Roberts and Phillimore covered each geographical area of aggression in turn. Their method was business-like, even brusque. They were thoroughly conversant with the relevant treaties and the diplomacy of the period, thanks to expert briefings from Jim Passant of the Foreign Office who had stayed in Nuremberg until their case was launched. No attempt was made to pad or plead. Carefully chosen evidence was placed in a brief, clear context. Where documents had already been read in court, they were simply referred to or quickly summarized before being submitted. The only colour came in 'Khaki' Roberts' presentation of the case on Belgium. Roberts was an exotic intrusion in the normally prosaic Nuremberg courtroom. He was the personification of the ripest Old Bailey style. Every paragraph began with an orotund 'My Lord'. The Tribunal had come to expect and welcome nothing extraneous from the British. When Roberts essayed a little hyperbole about the Nazi 'code of honour' and 'the acts of a common criminal' they cut him down to size. 'Mr Roberts' said Lawrence, 'I think we would like you so far as possible to confine yourself to the document.' 'Yes, My Lord . . .' and Roberts bowed to the rebuke with Old Bailey grace.

The British case could be presented so quickly and clearly largely because the thinking behind it had been deliberately simple. Should the Tribunal accept the British view that treaties make international law, then the count was not difficult to prove. The British presented to the judges the treaties which Germany had signed, the specific military plans which were put into effect to break them, and the historical facts of unprovoked invasions. It was a straightforward, limited concept; there was plenty of evidence to support it, all of it straight from archives. By adopting this approach, the British team had avoided the pitfalls pointed out by the eminent historian, E.L. Woodward, then working at the Foreign Office. His memorandum circulated the previous August argued forcibly that 'it is notoriously difficult to prove intentions from diplomatic documents'. (9) The British prosecutors had hardly discussed intentions; they had concentrated on plans which had actually been put into operation and the events which resulted.

In this, the British approach was in stark contrast to that of the Americans. The American count on conspiracy was by its very nature obliged to deal in vaguer concepts such as intentions. The Americans had not overcome the problems of vagueness. On the contrary, the way in which they developed their case had made it more dangerously diffuse and unspecific. The British stuck to documents and events that could not be contested; the Americans put heavy emphasis on documents open to challenge – Hitler's speeches, the Hossbach memorandum in particular. This opened their case to a double attack from defending counsel. They could and did challenge the actual authenticity of the documents produced, suggesting that the Hossbach memorandum was at worst forged, at best an inaccurate and unsubstantial summary; that the Schmundt minutes of Hitler's conference of 23 May 1939 existed in more than one version, with substantial discrepancies between them. They could then go on to show that Hitler had not in practice done exactly what he was reported as threatening. In Hossbach's memorandum of Hitler's conference of November 5 1937, the Führer was reported as intending to invade first Czechoslovakia and then Austria; and he had suggested 1943 as the earliest opportunity for aggression. The defence claimed that such speeches were never declarations of settled intent, but were merely explorations of available possibilities. Or they were largely hortatory, designed to goad lethargic and timid military and political subordinates to higher ambitions and greater efforts on Germany's behalf.*

Their arguments had a plausible ring to them because American prosecutors implied there was exact correspondence between Hitler's early statements and his subsequent acts. In other words they fell neatly into the

---

*Many historians would now agree with this defence interpretation. They see Hitler not as the long term strategist who stuck to his plans but as an opportunist, a genius of improvization. But Sir John Wheeler-Bennett deliberately included the Hossbach memorandum in the Anglo-American series of German Foreign Policy Documents of the inter-war years because he saw it as a valuable indicator of Hitler's broad aims which was supported by many similar speeches and policy documents -- aims whose details and emphases he adapted in response to practical situations. Recent historians, Joachim Fest and Norman Stone among them, quote the memorandum as an authentic record.

very trap against which Woodward had so accurately warned. The American evidence certainly suggested constant use of aggressive language by Hitler, readiness to contemplate aggression, and an early identification of the targets against which he did eventually move. It did not, however, actually prove conclusively the exact crime they alleged. It was no better than a prosecution of a man accused of strangling his wife on a given date relying on the evidence of a witness who claimed to have heard him threatening to shoot her on an entirely different day.

No such opportunities to the defence had been offered by the British case. As a result of the limited charges and the concrete evidence produced by the British prosecutors, the defendants began to look increasingly worried as point after point struck home and many of them found themselves directly implicated. (10) The Tribunal was impressed by the case, and no doubt relieved by its brevity. Birkett commented that Maxwell-Fyfe had tackled a potentially arid section with lucidity, and noted that Biddle considered Elwyn Jones' treatment of Norway and Denmark 'the best presentation we have yet heard'. (11)

But it is impossible to please all of the people all of the time. The Danes were not pleased. The story of how they had been attacked had taken so little time in court. It had been a terrible experience for the Danes; it was merely a bald recital for the court of a non-aggression treaty and a few facts of attack by the Nazis. The Danish government made an official protest to the British Foreign Office about what they saw as perfunctory, inadequate handling. Elwyn Jones pointed out that he had passed to the Tribunal the 'not very helpful Danish official report', and had tactfully suppressed a document which was not very creditable to the King. Danes in London and Nuremberg, he pointed out, had been very enthusiastic about the job he had done. Jim Passant drafted an official reply to the Danes. (12) He said that the bald facts were more than adequate to prove the point of unprovoked aggression and commented that the Danes did not seem to understand the need for relevance and avoidance of the merely corroborative. Probably his reply only went a little way to soothe bruised national feelings. It pleased the British team at Nuremberg, however, though Maxwell-Fyfe hinted that feelings other than Danish had been hurt. At the moment 'Elwyn has more sympathy for Canning than any rightminded Socialist should.' (13)*

After handling their case on Nazi aggression with such despatch, the British team were not active in court for a month. On either side of the Christmas recess, the Americans resumed the conspiracy charge, then introduced their case against the organizations.

The remaining British effort from mid-January went into the presentation of the cases against individual defendants. This was a confusing and unimpressive business, split between the British and Americans and seeming to

*As Tory Foreign Secretary, George Canning had sent the expedition which seized the Danish fleet and bombarded Copenhagen in 1807

be carried out at random either when there was the odd hour to spare during the organizations case or when the prosecutor responsible had his material ready. There was little dramatic about it: a few phrases were made about each man, relevant documents submitted with few extracts read, just serial numbers quoted. The public at large can have had litle idea of the nature of the cases against the men in the dock. The British, having been allocated the diplomats – Ribbentrop, Neurath and Papen – and the soldiers – Keitel and Jodl – had the chance to develop their case on aggression in further detail and to bind the defendants even more closely with the evidence. They were also responsible for the sailors – Raeder and Doenitz – which gave the further responsibility of presenting the case against the German Navy in mid-January.

The naval case was not so much a welcome opportunity as a constant problem to the British prosecutors. Both the admirals were charged on the first three counts. Raeder was relatively easy to prosecute – but only relatively. Under Counts One and Two it could be shown that he had held high command in the Navy and Cabinet rank. He had attended the key meetings where, it was alleged, Hitler had expounded his aggressive aims. There was evidence to suggest that he had been responsible for building up the German Navy in contravention of the limits imposed by the Versailles settlement. He had supervized the drawing up of naval plans for acts of alleged aggression and the use of the Navy in invasions of foreign territory. There was evidence too to link him with criminal orders and war crimes under Count Three.

The case against Doenitz, however, was much weaker. The British Admiralty had always opposed his inclusion among the defendants; he was in the dock because the Americans had put him there. There were only tenuous reasons to link him to Counts One and Two – he had been a relatively junior officer until he succeeded Raeder as commander of the Navy in 1943. Before that date his role had been limited to command of the submarine arm; he had not until then been a member of the indicted General Staff and High Command. He had not been personally involved in Hitler's strategy nor that of the Navy as a whole. His work and ambition had always been seen as that of a serving naval officer; his appointment as Hitler's successor seems to have come as a surprise to most people, including himself – it was thought of more as an attempt to unite the nation and secure relatively favourable terms from the Allies, rather than as a sign of Doenitz's high standing in Nazi circles. Given the weakness of the case against Doenitz on the first two counts, the emphasis of the prosecution had therefore to be placed on Count Three – War Crimes. The prosecutors had to show that German naval warfare had been criminal. Here their real problems began.

The British Admiralty had always been dubious about the desirability of a case against the German conduct of the War at sea. This was not because admirals wanted to avoid the precedent of putting admirals on trial. Rather, they knew that the laws of naval warfare were notoriously vague, and dangerously open to conflicting interpretation once sailors were faced with practical situations at sea. They still are. Furthermore, many of the laws of naval warfare were recognized as obsolete by the time of the Second World War. The 1907 Hague Conventions were not clear on the status and immunities of neutrals or those of merchantmen who were armed or who might use radios to transmit information on the whereabouts of warships. The conventions had dealt with the use of balloons in wartime, but not that of submarines. An attempt to regulate submarine warfare in regard to merchant ships was made in the London Protocol of 1936. According to this agreement, except in cases where a merchantman persistently refused to stop or actively resisted search, it must not be sunk until its crew, passengers and ship's papers had been put in a place of safety – which meant either being taken aboard another vessel or being provided with lifeboats and assured of safe weather conditions and the proximity of land. Such regulations already applied to the sinking of naval craft by surface vessels. However, existing law allowed that rescue of survivors need not be an absolute priority if it endangered the safety or the mission of the ship which had carried out the sinking. What the London Protocol had failed to take into account was that submarines on the surface would become as vulnerable as turtles on their backs. During the War the development of radar, the increased use of spotter planes and the introduction of improved radio communications for even the most primitive ships had endangered all vessels by 1939 and submarines especially. They could seldom afford to spend time securing the safety of others. Scrupulous attention to the rules on giving warning of attack and help to survivors was clearly in conflict with those aspects of the law which allowed consideration of one's own safety. All shipping – neutral, merchant, crippled – was a potential danger to submarines.

In October 1945, Humphrey Waldock, a legal expert at the Admiralty (and later President of the International Court at the Hague) had written a carefully reasoned memorandum explaining these and other legal problems. It was dismissed by the Foreign Office as: 'typical Admiralty whitewashing of the German Navy'. (14) But it was not whitewashing. It was the considered opinion of a distinguished lawyer, backed by the expert knowledge of experienced sailors who were well qualified to speak on standard practice in all navies. Its warning of legal difficulties in a case against the German Navy needed to be taken very seriously. The legal foundations of the British case were seemingly weak. Once they began to sift the evidence looking for specific examples of war crimes at sea, the whole structure appeared shaky. An obvious problem was that when ships and crews were suspected to have been destroyed, no evidence remained. Significantly, by the time the indictment was completed in October, the wording of the charges relating to the German Navy remained vague; the indictment alleged 'murder and ill treatment . . . of persons on the high seas' but gave no details, named no incidents. Doenitz spotted the absence of actual cases immediately and commented on it in his interrogations at the end of October. (15) He must already have been aware that the case against him on the first two counts was poor and taken comfort from this hint that evidence on war crimes was proving hard to find. He had every right to feel optimistic. By 13 November, Maxwell-Fyfe was complaining that the naval case in general seemed slight and that 'there was not much of a case against Doenitz'. (16)

It is, however, a most essential skill in any barrister to be able to make silk purses out of sows' ears. And the British did at least have the entire German Naval archive at their disposal in the citadel on Whitehall. A team under Major Kenneth Duke, assisted by WRNS and some ex-German sergeants in the Pioneer Corps, went to work on the documents. Gradually they gleaned enough to mount a promising case.

Evidence was found which suggested that Raeder might be linked with Hitler's plans to raze Leningrad to the ground. There was proof that he had passed on the Commando Order in October 1942, that two British commandos caught during the Bordeaux raid had been shot by a naval firing party, and that on other occasions the navy had handed commandos to the SS for execution. Other documents showed Raeder's cynical view of the laws of the sea and determination to fight the naval war by foul means if fair ones did not get the results he called for. In a memo in 1939 he had expressed the intention that '... measures which are considered necessary from a military point of view, provided a decisive success can be expected from them, will have to be carried out, even if they are not covered by existing international law' – which was very different from saying that naval law was ambiguous. He had added that in principle 'any means of warfare which is effective in breaking enemy resistance should be based on some legal conception, even if that entails the creation of a new code of naval warfare.' Raeder was prepared to invent law, or to invent practical justifications for action. In 1939 he had recorded that Hitler had given permission to sink neutral ships without warning in areas such as the Bristol Channel 'in which the fiction of mine danger can be upheld.' An even more blatant invention was uncovered in the archives in the citadel dealing with the sinking of the *Athenia* on 3 September 1939 on her way to North America. Nazi propaganda had claimed she had been sunk by a British submarine as a stratagem to lure America into the War (an attempt to update the *Lusitania* affair). Raeder had made public accusations to this effect against Churchill. Hawk-eyed WRNS, however, spotted that the log book of the U-boat which had in fact carried out the attack had been forged and that the official Naval War Diary had been falsified. Thereafter an affidavit could be obtained from a member of the U-30's crew and an admission from Doenitz that he had been aware, though disapproving, of the lies. (17)

Evidence against Doenitz was less easy to come by. When possible material was found, the Admiralty immediately applied wet blankets to the prosecutors' enthusiasm for it. The basis of their case under Count Three had to be the argument that although the laws of warfare at sea, especially those which applied to submarines, might be anachronistic, Germany had accepted them at the time. The detailed allegations against Doenitz were founded on incidents which could be interpreted as deliberate contraventions of naval law, such as the sinking without warning of the liner the *City of Benares* in September 1940 when 258 of the passengers and crew died; or the failure to attempt rescue following the sinking of the SS *Sheaf Mead* in 1940. The Admiralty had warned that sinking on sight might well be seen not as a crime but as an unpleasant fact of war, but the British persisted with the charge. (18) They argued in court that Doenitz's policy in regard to survivors began by interpreting existing law ruthlessly and ended by deliberately breaking it. The crucial moment in this development, they claimed, had come in September 1942 when he issued the so-called Laconia Order:* 'No attempt of any kind must be made at rescuing members of ships sunk, and this includes picking up persons in the water and putting them in lifeboats and handing over food and water. Rescue runs counter to the rudimentary demands of warfare for the destruction of enemy ships and crews ... Be harsh, having in mind that the enemy takes no regard of women and children in his bombing attacks on German cities.' The British Admiralty had suggested that this did not amount to an order to murder survivors deliberately and that it had in any case been variously interpreted by submarine commanders. (19) It was the prosecutors' contention however that even if the order was not a clear incitement to murder, it was at least ambiguous and that Doenitz must take responsibility for the fact that it had been defined as incitement on occasions. They quoted the case of the fishing trawler, the *Noreen Mary*, whose crew had been machine gunned as they tried to launch their lifeboats and that of the *Antonico* where survivors again came under fire as they put out in the ship's boats. (20)

To substantiate the allegation that the Laconia Order was intended to establish a policy of deliberate murder of survivors, the British produced two witnesses – the only two they used in their entire case. Both were U-boat officers. Neither could be termed an ideal witness. The first, Lieutenant Heisig, was in court to be examined on an affidavit that while a midshipman in 1942 he had attended a lecture by Doenitz in which the admiral had said that 'crews of ships like ships themselves were a target for U-boats' and pointed out that the Allies were finding it difficult to man their ships after U-boat successes. If true, Heisig's evidence clearly pointed to deliberate incitement to break naval law and commit murder. However, Heisig was a very young man at the time of the lecture – he might well have misunderstood. More significantly, he was the only witness to claim that Doenitz had ever expressed these views. Even more damaging to the ultimate value of his testimony was the fact that he had been interrogated at the time of the court-martial in Hamburg of Lt Eck and three of his crew from the U-boat 852 on charges of machine gunning and throwing hand grenades at the survivors of the *Peleus*, a Greek ship on charter to the British in the Atlantic. Eck had never claimed in his defence that he was acting on orders, but

*Details of the circumstances in Chapter 15.

186

Heisig might well have been led to believe that he could save Eck's life by putting the blame on Doenitz whose life was probably forfeit anyway. (Admiral Wagner was told that this suggestion was made to Heisig while he was being interrogated though Heisig's affidavit was signed after Eck's sentence had been passed and confirmed.) (21)*

The second prosecution witness, Captain Moehle, was equally unsatisfactory. He admitted he was testifying because when captured he had been accused of issuing the Laconia Order to others. A witness who might be literally talking to save his own neck cannot be seen as very reliable. From mid-1941 Moehle had been Flotilla Commander at Kiel, responsible for fitting out U-boats and for briefing commanders on their orders and missions. He claimed that when he asked his superiors about the Laconia Order he was told it was an instruction to kill survivors. He had passed it on but now maintained that he had always issued the caveat that 'everybody had to handle this according to his own conscience.' His evidence was not substantiated; everything was what a man in a tight spot might be expected to say.

Some of the weakness in the testimony of Heisig and Moehle appeared when they were cross-examined by Kranzbuehler, Doenitz's counsel. Heisig was forced to admit the difference between a prohibition against rescuing survivors (which could be proved by the available evidence and accorded with the law) and an order to kill survivors (for which the only evidence was his allegation). Moehle had no option but to agree with Kranzbuehler that naval standing orders urged taking of prisoners, on the grounds that they were valuable sources of intelligence, and that commanders disobeying the orders on the correct treatment of neutrals had been court-martialled. But these were relatively minor concessions, and just for the moment the case against Doenitz and on naval warfare in general seemed stronger than had originally been believed possible. For one thing, the British had presented it in court with reasonable assurance. More importantly, though, it had not as yet received a full attack from the defence. They were seemingly holding their fire and assessing the British position before revealing theirs. Once they questioned the legal grounds on which the case was based, once they examined and put into context the incidents adduced as evidence by the British, a dangerous number of leaks would be sprung. There was too big a gap between the British assertion that there had been a number of war criminals in the German Navy (as in any force of any nation) and the contention that their criminal behaviour

*At Hamburg Eck had claimed he used his machine guns and hand grenades to sink the *Peleus's* wreckage and life rafts – even though survivors were clinging to them – because their presence in the water would betray his position to enemy aircraft. The judge advocate pointed out that the best way to conceal a U-boat's position was to submerge and leave the area as quickly as possible, whereas the U852 had circled and attacked for five hours. It was an uncomfortable omen for the naval case at Nuremberg that he had stated the view that although the London Protocol had been signed by forty-eight nations it did not 'at present represent an effective rule of law.' Only three crew members of the *Peleus* had survived Eck's attack. They were picked up by a Portuguese ship after twenty-five days at sea. Eck, the ship's doctor and another officer, were executed at the end of November. Two other crew members were given prison sentences. (22)

had been ordered and directed by their commander. Kranzbuehler had given a hint of the power of his claws already. After his cross-examination of Moehle, Phillimore, whose witness he had been, had to announce that the British were dropping their charge that U-boats had attacked rescue ships. Kranzbuehler had shown that rescue ships were not legally entitled to protection. His knowledge of naval law was greater than the British team's – and he had plenty more up his sleeve. He had made the first defence breach in the prosecution case – albeit a fairly minor one. The prosecutors would experience even more substantial attacks once Kranzbuehler spoke in the defence case.

During the intricacies of the naval case, and the day and a half which followed devoted to listing documents used in the cases against individual defendants, the attention of the accused in the box often wandered unless they themselves were mentioned. Their attention quickened again, however, on 17 January when the French chief prosecutor, de Menthon, rose to open France's case on War Crimes and Crimes against Humanity committed in Western Europe. He spoke for four and a half hours and according to *The Times*, 'there were graver faces in the dock than at any time since the trial began'. (23)

It was a grave occasion for the French too. De Menthon was speaking on the eve of the anniversary of the declaration of the Second German Empire in the Hall of Mirrors at Versailles in 1871, a declaration which marked the unification of Germany, and was followed by a humiliating defeat for France and the loss of Alsace Lorraine let alone another war in 1914. The French had had a moment of revenge in 1919 when in the same hall at Versailles the peacemakers wrote German war guilt into their treaty and evolved a settlement intended to cripple Germany's military might for ever. But the treaty had failed to secure the peace. For the third time in less than a hundred years, France had suffered German invasion and occupation. De Menthon was to speak now for all those in the West who had experienced the degradations, privations and brutalities of Nazi rule.

Such experience could be expected to colour de Menthon's opening address, even to dominate it. German occupation had left destruction, death, grief in every country which had endured it. It had left a hatred of Germans. It had also created a festering sore of suspicion and vengefulness against fellow countrymen. Everywhere in Europe at the end of the War the people had turned on collaborators, be they politicians, profiteers, men who had betrayed Resistance workers, or girls who had had affairs with German soldiers. Everywhere there were court proceedings, lynchings, beatings up, smashed windows, shaved heads. In France an official purge had been launched. By the end of April 1945, the courts of justice had condemned 1,458 collaborators to death; official circles were then talking of investigating up to 100,000 cases. But already by July the momentum of vengeance was slackening, and there were complaints that whole groups were being spared – economic collaborators, the magistracy, police and

Armed Forces, the middle echelons of government. The complaints grew as prisoners-of-war and deportees at last came home and fanned the hatred for those who had helped Germany. In the view of an OSS report the main failure of the purge had been in not satisfying the French demand for justice; not providing 'the act of psychic catharsis' which had been hoped for to 'cleanse France of the corruption brought by four years of collaborationist intrigues and betrayals'. (24) Bitterness at this failure had come to the surface in the trial of Pierre Laval. He was sentenced to death on 9 October – the day Quisling in Norway began his appeal against his death sentence. But before Laval was sentenced there had been outbreaks of public hysteria and frenzied scenes in court as the judge and jury joined in the prosecution. The trial was being described in France as a heinous scandal in the history of French jurisprudence. There were calls for the overhaul of the entire French legal system. Foreign observers of the trial had feared that the Nuremberg Tribunal would inevitably sink to the same level of anarchy and lose any semblance of dispassionate justice in the screams for retribution.

It was therefore an extraordinary achievement and an immense relief that de Menthon's speech was characterized by great moderation. He himself had experienced occupation and exile; he had been closely identified with the Resistance; he was a politician and all too aware of the intensity of feeling of those who had suffered under the Nazis. Even so, he spoke calmly, avoiding any emotional appeals and attacks. His speech concentrated on clear summaries of the law of war crimes and crimes against humanity, and logical analysis of how they had been broken and by whom. He asserted the strength of international law as the basis of the Charter, the Tribunal's right to try Nazi criminals given Germany's loss of sovereignty, and the deliberate transfer of judicial power by individual states to this international court. Only twice did de Menthon show any of the feelings which had been masked by his thoughtful, thoroughly professional lawyer's work. Firstly, unlike Jackson, he was not prepared to make a rigid distinction between the Nazis and the German people as a whole. He identified the German people as sharing responsibility for Nazi war crimes. He accepted that no nation had a totally clean conscience, that war generates crimes by people of all nationalities. But he maintained that in examining the Nazi and German culprits, their former enemies could view their own consciences fearlessly – there was no common measure between them. Then, in his final words, he called on the Tribunal to make its judgement a decisive act in the history of international law, a preparation for a society which excluded recourse to war and which enlisted force permanently in the service of the justice of nations. By such a judgement, he said, the 'need for the justice of the martyred peoples will be satisfied and their suffering will not have been useless to the progress of mankind'.

'Ah, that is stimulating,' said Frank, as the speech ended. 'That is more like the European mentality. It will be a pleasure to argue with that man. But, you know, it is ironic – it was the Frenchman, de Gobineau, who started racial ideology.' (25) Frank was to be denied the pleasure of crossing swords with the French prosecutor. De Menthon left Nuremberg the next day to take up his duties with the French Consultative Assembly and the post of French Minister of Justice. His role as leader of the French team was taken by Champetier de Ribes – a lawyer, a former high-ranking civil servant and a man who had escaped from a German prison in 1941 and lived with the *maquis* until the Liberation. Francis Biddle discovered several years later that Champetier de Ribes' uncle had been the doctor in attendance at his birth in Paris. Champetier de Ribes was to become President of the Council of the Republic after leaving Nuremberg but died soon afterwards; even while at Nuremberg ill-health prevented him playing an active part in court.

A change of leadership in no way caused a change of tone in the French prosecution. It remained logical and dispassionate. More than any other case theirs was based on documents. It was reckoned that of the 2,100 finally submitted to the court during the prosecution case, 800 had been introduced by the French. The onslaught of their documents was inexorable. Nearly all of them were German – unanswerable. Backing them, providing the statistics of Nazi crime, were the national reports from each of the countries for whom France spoke.

The facts and figures of the economic spoliation of Europe told of theft and destruction almost beyond imagining – the more so because each report warned that the scale of pillage and havoc had been so great that it was still not possible to estimate the final totals. Some of the figures were difficult to grasp and they certainly made little impact on many in court or in the Press. For instance, it needed a degree of financial knowledge and understanding of each country's economy to absorb such figures as those for financial seizures over and above what was legally permitted for occupation costs: in Denmark the illegal seizures had been 8,000 million crowns, in Belgium 130,000 million Belgian francs. It helped when such figures were put into perspective: in France, the maximum sum which Germany could legally demand for the maintenance of her army of occupation was 74,000 million francs; yet the final French payment had come to 745,000 million, ten times larger. It was hard to picture information such as that the Germans had requisitioned without payment 70 million crowns worth of Danish agricultural produce each month or seized 1,100 million guilders worth of machinery and oil as they left Holland. The specific was easier to envisage: from Norway alone the Nazis had taken 30,000 tons of meat, 61,000 tons of dairy produce, 26,000 tons of fish, 68,000 tons of fruit and vegetables, 112,000 tons of fats, 300,000 tons of hay and straw, 13,000 tons of soap; in Holland they seized 600,000 hogs, 275,000 cows, 489 locomotives, 28,950 freight cars, and even 1 million bicycles and 600,000 radio sets.

As the torrent of statistics poured out, the mind tended to block off. Yet those who stopped to reflect realized what these figures had finally added up to. As J. Emlyn Williams, of the *Christian Science Monitor* put it, this part of the French case explained why Europe was now in 'such a gigantic mess. It is not simply as a result of the war but also the manner in which the Germans waged it, leaving those people they overran without means for their own recovery at the war's end and therefore of supplying help to the defeated Germans themselves.' (26) Bombing and fighting by both sides had done much to destroy Europe. But pillage by the Germans alone also wrought a terrible destruction and left a legacy of poverty and hunger.

The arithmetic of crime never held the popular imagination – there were too many figures, they were too big, there was no time to work out what they meant. The urge to present the details of crime in each of the western countries also lost the French the sympathy of the judges. Inevitably the French were not only repeating points already made by the Americans in the conspiracy charge; they were repeating their own points as they looked at each country in turn. The Bench grew restive. Already on the second day of their case Biddle was complaining in his notes: 'The French are going horribly slowly, step by step, with little new.' However, he added, 'we think we should be patient as it is a matter of national prestige.' (27) Patience wore thinner. Herzog and Gerthoffer on aspects of forced labour and pillage were both 'models of forensic brevity and succinctness despite the massive weight of the case they were called to present' thought the *Daily Telegraph* reporter. (28) But in spite of the fact that Biddle then admitted 'the lawyer, Faure, is doing a really first-rate job' on Germanization of occupied territories, he let off steam in a letter to his wife, seemingly written in court, and complained: 'The French are still on this morning, proving such highly important material as decrees in Alsace that the population must not wear berets, or hats that looked like berets, under penalty of going to concentration camps! I try to curb and shorten their endless zeal; but the Russians with an eye on their case which is to start next week, strenuously object to any interference!' (29)

The judges' patience finally snapped on 30 January when Dubost presented the case on the use of labour in concentration camps. Dubost was the victim of the French reliance on so many documents. He simply could not handle the quantity. He failed to produce the necessary certificates of authenticity for many of his papers, he had not indexed them, he confused their official numbers, and he had failed to realize that some languages take up more space than others, so the numbering of pages in document books would vary and no one could find passages he referred to. It was a muddle that had threatened many prosecuting counsel. They too had found the established procedures for presenting documents demanding and had frequently stumbled over them. A four-page play in heavy humour and lumpy alexandrines dealing with the confusion between Lawrence and Dubost over French documents was circulated among the prosecutors and aroused some wry sympathy. (30) But Dubost had reached an unparalleled level of incompetence, and at a time when the Tribunal was ready to burst from irritation and boredom with repetition and cumulative evidence. They burst over Dubost. His case was frequently interrupted, 'particularly at the instigation of the American judges'. (31) Such was the force of their frustration, they criticized him for mistakes he had not made; Lawrence, usually the most patient and careful of men, had to apologise when he found a marginal note on a document which he had claimed was missing. At one point Maxwell-Fyfe stepped forward to fight off another Tribunal attack and pointed out that Dubost (for once) had actually given verification of the source of a document he was presenting, for all the judges had assumed he had not. 'The French are very grateful for British help,' recorded Dean.

The French had so scrupulously avoided emotionalism that their presentation finally provoked the criticism by one observer that it was 'pedestrian and there seemed to be a lack of fire in their performance.' (32) On 6 February Birkett grumbled in his diary: 'this day, which is the hundredth session of the Tribunal, the French counsel, with a voice so toneless as to be without any meaning, presents a completely useless exposé of the looting of art treasures in France. This work had been done completely by the Americans, and even then it was a work of supererogation. But there is no disposition to stop him, and with complete murder in my heart I am compelled to suffer in silence, whilst the maddening, toneless, insipid, flat, depressing voice drones on in endless words which have quite lost all meaning.' (33)

This sort of reaction was a pity because, as Patrick Dean commented, so much of the French material was 'very striking'. (34) They had painted a picture not just of Nazi financial spoliation and the stripping of industrial and agricultural goods but of squalid organized looting of pictures and furniture, of libraries ripped out and sent to Germany. They had shown that where the Nazis could not obtain goods by requisition, by phoney financial transactions with fixed currency rates and worthless credit notes, or by outright theft, they had resorted to establishing a controlled black market in several countries – a black market officially suppressed in 1943 on the grounds that it corrupted the Armed Forces but which continued to function at a reduced level. The French had the material to bring to life the daily experiences of Nazi occupation: the acute insecurity resulting from the *Nacht und Nebel* policy by which French civilians disappeared without warning and with no indication to relatives of what had happened; the terrorization through the taking and shooting of hostages (29,000 in France) and the imposition of mass fines and reprisals for sabotage, as in Norway, or the introduction of 'protective' custody under which thousands had been tortured and 40,000 Frenchmen had died. The pattern of terrorization had varied in each country. In Denmark, the Nazi authorities had introduced a system of 'compensatory' murders: in retaliation for German deaths Hitler had ordered that Danes must be killed in the proportion of five for one. (In fact the occupying forces had only achieved a total which equalled about one for one.) Between the beginning of 1944 and the end of the war 267 Danes, nearly all well known, had been killed in their homes, their offices, on the street. In cases where the police had caught the murderers their prisoners received letters of congratulation from Himmler.

The French too had the details of chronic hunger that was imposed on the inhabitants of Nazi-occupied countries. In France where the population was accustomed to an average of 3,000 calories a day, the ration was limited to 1,800 calories from September 1940 and it fell to 900 by the end of the war (1,000 for those engaged in heavy labour, only 850 for the elderly). In Holland the situation was worse: the Dutch were fortunate to get 400 calories a day by April 1945 (and Dutch figures excluded those for the winter of famine). Goering had said: 'If famine is to reign it will not reign in Germany,' and food had indeed been stripped from occupied Europe for the use of the Germans. The results were summarized by Charles Gert-hoffer: 'The exhaustion is such that, despite the generous aid brought by the United Nations, the situation of the occupied countries ... is still alarming. In fact the complete absence of stocks, the insufficiency of the means of production and transport, the reduction of livestock and the economic disorganization do not permit the allocating of sufficient rations at this time.' He read the report of the Dean of the Faculty of Medicine in Paris which suggested that in their provision of rations the Nazis 'seemed as if they wished to organize the decline of the health of adolescents and adults' – babies, at least, had been adequately fed. (35)

The French had a tale to tell of the horrors of forced labour which would only be surpassed in nastiness by that of the Russians. In occupied western Europe men and women were drafted into designated industries. Many of them were forced to work, contrary to all international regulations, on military projects – 248,000 labourers were constructing the Atlantic Wall by March 1943. Worse than forced labour at home was deportation to work in Germany – 1,293,000 people were taken from the West by April 1943. In Germany, they worked on average eleven hours a day (twelve hours in one Krupp factory); for this they received the same daily wage as German workers. They were heavily taxed, they were fined for minor breaches of discipline, they might be deprived of ration cards for up to four weeks as a punishment.

The worst fate of all was deportation to concentration camps. Such was the scale, such was the official secrecy on the whereabouts of those seized that the prosecution could still provide no exact figures for those sent to the camps. It was guessed that 6,000 Luxembourgers, 5,200 Danes, 5,400 Norwegians, 12,000 Dutch, 37,000 Belgians had been sent. Of the 250,000 French deported, only 35,000 returned home; sometimes up to 25 per cent would die in the brutal transports on the way. The French brought witnesses to testify to the conditions in those camps. Maurice Lampe described Allied airmen worked and beaten to death at Mauthausen; 400 other prisoners there had been killed because the camp was becoming overcrowded. The defendants could not bear to hear his evidence; several of them removed their headphones. (36) Madame Vaillant Couturier gave details of her experiences at Auschwitz and Ravensbrueck. Her revolting story tumbled out so quickly that the interpreters could not keep up with her. Biddle could only note: 'It is hard to give the impression of the long monotony of horror.' (37) Dr Duport told of medical experiments at Buchenwald, so did Dr Balachovsky. Hans Cappeler described the tortures by the Gestapo, how his legs had been inserted into screws, how the flesh had loosened from his bones. On and on went the stories. Listeners could hear no more. The trial is 'being surfeited by the most murderous and revolting record of all time,' said *The Times*. Session after session they were hearing 'a hideous recital of crime'; every witness told 'something new in horror and misery'. (38) The long agony of Europe was being put on record, the witnesses were speaking for those who had suffered and died. But, said Birkett, 'from the point of view of the trial it is a complete waste of time. The case has been proved over and over again. Neither does the world need it any more, for all over the world the evidence has been published ... but it seems impossible to stop it, or to check the volume of it.' (39) It also seemed impossible that stories more appalling would be heard, that details more sickening, atrocities on an even greater scale could exist. But on 8 February the Russians opened their case on War Crimes and Crimes against Humanity in the East.

Goering had been looking forward to the Russian case. He thought it would concentrate on him, had looked forward to being the star. But in fact he looked depressed as he sat in the box on 8 February, waiting for the morning session to begin. The courtroom was packed for the first time in several weeks. 'Yes, they want to see the show,' he said scornfully. 'You will see, this trial will be a disgrace in fifteen years.' (40) As Rudenko gave the opening speech, Goering and Hess took off their headphones to show it was not worth listening to. They ignored Rudenko's legal justification for the trial, his insistence that international law is founded on treaty and that the Charter had been 'an unquestionable and sufficient legislative act' to create the Tribunal. They gave the impression that they had not heard his condemnation of 'the fiendish theory of the superior master race' by which the defendants had claimed the 'right' to act as they did. But in the afternoon Hess was absent, suffering from one of his frequent stomach cramps. All the other defendants, Goering included, 'appeared extremely downcast' (41) as Rudenko began a catalogue of the destruction the Nazis had wreaked in the East: 1,670 Orthodox churches, 337 Catholic churches, 69 chapels, 532 synagogues he claimed had been razed, 1,710 cities and over 70,000 villages almost completely destroyed, 6 million buildings ruined, 31,850 industrial establishments, 40,000 hospitals, 84,000 schools and colleges, 43,000 libraries. He calculated that 25 million people were now homeless. And they had starved: the Nazis had removed or slaughtered 7 million horses, 17 million head of cattle, 20 million pigs, 27 million sheep and goats, 110 million poultry. The Western official reports had admitted reservations about their final figures; the Russians admitted to no doubts. Their figures were confidently stated and satisfyingly round.

The Russian prosecutors began by presenting evidence on Nazi plans for aggression against the states of Eastern Europe and the intention to claim living space, food, industrial resources, and their determination to dominate the Slavs. The case was presented 'with great skill and clarity'; it had obviously been 'very carefully prepared' thought Patrick Dean. (42) It was, however, all old stuff. The Americans had already dealt with it thoroughly. There seemed no reason to expect that the Russians would hold the court's attention for long. But suddenly they staged a *coup de théâtre*. They began to read the interrogation of Field Marshal Paulus, the commander-in-chief of the German 6th Army at Stalingrad. The defence, who had already successfully protested against the use of a deposition by General Warlimont on the grounds that he must be brought as a witness – easily done since he was in Nuremberg – tried the same tactic again. It blew up in their faces. The Russians announced that they would produce Paulus in court that very afternoon. It was a total surprise to everyone, prosecutors as well as defence counsel. No one had even known that Paulus was in Nuremberg.

The court was packed that afternoon in anticipation of the Field Marshal's testimony. There was standing room only. Paulus was brought in, escorted by a white-helmeted MP. He was dressed in a blue suit and brown shirt. He looked pale but was calm and composed as he took the oath. (43) Once in the witness stand he never glanced at the defendants. They had shown concern as he entered the room. They hardly took their eyes off him as he gave his evidence. (44)

Objectively it could not be said that Paulus's evidence was as sensational as his appearance; it did not make a major contribution to the Russian case. He dealt with the technicalities of Army moves against Rumania, Yugoslavia, Hungary and Russia. He had clearly been carefully rehearsed in the best Moscow tradition for show trial. A blanket question from Rudenko: 'How and under what circumstances was the armed attack on the USSR carried out?' and Paulus spoke fluently and without prompting for many minutes. A statement that Nazi aims indicated 'the conquest of the Russian territories for the purpose of colonization with the utilization and spoliation of and with the resources of which the War in the West was to be brought to a conclusion with the aim of finally establishing domination over Europe' was neither elegant, nor spontaneous, nor indeed much more than unsubstantiated assertion.

But Paulus's testimony cut the defendants to the quick. Here was a man classified as a prisoner-of-war, not as a war criminal although he had been a member of the indicted General Staff. Here was a German soldier who had broadcast attacks on Hitler, Goering and National Socialism on Russian radio in 1944 and made accusations that the German Army had been callously sacrificed at Stalingrad. He was known to have joined the Russian-sponsored National Committee for a Free Germany. The defendants exploded after his testimony. The military men in particular shouted at everyone, argued with their lawyers, began to scribble urgent questions to be put in cross-examination. Goering bellowed to his counsel: 'Ask that dirty pig if he knows he is a traitor. Ask him if he has taken out Russian citizenship ...' (45)

The next day, Paulus had to face a three-hour barrage of questions from nine defence counsel. No other witness, thus far, had drawn such a heavy counterattack. He was not particularly impressive. He gave several of the stock, limp excuses the court heard so often: that he had protested against some orders, that he had the soldier's obligation to continue in his duty to his fatherland, and that only later did he realize he had been given criminal orders. When faced with specific questions on aggressive plans, or asked for details of troop numbers and deployments, Paulus constantly replied he could not remember. In the morning recess Goering sneered, 'He doesn't remember! Hess, do you know you've got a competitor?' (46) Paulus had to fight hard against repeated accusations that he had changed sides in captivity, that he had advised the Red Army and was actually teaching in the Moscow Military Academy. He did not, however, deny that in 1944 he had called on the German people to overthrow the Nazi regime. Nor, more importantly for the prosecution case, did he give ground on his fundamental point: the Nazis had deliberately planned a series of aggressive attacks in Eastern Europe. 'Physically trembling but mentally unshaken he left the courtroom with a scornful glance at the defendants – his first. (47) He soon recovered. Patrick Dean saw him that evening 'chatting and smoking in a friendly way with a number of Russian officers.'* Dean commented: 'It is not anticipated that the Russian prosecutors have any more unexpected witnesses up their sleeves, but it is interesting that they can apparently introduce prominent Germans into Nuremberg without the American security authorities or the Prosecution being aware of anything in advance.' (48)

Dean was right. The Russians would mount no more courtroom drama. From now on their case was founded on a mountain of documents of atrocity – atrocity compared with which the French accounts paled. They began with a section on the treatment of Russian prisoners-of-war. The order of the German High Command to the Army in Russia in January 1942 had stated: 'All clemency or humaneness towards prisoners-of-war is strictly condemned. A German soldier must always make his prisoners feel his superiority ... Every delay in resorting to arms against a war prisoner harbours danger.' (49) Soviet prisoners were to be branded. 'The brand is to consist of an acute angle of about 45 degrees with a centimetre of length of side, pointing downwards on the left buttock at about a hand's width from the rectum,' the official order carefully stipulated. Lancets were to be made available to all military units, Indian Ink would be issued to stain the scar. Russia had never signed the Geneva Convention on prisoners-of-war, 'consequently we are not obliged to supply Soviet prisoners-of-war with food corresponding in quantity or quality to the requirements of this

*Paulus returned to prison in Russia. He was released in 1953 and allowed to live in E. Germany where he died four years later.

196

regulation,' stated the High Command. Nor were they obliged, it appears, to accept any other normal decencies. Graevnitz issued orders to poison prisoners unfit for work. There were orders to liquidate political commissars. The Russian prosecutors read the German official figures on deaths from starvation and sickness in camps (from September 1941 to July 1942, 13,936 prisoners died from sickness in one Lithuanian camp; a total of 35,000 bodies had been found in mass graves). They read German official records such as those listing 130,000 prisoners-of-war tortured to death or shot in Stalag 350 at Maidanek.

Horrible as all this was, the judges became impatient as the hours of cumulative evidence dragged on. Birkett stopped taking any notes. 'I cannot comment more forcefully on the waste of time. The Soviet ideas of legal procedure are extremely primitive.' (50) At a closed session of the judges, Biddle raised 'a polite criticism of the terrific slowness of the trial.' He noted that he had been supported by everyone except Nikitchenko who said any attempt to hurry the Russians 'would look like prejudice against the Soviets.' (51) Whatever the view of the judges, an observer, Patrick Dean, had thought this section of the case 'well-presented and more horrible than usual.' He suspected the evidence on crimes against the civilian population would be 'even worse'. (52) He was right.

The court had to sit through more hours of documents, many of them reports submitted to the Soviet Extraordinary State Commission, recording the use of civilians as shields for the advancing German Army, the activities of the Einsatzkommandos with their gas vans and firing squads, the murder of hostages, and mass executions like Babi Yar involving multitudes of human beings which left the mind reeling. As if that were not enough, the Russians then submitted their evidence on the concentration camps. When the mind could take no more the Russian prosecutors handed to the judges samples of tanned human skin and soap made from human bodies. Most of those present in court had stopped listening long since. A journalist wrote of a Russian prosecutor's voice droning on: 'he was speaking about the murder of millions of men, women and children. The court yawned ... We were thankful when the court rose and we filed to the Tribunal cafeteria to sup tea and talk sweet nothings. Presently a little Russian captain entered. We saw him pay 1/6d for his snack and put down his tray. Suddenly he plunged his head into his hands and began to sob. "Oh mother, sweet mother, dear father, why did they kill you? ..." Then, with understanding in our hearts we went back to court.' (53)

Faced with the inconceivable weight and horror of the Russian case, natural revulsion all too easily turned into protective apathy. Even to suspicion. Birkett recorded that having heard so many Soviet official reports the 'impression created on my mind is that there had been a good deal of exaggeration but I have no means of checking this. But no doubt can remain in any dispassionate mind that great horrors and cruelties were perpetrated.' (54) It was probably at this stage too that Judge Parker could no longer believe what he was hearing. One evening he returned to his house and complained to an aide about the evidence being produced by the prosecution. 'You know, Jim, they're going too far in this trial. They claimed today that the guards threw babies up and shot them in the camps. You know no one would do that.' But soon afterwards Judge Parker took to his bed for three days. He had seen in court the Russian film on atrocities in Eastern Europe. (55)

It lasted for only forty-five minutes; its images stayed with anyone who saw it. It showed the warehouse at Maidanek where 800,000 pairs of shoes had been neatly stacked, the piles of skulls, broken bodies, mutilated corpses. There were sequences where naked women were driven to mass graves; they lay down and were shot; the guards smiled for the camera. The great bone crushers going to work on 150,000 corpses in Blagorschine Forest. The women bending over corpses stiffened by cold, trying to identify their husbands and children, patting the dead shoulders. The film surpassed in horror anything yet shown, anything envisaged from the evidence which had been heard. (56) It shattered the defendants. Most of them tried to hide their eyes. Only Goering maintained a pose of boredom, yawning from time to time and pretending to glance at a book. (57)

The film seems to have marked a watershed in the attitude of the judges. Having glimpsed something of the experience of Eastern Europe it was as if they could no longer insist on brevity, formal court disciplines in presentation of evidence. Whatever their desire for an expeditious trial, whatever their professional expectations of relevance, it was as if the judges had come to accept that the proceedings must fulfil a further need – to give release. They intervened not at all for the remaining six days of the Russian case. One day Archdeacon Lomakin of Leningrad gave evidence on the siege of his city and the desecration of its churches. The prosecuting counsel had no further questions for him, the defence counsel did not wish to cross-examine him. But Lomakin could not bear to stop talking, talking. The Tribunal gave him permission to continue until he had purged his spirit enough to leave the witness box. The judges sat on for six days in silence as horror was piled on horror.

Uninterrupted, the Russians gave their account of the spoliation and destruction of the occupied Eastern territories. (58) Robert Ley had expressed the attitude which governed in the region: 'It is our destiny to belong to a superior race. A lower race needs less room, less clothing, less food and less culture than a superior race.' So the Eastern Territories were not to be treated as geese which might lay golden eggs. 'The idea that order should be restored in the occupied territories and their economic life re-established as soon as possible is entirely mistaken.' Goering had written in 'Case Green' on plans for the region. 'Order should only be restored and industry promoted in regions where we can obtain considerable reserves of agricultural products or crude oil.' These reserves would be taken. The German Army would live off the land. 'In the occupied territories on principle only those people are to be supplied with an adequate amount of food who work for us,' said Goering in September 1941. Koch, the Reich

Commissar of the Ukraine, echoed him: 'We must aim at making the Ukrainians work for Germany and not at making the people here happy ... The Ukrainians will have to make good the German shortages. This task must be accomplished without regard for losses.' German appetites were not satisfied with food. 'It is urgently necessary that articles of clothing be acquired by means of forced levies on the population ... enforced by every possible means. It is necessary above all to confiscate woollen and leather gloves, coats, vests, and scarves, padded vests and trousers, leather and felt boots,' insisted an order from the General Staff. Local orders demanded the handover of scales, sacks, grain, salt, kerosene, benzine, lamps, pots, pans, oilcloth, window blinds, curtains, rugs. 'Anyone violating this order will be shot.'

What the Nazis did not want, alleged the Russians, they destroyed. The commander of the 98th Infantry Division ordered that 'available stocks of hay, straw, food supplies are to be burnt. All stoves in houses should be put out of action by hand grenades so that their further use can be made impossible.' This order was given in December – this was a sentence of death for a family. How could it survive a Russian winter without a stove? As the army left an area it razed it. It must be left a desert. 'In order to carry out a complete destruction, all the houses shall be burned ... Structures of stone are to be blown up, particularly cellars,' commanded an infantry colonel. Preparations must be carried out in secret. 'On the day designated particularly strict watch should be kept on inhabited localities so as not to allow any civilians to leave them.'

Surely, the Russians argued, orders such as this could not be justified as military necessity. The Nazis were on record as planning the ritual extermination of whole races. Himmler, for instance, had announced that only thirty million people would remain to live in Russia – but they must be left with no ties with the past, no science, no art and no religion in which they could seek spiritual solace. The Nazis had looted some art treasures in the East, but on the whole Slav art was not to their taste. Granted that after staying one night in the Hradschin in Prague, Hitler had left next morning with tapestries ripped from the walls (perhaps they were Gobelin and not Czech) but usually Nazis smashed and burned what they could find. They destroyed the houses of Pushkin and Tolstoy, they burned Tchaikovsky's manuscripts, they tipped others from monasteries and libraries into the rain, they paved a mud street in Kharkov with treasured books to ease the passage of army trucks. Professor Orbeli from Leningrad came as a witness to claim that the German Armed Forces had shelled the Hermitage Museum. Defence counsel tried to suggest that the museum had been hit accidentally, that the artillery was aiming for a nearby bridge. If so, said Orbeli, it was rank bad shooting; the bridge was hit once, the Hermitage was hit thirty times.

Remorselessly the Russians went on to produce evidence on the seizure and destruction of human beings. Much of their evidence about the use of slave labour came from captured Nazi documents. Frank told a conference in 1942 it must always 'bear in mind that it is much better if a Pole collapses than if the Germans are defeated.' So people were worked to death at home. Or they were deported to Germany. They were sent to build military defences, to work in munitions factories. A letter from a young German private described seeing women and children working fourteen or more hours a day until they dropped from exhaustion, then being whipped by guards. Other women became domestic slaves; they might only leave the house 'when on duty connected with the needs of the household' said official regulations. Perhaps they were lucky to be alive. An affidavit was read in court describing the writer's journey from Kursk. She and her sister were pushed into cattle wagons, with fifty to sixty people in each. 'In Lgov we had to get out and be examined ... In the presence of soldiers we were compelled to undress quite naked and have our bodies examined. The nearer we got to Germany the fewer were the people left in the train ... at nearly every station the sick and those dying from hunger were thrown out.'

The thrust of the Russian case on the concentration camps came from witnesses. Severina Shmaglerskaya who had spent three years in Auschwitz told of seeing women sent to work within minutes of giving birth, of babies taken away, of children driven to gas chambers. No defence counsel wanted to cross-examine her. Samuel Rajzman had been taken from the Warsaw Ghetto to Treblinka. He survived because he could speak Hebrew, French, Russian, Polish and German; he was needed to act as an interpreter. He described the arrival at Treblinka station. It looked like a station. There were signs saying 'restaurant,' 'ticket office.' There was even an arrivals and departures board but all departing trains left Treblinka empty. For on the platform prisoners were stripped, women were shaved so that their hair could be used for mattresses. Then they walked up Himmelfahrt Street, the 'Journey to Heaven', to the gas chambers. The whole procedure up to then had taken ten minutes. Rajzman believed they killed between 10,000 and 12,000 people every day at Treblinka. There were plans to increase the number of ovens from ten to twenty-five to keep up with the output of the gas chambers. He had seen the arrival at the station of his mother, his sister and two brothers. Friends, sorting the piles of clothes on the platform, found a photograph of his wife and child. 'That is all I have left of my family. Only a photograph,' he said. None of the defence counsel wanted to cross-examine Samuel Rajzman either.

Besides such witnesses, the Russians could produce documents of suffering too – documents on tortures, beatings, castrations, injections with poison, infections with cancer, typhus, malaria. They had too many documents. But how could the court refuse to accept in evidence the statement which Jacob Vernik, a Warsaw carpenter, had given his government? It described the year he had spent at Treblinka. The judges knew all too much by now about camps like Treblinka. But Vernik said that writing his statement had given him the only reason to continue his life. 'Awake or asleep I see the terrible visions of thousands of people calling for help, begging for life and mercy. I have lost all my family, I have myself led them to death. I have myself built the death chambers in which they were murdered. I am afraid of everything. I fear that everything I have seen is written on my face. An old and broken life is a very heavy burden, but I must carry on and live to tell the world what German crimes and barbarism I saw.'

At the end of a morning session, where the massacre of the Jews at Vilna was described and Severina Shmaglerskaya gave her evidence, Doenitz's counsel Dr Kranzbuehler asked him 'Didn't anybody know anything about any of these things?' Doenitz shook his head and shrugged his shoulders sadly. Goering turned round. 'Of course not . . . The higher you stand the less you see of what is going on below.' They all ate their lunches in silence that day. (59)

Their depression did not last long; they were soon able to brush away the impression left by the Russian evidence. A week after the end of the Russian case the defendants read newspaper accounts of Churchill's speech in Fulton, Missouri on 5 March. Churchill had announced that from 'Stettin in the Baltic to Trieste in the Adriatic an iron curtain has descended across the Continent.' He had condemned the creation of totalitarian governments by the Russians, the expulsion of millions of Germans from the states of Eastern Europe, the 'enormous and wrongful inroads upon Germany' made by the Russian-dominated Polish government. He had mourned the fact that 'this is certainly not the liberated Europe we fought to build up. Nor is it one which contains the essentials of permanent peace.' The defendants were delighted. Speer described their 'tremendous excitement. Hess suddenly stopped acting the amnesiac and reminded us of how often he had predicted a great turning point that would put an end to the trial, rehabilitate all of us, and restore us to our ranks and dignities. Goering, too, was beside himself; he repeatedly slapped his thighs with his palms and boomed: "History will not be deceived. The Führer and I always prophesied it. This coalition had to break up sooner or later".' (60)

All the defendants were excited, all felt vindicated. They had heard the entire prosecution case, heard thousands of documents and thirty-three witnesses on their crimes against peace and against people, heard evidence on their greed, their depravity, their inhuman cruelty. But they had not really listened. For them, it all paled into insignificance compared with the seductive abstractions of 'World Politics' and the 'European Balance of Power.' They seemed to think that the evidence would now pale for others too; that they would be released for new responsibilities, praised for their foresight. The prosecution evidence had left them unscathed. The history recounted by that evidence had left Samuel Rajzman with only a photograph of his wife and child. It had left Jacob Vernik and hundreds of thousands of others to live with a nightmare.

References for Chapter Nine

1 BWCE N/10
2 *Daily Express* Selkirk Panton, 4 December
3 *The Times*, 4 December
4 All quotations until further notice from IMT Vol. III
5 Neave *Nuremberg*
6 Defendants' reactions from *New York Herald Tribune* and *Daily Express*,
   December, and *Sunday Times*, 9 December
7 *Sunday Times*, 9 December
8 Dean to FO 4. December
9 Memo 29 August 1945. FO File 16 U6534
10 *The Times* and *Daily Express*, 7 December
11 Birkett, 6 February. Montgomery Hyde
12 Passant to Nuremberg, 25 January 1946. BWCE I/A
13 Maxwell-Fyfe to Passant. 1 February. BWCE I/A
14 FO File 16. 8620–8847
15 British prosecution minutes, 3 November
16 British prosecution minutes, 13 November
17 From information kindly supplied by Kenneth Duke
18 British prosecution minutes, 3 November
19 Ibid
20 All quotations from trial IMT Vol. V until further notice
21 From draft prepared for Sir John Wheeler-Bennett by Kenneth Duke
22 January 1946 report to UNWCC by Egon Schwelb, their observer at Eck
   court martial. FO 371. 57589
23 *The Times*, 18 January 1946
24 1945 Report by R and A Branch of OSS. Jackson Papers, Box 191
25 Gilbert
26 *Christian Science Monitor*, 24 January
27 Biddle Notes on Evidence Vol. III, 18 January
28 *Daily Telegraph*, 23 January
29 Letter to Mrs Biddle, 1 February 1946. Biddle Papers, Box 19
30 Lent to authors by Kenneth Duke
31 Dean cable to FO, 30 January. FO 371. 57537
32 Sir John Wheeler-Bennett
33 Birkett, 6 February. Montgomery Hyde
34 Dean cable to FO, 1 February. FO 371. 57537
35 Quotations from trial from Vol. VI from now on
36 *New York Herald Tribune*, 25 January
37 Biddle in Notes on Evidence Vol. III
38 *The Times*, 30 January
39 Birkett 28 January
40 Gilbert
41 *Daily Telegraph*, 9 February
42 Dean to FO, 11 February. FO 371. 57539
43 *Manchester Guardian*, 11 February
44 *Daily Telegraph* and *New York Times*, 11 February
45 Gilbert
46 Gilbert

47 *New York Times* 12 February
48 Dean to FO, 12 February. FO 371. 57539
49 Quotations from the trial from IMT Vol. III from now on
50 Birkett, 13 February. Montgomery Hyde
51 Biddle Notes on Evidence, 14 February
52 Dean to FO, 14 February. FO 371. 57539
53 Maurice Fagence. Feature in *Daily Herald*, 4 March
54 Birkett. Montgomery Hyde
55 Conversation with Jim Rowe
56 Film described in *New York Times, Daily Telegraph,* 19 February and *Daily Herald,* 4 March
57 *Daily Telegraph,* 19 February
58 Quotations from trial from IMT Vol. VIII from now on
59 Gilbert
60 Speer *Spandau Diary,* 11 May 1947

Chapter Ten

The prosecution case finished on Monday 4 March. It had lasted for seventy-three days. In that time many suspected war criminals had gone to ground in their own countries or fled abroad. All too many had been seized and lynched by angry mobs. Others had stood trial and been sentenced. National courts had conducted proceedings against their own countrymen or Axis prisoners. In Germany Allied courts had heard cases against military war criminals; seven people who had run a 'murder clinic' at Hadamar Asylum had been sentenced; so had the former administrators at Dachau and the commandant of Belsen. General Dostert had been tried and shot for ordering the summary execution of American soldiers in 1944; an American soldier had gone on trial in Monterey, California for killing prisoners-of-war. Proceedings had begun against Japanese leaders. Yamashita, 'the Tiger of Malaya' was sentenced to death in Manila on 7 December for a wide range of war crimes. On 20 January 1946, a permanent International Military Tribunal was established in Tokyo to deal with major Japanese war criminals. Civilian courts and military tribunals had already dealt with varying degrees of restraint and vengeance with hundreds of cases. But the trial of the major Nazi war criminals at Nuremberg was clearly set to continue for many more months. Before it began most people involved had cheerfully predicted that it would all be over in six weeks, or two months at the outside. Now they were more realistically thinking that they would be lucky to be home by the end of the summer. By the most optimistic estimate – that of David Maxwell-Fyfe – the trial could only end by mid-May given very hard work and a lot of luck.(1)

The pace of the trial was slow. Everyone admitted it. This was partly inevitable given the number of charges against so many defendants and the decision to read so much of the voluminous evidence into the record. It was also an unfortunate consequence of repetition of points and the use of too much cumulative evidence. The slowness of the trial was contrary to the Charter's call for an expeditious hearing and the wish of all concerned to maintain public interest. But most people involved had come to accept the pace. The judges and others had clearly decided there were priorities more pressing than professional neatness and brevity, public sympathy or the stipulation in the Charter for speed. The judges had made allowances for national pride and permitted the French and Russians to present cases fuller than the needs of the trial demanded; they had responded to intense personal feelings and allowed individual witnesses to lance their bitterness and grief. They were well aware of the context in which the trial was taking place. They knew it was no ordinary trial, either in the perspective of the law or in the history of Europe. It could not be hurried.

Norman Birkett wrote to a friend on 20 January about the difficulties, the hard work, the tedium with which the judges were faced. 'The thing which sustains me,' he said, 'is the knowledge that this trial can be a very great landmark in the history of International Law. There will be a precedent for all successive generations, and aggressor nations, great and small, will embark on war with the certain knowledge that if they fail they will be called to grim account. To make the trial secure against all criticism it must be shown to be fair, convincing, and built on evidence that cannot be shaken as the years go past. That is why the trial is taking so much time and why documents are being piled on documents ... The world must be patient (and so must I), for what is being done now assuredly belongs to history. But it will be late summer at the earliest, I think, before the final acts!' (2)

So the judges would not force the pace. They would continue to critcize poor presentation of cases, and would enforce procedures which avoided a flagrant waste of time. They had given a lot of opportunity to the prosecution to establish a full case. Now, to make the trial fair and convincing, they would have to be at least as tolerant and as generous with time to the defence. In the coming months the public would become increasingly bored with the proceedings at Nuremberg, increasingly irritated as they seemed to drag on. But the judges would only insist on expedition where it did not conflict with their primary wish to establish a full record and ensure a just hearing.

The judges' priorities were clear to observers of the trial. All of them, without exception, were impressed by the character they had stamped on the proceedings. 'Fair' and 'dignified' were the words nearly every reporter and visitor had used so far. A British MP, Wilson Harris, who had spent several days in the visitors' gallery of the court, commended the objectivity which the Tribunal was displaying. 'The whole setting of the Court is impressive and reassuring,' he wrote. 'Though the two Russian judges are fully justified in appearing in uniform, it is the plain black gowns of the other six that set the note – and no one can doubt that it is the right note. No Bench could be more impartial than this unprecedented body is showing itself to be ... The atmosphere of vengeance and retaliation is totally absent from the courthouse. The atmosphere is one of justice, stern but scrupulous and based on evidence which the defence has full liberty to controvert if it can to the court.' He recognized that the public was becoming impatient with the trial. 'The impatience is natural; but that does not mean that the Nuremberg method is wrong; in the main it is right.' (3)

It was not just Allied visitors who were impressed by the Bench's impartiality. Goering and others might continue to mutter derisively about 'victors' justice', but defence counsel who had at first feared a show trial were gradually reassured. As early as 25 November the British prosecutors reported to London that defence counsel were 'satisfied that the Tribunal will give the defendants a fair trial'. (4) The Tribunal's ruling on the Krupp substitution had given them that impression; other rulings had confirmed it. At the end of December, according to one American reporter, they conceded that the trial was much fairer than the defendants had expected. (5)

A factor in the defence's growing confidence in the proceedings – and an interesting indication of the general belief in their fairness – was undoubtedly the predictions circulating by Christmas about possible sentences for the defendants. Everyone had assumed before the trial opened that however impartial it might be, it would end with the execution of all the accused. But Wilson Harris had been given the impression that wholesale death sentences were unlikely. Indeed he repeated the view circulating in the Nuremberg corridors that they were undesirable since they would give colour to the idea that all the prisoners might just as well have been shot straight away. On 20 September the *Chicago Daily News* was quoting a prosecution confession that they were 'on thin ice' with Schacht, Doenitz, Papen, Fritzsche and Neurath, and it was confidently prophesying that sentences would not be uniform. (6) In February, Patrick Dean suggested that though Doenitz, Papen and Schacht would probably be convicted on the conspiracy charge, they would get lighter sentences than the others because the cases against them were so much weaker. (7) In the event, the guesses about who would be judged guilty of what were not proved fully accurate by the Tribunal's final judgement. As yet, no one could conceive of actual acquittals. But even before a word of the defence case had been uttered, it was freely acknowledged that the prosecution had only established degrees of guilt and that the Tribunal was bound to recognize this in their final decisions.

Before the trial opened, many had doubted the possibility of a dignified hearing and scrupulous impartiality in the general atmosphere of post-war Europe. Many had been sceptical about the ability to mount such a complex trial, to process effectively such a mountain of evidence, and to blend so many legal systems comprehensibly and acceptably. But by the time the prosecution case ended many of these doubts and anxieties had disappeared. Those who had vigorously opposed the whole idea of a trial or who had questioned its legal bases still continued to do so. Everyone, however, seemed to acknowledge that if trial there had to be, this was the way to conduct it. Kathleen McLoughlin wrote in the *New York Times* that the IMT had been 'launched with trepidation and misgivings' but by the second week it had 'taken on the tinge of success'. (8) Patrick Dean reported in February his impression that the 'trial has been a success to a far greater extent than I had dared to hope or most people had expected' – and he wrote as one who had been an earlier proponent of summary executions. (9)

Most of the credit for the success was awarded to the judges. Their rules of procedure had ensured efficiency. Their strict line over prosecution requests or sloppiness, their courtesy to defence counsel and the careful consideration given to their applications had gone far to gain the co-operation of the defence and show the public at large their determination that this was to be a fair trial. The judges had presented a model of international co-operation at a time when diplomatic alliances were strained or snapping. Their unity of approach and opinion was remarkable, given their very different national traditions and markedly different personalities.

In court and in the judges' private sessions, the French judges played little part. Even so, Papen, Schacht, and Fritzsche all felt special confidence in them and nurtured the bizarre belief that as Europeans they would somehow sympathise with German pre-war needs and policies; they felt confident they would give the defendants a fair hearing. (10) Falco, with sleek black head and moustache, smiled a lot. Donnedieu de Vabres, with wiry tufts of hair behind a bald dome and with the upper lip of a walrus, was inscrutable; his moustache and the headphones he wore in court reminded Biddle of pictures of Vercingetorix the Gaul. He seldom spoke in judges' sessions. When he did it was with the accuracy and knowledge of a scholar and the decisiveness and logic of a Frenchman. In court 'all he did was write for days, weeks and months on end', Papen recalled. (11)

Nikitchenko too was an incessant note-taker in court. The Russian alternate, Volchkov, had remained aloof, unknown, slightly sinister, making no contribution and giving no hint of his feelings or opinions, whereas Nikitchenko was increasingly an important figure behind the scenes and one viewed with respect and actual affection. Patrick Dean recorded that he was 'of the highest calibre and genuinely interested in Anglo-Saxon legal principles and in preserving the dignity of the court'. (12) Herbert Wechsler sums him up as a man of decent instincts and considerable sensitivity; a man – in his view – struggling in the coils of the Russian system. (13) Fritzsche viewed him through the eyes of national and political prejudice and assumed that any Russian judge must have decided the German defendants' fate in advance; he and his colleagues were just 'soldiers under orders', he thought. (14)

On the other hand all the defendants hoped for a fair hearing from the American judges. Parker, with his comfortable double chin and rimless glasses, gave an avuncular impression in court. Fritzsche thought he was the least enigmatic of any of the members of the Tribunal. In private sessions he was a great stickler for rectitude and scrupulous in his concern for the rights of the defence. He was probably the most conscientious of all the judges, dutifully reading the previous day's transcript every night. (15) He was a compassionate man and Dean correctly guessed that he 'clearly finds it difficult to appreciate the full extent of the crimes and suffering which have taken place in Europe in the last ten years'. (16)

Biddle, an elegant figure with Clark Gable moustache, tense and alert as he perched over his notes, was the more dominant figure in court and outside. He sat next to Lawrence. They whispered frequently. 'It was plainly his impatience with verbosity that inspired many of the President's sharp interventions, especially in the American case,' thought Bob Cooper who reported the trial for *The Times*. (17) And these interventions contributed to the rapid deterioration of the relationship between Biddle and Jackson.

The reversal of their roles and relative authority had created a situation requiring tact from Biddle and some humility and acceptance from Jackson. These were not forthcoming. Biddle was all too obviously behind the Tribunal's criticisms of the American presentation and a supporter of decisions on procedure which went against the arguments presented by Jackson. There could be little doubt about it – Biddle's whisper during Bench consultations was of the stage variety and penetrated to every corner of the room. Outside the court, the criticisms he expressed of several American prosecutors verged on the downright rude. Jackson took these criticisms personally. He saw the man who had once been his subordinate as uppity and he became rancorous in return. After so many of his requests on procedural matters had been rejected in the early weeks, Jackson retired to sulk. 'There is antipathy between Jackson and Biddle,' Dean reported, 'so usually legal points are put by the British to the British judges.' (18)

It was the British judges who had made the greatest impression and contribution of all. Birkett's 'long, lean, red face and bristly reddish hair, his angular gestures and owlishly blinking eyes aroused kindly feelings amongst us', said Fritzsche. (19) He concealed his bitterness at being only the British alternate and instead displayed his great energy and capacity for hard work. Whatever his resentments may have been, they were bottled up; what was seen was his humour and his friendly manner. Personal relationships between the judges were greatly assisted by the friendship Birkett established with Biddle and by the fact, gratefully acknowledged by Maxwell-Fyfe, that he was 'a constant and understanding liaison with the Russian judges'. (20) As a barrister, Birkett had been one of the greatest orators of his period. As a judge he revealed his mastery of the written word. Most of the Tribunal's public pronouncements and the rulings delivered in court were drafted by Birkett. Even more importantly he had an amazing grasp of the thousands of documents put into evidence. 'He seized on them like a hawk,' wrote Cooper. (21) A reader of the transcripts of the trial is astonished at how often the Tribunal noticed if a document had been read two months previously, how it could spot that a passage four pages further on was relevant and should be read, and could instantly correct dates or names. Most of these interventions were in fact inspired by Birkett. His eye and memory were as keen as his intelligence.

The different skills, and the individual approaches which the judges brought to their work were not apparent to most observers. For them the trial was personified, all its virtues were embodied in one man – the President. Sir Geoffrey Lawrence came into court each session with a brisk stride, made a formal little bow to the counsel, then sat at the centre of the bench. He had set the tone of efficiency and dignity at once. His was the voice of the Tribunal. It was he who delivered the judges' opinions, he who pulled back straying counsel, courteously encouraged witnesses to sit or called for prosecution or defence views on procedural requests by their adversaries. He might only have been expressing the opinions of his colleagues but the manner in which he did it gained the admiration of everyone and won respect for the trial itself. He had been given a gavel to assert the judges' authority. It disappeared within a few days (perhaps into the pocket of a souvenir hunter). Lawrence did not use its replacement. He simply tapped with his pen. That was enough. 'I have rarely met a judge of such authority and skill presiding over a case,' said a defence lawyer. (22) His control and authority were gifts; he had no need to strive to assert them. His voice was quiet but firm, his dignity modest and natural. He was a man free from all pomposity, who never confused the importance of his office with his own. Without effort he projected his firm belief in the highest standards of impartial justice. He would have conducted the trial of a burglar with the same firm, scrupulous, considerate approach he brought to Nuremberg.

Behind the scenes, Lawrence maintained the same impartiality in the judges' discussion. Others – Birkett and Biddle especially – undoubtedly thought they were infinitely cleverer than Lawrence. He let them speak, he listened. Maxwell-Fyfe thought he 'personified the great tradition of the English Common Law that the judge should hold the ring and not descend into the argumentative area'. (23) As chairman, Lawrence let others take the front of the stage and left the limelight to stronger egos. If a consensus seemed possible he left it to emerge; if tempers got short or views were polarizing, he tried gentle tact to find common ground. In private life Lawrence was a collector of china, a passionate and expert breeder of Guernsey cattle who knew the pedigrees of all his cows by heart. He was a devotee of the Turf and had been counsel to the Jockey Club. In court he was exactly what everyone expected a judge to be. 'Hollywood would have cast him,' said an American lawyer; 'he was like God,' said an interpreter. Physically a short, stocky figure, Fritzsche thought he was 'like a giant'. The first impression everyone had of Lawrence was that he was stern, the image of the severity of justice. Once, when he sharply cut short a dispute in court, Goering mumured: 'Do you hear the wings of the Angel of Death?' (24) But then suddenly Lawrence would smile. 'His rare smile was a joy,' wrote Cooper; it was 'so humanly kind that you found yourself smiling with him, and looking over the long dock and its strained, sombre men you saw that some of them were smiling too'. (25) Lawrence's character and manner, thought Maxwell-Fyfe, 'gave the trial a humanity which brought it up to the level required by a civilized concept of justice'. He imprinted his outlook and standards on the entire proceedings.

The judges' firm control and insistence on fair procedures had been seen most clearly thus far in their attitude towards the prosecutors. The prosecution might believe it was presenting an open and shut case, but the judges required convincing and they were not going to have their decisions dictated to them. They would run the proceedings in the way they saw fit. Their attitude was first announced in their refusal to accept the Krupp substitution. Thereafter they listened to prosecution and defence arguments on procedural questions and reached their decisions guided by their Rules of Procedure, the Charter and their respect for judicial proprieties. They were remorseless in demanding that the prosecution must provide adequate numbers of copies of documents to be used in evidence, regardless of the administrative problems involved. Jackson's complaint that the defendants were getting more by way of documents and transcripts than an American citizen might expect from an American court was ignored. (26) In this court everyone must meet the expectations of the Tribunal. It was no good the French making breezy references to incidents which had occurred during the Nazi occupation of Western Europe. The Tribunal would not accept they were 'of common knowledge'; the French must produce evidence to support their allegations. (27)

Many of the judges' rulings were accepted with little complaint by the prosecution. There was no protest when the Tribunal requested the General Secretary to obtain for Seidl the forty volumes of Frank's diary which the prosecutors had been extremely laggardly in handing over. (28) Jackson did not grumble when permission was given to call Dr Schuschnigg, the Austrian Chancellor at the time of the Anschluss, as witness, so that he could be cross-examined on an affidavit he had provided for the prosecution. (29) It could have come as no surprise when the Tribunal assured the defence that whole documents and not just excerpts read by the prosecution would be taken into account by the judges; nor that they emphasized the right of the defence to cross-examine witnesses. These rulings could have been expected in any court of law. They had to be emphasized at Nuremberg to confirm to the defence and to the public that the accused would be given adequate opportunity to conduct their defence.

But Jackson, more than anyone, was infuriated by many other rulings. He expressed anger at the decision that parts of documents on which the prosecution wished to base its case must be read in court, rather than merely deposited. (30) He saw this as a waste of valuable time; he had no sympathy with the judges' arguments that a full record must be maintained, especially at a time when copies of documents which the defence might wish to consult were in short supply. (31) He was angry too at the ruling that affidavits would not be accepted if their deponents could be found to give evidence personally. (32) Again, his argument ran that the examination of witnesses would waste time; finding them might cause endless delays, certainly make a break in a case. What he did not admit in open court was his belief that witnesses were much more vulnerable to cross-examination than documents. Nor did he express publicly what he admitted to other chief prosecutors – that General Halder, for instance, whose affidavit was a series of limited answers to carefully framed questions, looked convincing prosecution evidence on paper but might well use an appearance in court as a chance to speak up for the General Staff, (33) and lose his value to the prosecution. Jackson smouldered as Tribunal decisions like this went against him. He lost the ability to see that legitimate counsel's tactics are not necessarily the same as the weapons of justice. He was too readily convinced that rulings were being made in order to attack him personally, and that they stemmed from Biddle's spite. He lost a sense of proportion and came to believe that chips from the surface of the American case would sink the entire vessel.

A more objective observer, however, could have seen that the judges were not partial. They turned down Stahmer's application for defendants to cross-examine witnesses personally (Goering was itching to get at Lahousen). (34) They rejected the suggestion that the prosecution should be obliged to produce exculpatory evidence – though this was Continental practice and has since been introduced in America. (35) Once the flow of document copies was steady and the daily transcript had caught up with the proceedings in court, the judges became much less sympathetic to defence demands for advance access to prosecution evidence and time to study it. When Seidl and Sauter complained at the sudden appearance of a document book on 9 January and grumbled about the strains imposed on their time by the need to absorb all this evidence, they were told they were fortunate indeed to be given copies of what was actually an American trial brief which the prosecution was under no obligation to supply. And Lawrence wryly pointed out: 'You have, I regret to say, a considerable time before you will have to get up and call your own evidence and ultimately argue upon the documents which are now being put in.' (36)

The judges too could be very sharp with defence counsel when they thought they were behaving unreasonably. The epitome of the unreasonable was Dr Babel. He was the leading member of the small defence group which did not so much fight for defence rights as keep up what can only be called an incessant whine. When he asked for a day's notice before being called to cross-examine a witness, Lawrence told him that as counsel for the SS he should have anticipated evidence on conditions in concentration camps – he had actually had forty days to prepare his cross-examination. (37) Babel also lapsed rather easily into hysteria. One day when three witnesses had been guided through their testimony by French counsel, he suddenly grabbed the microphone and shouted: 'I protest against the prosecution's declaration that I tried to confuse witnesses with my questions.' No such declaration had been made; he had not asked a question for hours. 'This war has brought me so much misfortune and sorrow that I have no reason to vindicate anyone who was responsible for this personal suffering or for the misfortune that fell on our people.' Lawrence told him he was not to make a speech and asked him to sit down. But Babel raged on about needing protection from prosecution attacks and not understanding this court's procedures until Lawrence, like an experienced nanny, distracted his attention with the offer of a witness to examine. (38) On this occasion the ploy worked.

But unfortunately witnesses did not always have a soothing effect on Dr Babel. When cross-examining the General Secretary of the University of Louvain he suddenly announced that the witness claimed to have lost fifteen kilos during the War: 'Well, I have lost thirty-five.' Very upsetting for him no doubt; so upsetting that when Lawrence told him the court was not interested in his own experiences and suggested he carry on with his cross-examination, Dr Babel could think of no more questions. At the end of the session, though, he did think of another complaint: actions by the German Army had often been provoked by the illegal acts of civilians in occupied countries, but no one had condemned the behaviour of Resistance groups. Lawrence pointed out that there were twenty defence counsel in court and 'if they are all going to get up in the way you do and make protests we shall never get to the end of the trial.' (39)*

The trial would undoubtedly have dragged on much longer if the Tribunal had allowed the defence the opportunity it craved to deal fully with each point in a case as it arose. Dr Thoma, for example, wanted to answer each accusation against his client Rosenberg as the prosecution made it. (41) Several times Kauffmann insisted that unless prosecution evidence was challenged straightaway, it would leave an indelible impression. Several counsel demanded that where sections of documents were taken out of context by the prosecution, the documents must instantly be read in full to set the record right. The Tribunal's answer to these complaints was always the same: the defence would be given ample opportunity to answer points and challenge evidence during its own case. However suspicious counsel might be that they would not be given ample time, however uncomfortable they might feel with an unfamiliar adversary process and its sharp division between prosecution and defence time, the method did undoubtedly prevent the trial from bogging down in unnecessary detail and endless nitpicking. Furthermore, it gave the defence major theoretical advantages; the prosecution had to reveal its full hand before the defence case began, the defence had months to prepare their cases, and they would get the last word. It took a long time to learn that the Tribunal would apply its rules impartially. Some would still deny that the rules were fair, many would complain that they suffered because the rules were strange to them. It does

*Dr Babel did not quite get to the end of the trial himself. It was discovered by the Tribunal in April that he was collecting money from SS internees in camps to fund his work. The General Secretary was asked to investigate; the Nuremberg Bar began enquiries in July. When a report on his finances was received from the President of the County Court Nuremberg-Fürth, in August, the Tribunal decided to dismiss Dr Babel and pay him no further fees. (40) He probably felt very hard done by.

not seem to have occurred to them that several of the procedures improvized for this unprecedented trial were equally unfamiliar and galling to the prosecution.

The suspicions and resentments of defence counsel are not surprising. They had a long time to wait before the concern of the Tribunal to give them a fair hearing could be demonstrated; they were in an invidious position, caught between the expectations of their clients, those of the court, and their fears of the reactions of the German public. Their confidence took time and patience to acquire; it needed constant reinforcement by the Tribunal. At the preliminary briefing for defence lawyers on 15 November, the judges had told them: 'The services which defence counsel are performing are important public services for the interests of justice and they will have the protection of the Tribunal in the performance of their duties.' (42) The Tribunal had to show, later, that this statement had not been merely a bland formality. On 2 February the *Berliner Zeitung* published an article critizing Dr Marx, Streicher's lawyer, on the grounds that he had cross-examined a witness in an improper manner and expressed his personal views. The attack was brought to the notice of the Tribunal. In court on 5 March Lawrence delivered the judges' condemnation of the article. (43) He pointed out that it had gone on to threaten Marx with 'complete ostracism in the future' and that it did so 'in language both violent and intimidating'. He read their decision that such attacks would not be tolerated. 'Counsel is an officer of the Court and he must be permitted freely to make his defence without fear from threats or intimidations ... The Tribunal itself is the sole judge of what is proper conduct in court and will be zealous to insure that the highest standard of professional conduct is maintained. Counsel in discharge of their duties under the Charter may count on the fullest protection which it is in the power of the Tribunal to afford. In the present instance the Tribunal does not think that Dr Marx in any way exceeded his professional duty.' The Allied Control Council was asked to investigate and report on the matter.

The judges' statement had been timely. It may well have prevented an outbreak of Press attacks on German counsel. On 16 February, the *Taglische Rundschau* had struck at Kauffmann, criticizing his voice of 'unctuous pathos', sneering at his claim to speak 'in the name of human justice – he, the advocate of Kaltenbrunner'. The article and a letter from Kauffmann asking for the Tribunal's protection, were forwarded to the judges. (44) Again, the Control Council was asked to take action. (45) The judges' public statement and the readiness of the ACC to take up such matters, seem to have been enough to curb the German Press. No more attacks were reported. The firmness with which the judges had acted convinced one German lawyer at least that 'The Court was behind us 100 per cent'. (46)

The Tribunal could be just as firm when counsel from either side tried to manipulate the Press instead of suffering at its hands. From 4 December, the American Armed Forces newspaper *Stars and Stripes* had begun to publish the answers of the defendants to an Associated Press questionnaire on general matters such as their views on the running of the war and on specific concerns of the trial such as their reactions to the American film, 'The Nazi Plan'. Almost full-page coverage was given each day to the opinions first of Goering, then Hess, then Keitel. The *Stars and Stripes* was not the only paper to carry these stories. On 12 December Rudenko protested at a chief prosecutors' meeting about an interview Stahmer had given to the *Neue Zeitung* on 7 December about Goering's answers and about the publication of Hess's views on 10 December. Rudenko wanted a court ruling that such interviews were improper. His argument created a moment of unease. Maxwell-Fyfe agreed with him, but had to point out that the prosecution too had given interviews. Jackson, an enthusiastic interviewee, insisted as he always did, that in the United States the Press was invariably given the widest facilities. In this case he felt that if the court now intervened it would be accused of trying to muzzle the defence. The prosecutors finally decided to consult the judges privately. (47) The judges' response was unequivocal. Interviews with defendants through their counsel 'cannot and will not be countenanced', they said; such behaviour conflicted with the impartial administration of justice. (48)

Defence interviews stopped, for the time being. Jackson took the hint from the judges' statement and on 7 January issued a general memo to his staff prohibiting Press interviews with defendants and witnesses. (49) But this did not gag officials. The steady flow of stories from Gilbert and from members of Andrus' staff continued to be a staple of Press coverage of the trial. And actual documents were leaked to journalists by some of the American lawyers. At a meeting on 5 February, all the chief prosecutors expressed concern at the number of documents the Press was obtaining – and particularly at the interpretations they were putting on them. It was agreed, however, to avoid a confrontation. Everyone preferred to maintain reasonable relations with the Press in view of the desire to get full coverage for the trial and to inform the public. (50)

Matters such as relations with the Press, the inviolability of counsel from intimidation, the procedures to be followed by the adversaries in a trial, do not normally require much attention. In most trials the participants share a common tradition, know the established forms of behaviour, slip naturally into the expectations and habits of a professional lifetime. When individuals step over the locally drawn line, intentionally or not, it is a relatively simple matter for the court to pull them back into place. At Nuremberg, however, there were no precedents, no shared assumptions, no commonly accepted codes to guide behaviour from the beginning. Everything had to evolve. Similarly there had been no machinery in existence for running the proceedings. This too had to be devised. It took time before it was in good working order.

The processing and provision of access to documents had posed a major problem of organization. Within a few weeks of the start of the trial the problem had been eased, but it was never settled to the complete satisfaction of everyone. Defence counsel in particular continued to suffer spasms of suspicion that material was being concealed by the prosecution. Even their complaints, however, diminished in number and intensity from early December, as the machinery for handling documents was tuned up. On arrival in Nuremberg, documents were taken to the Document Room in the Palace of Justice. Such was the torrent, they were still flowing in steadily when the trial finished. Each document would only be acceptable to the Tribunal if it were accompanied by a certificate as to its source and probable authenticity. In the Document Room a staff of about five logged the arrival of each document and allocated to it a serial number. There were several series; each set of numbers was prefaced by initials to indicate the source (for example the 'PS' series, one of the biggest, came from Paris, where it had been collected by Storey). The originals were put into safes, only to be removed for submission in court. Once formally submitted they remained in the possession of the Tribunal. Only on the rarest occasion did the Tribunal accept copies – in the case of the Hossbach memorandum the original was lost. Any copy had to have a further certificate to attest its genuineness. In the Document Room, photocopies were taken of all documents and these were then translated into the languages of the trial. Next, a Staff Evidence Analysis (SEA) sheet was compiled giving each document a title, listing the defendants implicated, the sections of the indictment involved and providing a short description of its contents. One copy of the SEA sheet contributed to an index of all the documents available; others were sent up to the Defence Room for information, and were circulated to the prosecution. Those who wished to see a particular document could then come to the Document Room and apply for it at the counter. The room was packed with shelves from ceiling to floor; staff and porters needed ladders to reach the top shelves. As the trial went on new rooms had to be found for the overspill. In the early weeks the staff had laboured from 8.30 in the morning until late at night; as the pace of input and demand slackened so did their hours of work. (51)

The Document Room was the hub of the trial. It also became a resource centre for the outside world. Governments and legal authorities from all over Europe began to send requests for copies of documents to be used in evidence in their own trials. The general public wrote too, requesting information: heart-rending letters, very often, asking for any hint of the whereabouts of missing relatives.

There were other letters too, giving details of conditions in concentration camps or atrocities witnessed, and offering documents or photographs to be used as evidence. Many letters suggested defendants for future trials or denounced the accused and witnesses in the present proceedings. Gypsies wrote asking to be allowed to submit affidavits since they felt their sufferings had been overlooked at the trial. Many people asked to be called as witnesses; nearly all of them wanted to appear for the prosecution. Practically no one wrote as did one woman asking what was wrong with being a Nazi; she was one and proud of it; and what should the Germans have done with Jews during the War – fed them? (52) All these requests and applications were channelled to the Court Contact Committee.

When the Committee was first mooted it was intended to be a liaison group of prosecutors to deal with problems such as the provision of documents, agreements on the use of witnesses and relations with the Tribunal and defence. (53) In the event those functions were carried out less formally and the grand title of Court Contact Committee was applied to a single German-speaking member of the British team, his desk and his telephone (and sometimes a temporary secretary). Major Alfred Wurmser reviewed the correspondence, decided if the questions it raised should be pursued, and passed on anything relevant to defence or prosecuting counsel. He consulted with the General Secretary, or any other official who might be involved, on matters such as outside requests to interrogate prisoners held in Nuremberg or information on the whereabouts of Hitler, just seen 'alive and well'. He acted as a post office for internal matters, receiving applications from defence counsel, forwarding them to the relevant prosecution or tribunal staff and reversing the process when need be.

It was an *ad hoc* arrangement which worked admirably thanks to Wurmser's hard work and encyclopedic knowledge of the responsibilities and abilities of everyone with authority inside and outside the court. His role developed as the need for it became more apparent. He became essential to the machinery which had to be invented to ensure the smooth running of the proceedings.

A glaring example of how this machinery was only developed as the need for it arose occurred over the question of payment to defence counsel. In any ordinary trial either the defendant pays his lawyer, or the court can set in motion the local means for providing legal aid. At Nuremberg all the defendants, like any Germans awaiting de-Nazification proceedings, had had their bank accounts and assets frozen. There was no extant German state, so the state could not pay. The Tribunal had decided at the end of October, before the trial began, that they would make an advance payment to the German lawyers, and then decide on further allowances when the trial ended. At that stage they considered 4,000 marks an adequate advance; no one thought the trial would last more than a few weeks. It was hoped, but not yet known, that the Allied Control Council would ultimately take on the costs of the trial. Meanwhile Biddle approached General Eisenhower, the American representative on the Council, and asked him to raise the matter with his colleagues. Until a decision was made, Eisenhower established a fund out of the American occupation budget to cover running expenses, including defence fees. (54) By 8 November, he had provided a float of 50,000 marks for the Tribunal. (55) Since the defence counsel had not pressed for payment, the decisions on what to pay and when were postponed until, on 21 November, an interim payment of 2,000 marks to each was agreed upon. (56) There the matter rested for nearly a month. The judges had many urgent problems to settle; judges are not usually asked to bother themselves with counsel's fees. And it seemed to have occurred to no one that as the proceedings stretched into months rather than weeks the German lawyers might find themselves acutely financially embarrassed.

Not until their anxious letters began to arrive in December. The defence lawyers had every reason to feel anxious. The Tribunal might feel benevolent, they might have funds available, but no one had told the lawyers. Two payments had been made, but there had been no announcement that there would be any more. As Dr Dix pointed out in his letter, he had accepted a defence post at Nuremberg because the authorities in Berlin had assured him that arrangements for salaries had been made; 'otherwise it would have to be considered my financial ruin'. He, as well as Luedinghausen and Pannenbecker, complained that though stuck at Nuremberg they still had to pay the rents of their houses and offices at home; there were the salaries of their private staffs to consider; in their absence their private practices were shrinking. Dr Kraus was only on leave of absence from his university post and not receiving his salary. (57) Since money could not be moved from Zone to Zone, many counsel could not draw on their own reserves. Most counsel appealed to the Tribunal for assistance. Typically Schacht wrote directly to the Property Control Division of the US Military Government asking them to unfreeze his assets in Munich and Berlin so that he himself could pay 50,000 marks in monthly instalments of 10,000 to be shared between Dix and Kraus.

The flurry of letters stung the Tribunal into action. On 15 December they awarded an immediate payment of 3,000 marks to each counsel and promised a further grant in three months' time. (58) At last on 17 February the Financial Directorate of the ACC agreed to take over the financing of the Tribunal, the costs to be shared between the four Zones. (59) So on 19 February the Tribunal had the money available to pay 5,000 marks to each German lawyer (60) and to pay a further 7,000 marks in July. The ACC had decided by March on a monthly fee of 3,500 marks to each counsel (with extra where a lawyer was working for a second client or representing an organization). A Foreign Office official, secure in a larger salary and a guaranteed pension, unpleasantly commented that the defence counsel seemed dissatisfied with this rate so there might be 'a welcome shortening of the proceedings'. (61) (Dix had in fact suggested 50,000 marks for the first three months plus refreshers of 10,000 for each subsequent month.) (62)

Problems of payment were strange to the Tribunal, but once aware of any problem, they did try to tackle it. When Kranzbuehler wrote to the General Secretary pointing out that his employers were the German Minesweeping Service and not the court and that the Navy could hardly be expected to pay for his secretarial help, they quickly reimbursed him the 2,000 marks he claimed in expenses. (63) It might have cheered defence lawyers if they had known they were not alone in penury. On 6 June

Thomas Dodd had to pen a tactful note to Jackson to say that up to 31 December he had been paid a daily rate by the OSS. But the OSS had then 'gone out of business' and Dodd had not been paid for six months. (64)

Such nuts and bolts were important for the smooth running of the trial, but they were imperceptible to outsiders. What outsiders noticed and marvelled at was the vital cog in the machinery – the simultaneous translation system. It was truly simultaneous. As long as speakers maintained a steady hundred words a minute, the translators in their glass booths could provide an almost current version of the trial in any language. Given documents in advance, so that there was time to prepare, the translators could be synchronized even more exactly with the speakers. It was an extraordinary achievement and it staggered all visitors to Nuremberg. The art of simultaneous translation was virtually unknown at the time. Of the teams of interpreters at Nuremberg possibly only two members – Haakon Chevalier and Eduard Roditi – had ever practised it before on the new IBM equipment. The others had had scarcely any time to learn: the equipment went astray and only turned up five days before the start of the trial. This allowed merely five days of rehearsal: reading documents to each other to see if it was going to be possible to talk in one language while listening through headphones to the court proceedings in another. (65)

Colonel Dostert, the head of the translation section, had grouped his simultaneous translators into three teams of twelve: one team had to sit in court and work a shift of one and a half hours; another to sit in a separate room, relatively relaxed, but still wearing headphones and following the proceedings closely so as to ensure continuity and standard vocabulary when they took over; the third having a well-earned day off. The work was exacting. It needed great linguistic skill and total concentration. For many of those involved the subject matter imposed a further emotional strain. Working conditions were uncomfortable: the translators were cramped in their booths, even hotter than others in the courtroom. They spoke through a lip microphone to try to dampen their sound (the booth was not enclosed at the top) but not even the use of the microphone nor the huge headphones they wore could deaden the noise made by their colleagues. As they worked they had to fight the distractions of other versions and other languages. The elaborately coiffured woman universally known as the Passionate Haystack produced the most inescapable and nerve-wracking sound – a penetrating twang which provided a steady background screech on many of the sound recordings of the trial and sometimes gives the impression that a particularly incensed charwoman had come into the courtroom to stage a protest about working conditions.

Colonel Dostert was a hard task master – woe betide anyone he found in the rest room without headphones. He imposed high linguistic standards; everyone had to acquire the jargon and technical terms required by the evidence. But Dostert was universally respected. Though he demanded more than most people would have believed they could give, he always estimated exactly how much strain they could bear. The efficiency and accuracy of the translations owed everything to his planning and expectations. Accuracy was essential both to avoid confusion in court and to provide an impeccable record of the trial. Each team had three monitors and a chief interpreter attached to supervize its version. The monitor sat outside the booth, maintaining the flow of documents to the translators and controlling the speed of speakers with the red and yellow buttons. Every day the sound recording of the translators was checked against the verbatim shorthand account of the court reporters. Any discrepancies were discussed and resolved; if they involved the interest of the defence, their lawyers were consulted and asked for permission before changes were made.

Though the printed record was to be as impeccable as possible, inevitably the simultaneous translation heard in court had its imperfections. On the whole it avoided confusion, such as that caused one morning when a German witness was asked by his American cross-examiner whether he had been kept for eleven weeks in 'Ashcan' and he bewilderedly explained that he had been imprisoned in Mondorf in perfectly humane conditions and never locked 'in a refuse bin'. (66) But there was criticism of the linguistic abilities of some of the teams. The Russians had insisted on bringing their own staff for work into Russian and native speakers thought their translations were poor. (67) Experience proved that good translation depended on perfect mastery of the language from which, rather than into which, the translator was working. Most of the Americans did not speak German as their first language and their lack of fluency, let alone vocabulary, was particularly aggravating to Germans. Birkett was ruffled too. To be fair to the interpreters, Birkett used language of a rare exactitude and purity, but he could not abide their use of what he considered 'American' rather than 'English'. He condemned as 'crimes against humanity' such words as 'argumentation', 'orientation', 'activated', 'motivation', 'finalize', 'visualize', 'concrete observations' and 'reprivatization'. (68) Other people were irritated by the tendency of some interpreters' voices to 'colour' testimony through vocal inflection. No one ever came to accept women's voices speaking the words of a German general, let alone a thick Brooklyn accent delivering the speech of a German aristocrat.

Such criticisms, however, were matters of taste, of superficialities rather than of substance. The unanimous judgement on the simultaneous translation system was that it was a miracle like Pentecost. No one was ever unreasonable enough to expect all the translators to reach the standard of the ace of them all – Wolf Frank. He was a German and at the same time an English officer. His use of German and English was noticeably better than that of most native speakers. His voice and manner, the nuances of his vocabulary, the ability to convey the character of the person for whom he was translating were all outstanding. Dostert actually broke his shift system to take advantage of them. It was Frank who translated into German the judges' sentences on the defendants. And Frank who performed one of the most extraordinary feats of the whole trial. Singlehanded he translated into English the whole of Goering's performance in the witness box, a total of twelve hours.

By the end of the prosecution case, outside judgements on the Nuremberg Tribunal were favourable. There was approval of the tone of the trial and the deportment of its participants. The more that was understood of its machinery, the more it was admired. But much more important was the response to the content of the trial. What had been the impression made by the case against the defendants?

There was no question in anyone's mind that the case had been devastating. Experts might ponder whether the prosecution evidence had been equally effectively used against all the defendants; no one doubted they had heard an appalling indictment of the Nazi system as a whole. It is not surprising that the Allied public had been shocked at so much of the evidence produced in court – much of what they were now able to read had happened behind the scenes, much of it concerned foreign affairs which always tend to attract limited public interest.

Before the War, a combination of apathy and escapism had enabled people to avoid thinking about events in Germany and allowed them to hope that unpleasant facts would simply 'go away'. During the War, reports of Nazi atrocities were often dismissed as propaganda and in any case had to take second place to the overriding necessity of defeating Germany. What is surprising, however, is that professional observers of the Nazi era who had personally experienced some of the events described in court, or who had seen many of the documents submitted, could be shocked too when they assessed the evidence. Even William Shirer, a journalist who had been based in Berlin before the War and written perceptive and well-researched accounts of Nazi politics, sat in court for part of the prosecution case and described himself as rocked by it. 'The deceits, lies, trickery, and double-crossing of these Germans as their records unveil them are even more fantastic than was realized at the time they were perpetrated ... One is still shocked to read in cold type the script drawn up by the Hitlerites themselves.' He well knew that the American public had been insulated from much of what was described, and had tended to dismiss many of the stories they had heard as émigré exaggeration. Now, he told them, 'the sceptical – folk from Missouri – must bow to the crushing blow of the facts.' (69) Patrick Dean, too, whose work with the British prosecution team had already acquainted him with much of the evidence, could still react with horror and surprise to what he heard in court. In his report to the Foreign Office on 11 February, after listening to French and Russian figures in court, he recorded his appalled estimate that over ten million civilians must have died in Europe; this equalled one in four of the population of Britain or more than the total of Scotland and Wales. The trial had brought home for the first time to Dean, as for so many others, the realities of the slaughter. He was suddenly understanding the suffering of those who had experienced bestial treatment or the loss of loved ones. (70) (It is significant that soon after this report was received, the Foreign Office began to contact governments in Europe, the Commonwealth and elsewhere asking for detailed figures of death and deprivation. Evidently the true statistics of the war were still not known by mid-1946. Once compiled, Dean's estimate would be seen to be tragically short of the mark.)

The impact of the evidence on the German public had been rather different. Many people had prophesied before the trial began that the German people would be too war-weary and preoccupied with the problems of daily existence to care much about it. The *Christian Science Monitor* had pointed out on 20 November that German newspapers had already condemned the accused; most people assumed that the trial would only confirm this verdict. So far the Germans were only criticizing the loss of the War, not the starting of it. (71) A week later the *Chicago Daily News* suggested the trial was failing to prove to the Germans the criminality of the Nazis and their own share of the blame for supporting Hitler. (72) But this was surely rather early in the day for any dramatic results from the trial – and no one in it had yet indicted the German people as a whole. Indeed the *New York Herald Tribune* noted that Berliners had welcomed Jackson's emphasis that the Germans themselves were not incriminated. (73) The impact of the trial on the Germans was bound to be muffled. They were struggling to live in ruins, ekeing out an existence on scanty rations, anxiously searching for daily necessities such as soap, cooking fat, fuel. They too had griefs – relatives to mourn, loved ones in prisoner-of-war camps or on the lists of the missing. They had the further bitterness of having lost the War; many felt bewildered or betrayed. If many outsiders had doubted the possibility of a fair trial, no wonder most Germans continued to believe that the Nuremberg Tribunal was a kangaroo court for the defendants and a refinement of humiliation for themselves.

A major problem in winning German interest in the trial and in proving its impartiality arose from the way it was reported in Germany. Jackson had insisted 'one of the primary purposes of these trials is to convince the German people that they were the first to be betrayed and to prevent, if possible, the building up of a legend which will revive hostilities in the future.' This story must be got to the German people by their own journalists, who must not suffer discrimination, but be helped with the fullest courtroom facilities. (74) But many German journalists were reluctant to go to Nuremberg. An official communication assured them as late as February 1946 that they would be provided with an office, telephones and even typewriters – something not provided for foreign correspondents. It lauded the advantages of lunches on American rations in the courthouse, though had to admit that an UFSET regulation made it impossible to feed German civilians at other times from Army stocks. (75) Still German journalists tried to avoid the trial. The public was already cynical about the Press and radio after years of control by Dr Goebbels. Now they knew their media were licensed by the occupying authorities, they found it hard to believe they were not tightly controlled in the Allied interests. In the American Zone it was calculated that four million copies of various newspapers were available to twenty million people; in the British Zone there was one copy for every five inhabitants. (76) By early December Brigadier General Roberts, Chief of Information Control Division, US Forces in Europe, reckoned that some 19 per cent of the news columns in the American Zone were being given over to coverage of the trial. But, as the *Christian Science Monitor* pointed out, this coverage was patchy: *Suddeutsche Zeitung* in Munich was only giving 5 per cent of its space to reporting the IMT, whereas the *Darmstadter Echo*, the *Marburger Press* and the *Wiesbaden Kurier* were regularly allocating 30 per cent (77) (an indication at any rate that editors had some control over the contents of their papers).

Could the number of column inches really change the attitude of the German public to the trial? At the beginning of December various Allied correspondents joined together to undertake a survey of public opinion. The impression they gained was: 'Germany is bored and cynical with the trial'. Some of those questioned replied they found the daily accounts unpalatable; many said 'why not hang the lot of them and be done with it.' Some had added the criticism that there was no justification for trying military men who were merely carrying out orders. Others had also argued that Allied bombing had been worse than anything that had happened in the concentration camps. A few condemned Hitler 'for bringing all this on us'. (78) Later in the month *Reynolds News* questioned 150 people about their reactions to the trial. Sixty-one said the defendants should all be shot; forty-five expressed disbelief at the evidence which had been reported; thirty-two thought their leaders had had 'the right to act for Germany'; forty-two said 'this is horrible, I did not know'; seventy-two replied 'not interested'. (79)

Confirmation of the findings of the press straw poll came from a German defence counsel, Dr Bergold. He wrote to Robert Kempner of the American prosecution team describing conversations with family and acquaintances during the Christmas recess. These had convinced Bergold that many regarded the trial as something 'taking place on the moon'; if they stopped to think about it at all they could not believe the evidence. They thought 'the whole trial is exaggerated propaganda, they all refuse to believe in the atrocities revealed. In some cases they even believe that the defence counsel will be imprisoned by the American military authorities as soon as the Trial is over ... To use an oft repeated word in Germany, the entire Trial is considered a swindle.' (80)

Bergold suggested it would be beneficial if seats in the Visitors' Gallery were allocated to Germans – no matter what their political beliefs. Up to Christmas it had seemed to him that it had contained merely 'men in uniform who in many cases are only satisfying their private curiosity'. This idea had occurred to others – Drexel Sprecher, for instance, an American prosecutor who had worked on German Trades Union affairs for the OSS, had strongly recommended to the authorities that unionists should be invited to Nuremberg. (81) The idea was put into effect. Reserving seats was easy; it was more difficult to persuade Germans to occupy them. But some did. It was, however, less the presence of particular individuals than the steady drip of news and evidence which produced the relatively favourable results of a poll held in Frankfurt in February. Eighty per cent of those questioned thought the trial was being conducted fairly; seventy per cent thought that all the defendants were guilty (Hess was most often named as innocent). A majority of the sample resented the prosecution of the military representatives and the General Staff who were 'only doing their duty'. (82) A frightening indication of the failure to inform the public about the trial was that this latter group was totally unaware that a major charge in the trial was that of planning aggressive war.

But whether they were ignorant, apathetic or plain hostile to the trial, nothing could alter the fact that the German people had gradually become part of it themselves. That had never been Jackson's intention. He, like many others, had hoped to prune out Nazism and induce healthy growth in remaining Germany. The idea of German guilt had not appeared in the indictment. It had emerged during the trial. De Menthon had first suggested it in his opening speech. Several witnesses had then gone out of their way to allege that thousands of ordinary soldiers in the Wehrmacht were fully aware of the activities of the SS, the Einsatzkommandos and the like. They had argued it was impossible to remain unaware of the concentration camps and their degradations: the ragged, bony inmates had often been sent to work in local factories and had spoken to their fellow workers; around the extermination camps foul miasmas had lingered and thick columns of black smoke were plainly visible. By 20 January Norman Birkett was writing: 'There are, in truth, two trials going on at the same time, the trial of the defendants in the dock and the greater trial of a whole nation and its way of thought.' (83) Dean commented to the Foreign Office in February that 'it is quite impossible for the German people to say that they were unaware of what was going on' – the scale of atrocity was too great. His point was seized on by the Foreign Office. Minutes flew back and forth suggesting ways to make the Germans face this unpalatable fact. E.L. Woodward insisted that though the question of calling aggressive war criminal might continue to be debated, there must be 'no comeback on the question of crimes committed before and during the War'; it was essential that the Tribunal make a pronouncement on the share of all Germans in responsibility for them. (84)

But this was not really a judicial function: it was a political decision, part of the general policy for the reconstruction of Germany. It was also a personal, moral decision for the Germans themselves. If the issue of general guilt occasionally surfaced in the minds of counsel at Nuremberg, it was quickly sunk again. They were concerned with the immediate, practical problem of fighting their cases, with specific charges against the actual defendants in the dock, and not with even more tangled questions of the guilt of a nation.

This was more than enough to keep counsel occupied. The routine of the court was time-consuming. Hearings generally took place on five days a week, but frequent Saturday morning sessions were introduced to consider administrative matters or when it was decided not to break the flow of a case or a cross-examination by a full weekend. The sessions began at 10.00 a.m. The mid-morning break only lasted for ten minutes. Lunch was from one till two, and the afternoon session then ran from two till five, broken only by another ten minute interval. During the prosecution cases, the Allied teams thought it necessary to maintain a presence at their tables in court, even though so many staff were needed for preparations behind the scenes. Constant presence by the defence counsel was obligatory; only when the defence case opened were counsel given permission to absent themselves for a couple of days just before they presented their client's defence. Work did not stop when the afternoon session ended. The judges almost invariably held a private meeting. Prosecution counsel might gather to prepare or polish presentations for the future or plan counter-attacks to moves by the defence. Defence counsel had to read the accumulation of evidence, try to acquire their own, and consult their clients.

Strong differences of national approach had begun to show in the way the lawyers worked. In the federal structure of Germany there was no unified Bar; in the Nuremberg courtroom there was no co-ordinated defence. A German lawyer might discuss his client's case with a colleague if his experience was relevant or if their clients' cases overlapped. On occasion they might all meet to frame a request or a protest to the Tribunal. But such meetings were rare. The defence campaign took the form of a series of dog fights. It undoubtedly lost effectiveness as a result.

By contrast the British brought to Nuremberg the traditions of a cohesive national Bar and the habit of playing team games. They had the inestimable advantage of being a small team of barristers. When need be, Maxwell-Fyfe could group them all around his desk for 'morning prayers' at 9.0 a.m. before the court session. (By 11 December, the pressure of work had diminished and the morning assemblies could be cut to Tuesday, Thursday and Saturday. On 12 January they were cancelled for a fortnight to get everyone fit and keen for work during the defence cases.) (85) While preparing the British case, Maxwell-Fyfe had insisted on a double approach – evidence must be amassed 'horizontally' to cover the charges in the indictment, and 'vertically' to cover each defendant. (86) The business of preparing a case from scratch was a new experience for the whole team. As Maxwell-Fyfe put it they 'were acting as solicitors as well as doing their own job' as barristers. (87) Sections of the case were allocated to the barristers who would usually present them in court. Maxwell-Fyfe left them to work up their areas of responsibility – but then checked their preliminary drafts and made suggestions for adjusting them to fit the overall case. He insisted on everyone participating in the discussions on the drafts and maintained a strict rota for attendance in court. Everyone must be aware of the case as a whole, both to co-ordinate their own efforts and to be ready to take over any aspects should a colleague fall sick. One observer, used to government interdepartmental meetings, was astounded at the drive Maxwell-Fyfe could generate by the most silky means: 'I wonder if I could ask you, Khaki?', 'Would it be possible, Mervyn?' He did not give orders – but everyone leaped to. He was a methodical organiser. He was not addicted to paper, but when appropriate he laid out his ideas on future plans in concise, logical memos, and gave an opportunity to discuss them. (88) He was clearly a believer in timetables: setting out deadlines for the preparation of briefs against defendants, the completion of document books, or notes for the cross-examination so as to galvanize the energy of his team and be certain that adequate preparations were made well in advance of need. (89) Harry Phillimore, the secretary to the team, acted as his staff officer and made a first-class progress chaser. Thanks to Maxwell-Fyfe's methods the British worked harmoniously; their efforts were neatly dovetailed, so was their case. They were a business-like, purely practical group. Nearly all of them had been practising criminal lawyers. There was little or no discussion of broad issues, legal philosophy; they concentrated on winning their case. (90) The British were, as a member of their team put it, like barristers on a murder case at Winchester Assizes. (91)

This was a very different style and attitude from that of the Americans. A member of their team described it as tackling its case as if arguing before the Supreme Court; that is to say, as if involved in appellate work rather than in a trial of first instance. (92) Inevitably so. In the American legal tradition, the able lawyer rises above the seamy criminal court; he writes briefs, advises institutions, aspires to present issues to the highest court. There were few, if any, practising criminal lawyers on the American team, and Jackson himself had lived for years in rarefied legal air. Some of his insistence on relying mainly on documents might be traceable to the work he had been engaged in for so long. Experience and personality together produced in him a demand for the widest possible definition of terms for his case and the greatest possible accumulation of facts. At best this could result in every imaginable point being meticulously covered. At worst, no one could see the wood for the trees.

The American approach lacked intellectual clarity and forensic sharpness. Characteristically, Jackson liked to be provided with what he called 'self-proving' briefs purely for his own information. These were devoted to particular aspects of the case or a defendant, were backed by the relevant documentary evidence, were introduced by a historical background and might well extend to one hundred pages. (93) These briefs were no doubt very educational, and they might serve as useful source material for anyone building a case. But they consumed a vast amount of staff time and were far too diffuse and general to be of immediate use in court.

The full extent of the resulting mental confusion was revealed at Christmas. Up till then, the American case had been devoted to the big issues – slave labour, the Jews, aggression, and so on. Late in the day Jackson had a revelation that the cases against the actual defendants had not been co-ordinated with the main thrust of the case. He went to Robert Kempner and dramatically confided to him his new found awareness that Hitler and the Nazi regime were not before the court; Goering and Ribbentrop and the rest were, and the American case had to take this apparently startling fact into account. Kempner found himself made Chief of Division responsible for preparing the cases against the defendants. (94)

Jackson lacked many of the talents needed for a team captain. He could not organize the allocation or co-ordination of work effectively. His staff too often worked in the dark. The American group was far too big for anything like the British morning prayers, but Jackson introduced no suitable alternative method for giving it a sense of direction, any understanding of the overall progress and needs of the case. He closeted himself with his close advisers, Alderman and Kempner in particular, and seemed aloof from the rest of the team, many of whom never actually met him. Which was a shame. The delightful letters of thanks he wrote to departing members show a warmth and an appreciation of individual contributions and difficulties which, if expressed earlier, would have gone a long way to cementing the group and ensuring its cheerful work. (95) Most people agree that he hated detail, and this made him a bad administrator. He delegated too much, and lost control; he 'tended to run away from administrative and executive difficulties' but they remained to bedevil others. (96) He ran away too from the need to settle the personal feuds and misunderstandings in a team which often showed acute symptoms of bastard feudalism with a weak centre and internecine wars between mighty barons. (97)

Jackson's personal failings and his lack of interest in administration lost the Americans the control of the whole prosecution which he had always intended to assert. The daily grind of court attendance which Maxwell-Fyfe thought vital to understanding and directing the case became irksome to Jackson; he left it to Thomas Dodd. The rebuffs he had received from the Tribunal over procedural points and his growing resentment at Biddle's attitude, together with his impatience with business matters, led him to withdraw from detailed overseeing of the prosecution, leaving a vacuum which was filled by Maxwell-Fyfe. Gradually he began to co-ordinate administration, suggest timetables and fruitful lines of work. He increasingly took over liaison with the defence lawyers over problems of acquiring evidence and witnesses. He did it most tactfully and competently. Jackson does not seem to have resented the loss of control; rather he appears to have welcomed the shedding of irksome responsibilities. Maxwell-Fyfe won the respect and confidence of the Germans and of the Allied teams by his conscientiousness and obvious concern for fair play and efficiency. On most occasions they were glad to let him speak for them. (98)

By Christmas, Maxwell-Fyfe had been cast as the chief chief prosecutor. The exchanges in court between him and Lawrence, both using the language and little graces to which they were accustomed, gave the trial a strangely English air.

The Congress of Vienna in 1815 was said not to have worked but to have danced. The IMT at Nuremberg managed to do both. After hours there was a great deal of dancing, as well as sporting activity, flirtation and certainly a great deal of drinking. People busy during the day, strained by the nastiness of the subject matter they were dealing with, were all too glad to unwind when they could. The War was over; it was natural to celebrate. Elsewhere men and women were being demobbed, going home, settling down to civilian life. At Nuremberg, those working on the trial were still mopping up the War, subject to a military atmosphere and far from home. If they were to be denied the satisfactions of repatriation, family, and peacetime careers, they would wring what pleasure they could from the situation they were in.

It was a frenetic pleasure. It was induced as an escape from the evidence which filled working hours and was chased through a devastated city where the stench of corpses never dissipated, where sullen inhabitants avoided the eye and ignored a greeting. Genuine relaxation was hard to find. There was constant edginess in Nuremberg, constant security precautions. Everyone continued to believe that snipers waited in the ruins; everyone stuck to the few buildings controlled and guarded by the US military and did not leave the tracks cleared for traffic through the rubble. Judges and many leading counsel were obliged to accept armed escorts. One evening those living at the Lawrence house returned home to find the place was freezing and there was no dinner. The American military authorities had arrested the whole staff. The boiler man had been discovered to be an ex-SS man; he, and his wife and daughter who ran the house, had been whisked away. (99) (To everyone's pleasure they were later able to return, since military edicts did not forbid an SS man to work *outside* a requisitioned house. He was reckoned safe with the boiler and the garden. His wife and daughter seemed to have spotless pasts.)

In mid-December Brigadier Watson, who was responsible for security, combed the courtroom staff. The caretaker who had held his job since 1914 and been retained because he knew the buildings so well was sacked; he had been a minor but active Nazi. There were suspicions about one of the defence counsel's assistants; he was dismissed. Watson said: 'We can't get at the Nazi counsel, as they have been approved but we can get at the others and we are going to root them out.' (100) There was a further tightening of security later that month when the petrol tanks of several official cars suddenly froze. Sabotage was suspected; it was reported that their tanks had been filled with water overnight. (101) A major alert followed in February. A rash of machine guns appeared on the roofs of the Palace of Justice and the jail, guards were ordered to carry small arms at all times, military units closed all roads leading to the city. It was a response to rumours that SS men in nearby internment camps were going to stage a mass breakout and attack to release the defendants. (102) The rumours seem to have been untrue. After thorough investigation, the most un-covered was a dump of dynamite on Fürth Station – and that had undoub-tedly been there since the end of the War but overlooked in previous searches. (103) But this sort of flap fed the nervousness and suspicion which always lurked in Nuremberg.

Against that background, those who worked at Nuremberg clustered for their social life in an isolated island of safety and entertainment – the Grand Hotel. In a city blacked out at night it was a beacon. Sir John Wheeler-Bennett stayed there for a while. 'In its palmy days it had been one of the leading hotels of the city and one in which foreign VIPs invited to the Nazi Party Rallies were housed. It had been badly damaged, however, and its resuscitation was another of the miracles performed by the American Army. It was clean and, though sparsely furnished, was tolerably comfortable. The food was plentiful and, by American Army standards, well cooked. It also sported a not undistinguished cellar ... and one was grateful for this because every mouthful of water was so heavily chlorinated that a spoon placed in a glass of it would stand alone ...' (104) The public rooms were open to officers and to anyone with a courtroom pass. The only place to sit and talk was the reception hall, which Wheeler-Bennett thought looked like 'a Hollywood set for an international spy drama. There was a great deal of red plush and artificial marble and tar-nished ormolu.' It was an appropriate setting for the incident when a Russian staggered through the door and collapsed in the middle of the marble with a bullet wound next to his heart. (Old Nuremberg hands swear that no one stopped drinking or even blinked.) He was rushed to hospital but died before anyone could be found who spoke Russian and could discover what had happened. The Russian delegation knew him, he was one of their chauffeurs, but they were certainly not going to reveal any details of the shooting. (105)

Dancing in the Grand Hotel took place in the Marble Room. Delicate European eyebrows were raised at the scandalous sight of jitterbugging. And there was a cabaret, with innumerable changes of performers: singers, dancers, acrobats and a boy juggler or a midget who piled half-a-dozen cups and saucers on his head and then threw in lumps of sugar and a spoon. Seemingly good clean fun. But Wheeler-Bennett found 'something in-finitely tragic in those underfed entertainers in their pathetic and tarnished finery, singing their songs of the pre-Nazi period with desperate nostalgia ...' (106) Bob Cooper acknowledged that the Grand Hotel was an antidote to the monotony and depression of the city, but thought 'its strident blare, its forced cynicism in the midst of so much suffering, even of a beaten enemy, were often shocking.' (107)

Wheeler-Bennett moved out of the Grand Hotel. He had found his stay disagreeable. 'Outside the hotel, often flattening their noses against the cracked glass panels, were starving or at any rate underfed Germans. Inside we, the conquerors who had brought their leaders to trial, were disporting ourselves in a manner certainly vulgar and virtually callous.' He went to live with Judge Biddle. Others had no alternative accommodation. They lived on the upstairs floors to which there were no lifts, or in the annexe, the 'Guest House wing'. The entire outside wall leading to the annexe had been blown off during a raid. It was never replaced, so access to the rooms was along exposed catwalks – vertiginous, and, in winter, bitterly cold. It was a bachelor establishment. General Patton had decreed that since the American Zone could not accommodate the wives of his men, no one could have wives. He could not deter one married couple – the Margolies. Harriet, like Sweet Polly Oliver, had listed as a lawyer to follow her husband Dan, first to London, where she had worked with the Americans on the Indictment, then to Nuremberg, where she was on their prosecution team. She was the only woman lawyer in Nuremberg. General Patton may have spoken against happy married life. Fortunately he had said nothing about Sin. So Harriet Margolies dropped her married name and the Margolies lived 'in sin' in the Grand Hotel. They were probably not the only ones, but they were the most respectable – the only sinners with a marriage certificate. (108)

Six miles outside Nuremberg was an alternative pole for social life, the 'castle' of the Fabers, the pencil manufacturers. Here lived the Press. The house was repellent. Harriet Margolies explained the thinking behind the interior decorations: 'First you hang a tapestry on the wall, then you put a painting on that, and in front of the painting you set a large statue. Any bits of wall space that are left over you fill with cabinets stuffed with *objets d'art*. You cover every inch of the floor with thick carpets, liberally sprinkle with mahogany furniture and tables, cover every table surface with elaborately embroidered cloths and light with chandeliers dripping with crystal.' (109) The décor alone justified calling the house 'Schloss Schrechlich'. And there must have been something else about the living conditions to explain the fact that at the beginning of December over 300 journalists had dysentery. (110) They paid rent to squeeze into dormitories somehow fitted into the small spaces left between furniture. Each dormitory shared a bathroom – one bath and five washbasins – between twelve correspondents. The beds were cramped and drunks clambered over them when they returned in the middle of the night. There were compensations: extensive grounds, American rations and PX cards, and a huge bar with unlimited quantities of cheap drink. So the inhabitants drank, threw parties and staggered out on to army lorries every morning to be driven to the court. (111)

There, the journalists were well provided for. They had seats in court or in a room where they could listen to the proceedings over loudspeakers. The Russians, Americans and British had all provided facilities in the Palace of Justice for transmitting Press copy. The British transmission centre had been set up by 21 Army Group HQ and was headed by two journalists in uniform and staffed by the Royal Corps of Signals – a complement of about thirty in all. It served any journalist who used Roman characters. There was a fixed rate of charges: 1½d a word for British, 2½d a word for foreign correspondents and 2½d a word for service messages from journalists to their offices. Seven teleprinters were linked to the London GPO and to the War Office so that copy could be picked up or re-routed. An M-set was available for wireless transmission and the BBC maintained its own Golden Arrow broadcasting van. Copy was brought to the centre in all forms and conditions: typed, in pencil, on any paper that came to hand. Hot news flashes were jotted down in the Press Gallery and passed to the Irish Guardsmen on duty to be rushed down to the copy room. Pressure of work there varied: when public interest was high, 120,000 words a day were being dispatched, and when American or Russian equipment broke down there were even more. In December the centre was bringing in £700 a day in revenue. The centre's staff probably had as wide an understanding of the varied views of the trial as anyone in Nuremberg or outside. They studied and discussed the copy; they looked forward to getting the newspapers to see how editors had treated the stories. (112)

Not that newspapers were always easy to come by. The British team at Nuremberg grumbled at the considerable delay in getting papers and letters from home. A parachute drop at Fürth was considered for a time but was ruled out. (113) Any form of communication with the outside world was difficult. Roads, railways, bridges were only slowly repaired. Air transport was the most reliable, but even that was far from regular. The BWCE used RAF Transport Command when possible and documents could be despatched by Mosquito. But as Transport Command began to wind up, civil aviation was slow to take over; there were not enough planes to charter from Croydon to ensure constant links. (114) Lack of contact with the outside world, the difficulty of moving even to other parts of Germany, led to a sense of isolation, to a feeling that everyone was living on top of each other.

This arose partly because everyone was marooned in Nuremberg, but even more because fraternization with Germans was forbidden by the military authorities. Army orders were not enough to stop some contacts, but they were few, given the suspicion with which civilians and occupying forces tended to view each other. In any normal trial, lawyers from both sides would be expected to mix freely in private. Not so at Nuremberg. Some Germans were invited to play table tennis, some counsel came to an American Thanksgiving dinner, but on the whole the defence lawyers lived their own lives and few feelers were put out to them. Most contact with Germans was probably established at the NCO's black market. A British soldier described the scene every Friday afternoon in the barracks he shared with GIs. 'On the beds, the GIs would take out their purchases from the PX stores, everything from toothpaste to cigarettes and canned peanuts, and lay them out with the expertise of professional display men. At a precise time, a GI would pull open the door and in would troop 'our

Germans', the people in American employment. They went from bed to bed until they got the best value for money. Competition among suppliers was keen. There was sometimes a bloody nose when one dealer cut his prices below another's.' (115) At Christmas other soldiers took toys and rations to German families.

Those working at Nuremberg were not only cut off from the local citizens. They were stratified by rigid class divisions. The Grand Hotel was for officers only. The Faber house was technically off limits to NCO's, even though many were smuggled in to parties. National divisions remained too. The Russians lived in their requisitioned houses literally behind barbed wire. Sounds of singing, dance music, revolver shots in the night suggested that they held parties but no one was asked to them. (116) They seldom appeared at the Grand Hotel. The Russians might occasionally appear at parties elsewhere, but they were never off guard. When two British officers tactfully escorted Rudenko into the fresh air after he showed the effects of an excessively energetic celebration, he was grabbed from them by Russian guards the moment they opened the door and driven away in an official car. (117) The French too tended to live apart. Everyone had the impression they were tired rather than anti-social. They were happy to invite others to their Cercle Français where they imported singers and speakers and held concerts, but seemed too drained by the War to want to launch into more hectic entertainments. The British were more social, but potentially isolated by geography. The lawyers lived out in the village of Zirndorff. Even today the drive on good dual carriageway takes nearly half-an-hour. Once there, they often preferred to stay. Maxwell-Fyfe amused himself at weekends plotting Wallenstein's fortifications nearby. He enjoyed military history. He once gave a lecture to all those interested or loyal enough to attend on Gustavus Adolphus' campaign in the Thirty Years War. (118) The others led the life of country gentlemen. There was plenty of shooting and fishing, and quite the best introductions to it. Major Wilkinson, an ADC to the British judges, was stopped in court one morning by Goering, the former Chief Game Warden of the Third Reich, and asked whether he had found good fishing. When Wilkinson lamented his lack of success Goering gave him the name and address of a water bailiff: 'Just mention my name ...' It still held the old power. Wilkinson never lacked for sport or trout again. (119) Those who preferred shooting were more alarmed than pleased by an invitation to join Lawrence. He tended to use them as beaters and since his shooting was more enthusiastic than accurate, they used to find the excitement too much for them. (120)

The judges seldom mixed socially with prosecution staff, except for the occasional drinks party or the odd picnic. But to maintain and demonstrate impartiality, they usually kept them at arm's length. Total claustrophobia was warded off by the daunting programme the judges set themselves for entertaining VIP visitors. Many people wanted to experience the trial at first hand, many judges felt it important that it should be seen by as wide a spectrum as possible. So court sessions and judges' meetings were followed by an incessant round of parties and official dinners. With luck these might be entertaining; with the wrong mix of guests they might be an alternative form of hard work. One party was simply embarrassing. It was a dinner given in honour of Andrei Vyshinsky. In 1945, Vyshinsky was the Soviet Deputy Foreign Minister and principal delegate to the United Nations. In the 1930s he had been Chief Public Prosecutor in Stalin's purge trials. His arrival in Nuremberg caused a shudder; in western eyes, any connection between him and true justice was entirely notional. He had come unheralded; he just turned up in court on 27 November and it was announced he had joined the Soviet prosecution team. At the dinner, where the usual marathon of Russian toasts had been endured, Vyshinsky proposed his own in Russian: death as soon as possible to the defendants. Raising the elbow and downing the contents of the glass were so automatic by this stage of the evening that no one waited for a translation before drinking.

Once they realized what had been said, they were aghast. As Maxwell-Fyfe noted, the incident was open to serious misconstruction: it could be seen as collusion between judges and chief prosecutors. Judge Parker was particularly upset at the idea that American judges might have been thought to have proposed death sentences for men they were supposed to be trying. Judge Biddle soothed him by saying the matter would blow over and that continued fairness in the trial itself was all that really mattered. Dean however reported his impression that Biddle was not pleased by the incident and added that Jackson looked 'rather alarmed'. (121) Whatever Vyshinsky's motives for coming to Nuremberg – and the month of his stay aroused intense speculation – they were probably quite straightforward: to judge progress for himself. He confided to Patrick Dean that he found the trial too slow but felt that if he tried to speed it up, he would 'run into problems with the Americans'. On his return to Moscow, Vyshinsky told the British Ambassador that he had a favourable impression of progress and was pleased by the way the Soviet judges were co-operating with their colleagues. (122)

The quasi-diplomatic role that the judges took on with their evening entertaining of visitors did not alter the fact that for the most part they lived in a closed world. During the first few days of the trial, the judges had lunched in the court cafeteria, queueing with trays at the counter where food was sloshed into their dishes. It was decided, largely at the instigation of the British, that this was hardly dignified. A separate room was soon found for them. At home, they lived with their staff. Birkett defied Patton and Lady Birkett was brought out. Lady Lawrence's presence at Nuremberg had almost been a main condition for Lawrence's acceptance of his post. She sat in court nearly every day and joined the judges for their evening entertainments. Francis Biddle thought she was the best dancer in Nuremberg. (123) Nikitchenko, next to whom she usually found herself at dinner, never broke his rule of not speaking English. Instead he entertained her with drawings on menu cards and scrap paper. He was enchanted by the two Lawrence girls when they came out to stay – pretty, lively young creatures must have come as a welcome contrast to all the VIPs – and invitations were issued to tennis parties at the Russian judges' house.

Biddle and Parker lacked the comforts and pleasures of some kind of home life. Mrs Biddle came over for a couple of months in the spring of 1946 but she could not stay long. Their son, Randolf, was ill, seemingly suffering from chronic malaria and a nervous breakdown precipitated by his war service. Anxiety over his condition kept Mrs Biddle in America and always wracked her husband. For the most part Biddle and Parker lived together, without major rows but with little mutual satisfaction. Biddle grumbled in a letter to his wife about being 'pretty fed up with this communal life, with Parker's "tone"'. (124) What he called 'the fraternity life' cannot have been much fun for the four judges' aides either. They were of a younger generation and although talking shop every evening was no doubt going to be of great benefit to their legal careers, it cramped their social lives.

Escape from Nuremberg and its tight circles of judges, prosecutors, journalists and national groups was rare. There was too much work to do and too little transport available. Once a train was hired to make a trip to Paris, occasionally cars might be obtained for visits to Prague – so beautiful and so cheerful by contrast with ruined, sombre Nuremberg, and with unparalleled black market provisions. Skiing trips were more common. The Americans advertized skiing weekends in 'Berchtesgaden, the Switzerland of Germany'. It was the skiing bargain of all times – for the five day trip with hire of skis, the cost was eight marks a day for officers and civilians, three marks for enlisted men. (125) And skiing was a welcome means of thrashing out tensions. The longest break the staffs ever had was two weeks at Christmas. Many of the British and French were able to go home. Jackson went to Cairo and Jerusalem. Birkett took Biddle home with him, and they spent evenings reading poetry aloud and listening to gramophone records. Nuremberg was a gloomy place that Christmas. It had once been something from a child's dream – famous for gingerbread and wooden toys. In 1945 *Stars and Stripes* prophesied 'Slim Yule Ahead' and the only treat for the citizens of Nuremberg was a special ration of a pound of sugar, two small bags of egg substitute and a can of condensed milk. (126)

For the defendants, Christmas meant unrelieved confinement in the jail. The daily sessions in court had taken on their own monotonous routine, the piling up of evidence had become as tedious for the defendants as for any spectator. But at least sitting in court meant an escape from the cells. There Hess pounded his typewriter, Ribbentrop covered quires of paper with verbose and ill-argued attempts at a defence, Streicher played games with matchsticks, and most of the others read library books or studied documents for their cases. Speer had decorated his cell with drawings in black, red and blue crayon. To pass the hours in court he drew landscapes

– mountain peaks with castles towering over deep valleys. Schacht wrote poems. Light verse was the rage in court; defendants, lawyers, judges and visitors scribbled incessantly and a keen competitive spirit was aroused. Many of the others furtively read books or newspapers, wrapped in legal papers – anything spotted by a guard was confiscated. Frick was hopelessly bad at concealing his reading matter in spite of all Fritzsche's attempts to teach him ways of concealment; he seldom had anything to read by mid-morning. (127) The sessions in court had not only become boring, they were increasingly physically uncomfortable. The bench was hard; it even wore out the trousers. First Fritzsche brought in a blanket which he shared as a cushion with Neurath, then the others took up the idea. The morning and afternoon recesses were a welcome chance to stretch the legs. The prisoners were escorted to the lavatories down a corridor lined with military policemen and packed with people smoking. Cigarette ends were delicately extinguished to leave something for the German cleaners to collect. (128) In the court corridors, in the jail, there were sudden blasts of music. The guards were addicted to the wireless. It was maddening for the defendants. The hit of the year was 'Don't Fence Me In'.

But for a fortnight at Christmas there were no trips to court, no visits to counsel. The defendants sat in their cells with only a walk in the exercise yard to look forward to. They were not allowed to receive visitors or parcels. The prevailing depression was made worse by the news on Christmas Eve that the wife and daughter of Dr Lammers, a witness for Keitel who was being held in another wing, had committed suicide. (129) The only seasonal celebration came with the issue of a cigar or an extra two ounces of tobacco. Lest anyone think that Colonel Andrus was becoming sentimental, he told the Press that this was to keep the defendants' 'nerves normal while working on their cases'. (130)

On Christmas Eve many of the defendants went to a service in the double cell on the first floor which had been converted for use as a chapel. Hess never went to services in case 'it will be thought I am doing so because I am frightened'. (131) Nor did Jodl or Frick who said they believed in God but not organized religion. Goering was there, however. He was said to have tears in his eye as he sang 'Silent Night'. (132) At the first service he had attended in the gaol, he had been indignant at the absence of an organ and staged a protest by refusing to say the Lord's Prayer; Goering had vowed never to go to the chapel again. But on 8 December he told the Protestant chaplain, Pastor Gerecke, that he would go to services as a personal favour: 'As ranking man of the group, if I attend the others will follow suit'. The extent of Goering's religious devotion never increased, in spite of all Pastor Gerecke's patient and determined campaigns for his soul. He consistently maintained that he found all religious teaching unacceptable. He went to services regularly, but he confided to Dr Gilbert: 'Prayers, hell! It's just a chance to get out of this damned cell for half an hour!' (133)

Pastor Gerecke had thirteen nominal Protestants in his flock. He had been born and bred on a farm in Missouri and although he came from a German immigrant family his German was far from fluent and writing a sermon demanded a painful effort. When he first arrived Gerecke made little impression. Fritzsche described him as 'insignificant-looking' and 'unassuming'. But he soon won respect and all hearts. Everyone was comforted by his conviction that God alone could judge and that his only duty was the care of souls. (134) Schacht, not a man given to admiration let alone affection, said of him there was 'a most moving quality in Pastor Gerecke's zeal and devotion to his task. He was a dear, thoroughly well-intentioned man, possessed of great personal tact.' (135) When Gerecke was due to return to the States in mid-1946, Fritzsche drew up a petition for the extension of his ministry and it was signed by Catholics as well as Protestants. (136)

The Catholic chaplain was a New Yorker, Father Sixtus O'Connor. He was young and energetic, and he was popular – not least because he was prepared to break prison rules, which Gerecke was not, and help the prisoners to contact their families. (137) The only baptized Catholic who refused to have anything to do with him was Streicher. Frank, on the other hand, could be seen as a triumph for Father O'Connor – or perhaps something of an embarrassment. Frank was a lapsed Old Catholic who announced his conversion to Roman Catholicism in prison. This conversion had resulted in a state of abject penitence which was not always theologically distinguishable from maudlin self-pity. Furthermore, Gilbert clearly suspected it had enabled Frank to cut himself off from his past; he often spoke of his life before conversion as if it were the existence of someone else. 'It is as though I am two people. Me, myself, Frank here – and that other Frank, the Nazi leader. And sometimes I wonder how that man Frank could have done those things ... Isn't that interesting ... Just as if I were two different people ... Fascinating, isn't it?' (138)

Frank was certainly a fascinating case for a psychologist, but then so were the other defendants. And they also presented interesting case studies in moral attitudes. By February they had heard three months of evidence against the regime in which they had held posts of high responsibility for many years. They had also heard detailed evidence on their own individual policies and acts. Much of it was in their own words; the rest came from documents written or signed by their colleagues or by their former leader. No doubt they could pick holes in some of the law being applied in the trial; it was not difficult to spot weaknesses in the structure of some of the individual cases, moments where the evidence was tied to individuals too loosely. But the prosecution case against the Nazi regime and against its leaders in the defendants' box had been massive, it had been in the Nazis' own words, and it had given a picture of unrestrained cruelty, cynical contempt for human values, let alone the norms of civilized political and diplomatic behaviour. Was it really possible for them after such an indictment, such evidence, not to question their own part in the history they had heard? Though a fair judicial process would allow them to challenge aspects of the case against them, and mount a defence, could men who had wielded such power in the state not sense some responsibility for the crimes and atrocities which that state had perpetrated? Could they not acknowledge a sense of moral guilt for such a regime? Or, if that was asking too much, at least a degree of embarrassment at being associated with it?

It is true that during the three months of prosecution evidence, the defendants had all, at some point or another, been appalled at what they heard. Few of them could watch the films and face the degradation and suffering they showed. Each of them, on occasion, described the persecutions, the tortures, the murders as 'terrible', 'shocking'. But the shock they experienced was short-lived. They soon recovered. They had a resilience to what they heard day after day which can only be attributed to a total lack of moral sensitivity. They could listen to three whole months of analysis of Nazi policies, details of their own crimes, the facts of the suffering of their victims and remain impermeable. Not only did few of them sense a moral responsibility for the part they had played, few of them thought to question whether they should.

Dr Gilbert tried to keep a verbatim record in his diary of the defendants' reactions to the evidence in court and of their judgements of their own pasts. Gilbert's entries from November to the end of February show how little impact the prosecution case had made on them and suggest why they had been so little moved. The diary, in essence, lists a variety of protective barriers erected by the defendants against the reality of their lives. Frank was not unique in finding an escape from the need to face his past. They all did. The language they used is in itself significant. They seldom used such words as 'murder', 'torture', 'starvation'. They slithered away from the specific and hid in euphemisms, cloaking facts in vagueness: 'such things', 'those horrors'. The defendants had always avoided the nasty words. All their documents spoke not of their hatred or jealousy or ideological ambitions for the Jews, but of 'the Jewish Problem' (just as they never wrote of ambitions or even fears when dealing with Poland, but of 'the Polish Problem'). This terminology conveniently implies that since others have caused the difficulty, others must pay the price for solving it. From this starting point they could bypass the need to say 'we want to get rid of the Jews' or 'we want to invade Poland' and instead say 'the Jewish problem must be solved' or 'the Polish problem cannot be allowed to continue' (faced with a problem after all it is only right and proper to try to solve it). It was a simple linguistic dodge to skirt round the harsh black and white of 'we have decided to kill all Jews' or 'we will invade Poland', and to resort to the more euphonious 'it has been decided to implement the Final Solution' or 'steps are to be taken to secure Germany against the Polish menace.'

The military defendants continued to use the vocabulary which had always saved them the trouble of thinking. Their words turned moral apathy or weakness into virtues. Keitel summed up the standard military line: 'I can only say I was brought up in the Prussian officer's tradition to obey orders with honour and loyalty'. 'Obedience', 'honour', 'loyalty' are fine things – in some contexts. But the Nazi generals and admirals used the words as bolt holes where they were secure from the need to ask themselves 'obedient and loyal to whom and to what orders?'; 'can a man claim honour when he fights in a dishonourable cause and for a criminal?' Such questions were avoided. 'Don't you see,' said Keitel, 'if Hitler ordered it that was good enough for me? After all I was only his office chief.' That 'only' was a staggering piece of self-revelation. It indicated Keitel's wish to imply that he was nothing more than a filing cabinet or a typewriter; that he could only be expected to obey and perform; that it was not his function to make moral judgements and decisions. Objectively, Jodl more than Keitel could recognize the difference between right and wrong. He expressed moral outrage at the evidence he heard in court about Hitler's ruthlessness and aggressive ambition. But he could contemplate his own part in carrying out Hitler's plans with equanimity. 'Perhaps it's just as well I didn't know (about the plans) . . . At least I fought with conviction and honour.' It is doubtful that he knew nothing about Hitler's plans; there is no doubt at all that a thinking man ought to feel some shame at having been either duped or used for such ends.

Jodl had demonstrated one of the commonest devices for evading any share of responsibility: 'I did not know.' This device allowed them to pose as moral human beings who recognized the wrong, acknowledged that crimes had been committed but at the same time to maintain they had lived in a vacuum which had isolated them from all contamination. 'I knew absolutely nothing of these things and I certainly had nothing to do with it,' said Sauckel. 'Do you think I had the slightest notion about gas wagons and such horrors?' asked Funk. He then added that he had saved the French from the devaluation of their franc during German occupation – a typical example of a defendant's resort to any claim of virtue as if it exactly counter-balanced whatever moral turpitude was under discussion (Frank for example clearly believed that the act of handing over his diaries to the Allies had magically wiped out all his crimes which the forty volumes recorded). The inability to make moral connections, to see that there might be some share of guilt or responsibility, meant that Rosenberg, the Party ideologist who had done more than most to evolve and spread the doctrine of anti-Semitism, could make a demonstration of injured innocence after days of evidence on concentration camps and the extermination of the Jews: 'Of course it's terrible, incomprehensible, the whole business. I would never have dreamed it would take such a turn . . . We didn't contemplate killing anyone in the beginning, I can assure you of that. I always advocated a peaceful solution.' Ribbentrop could tell Gilbert: '. . . all the persecutions and atrocities are revolting to all of us . . . Can you conceive of me killing anybody?.. Tell me frankly, do any of us look like murderers?' Perhaps not, not now, if like Ribbentrop they were perpetually trembling in terror. Perhaps Ribbentrop and many of the others would never have been prepared to kill anyone themselves. But they should have been prepared at this stage to ask themselves whether they had ordered others to kill, whether they had condoned murder, whether their policies had led inevitably to the deaths of others. After the months of evidence on what they had done and what effect they had had on millions of human beings, they might have questioned whether 'I didn't know' and 'I never meant that to happen' sounded like the defence of a moral, dignified, thinking man or the plaintive wail of an infant.

Ribbentrop continued his self-justification to Gilbert by pleading: 'why can't the victors accept this as a historical tragedy that was inevitable and try to work to a peaceful solution' (presumably he did not mean 'peaceful solution' in Rosenberg's terms.) In talking of historical tragedy, did Ribbentrop mean to star as the hero or was he using Fate to stress his own powerlessness when caught up by an irresistable force? Since he had the woolliest mind in Nuremberg jail it would be typical of him to use the vaguest of excuses to shift blame elsewhere. Others were more specific. Speer, for example, blamed the War entirely on the British: they should have told the Poles to accede to German demands, then 'the whole War could have been avoided. Our demands were so reasonable. It wasn't necessary to go to war over it.' Schacht predated the guilt and extended it. He said the Weimar Republic was 'so willing to do anything for peace. We were so modest in our demands. All we wanted was some possibility for export, for trade, to live somehow ... and to every little suggestion the Allies said "No".' So Hitler came to power and 'those fools Daladier and Chamberlain dropped the whole thing in his lap'. Many historians will now argue that Allied policy weakened the Weimar Republic, helped the rise of Hitler, and played into his hands. That is a far cry, however, from saying that the Germans themselves played no part, or from saying that all German complaints and ambitions were and remained reasonable. But blaming another Power was an excuse for washing one's own hands, whether the Power was Fate or the British.

One of the commonest targets for blame was Himmler. He was well chosen: a man who had genuinely held great power, a man who had frightened them all and who was not there to argue or return blame. Himmler had undeniably created much of the Nazi state within the German state. It was all too tempting to argue that all crimes were committed by his apparatus; it was another device for claiming to have been distanced from 'those things', and unspotted by them. When Schirach asked Goering who had given the orders for the brutal wiping out of the Warsaw Ghetto the answer was inevitable: 'Himmler, I suppose.' Then Goering added: 'Himmler had his chosen psychopaths to carry these things out and it was kept secret from the rest of us. But I would never have suspected him of it. He didn't seem to be the murderer type.' Ribbentrop claimed rather more perception – and in so doing for once defended others as well as himself: 'Himmler must have ordered those things. But I doubt if he was a real German. He had a peculiar face.' Streicher shared his belief that Himmler was not a true German. He too blamed Himmler for things for which he might have blamed himself. 'That was all done by Himmler. I disapprove of murder.' Then he pointed out that Himmler boasted of being an authority on race. But 'he didn't know anything about it. He had Negro blood himself . . . I could tell by his head shape and hair. I can recognize blood.'

In blaming Himmler some of the defendants were not just trying to avoid blaming themselves. They were also trying to avoid naming Hitler. They had helped him to power, worked for him, glorified him. Could they now see him as the source of all 'those crimes'? Some of them could not, some of them would not. Ribbentrop unconsciously expressed the dilemma they were in: 'I can't conceive of Hitler ordering such things. I can't believe he knew about it. He had a hard side I know, but I believed in him with all my heart. He could really be so tender. I was willing to do anything for him.' If you admit to having believed in a man, it is uncomfortable to accept him as a criminal; if you know you would have done anything for him, others will ask whether that included crimes. Ribbentrop preferred to put all the blame on Himmler. Others were uncertain whether Himmler was carrying out Hitler's orders. 'Well, it's hard to say,' Sauckel told Gilbert. 'We are of different opinions whether Hitler knew about those things . . . But there is no doubt Himmler did those things and they cannot possibly be justified.'

Frank was more prepared to pin blame on Hitler: 'At some moment Hitler and Himmler must have simply sat down and Hitler gave him orders to wipe out whole races and groups of people.' Neurath reached a rather similar conclusion, a comforting one since it implied that no one else bore any responsibility, even knew what had been decided. Hitler – thought Neurath – 'must have done his conspiring with his little group of henchmen late at night. But I couldn't stay up so late. Sometimes he would call up at one, two or three in the morning. That is probably when these secret discussions with Himmler and Bormann took place.' How very nice to sleep the sleep of the just while four million slave labourers work for your country, five million Jews die for your ideology, while huge resources are expended to construct camps, guard prisoners, extract the gold teeth from the dead, organize peripatetic death squads to follow your armies and plan the routes of trains to loot the treasures of Europe for your delectation. All the defendants claimed to have known nothing of the unpleasant policies of the government which they served, not to have noticed the huge sums for extermination which appeared in the budgets they passed as ministers. But, after three months of detailed courtroom evidence, there was no longer any question of not knowing now. All the defendants, without exception, accepted the evidence they had heard, and never denied that 'these things' had happened. But they could not accept that the evidence implicated themselves, not just legally, but even more clearly morally.

There was something else they could not accept – that the evidence always led back to Hitler. Hitler was the central figure at the Nuremberg trial. His was the name most often heard in court; his were the policies, the orders, the speeches most often quoted in evidence. He was the obsessive subject of the defendants' conversations, just as he had been the centre of their lives for so many years – inspiring, bullying, giving them immense power, reducing them to snivelling suppliants, and dazzling them until they could no longer see what they were doing. They were still dazzled. 'The Führer had a terrifically magnetic personality,' said Ribbentrop. 'Do you know, even now, six months after his death, I can't shake off his influence.' Stronger personalities than Ribbentrop shared those feelings. As they saw their Führer in 'The Nazi Plan' film, they were magnetized again. Some were trying to shake off the influence. Neurath called Hitler a liar: 'He simply had no respect for the truth,' but he added that Hitler had been 'a fascinating demagogue'. Papen vehemently denounced the moral corruption of Nazism and blamed Hitler for Germany's present plight, but even he spoke with awe of Hitler's pre-War successes: 'he seemed to be accomplishing so much without spilling a drop of blood.' Keitel too: 'Just imagine, we reoccupied the Ruhr with three battalions.' Then he added: 'It would have been so much better if Hitler hadn't got away with so much.' But he had, and his subordinates had revelled in his success. Success had justified every action and getting away with it had formed their moral attitudes.

Now the success had evaporated. Germany had been defeated. Her former leaders were on trial. The policies which had contributed to all that success were now labelled criminal, and Hitler, the wizard who had bewitched them, was gone. Surely, they thought, he could have explained everything if he had been there. Surely he could have explained that he as Führer had made all the real decisions, given all the orders. Could he not have taken all the responsibility? Was his suicide the escape of a coward?

These ideas worried them for many weeks. Keitel seems to have been the first to express them, at lunch on 14 December. Goering, *Treue Hermann*, tried to crush him: 'You men knew the Führer. He would have been the first one to stand up and say "I have given the orders and I take full responsibility." But I would rather die ten deaths than have the German sovereign subjected to this humiliation.' Keitel fell silent, but Frank was not crushed: 'Other sovereigns have stood before courts of law. He got us into this . . .' Keitel, Doenitz, Funk and Schirach suddenly got up and left Goering's table.

This row at lunch brought to a head the simmering crisis in the ranks of the defendants. There were pressures to break ranks, denounce the Nazi regime; hopes of winning clemency or just cleansing the conscience. But there were many practical reasons why they should maintain a united front and present a consistent defence. Furthermore Goering was determined that they should do so, less because he hoped for practical gains than because he had cast them as the heroes of old who must remain true to the end. He made it clear that he was not afraid to die: 'That doesn't mean a thing to me, but my reputation in history means a lot. That's why I'm glad Doenitz got landed with signing the surrender.' He urged his colleagues to stand by their policies in court, as he intended to do. 'Of course we rearmed. Why I rearmed Germany until we bristled,' he told Gilbert. 'Of course I considered your treaties so much toilet paper. Of course I wanted to make Germany great. If it could be done peacefully, all well and good; if not, that was fine too.'

He tried to inspire the others with the same defiance. Where they were too frightened he offered them protection. 'Don't worry,' he told Funk, 'you were only taking orders from me. I'll take full responsibility for the Four Year Plan.' Where he suspected willingness to admit a degree of guilt he tried doses of contempt; he said of German witnesses for the prosecution: 'It makes me sick to see Germans selling their souls to the enemy. I just detest anything that is undignified.' He told two who had given up hope that they must face a martyr's death in the confidence that the German people would rise again and move their bones to marble caskets in a national shrine (an ill-chosen bribe, perhaps, for someone as terrified as Funk, but rather more effective for Schirach). Such was the strength of Goering's personality, the fertility of his imagination in finding ways of threatening, cajoling, that it seemed almost possible that he would maintain his dominance and hold all the defendants to the line he had chosen.

Not that they all accepted his influence over them willingly. The old Flensburg group under Doenitz still saw him as flashy and vulgar, but for reasons of dignity and old-fashioned pride they wished to remain united and preserve a front in court. Many could accept Goering's criminal policies and his cynicism but had been appalled by the evidence on his looting. Schacht had said: 'Stealing is in a way even worse than killing; it shows a man's character.' Frank said he really did not know what to think of Goering: 'He can be so charming at times. But how could he steal those treasures for himself in wartime?' But those most likely to reject the Goering line and to condemn in open court the regime they had served were Schirach and Speer.

When Schirach first arrived in Nuremberg jail he told Gilbert he intended to write a denunciation of Hitler's 'betrayal' of German Youth. But Gilbert noted in mid-February that the 'essential moral weakness of this narcissist had been clearly shown in the manner in which he had subdued his indignation at the betrayal ... under the influence of Goering's aggressive cynicism, nationalism and pose of romantic heroism.' Gilbert, however, suspected that Schirach was weak enough to give way to the strongest pressure and felt that he and Kelley between them could act as a countervailing force to Goering. He wanted a public denunciation by

Schirach. His other hope lay in Speer. Speer's counsel had actually announced in court on 3 January that his client had attempted to assassinate Hitler in February 1945. (Details would emerge during Speer's appearance in the witness box.) The announcement had caused first bewilderment among the other defendants, then an explosion of rage from Goering. 'Damn that stupid fool, Speer,' he said in his cell that evening. 'Did you see how he disgraced himself in court today?.. How could he stoop so low as to do such a rotten thing to save his lousy neck?' In his own cell Speer told Gilbert: 'It shows that somebody did try to do something ... instead of obeying that destructive maniac to the very end.' Gilbert decided to play on Speer's rejection of the destructive. In mid-February he took a book with pictures of Speer's work as Hitler's architect. He stressed how much was now in ruins. Speer condemned Hitler for destroying not just his own work but much of what Germany had built up over 800 years. Then he burst out: 'Some day I would just like to cut loose and give a good piece of my mind about the ... whole damn Nazi mess and ... let the German people see once and for all what rotten corruption, hypocrisy and madness the whole system was based on.'

But only 'some day' – Gilbert wanted it one day very soon. His diary is extremely coy about any backing he may have had from others in authority in his plans to wring denunciations from Schirach and Speer. It seems clear that he had Andrus's co-operation. There is no evidence whatsoever in any source that he discussed his ideas with the prosecution. Acting alone or with approval, however, he set about breaking Goering's control over the defendants and rendering them more vulnerable to gentle persuasion from other quarters. First, on 15 February an order was issued imposing strict solitary confinement in jail. No official reasons were given, but Goering spotted immediately that he lay at the bottom of it: 'Don't you see that all this joking and horseplay is only comic relief ... If I didn't pep them up a couple of them would simply collapse.' Then a week later Gilbert drew up new seating arrangements for the defendants at lunch (he says in his diary that this was at Andrus's suggestion). Under the new arrangement, instead of sitting together in one room, where Goering could dominate them all, he was to be separated and must lunch alone. The others were then divided between five other rooms, the groups being composed to fit Gilbert's theories on their personalities. In the 'Youth Lunchroom' Speer, Fritzsche, Schirach and Funk were to eat together – Gilbert reckoned that Speer and Fritzsche together could wean the other weaker characters away from Goering's influence. In the 'Elders' Lunchroom' he put all the old Conservatives, Papen, Neurath, Schacht and Doenitz, those always fastidious in their judgement of Goering, whom he hoped would be won over by Schacht's contempt for Hitler and Ribbentrop. Frank, Seyss-Inquart, Keitel and Sauckel were grouped together to encourage the feeble flickers of personal guilt that each of them had shown on occasion. Raeder, Streicher, Hess and Ribbentrop were put together because Gilbert thought they would hardly find anything to say to each other and this would neutralize them. Which left Jodl, Frick, Kaltenbrunner and Rosenberg to share a lunch table. Gilbert offers no reason for this grouping; presumably they were just remnants for whom he had no ambitions and who would not actually do each other any harm.

The results of the experiment were seen almost immediately. Within a day Schacht was regaling his lunch companions with his contemptuous opinions on the Nazis as gangsters destroying the economy he had built up – in spite of a glowering Goering looming in the doorway. By the weekend Speer was admitting to Gilbert that the new arrangement made him feel freer to develop the plans for his defence along the lines he preferred; he wanted the German people to realize that Hitler, not the Allies, had been responsible for their present suffering. It was a small step forward for Speer. Perhaps the other defendants too might begin to ponder questions of their own responsibility. It was a slim hope. If three months of prosecution evidence had affected them so little, it was hardly likely that even the ingenious plot of separate tables would arouse a sense of moral responsibility during the next five months of the defence cases.

References for Chapter Ten

1 Dean to FO, 11 February. FO 371. 57539
2 Birkett to Mrs Cruesmann, 20 January. Montgomery Hyde
3 Feature by Wilson Harris, *The Times*, 21 February
4 BWCE Report 3, 25 November. N/40 Cornwall Gardens
5 *Chicago Daily News*, 20 December
6 Ibid
7 Dean to FO, 11 February. FO 371. 57539
8 *New York Times*, 24 November
9 Dean to FO op. cit.
10 Papen, Schacht, Fritzsche
11 Papen
12 Dean op. cit.
13 Conversation with Herbert Wechsler
14 Fritzsche
15 Conversation with James Rowe
16 Dean op. cit.
17 Cooper *Nuremberg*
18 Dean op. cit.
19 Fritzsche
20 Kilmuir
21 Cooper
22 Conversation with Dr Seidl
23 Kilmuir
24 Fritzsche
25 Cooper
26 Reported *New York Times*, 1 December
27 24 January, Vol. II IMT
28 Tribunal minutes, 29 November

29 29 November, Vol. II IMT
30 Minutes of Chief prosecutors' meeting, 5 December. BWCE N/10
31 Ibid
32 Ibid
33 Ibid
34 1 December, Vol. III IMT
35 14 December, Vol. III IMT
36 9 January, Vol. V IMT
37 28 January, Vol. VI IMT
38 29 January, Vol. VI IMT
39 4 February, Vol. VI IMT
40 Tribunal minutes, 15 April, 3 July, 17 July, 27 August
41 12 December, Vol. III IMT
42 15 November, Vol. II IMT
43 5 March, Vol. VIII IMT
44 Court Contact Committee File 60. Cornwall Gardens
45 Tribunal minutes, 20 March
46 Conversation with Dr Merkel
47 Minutes of Chief prosecutors' meeting 12 December. BWCE N/10
48 Tribunal minutes 17 December
49 Jackson Papers,. Box 211
50 Minutes of Chief prosecutors' meeting 5 February
51 Conversation with Donald Spencer
52 Court Contact Committee files *passim*
53 Minutes of Chief prosecutors' meeting, 26 and 27 October
54 Tribunal minutes, 30 and 31 October
55 Tribunal minutes, 8 November
56 Tribunal minutes, 21 November
57 All letters dated 4 December and sent to General Secretary. Court Contact Committee File 62
58 Tribunal minutes, 15 December
59 FO 371. 57558
60 Tribunal minutes, 19 February
61 FO 371. 57558
62 Letter to General Secretary, 29 December. BWCE N/16
63 Letter to General Secretary, 3 January. Court Contact Committee File 62 and Tribunal minutes, 5 January
64 Dodd to Jackson, 6 June. Jackson Papers Box 201
65 Conversation with Wolf Frank
66 27 March, Vol. X IMT
67 Vassilichikov – conversation with Wolf Frank
68 Quoted by Montgomery Hyde
69 *New York Herald Tribune*, 2 December
70 Dean to FO. FO 371. 57539
71 *Christian Science Monitor*, 20 November
72 *Chicago Daily News*, 26 November
73 *New York Herald Tribune*, November
74 Jackson to Director of Public Relations Division September. Jackson Papers, Box 213
75 Brigadier General Leroy Watson, 14 February. Jackson Papers, Box 213

76 *Christian Science Monitor*, 3 December
77 *Christian Science Monitor*, 18 December
78 *Daily Herald*, 5 December
79 *Reynolds Daily News*, 16 December
80 Bergold to Kempner, 7 January. Jackson Papers, Box 231
81 Conversation with Drexel Sprecher
82 Reported in *Stars and Stripes*, 12 February
83 Birkett to Mrs Cruesmann. Quoted by Montgomery Hyde
84 FO 371. 57539
85 British prosecution minutes, 13 December and 12 January
86 Kilmuir
87 British prosecution minutes, 5 November
88 For example memo of 11 December attached to British prosecution minutes
89 *Passim* in British prosecution minutes
90 This section based on conversation with Kenneth Duke and Anthony Marreco
91 Conversation with Anthony Marreco
92 Conversation with Harriet Margolies
93 Conservation with Drexel Sprecher
94 Conversation with Robert Kempner
95 Jackson Papers *passim*
96 Telford Taylor. *The Nuremberg Trials* Columbia Law Review Vol. 55 1955
97 Based on conversation with Robert Kempner, Dan and Harriet Margolies and Drexel Sprecher
98 Based on conversations with above and with John Phipps
99 Letter from John Phipps to his wife, 27 November
100 *New York Times*, 15 December
101 *News Chronicle*, 17 December
102 *New York Times* and *Stars and Stripes*, 12 December
103 Cable from Phillimore BWCE N/30
104 Wheeler-Bennett
105 *Star and Stripes*, 12 December
106 Wheeler-Bennett
107 Cooper
108 Conversation with Dan and Harriet Margolies
109 Letter from Harriet Margolies, 20 November
110 *New York Herald Tribune*, 4 December
111 Conversation with Norman Clark
112 Letter from Bill Lynn
113 BWCE cable, 4 December
114 Conversation with Major Wilkinson
115 Information supplied by Bill Lynn
116 Neave
117 Conversation with Major Wilkinson
118 Kilmuir
119 Conversation with Wilkinson
120 Wheeler-Bennett
121 Dean cable, 27 and 28 November
122 BWCE N/30
123 Letter from Biddle to his wife, 24 March. Biddle Papers, Box 19

124   Letter from Biddle to his wife, 4 February. Biddle Papers, Box 19
125   Jackson Papers, Box 201
126   *Stars and Stripes*, 24 December
127   Fritzsche
128   Schacht
129   Fritzsche
130   In several newspapers
131   *Manchester Guardian*, 5 December
132   Several newspapers
133   Gilbert
134   Fritzsche
135   Schacht
136   Fritzsche
137   Schacht
138   This and all quotations until end of chapter from Gilbert

Chapter Eleven

The defence case began on 8 March 1946 – in spite of an attempt by the defence lawyers to delay it for three weeks. On 4 February, Dr Stahmer had written to the Tribunal on behalf of his colleagues pleading for a recess at the end of the prosecution case to give defence counsel time to prepare. His request was repeated in court by Dr Kraus on 18 February. The judges decided to refuse a three week recess. (1) They pointed out that at the end of the prosecution three days would be devoted to hearing argument on the case against the organizations, with a further four days hearing applications for defence witnesses and documents. This should give ample time to prepare the cases for the defendants – even for Dr Stahmer whose client would appear first. (2)

The prosecutors, on the other hand, might well have been more ready to grant a delay. When they discussed the matter in meetings on 12 and 15 February, Maxwell-Fyfe and Dubost were quite willing to consider a recess of anything up to a week, and they talked the Russians round from total opposition to any delay to acceptance of two or three days for defence preparations. Jackson had argued most forcibly for allowing an adjournment of at least a week, maybe more. He had urged the need 'to avoid any risk of marring the long-term effects of the trial', and quoted the criticisms by the New York Supreme Court that the trial of Yamashita had been rushed. Jackson stressed that the prosecution was indebted to the defence for their conduct thus far; it would be wrong to be too hard on them over this matter. He even expressed the fear that to refuse the defence request might result in them 'throwing up the case'. (3)

The Tribunal, however, did not consult the prosecutors, and it was unanimous in rejecting the defence request. Underlying the judges' insistence that the defence case should start promptly was undoubtedly a concern that an already lengthy trial might be intolerably dragged out – either by an impractical desire for perfection or by deliberate obstructionism. The judges were not seeking to skimp on the defendants' cases; on the contrary they were determined to examine them thoroughly. But they were anxious that public respect for the management of the trial should be maintained. Attention at this stage to the Charter's call for a 'prompt and expeditious' trial would both satisfy public expectations and serve notice that the Tribunal intended to keep a firm control over the proceedings and to discipline its participants. Yet the Tribunal's subsequent handling of the defence case would clearly demonstrate its readiness to grant a fair and full hearing and its view that saving time was not the sole priority.

Furthermore, the Tribunal had already shown some impatience with defence complaints about inadequate time for preparation. Their reprimand to Babel who had asked for a day's notice before cross-examining a witness had been but one example of several. Too many of the complaints about lack of time had turned out to be unsubstantiated. Dr Seidl might believe, then and now, that the defence had been denied fair warning of the case they must answer because the Continental practice of presenting all prosecution documents with the indictment had not been followed; (4) Papen might write in his memoirs that it was difficult to work up a defence because he 'did not know what documents the prosecution possessed'. (5) But, in fact, the defendants had known the charges they faced since they received the indictment on 19 October; thanks to the compromise reached at the London Conference, that indictment had been accompanied by a selection of documents indicating the nature of the evidence on which the charges were based. All the German lawyers had been appointed by 10 November. They could have started work immediately on a general defence – indeed some of them had had a clear enough idea of the lines they would pursue to start applying for witnesses and documents by the end of that month. (6) Though the bulk of prosecution evidence accumulated only gradually as documents were presented during its case, the defendants and their counsel had sat in court every day since mid-November and heard extracts read and received document books. *Pace* Papen, he had begun to know what documents the prosecution held from the day he read the indictment; by March the defendants knew only too well the evidence on which the prosecution case rested – and what a terrifying quantity of it there was. Even by Christmas, the American and British counts had been completed; it was possible to start work then on a defence against accusations of conspiracy and waging aggressive war. For anyone still needing clarification of these accusations, summaries of cases against individuals on the first two counts had been presented in court in January; the evidence against each had been collated, printed and circulated. There was plenty for the defendants and their lawyers to be getting on with before the French and Russian cases began. With such possibilities open to the defence, the Tribunal could well believe that lawyers who had been so dilatory did not deserve three weeks' grace, though some undoubtedly needed it.

Defendants or their counsel, however, have seldom mentioned these opportunities in memoirs or interviews. Instead they have tended to concentrate on allegations of unfair practice hampering the possibility of an adequate defence. Many give the impression that they never had access to essential prosecution material. But in fact after the initial muddle and incompetence of the early weeks, a steady flow of documents had been established. Before long, defence lawyers had been able to get the transcript of a day's court proceedings within forty-eight hours. Though only extracts from documents were read in court, each document was given an index number. It was easy to go to the Document Room and ask for a copy of the whole. Even when the demands on the copying equipment were heaviest the request would be met after a week. (7) Dr Seidl has gone so far as to register indignation that the defence was only allowed to see a mere photostat of an original document. (8) He seems unaware that that rule applied to the prosecutors too; originals were reserved for the Tribunal alone. No one has shown that copies were not genuine or complete. Ribbentrop complained in his memoirs, written in Nuremberg jail, that one of the diaries of the Italian Foreign Minister, Ciano, which was used against him was 'certainly a forgery' and that he could never find out whether the photocopies were based on the real or the faked version. (9) He might have noticed in all the months he sat in court that every document submitted had to be accompanied by a certificate of its source and authenticity. Where there was real doubt counsel could challenge authenticity in court. They frequently did so, sometimes successfully. The proper and effective time to complain was in court, not in memoirs.

Besides, the complaints do not always stand up to examination. A recent German author, Werner Maser, has suggested that several defence counsel were horrified that so many prosecution documents were 'untranslated'. He does not point out that though extracts might be read in court in English, French or Russian, they were translated into German by the simultaneous translators; they were printed in every language in the transcripts and document books. In any case, nearly all the documents were in German in the first place. If anyone should complain about lack of translations – and then only at the stage of preparation – it is the prosecutors. Maser is also ready to retail an accusation from Doenitz that 'thousands of documents which seemed likely possibly to incriminate the Allies and exonerate the defendants suddenly disappeared'. Even if one ignores the folly of presuming that the court would have accepted *tu quoque* evidence (whatever others might have done it did not legally cancel out or excuse criminal acts by defendants) it is significant that Maser does not name a single document allegedly suppressed in this way. Any confidence in the accusation is destroyed when he goes on to say that they could only be removed by officers who were under the command of Colonel Andrus. Agent of Sinister Powers does not seem type casting for Andrus; nor does Maser show any understanding of Andrus's actual powers and limits of authority in the court house. The whole story collapses when Maser repeats Doenitz's claim that his accusation was finally proved by what the author calls 'a source in Tahiti whose name cannot be given for obvious reasons'. (10)

Too many of these complaints and allegations are either silly or actually dishonest. They do grave disservice to their cause because they detract from the sympathy which ought to be felt for the serious problems the defence experienced. Many of these stemmed from the handicap of working with such tiny staffs. Prosecution teams added up to hundreds. Defence lawyers, on the other hand, were lucky if they could summon an assistant and a secretary. Thanks to their large pools of manpower the prosecutors could both maintain a presence in court and find ample staffing for the work in their offices. The German counsel, by contrast, were obliged to sit in court all day, every day – the Tribunal insisted they be available to guard their clients' interests and cross-examine relevant witnesses. Meanwhile, an assistant or secretary would be left to struggle with the hundred and one jobs occasioned by the prosecution charges and evidence and the practical needs of the defence. Court attendance prevented daytime consultations with clients, while in court the lawyers could only exchange brief scribbled notes with defendants on matters of immediate concern. At lunchtime counsel and defendants had to go their separate ways to their own canteens. This left only the hours after 5 o'clock, hours when everyone was tired and strained, for lawyers to consult their clients, to log the transcripts, plough through the stacks of documents used by the prosecution and to try to find their own evidence. Maxwell-Fyfe told them when they requested a three week recess that no one could work up a case without burning some midnight oil. (11) The German counsel undoubtedly had to burn very much more than their prosecution counterparts who could call on so many assistants, researchers and secretaries.

Their use of midnight oil would have been more economical, the time available for preparation would have seemed longer, however, if defendants and their counsel had anguished less and put more thought into a practical approach to the needs of their defence and had exploited the real advantages they possessed. The prosecution had clearly laid out the charges to be answered and the evidence on which they were based. The defence had been given lines to work along, limited areas which must be covered. They were not starting from scratch or thrashing around in the complete archive of the Third Reich, as the prosecutors had been, before they could determine what matters were relevant. More importantly, they were not shackled by the abysmal ignorance which had so impeded the prosecutors. They were Germans, working with their own history and on material in their own language. Their clients were the men who had shaped the policies and made the decisions against which prosecution allegations were directed; they were in the best position to give alternative explanations and analyses. Unlike the prosecutors, these men knew the chain of command, the machinery for decision, the distribution list for memos and orders. The prosecution had groped and blundered for months trying to understand the structure of Nazi government and the armed forces; they had stumbled in and out of blind alleys before they could assemble a picture of Nazi policies and the involvement of individuals in them. Often it had been sheer chance rather than understanding which had enabled them to discover the minutes of meetings or documents recording orders. Knowledge painfully and sometimes only partially acquired by the prosecutors was already possessed by the defendants.

Unfortunately the defence seems to have insufficiently appreciated such advantages, and they did not develop what resources they had. Rather than concentrate on rebutting the specific allegations which had been made, too many defence lawyers devoted their time and zeal to obtaining and trying to use documents which they must have known would be declared inadmissible. They wanted Nazi government White Books – official justifications for policies backed by carefully selected and edited Allied documents. They chased evidence of crimes by others such as the secret protocol to the Nazi-Soviet Pact, or British plans for an invasion of Norway. Such material was all too obviously intended for a plea of *tu quoque* and would never be accepted by the court. In spite of the prohibitions expressed in the Charter and repeated rulings by the Tribunal, they put it into their document books and tried to slip it into the proceedings – even when permission to use individual documents had been refused after application. They then expressed outrage when the Tribunal would not accept such evidence. Too many counsel relied on elaborate defences constructed on German grievances about the Versailles Treaty and claims that it had ceased to be binding in any respect since others had failed to comply with its requirements on disarmament. This was to imply *tu quoque* and to stretch a single debatable point which – even if conceded – could in no way excuse the wide variety of alleged subsequent crimes.

Papen recognized in his memoirs: 'It is true that *tu quoque* is a bad defence,' (12) but went on to say that it seemed necessary to show whether certain international laws were respected at the time of his alleged crimes. This suggests a belief that if everyone breaks the law it ceases to exist. Legal theory and practice have always shown otherwise. If, instead, Papen and others had argued that there was no law to guide their behaviour or that existing law was too vague and ambiguous to be effective, they might have established a much sounder defence against some of the charges they faced. After all, several of the participants at the London Conference had not been convinced that aggressive war was a crime in international law, even though they had succumbed to pressure to make it a charge. Those defendants who were to press this fundamental point of law in their cases were to make an effective showing.

The fruitfulness of questioning what international laws existed to govern the defendants' policy and how their ambiguities had been open to different interpretations was demonstrated in the winning strategy devised by Kranzbuehler, counsel for Doenitz, who also worked on the legal bases of the naval case as a whole. He asked the Tribunal's permission to send an interrogatory to the American Admiral, Nimitz, to ascertain what had been the actual practice of the American Navy in the Pacific. He got it. His request had been skilfully framed to avoid implications of *tu quoque* and to stress the need to establish current interpretations of uncertain naval law. (13) Similarly he convinced the Tribunal of his right to apply to the British

Admiralty for both German captured documents and for British naval papers. Again, he had based his request on the argument that where the law was acknowledged to be vague or disputed it was necessary to examine actual practice. This application received backing from Maxwell-Fyfe who pointed out to the Admiralty that it would be helpful if Kranzbuehler's assistant were allowed to look for the material he wanted in person. Otherwise, he suggested, no one would be convinced that Doenitz and Raeder had been given reasonable facilities to defend themselves. 'Nothing short of this will really be fair to the defence or will completely satisfy them or the Tribunal that justice has been done.' (14) The Foreign Office, often leery of revealing its own documents, seconded his request, though Mr Troutbeck querulously enquired whether, 'if Ribbentrop's defending counsel asks permission to come over and examine the whole of the diplomatic documents in our possession, will he be allowed to do so?'

The Tribunal's answer to such a request from Ribbentrop would have been 'no'. They were sympathetic to requests for evidence which could be shown to be relevant but they were not prepared to countenance what became known as 'fishing expeditions'. They might well have permitted a trip to examine a limited number of documents in a few clearly specified areas, but it seems doubtful that Ribbentrop would ever have been capable of framing a sufficiently uncloudy and concrete request. Kranzbuehler had set an example of how to get what was wanted by approaching the Tribunal using the forms which they accepted. Other counsel were much too vague. They requested facilities provided by the General Secretary to copy mountains of documents on the off-chance they might discover the odd nugget in them. The Tribunal had to remind them that 'in order that time should not be wasted and money should not be wasted it is necessary to show whether witnesses and documents have any shadow of relevance to the issues raised.' (15) All they asked was to be shown 'a shadow of relevance'. They interpreted the rules of evidence very broadly.

Not broadly enough for some people. Papen complained he was not allowed a complete set of Cabinet minutes. Perhaps if he had asked only for those meetings he himself attended and shown why they were necessary he would have got them. He also complained he was not given his private papers which had been left in Berlin and at Wallerfangen. (16) Schacht too denounced the fact that he was 'not allowed access to the complete material which the Allies had confiscated' from his personal archive. (17) Again, a specific request might well have elicited a different response. Yet neither man actually names in his memoirs a single document from these ample stores which would have significantly improved his case. Conceivably, to be padded round with one's private papers at such a time might give a sense of security; some might jog the memory or ease the process of seeing the design of a lifetime's work. It is however a sad possibility that those defendants and counsel who could never see the wood for the trees would have become even more confused if surrounded by a forest. All too many defendants registered grievance about lack of access to papers. But

Fritzsche, for example, never thought to mention the help he received from the prosecution and the General Secretary when he was looking for letters he wrote to Himmler enquiring about rumours of extermination of the Jews. Nor did he record that every effort was made to obtain BBC recordings and transcripts of speeches he had made between 1933 and 1945. (Unfortunately the BBC could never afford to keep discs on which such recordings were made and only began to monitor Nazi broadcasts in 1939 and then only kept brief summaries.) (18) This lack of evidence on the Fritzsche case was to prove as frustrating to the prosecution as to the defence. Not surprisingly no one since the trial has put into writing what one defence lawyer told Robert Kempner at the time: that he was afraid to look too thoroughly into his client's papers in case he turned up yet more incriminating material. (19)

The defence has, however, very properly recorded a genuine impediment to their work – the need to apply openly to the Tribunal for documents and witnesses and to submit their requests to argument from the prosecution. This procedure undoubtedly saved time and trouble later in court, but it robbed the defence of the element of surprise. It forewarned the prosecution of the line the defendants would take and showed them the exact contribution which the evidence was intended to make. The prosecution thus had time to prepare their counter-attack, to study defence documents and find their own to challenge them, to research the backgrounds of witnesses and design effective cross-examination. Since so many potential defence witnesses were prisoners-of-war, they could be interrogated. The system of open application resulted in the defence having to reveal most of its cards before playing its hand.

Not all defence complaints about Tribunal processing of defence requests are justified, however. Maser expresses indignation that only four of Jodl's nineteen applications for witnesses were granted – on 'grounds of time', he says. (20) Concern about time was not at the root of the Tribunal's decisions. The rule which they stated again and again was that the evidence to be given by a witness should neither be cumulative nor irrelevant; exactly the same rule had been applied to the prosecution. Witnesses must also present evidence on matters germane to the issues of the trial. When Seyss-Inquart's counsel applied for thirty-seven witnesses to show his client had averted atrocities and mitigated the severity of Nazi occupation of the Netherlands, the judges pointed out that the prosecution had not actually offered any evidence on crimes there. If he insisted on dealing with Seyss-Inquart's governorship he 'must select a reasonable number of witnesses who have general knowledge of the conditions he wishes to prove'. To request thirty-seven for this purpose was hardly reasonable. (21)

Nor were many of the requests made by Ribbentrop. They gave the impression he was arranging one of his smart cocktail parties in his London embassy rather than preparing a defence. He wanted to call the Duke of

Windsor, the Duke of Buccleuch, Lord Derby. (22) Since he could think of no good reason for their summons he was not allowed to issue it. His application for Winston Churchill was turned down too. Ribbentrop was not the only defendant to want the former Prime Minister, and like the others he failed to counter the prosecution argument that he could not provide any relevant grounds for Churchill to appear. There was no argument over his requests for Lord Dawson of Penn or Geoffrey Dawson, once the editor of *The Times* – both were dead. But there was some debate about his wish to call Lords Vansittart, Londonderry, Beaverbrook and Kemsley. For once Ribbentrop's interest was less in their titles than in what he hoped they might say about his 'desire for Anglo-German co-operation' and 'hopes for peace' which he claimed to have shown both as ambassador and Foreign Minister.

Maxwell-Fyfe warned the Foreign Office that these requests might well be granted by the Tribunal and asked for guidance. (23) The Foreign Office view was the same as the one they expressed when Goering applied for Lord Halifax, Sir Alexander Cadogan and Sir George Ogilvie-Forbes, once counsellor in Berlin. They saw no reason to prevent those in private life giving evidence for the defence. Although they felt there might be a chance to plead 'public policy' to prevent serving officials having to attend the trial, 'when a man was on trial for his life it would be unreasonable' to deny him such witnesses. (24) But appearances in court could be avoided if all the eminent gentlemen agreed to answer defence interrogatories. They did so. The questions were forwarded to them, often with 'helpful suggestions' from Professor Woodward as to their answers. (25) There was consternation when those of Lord Londonderry were returned together with a bill for £5 6s from a notary who had come to his home to witness his signature. After a frenzied exchange of minutes and memos, the Foreign Office reluctantly agreed to pay it on the grounds that his Lordship was too old and ill to go the notary's office in person – but they warned that this should not establish a precedent. (26)

The real difficulty faced by the defendants was not in getting well-chosen witnesses accepted by the Tribunal but in finding any witnesses at all. Many of their former colleagues were dead, others had fled abroad or gone into hiding in Germany. Not surprisingly many old Nazis and former officials were trying to keep their heads down in 1946; they had no wish to draw attention to themselves in a highly publicized trial nor to risk damaging their chances of settling into anonymity or getting through their de-Nazification proceedings. A system resembling the use of the subpoena had to be introduced to coax the unwilling into court. This could only be applied if a possible witness could be traced – a formidable task for the occupation authorities in the chaos of post-war Germany. The complications were increased by the fact that so many requested witnesses were lost in the jumble of prisoner-of-war camps or internment centres and had to be sought in the records of four different Zones.

Even when documents could be found and witnesses traced, the defence were further troubled by various unfamiliar procedures for presenting their cases. German lawyers were accustomed to judges playing a much more active role in a trial, examining defendants and witnesses. The court insisted that witnesses answer questions, whereas in German law they had the right to refuse. In re-examining witnesses, defence lawyers could deal only with points already raised by the prosecution's cross-examination rather than raise an endless series of new matters. Further, the German counsel had had no experience of the Anglo-American adversary process where the job of counsel is not to establish facts with the Tribunal, but to undermine the validity of their opponents' evidence. Not until this trial had they practised the art of cross-examination which can so effectively lead witnesses into pitfalls and shake confidence in their testimony as a whole.

The defence counsel, however, seem to have been unduly shaken by the unfamiliarity of the procedure they were asked to follow and to have allowed themselves to be hamstrung. They and their clients have since accused the system of being unfair because it was new to them; they sometimes imply it was rigged against them. But, after all, the procedure was new to all the participants in the trial. The Charter and the judges' rules were hybrids of Continental and Anglo-American practice. The prosecution had to struggle with unwelcome novelty too. The defence had had nearly four months to observe the ways in which counsel can examine witnesses. Most of them had practised cross-examination on prosecution witnesses, and some of them had shown a natural aptitude for it – which is more than can be said for some of the prosecutors. The French and Russians were as untrained as the Germans, the Americans were out of practice if they had ever had any. The Germans could have taken comfort and learned a lot more from the examples and failures of their adversaries.

They could also have relished a right denied them under German law but secured for them by the International Military Tribunal. At Nuremberg each defendant might give evidence in his own defence – though if he chose to do so he must take the oath and submit to cross-examination by the prosecution. This was standard practice in British and American courts but not on the Continent. But awareness of the right seems to have come as a bombshell to the Russians in February. They behaved as if they had never read the Charter, or at least had failed to realize what it meant. They said they were appalled by the prospect of defendants testifying under oath. In a private session of the judges on 20 February they refused point blank to allow it. Biddle recorded that the session developed into a 'terrific fight'. Nikitchenko maintained a vigorous objection to the procedure; Parker was so shocked at the thought that defendants might be robbed of a right that he threatened to resign. Biddle issued a stern rebuke to Parker for considering such extreme protest. Finally enough order was restored for a vote to be held – and the other judges voted the Russians down. (27)

But that was not the end of the matter. The Russians would not be pacified. They next refused to countenance the idea that defendants and their witnesses would sit in the very same box as that used by the prosecution witnesses. They reacted as if sacrilege was about to be committed on sanctified fabric. There was no reasoning with them. The meeting broke down with no decision and a deal of bad feeling on both sides. It was a rare example of the judges failing to settle arguments amicably and with common sense. Lawrence had to repair unity and broken tempers. He tried a private approach to Nikitchenko and the suggestion that the real issue to be settled was one of security: the witness box stood near the end of the Tribunal's bench and a defendant might be able to aim a blow at a judge. (Presumably the handiest target would have been Volchkov.) Why not move the box to a safer position? Once moved would it really be occupying the prosecution's ground? So might it not be seen as a rather different box? The security argument was thin, the symbolism of the move was threadbare, but they were enough for Nikitchenko. He must have recovered his temper and been pleased by any opportunity to display his usual practical and co-operative spirit. He seized the proffered olive branch and good relations between the judges were restored. (28) Anglo-American rights and obligations had been conferred on the defendants. Ribbentrop's counsel was none too pleased. He protested that the procedure was unfair to his client. (29) (If he meant that his client would be incapable of standing up to cross-examination or even working through a prepared defence in court, he was right.) But others welcomed the chance for defendants to present their cases personally and with the guidance of their counsel.

Whatever the advantages or disadvantages of the procedure evolved for the Nuremberg trial, whatever the grounds for complaints about it, there is little doubt that the physical conditions in which the defence had to be prepared were far from comfortable. Defendants and their counsel met in Room 55 in the Palais de Justice – the Defendants' Visitors' Centre. It was a large room, originally simply furnished with rows of tables and chairs. Inevitably it was noisy; concentration was difficult against the background hubbub from twenty other discussions. It became even harder when those responsible for security exclaimed in horror at the sight of open tables and insisted on putting the defendants into separate booths and cutting them off from their counsel with mesh grilles. The partitions were flimsy and did not reach the ceiling, so did nothing for sound insulation. The fine wire mesh made people feel sick or giddy and eventually one central section had to be replaced with a glass panel. But everyone then had to raise their voices to penetrate to the other side, making the room even noisier and the strain of working there even greater. Rivalry broke out as defendants staked claims to booths thought to be quieter. Goering asserting his position as Number One Survivor of the Reich and Number One on the Indictment grabbed Booth Number One – it abutted on to the wall of the outer office so was only exposed to sound from one side. He did not keep his privileged position for long. Emma Schwabenland, who was in charge of the Defendants' Visitors' Centre, soon established a rota for the use of the booths; everyone was to have a chance of enjoying relative calm and quiet.

Emma Schwabenland was an outstanding example of how individuals could do something by small gestures to ease the unpleasant lot of the defence. It was possible to maintain the consideration and good manners which would be expected in the outside world, but which were too often forgotten in Nuremberg in relations with former enemies and potential security risks. Miss Schwabenland was an American schoolteacher who had learned German when she spent a year as an exchange teacher in a German school. She had come to Nuremberg as a translator of documents, but Colonel Dostert who always possessed a good eye must have soon recognized her as conscientious and sensible. He asked her to take over the Centre, originally just to help those German counsel who did not speak English – and insisted that they be treated with every courtesy. There was no need to insist. Miss Schwabenland would not have behaved in any other way. Her role and usefulness soon expanded. She imposed proper behaviour in the Centre as she would have imposed it in her classroom. She was firm but not a martinet. Defendants drilled to stand to attention when Allied officers appeared were allowed to remain seated as Miss Schwabenland popped in and out of their room. By small acts of concern and sensitivity she soothed the irritations of their counsel. For instance she kept matches for them. Lawyers were allocated a cigarette ration but matches were unobtainable. She got them shoe laces and saved light bulbs thrown away by profligate electricians. Where there seemed no sense in sticking to the rules she bent or broke them. Defence lawyers, like all Germans, were forbidden to write to relatives abroad. This was a source of anxiety and distress. Miss Schwabenland was prepared to accept a few letters from trusted counsel, vet them, and forward them through her own relatives to the States. She defied the prohibition on fraternization and invited favourite counsel to parties. Gradually her help was extended to the prison chaplains who were responsible for reading most of the prisoners' incoming mail. Her knowledge of German and her tact were useful to them when large numbers of letters were arriving. There was no gossip about what had been read. When letters were vitriolic or threatening, which they often were, they were simply dropped in the wastepaper basket. (30)

Whatever problems and discomforts the defence faced, they could not overlook for long the fundamental inescapable worry – how could they counter the prosecution case? They had heard grave charges, backed by telling witnesses and damning documentary evidence often quoting the defendants themselves. It was a frightening challenge to find holes in such a case. What could the defence hope to find that might extenuate their clients, let alone disprove the charges? The defendants had met daily until the imposition of separate lunch rooms and solitary confinement. The record of their discussions during these months suggests that few of them had begun to entertain the possibility of a genuine defence. There was little doubt that the alleged crimes had taken place, merely assertion that others had born even greater responsibility for them. Such scraps of favourable evidence as they found challenged only details of the prosecution case and did not amount to a real counter attack against the whole. The best the defendants could do was to agree to pass on any useful documents which might turn up (though Fritzsche suggests that the military were reluctant to do this) and promise not to save their own skins by turning against each other. Blame could be hurled at the dead, at Himmler and Goebbels (though preferably not Hitler), but not at fellow defendants.

Some of the American staff had hoped to drive wedges between defendants by coaxing individuals to turn King's, or State's, evidence. The Russians had prepared denunciations for Fritzsche to sign when he was in the Lubianka. Several American counsel wanted to develop contacts with German lawyers to test the willingness of their clients to 'co-operate'. Goering would have been the most desirable prey. It was argued that his vanity would make him vulnerable to an approach from the prosecution and that his desire to play the hero would lead him to give a full account of Nazi policies in the belief that he was defending and promulgating them. Robert Kempner was sent to make contact – a German native, even once Goering's subordinate in the Prussian Ministry of the Interior, if only for a few days. Stahmer, Goering's counsel, nosed the bait, nibbled briefly and suggested that Goering might lend assistance in return for a promise that he would be shot by a firing squad rather than hanged like a common criminal. The Americans would make no promises. They got no statement. Kempner himself says he had undertaken the negotiation reluctantly – he felt that no one should deal with such a man; no one should sup with such a devil however long their spoon. (31)

Jackson too, was resolutely set against the idea. He thought that any bargaining or backstage negotiation with the defendants was outrageous in a great trial involving profound moral and legal issues. If his hopes for a major and lasting development in international law were to be realized he felt that the Tribunal's judgement must be based on law and on the evidence it had weighed, not on lawyers' tricks and testimony extorted from the frightened hoping for leniency. (32) Furthermore, he had too much confidence in the strength of his case to need to resort to trading and enticement. Some of his colleagues were not convinced. Bill Donovan in particular wanted to pursue the line of getting defendants to denounce their regime or their colleagues. Paradoxically the possibility of splitting the defence resulted in an irreparable division in the prosecution team.

Donovan was taken by a subtle approach from Schacht in November 1945. Schacht's lawyer wrote Donovan a flattering letter praising his 'high standing', 'experience' and 'wisdom'. It suggested that his client might consider providing a 'brief summary of the underlying reasons and conditions of the Nazi regime'. It was the most delicate of hints. If challenged, Schacht could easily assume righteous indignation (one of his great talents) and deny he had offered real co-operation. Donovan was excited by it, however, and urged Jackson to follow it up. He argued it was unnecessary to give any promises or make any bargains. Jackson was not to be persuaded. His refusal and Donovan's continued enthusiasm for the attempt finally severed their already strained relations – the result of Donovan's resentment of Jackson's authority in the team and his failure to make witnesses rather than documents a major part of the case. Jackson was emphatic: 'We do not see alike about the defendants such as Schacht. I do not think he will help us convict anyone we do not already have convicted on the documents.' Riled by Donovan's insistence he now refused to allow him to cross-examine any defence witness. This was the last straw. Donovan replied with a strongly-worded memo criticizing Jackson's handling of the whole prosecution case and stating his intention to leave Nuremberg. He did so soon afterwards. (33)

Schacht had not been alone in sounding out the prosecution's attitude. Keitel had pondered the possibility of salving his conscience. He had discussed the idea of making an offer to the prosecution in his early interrogations with Thomas Dodd. (34) Dr Nelte, Keitel's lawyer, then told Robert Kempner of his client's willingness to assume full responsibility for his orders so as to relieve his subordinates of blame. Kempner made no promises; he just sent the message to Keitel to go ahead and confess if he wished. Keitel, however, got cold feet. Never in his life had he acted willingly on his own initiative. His counsel might have suggested that a confession could produce some mitigation of sentence, make the task of defending the General Staff easier, but Keitel was used to acting not on suggestions but on orders from superior officers. He consulted Goering. Goering's views were predictable: on no account were the defendants to break rank and weaken the united front. Keitel wrote to Kempner to explain that after a sleepless night he had changed his mind. There would be no confession. (35)

Denied co-operation from the defence, the prosecutors had to rely on their own wits and on carefully prepared cross-examinations to fend off counter attack during the defence case. As early as October they had tried to anticipate the approach the defendants might take. Jackson had warned that they must expect applications for such witnesses as Churchill and Molotov; he had been ready to urge the Tribunal to ask for proofs of relevance before such prestigious witnesses were obliged to appear in court. In the event, the Tribunal needed no urging to establish its rules for granting defence witnesses and documents. At the meeting of chief prosecutors on 30 October, Jackson and Maxwell-Fyfe reached the same conclusion from Jodl's requests for records of war crimes committed by the Allies – namely that the defence was preparing a case based on *tu quoque* and the right of reprisal. They agreed to invoke the Charter to stymie the use of *tu quoque* and Maxwell-Fyfe suggested reminding the Tribunal that at the Leipzig trials after the First World War the German judges had ruled it out of order. Even so, all agreed to prepare lists of possible defence allegations and to draw up lists of answers to them. (36)

In particular, the British, Americans and Russians were continually worried that the French would be accused of mistreatment of German prisoners-of-war. There had been plenty of publicity about the conditions in which these prisoners were kept, and a highly critical Red Cross report on the matter which had given rise to a blazing row between the French authorities and General Eisenhower. The French prosecutors, however, seemed oblivious to the dangers of the topic. In December they blithely announced their intention of bringing witnesses in their case to the shackling of Allied prisoners. Maxwell-Fyfe was aghast. (37) Someone must have talked them out of their folly – though prosecution minutes do not record how it was done – because the matter was not raised in the French section of the prosecution.

By mid-November, the British were worried that they would be accused of condoning breaches of the naval clauses of the Versailles Treaty by signing the 1935 Anglo-German Naval Agreement. Maxwell-Fyfe thought it would be possible to argue that the Treaty still stood *vis-à-vis* its other signatories and that British assent to the Agreement was only obtained because the Germans gave false information about the size and condition of their existing fleet. To be on the safe side, however, requests were sent to the Foreign Office for help in establishing the details. (38)

All the prosecutors feared the defence would argue that the foreign policy of others had encouraged that of Germany. The defendants might claim that other nations had condoned breaches of the Versailles Treaty from the occupation of the Rhineland to the take over of Czechoslovakia; had indeed been ready to negotiate over such questions as the incorporation of the Sudetenland. Furthermore, the defence could trade on the fact that although the Allies now accused the Nazi government of crimes against its own citizens, every one of their own governments had recognized that regime in 1933 and had continued to maintain diplomatic relations with it up to the outbreak of War. The chief prosecutors appeared not to realize that the argument was fallacious – recognition never implies approval. At the chief prosecutors' meeting on 30 October Pokrovsky dismissed their fears on other grounds, that 'the judges did not assemble to hear their own governments criticized'. The others were less optimistic. Maxwell-Fyfe and de Menthon preferred the argument that their governments had acted in good faith but had been deceived by the lies and false assurances of the Nazis. (39)

A more acute and time-consuming cause for concern for the British prosecutors arose from their belief that the naval and military defendants were preparing to claim that Germany had invaded Norway only to pre-empt a planned British attack. Requests for documents by Goering and Raeder pointed to Norway as a topic they intended to stress; the questions prepared by Keitel for an interrogatory for Churchill's nephew, captured at Narvik, indicated that he intended to examine British invasion plans.

Defence counsel were known to have obtained the White Books on Norway containing documents said to have been captured during the German invasion, showing that the British carefully prepared plans which the Germans had only narrowly averted. Given this clear warning of defence targets, the British prosecutors wanted full information and all the help they could get on the matter. Instead they met point blank refusal from their own government. Attlee, now Prime Minister, snapped 'we are not on trial' and opposed sending any government documents to the prosecutors. (40) The Foreign Office began a campaign of prevarication. Officials there delayed response to any request for information, then, when pushed, forwarded wordy briefs which evaded all the questions put. British prosecution files preserve several of them. The kindest conclusion which can be drawn from the line they take is that officials who sent them did not really understand the Norwegian policy and were retailing their own confusion. Once confused they may have obfuscated the issues further, fearing that departmental interests and international diplomacy were involved. Whatever the reason for Foreign Office policy, the result was to involve the British prosecution for months in anxiety which could have been allayed in a week, and to create the fear that the British government really had something very nasty to hide. In fact, for the specific purposes of the case at Nuremberg and indeed in the long-term perspective of international law and diplomacy, they did not.

Foreign Office circumlocution for a long time muddied a history of policy towards Norway which in fact fell into two distinct phases. The background to both was British awareness of the advantages which the capture of Norway could secure for the Germans and the desire to deny them those advantages. Norway's coast provides a complex series of channels stretching for 400 miles, known as the Leads. These channels, protected and concealed by innumerable islands, could offer the German Navy safe routes into the Atlantic and secure hiding places from which sorties could be launched on Allied shipping. Possession of Norwegian ports would facilitate any attack on the Soviet Union and would prevent the German Navy being bottled up in the 'Wet Triangle' as they had been during the First World War. In British eyes the most vital of these ports was Narvik; it was ice-free in winter and furthermore Sweden used it to export about one tenth of her shipments of high grade iron ore to Germany. The British and Nazi leaders tended to see these shipments as crucial, believing that they were Germany's only source of material suitable for munitions and that without them Germany would be reduced to a mere year's campaigning requirement. (Some recent research suggests its importance was exaggerated.) Seizure of Norway would have been a relatively simple matter. The Norwegians had been firm neutrals since 1918; they had been devoted adherents of the League of Nations and having put their trust in collective action had reduced their armed forces to the minimum – their navy still had two pre-Dreadnought ironclads.

In the first stage of their policy towards Norway, the British had indeed planned to seize strategic Norwegian areas. But that plan had been drawn up in response to the Russo-Finnish War which began on 30 November 1939. The Russian invasion of Finland had transgressed League rules; members could show their devotion to its principles by going to the aid of the Finns. The British intended to do so by crossing Norway (who was obliged by League regulations to permit transit), disingenuously leaving on the way enough troops to secure the Swedish routes to Narvik. Over 15,000 combat troops were at the ready, a further 42,000 were being prepared. The French were egging them on in the hopes of diverting Germany from France. All that was needed to launch the action was an official Finnish request for help. It never came. On 12 March, the date set for the British expedition, the Finns were obliged to make peace with Russia. Plans for the expedition were not immediately cancelled but troops were soon dispersed. This British scheme as regards Norway had been of doubtful morality and tenuous legality. Obviously in 1945 the Foreign Office would prefer it should not come to light. But the essential fact was that it had never been implemented. No actual crime had been committed. And an old, abandoned plan could not be effectively quoted to justify a much later German invasion.

Instead the defendants would have to prove that this invasion was prepared and launched to prevent a known attempt by the British, and here they were on much weaker ground. The British had certainly decided on 28 March to order the mining of the Leads – they might be territorial waters of a neutral country but they had already been violated by the German military as had been proved in February when the British rescued prisoners of war from the *Altmark*. Should the Germans retaliate for the mining by attacking Norway, then British troops were to be sent for her defence – but only if the Norwegian government requested aid. Warning of minelaying was sent to Oslo on 8 April. The Norwegians robustly announced their intention to sweep them. But on that very day, the German Navy was already at sea, prepared for a synchronized landing and the seizure by force of several ports. This attack had been planned for many months and had received Hitler's approval on 26 March. (41) British noses were clean on this matter; there had been no time to collect even the slight smuts which might have been noticeable in their intentions.

But the Foreign Office saw neither the distinction between the two policies nor the legality of the second. As late as March 1946 their minutes commenting on the increasingly desperate prosecutors' pleas for enlightenment about British policy record their wish to avoid any discussion about Finland. One official candidly noted that in this stage of policy the British 'had not been deterred by any moral grounds from commiting an act which we have denounced . . . as a most criminal breach of international law' in others. It was an attitude summed up more succinctly by a colleague who wrote that 'there was a lot of funny business at the time' which they would prefer to conceal from the Tribunal. The minutes also show the fear that any mention of Finland might 'tend to stir up old rancours and suspicions in the Russians'. (42) They show that the Foreign Office could hardly work out the details of the Norwegian policy themselves, even if they had wished to explain it to the team at Nuremberg. There was no central file on Norway, documents were scattered among different departments and were difficult to track down since each department had given a different code name to each step of planning. Only in late March when an official was sent to Paris to confer with the Quai d'Orsay did anyone stumble on the vital discovery that most of the documents in the White Books on which the defence seemed likely to lean had not been captured in Norway but from General Weygand's archives in France well after the invasion of Norway – no kind of justification for an attack. (43) Caught between well-earned embarrassment, bureaucratic confusion and intellectual muddle about the true issues involved, it was not surprising that the Foreign Office preferred to stall and leave the British team in Nuremberg in the dark.

Sir Hartley Shawcross, however, wanted the whole matter thrashed out openly. He had clearly been able to put two and two together from the skimpy information the Foreign Office had sent and could see that from the legal point of view they had nothing to hide. On 15 March he sent a strongly worded request for full, honest and accurate information at last. (44) Perhaps it began to dawn on the Foreign Office that highly skilled lawyers were well qualified to dodge around any distasteful subjects which were not really essential to the case in hand; that the Tribunal would not wish to hear old stories about Finland which had no real bearing on the question of the German invasion of Norway. Anyway, gradually, if all too slowly, the Foreign Office overcame its reluctance to allow the British prosecutors to understand its policies, and a steady trickle of useful government documents began to arrive at Nuremberg in April. With proper information the lawyers now found it relatively easy to prepare an adequate case against expected defence allegations.

Norway and similar embarrassments were chronic irritants rather than major problems. The main concern of the prosecutors before the defence began was to prepare their cross-examinations of defendants and witnesses. In December they had decided who would take major responsibility for dealing with the first thirteen defendants. (45) Patrick Dean had told the Foreign Office that the British wanted 'a good share of the more prominent' – certainly Ribbentrop and the admirals, and preferably the generals too since they felt they had assembled some damaging evidence for the military case. (46) It was taken for granted that the Americans would deal with Goering and assumed that the Russians would press for Hess since they saw him as the enemy who had tried to ease the attack on the Soviet Union by persuading the British to keep out. Dean noted that Jackson was broadly in agreement with British suggestions about dividing up the list but was worried about allocating defendants to the French and Russians; he feared they would 'make a mess of it'. By May the prosecutors had distributed the remaining defendants. The Foreign Office was pleased with the final British clutch: 'we have the pick of this bunch', noted one official. (47)

Once responsibility for defendants had been distributed the prosecution teams could begin to assemble documentary evidence to use against them. There was plenty left from the prosecution cases and new material had continued to flow to Nuremberg. Requests were sent to governments and military authorities for information on potential witnesses, hoping for clues as to the areas they would cover and incriminating information to destroy the court's confidence in them. Above all, the prosecutors had to prepare the actual cross-examination schemes. The approach to this work reveals the contrasting styles of the Americans and the British – and gives early warning of their failures.

Both teams set about their task using methods similar to those adopted for their prosecution cases. The Americans used the combined efforts of their huge team; everyone threw in ideas and evidence. There was consequently difficulty in evolving a clear line. The British, on the other hand, started with their small team and stripped it down even further: one lawyer was given full responsibility to prepare the cross-examination and to carry it out in court. He occasionally got an assistant, but only as a dogsbody. It was that lawyer's job to chase up and sift evidence and to frame the shape of his cross-examination and the questions he would put. The format for his work was laid down by Maxwell-Fyfe. The major points he wished to establish had to be decided, then questions prepared to lead to them. Each main point had to be backed by a list of documents, which could be used to emphasize a question or counter a defendant's denial. This projected cross-examination was presented to the whole team like a paper at a seminar. Others criticized, pointed out problems and weaknesses, suggested amendments or alternative material. This sort of meeting was an excellent testing ground. All the British members were experienced criminal lawyers and cross-examination was the honed tool of their trade.

Maxwell-Fyfe set a rigorous standard for his work and expected others to match up to it. He had not been one of the noted cross-examiners of the English bar; there were plenty more brilliant. But he compensated for lack of talent by sheer hard work. Even at this stage of his professional life he prepared his work with all the conscientiousness of a young barrister with a career to build up. His homework was thorough: plenty of background reading to provide context, so that he would not stumble on basic history. Where the reading raised problems he called in the historian, John Wheeler-Bennett, to answer them during lunch in his office. He well knew that any psychological advantage over a defendant would be lost if a lawyer could be tripped up over minor points. So he swotted up on tiny details: in court he would always use the exact German title for an official post, employ German terminology or toss in the number of a department or the prevalent abbreviation used in some technical jargon. He was even prepared on one occasion to refer, as if casually, to a film being shown in

Vienna at the time under discussion and to name its star. Any defendant who had hoped to patronize Maxwell-Fyfe as an ignorant foreigner and sidetrack the cross-examination soon gave up.

Jackson, by contrast, lacked recent courtroom experience and failed to realize the need for sheer grind in building up an effective cross-examination. He relied heavily on ideas and information supplied by others. His work was never scrutinized by skilled eyes, its strengths and imperfections only became apparent in court. It is also possible to question whether his preparation was not hampered by too great a confidence in his own case. He seems to have been inadequately prepared for any denial or argument, let alone for the tricks which might be played by an intelligent witness.

Scattered among Jackson's papers in the National Archive in Washington are some loose sheets of paper on which he had planned the cross-examination of Goering and Schacht. (48) They are probably early drafts; they certainly are not the scripts from which he worked in court. Even so the style is near enough to make them revealing as indications of Jackson's weaknesses as a cross-examiner. Much of the success of a cross-examination depends on framing questions in such a way that the defendant is obliged to give the desired answer. Yet Jackson did not, in fact, prepare many actual questions. The notes contain statements: to Goering, for example, he considered saying: 'Before march into Austria, when talked Czechoslovakian ambassador, you knew you were soon to make demands about Sudetenland.' 'Both this and Ribbentrop conversation intended to create assurance known to be false.' 'Did intend to use force if resisted.' These are assertions. They hope to make the points which in a textbook cross-examination would only be deduced later from the answers of a defendant.

Occasionally Jackson had put in brackets the number of a document which could emphasize his point, but even so the very approach left his bald assertions wide open to challenge or outright denial. The same risk is shown in his sheets of preparation for Schacht. He says, for example: 'You have also testified that you were never told about the type and speed of rearmament. This is directly contrary to the statement of General Blomberg.' Maybe, but what was Jackson going to do if Schacht questioned the truth of Blomberg's statement or suggested the General was in no position to judge his knowledge? Even where Jackson did actually draw up questions they are like those in Latin grammar books which assume a standard form of answer; in court there is no logical necessity to give it. He was thinking of asking Goering: 'Just how long was your word of honour for? Good for that manoeuvre only?' It implies that Jackson expects his witness to reel back defeated while he sweeps on in triumph to the next question. Instead it was much more likely that Goering would try to argue the toss – and Jackson had listed no documents to show how often the man gave his word then broke it. What is all too apparent in these notes is that Jackson is trying to establish opinions, not facts. This is dangerous ground

– opinions are debatable and witnesses should never be given the opportunity to argue.

By contrast, notes for the cross-examination prepared for Doenitz (in the event not one of the most remarkable of achievements) shows the care and detail with which such work must be prepared – though unsigned, it is presumably the work of Maxwell-Fyfe who did the cross-examination. Points must be built up step by step and made secure against counterargument. (49) The first point Maxwell-Fyfe wished to establish was that Doenitz had taken part in and was fully aware of the criminal plans of the Nazi government. To do this he is prepared to use at least eighteen questions. They begin blandly, then creep slowly and logically towards more threatening areas, though their final intention is concealed. He was thinking of starting with the incontrovertible: 'As Commander-in-Chief of the Navy you had the equivalent rank of Minister of the Reich and the right to attend meetings of the Reich Cabinet?' It was hardly likely that Doenitz would deny this; should he try to, Maxwell-Fyfe had obtained the decree relating to the status of Supreme Commanders. He would then creep to the fact that Doenitz saw Hitler 119 times in just over two years – again, should this be denied the minutes of the meetings could be submitted and counted. There were then questions to show how many times Doenitz had met Speer, questions on how often he saw Jodl and Keitel – records of all these encounters were available. Only at this stage would something of the thrust become apparent – surely at these meetings general strategy must have been discussed. If Doenitz admitted the point, all well and good; if not, Maxwell-Fyfe was equipped with Doenitz's own interrogation admitting that when at Hitler's headquarters 'I listened in to all those military conversations of the generals.' Only after going through the same cautious, detailed procedure over meetings with other ministers and officials would Maxwell-Fyfe reach the point he was trying to establish: 'Although you were present at all these meetings with all these ministers over two years, do you say you were ignorant of . . .' then a list of charges against Doenitz: his involvement in the slave labour policy, the use of concentration camp labour, the planning and waging of aggressive war. With luck Doenitz would admit the point. If he did not, the rest of the cross-examination was constructed to deal with each of these charges in turn, showing the exact responsibility of Doenitz in each. Every section was as carefully drawn up and as thoroughly documented as the first.

The style, the method, the logic of this plan are typical of standard crossexamination. So too is the thoroughness with which evidence was provided at each stage, to be kept in reserve if not needed. Ideally the lawyer in a cross-examination should drive it through at the speed he dictates, not allowing the witness breathing space or a chance to draw red herrings across his line of questioning. If unforeseen denials or tricks are suddenly produced he must bring the witness back into line as quickly as possible. Some can manage this *ex tempore*. Maxwell-Fyfe made meticulous preparations for all eventualities. Wheeler-Bennett watched him preparing a cross-examination not just with questions which were virtually certain to elicit an inevitable response but with diagrams indicating questions which would tackle alternative replies and lead the witness back to the central issue by as short a route as possible. (50) The immense difference which care and effort could make to a case and to the morale of those presenting it was first seen in the cross-examination of the first defendant at Nuremberg – Goering.

References for Chapter Eleven

1 Tribunal minutes, 18 February
2 IMT Vol. VII
3 Minutes of chief prosecutors' meeting. BWCE N/9
4 Conversation with Dr Seidl
5 Papen Memoirs
6 Tribunal minutes
7 Conversation with Donald Spencer and Dr Merkel
8 Dr Seidl
9 Ribbentrop: Memoirs
10 Werner Maser *Nuremberg: A Nation on Trial*
11 IMT Vol. VII, 18 February
12 Papen
13 Tribunal minutes, 10 April
14 FO 371. 57537
15 IMT Vol. VIII, 23 February
16 Papen
17 Schacht *My First 76 Years*
18 FO 371. 57546
19 Conversation with Dr Kempner
20 Maser
21 Tribunal minutes, 15 December
22 BWCE N/30
23 FO 371. 57539
24 BWCE N/30
25 For example FO 371. 57541
26 FO 371. 57544
27 Biddle Notes on Evidence Vols. II and III. Box III
28 Conversation with John Phipps
29 Biddle op. cit.
30 Facts from a conversation with the former Emma Schwabenland
31 Conversation with Robert Kempner
32 Telford Taylor
33 Bradley Smith
34 Conversation with Dan Margolies
35 Conversation with Dr Kempner: also recorded by Gilbert
36 Minutes of chief prosecutors' meeting, 30 October
37 British prosecutors' meeting minutes, 18 December
38 British prosecutors' meeting minutes, 16 November
39 Chief prosecutors' meeting minutes, 30 October

40 FO 371. 57545
41 Background information taken from two books by T.K. Derry: *A Short History of Norway* and *A History of Modern Norway – 1814–1972*
42 FO 371. 57543
43 FO 371. 57544
44 FO 371. 57543
45 British prosecution minutes, 11 December
46 BWCE N/30
47 FO 371. 57547
48 Jackson Papers, Box 195
49 Kindly lent to the authors by Kenneth Duke
50 Wheeler-Bennett

Chapter Twelve

The Goering case was vital to the prosecution; it was almost a microcosm of their entire indictment. The man himself had for most of the Third Reich held power in Germany second only to that of Hitler. He had played a significant part in extending the Party's grip on the nation and in the terrorism which had quelled opposition to it – the Roehm Purge, the Reichstag Fire, 'Kristallnacht', and so on. His mind had been employed in nearly every field. Goering had built up the Luftwaffe in contravention of the Versailles Treaty and sent it into action in every area attacked by Germany. He had played his part in all military planning, been present at all the conferences which the prosecution alleged proved Nazi aggressive intent. He had been involved in economic planning too. His work with the Central Planning Board, the Four Year Plan and with the policies for exploiting the Eastern Occupied Terrorities had been crucial to Germany's preparations for war and for the administration and spoliation of the areas conquered. He had still found time for diplomatic activity as well, supervizing the Anschluss and prostituting his charm to give assurances to the Czechs and others that they would never be attacked. If the conspiracy count was to be proved, then Goering's part in it had to be established beyond any reasonable doubt. If he was not a conspirator, no one was.

Goering was accused of playing a major role in all the other three counts as well. Massive evidence had been presented on his contribution to the waging of wars. The illegality and viciousness of their conduct were also attributed partly to his policies and influence. He had to answer general charges on his encouragement of war crimes such as the lynching or execution of captured airmen, and more personal charges concerning the atrocities committed by the Hermann Goering Division and the murder of the fifty British airmen who had escaped from Stalag Luft III in Sagan. There was evidence that Luftwaffe factories had been increasingly dependent on the use of prisoners-of-war to manufacture planes and weapons. Goering's activities too had allegedly covered a wide range of crimes against humanity. Though he had passed his responsibility to Himmler, it had been Goering who had invented and developed the Gestapo and concentration camps while he was Prussian Minister of the Interior. His administration of the Four Year Plan had countenanced the use of slave labour. His personal looting had been on a scale more than adequate to justify charges of criminality. But he had not been content with stealing paintings for his own collection at Karinhall. Goering as much as anyone was alleged to have stripped Europe of its artistic inheritance, its food, its industrial resources and its people for the sake of the Nazi Reich.

In the view of the prosecution, Goering's cynicism, the brutality which lay just below his genial skin, his avarice, all had characterized Nazi policies. To expose the nature of the man and to expound his crimes in court would be to vilify the entire Nazi regime. To fail would be inexcusable; the evidence was monumental. But the Goering case was equally vital to the defence. Any breach they could make in the prosecution charges could be used by future defendants; any blemish which would be found in prosecution evidence might shake confidence in the whole. Any success in the Goering case would serve to show other defendants that there was still hope. Many of them needed borrowed courage, so did their former colleagues and followers outside Nuremberg. Goering had plenty of courage to spare. He had prepared a defence not just for himself but for others in the dock and for the whole history of Nazism. His case might well be a turning point in the trial and in much more besides.

The importance of the Goering episode in the drama of the Nuremberg trial was apparent to many outside observers as well as to the participants. The day the defence case began – Friday, 8 March – the courtroom was crowded for the first time in many weeks. There was a mood of keen anticipation. Something of the theatrical atmosphere of the opening of the trial was revived as visitors crowded into their gallery and cameras flashed in the well of the court. (1) There was a revival of anxiety too. The military authorities had set up new sandbagged gun positions in the corridors and round the building. They feared an attack to rescue Goering. (2) Goering himself was clearly aware of his crucial role, but for once he showed no sign of relishing the centre of the stage (he always seems to have had stage fright before a major appearance). Before the session began he sat hunched in the dock, looking 'the picture of misery' and clutching a grey Army blanket round his knees. His customary red, polka-dotted scarf, usually so jaunty, today seemed only to emphasize his pallor. (3) He fidgeted uneasily. As his counsel, Dr Stahmer, made a few introductory remarks, claiming that the Versailles Treaty had ceased to be binding since others had failed to disarm, and encountered the wrath of the Bench by trying to introduce two speeches and a book already ruled irrelevant, Goering tried to write some notes. But his hands were trembling so violently that he gave up the attempt and folded his arms to trap the hands which betrayed him. (4) The former Reichsmarschall recovered some of his self-control and bravado as his witnesses appeared on the stand. He beamed to encourage them; nodded or frowned to prompt them. Their eyes slid constantly to him and they were coaxed through their testimony more by the actor-manager than by Stahmer. (5)

Even under Goering's skilled guidance, however, his witnesses played their parts badly. Bodenschatz, the liaison officer between the Luftwaffe and Hitler's headquarters until he was wounded in the July Bomb Plot, was seen by several journalists to be sweating heavily. He literally read his lines – and the Tribunal overruled Jackson's protest and allowed him to continue to use his prepared script. He plodded through the encomium he had been given. Goering knew nothing of the plans for 'Kristallnacht' on the night of 9-10 November, said Bodenschatz; he knew nothing of the conditions in the concentration camps or the extermination of the Jews – such things were never discussed at headquarters. Goering, he went on, had rearmed only to give Germany parity with other nations; had drawn up the Four Year Plan to secure vital raw materials which others sought to cut off; had worked for peace and opposed the attack on Russia. As if his version were not implausible enough, Bodenschatz summed up Goering as 'a benefactor to all in need'. (6)

The hollowness of his testimony was soon revealed by Jackson's cross-examination. Bodenschatz admitted knowing that a meeting he had quoted had taken place because 'Dr Stahmer told me so' – and spectators burst out laughing. (7) He was led into recalling Goering's promise to protect Germany from air attack – and Goering was furious that his failure had been publicized. 'He gnashed his teeth and his eyes blazed with fury,' a reporter noticed. (8) By lunchtime some of the defendants, Jodl and Schacht especially, were expressing malicious satisfaction at the sight of Goering's discomfiture, but others became insecure as they realized the damage a cross-examination could inflict. Goering, though, was not going to admit to anxiety: 'Wait till he (Jackson) starts on me – he won't have any nervous Bodenschatz to deal with.' (9)

In the afternoon the testimony of Field Marshal Milch was even more of a failure. He expanded several points made by Bodenschatz about the Luftwaffe and Goering's wish for peace, and added some new ones of his own about 'terror fliers' always being treated as 'comrades' and Dachau being a clean, well-run place, providing excellent food for those staying there. Under cross-examination, the extent of his lying became all too apparent and Milch was too lumbering to avoid the numerous pitfalls dug for him. He denied to Jackson that the Central Planning Board dealt with labour problems, and then had to listen to readings from its minutes where Speer suggested that slackers should be sent to concentration camps. He denied that the Board used prisoners-of-war, then suffered quotations from his own complaints at a meeting that the prisoners they were sent were all too often unfit for work. Confronted with his own words – that it was 'amusing' to think of prisoners-of-war manning anti-aircraft guns – Milch could only mumble that the minutes must be inaccurate, that the Board would never have released such prisoners from industrial work, although minutes before he had denied that they were ever employed. Presented with evidence to show that the Luftwaffe used concentration camp labour in its factories, he could not deny it – only deny that he knew about it. Having asserted that he believed all foreign workers were volunteers, he could not deny he was present when Sauckel had boasted that of the four million of them in Germany, only 200,000 had come voluntarily; he merely said he could not remember this meeting.

The excuses got even feebler as 'Khaki' Roberts ran rings round him. Milch 'knew nothing' about plans for aggression, though he had been at the 23 May 1939 conference on Poland. Whatever planning for invasion was mentioned by Roberts, Milch always claimed to have been on leave at the time. When shown his correspondence with Himmler about the experiments performed for the Luftwaffe on prisoners in concentration camps to test theories on high altitude flying and the effects of exposure, he could only insist he had forgotten Himmler's missives and signed his own without reading them. The *New York Times* reported that Milch left the box 'a confused and wilted witness who had contributed as much to the prosecution case as he had tried to detract from it.'* (10)

The same could have been said of Goering's subsequent witnesses. Brauchitsch, Goering's old adjutant, tried to maintain that no one knew anything about any unpleasant matter – except the orders to lynch enemy airmen, and these were 'ignored'. Korner, once State Secretary in the Prussian Ministry, also pressed the line that everyone had seen, heard and spoken no evil, even arguing that since Germany had built up agricultural production in countries she occupied, she had a right to take a little of 'the surplus'. As Dean said in a cable to the Foreign Office that evening, both Korner and Brauchitsch had 'made a very bad impression' and were too obviously lying. (11)

For a brief moment Field Marshal Kesselring made a slightly better impression. He was helped by looking 'trim and confident' in his Luftwaffe uniform, and his answers to Stahmer and other defence counsel were refreshingly direct and assured. (12) Jackson's cross-examination made little headway against his authoritative manner. It was only when Maxwell-Fyfe took over that it became clear that Kesselring was, in Dean's words, 'a decent man according to his own standards' but that 'his standards were those of a murderer and a liar whenever any German military advantage could be gained.' (13) Maxwell-Fyfe confronted him with evidence of the bombing of Rotterdam after negotiations for surrender had begun, of the brutal treatment of hostages and partisans, of the involvement of the Luftwaffe in plans for attacks on Poland and Russia. Kesselring collapsed. *The Times* reported the short but devastating assault by Maxwell-Fyfe as being 'as masterly a piece of cross-examination as the court has heard'. (14)** He was to be equally effective with Goering's last witness.

Birger Dahlerus was a Swedish businessman who had known Goering's first wife and had used the contact to arrange a meeting between Goering and seven British industrialists in July 1939 at his own wife's house in

*In 1947 Milch was sentenced to life imprisonment as a war criminal by a Military Tribunal at Nuremberg. In 1951 his sentence was commuted to fifteen years. He was in fact released in 1954, and died in 1972.

**Kesselring was sentenced to death by a British military court in Venice for ordering the execution of Italian hostages. His sentence was commuted to life imprisonment, but he was released in 1952 because of ill-health. He died in 1960.

Schleswig-Holstein. Dahlerus hoped to persuade the Nazis that the British would tolerate no more aggression by Germany. He had followed up the meeting with conversations with Lord Halifax and several British officials, approaches to Ribbentrop and Goering, and even a meeting with Hitler himself. In the autumn of that year he had written a book about his efforts, *The Last Attempt*. Goering had read it in his cell at Nuremberg and had been keen to call Dahlerus as a witness to his peaceful intentions. Dahlerus had been most reluctant to appear for the defence – but in the end proved a most valuable prosecution witness. As Maxwell-Fyfe guided him through the events of this period Dahlerus was patently appalled to realize that while he thought he was engaging the Nazi leaders in negotiation, they were already fixing the date to invade Poland and using him to conceal their aims. Even more embarrassing for the defence, it became clear that Goering must have read Dahlerus's book very cursorily and that Stahmer cannot have read it at all. Extracts read by Maxwell-Fyfe described Goering's 'obsequious humility' as Hitler ranted and screamed about 'planes, planes ... tanks, tanks', and 'exterminating the enemy'. They described how by 1 September Goering was 'in some crazy state of intoxication'; how he demanded huge chunks of the Polish Corridor, then called his demand 'a magnanimous offer'. The book not only damaged Goering; it recorded that Dahlerus had been warned by Goering that Ribbentrop would try to sabotage his plane and added the impression that the Foreign Minister had done everything in his power to prevent the success of the negotiations. As the cross-examination continued, Goering fumed, and pulled at the cord on his headphones until a guard took it out of his hands before it was ripped off. That evening Ribbentrop whimpered to Kaltenbrunner: 'I don't know who to trust now.' (15)

Though defendants had been shaken, testimony cut to pieces, and the case against Goering considerably hardened, the prosecutors had little reason for self-congratulation. With witnesses of such low calibre, their task was all too easy. Even so, though the British had shown competence of a kind taken for granted in a minor trial at home, Rudenko and Jackson had shown a worrying lack of skill; what little success they had achieved had resulted not from their own talents but from the ineptitude of the witnesses. Jackson had taken the main responsibility for the cross-examinations and had already shown some of the weaknesses which were soon to prove fatal. He was long-winded, leaving time for his points to be spotted and replies to be framed. On some occasions it was not always clear what point he was trying to establish or whether it really mattered – as the *New York Times* was quick to notice. (16) He was not always in control of his material and more than once had muddled documents or been caught out on small details. Many defence counsel on the other hand had taken full advantage to examine witnesses in the interests of their own clients and had made a relatively good job of it. Furthermore the testimony they had extracted had not been challenged as prosecution counsel concentrated on the Goering case.

The prosecutors do not seem to have been troubled, though. Perhaps they could dismiss their poor performances as dress rehearsal failures. What did cause them anxiety was the time being taken by the Goering case. Stahmer had encouraged his witnesses to make long statements, the number of questions from other defence counsel had dragged out the testimony even further, the prosecution cross-examinations had been unduly prolonged. All four teams had cross-examined Milch, an experience which brought home to them that they were taking far too long. They met the following morning to discuss ways of shortening the proceedings. The British successfully argued that future cross-examinations be conducted by one prosecutor only, with short supplementary questions from others solely when national concerns were involved. (17) They were not yet prepared to make official complaints about the time being taken by the defence, though it was already causing irritation. It had been noted with some alarm that though there had been a few tart comments from the bench, the judges had on the whole left the proceedings to run uninterrupted. The defence was being given ample leeway – the prosecutors thought too much.

The judges had, however, intervened on one crucial point: they had ruled against defence questions on violations of international law by the Allies. Laternser had tried to introduce *tu quoque* evidence in his examination of Kesselring; Rudenko and Jackson had been quick to protest and argue that violation by one side never excuses violation by the other. Stahmer had pleaded the need to examine matters which 'may contribute to a more lenient judgement of German behaviour' – in other words the hope of establishing mitigating circumstances only, but he had not convinced the judges. Beaumont at the Foreign Office expressed some anxiety that the judges' ruling might be seen in the future as wrong, unfair. He was aware however that it would speed up the trial and prevent it bogging down in ding-dong battles over particular incidents – the Tribunal, after all, was concerned not with individual acts but with the allegation of a deliberate Nazi policy of atrocity. (18) Though the ruling had been expected by the prosecutors, it was useful to have it on the record at this early stage. With this comfort and with teeth sharpened on witnesses, they felt ready to deal with Goering himself.

Goering went into the witness box on the afternoon of Wednesday, 13 March. For a moment he looked nervous; his face was very flushed and his hand shook when he raised it to take the oath. (19) 'We stirred with expectation,' *The Times* correspondent Bob Cooper remembered, 'when Goering left his corner seat in the dock and walked boldly to the witness box, his baggy trousers falling over high jackboots, a thick sheaf of papers under his arm. Not the Goering of pomp and power, but still a considerable figure.' (20) He was not the Goering of the newspaper cartoons and the Allied propaganda either. It had been all too tempting in recent years to believe that Goering was little more than the 'hail-fellow-well-met' old air ace, now run to seed. He had been caricatured as 'Fatty Hermann', dismissed as merely the smiling face of Nazism. He had been grossly underestimated. He was a man of great intelligence, nimble wit, wide grasp and immense energy. The Reich had employed all too many third-rate incompetent time-servers – Goering had shone by comparison. Even in 1946, after amassing the horrific evidence against the man, it was still dangerously possible to assume that he was now nothing more than the self-indulgent, pleasure-seeking, drug-impregnated bag of lard with whom Hitler had lost patience and who had sat in Karinhall for two years painting his face and changing his jewellery.

In fact, captivity had transformed the man. His trousers were baggy because prison food and some exercise had made him fitter than he had been for years. Weaning him from drugs had restored the clarity of his intellect and memory; his mind was fitter than ever. His courage was as great as it had ever been. He was not trammelled by false optimism or distracted by an urge to scrabble for loopholes of extenuation. 'Goering is certain he is going to be hanged,' said Werner Bross, one of his assistant counsel. 'But he says he will die like a man.' (21) Goering's vanity, which had handicapped his career, was now transformed into a possible strength. He was resolved to pass into history as the hero who had remained true to his cause and given his powers and his life to defend it. He had decided to print his self-image on the future, to rally his faltering colleagues and reassure his nation, degraded by defeat and wounded by calumny. Bross was known as an opponent of Nazism, yet there were tears in his eyes, thought his interviewer, when he spoke of Goering. 'After all, Goering is a fellow German and even if he has done wrong, one cannot help feeling proud that he is living up to the best German traditions of courage and loyalty.'

Once Goering settled in the witness box his stage fright went and he seemed almost relaxed. The official films show him quite still for the most part, reserving gestures with his right arm to colour key passages in his statement. Only before the start of each session can he be seen taking deep breaths, rubbing his hands and licking his lips. His voice was full and confident, projected without effort. There is a noticeable lack of theatricality in his testimony: the underplaying perhaps of a good actor. Throughout his examination he directed few glances at the Tribunal; he addressed most of his answers to his lawyer. Only occasionally did he look round the room to check the response and to involve his audience. He carried his thick wad of notes, but needed no more than a quick reference to prompt his next passage or refresh his memory on details. He was proud of this: 'It is all from memory. You would be surprised how few cue words I have jotted down to guide me.' (22)

Fluent and assured, with only rare feeds from Stahmer, Goering delivered a carefully prepared statement for the whole afternoon – then the next day, and the next. The tone was one of candour – it might alternatively be called a shameless confession of facts and attitudes that most men would have worked hard to deny. He not only acknowledged his position in the Nazi party, the Luftwaffe, the Four Year Plan, the Cabinet, in Hitler's inner coterie, he positively boasted of the authority he had wielded and the influence he had exerted. He was proud of the role he had played in destroying opposition to Nazism: what he called crushing 'so-called freedoms; obstacles to progress'. He was proud of his role in foreign affairs, helping 'to fulfill an old, old longing of the German people . . . (to) become a unified Reich'; acquiring living space to establish 'the proper relationship between a population and its nourishment, its growth and its standard of living'. He cheerfully admitted that he had organized black markets in occupied countries: 'a black market is inevitable in times of scarcity, it is again flourishing in Germany today.' He had no qualms about discussing many of his policies towards the Jews: their influence, he said, had been out of all proportion to their numbers; it was National Socialist policy that 'Germany should be led by Germans'. The Nuremberg laws were 'to bring about a clear separation of the races'.

Throughout his testimony Goering savoured the opportunity to make jibes at his adversaries. Hitler had become Head of State, Government and the Armed Forces, he explained, 'following the example of the United States'. He was accused of using Russian resources for German ends. Well, he replied, that was 'just as natural, just as much a matter of duty for us as it was for Russia when she occupied German territories, but with this difference: that we did not dismantle and transport away the entire Russian economy down to the last bolt and screw as is being done here' (an arguable point but one which hit a sitting Russian target). Germany was criticized for seeking living space. Perhaps the situation is different for the Four Powers, he sneered, who 'call more than three-quarters of the world their own'. He was being charged with war crimes, crimes against humanity. Was it not Churchill, he inquired pointedly, who had said 'in the struggle for life and death there is in the end no legality'?

But the main theme of his speech was complete acceptance of his own personal responsibility. Goebbels or Hitler might be blamed for the outrages of 'Kristallnacht' but as for the subsequent fines and economic laws against the Jews, 'I issued them and consequently am responsible and do not propose to hide in any way behind the Führer's orders.' Then: 'I was responsible for the rearmament, the training and the morale of the Luft-waffe.' As for the negotiations and trickery which led to the Anschluss: 'Not so much the Führer as I personally bear the full and entire responsib-ility for everything that happened.' There was no hesitation in admitting to the measures for stripping the Russian economy: 'I naturally take com-plete responsibility for them.'

Where appropriate Goering could reconcile his own responsibility with his praise for the *Führerprinzip* – the 'Leadership Principle' – according to which power and policy flowed from Hitler. He made no attempt, as others had done and would continue to do, to suggest that the *Führerprinzip* removed from individuals their own obligations. Nor did he accept the prosecution accusation that it had constituted a tyranny. 'I upheld this principle and I still uphold it positively and consciously'; it had always existed in Germany, was especially necessary when a country was at low ebb or in danger. In upholding it, Goering was proffering an umbrella to his colleagues in the dock: the Reich Cabinet did not meet after 1937 because 'the Führer did not think much of Cabinet meetings'; the Führer quite properly never asked for the opinions or approval of his generals – it was up to the leader to make the fundamental decisions. He himself avoided using the shelter set up for him by Bodenschatz: the idea that his worsening relationship with Hitler had cut him off from policy making. He was too vain about his influence with the Führer to avail himself of that defence. He preferred to stress how often he had been consulted – the one significant exception being over the Stalag Luft III affair.

For all his skill, staunchness to old values and sheer brass neck, Goering was not prepared to grasp some of the nettles standing in his path. He dodged quickly round matters like the Roehm Purge, the burning of Reichstag and other cases of terrorism; he dismissed them as rare examples of other people getting out of hand. He would only talk of concentration camps being established for 'protective custody' and 'a political act for the defence of the Reich'; he fell back on the usual claim that after Himmler took control in 1934 no one knew what happened in them. He denied point blank that free workers were enslaved or that the Four Year Plan had an aggressive purpose. He stretched credibility to the very limit in arguing that Yugoslavia was mobilizing before she was attacked, that only military targets were bombed in Poland, that all bombing in Holland was intended to end the campaign as quickly as possible so as to save lives. Goering asserted that Leningrad was the only Russian city to suffer starvation and that was because of the siege, that Russian agriculture and industry were built up not destroyed, that prisoners in underground Luftwaffe factories were happier than in their camps – 'given what is known now' – and that all prisoners-of-war engaged in anti-aircraft operations were volunteers, mainly Russian, he said. He was adamant in denial of knowledge of Sagan, of any order to lynch Allied 'terror fliers'. Almost pathetically he kept coming back to the allegations about his looting – a taint on the heroic character he was trying to create. He described all art treasures as having been 'rescued' from destruction or 'deserted' by their owners. Perhaps, he conceded, 'my collector's passion got the better of me' when some French paintings were taken to North Germany. But 'I meant to pay for those objects which I wanted to have' – even to give the money raised by the sale of the others to families of French war victims. But alas, that kindly intention had been frustrated by the Party Treasurer.

After completing his statement, Goering was examined by nearly all the defence counsel in turn. He rose to the occasion with seigneurial generosity and genuine cleverness. Everyone was afforded some protection; everyone was presented with a suitable line of defence to develop, in some instances better than anything they were to manage later for themselves. Even so, to be defended by Goering was not a source of unalloyed satisfaction. His favourite means of parrying charges against his fellow defendants was to employ disparagement. Keitel, he said, could make few decisions of his own; he 'came between the millstones of stronger personalities'. The General Staff had little influence on military planning; they always showed such a 'very reticent and timid attitude'. Ribbentrop and Rosenberg were too little respected to be given any say in foreign policy. Schirach and Seyss-Inquart were not dependable enough to be given much rein in their own spheres. Jodl's diary might say Germany was looking for an excuse to invade Norway but that was just a typical example of his ignorance and poor judgement. In stressing the insignificance of the others, Goering was exalting his own position: he, not Papen, had negotiated the formation of the Nazi government in 1933; he, not Funk or Schacht, had been responsible for most economic decisions. No one had been privy to the Führer's plans in foreign policy – but Goering alone had sometimes been admitted to the private realm. In this and other matters 'at best only the Führer and I could have conspired'.

Goering's performance so far had made a tremendous impression. Dean praised his 'mastery of facts and persuasive manner'. (23) Several newspapers commented on the sustained note of sweet reasonableness by which he had secured the Tribunal's non-intervention. They noted his subtlety and mental agility, and expressed grudging admiration for his magnanimity to the other defendants in fighting their cause. These colleagues had certainly viewed much of the statement with delight. On the first evening they had greeted his return to their box 'like fellow schoolboys greeting a classmate leaving the examination room'. (24) After the examination in chief, 'the handshaking and plaudits, the bright eyes and smiles of his comrades in the dock, happier than they have been for months, are proof that he is winning them over to his last ditch stand of the Nazi regime in history'. (25) The praise had certainly continued below stairs. Speer said he had found the examination in chief 'gripping'; even Doenitz was impressed by Goering's control and commented that 'Biddle is really paying attention. You can see that he really wants to hear the other side of the story.' Frank had been delighted (and no doubt relieved) by the way Goering was prepared to take responsibility for so much; he only wished he had always behaved so well. So did Neurath. Schirach was so swept away by his hero's performance he believed it would be madness now to convict him because 'he is so popular, even in America – and you can see now why he was so popular'. (26)

But where there was public praise it was for the style of Goering's statement and not for its content. In spite of all his care in preparation and the brilliance of his performance, Goering had failed to convince. It was acknowledged he had eased the defence for some of the others, but it was not felt he had succeeded in absolving the Nazi regime in any way. The general judgement was summed up in Dean's words: 'His story amounted almost to a plea of guilty' – personal and national too, he might have added. (27) The case for National Socialism might have been put forcibly, but it had been made with too blatant a demonstration of the callousness and disregard for restraints and decencies on which that regime had rested. And where he could not brazen or slither, Goering had too often relied on lies – lies which laid him open to prosecution attack and which could impugn the rest of his testimony.

He had given twelve hours of evidence, a remarkable physical and mental achievement if nothing else. He had spoken with hardly an interruption from the Bench, delivering what was as much a plea to posterity as a defence – and he had been allowed to get away with it. Birkett was horrified by the Bench's tolerance of this approach: 'If this procedure is followed in the case of all the defendants, and long detailed statements are made covering important and unimportant points alike, then the time taken will be so great that the trial will be written down as a failure. It will have done much to restore German faith in their leaders, and the verdicts against the leaders will be regarded by the German people as excessively unjust.' (28) But at least a performance of this length had given the prosecutors ample time to get the measure of the man, and to sense something of his formidable powers. Any good impression Goering had made in his examination in chief must now be wiped out by the cross-examination and it was essential to pull him away from his broad generalizations and towards those specific charges on which the prosecution case was founded.

This was the challenge faced by Robert Jackson when he opened the cross-examination on 18 March. Goering, who had been clearly exhausted when he left the stand on Friday, had had a weekend to recuperate. He was in fighting trim. As Jackson's sturdy, pugnacious figure crossed to the microphone, Goering cast a glance of reassurance at the defendants' box, then sat forward, a hand on each knee. He was hunched, alert, expectant. His eyes stayed fixed on Jackson's face like a swordsman looking for warning of the thrusts that would come. (29)

Jackson began slack and slow on his feet. He dragged through the early history of Nazism, the policies with which the Party had gained control over Germany, the incidents with which he no doubt hoped to illustrate its criminality. *The Times* correspondent and others were amazed that he should spend so much time on such side issues: it seemed a clear tactical mistake to allow Goering to warm up before introducing the more vital charges on which the main case was based. But then Jackson had always seen the entire prosecution case teleologically – the final crimes being implicit in the very origins of the regime. Whether the issues were well-chosen or not, Jackson did not use them effectively. He skipped from one topic to another, using little or no documentary evidence to support the allegations he was making. His questions were general and imprecise. Goering seized them, condescendingly divided them into more specific sections, then dealt with each at great length. He was parrying Jackson with ease and taking an opportunity to repeat all the justifications, all the boasts he had made in his examination in chief. Jackson became increasingly irritated as Goering avoided direct answers. The official film shows him jabbing his pen into the rostrum or turning it over and over in mounting agitation as Goering's rhetoric gained force. He played into Goering's hands with questions on the Roehm Purge and the burning of the Reichstag. Strong suspicions there might be, but Jackson had no conclusive evidence to prove Goering's connection with either incident. Goering could flick away with ease affidavits from three SA men that he had provided materials for the Reichstag Fire; he then had the confidence to add that he had no regrets about its destruction 'from the artistic point of view'; he only lamented having to replace the building with 'My Kroll Opera House ... the opera seemed to me much more important than the Reichstag.' Jackson did not even use the documentary evidence which undoubtedly existed on Goering's aggressive intentions towards Austria and Czechoslokavia; he left him to counter the accusations with contentious statements about policies in these areas having followed the principle of self-determination established by the Versailles Treaty. When at last Jackson began to introduce evidence, Goering threw it back at him, pointing out, for example, that the minutes of a meeting where Jackson alleged he began the process of rearmament in 1933 merely said that the policy had been 'discussed' not 'begun'. By the time the session finished, it was all too clear who had won the bout. 'Well,' said an American reporter, 'I guess Jackson has been saved by the gong'. (30)

Goering's performance had impressed Birkett. He wrote: 'He reveals himself as a very able man who perceives the intent of every question almost as soon as it is uttered. He has considerable knowledge, and has an advantage over the prosecution in this respect, for he is always on familiar ground ... he has therefore quite maintained his ground, and the prosecution has not really advanced its case at all. Certainly there has been no dramatic destruction of Goering as had been anticipated.' (31) Several newspapers too noted that Jackson had failed to extract a single admission which had not already been made in direct evidence and had not even drawn attention to the guilt they exposed. (32) Dean had checked on the professionals' judgement of Jackson's performance. Among the lawyers it had been 'severely criticised'; he reported their complaints that Jackson had failed to reveal Goering's frequent lies and had not used the good material which everyone knew was available. (33)

It was bad enough to have mis-handled the first day of cross-examination in such a vital part of the case. It was more serious that the experience had enabled Goering to return to the dock 'in a state of obvious self-satisfaction' (34) and that the other defendants and their counsel seemed to have a glint of triumph in their eyes. (35) It was, however, a greater, irreparable disaster that his first day of cross-examination had shattered Robert Jackson. He would never recover.

It was not realization of professional inadequacy which caused his disintegration; it was his reaction to the way the Tribunal had conducted the day's proceedings. They had let Goering rip; they had left him to make prolonged speeches without rebuke; they had allowed him to treat Jackson's questions in any way he chose. Jackson expected 'yes' and 'no' answers, and expected the Tribunal to insist on them. When he made an angry appeal to the judges for limits to be imposed on his witness, they replied they wished to hear what Goering had to say. Given such overt encouragement Goering had become even more long-winded, yet more insolent – he even had the effrontery to criticize Jackson's questions as too broad and inconclusive. Still the Tribunal had issued no rebuke. Given Jackson's history of resentment of Tribunal rulings against him, he was in no mood to endure what he could only see as new vindictiveness, threatening virtual destruction of the most important part of his case. He must have blamed the humiliation of the day not on his own shortcomings but on the conditions the judges had created for him to work in.

Consequently, when Jackson resumed the cross-examination next day he was hardly in the frame of mind needed to get a grip on Goering; at least, that is the only charitable explanation for the intellectual mess that followed. Surely no man capable of dispassionately judging his previous day's work would have seemed so inadequately prepared and so out of control of his material. Yet a wonderful opportunity awaited him. Dahlerus had opened the day, and by mid-morning Maxwell-Fyfe had turned him into a prosecution witness. But even with Goering softened up by Dahlerus's revelations, Jackson could do nothing. Yet again he chose to make a major issue of a minor point – and adopted a weak position which he himself then undermined. He challenged Goering's claim never to have taken part in a meeting of the Council for the Defence of the Reich by using a document purporting to show that he had chaired such a meeting. By the time defence counsel had grumbled about not being given advance copies of the minutes, Goering had had ample time to read them (which seemingly Jackson had not). He immediately drew attention to the fact that the document described a group much bigger than the Council and that it actually stated that the Council never met. Jackson then embarrassed himself still further by producing a document intended to demonstrate the damaging charge that in 1935 Goering was planning 'the liberation of the Rhineland'. One glance and Goering knew he had Jackson on the ropes. No, he said, the document was talking about the 'cleaning of the Rhine' – removing obstacles in the river, such as tugs, which might impede navigation in case of a sudden mobilization. He was right. Jackson complained bitterly that evening to Colonel Dostert that he had been given a wrong translation. Dostert leapt to the defence of his staff: he called the use of 'liberation' for 'cleaning' an easy but unimportant slip. (36) And indeed the bigger slip was surely Jackson's – he had read 'Rhineland' for 'Rhine', or someone on his staff had. He was winded by Goering's quick counter, stammered for a moment, then snapped that at least the document showed planning 'which had to be kept entirely secret from foreign powers'.

Secret planning is never in itself a crime – and Goering was delighted to point it out: 'I do not think I can recall reading beforehand the publication of the mobilization preparations of the United States.' Jackson could stand no more. 'This witness is not being responsive ... It is perfectly futile to spend our time if we cannot have responsive answers to our questions ... the witness is adopting an attitude to the Tribunal which is giving him the trial which he never gave to a living soul, nor dead ones either.' As he lapsed into incoherence, Lawrence came to his rescue. 'Perhaps we had better adjourn now at this state'; 'state' was a verbal slip, but an accurate description of what Jackson was in. He had been saved by the gong again. But he finished this second round of the bout infinitely weaker and more severely mauled than by the first. Goering, however, left the witness box jubilant after an afternoon of delight in playing to the gallery.

Again, the Tribunal had not intervened to protect Jackson or to discipline Goering. Some observers thought the judges must now act to preserve some dignity for Jackson and to assert its control over the proceedings. Maxwell-Fyfe went privately to Birkett to warn that Jackson was 'in a terrific state'. (37) Birkett was only too anxious to restore to the trial the conduct he considered proper and efficient. He drafted a notice to be read from the bench next morning stating that the trial was 'in danger of becoming unduly and unnecessarily prolonged because of the non-observance of the rules of giving evidence and the Tribunal gives clear and firm notice that no irrelevancy in the answering of questions will be tolerated'. (38) But his suggested course of action was not followed. Biddle and Parker opposed the idea and Lawrence drifted to their view. Birkett was convinced that the American judges were unwilling to intervene 'for reasons personal to Jackson'; (39) Biddle only noted that they decided 'it wiser not'. (40)

So Jackson had to face a third day without the procedural framework which he so strongly felt the Tribunal should have constructed. He began it angrily with what Biddle criticized as 'a silly speech', (41) condemning Goering's snide remarks and propaganda, the way 'the control of these proceedings is being put in the hands of the defendant', the degeneration of the trial into what he described as a 'bickering contest'. What he was trying to say was not silly. It would have been possible to argue cogently the need to prevent propaganda, to ensure expedition, to apply standard rules for giving evidence. But Jackson was too angry to be cogent, and his continuing resentment at Goering's parting shot at America obscured his more appropriate points. As a result Lawrence took no notice of the underlying principles and kept trying to pacify Jackson with suggestions that '... surely it would be wiser to ignore' the defendant's asides. The best Jackson could get was Lawrence's statement that defendants must answer 'yes' or 'no' whenever possible and might only add brief explanations when necessary, not speeches. It was not a very firm statement, and 'brief explanations' did not make limits clear.

Jackson was therefore not soothed by the time he resumed his cross-examination. With incredible clumsiness he came back to a matter which had been so irrelevant and mishandled the previous day – the Reich Defence Council. Not only was he flogging a dead horse, he was doing it with a rashly untested implement; a new document of which he could only say 'I do not know what it says, except that it is the minutes of a meeting.' Goering knew right away: it stated that he was not present at the meeting, only represented by the two State Secretaries. Having won that point so quickly, Goering could now adopt a new and disarming tactic, that of bland co-operation: agreeing with all Jackson's points about excluding Jews from industry, agreeing that he promulgated anti-Jewish legislation. Even when he could no longer remember particular decrees he graciously accepted that he must have issued them. Of one document he was even ready to say: 'If you have it there before you then it must be correct.' It was a form of co-operation so patronizing that it was barely distinguishable from contempt.

It was a bad start for Jackson, but he fought back. At long last he began to deploy some of the solid evidence he held, though still not on the really central charges. Most effective in the view of journalists were his documents covering the events of 'Kristallnacht' on 9-10 November 1938. Goering still denied planning and taking part in the actual terrorism, but his behaviour afterwards was enough to damn him, and it was fully documented. He had denied the Jews the right to claim insurance payments for the damage they had suffered and insisted that the State would fix as low a compensation sum as possible, then give preference to claims by Party members. Jackson read Goering's interview with an insurance expert who was told that since his profession was being saved millions of marks by the settlement 'I should like to go fifty-fifty with you' – a jocular remark, perhaps, but one from a patently venal and coarse man. More of Goering's crudity was shown by the verbatim record of a disgusting dialogue when Goebbels complained that Jews took up too many seats in trains and Goering replied that this was easily remedied: kick them out and they 'will have to sit alone in the toilet'. Goering might now try to explain that away with the comment to Gilbert: 'I was getting irritated with Goebbels' small details'. But next day many newspapers printed the whole conversation, with Goering replying to Goebbels' demand that Jews be banned from holiday resorts with the fantasy that they should be given enclosures to share with 'the various animals which are damnably like the Jews – the elk too had a hooked nose'. Documents like this wiped out the impression of the urbane Goering. They were not enough to hang the man – bad taste is not a crime, vulgarity is far distant from planning genocide. But Jackson had effectively damaged the image Goering had tried to project and had done so by employing one of the classic devices of cross-examination – luring his witness into denials and false assertions before using his evidence to expose him.

Once Goering was unbalanced Jackson could drive him back, first with crushing evidence on his part in the extermination of the Jews. No amount of wriggling by Goering about 'total' being mistranslated as 'final', and 'complementing' as 'completing' could make these documents look any better. Today Jackson could not be shaken by linguistic details. Nor could he be swayed over his evidence on Goering's looting. Again he trapped Goering into denials, then felled him with records of whole goods trains trundling art treasures to the Field Marshal's private collection. He followed up his advantage with good material on the stripping of Russian resources. For almost the whole day Jackson demonstrated how easily Goering could be tackled if pressure was applied in the right places and with some expertise.

But then he threw away his advantage by entangling himself in a matter which, unless it was part of a hidden strategy of which this was the first tactical move, was surely petty to the point of being ludicrous. Jackson set out to prove the intention to destroy the American ambassador's house during the bombing of Warsaw. This was hardly a matter of great concern – except to the ambassador, perhaps – but it gave Goering a wonderful chance to show off and turn the tables on Jackson. The allegation relied on what Jackson believed were Luftwaffe aerial photographs. Perhaps they were, but Goering soon disabused him of the idea. He was, after all, a flier from the First World War, the founder and head of the Nazi Luftwaffe; aerial photography was something he knew a lot about. So he pointed out that the angle of the pictures suggested they were taken from a steeple, certainly not from the air; he explained how such aerial shots are taken; worse still he turned the pictures over and discovered they were undated, and bore no departmental stamp. He blinded the court with science, until he felt cocky enough to say: 'However, let us assume that they were taken by the Luftwaffe so that further questions will be facilitated.' Jackson had to give up. He switched his attack to questions on terrorism, the killing of hostages and the shooting of parachutists. But these points were made as shallowly as in the previous days of the cross-examination.

Observers such as Dean were prepared to concede that this day had been 'better conducted than before', (42) and the *Christian Science Monitor* spotted that in mid-afternoon 'for the first time since he took the witness stand a week ago Goering appeared uncomfortable'. (43) But this was small comfort. So far no major target had been hit by the prosecution, huge resources of evidence had been neglected, and Goering had emerged relatively unscathed. He was able to tell his colleagues: 'If you all handle yourselves as well as I did you will do all right.' (44) Jackson's cross-examination had been a disaster – for his own prestige and confidence and for the case in general. The real blow to the prosecution came from the fact that the Tribunal had already ruled that further cross-examination could not cover ground already touched on. Golden opportunities had gone forever.

The situation created by Jackson was hardly an enviable one for the British to inherit. Since they had successfully pressed for restriction of the number of cross-examinations, they had only expected to deal with a small number of topics – Dahlerus, the Stalag Luft III case and any matters of foreign policy left by the Americans. They had always assumed that Jackson would take on the bulk of the case. Their preparations for the cross-examination of Goering had therefore been deliberately limited. On 21 February, when they first discussed the lines to pursue, Roberts thought there was no evidence to connect Goering with the murder of the fifty British airmen who had escaped from Stalag Luft III at Sagan. It was fortunate that he decided to check his impression. (45) It was even more fortunate that after hearing Goering claim he was on leave when the British prisoners were murdered, Maxwell-Fyfe, meticulous as ever, asked Roberts to look for any evidence which might refute the claim. (46) At least the Sagan atrocity had been carefully researched. Furthermore Maxwell-Fyfe had decided a week later to concentrate his attacks on foreign policy to the six brief points where he thought they had the best documentary evidence. (47) This area too had been thoroughly prepared. But faced with Jackson's failure and the realization that they must now save the day, the British team scoured the rest of their evidence for further material which would not be cumulative to matters already raised by Jackson but still adequate to hang Goering.

Maxwell-Fyfe took over the cross-examination at an inconvenient time – 4.50 p.m., ten minutes before the session was due to finish. Goering, who had been looking tired, glanced at the clock. (48) He may have hoped to be out of the box in ten minutes and back in his cell to rest before facing a new adversary. If so, his hopes were dashed. The Tribunal ordered the session to be extended for a further half hour. This was little enough time for Maxwell-Fyfe to get very far with Goering, but he did not adopt the role of night watchman, simply playing out the remainder of the day.

Instead, he played one of his strongest strokes, Stalag Luft III. It was a textbook example of cross-examination: short, precise questions on facts, winning brief affirmative replies. The manner was calm, the approach was deceptively simple and concealed its purpose. Before long Goering had repeated that he was on leave when the killings took place and admitted that he was still accessible by telephone. It was possible for him to believe that this was the only admission Maxwell-Fyfe was looking for. But having handled his witness delicately so far, Maxwell-Fyfe now made a more brutal thrust. He came back to Goering's claim to have been on leave and lured him into a casual statement that the leave had ended a few days before Easter. Then he struck. Easter had been about 5 April, so Goering's leave must have ended between 26 and 29 March; but 'these shootings of these officers went on from 25 March to 13 April, do you know that?'

Once hit, Goering began to stagger. Suddenly the man who had made such a display of comprehensive grasp of detail, such a parade of accurate memory, was saying he could not remember the name of the commandant of Sagan, or the name of the head of Inspectorate 17 of the Luftwaffe, or to whom each man reported. Maxwell-Fyfe could remind him; he performed a sparkling little cadenza on German titles, the minutiae of Luftwaffe bureaucracy. It was the turn of the prosecution to blind with science. It was still possible, though, for Goering to believe that he had merely been caught out over dates, that there was no further evidence to connect him with the Stalag Luft III murders. Maxwell-Fyfe left him with that illusion, perhaps because time was running out, and turned aside to the briefer topic of *Aktion Kugel* and the Luftwaffe policy of handing over all escapers except British and American to the police to be shot at Mauthausen, using guns concealed in the measuring equipment when they went to collect their prison uniforms. By the end of the afternoon journalists saw that Goering's face had blanched. His lips were drawn into a thin line and his hands were nervously gripping the sides of the witness box. He was rattled.

And Maxwell-Fyfe was able to start the next day with the evidence he had held back on Sagan. This cross-examination was remorseless – detail after detail of Goering's involvement was established by document after document. If Goering challenged a piece of evidence Maxwell-Fyfe would say: 'That is a perfectly fair point,' then produce another on the same detail – this one more damning. Goering stopped challenging. Maxwell-Fyfe then turned on Goering his own weapon of accepting responsibility: given his position in the Luftwaffe he now had to accept ultimate responsibility for the murders – in principle, just until it was proved in fact. Maxwell-Fyfe's manner was suave, almost detached. Only occasionally did observers notice a quick smile when a lie was revealed. He exploited Goering's previous ploy of co-operativeness: 'Now, would you like to help me – you were most helpful last time – to find the place?' Then he led Goering to finding extracts in documents which said 'the Reichsmarschall was fully informed' about the Sagan murders, and into reading affidavits that Milch had forwarded to him information and several protests about the killings. When Goering thought he had found a gap and suggested that the donor of an affidavit had never been asked whether he checked if this information had really been handed on, Maxwell-Fyfe was ready for him: 'Oh yes he was' – and read the reply. Goering was allowed no time to recover his balance or to divert the proceedings with long statements. The moment he tried to add to the barest explanation Maxwell-Fyfe cut him short: 'I have put my question . . . I pass on to another point.' That morning Goering behaved like the school bully confronted by a Tom Brown. For months he had bragged, hurled threats at witnesses, alternately terrified or cajoled his timid henchmen. Suddenly the essential childishness and vulnerability of the bully was exposed; when challenged he first resorted to bluster but rapidly became abject. He had no answer to accusations and evidence on aggression towards Poland, and it took only minutes to trap him into saying first that Ribbentrop knew nothing about the negotiations with Dahlerus, then that he had resented them.

'Well, now,' said Maxwell-Fyfe after calling attention to this particular tangle, 'I want you just to help me on one or two other matters,' and he bombarded him with documents on the deliberate violation of the neutrality of Holland and Belgium. Goering had no defence. Next he was snared into asserting that Germany had always maintained the best of relations with Yugoslavia before being shown incontrovertible evidence of long-standing intentions to invade. Goering had no answer to that, nor to evidence of his knowledge of atrocities against partisans. He scored one small point – he noticed that one document was marked 'copy' and had only a typed signature (the Tribunal finally ruled it inadmissible and it was struck from the record). Then he faced a barrage of documents on Auschwitz and on the use of slave labour. The documents were too convincing for anyone to take seriously Goering's plea that he knew nothing about such matters. At worst Maxwell-Fyfe had proved that the head of the Four Year Plan was guilty of criminal negligence if he did not know what crimes were being committed in its name; at best he had shown beyond reasonable doubt that Goering had been fully aware of the barbarity.

Goering's fists remained clenched, his face became 'strained and congested'. (49) 'Goering's denials,' said *The Times*, 'sounded far less plausible than at any time ... he had never sounded less sure of himself. (50) He struggled to return to ground on which he felt more secure, asserting his loyalty to Hitler. 'I believe in keeping one's oath not in good times only but also in bad times when it is much more difficult,' a noble sentiment, but one implying less confidence in his Führer and himself than he had previously maintained. Again and again Goering insisted that Hitler had known nothing about the extermination camps, that Himmler kept such things secret, that the Nazis were following 'a policy of emigration, not liquidation'. To no avail. Maxwell-Fyfe read Hitler's comments to Admiral Horthy in 1943. The Jews, said the Führer, had been treated as tuberculosis bacilli with which a healthy body might have been infected. Ribbentrop had added the recommendation to the Hungarians that all Jews be exterminated or sent to concentration camps; 'there was no other possibility.' Maxwell-Fyfe read him the minutes of a meeting in 1942 when he had been told, with some mathematical inaccuracy, 'there are only a few Jews left alive. Tens of thousands have been disposed of.'

Maxwell-Fyfe wrote later that Goering had been 'the most formidable witness' he had ever examined. (51) But he had had years of experience, and the professional expertise and the tricks of the trade which are second nature to a competent barrister had served him well. He was not one of the great practitioners of the art and this was not even his best performance at Nuremberg, but thanks to thorough preparation and the ability never to lose ascendancy over his witness he had scored a success at a crucial moment of the trial and in difficult circumstances. Faced with sustained and methodical competence rather than brilliance, Goering had crumbled. Curiously Maxwell-Fyfe's performance got a muted reaction. The American Press was virtually silent. Dean's report was not rapturous, but it was, perhaps, realistic: 'The effect of the British prosecution has been to knock Goering off his perch. He will not find it easy to re-establish himself.' (52)

And, indeed, by the time Goering had undergone cross-examination by Rudenko for an afternoon and part of the following morning he left the box 'with a wilted and bedraggled air'. (53) Rudenko's courtroom style had been in noticeable contrast to that of Maxwell-Fyfe. It comes as a surprise to hear his voice, soft and gentle, rather mellifluous. What he actually said, however, was harsh, assertive and harassing. All the Russian prosecutors went into attack, as Wheeler-Bennett described them, like a heavy armoured column. Rudenko's questions to Goering were typical: slightly rephrased assertions expecting crushed confession. They were often hammered: 'Have you forgotten that document? Have you forgotten about that?' Given this approach Goering seemed to perk up for a time, and quite enjoy himself again, drawing attention to sections of documents which had not been read, sneering at Rudenko's lack of German, needling him with the charge that 1,680,000 Poles and Ukrainians had been transported by the Russians. Even so, the documents on his aggressive intent towards the USSR and the vicious exploitation of the territories Germany conquered were more than strong enough to withstand Goering's restored panache.

Back in his cell, Goering was far from jubilant about his performance, though he tried to put a good face on it. 'Well,' he kept saying, 'I didn't cut a *petty* figure, did I? Don't forget I had the best legal brains of England, America, Russia and France arrayed against me with their whole legal machinery – and there I was alone.' (54) Others would have agreed with him. He was certainly not a petty figure, indeed a most impressive if rebarbative one. As *The Times* put it: 'If nothing but his subtlety and powers of reasoning were involved, Goering would leave the box a far bigger figure than when he entered it.' (55) But it went without saying that Goering's deeds had been on trial, not his personality. The concern of the court was not with his strength of character but the strength of the evidence which supported or rebutted the allegations against him.

In the tight little legal world of Nuremberg, however, this fundamental issue was temporarily forgotten. The actors on the courtroom stage became so obsessed with details of professional skill that they lost track of the purpose and quality of the play. In recent days all the talk had been not of evidence and admissions but of failure and success in presentation. In particular the topic endlessly debated had been that of Jackson's cross-examination.

All the reviews of Jackson's performance were hostile – he had never mastered his witness or his material, lacked the essential skill to frame questions so as to allow a witness only one answer. For some critics, Jackson's failure had been entirely the result of his inadequate technique: moving advocate, able judge, inspiring crusader for international law he might be; cross-examiner he was not. Perhaps he never had been, or perhaps his skills had fallen into desuetude. Whatever the reason, he lacked what Maxwell-Fyfe called 'the sixth sense of the cross-examiner which subconsciously anticipates the workings of a witness's mind.' (56)

Other critics, however, thought that professional inadequacies were less of an explanation of the failure than psychological factors. Some pointed out that Jackson could hardly expect to keep control of Goering when he could not keep control of himself. Goering had driven him into loss of temper – the result had been the loss of the cross-examination. Jackson's temper certainly had a short fuse. It had been noticeable in the days of the London Conference that he found it bewildering, indeed intolerable if others did not share his moral convictions. Faced with the cynicism of Goering, with the man's pride in his turpitude and shameless justification of so much that Jackson found abhorrent, it is possible that Jackson's fuse simply detonated. Furthermore, others considered that he had been at a great psychological disadvantage in coming to Nuremberg from the protected environment of the United States. He had not lived with the Nazi mentality, had never been obliged to question and temper his own political beliefs to counter it; the first major encounter with Nazi thinking had overwhelmed him. Several observers had noted Goering's infinitely greater knowledge and understanding of everything they had battled over – perhaps more homework would have enabled Jackson to challenge him, or at least give the impression of depth which Maxwell-Fyfe could simulate. Some, like Beaumont at the Foreign Office, believed that a European would have found Goering an easier task, though he had to admit that 'politically the advantages of having the USA in the forefront of this trial are overwhelming,' and that since the Americans had been so instrumental in setting up the trial and had provided the resources to run it, there could have been no possibility of denying them the leading defendant. (57)

But as the inquest on the Goering cross-examination went on, argument increasingly raged on whether Jackson's failure had not been caused by the Tribunal itself. Should the judges have intervened at the very beginning to insist that Goering give brief, factual answers? In which case, it was argued, Jackson would never have been reduced to loss of temper and control. Maxwell-Fyfe thought it was wrong to blame the judges. 'If Goering – who after all was on trial for his life – could run rings round prosecuting counsel, that was a matter for counsel to put right without assistance from the Tribunal.' (58) But this uncompromising view was rare. Most people, in varying degree, attributed blame for Jackson's problems to the judges. Hartley Shawcross criticized 'the weakness of the Tribunal in allowing excess latitude to Goering.' (59) Birkett said in private that Lawrence should have controlled the witness, and he continued to maintain that his draft ruling should have been read and applied. (60) Had his advice been taken, Goering 'would certainly have been much more under control and the lost confidence of Mr Justice Jackson would have been restored for the ultimate benefit of all concerned in this trial.'

American commentators and lawyers in particular stressed that in their own courts judges would never have permitted a witness to avoid direct replies and to romp into lengthy and often irrelevant explanations. This was certainly Jackson's view. It was expressed in his angry demands to the Bench for a ruling and to his son, William, who remembers his father's belief that Lawrence's refusal to intervene had made an effective cross-examination impossible. (61) There were those who said it was Lawrence, not Jackson, who had not done his job properly. Yet the extent to which any judge should intervene and shape court proceedings is a matter of personal judgement and style, whatever formal procedures are laid down. It may be desirable to assert the Bench's authority and establish limits; at the same time it is also desirable to avoid any accusation of intervening to shackle one side or another. Those intimate with Lawrence say that he was determined above all that the Nuremberg Tribunal should give a fair hearing to the defence – on that its final success or failure would be judged. If Lawrence was thought to have erred in giving too much scope to a defendant, then he would have felt he had erred on the right side; better to shoulder some personal criticism than have the whole trial dismissed as partial to the prosecution. As chairman of the Bench and spokesman for its views, Lawrence often drew the fire of the Tribunal's critics and sheltered his colleagues. With the exception of Birkett (and the Russians seem to have found themselves in strange company on this occasion) none of them had wished to impose rigid restraints on Goering's testimony.

No single explanation will finally settle the question of what went wrong with Jackson's cross-examination of Goering. The answer consists of a blend of the possible ingredients according to individual taste. It is, however, clear that the impact of his failure was a personal tragedy for Robert Jackson, overshadowing the rest of his time at Nuremberg. Only in his final speech did the old mastery and passion revive. Until then he behaved like Achilles in his tent, bitter, impatient with the trial and irreconcilably estranged. Biddle, in a letter to his wife, noted Jackson's mood during Maxwell-Fyfe's cross-examination of Goering. It is a letter which shows the limits of his sympathy for Jackson, who always nurtured a suspicion that Biddle bore personal malice towards him. Biddle wrote of Jackson 'sitting by, unhappy and beaten, full of a sense of failure ... I know he has it in for me .... He knows that the Court are apt to follow me, at least to an extent, and he thought we should have "protected" him. But I have felt his opposition from the beginning, and it springs chiefly, Herb [Wechsler] thinks, from the reversal of our positions. Where I have been opposed to him [in court decisions] ... I am certain that I was right. I have repeatedly asked Bob to the house, but he never comes – and I am afraid we are no longer friends.' Then he added a not untypical feline comment: 'Just now I hear he is doing his best to prevent Tel Taylor's wife from coming back with him; and one cannot help suspecting that the reason for this is because he doesn't want his own! Why else?' (62)

The wrangles between the two men now became more frequent, and more acrimonious. Biddle jotted in his notes in the second week in April that Jackson 'came to see Parker and me after lunch in a very wild and uncontrolled mood. Apparently the criticism of his cross-examination of Goering had got way under his skin. He threatens to resign – this is not new.' He recounted Jackson's complaints – a weird assortment of technical arguments about whether defence counsel could print all the documents they wanted, old resentments about Biddle getting a new house, fresh criticisms of Lawrence's tolerance towards defendants. 'Parker and I had to cool him off,' wrote Biddle. 'He's very bitter. He seems to me to be very unfair and unhappy. I am sorry for him.' (63) It was hard not to be. Jackson's heart was always on his sleeve. Birkett noticed how his behaviour in court showed his continuing misery in mid-April. 'He is a thoroughly upset man because of his failure in cross-examining Goering from which so much was expected. He has taken it very badly indeed and his instinct is to run away from the scene of his failure ...'

Birkett then added a comment which puts the whole matter into perspective: 'This trial is regarded as a spectacle, a kind of gladiatorial show, with the prominent Nazis like Goering taking the place of the wild beasts and prosecuting counsel as the gladiators and baiters.' (64) This was all too true. Any trial can become a spectator sport, and this one was drawing the attention of the world. The general public was too little versed in legal matters, too impatient to read the evidence carefully. Consequently it judged the proceedings at the most superficial level – goodies, baddies, stars and flops. In this atmosphere it was not always possible for those working at Nuremberg to keep a sense of proportion. The controversy over Jackson's cross-examination and the Tribunal's handling should not have concealed the paucity of Goering's defence, but it did. Prosecution and defence counsel talked as if there had been a disaster, with irreparable damage done to the entire prosecution case. Even Birkett thought the trial as a whole would never recover since the defence would all now follow Goering's unrestrained manner in the witness box. A feature in the *New York Times* on 23 March which smacks of briefing by American counsel spoke of Jackson's fears of Nazis at large taking heart, of defence counsel becoming increasingly insolent and defendants planning to spin out the trial to farcical length, and of the Allied Control Council being deeply disturbed by the turn of events. (65) The Cassandras who had always warned that a trial would be a platform for Nazi propaganda, or that it would degenerate into protracted farce, looked as if they might be vindicated.

But reactions like this were merely adding gusts to what was already only a storm in a tea cup. The cross-examination of Goering was a disaster for Jackson personally, but not for the prosecution case, nor the trial as a whole, still less for the future of Germany. It had at least been valuable in demonstrating lack of partiality by the Tribunal to the prosecution. Those defence counsel who wished could take comfort in Jackson's discomfiture;

those who wanted to continue to complain about the unfairness of the proceedings now did so with less chance of winning sympathy. It was not inevitable that the trial would drag on interminably. On 22 March, the Tribunal announced that no defendant would be allowed to go over ground already covered by Goering. There must be no repetition of the history of Nazism or the justification of its policies. The decision mirrored the prohibition placed on the prosecution not to cover matters already dealt with by colleagues. However heroic a stance Goering had tried to adopt, it had not wrought political miracles in his country – those who affirmed Nazi beliefs stuck to them, those who were apathetic or too exhausted or hungry to respond had not been roused. It had not even had a permanent effect on his fellow defendants. Some who had always loathed him and shrugged off his influence still did so, with a little grudging praise for his acceptance of responsibility; others who had always been apprehensive about their own defence tended to measure themselves against Goering's stature and feel even smaller. Counsel might wish their clients had something of Goering's fighting spirit, but what they most needed was convincing evidence to break the prosecution case – and that was difficult to find. Seyss-Inquart summed up the whole Goering affair – and the trial itself – most accurately and concisely: 'All that talking isn't going to do him any good. They have it all in black and white.' (66) The decisions of the Tribunal, the final judgement of the trial, as opposed to the assessment of the general public, would in the end be based on the black and white of the documents, not on the colour of personalities.

References for Chapter Twelve

1   Several newspapers
2   *The Times*, 8 March
3   *Evening Standard*, 8 March
4   Gilbert
5   *New York Times* and *Daily Express*, 9 March
6   From IMT Vol. IX – as are all quotations from the trial in this chapter
7   *Daily Express*, 9 March
8   *Evening Standard*, 8 March
9   Gilbert
10 *New York Times*, 11 March
11 FO 371. 57542
12 *New York Herald Tribune* and others
13 FO 371. 57542, 14 March
14 *The Times*
15 Gilbert
16 *New York Times*
17 Dean cable, 11 March. FO 371. 57542
18 Minute, 12 March. FO 371. 57542
19 *Daily Telegraph*, 13 March
20 Cooper
21 Interview with Selkirk Panton *Daily Express*, 17 March

22 Gilbert
23 FO 371. 57542
24 *Manchester Guardian*, 13 March
25 *Daily Express*, 17 March
26 Gilbert
27 FO 371. 57542
28 Quoted by Montgomery Hyde
29 Several newspapers
30 *Daily Express*, 18 March
31 Quoted by Montgomery Hyde
32 *The Times* and others
33 FO 371. 57542
34 *Daily Telegraph*, 14 March
35 *The Times*, 14 March
36 Dostert memo, 20 March. Jackson Papers, Box 231
37 Biddle Notes on Evidence. Vol. III. Biddle Papers, Box III
38 Quoted by Montgomery Hyde
39 Quoted by Montgomery Hyde
40 Biddle op. cit.
41 Ibid
42 FO 371. 57542
43 *Christian Science Monitor*
44 Gilbert
45 British prosecution minutes, 21 February
46 British prosecution minutes, 16 March
47 British prosecution minutes, 19 March
48 *Daily Herald*
49 *Daily Telegraph*
50 *The Times*
51 Kilmuir
52 FO 371. 57542
53 *New York Times*
54 Gilbert
55 *The Times*
56 Kilmuir
57 Minute, 20 March. FO 371. 57542
58 Kilmuir
59 Shawcross
60 Quoted by Montgomery Hyde
61 Conversation with William Jackson
62 Letter to Mrs Biddle, 24 March. Biddle Papers, Box 19
63 Notes on Evidence Vol. III. Biddle Papers, Box III
64 Quoted by Montgomery Hyde
65 *New York Times*
66 Gilbert

Chapter Thirteen

No matter what dramas were played out at Nuremberg, the tension broke, the mood changed abruptly when Rudolf Hess came on the scene. Hess was a clown – but a Shakespearean clown. He was a grotesque figure, gaunt and with angular projections from a baggy, grey tweed suit. Everyone watched with fascination his contrast grimaces and gesticulations, his sudden paroxysms of laughter. His rabbity grin expressed no comprehensible delight. When people laughed at him – and they sometimes did – they immediately became uneasy. For hours on end Hess would show no interest in what was happening in court; he seemed to have no contact with reality. Suddenly he would shoot a piercing glance at the visitors in the gallery and smile sardonically, and spectators would feel a chill. At such moments, those who felt pity for this scarecrow, thin, miserable and old, those who believed the experts must be wrong and that Hess was too mad to be on trial, were shaken. There was a knowingness, a cunning, a shielded strength in the man. So perhaps after all he was a hoaxer; perhaps this pathetic, ill-co-ordinated figure concealed someone capable of the influence and the crimes of which he was accused. Like the Shakespearean clown, his presence was always disturbing, and challenged certainties. His lurches into the limelight were disrupting, and there was a recurrent suspicion that Hess might be calculating his effects.

As the Goering case finished, Hess seized public attention and the newspaper headlines. Would his memory be adequate to cope with his defence? Would he even testify? Dr Gilbert had been anxious about Hess's mental fitness for some days. During the weekend of 9–10 March, Schirach had drawn his attention to signs that Hess was lapsing deeper into amnesia. Gilbert probed to determine the extent of the blackout. He told Hess that General Blomberg had just died; Hess had a vague recollection that Blomberg had been a general but no other reaction. When told later that Professor Karl Haushofer and his wife had committed suicide, he remembered he had called the man as a witness but seemed to have no memory of why. (1) Yet Haushofer had been the theorist behind Hess's views on geopolitics, and he and his son, Albrecht, are credited with inspiring Hess's flight to Britain. Gilbert's testing had answered none of the questions Hess's case always raised: would pressure and challenge revive his mind? How genuine and how relevant to the trial were its gaps?

These questions began to seep through into public awareness. On 24 March the *Sunday Express* carried an interview with Hess's counsel, Seidl. Seidl put forward the view that Hess would go into the witness box but he was pessimistic about his client's ability to defend himself adequately: 'He may be slow in answering questions,' he said, 'especially those of the prosecution as he is again having "difficulties" – his mind is wandering and he may not be very lucid ... Anything can happen. I hope there will not be a scene.' (2) Seidl was building up the drama and undoubtedly preparing excuses, if not a defence, for his client. What was surprising was that he had said Hess would go into the box. This had never been certain. In January, Hess had dismissed his first lawyer, Rohrscheidt, who had broken his ankle and expressed doubts about his physical capacity for continuing to work on the case. In his letter of dismissal, Hess had stated firmly: 'I do not want any affidavits or documents. I do not want any lawyers. I do not want any defence.' (3) Within three days, however, Hess had written to the General Secretary protesting that he was undefended. The Tribunal insisted that he must not be left to defend himself and Airey Neave was sent to persuade him to accept another lawyer. (4) Hess named Seidl – somewhat to Seidl's embarrassment since he did not wish to give the impression of poaching clients and was already representing Frank. (5) His scruples were overruled by the Tribunal. Whatever Seidl may have said to a journalist on 24 March, he now says that Hess never intended to go into the witness box, and indeed that he was not even prepared to recognize the court. And Gilbert recorded in his diary for 24 March that Hess told him he would not appear because he did not want to suffer the embarrassment of not being able to answer prosecution questions. 'He insisted that this was his own decision,' Gilbert added, 'but I know that Goering and Doctor Seidl have urged him not to take the stand.' (6) But whatever had been going on behind the scenes, whatever the doubts about when and by whom decisions had been made, one was reached by 25 March. The defendants were told of Hess's resolve to remain silent, and Seidl told the *Daily Express* that Hess would not recognize the Tribunal and quoted him as saying: 'I am not going there to be asked a lot of silly questions by people I don't like.' (7)

If this was his client's attitude, Seidl had to fight the prosecution charges on his own. He set about it with a campaign of diversions – noisy enough to distract from the charges against Hess, explosive enough to shake the Tribunal. The first had come during his introductory remarks on 22 March. He announced: 'Hess contests the jurisdiction of the Tribunal ...' (8) Hess would recognize the court as qualified to judge on matters relating to war crimes and was prepared to take full responsibility for all laws and decrees he signed and orders he issued. But he would not accept the Tribunal's authority to deal with charges relating to the foreign policies of Germany as a sovereign state, or indeed much else. Seidl announced only this bald decision in court. He now says he had decided that the evidence against his client on Counts Three and Four was minimal and that it could be shown that Crimes against Peace were not punishable under international law. (9)

This challenge to the legal basis of the trial was not made at this stage, however, only Hess's challenge to the Tribunal's competence. It was quickly brushed aside. The Tribunal pointed out that the Charter ruled out any argument over its authority. The court would continue to hear Hess's case whether he approved it or not. Seidl then publicly declared Hess's refusal to take the stand.

He had already prepared another diversion with his third document book, a volume largely composed of quotations from newspaper articles and politicians criticizing the Versailles Treaty. As the prosecution had long feared, he and others intended to use Versailles to justify Nazi policies, and threatened to pull the trial away from the immediate charges in the indictment and into remote and muddy waters: incessant debate about international diplomacy from 1918, allegations of misconduct by others and lengthy discussions of infractions of a few clauses in an exceedingly long and complex treaty. The Tribunal took a little longer to deal with this distraction – but not very long. Maxwell-Fyfe forced the matter on their attention on 26 March. He described the third document book as a 'collection of polemical and journalistic' opinions on Versailles, (10) and insisted that the Treaty was an issue too remote for consideration. Dix, for the defence, urged that it must be taken into account if German policy were to be understood. Horn went further and said it had been signed under duress and that in international law such treaties 'have grave deficiencies and are infamous'.

The argument between the counsel began to centre on the question of whether failure by others to disarm had precipitated and excused German rearmament. Biddle intervened to cut it short. He asked for Maxwell-Fyfe's views. Sir David, whose reply had been long prepared and was based on Foreign Office briefing, maintained that the Treaty had 'looked for' (this is presumably different from 'insisted on') a general disarmament once Germany had complied with the clauses on her own disarmament. He gave his opinion that by 1927 Germany had met those requirements so the Disarmament Commisson had left. International conferences on disarmament had taken place as hoped, but had failed to achieve a total renunciation of arms.

Biddle found the argument satisfactory and announced that in his view Seidl's third document book did not seem relevant. For a moment, however, the contest between the counsel continued until Lawrence interrupted and showed how far they were straying not just from the immediate issue – that of the admissibility of documents – but from the fundamental question. He bluntly asked Seidl if the provisions of the Treaty, however unjust they were alleged to be, and their infraction by others actually justified the waging of war by the Nazis and the horrors that followed. Not surprisingly, faced with such precision Seidl sank into vagueness; he became so muddled that Lawrence warned him he could not be 'understood in the least'. Since there was no possible way in which resentment over Versailles could ever justify subsequent Nazi atrocities, the Tribunal announced in the afternoon session that all discussion of the Treaty was ruled inadmissible. The prosecution was mightily relieved. As Dean commented, the Tribunal's ruling was 'an important decision and if a contrary view had obtained, the position here would have been impossible'. (11) The length of the discussion and the way in which it had rapidly lost all track of relevance had indeed been a depressing reminder of the dangers of plunging into such broad and unanswerable issues. The Tribunal's ruling should keep the trial on the strait and narrow; it undoubtedly muffled Seidl's second explosion.

His third occasioned much more alarm. He was determined to introduce evidence on the Nazi-Soviet Pact and in particular to compel the court to consider the Secret Protocol. For a long time he had no copy of the Pact. Nor, it seemed, did anyone else. On 29 March, the Foreign Office at last admitted to having one they had captured from the Germans, but they preferred to keep it up their sleeve since they believed the Russians did not know of its existence and assumed they would rather no one did. (12) But the British were probably not alone in possessing a copy. Dr Seidl at last obtained one. He, and others, believe it was deliberately passed to him by American lawyers (anti-Russian, Cold War sentiments were strong in some quarters of the team). (13) But Seidl now faced a new problem – how to get the Protocol into evidence. Provenance and authenticity of documents had to be certified and it would be too embarrassing all round to admit where this one had come from. So instead of a frontal approach, Seidl had to try dodging in at the side. On 25 March he attempted to slip into evidence an affidavit by Gaus, the head of the Legal Department of the German Foreign Ministry in 1939, and the man who had actually drafted the Pact. The Tribunal jumped on Seidl. He had not even applied for an affidavit from Gaus, let alone received permission for it, and the only version he was offering was in German. After strenuous objections from Rudenko about standard procedures being ignored by a defence lawyer, the Tribunal agreed to wait for translations before deciding on admissibility.

They had to wait and wait. Whenever the matter was raised in court the affidavit had still not been translated. Every time Rudenko would leap up and call the attempt to introduce it an 'act of provocation' or 'an attempt to divert the Tribunal from the issues we are investigating'. In private the judges had to wrangle with their Russian colleagues. Biddle recorded that on 28 March they had an hour's fight over the matter, Nikitchenko vigorously objecting on the ground that 'the treaty is irrelevant and nothing but propaganda. Finally we permit the witness (Gaus) to be questioned, but at Nik's suggestion say nothing about the right to introduce the treaty itself, for obvious reasons.' (14) Ultimately the judges reached a curious compromise – the Protocol would not be read in court, but it could be referred to. For the moment the affidavit would be enough, and Gaus himself need not appear unless the prosecution required him – which they did not.

On 1 April, the Tribunal at last heard the Gaus affidavit. It was rather disappointing. The Foreign Office had studied a copy of it on 15 March; significantly they offered no comment, for there was nothing in the document to cause any anxiety. Most well-informed people already knew what was in the Protocol; any acute observer of the international scene might have guessed. Gaus spelt out the details of the agreement to carve up Poland and the Baltic States and added some more about discussions on the Balkans and Russia's interest in the Skaggerak and Kattegat. The only revealing and enlivening moment in an otherwise dull work came when he explained that the text of the Pact had been agreed quickly, all except the preamble in which he had drafted a sentence about friendly relations between Germany and the Soviet Union. 'Mr Stalin objected to this,' he wrote, 'with the remark that the Soviet Government could not suddenly present to the public German-Soviet assurances of friendship after they had been covered with pails of manure by the Nazi government for six years.' So the phrase had been omitted. It was interesting to learn of Stalin's concern for public opinion. For the rest, Seidl's third would-be explosion had proved to be a damp squib. But at least the Tribunal's decision to listen had shown its willingness to risk political disapproval and its preparedness to bend its rules on the acceptability of evidence about the behaviour of others. Today Dr Seidl might still question the legal bases on which the Tribunal was founded but he must surely admit that on this occasion they were willing to bend over backwards for him.

What remained of the case for Hess took barely a day. There was an affidavit from his former secretary expressing her conviction that Hess had flown to Britain with the sole desire of promoting peace. Another affidavit and two witnesses claimed that the Auslands Organization which operated under Hess's auspices was not a Nazi Fifth Column in countries abroad. This view could not be sustained after the submission of new prosecution evidence showing the numerous occasions on which the AO had provided Berlin with intelligence and the places in which it had shared accommodation with the Abwehr.

Throughout the case, Hess actually managed to drag his attention away from the novels he read in court. Mostly he occupied his time making caustic comments to his neighbours or sending off a stream of messages to Dr Seidl. On occasion he followed the proceedings with strained attention; twice he was seized with inexplicable laughter. (15)

Since Hess refused to enter the witness box, the prosecution had been robbed of the chance to cross-examine him. Thanks to the very narrow target presented by the two witnesses they had also been denied an opportunity to introduce much new evidence. When the British had discussed the Hess case in February, Griffith-Jones had thought there were few 'killing documents' against him; the prosecution case would have to rely on emphasizing the important posts he had held and the nature of the laws for which he had been responsible. (16) By 23 March, when it was clear that Hess would accept responsibility for his legislative acts and orders,

Maxwell-Fyfe decided to list them and get Seidl's acceptance of their accuracy so as to limit the time taken by cross-examination. (17)

In the event, since there was no cross-examination, the case against Hess remained where it had rested since its presentation in February. The argument ran that Hess was a major contributor to the Nazi conspiracy. He had joined the embryo Party in 1920, introduced the concept of *lebensraum*, and influenced Hitler from 1924 when he had taken dictation of *Mein Kampf* in the Landsberg fortress right up to May 1941. Photographs had been submitted to show that he was Hitler's constant companion. His very titles were said to establish his importance in the Reich: from 1933 he had been Deputy Führer and Reich Minister Without Portfolio – but with a seat in the Cabinet. In 1939 he had been named successor to Hitler and Goering; from then he had been the third man in Germany. In such a position he had undoubtedly shaped and directed policy and criminal activity. But the prosecution case did not rest entirely on Hess's formal position. As he himself admitted, he had signed the Nuremberg Laws for the Protection of Blood and Honour in 1935; he had been responsible for issuing and carrying out all the Nuremberg Decrees on which persecution of the Jews was based. He had signed the decree for compulsory military service in 1935, and so made a significant contribution to Nazi preparations for war. He had signed the laws to incorporate Austria, Danzig and Poland into the Reich. Whatever Hess's declared reasons for his flight to Britain, he knew that the date for the attack on Russia had been fixed days before, and it was the prosecution's contention that his only motive was to enable Germany to fight on one front only.

The case on the first two counts had been adequately compiled and forcibly argued. Whether it would convince the judges, however, depended on the view they would take of the conspiracy charge, the importance of pre-war Nazi crimes, and the validity of the prosecution's belief that aggressive war was a crime in international law. Where the case against Hess was weakest was in the last two Counts. There was little evidence suggesting involvement in war crimes or crimes against humanity once the war began. The prosecution had submitted a vague statement about the desirability of sending Waffen-SS units to the Eastern Territories in view of their 'intensive National Socialist training' (which might just possibly imply intended persecutions). They had also used a complaint from the Ministry of Justice in 1941 that Hess was urging corporal punishment for Poles on the grounds that they were not susceptible to ordinary punishments. But they had produced nothing more concrete than these hints at his attitude, and when all was said and done Hess had left Germany too soon to be involved in most of the war crimes and crimes against humanity. If he were to be convicted it would have to be on the first two Counts.

The case against the next defendant, however, Joachim von Ribbentrop, was very much stronger on all four Counts. As with Hess the prosecution had founded the case on his position in the Nazi hierarchy – Foreign

Minister and Cabinet minister. That and his presence at so many of Hitler's key conferences had given him a thorough knowledge of Nazi planning and action and, it was alleged, were enough to prove his complicity. Ribbentrop was to claim – as Goering had already argued for him – that he had had no influence on Hitler's foreign policies. No matter; it was the prosecution's contention, originally set out in January, that he knew what they were and had carried them out. Furthermore, the lying, chicanery and duplicity of Nazi diplomacy, they claimed, bore Ribbentrop's personal imprint even though Hitler might have cast them. They had produced plenty of evidence to support their view, and they had more than enough evidence to show Ribbentrop's involvement in war crimes and crimes against humanity. Minutes were submitted of a conference where he had opposed suggestions that only enemy airmen who had attacked civilians should be lynched; he had wanted all captured pilots to be handed over for instant execution. Documents by the dozen were put into evidence to show he had urged foreign politicians to exterminate their Jews; and proofs of connections between his Ministry and the pillaging of art treasures and the deportation to Germany of workers. Ribbentrop might have been a mere lickspittle, but he had been a willing, devoted, conscientious one. In his cringing desire to serve his Führer, he had been delighted to take on any dirty work and do it to the best of his somewhat limited abilities.

With such a case to answer, it was no wonder that Ribbentrop was such a frightened man. The prospect of finding a defence was daunting, and Ribbentrop's immediate reaction to any challenge was to lie down and quiver. Whatever vestigial backbone he had once possessed had disintegrated as the Reich collapsed. His mind had always been flaccid; faced now with the need to use every mental resource to prepare a defence, it deflated entirely. His only resort was to panic. He fired off requests for scores of improbable witnesses; even before his applications were refused, he changed his mind and prepared even more ludicrous lists. He covered reams of paper with self-justification and urgent instructions to his counsel, then threw them on to the floor and lapsed into torpor. He spent hours gazing morosely at the mounds of documents he had first seized avidly, then thrown on one side because they offered no hope. Frantically looking for anyone else to blame, he had sacked his counsel in January. Dr Sauter had done his best for Ribbentrop – got him the help of his old secretary for a few weeks, and passed on his complaints to the Tribunal that he could not cover the foreign policy of a lifetime with 'only a pencil and a block of paper'. (This was lawyer's rhetoric. Ribbentrop must have consumed more paper and pencils than the rest of the defendants put together.) (18) But Sauter had found no magic solutions to Ribbentrop's problems – he had to go. He was replaced by Horn, an egregious man whose manner aroused impatience and hostility from the judges. Horn at least won spasmodic approval from Ribbentrop; their thought processes were not dissimilar. It was only spasmodic approval; Horn's woolly mind sometimes produced what seemed like a possible defence, for the rest Ribbentrop had to cheer himself with the delusion that the trial would be called off, or at least that his own case would be postponed indefinitely.

Pathetic though Ribbentrop was he aroused no pity and attracted no sympathy. Andrus found him infuriating. The man's slovenliness and messy cell would have been enough to drive the Colonel to distraction, but in addition he could not tolerate someone so 'full of self-pity', a man 'who never looked me in the eye'. (19) Papen said that Ribbentrop in jail was revealed as 'a husk with no kernel and an empty façade for a mind'. (20) His contempt came partly from the grovelling spectacle Ribbentrop was presenting, partly from snobbery. Papen had always resented the success of a man with none of his own aristrocratic background, none of those diplomatic skills which he believed he himself possessed in rare abundance. Ribbentrop, the arch-snob, aroused counter-snobbery in others; a vain man, he sparked off everyone else's vanity. Goebbels, a product of the working class, had sneered years ago that 'he bought his name, he married his money and he swindled his way into office'. (He himself of course had risen merely by manipulation and venom.) The sycophants round Hitler had resented Ribbentrop's ability to fawn more than themselves and had jeered at his phoney 'von' and his past career as a champagne salesman. All were jealous when the parvenu Nazi who only joined the Party in 1932 was called by Hitler 'greater than Bismarck'. Schacht, revealing his own particular conceit, told Gilbert that Ribbentrop 'should be hanged for his stupidity; there is no worse crime than stupidity'. Goering, on the other hand, picked on Ribbentrop's inability to emulate the Führer: 'I'm sorry to see Ribbentrop breaking down ... I hate to see him wavering like this, excusing himself with endless memoranda and verbose explanation.' He would then give an impromptu rendition of how he himself could nobly defend Nazi foreign policy. (21)

Robbed of any support from colleagues, bereft of any moral fibre, hopelessly adrift on uncharted seas of paper with no mental rudder to steer by, Ribbentrop lapsed deeper and deeper into despair as the day for his defence drew nearer. There was a touching indication of his frame of mind on 14 March when he came into court with his usually crumpled appearance made worse by the absence of a tie. He told Gilbert that his tie had been feeling strangely tight recently. (22) It did not need a psychologist to infer that Ribbentrop was feeling the noose tightening already. By 25 March, when the end of the Hess case was expected, Ribbentrop rushed to the only escape route he could find – illness. He announced he was too sick to take the stand. 'Well, now,' said his former counsel, Sauter, 'isn't that strange. Ribbentrop is sick on the day his defence is supposed to begin. What an unfortunate coincidence. He drove me crazy with his doubletalk' and constant changes of mind. 'I am glad I washed my hands of the whole thing.' (23) (An interesting way to say 'I was sacked'.) In court on the 26th, Horn told the Tribunal that his client was suffering from 'vasomotor disturbances in his speech' as a result of heart trouble. As ever, Ribbentrop evoked no sympathy. Dodd reported that Andrus and the prison doctor agreed that he was 'nervous and appears to be frightened but he is not disabled in any sense and is capable of testifying'. The judges insisted that he appear. Ribbentrop's last bolt hole was sealed.

Before Ribbentrop went into the witness box, however, Horn intended to submit documents and introduce witnesses on his behalf. The presentation of the documents was confusing and incompetent; many of them were not yet translated. This was not surprising since Horn had intended to use 313. A memo from Drexel Sprecher on the 26th drew attention to the prodigious number and the fact that the index alone took up thirty-one pages; its author was 'absolutely flabbergasted' at the number of *tu quoque* pieces of evidence Horn was trying to employ. (24) Horn's technique with such documents as he had ready was to read out large chunks without any explanation of purpose or relevance. He soon ran foul of the Bench, with Lawrence pulling him up time and again. As the muddled piles of paper accumulated, Lawrence asked him to present them 'if I may use the phrase, in bulk'. But Horn was no more capable than his client of spotting relevance or even arranging information under headings.

He abandoned the task. When he took it up again on 27 March, the Tribunal was no more pleased with his method. The judges' irritation was undoubtedly increased by Horn's manner. One newspaper pointed out that he was 'apt to be arrogant' (25) and Dean called him 'exceedingly obstinate and sometimes insolent'. (26) Two days later Horn had to admit that he could still not provide English translations of his remaining documents. That did not matter – the prosecutors had worked through enough of them in German to know they objected to most, and said so. By 2 April when the matter was finally thrashed out, they were well-armed with complaints. The number had vastly increased since Horn now wanted to put in nine document books, and the last two volumes alone contained 350 documents. The prosecution pointed out that most of the evidence in them was vague, cumulative or irrelevant. Some documents were not even originals; some, especially those from White Books, had no proof of authenticity. Horn spluttered for a while and Dix subjected the court to lengthy definitions of 'cumulative' and 'irrelevant'. To no avail. Next morning the Tribunal refused to accept well over half of Ribbentrop's documents

Horn was no more successful with his witnesses. Steengracht had been Ribbentrop's adjutant and was then promoted in 1943 to State Secretary at the Foreign Ministry. An interrogation report described him as 'an extremely dull-witted person, lazy and with little interest in his work' but noted that he had been clever enough to send his wife and children to Switzerland at the end of 1944. (27) Steengracht gave an entirely predictable testimony and at the same time provided a virtually complete compendium of the stale arguments of all Nazi bureaucrats. His defence of Ribbentrop consisted of creating a picture of a man of 'soldierly obedience' who stood in a certain hypnotized dependence on Hitler. According to Steengracht, Ribbentrop had been kept in the dark about everything and had no influence, in spite of which he had somehow been able to check excesses by others. His defence of everyone else retailed the usual stories about staying on and mitigating the nasty policies and not resigning because worse men would get the job. He blamed everything on Hitler and Himmler or on other states who had sinned by recognizing and then treating with respect the Nazi government.

It was a poor testimony, made worse by the fact that Steengracht read every word of it – and was told off by the judges for so doing. The only interest in his evidence lay in confirmation of a point which had appeared in the prosecution case and would be stressed by the defence – that the Nazi state, co-ordinated by Hitler, had consisted of innumerable overlapping, competing, antagonistic agencies. He was undoubtedly right to say there were at least twenty different organizations which ran foreign bureaux and that Himmler, Goebbels, Bormann and Goering all struggled to influence foreign policy. He could have added that Ribbentrop himself not only ran the official Foreign Ministry, into which he infiltrated Nazi toadies, but also incredibly set up a rival to his own department, an even more obsequious agency for foreign affairs, the Büro Ribbentrop. Other witnesses would show similar duplications and confusions of authority in other spheres. Increasingly listeners would question the stereotype of German bureaucratic efficiency, and indeed wonder how the Nazi government ever survived so many back-biting officials, non-communicating departments and fights over resources.

Ribbentrop's next witness, his old secretary Margarete Blank, was hardly worth calling. She was only capable of exuding sentimentality about Ribbentrop's efforts 'to enjoy the Führer's confidence, to justify it by his conduct and work', and giving an embarrassing picture of how he 'suffered physically and mentally' if he did not see Hitler for several days. Paul Schmidt, on the other hand, was a defence disaster. A Foreign Ministry interpreter since 1923, Schmidt had accompanied Hitler abroad and been present at most of his important meetings with foreign politicians and diplomats in Germany. What Schmidt knew would have been better concealed. Certainly little of it was revealed by Horn's vague questions. Much more emerged during cross-examination by Maxwell-Fyfe. For a start, the statement Schmidt had given to the prosecution the previous November in which he had said that Nazi aims had always been clear: they sought domination in Europe – first by incorporating those areas where German was spoken, then by expansion elsewhere under the slogan of *lebensraum*. This strategy, said Schmidt, was laid down clearly; only the tactics to implement it had been improvised. How very gratifying for the prosecution to have confirmation in open court of one of the most basic points they had wished to establish – the more so to have it come from a defence witness. As if that were not enough, Schmidt now agreed that though Hitler alone spoke at conferences, it was at those conferences that the government of Germany had taken place. Again, he had substantiated a fundamental prosecution argument: that there had been silent approval, full understanding of Hitler's policies by those present, many of whom were in the dock.

Characteristically, Ribbentrop, who had insisted on calling Schmidt, then complained to his counsel in a note printed with his memoirs that Schmidt knew nothing about policies or plans. Was that why he called him? He went on to complain: 'It is one more very sad personal experience to see Schmidt allowing the Allied prosecution to call him as a witness against Germans.' (sic) (28) Everything for Ribbentrop was seen through the prism of self-pity – and it was amnesia of Hess proportions to believe within weeks that his own witness had in fact been brought by the prosecution. It was an almost forgivable mistake. Schmidt had given valuable evidence for the prosecution case, and the disastrous impression made by all Ribbentrop's witnesses thoroughly scared the whole defence. Dean noted in a cable on 28 March that many defendants were 'beginning to cut out some of the witnesses for whom they had asked'. (29) No one else wanted to be saddled with a Dahlerus or a Schmidt.

By the time Ribbentrop began his own testimony on the afternoon of 28 March, the weakness of his defence was already apparent. He himself delivered the fatal blows. The *Daily Telegraph* reporter described him as he moved to the witness box: 'His face was drawn, his cheeks were sunken and pallid ... His gait was halting as he walked to the witness stand clutching a file of papers.' (30) He might just as well have clutched a handful of straws. He began to work his way through his prepared statement in a lifeless voice, sounding tired and already defeated. He rambled on about the iniquities of the Versailles Treaty, the horrors of Germany's economic collapse, and tried to recreate the mystic experience of his first meeting with Hitler in 1932: 'this man, if anyone, would save Germany from these great difficulties and that distress'. It was all pointless and irrelevant.

Next morning Lawrence issued a stern rebuke and warned Ribbentrop against reviewing the history of Nazism and reverting to the inadmissible topic of Versailles. Though speeches were forbidden he continued to make one: praising his own ardent hopes for peace, denying any knowledge of the Anschluss and the incitement of the Sudetenlanders. He hit a long, deep purple passage about his attempts to meet world aspirations for peace at Obersalzberg, Godesberg, and Munich and drove Lawrence to complain that there was no point in describing negotiations aimed at reaching agreement when the case he had to answer concerned the breaking of those agreements. So Ribbentrop launched into an alternative saga: of Germany's 'protection' of Sudetenlanders, Bohemia and Moravia, and Germans in the Danzig Corridor. He bemoaned the beastliness to the Germans of everyone, especially the British and French whom he accused of egging on Germany's enemies and forcing her to take 'defensive measures'. It was a poorly argued section and delivered at a length which was exhausting rather than exhaustive. Lawrence issued another warning: 'this exaggerated going into detail does not do the defence case any good in my opinion.' Even so, next morning Ribbentrop resumed the endless plaint, berating every other nation for mistreating Germany and driving her to 'protect' the peoples of Europe.

The *Daily Telegraph* summed up Ribbentrop's testimony as 'a nebulous apologia which only narrowly escaped the stigma of cowardice'. (31) *The Times* said its verbosity, illogicality and speciousness explained why diplomatic intercourse with Nazi Germany had become virtually impossible in the years before the War. (32) Fritzsche wrote later that the other defendants had hoped that Ribbentrop would show that Nazi foreign policy had not been the succession of broken treaties and criminal adventures alleged by the prosecution. (33) These had been faint hopes indeed and Ribbentrop had dashed them. Already on the evening of the 27th Schacht had been pessimistic: 'Such a wash rag for a Foreign Minister.' By the 29th Papen and Neurath were saying Ribbentrop's evidence showed he had no conception of foreign policy (a fair comment), and on the evening of the 30th Goering was seething with contempt: 'What a pitiful spectacle. If only I had known, I would have gone into our foreign policy a little more myself.' (34)

Goering had done his best to rally Ribbentrop. He had been horrified by the spectacle of Ribbentrop's witnesses. Before the session on 27 March, to show his feeling, he turned his back on Ribbentrop, then gave way to the urge to berate him for the mess he was making of his defence. There was a noisy altercation between the two of them lasting for ten minutes, which was avidly followed by spectators in court. Ribbentrop actually managed to stand up for himself for several minutes on end, until the court was called to order. Thereafter Goering sought refuge from the embarrassment of Ribbentrop's defence in a book, but was prodded by Andrus himself: 'Stop reading that book. It is an insult to the Tribunal.' He had then adopted a new tactic, giving vent to his feelings by sneering to his neighbours while Ribbentrop was giving evidence, then leaping up to congratulate him as he returned to the dock at the end of a session. (35)

It had all been fruitless. Nothing could stiffen Ribbentrop, and his defence was so ramshackle that it only required a few prods from Maxwell-Fyfe for it to collapse. It was a Maxwell-Fyfe on particularly good form, well prepared for cross-examination since the British had handled the prosecution case against Ribbentrop and against Nazi foreign policy as a whole. Maxwell-Fyfe had known for some time he would be responsible for the main attack on Ribbentrop on the stand. He had decided to keep it short, 'even if that means throwing some good points away'. (36) After two and a half days of exculpation from Ribbentrop, Maxwell-Fyfe took only five hours to demolish him. Ribbentrop probably came nearer to drawing sympathy during those hours than at any time in his life.

The prosecution case against Ribbentrop on matters of planning and waging aggressive war was already weighty. Maxwell-Fyfe now added to it with new documents. Ribbentrop wriggled and denied, but his evasions and lies were ruthlessly exposed by the evidence. There on paper were his own words laying out policy for the German Sudetenlanders; the minutes of conferences he had attended where military preparations were discussed for taking over Bohemia and Moravia should threats fail, and where the campaign of pressure on Poland was evolved. But Ribbentrop still maintained he could not remember ever knowing any of the details of these policies. ('It was a very long conference,' or 'I think I arrived late,' he explained.) He again tried to argue that he had never wanted war. Maxwell-Fyfe read him his own words about Danzig: 'We want war,' and later, once he got it: 'I am glad now about the course of events.' Damned out of his own mouth, Ribbentrop could only say: 'It is quite clear that this is nothing but diplomatic talk.' What an admission! Maxwell-Fyfe seized it: 'Don't you think that there is any requirement to tell the truth in a political conversation?' When Ribbentrop could only bluster in reply, Lawrence intervened: 'Your explanations are too long, too argumentative, and too repetitive.'

But long-winded repetitions were all that Ribbentrop had available. And they were often repetitions of lies, lies which were all too easily revealed by Maxwell-Fyfe's evidence. Some were silly, unnecessary lies, as when he claimed to have been taken by surprise that Hitler had obtained an honorary rank for him in the SS. The court was shown the actual letter of application written by Ribbentrop personally, as well as the anxious hint he had sent later that he would like an SS Death's Head ring – size seventeen. (For a moment, the SS, an organization of thugs run by psychopaths, sounded like a small boys' secret society run by a cornflake manufacturer.) Ribbentrop continued to maintain that he had never known anything about concentration camps, though he admitted that his ignorance might sound amazing. Maxwell-Fyfe had asked two of his witnesses about the location of Ribbentrop's six houses. They had been puzzling questions at the time, but now their point was revealed. Down from the wall came a map, with Ribbentrop's six residences marked on it – and all the concentration camps nearby. Mauthausen, for instance, with thirty-three separate units and up to 100,000 inhabitants at a time, was a near neighbour of his house at Fuschl; Ribbentrop must have flown over it frequently when going to stay. Several newspapers reported there was complete silence in the courtroom as the significance of the map sank in. Ribbentrop had also pleaded ignorance about the harsh treatment of partisans, and forgetfulness about the deporting of foreign labourers. Well, said Maxwell-Fyfe, 'here fortunately I am in the position of assisting your memory with some documents', and there were Ribbentrop's very words urging the extermination of partisan groups, 'including women and children', and enthusiastically promising his Ministry's support for the transportation of workers.

Maxwell-Fyfe's ruthlessness reduced Ribbentrop to hysteria. He returned to the dock literally gasping and squealing. His knees gave way and he had to be helped back to his cell. (37) The cross-examination had been so lethal that it hardly needed to be followed by others. Indeed the Tribunal became restive and interrupted frequently as Rudenko and Edgar Faure submitted evidence too obviously cumulative. Ribbentrop's replies were inevitably repetitious too. But there was one which might damn him in the eyes of others but redeemed him at least in the judgement of his fellow defendants. He told Faure: 'I was a faithful follower of Adolf Hitler,' – after that his colleagues forgave him the rest. Amen picked up the idea of the faithful follower and servant. He asked Ribbentrop if he knew what a 'yes-man' was. Yes, said Ribbentrop, in German it means 'a man who obeys orders and is obedient and loyal'. Unwittingly he had produced an epitaph for Nazi officialdom.

It was an epitaph equally suitable for the man who followed him into the witness box on 3 April – Wilhelm Keitel. From 1938 to 1945 Field Marshal Keitel had been Chief of Staff of the High Command of the Armed Forces (OKW). He tried to write his own epitaph within minutes of taking the stand. 'I can say that I was a soldier by inclination and conviction,' he announced. 'For more than forty-four years without interruption I served my country and my people as a soldier.' That statement was a source of pride for Keitel; for others it was a source of questions. What kind of soldier had he been? What kind of service had he rendered? What influence had his service and convictions had on other soldiers?

It had been the prosecution's contention when presenting their case in January that Keitel had been the epitome of the 'political general' – a devoted Nazi, though never a Party member, since serving officers were not allowed to join until 1944. It was alleged he had been the lynch pin in Hitler's military planning and operations, drawing up and issuing every vital order. It was argued that Keitel's high position in the military hierarchy and his devotion to Hitler had forced or persuaded other commanding officers to comply with Nazi policies, that his standing and authority had legitimized the regime they were expected to support. Keitel was on trial in his own right and charged on all four Counts. He was also a key figure in the charges against the General Staff and High Command and one of their representatives in the dock. In addition, accusations against Keitel could, by implication, impugn the whole German Army. He prided himself on being a soldier, he boasted the military virtues of obedience and loyalty. But what did they add up to? For soldiers, let alone civilians, Keitel had been the supreme military yes-man. His colleagues had always called him '*Lakeitel*' – the lackey, Hitler's lackey. Others knew him as '*Nickesel*' – a toy donkey with a constantly nodding head. Bob Cooper, sitting in the Press Gallery, remembered being told by two shorthand writers who regularly attended military conferences that they never bothered to write down Keitel's first sentence – it was always identical to Hitler's last. (38)

An undignified picture, and one at first sight difficult to reconcile with the dignified military figure in the witness box. Keitel had greying hair cut *en brosse*, a short clipped moustache. His uniform was stripped of insignia, but as spotless and as carefully pressed as the most fastidious batman or

Colonel Andrus could have wished. In repose he sat tight-lipped, but he was confident and emphatic when he spoke and he deliberately turned to address himself to the judges, the dock and the spectators as if lecturing at a Staff College. The films show that as each session wore on he would lean to rest his right elbow on the front of the box. This was not a slouch; Keitel would never slouch. It was to keep his back as rigid as ever. The audience was impressed. After the shambolic figure of Ribbentrop shaking and scuttering into evasion, here was a defendant whose appearance and whose air of telling a frank, straightforward, soldierly story seemed admirable. But spectators were only impressed by the contrast and only for a short time at that. What Keitel was actually saying was that he saw himself as a piece of office equipment, proud to be used by others. He did not present himself as a dignified human being with a mind and a moral sense, but as an efficient, hard-working, constantly available, versatile instrument.

Keitel's examination in chief lasted for two and a half days. It amounted to variations on a few simple themes. One – the theme for the Armed Forces – ran: 'that was a political decision.' Keitel saw policy as divided into watertight compartments. As he told the story, politicians decided to invade Czechoslovakia, soldiers drew up the invasion plans; politicians decided on aggression towards neutral countries because that was 'a foreign policy matter', and soldiers then attacked them; politicians decided to launch wars without warning or ultimatum, soldiers fought them. He was painting a picture of magnificent military obedience, admirable soldierly efficiency. He was simply missing out the vital detail – that soldiers too are bound by international and moral law. But Keitel's concept of a soldier made this omission logical: he revealingly called the Armed Forces 'a tool of the politicians', for him a term of praise, which by definition excluded any legal or moral obligations on the part of the military.

The theme in relation to his own defence was by now banal and overused. It was 'I never knew.' Keitel claimed to have known nothing about conditions in prisoner-of-war camps (though the OKW had the right to inspect them); about any military plans up to the last minute (as if it made it better to put them into effect when taken by surprise); about the handover of prisoners to the SD (though as he was later reminded, he had been the one-man court of appeal for those in SD captivity).

The theme which recurred most insistently was what might be called that of the office machine. He clearly believed he only had to say it was Hitler who had asked for information, evolved strategy, or asked for orders to be drawn up and it would then be inconceivable for anyone to blame Keitel for the information he supplied, the strategy he accepted, and the orders he issued. He stated continually that he, the Field Marshal and the OKW he headed had 'no power of command'; only Hitler, the Supreme Commander, could give orders. So hundreds of orders signed 'Keitel' were in fact 'Führer orders'. Keitel had put his name to invasion plans, policy documents on stripping food and looting in occupied areas, orders for sending prisoners-of-war to industry, transporting foreign workers to Germany, seizing and executing hostages, but could not see that he bore any moral responsibility for them. Not for Keitel the old cliché 'I was only obeying orders': for him it was 'I was only writing orders.' For some orders he did accept bureaucratic responsibility – the *Nacht und Nebel* Decree for instance, instructions on how to carry out the Commando Order and the Commissar Order, the formalities for the lynching law. These orders, drafted and issued by Keitel, might have set in train some of the most appalling of war crimes. Even here Keitel appeared to see no difficulty; it was enough that he had disapproved of the policies for his conscience to be clear. He could see no connection between his acts and the horrifying crimes which had followed from them.

It was quite clear, however, during his own testimony and under cross-examination that Keitel had some perception of right and wrong (though not in himself); he was able to see that crimes had been committed (though he felt personally innocent); he was even able to say that the Armed Forces had on occasion 'overstepped the mark', as he put it. But he could not blame them; they had acted out of military necessity, he thought, or by mistake, or because of the orders they had received (and of course most of those orders were not his). The leaders could not shift their responsibility on to the men in the field, he insisted; 'the large mass of our brave soldiers were really decent'. So if most soldiers were decent and Keitel himself was guiltless, where did the blame lie?

Keitel's answer was unambiguous and logical: with Hitler. It was Hitler who had worked out strategy, decided on methods. It was Hitler the Supreme Commander who had compelled others to apply them. So, argued Keitel, 'the traditional training and concept of duty of the German officers which taught unquestioning obedience to superiors who bore responsibility, led to an attitude – regrettable in retrospect – which caused them to shrink from rebelling against these orders and these methods even when they recognized their illegality and inwardly refuted them.' What a startling series of admissions! Keitel had used words like 'regrettable', 'rebelling', 'illegality'. While defending his subordinates and praising military obedience he was confessing that crimes were committed, that it had been wrong to obey. And he went further, further than any defendant or witness had yet dared to go: 'The Führer,' he declared, 'Hitler, abused his authority . . . in an irresponsible way with respect to us.' Hitler had been loaded with responsibility before, but no one else had ever dared to denounce him and regret obedience to him.

Keitel created an unpleasant picture of how Hitler had been able to assert his authority against the better judgement of his subordinates. He summed up his claim that no one had played any part in military conferences and so bore no blame for decisions in one pithy phrase: 'the Führer arrived, spoke and went out.' He brushed aside any suggestion that he could have argued with his commander: 'one could never get beyond the second sentence of a discussion with Hitler.' Arguing that he was driven against his will to issue the Commando Order he explained Hitler's wrath at the rate of sabotage in occupied areas and added: 'We heard Hitler's outbursts of temper on this subject almost every day.'

Yet in spite of all Keitel's grumbles and his readiness to condemn, the admiration for Hitler which had kept him a docile slave and flatterer for so many years shone out from time to time. When explaining that much of his pre-war work had been concerned with using threats of force to obtain negotiated settlements (something a more morally sensitive man might have been ashamed to admit), he could not resist paying the usual military tribute to the Führer who had obtained so much 'without a shot being fired'. When being cross-examined by Rudenko, he said that Hitler was self-taught in military matters but his knowledge was 'amazing'; everyone felt 'only a genius can do that'. 'I was the pupil and not the master,' he added in awe. Under re-examination by his counsel, Keitel struggled to win understanding for his constant subservience. 'You had to know the Führer ... you have to know in what atmosphere I worked, day and night for years.' He painstakingly tried to recreate the Führer and to show why he had won such devotion. Hitler had been so decisive, he explained, he had such forceful arguments, showed so much concern for the welfare of his soldiers and the future of the people. Faced with all this 'never did it enter my mind to revolt against the Head of the State, the Supreme Commander of the Armed Forces.'

Keitel's examination in chief left an unpleasant taste in the mouth. He kept his dignified demeanour and intermittently impressed on the occasions when he tried to tell the truth. But, as Dean decided: 'Like Kesselring he is truthful and decent according to his own standards, but his standards are those of a savage.' (39) Keitel may have claimed to be a mere typewriter, but it was impossible to forget the words he had written. Though the ideas and the literary influence may have been Hitler's, the words had been Keitel's own. He himself had composed the note in the margin of a protest by Canaris about the bestial treatment of Russian prisoners of war: 'These objections arise from the military conception of chivalrous warfare. We are dealing here with the destruction of an ideology and I therefore approve such measures and I sanction them.' The *Nacht und Nebel* Decree had been his: 'Effective and lasting intimidation can only be achieved whether by capital punishment or by means which leave the relatives and the population in the dark about the fate of the culprit. Deportation to Germany serves this purpose.' His were the words of the order to suppress insurrection in the Occupied Eastern Territories in 1941: 'Every case of insurrection against the German occupying powers is to be attributed to Communist initiative irrespective of the particular circumstance. It must not be forgotten that in the countries in question human life often means nothing and that intimidation can be achieved only by unusual severity ...' Keitel had spent much of his working life considering ways of intimidation. He had been a bully; perhaps a lower grade one than Hitler, one who hid behind the skirts of his Führer's greatcoat, but a bully all the same. During an interrogation in the previous October, Keitel had laughed in delight at the memory of an incident (of which he denied all recollection in court). He had described the visit to Berchtesgaden of the Austrian Chancellor, Schuschnigg. He himself had been summoned by a shout from Hitler: 'Keitel, come here.' 'Yes, my Führer. What do you wish, my Führer?' 'Nothing,' replied Hitler, 'I just wanted to scare Schuschnigg'. There, in a brief dialogue, was Keitel the lackey, Keitel the bully's tool. And how happy he had been to remember it all. (40)

Cross-examination by Rudenko and Dodd added little to the case already thoroughly documented by the prosecution and virtually conceded by Keitel. Rudenko merely went over ground previously covered in meticulous detail about the invasion of Russia. He used his usual hectoring manner and riled Keitel by addressing him throughout as 'known as Field Marshal' or 'Defendant Keitel, Field Marshal of the former German Army'. Keitel tried to put him in his place. Asked about his relationship with Hitler, he snapped back: 'I have stated here that I was a loyal and obedient soldier of my Führer. And I do not think that there are any generals in Russia who do not give Stalin implicit obedience.' Dodd asked only one question: did Keitel admit he had carried out criminal orders? Keitel had admitted that more than once in his testimony – he could only repeat himself.

Maxwell-Fyfe's approach was different. (41) In large part he relied on detailed questions on the events of Sagan and the lynching of Allied airmen, and at once brought the wrath of Lawrence on his head: the Bench was restive at the minutiae and repetition. For the rest, Sir David tore aside the veils of euphemism behind which even Keitel sometimes hid. After a phrase of Keitel's implying that hand-over to the SD meant being put into police custody, Maxwell-Fyfe rebuked him: 'You have been at this trial too long to think that handing people over to the SD means police custody. It means concentration camps and a gas chamber, does it not?' When Keitel proffered a kind of apology for his orders to punish families of Frenchmen found fighting with the Russians, and expressed regret that these relatives had been held responsible for 'the misdeeds of their sons', Maxwell-Fyfe cut him short: 'If you think that is a misdeed, it is not worth our discussing it further.' This was a new style for Maxwell-Fyfe, much more brutal than his usual urbane manner. The *New York Times* reported that Keitel began to stammer, and was forced to agree that orders he had issued were cruel and despicable. Before the end 'he was leaning back groggily in his chair, groping for words'. (42) Maxwell-Fyfe aimed one last savage kick where he knew it would hurt: 'You were a Field Marshal, standing in the boots of Blücher, Gneisenau and Moltke. How did you tolerate all these young men being murdered, one after another without making any protest?' There was no real answer.

Before Keitel left the witness box, Lawrence more or less repeated the question, almost offered Keitel a moral lifeline. He asked whether Keitel had ever tried to protest formally against policies he said he abhorred: had he ever put his views in writing? Keitel could not see the salvation that beckoned. He thought (only thought) that he might once have penned protest, perhaps some time in the winter of 1939–40. He had asked to resign 'for the reasons I was quoting' (he did not quote them now) and 'on account of accusations made against me'. How typical that personal grievances had played as large a part as moral outrage in his desire to resign. How characteristic of all the office holders who appeared at the trial that he had a detailed memory for facts and figures, but only the most blurred recollection of the brief instant in which he had recognized that what he was doing was wrong.

Keitel's testimony had done nothing to rebut any of the charges against him. His witnesses did nothing to help him. Lammers, the Chief of the Reich Chancellery from 1933 to 1945, had been Hitler's legal adviser and his liaison with his ministers. He had also been his doorman – access to the Führer tended to be in his gift. Lammers, if anyone, knew the tangled ways through the web of Nazi departments, knew the powers and reputations of their staffs. He knew Hitler, and he paid generous tribute to him as an administrator: 'the Führer had an extraordinarily quick power of perception and almost always a correct evaluation of affairs.' Conversely, Lammers belittled the abilities of everyone else. Nearly all the defence counsel questioned him and he provided the desired low estimate of their clients' influence. An interrogation report on Lammers had described him as 'this rather revolting old man'. (43) Bob Cooper recorded that he was 'coldly repellent, snake-like' and that some of the women court reporters sitting near the witness box were afraid of him. (44) His very appearance might have weighed against his evidence, but then under cross-examination the authoritative, contemptuous bureaucrat gave way. He was so desperate to save himself that he shovelled blame on to Hitler and Bormann – all the time failing to notice or even not caring that every word backed up prosecution charges of criminal policies.*

Two witnesses Keitel had tried to drop – General Westhoff and Max Wielen, once in charge of the criminal police in Breslau – were called by the Tribunal to be questioned on affidavits they had given on the Stalag Luft III murders. Both confirmed their statements and added fresh details to implicate Goering and Keitel among others.

By the time Keitel's lawyer, Nelte, submitted his remaining documents, it was the end of the session of 10 April. The Keitel case had run for seven whole days (a full Saturday sitting had been inserted). Seven days of court time had been consumed when every word Keitel had to say already existed in a written statement presented to the judges. It had taken seven days to go over a case which the prosecution had previously firmly established with documents and which Keitel more or less admitted. For many people the Keitel hearing had been the last straw of mounting frustration at sheer waste of time and of fear that the trial was doomed to drag on interminably.

*At a subsequent trial in Nuremberg, Lammers was sentenced to twenty years imprisonment. The US High Commissioner halved the sentence; even so he was released at the end of 1951. He died in 1962.

Birkett, who had lamented the lack of control over Goering, had plunged deeper into despondency during the Ribbentrop case. On 30 March he had written: 'The trial is now completely out of hand. (Ribbentrop) continues to make very long answers on matters which are only indirectly relevant to the issues in the cases.' During the cross-examination of Keitel he had drafted an intervention to be read by Lawrence: 'I don't want to interrupt your cross-examination, General Rudenko, but many of these matters have already been gone into most exhaustively and I am not sure how far a repetition of them is helpful to the Tribunal.' The notice was not read. Quite rightly Birkett grumbled at how often the same matters were analysed: 'Does the Tribunal really need any further evidence about the German attitude to the Jews?' He pointed out that very little cross-examination was needed; 'all prosecutors should limit themselves most rigidly in the interests of time.' (45)

Birkett distributed blame with an even hand; in his view the Tribunal had lost control and the prosecutors were not doing their job properly. This was not the way the prosecution saw the problem. They were furious at the time being taken by the defence case, blaming the Tribunal and the defence, but blind to their own contribution to the length of the proceedings. On 3 April they discussed at the chief prosecutors' meeting a hint from the judges that they should limit their cross-examinations of defendants and witnesses: one nation ought to be enough was the suggestion. The prosecution dug in their heels. Strictly between themselves they were prepared to concede that two cross-examinations were usually enough, if others could be added in special circumstances, but they were not prepared to bow to a formal ruling. They insisted on every nation maintaining a right to cross-examination. They would not meet the judges' wishes but might observe self-denying ordinances. (46) The logic of the position they had adopted was that the Tribunal must assert its authority – but only at the expense of the defence. The most they were ready to do was to make private approaches to defence lawyers in the attempt to find quicker administrative procedures.

There had been constant prosecution complaints about the number of documents requested by the defence, the sheer volume of paper which had to be translated and printed, then the time taken in court by hearing argument on its admissibility and even by the reading of extracts and summaries during cases. By 4 April Maxwell-Fyfe had decided to meet Dr Dix, Schacht's counsel, to hold a preliminary discussion on the documents for his case and try to work out an amicable agreement as to which were necessary and acceptable. (47) By holding discussions at this stage, at least translation and printing might be avoided and lengthy arguments in court prevented. Given the two sensible and co-operative men involved, it indeed proved a useful meeting. Both expressed their satisfaction with the system in court on 6 April. They suggested it might be expanded to other cases and to applications for witnesses. But this was a long-term solution, and it depended on goodwill. Goodwill was absent in some defence lawyers, and many enormous documents had already been sent to the translators and printers.

So prosecution hopes were not high that this new procedure alone could speed up the trial. They wanted action by the judges. They discussed the possibility of getting it at a chief prosecutors' meeting on 5 April. Maxwell-Fyfe was gloomy. He felt the trial would now last until the end of August, and that 'the Tribunal had not been entirely co-operative in this respect'. Rudenko complained bitterly at the judges' general lack of firmness (perhaps he would have complained more if Birkett's reproof had been read) and at the time being taken by Keitel. He wanted a joint protest from all the prosecutors to the judges. Jackson was pessimistic about the judges' reaction; he pointed out they had not so far accepted any prosecution suggestion for shortening the time taken by the defence. He could only hope the Press would bring pressure to speed things up. He bemoaned the fact that the Tribunal seemed to have no appreciation of the political consequences of allowing the trial to stretch out – the loss of public support and respect – and added morosely that it was 'difficult to instruct (the judges) in public and improper to attempt to instruct them in private'. (48)

Given Jackson's anxiety at the prolonged hearings and his long-standing hostility towards the Tribunal, it is hardly surprising that he suddenly lost his temper at the start of the morning session on 9 April. The catalyst for his rage was Rosenberg, and Rosenberg was in himself enough to try the patience of any reasonable man. What had proved intolerable for Jackson on this occasion was Rosenberg's requests for documents. They covered 25,000 sheets, and paper as Jackson pointed out was 'a scarce commodity today'. Furthermore, the previous evening Rosenberg's counsel had asked for 260 extra copies of his document books to be printed, many of these for distribution to the Press. Jackson could swallow no more: 'This matter of printing documents has proceeded in its abuses to such an extent that I must close the document room to printing documents for German counsel,' he shouted. As if Rosenberg's documents were not indigestible enough in quantity, their content was unpalatable too – anti-Semitic 'rubbish' said Jackson; extracts from 'recognized scholars' and Rosenberg's philosophy 'based on the new romantic philosophy', replied Thoma, his lawyer. Jackson protested that a huge proportion of the documents was in contravention of Tribunal rulings on relevance and admissibility and that 'the United States cannot be acting as Press agents for the distribution of this anti-Semitic literature'. He demanded that Masters be appointed to scrutinise documents before they were even translated let alone printed. (Jackson had been keen on the use of Masters ever since the London Conference but no one else shared his enthusiasm and they were reluctant to delegate the authority of the court.)

As he seethed, others rushed forward to still the troubled waters. Maxwell-Fyfe and Lawrence worked out that most of the Rosenberg documents had been processed before the recent Tribunal rulings on the need for argument and approval; Dr Thoma assured everyone that he always told Rosenberg: 'I cannot defend your anti-Semitism; that you have to do yourself.' Dix – always ready with balm, soothing and sticky – urged that everyone must work together, lauded the new consultative procedure between counsel, said that mistakes will always happen, and suggested that the 'tribunal have more important tasks than that of continuously protecting the defence' (in a context which made clear that he meant protection from Jackson).

The row seems to have let off Jackson's steam for a while. Gradually in the coming weeks, the methods for processing documents were tightened up and the meetings between counsel increased in number and efficiency. The machinery began to operate more smoothly. What did not change was the basic attitudes of its operators. Though the Tribunal minutes do not record the judges' opinions on any matter, on this problem they seem to have followed their usual line, preferring to attract opprobrium rather than crack the whip at the defence. Lawrence was to interrupt rather more frequently to criticize irrelevance and cumulative evidence from now on, but plenty of both crept in. The obverse of the judges' leniency to the defence was some attempt to discipline the prosecution. This merely provoked further obstinacy from the prosecutors. They were furious at a meeting on 16 April after the Tribunal had refused to allow the Russians to cross-examine a witness. Again they asserted their right as sovereign nations to cross-examine when they chose; again they spoke of reaching a voluntary limitation. (49) But they did little about it; and the judges abandoned the attempt at a formal ruling. Instead on 27 April representatives of the prosecution and Dr Dix were called before the judges to discuss ways to shorten cross-examination. (50)

The fact that the British had joined the other prosecutors in their stand concealed a practical motive (or others might consider it a fine conceit of themselves). Patrick Dean, who was attuned to British views, wrote to the Foreign Office on 31 March admitting that the most sensible solution to the cross-examination problem was to divide up all the defendants and witnesses, then give each team sole responsibility for them. But, he said, the British were easily the best cross-examiners. If they were restricted to asking only supplementary questions then they would be unable 'to destroy the effect of the preceding ineffective cross-examination'. As he pointed out, there was plenty of room for improvement in everyone's technique if 'they would stick closely to the documents which are in almost all cases overwhelming, but for some reason they are unwilling to do this'. (51) Perhaps some of them were unable to see that point. Undoubtedly others were reluctant to lose an opportunity for themselves and their country to shine.

It was no change of heart by the prosecutors nor any improvement in skills which led to the next case – that of Kaltenbrunner – lasting only two and a half days. The French followed their usual habit of remaining silent. The

British had already decided on 2 April to leave the case to the Americans; they handed over documents they thought might be useful and took a back seat. (52) Thereafter, much of the speed of this case was the result of efficiency by Kaltenbrunner's counsel, Kauffmann. He proved orderly, he was able to summarize prosecution arguments succinctly, and he insisted on brief answers from his client. Brevity came easily to Kaltenbrunner. Faced with any allegation, any evidence against himself, and he simply denied it.

Had Kaltenbrunner faced a jury, one fears that the twelve good men and true would not have bothered to listen to the evidence. One look at him would have convinced them that he was guilty. He was a huge man, towering over everyone in the dock, his bulk increased by massive shoulders and gorilla arms. His jaw jutted forwards, his great ears sprang out at the sides, looking even bigger because exposed by the close crop of his hair. His eyes were narrow, his lips thin, his face pock-marked; on his left cheek there was a scar. He was everyone's nightmare of a Gestapo brute. But he had crumbled with fear in captivity. His brain haemorrhage had been attributed by the doctors to hysterical panic. Andrus, who hated a sniveller even more than a sloven, noted that 'he had come into my custody sick with fear' and noted with approval Gilbert's judgement that Kaltenbrunner had 'a weak vacillating will and an emotionally unstable schizoid personality'. 'Stripped of his power,' Gilbert had told the Colonel, 'he now cringes and complains that he was only a tool of Himmler and an unimportant one at that.' (53)

Perhaps Kaltenbrunner's only virtue was consistency. He continued to call himself an unimportant tool when he was in the witness box. It was not a convincing defence. Born near Braunau (Hitler's birthplace), at school with Eichmann, he had trained as a lawyer but devoted his time and skills to the Austrian SS. He had worked with Seyss-Inquart to bring about the Anschluss, then organized the Nazi police in Austria. His particular interest, however, was in intelligence work. His abilities in this field seem to have brought him to the notice of Himmler and, rather to everyone's surprise, he was suddenly brought by Himmler to Berlin in 1943 to head the RSHA (Reich Main Security Office). This position gave him control of the Gestapo and the SD, and also responsibility for the concentration camps and the administration of the 'Final Solution'. His lawyer claimed that Kaltenbrunner was only given this job because he was 'the least dangerous man for Himmler'; affidavits maintained that he was less of a rival than his predecessor, Heydrich. But a witness was to suggest that the activities of the RSHA got nastier once Kaltenbrunner took over and 'we learned that perhaps the impulsive actions of a murderer like Heydrich were not so bad as the cold, legal logic of a lawyer.'

Kaltenbrunner himself took the line that his only interest had been in intelligence and that he had ignored the police and executive tasks for which his office was responsible. But it was inconceivable that a man in his position was unaware and guiltless of the full range of policies the RSHA had carried out. And indeed, the prosecution evidence had already clearly established Kaltenbrunner's day to day control over the multifarious criminal activities of his subordinates and his intimate working relationship with Himmler, Eichmann and Heinrich Müller, head of *Amt* IV in the RSHA, who had zealously organized the delivery of Jews to Auschwitz.

The indictment against Kaltenbrunner was massive. As one newspaper put it: 'probably more appalling crimes have never been charged against any man'. (54) It would not be enough, however, for the prosecution just to secure the conviction of Kaltenbrunner personally. They had realized in the previous September, with some concern, that they must have in the dock a major Gestapo figure as representative of the organization against which they sought a declaration of criminality. Himmler was dead, Eichmann had disappeared, Müller was probably dead and Goering could not be named as the representative of the Gestapo – he had headed only the Prussian branch which he had then handed over to Himmler. Nor could Frick – the Gestapo had reported to him as Minister of the Interior but was not subjected to his regular control. Kaltenbrunner remained the only feasible prosecution candidate to represent the Gestapo. Only his formal position as Head of the RSHA linked him with the organization and, as an American staff memo pointed out, to establish a stronger connection would require 'a very liberal interpretation and actually an extension of Article Nine of the Charter. To say the least it will give the defence a strong point for argument.'* And the prosecution faced a further difficulty: Kaltenbrunner could argue that since he only took office in 1943 he could not be held responsible for policies and acts before that date; the prosecution would have to fall back on the contention that he took over with full knowledge of the Gestapo's criminal nature and in so doing ratified its previous acts. (55) Given these early doubts the prosecution had been fortunate in obtaining concrete evidence against Kaltenbrunner in his capacity as administrative head of the Gestapo which was both hard enough and disgusting enough to cover the technical crack which ran under their case, a crack that had widened with the decision to split the Gestapo and SD and hold separate hearings against each. Kaltenbrunner was now the sole representative in the dock for both organizations.

Once he took the stand on 11 April, however, any prosecution worries about the organizations' case began to disperse. Kaltenbrunner made no attempt to deny the crimes of the Gestapo and the SD. As Dean observed in a cable with some understatement: 'this should prove useful in the case against these organizations.' (56) Indeed Kaltenbrunner denied no crimes. Like Keitel he simply denied he had any connection with them. But he extended this line of defence to an unparalleled length and thinness. It was no wonder he looked pale and nervous as he gave evidence and stretched credulity, that he twitched incessantly as he tried to maintain the untenable.

*Article 9 stated: At the trial of any individual member of any group or organization the Tribunal may declare (in connection with any act of which the individual may be convicted) that the group or organization of which the individual was a member was a criminal organization.

Keitel had at least admitted to drafting orders, even to signing them. Kaltenbrunner would admit to nothing. He claimed that orders were issued in his name without his knowledge; that he was constantly bypassed in the chain of command; that he was never informed of policies in operation when he took office and remained unaware of them. His examination in chief took only a morning. It had been a session of breathtaking high-wire lying, made all the more amazing because he was such a clumsy performer. The *Daily Telegraph* thought Kaltenbrunner must be 'surely the most inept Nazi apologist to enter the witness box'. (57) *The Times* thought he had 'put forward the ugliest defence yet heard at the Nuremberg trial ... a flood of clumsy denial that would look stupid were it not a sorry attempt to hide behind dead men' – Himmler and Müller in particular. (58) Birkett, like everyone else, had to accept that 'it is impossible to think of the position occupied by Kaltenbrunner and at the same time to believe that he was ignorant of so many matters'. Yet Birkett suffered from the problem experienced so often by those at Nuremberg: 'It is always difficult to imagine that one human person can have been the head and fount of such scenes of misery and bloodshed.' (59)

But once the cross-examination of Kaltenbrunner began, it became certain that he had indeed been the originator of so many of the most loathsome of all Nazi crimes. For a day and a half Amen laid bare his lies. Amen had collected damning affidavits and documents and he used them with remorseless efficiency. Out came example after example of Kaltenbrunner as the vital cog in the machine by which Himmler had processed arrests, punishments, executions. There in court were Kaltenbrunner's own orders for British and American commandos to be shot, for anti-Jewish measures to begin in Denmark, for SD members to be drafted into Einsatzkommandos, for 65,000 prisoners to be murdered in Mauthausen, for Hungarian Jews to be worked to death. Kaltenbrunner denied them all, of course. He tried to claim that his signatures were only facsimiles; when that failed, he claimed they were forgeries. He attempted to explain that he had negotiated with the Red Cross for the hand-over of prisoners, that thanks to his efforts the extermination of the Jews had stopped in 1944. He swore he had only ever seen one concentration camp and that was Mauthausen, which he called a labour camp where stone was quarried for the pavements of Vienna. He declared he had never even heard of Auschwitz until 1943 when Himmler told him it was an armaments factory; that he never saw a gas chamber; that he had never heard of a policy to kill Jews – it was all settled when he took office (and this minutes after he had claimed to have stopped extermination).

But all Amen's evidence made nonsense of Kaltenbrunner's disclaimers. Affidavits told of his three visits to Mauthausen, of how he 'went laughing into a gas chamber' and enjoyed demonstrations of the three methods of execution; hanging, gassing and shooting in the back of the neck. 'Lies,' said Kaltenbrunner. Another affidavit explained that SD units engaged in wiping out the Warsaw Ghetto got their orders direct from Kaltenbrunner.

The man who wrote it, said Kaltenbrunner 'comes from North Germany and knows nothing about history or politics'. As Amen pressed his case, Kaltenbrunner became hysterical: 'For a whole year I have had to submit to this insult of being a liar,' he screamed. Then in a characteristic flash of self-pity he whimpered: 'My mother who died in 1943 was called a whore and many similar things were hurled at me.'

The other defendants thought it a contemptible exhibition. They all expressed horror at the lies the man was telling – though they were all prepared to perjure themselves, they could not stomach the sheer quantity of brazen perjury Kaltenbrunner was indulging in. Nor, in spite of their own proclivities, could they countenance such gross claims of ignorance and lack of responsibility. (60) From the first session in Kaltenbrunner's defence 'his fellow prisoners in the dock began to look embarrassed', *The Times* reported. 'Goering absented himself in the afternoon with a slight cold.' (61) When Kaltenbrunner returned to the dock on the second day, Jodl 'was the only co-defendant who said a word to him'. (62)

Kaltenbrunner's chief witness came into court on 15 April. He was a strange choice for anyone's defence, but at least he was willing, indeed proud to take responsibility and so shift it from Kaltenbrunner. He was Rudolf Hoess, a man who from 1934 had made a profession of running concentration camps. He had learned his trade at Dachau and Sachsen-hausen; he had finished his career as deputy to the Inspector General of Concentration Camps. He was a devoted father and husband and an animal lover who told Gilbert that he had spent the happiest days of his life at the end of the war when he was hiding on a farm with only the horses for company. (63) Perhaps his sensibilities would have prevented him from running a knacker's yard. Instead, from 1940 to 1943 he had killed two and a half million people as commandant of Auschwitz. Not that Hoess was quite certain how many deaths he had organized and supervized. But Eichmann had told him it was two and a half million and Hoess always accepted everything a superior told him. Here, if in anyone, was a fount of inexpressible human misery. Here, in Hoess, were personified all the Nazi virtues of duty, hard work, obedience; and all the worst of Nazi callousness and bestiality. Here was a human being who had unleashed horror on a scale beyond the imagination.

Hoess was first and foremost a technician. In court he described in a flat, matter-of-fact voice and with carefully chosen details his supreme organizational achievement – the murder of two and a half million people. With a certain pride he explained the planning which made it possible to bring up to one hundred wagon loads of people a day to Auschwitz; to inspect them and arrange for some to be put to work for a while and the rest to immediate death. He explained the neat system by which the bodies were disposed of, the gold teeth and rings sent to the SS in Berlin and the women's hair sent to upholsterers. It was an organizational triumph. It had been made possible because Hoess was conscientious, measured himself against the best in the business and was always ready to learn. He had visited Treblinka and was not impressed. At Treblinka the gas chambers were inadequate, they only took 200 at a time; his own gas chambers at Auschwitz were built to deal with 2,000 each. Nor had he a high opinion of the monoxide gas they used at Treblinka. Hoess himself had introduced Cyclon B – it only took between three and fifteen minutes to do its work. He was pleased to say that thanks to his impeccable arrangements, few of the victims had ever realized they were about to die: notices gave the impression they were going for delousing or showers. This was again an improvement on Treblinka where there were frequent panics and things 'got out of hand'. He prided himself on the discipline at Auschwitz. Cases of 'ill-treatment' and 'excesses' by guards (by which he presumably meant hurting rather than killing people) were punished by detention in a dark cell, chaining or strapping.

Not that Hoess was complacent about his achievement. He was a man who set high standards for his work. He expressed dissatisfaction that up to half a million people at Auschwitz must have died from starvation or disease – those, after all, were not the deaths he had been ordered to administer. Furthermore, he regretted he had been unable to maintain the total secrecy he had aspired to. The medical experiments he ran were supposed to be secret (he himself had only told his wife) but 'of course the foul and nauseating stench from the continuous burning of bodies permeated the entire area and all of the people living in the surrounding communities knew that exterminations were going on.' Those in the courtroom listened to Hoess in silence. It was almost impossible to take in what was being said. The defendants at lunchtime were silent too. Only Doenitz and Goering managed to make any comment to Gilbert. It was the same comment from both of them – that Hoess was obviously a South German; a Prussian could never have done such things. (64) (Goering had in fact been born in Bavaria but after military training in Prussia thought of himself as an honorary citizen.)

Hoess left the witness box. Suddenly, after peering into a fathomless pit of obscenity, those in the courtroom experienced the shock of total contrast. With Kaltenbrunner's defence completed, the Nuremberg court on the afternoon of 15 April became the reluctant audience for an outpouring of philosophical thought that sounded altogether meaningless after the terrible evidence of the slaughter of millions. Alfred Rosenberg had taken the stand. 'Philosophical thought' was only a courtesy title for the jumble of prejudice, irrationality and half-understood plagiarized ideas which stuffed Rosenberg's head. He believed he approached the question of race scientifically – in fact he had too many preconceived ideas for any of the objective assessment of evidence required by science, and scientists had provided him with no data to back his theories. He also boasted that he provided a historical perspective for his views – but he merely picked at historical events like a myopic jackdaw, then crammed the bits and pieces, with a vain attempt at a fit, into the rickety pile he called an ideology.

Rosenberg had been the editor of the Nazi newspaper the *Völkischer Beobachter*. He was the author of such early turgid claptrap as *The Tracks of the Jew through the Ages*, *Immorality in the Talmud* and *The Crime of Freemasonry*. These works had made him the leading Nazi theoretician on race. His *Myth of the Twentieth Century* had become a Nazi Bible. Its sales were second only to those of *Mein Kampf*. The book may have been a bestseller but few could read it. Goering had called it 'junk' and Goebbels said it was 'philosophical belching'. Hitler had little critical comment to make since he confessed he found it too obscure to work through. Never mind – if it was too difficult for the Führer, the author must be a most profound thinker. So Rosenberg became Hitler's Delegate for the Entire Intellectual and Philosophical Education and Instruction of the National Socialist Party in 1934 and from 1933 he was head of the Party's Foreign Affairs Department with responsibility for liaison with Nazi parties abroad. He was encouraged to set up his Institute for the Investigation of the Jewish Question in 1939, which opened with his resounding words: 'Germany will regard the Jewish Question as solved only after the last Jew has left the Greater German living space.' And since the source material of the Institute was Jewish archives and art, it was logical that the scholar/scientist Rosenberg should extend his researches and establish the Einstab Rosenberg – a task force to confiscate the Jewish art treasures of Europe and cart them back to Germany

There were opportunities to apply his racial theories and pursue his cultural interests when he became Minister for the Occupied Eastern Territories in 1941. Proving that his ideas were not merely anti-Semitic, he had set about the persecution and murder of Slavs and Jews alike. Checked only by the superior taste of rival connoisseurs such as Goering and by the incompetence of his own Einstab staff, he had pillaged anything he could lay his hands on. He had broadened his collector's mania from art to food. Russia must feed Germany, he had declared. 'We see absolutely no reason for any obligation on our part to feed also the Russian people . . . We know this is a harsh necessity, bare of any feelings.' Nor did he see any obligation to accept limits on the methods of government employed in the area. Rosenberg had been quick to point out that Russia had not signed the Geneva Convention and he had argued that the Hague Conventions no longer applied 'since the USSR is to be considered dissolved . . . Therefore any measures are permitted which the German administration deems necessary and suitable.'

For a day and a half Rosenberg gushed hot air in the dock. An explanation for his wobbly mind began to occur – it was set in a wobbly head; he had to keep seizing his chin with his right hand to jam his head still. If he had ever been capable of a clear thought he might have realized that it was possible to mount a defence based on the undoubted fact that few Nazis had ever taken him seriously and that he had always been bypassed by more able competitors such as Goering, Goebbels, Bormann or Himmler. But Rosenberg took himself too seriously and had too high an estimate of his work to assess let alone admit his own insignificance. So for a day and a half, slumped in his chair, he more or less admitted the charges against him. Having accepted the charges, he had plenty of time left to browbeat a new audience with his Great Thoughts. For hours he maundered on. It was no more possible to grasp what he was saying than to seize a handful of cloud. Those who could went to get coffee or took an early lunch; others such as guards and messengers had to fall asleep. (65) Birkett had been blessed with a cold, so missed the second day of Rosenberg's philosophy. Anyone who has read his testimony must sympathize with the desire to escape. Yet it seems rather a pity that so many people missed a unique opportunity to study what passed for thinking in Nazi circles.

Since Rosenberg patently had no defence, since the prosecution case was already adequately documented and the defendant had produced no evidence in rebuttal, it would have made sense for the prosecutors to pray that he would leave the witness box eventually, and sit in silence. Unfortunately, however, the Americans had obtained several excellent new documents since presenting their case against Rosenberg and could not resist the temptation to use them in court. So for a whole morning on 17 April Dodd conducted a cross-examination. He did it very well; his evidence was impressive and he deployed it with skill. All Rosenberg could do was to slump lower and try to explain that 'exterminate' does not mean 'kill'. But it was a work of supererogation. At a chief prosecutors' meeting Rudenko pointed out that if Dodd had not intervened the whole case would have been over and a day saved. (66) Seemingly he did not expect anyone to draw attention to the fact that he himself had asked a pointless question about the invasion of Russia.

The same argument about leaving well alone could have been applied to the next case – that of Hans Frank, the star defence counsel of the Nazi Party in its early days, Hitler's personal lawyer, once Reich Minister of Justice and finally Governor General of Poland. The forty-odd volumes of his diary on his work in Poland which he had donated to the Allies would have been ample evidence on which to hang him. In addition, however, the prosecution had collected more than enough alternative documents to build a sound case against him. There was his description of his mission as Governor General in Poland: 'This territory in its entirety is booty for the German Reich.' (67) The booty included its people. On another occasion Frank had stated 'the Poles shall be the slaves of the Greater German world empire.' And there were details on how that enslavement had been carried out, such as his letter to Sauckel in 1942: 'I am pleased to report to you officially that we have up to now supplied 800,000 workers for the Reich ... Recently you have requested us to supply a further 140,000. I have pleasure in informing you officially that 60 per cent will be supplied by the end of October and the balance of 40 per cent by the end of the year ... You can, however, next year reckon upon a higher number of workers.' The slaves who remained in Poland were not to be given subsistence if food was

322

needed elsewhere. The prosecution had read Frank's speech in 1942: 'Before the German people suffer starvation, the occupied territories and their people shall be exposed to starvation.' He announced that six times as much Polish grain as the previous year would be sent to Germany. This created a problem: 'can we,' asked Frank, 'cut two million non-German inhabitants of the region out of the general rationing scheme?' Indeed they could. For instance the Polish intelligentsia and nobility could be murdered, the export of Polish workers increased. And the actions against the Jews could be stepped up. Already by mid-1942 Frank had expressed pleasure that in a tour of major Polish cities he had noticed 'that the efforts of the German administration have been crowned with real success, as one now hardly sees any Jews'.

As if all this evidence were not enough, Frank had no intention of defending himself. In 1943 he had told a labour conference: 'we who are gathered here figure on Mr Roosevelt's list of war criminals.' He had echoed Goebbels' boast: 'I have the honour of being Number One. We have, so to speak, become accomplices in the world historical sense.' No matter if 'world historical sense' is incomprehensible. For the purposes of the Nuremberg trial, the prosecution alleged it meant 'in the sense of Count One'. Frank was not charged on Count Two; his war crimes and crimes against humanity were the main focus of the prosecution case. And in the witness box on 18 April, Frank admitted his guilt in them all.

He took only two hours and fifteen minutes. One newspaper called it 'a record for brevity and candour'. (68) He did not behave with his usual grovelling self-pity; he spoke in a loud and clear voice, waved his hands, expressed himself with 'almost religious fervour'. (69) Quite correctly Frank pointed out that his office in Poland had given him no control over the activities of the SS; that Himmler, Bormann and others had frequently ignored or countermanded his policies. He also said he had often tried to resign (fourteen times, he reckoned) but added his probable motive: Hitler, in his heart, 'was always opposed to lawyers and that was one of the most serious shortcomings of this outstandingly great man.' He even praised his own efforts in founding a Government General Philharmonic Orchestra and a Chopin Museum (did he hope people would think he had left Poland a better place than he found it?). Nevertheless, he confessed that 'having lived through the five months of this trial ... now I have gained a full insight into all the horrible atrocities which have been committed, I am possessed by a deep sense of guilt.' He admitted that he personally had played a part in the extermination of the Jews: 'my conscience does not allow me to throw the responsibility solely on minor people.' And he expressed his conviction that 'a thousand years will pass and still this guilt of Germany will not have been erased.'

What more could the prosecutors ask? Yet both Dodd and Smirnov insisted on cross-examining. All they achieved was a certain amount of backpedalling by Frank: claims to have learnt of murders in Auschwitz and Maidanek only in 1944; vague stories of efforts to secure the release of several Krakow professors. Frank's witnesses added nothing significant: small details of criticism of aspects of Nazi policy and that was all; certainly no suggestion that Frank had opposed policies in principle.

The defendants in the dock had listened to Frank's testimony intently, leaning forward and following every word. At lunch, Papen and Seyss-Inquart gave him some words of encouragement. But most of the others had been horrified by what they heard. Fancy saying that Germany had been disgraced! Frank, however, was delighted with his testimony, proud that he had stood out from the other defendants who always claimed ignorance of what was going on. 'I *did* know what was going on. I think that the judges are really impressed when one of us speaks from the heart and doesn't try to dodge the responsibility.' Schirach had certainly been impressed. Having wavered for so long he was now inspired to make a clean breast of things himself, to declare that everyone had been misled by Hitler on the racial question. As Schacht noticed, Schirach's mood was the first sign that Goering had lost control over the other defendants. Frank had damaged the united front. Schacht himself was preparing to go further. He wanted to make accusations against fellow defendants – Goering, Ribbentrop, Keitel and Raeder were his chosen targets. 'My people must be shown,' he declared 'how the Nazi leaders plunged them into an unnecessary war.' (70)

So by mid-April the defendants were clearly divided. Their counsel had shown little ability to construct defences for them or find evidence to counter prosecution charges. The prosecution case was as solid as ever – in some areas it had been strengthened recently with new documents. The Goering performance might have shaken the prosecution's confidence but he had only exposed gaps in their professional skills, not in their allegations. The six defendants that followed him had offered no challenge. The only doubt in anyone's mind so far must be whether Hess was sane enough to be found guilty. The prosecutors had reason to smell victory. The greatest criticism they had to face was that they were taking such an inordinately long time.

References for Chapter Thirteen

1 Gilbert
2 *Sunday Express*, 24 March
3 *Stars and Stripes*, 27 January
4 Neave *Nuremberg*
5 Conversation with Dr Seidl
6 Gilbert
7 *Daily Express*, 25 March
8 From IMT Vol. IX
9 Conversation with Dr Seidl
10 Quotations from the transcript are from IMT Vol. X until specified
11 Cable to Foreign Office, 26 March. FO 371. 57544
12 FO 371. 57545

13 Conversation with Dr Seidl and information in Bradley Smith
14 Biddle Notes on Evidence. Vol. III. Biddle Papers, Box III
15 *Manchester Guardian* and *Daily Telegraph*, 25 March
16 British prosecution minutes, 21 February
17 British prosecution minutes, 23 March
18 IMT Vol. II
19 Andrus
20 Papen
21 Gilbert
22 Ibid
23 Ibid
24 Memo kindly lent to the authors by Drexel Sprecher
25 *The Times*, 26 March
26 Cable to FO, 31 March. FO 371. 57544
27 Jackson Papers, Box 210
28 Ribbentrop memoirs
29 Cable to FO, 28 March. FO 371. 57544
30 *Daily Telegraph*, 28 March
31 *Daily Telegraph*, 29 March
32 *The Times*, 2 April
33 Fritzsche
34 Gilbert
35 *Daily Express*, *Daily Telegraph* and *The Times*, 27 March
36 British prosecution minutes, 26 March
37 *Daily Herald*, 1 April and *Manchester Guardian*, 2 April
38 Cooper
39 Cable to FO, 6 April. FO 371. 57544
40 *New York Times*, 14 October 1945
41 All quotations from the trial from IMT Vol. XI until specified
42 *New York Times*, 6 April
43 Jackson Papers, Box 210
44 Cooper
45 Quoted by Montgomery Hyde
46 Chief prosecutors' minutes, 3 April. Court Contact Committee File 60
47 Tribunal minutes, 4 April
48 Chief prosecutors' minutes, 5 April. Court Contact Committee File 60.
49 Chief prosecutors' minutes, 16 April. Court Contact Committee File 60.
50 Tribunal minutes, 27 April
51 Cable to FO, 31 March. FO 371. 57544
52 British prosecutors' minutes, 2 April
53 Andrus
54 *The Times*, 12 April
55 Memo to Storey, 29 September 1945. Jackson Papers, Box 192
56 Cable to FO. FO 371. 57545
57 *Daily Telegraph*, 11 April
58 *The Times*, 11 April
59 Quoted by Montgomery Hyde
60 Gilbert
61 *The Times*, 11 April
62 *Manchester Guardian*, 12 April

63 Gilbert
64 Gilbert
65 *Manchester Guardian*, 15 April
66 Chief prosecutors' minutes. Court Contact Committee File 60
67 All quotations from the transcript from IMT Vol. XII from now on
68 *Evening Standard*, 18 April
69 *New York Times*, 18 April
70 Gilbert

Chapter Fourteen

The defence front continued to crumble and the anticipation of a total prosecution victory was heightened during the next case heard at Nuremberg – that of Wilhelm Frick. Frick had been Minister of the Interior from 1933 until 1943. In that post he had played a major part in crushing opposition to Nazism; he had devised and directed measures for the suppression of trades unionism, the silencing of Christian critics and the elimination of alternative political parties and the provincial legislatures. By 1935 he had sent over 100,000 opponents of Nazism to concentration camps.

The Jews had been victims of Frick's policies: he had drafted and put into effect laws which excluded them from economic activity and public life. Other hapless victims were the mentally sick, the incurably ill, the severely handicapped. In Frick's eyes these unfortunates were not objects of compassion but 'useless eaters'; they must be removed. So he had prepared the law on euthanasia. (He had been delighted in the mid-1930s to send details of this policy to Robert Kempner, once an employee in his Ministry, then in exile in the United States, finally his prosecutor at Nuremberg.) (1) One of Frick's contributions to Nazism was to envisage the monstrous and cloak it in 'law'. The basis of this law was the belief that 'Right is what benefits the German people, wrong is what harms them.' He had applied no other principle, moral or legal. Frick, in the prosecution's view, had used his talents and training to abuse law and pervert justice in the interests of Nazi domination. He had provided the legislative framework for state criminality.

But he was more than an invaluable lawyer for Hitler, he was a sedulous bureaucrat. Frick had set up the administrative structure of the police state by organizing the police network and laying down the procedures for the Gestapo and the concentration camps. He made sure the police were available for drafting into the armed services when war began. As territories were incorporated into the Reich or conquered, it was Frick who worked out the details of their control and administration. In 1943 he had moved from theory and planning to the practical, and became Protector of Bohemia and Moravia.

Frick had undoubted abilities as a bureaucrat, but also embodied all the bureaucrat's possible weaknesses. These came to the surface in Nuremberg jail. He was pernickety. A psychologist told the *Chicago Daily News*: 'He is like a little old woman, worrying about trivial little things all the time.' (2) He had lived his life with facts and figures, diagrams and the minutiae of bureaucratic systems. Andrus had received a report from Gilbert which called Frick callous and unimaginative. (3) His fellow defendants found him taciturn and totally cold. He shared their general inability to see connections between his acts and what had happened outside his office. Just before his case began he told Gilbert: 'The mass murders were certainly not thought of as a consequence of the Nuremberg Laws ... It may have turned out that way, but it certainly wasn't thought of like that.' (4) He felt no responsibility or regret. Frick seemed incapable of feeling, except for himself. He was the most constant and bitter complainer about prison conditions. He was not sybaritic, just totally selfish, and this selfishness must ultimately explain why Frick decided not to go into the witness box.

He had decided that there was little to be said in his defence. He accepted the prosecution charges in the main, just wanted to make a few corrections of detail. He wished it to be made clear that he had not seen Hitler after 1937, and that he had never approved of atrocities. Lammers had already given evidence that Frick submitted several requests to resign. (5) As Frick told Gilbert: 'Hitler didn't want to do things my way. I wanted things done legally. After all, I am a lawyer.' (6) He also wished to emphasize that his control over the police in Germany had been limited by Himmler's interference and that he had had no authority over police in occupied territories where Himmler's power had been total. He hoped it would be understood that in Bohemia and Moravia, though he held the title of Protector, the day-to-day running of the area had been in the hands of Karl Hermann Frank, a Sudetenland Nazi of quite extraordinary ruthlessness and cruelty. All these points, thought Frick, could be adequately dealt with by his lawyer and a witness. He could leave it to them to tidy up the record; why bother to go into the witness box? There was another possible motive for his non-appearance – an expression of his overwhelming preoccupation with his own interests and comfort. Both Fritzsche and Robert Kempner were convinced that he wished to avoid any questions about money he had salted away in three bank accounts in Germany – money he had undoubtedly purloined in Czechoslovakia and which would provide for his wife and children after his death. (7)

It would have been typical of a Nazi bureaucrat to use his official position to feather his nest. It would have been characteristic of Frick to safeguard a hoard and ignore the interests of anyone else. But, by not going into the witness box, Frick was letting down his fellow defendants. He was dodging the chance to speak on their behalf, to take responsibility for measures which might otherwise be attributed to some of them and defend legal and administrative aspects of the regime they had all served. To make matters worse for them, the one witness he intended to call was an inveterate opponent of Nazism and a doughty fighter against Hitler and his henchmen. It was certain that this witness would use his appearance in court to attack those he had regarded with implacable hatred for years.

Frick did not care what his witness said, who he implicated, or what crimes he exposed. All that concerned him was to make slight adjustments and corrections in the prosecution case against him. Let the rest, quite literally, go hang.

So it was that on the morning of 24 April Frick's counsel, Pannenbecker, denied no prosecution allegations against his client and simply ran through a group of documents to support Frick's point that there had been a difference between his formal positions and the actual authority he could wield in police matters. Then, in the afternoon, he called his witness: Hans Bernd Gisevius. (8)

Gisevius was in Nuremberg to give evidence for Schacht as well as Frick. All the other defendants were fearful of what he would say. They knew he had recently published his memoirs and that the story he could tell in court would damage them all. Gisevius had set out in life to be a civil servant. In 1933 he found himself in the Gestapo. Within a few weeks, he realized that the organization was criminal to the core and began to collect dossiers of its crimes and to circulate them among his superiors with calls for action to restore law and order. Inevitably he was threatened with arrest. He wriggled away – first to the Prussian, then to the Reich Ministry of the Interior, where he worked under Frick. He did not give up his fight. Still he compiled dossiers on Gestapo illegal activities; still he called for official action to stamp them out. He was sacked. He found other jobs and continued his campaign to bring official criminals to book. Gisevius was sacked time and time again. He joined successive groups of anti-Nazi plotters who hoped to bring the regime down by an Army coup. He worked to warn the French and British of Hitler's aims in Czechoslovakia. Just before the outbreak of war, Field Marshal Witzleben had provided him with forged mobilization papers so that he could be brought into the OKW without going through a preliminary vetting by the Gestapo. There he worked with high-ranking officers who were planning to overthrow the regime and who hoped to prevent a war. But the Gestapo was hot on his trail. In 1940 Admiral Canaris saved his life by sending him to Switzerland – ostensibly to do routine intelligence work, in reality to act as his liaison with Allen Dulles of the OSS. Gisevius maintained his contacts with the resistance to Hitler and went back to Germany briefly at the time of the July Bomb Plot against Hitler.

This extraordinary story in itself made Gisevius a fascinating witness. It also made him a damaging one for the defence. The defendants and Nazi witnesses had always stuck to the claim that protest in the Third Reich was impossible. Yet here was a man who had protested constantly – and survived. Many had claimed ignorance of criminal activities. Here was a man who had collected files on them, sent the evidence to those in authority and could prove they had chosen to take no action. Evidence by Nazis so far might have given the impression that moral corruption in Hitler's Germany had been so extensive that it was impossible for anyone to retain the slightest sense of right and wrong. Yet here was a man who had known the difference and risked his life for what he knew to be right. Gisevius said in his evidence 'everything was possible in the Third Reich.' To be fair to the defendants, their witnesses, and to Germans outside the court, it might be unreasonable to expect them all to come up to Gisevius's standards of rectitude and courage. But once these standards were declared, once the range of possible actions was available for consideration, then everyone could be measured against them. All too many had to be found sadly wanting.

But Gisevius had more concrete contributions to make to the trial. As witness for Frick he did the task required of him, calling Frick 'a minister with no personal executive power' and explaining that he had had no influence over Hitler and indeed no access to him. He corroborated Frick's story that Himmler interfered in police matters, but that was as far as Gisevius was prepared to go. He would not eulogize or conceal, and under cross-examination he made no bones about his belief that Frick bore ultimate responsibility for the administration of concentration camps. As witness for Schacht, Gisevius spent more time, clearly because he believed there was much more to be said in Schacht's defence. With obvious sincerity and without forcing conclusions, he drew a picture of Schacht as an opponent of Hitler and frequent collaborator with those plotting to overthrow the regime. He had made a major contribution to Schacht's defence. Once Schacht took the stand it would be difficult not to see him without something of the rosy tint Gisevius had lent him.*

These formal duties performed, Gisevius seized the chance to continue his personal crusade against Nazism. He explained that had any of the conspiracies he joined succeeded, he would have been put in charge of police in Germany. Then, he told Jackson, everyone in the dock would have been put behind bars – with the exception of Schacht (and if that was the only exception then presumably Frick too would have been treated as a criminal). Now, from the witness box, he was seemingly doing his best to make sure that these same men went behind bars, or better still to the scaffold. Contrary to their claims, he asserted that Ribbentrop, Jodl, and Funk had all had great influence with Hitler. He was certain that Neurath and Papen, however aloof they might have seemed, were fully aware of Gestapo activities and chose to countenance them. He emphasized Keitel's immense influence over the OKW and Army and his full knowledge of the extermination of Jews, the enslavement of foreign workers and atrocities carried out by the SS and Armed Forces.

Gisevius's main target, however, was Goering. He told the story of the Reichstag Fire and insisted that, though Goebbels had planned it, Goering had been informed. Further, Goering himself had arranged the murder of one of the SA men responsible who had confessed to a magistrate out of resentment at not being paid. Goering listened to the story, 'motionless, staring at Gisevius in cold rage'. (9) Gisevius lingered over the details of

---

*Gisevius's account of Schacht as a plotter is summarized in the section on Schacht's case.

the Roehm Purge (he had investigated the affair at the time), drawing attention to Goering's involvement. Goering, he alleged, with Hitler and Himmler had drawn up the lists for those to be killed. As this testimony continued, Frick remained as cold and unmoved as ever. Schacht was delighted: 'Now all the rotten business is coming to light,' he said to Gilbert as Speer and Fritzsche beamed with satisfaction in the background. 'It was so stupid of the prosecution to indict me. My witness is their best witness.' But Gisevius's account of the Roehm Purge had provoked most of the other defendants to uproar. They were appalled by the details of the sordid fight between two sets of Praetorian guards. Jodl was purple in the face and nearly in tears: 'It is a disgrace for the decent people who followed in good faith into this *Schweinerei* ... They were a bunch of dirty swine on both sides.' Goering was so incensed that he stood in the dock at the end of the session, resisting all attempts to move him, and harangued everyone within earshot until at last he could be shoved into the lift. (10)

But even more anguishing for Goering was to be Gisevius's extraordinary account of the Blomberg and Fritsch scandals. Field Marshal von Blomberg had sworn the oath of allegiance to Hitler and imposed it on his fellow officers, becoming commander-in-chief of the Wehrmacht as a reward. Goering had probably hoped for the command himself; Himmler feared in Blomberg a rival to the power of his SS. Blomberg fell into their hands as a result of his second marriage in 1938 – a ceremony at which Hitler himself had been a witness. Blomberg had married a former prostitute with a criminal record and Goering knew it. He let the wedding take place and then colluded with Himmler to show the files on her to Hitler. The Führer, that model of bourgeois respectability, promptly sacked Blomberg. The replacement, however, was even less acceptable to Goering and Himmler. Field Marshal von Fritsch was a conservative by nature but an unpolitical soldier; he had been shocked by the aims revealed at the Hossbach conference and opposed the war which others seemed determined to wage. Goering and Himmler decided to ruin him, too. As Gisevius finally told the story in court, they had gone to Hitler with documents to show that in 1935 Fritsch had narrowly escaped arrest as a homosexual. (He omitted the detail that they had confonted Fritsch in Hitler's presence with a male prostitute who swore that the Field Marshal had been paying him since that date to keep his mouth shut.) Gisevius thought that Hitler was convinced by their evidence. It is more probable that he was merely glad of an excuse to get rid of Fritsch. He was forced to resign 'for reasons of health'. In fact, said Gisevius, the documents which drove him out of the Army had been forged by the simple expedient of substituting Fritsch's name for the real subject of the files, a Captain Frisch.

Goering had done his level best to prevent these squalid stories being told in court and Gisevius, as ever, fought him. Soon after going into the witness box on the afternoon of 24 April, he told the court that while waiting in the room used by defence counsel that morning he had overheard a conversation between Goering's lawyer, Stahmer, and Schacht's counsel, Dix. Stahmer had passed on a warning from Goering that if Gisevius mentioned Blomberg's marriage he 'would not spare him'. Up leapt Stahmer to protest that he had only passed on Goering's remark 'for reasons of professional etiquette ... I am really surprised that Dr Dix has in this manner abused the confidence which I placed in him.' Dix, understandably, hardly saw the matter in that light. He told the court that Stahmer had added that if Gisevius raised the Blomberg affair, Goering intended to disclose everything he knew about Schacht – and 'he knows lots of things against Schacht which may not be very pleasant for Schacht.' Goering listened to the two counsel with the colour drained from his face; he looked, thought one reporter, 'enraged and thwarted'. (11) It is odd that the Tribunal passed no public comment on this blatant attempt to intimidate a witness. There is no hint in the minutes of their private sessions that they discussed taking action, concluding perhaps that the speed with which the business had come to light was warning and punishment enough. On the morning of 26 April, however, Pannenbecker gave voice to the shock of many of his colleagues at the incident in their room and expressed their pleasure that Gisevius had described conditions in Germany so openly. Gisevius accepted the apology, hinted that there had been a further incident which he preferred not to discuss and emphasized that he had no wish to criticize most defence counsel who in his opinion were engaged in 'a difficult task'.

On 24 April, however, Gisevius stuck to testimony on other matters, beginning his scandalous revelations on the Blomberg-Fritsch affairs only on the next morning. Lawrence tried to stop him on the ground that this story was irrelevant to all the cases in hand, but Dix insisted – as did Jackson – that the matter must be established. All the dirt came out. That evening Goering tried to wave the whole thing away; he dismissed it as old gossip. But Keitel was upset. No wonder; his son had married Blomberg's daughter by his first wife. Keitel too might have preferred to hush up the Blomberg family history. (12)

Those defendants who habitually despised or hated Goering had enjoyed his discomfiture during the Gisevius testimony. But few of them enjoyed Gisevius's accounts of the Army's attempted coups against Hitler, both before and during the War. He went into great detail, much against the wishes of Lawrence, but with encouragement from several defence counsel. He named many prominent German generals as plotters, and pointed out that Rommel had even seemed likely to join them, but wrote him off as 'a typical Party general' who had been afraid to commit himself to the fight until it was proved successful – unlike other senior officers he described who 'from the beginning stood for decency and honour'. He fuelled the hatred among many defendants for witnesses who had appeared for the prosecution: Paulus, for example, whose surrender had aborted one coup; Lahousen, who had supplied the bombs for several attempts on Hitler's life. Inevitably, the military defendants were most disgusted by what they saw as treason in their ranks, but others were uneasy at the idea of plotting, especially during the War. Even Fritzsche wished that Gisevius had avoided so much detail – but in Fritzsche's view the mistake had been to risk creating a new 'stab in the back' legend around Hitler and Germany's defeat. (13)

The anger of so many defendants must have inspired the particular virulence with which several of their counsel questioned Gisevius about his contacts in Switzerland with Dulles and the OSS. Birkett noticed that Seidl 'spoke with unusual passion', suggesting that Gisevius had worked with foreign powers against Germany. 'It was most revealing,' Birkett thought, 'and showed the depth of national feeling whatever the evil record of the nation.' (14) Other counsel insinuated that Gisevius had taken money to betray his country. Gisevius was unshaken by the attacks. 'I was in the service of a good, clean, German cause,' he stated proudly. As his cross-examination by Jackson finished, he had said: 'I want to thank you, Mr Prosecutor, for giving me an opportunity to testify emphatically on behalf of the dead and the living.'

Frick, by refusing to enter the witness box, had done nothing to help himself or his fellow defendants. Gisevius's testimony had done a great deal to improve already good prosecution cases against several of those on trial. Morale in jail now dropped even further and splits between the defendants were widening. Even so, there were no grounds yet for prosecution complacency, no reasons to believe that all their cases would have such an easy passage through to judgement. After eight relatively straightforward cases the prosecution now had to tackle a handful of trickier ones, cases which raised real difficulties and needed skill and some luck to win.

The first of these – that of Julius Streicher – gave an appearance of simplicity which was highly misleading. The misconception arose from assuming that someone so immediately repellent must be found guilty. Any spectator in court had an instant desire to go and wash thoroughly after being in the same room as the man. The sight of Streicher doing his daily exercises in prison soured the breakfast in the stomachs of prisoners and guards alike. He exercised stark naked. He was revolting. Everyone complained about the spectacle. Fritzsche tactfully presented him with a pair of shorts made by cutting down a pair of old trousers, but Streicher refused to wear them. (15) He had driven the other prisoners distracted in the early weeks in jail by bellowing in the night. Andrus stopped that – he threatened punishment and Streicher fell silent. Andrus could not, however, stop Streicher telling him incessantly that General Eisenhower was a Jew (and that was why he had attacked Germany) and that Jackson was a Jew (whose real name was Jacobson). Andrus did not need a report from Gilbert to tell him that Streicher was 'rigid, insensitive and of obsessive mentality'. That was plain for all to see. He was also well aware that Streicher was 'the least intelligent and least amenable of all defendants'.

It was, however, possible to extract occasional entertainment from Streicher's stupidity and one-track mind. Andrus once sent interrogators to him accompanied by a blond, blue-eyed Jewish interpreter. Streicher, always susceptible to a handsome young man, had been thrilled. He called the interpreter 'a perfect example of a German Nordic'. Gilbert told Andrus that such was Streicher's fastidiousness on racial questions that he 'considers the Bible pornographic literature and has no use even for Christ because he was a Jew'. (16) Streicher considered himself an expert on pornography. He had a huge collection. In October 1945, *Stars and Stripes* had trumpeted the headline 'Streicher's Lewd Books May Figure in Trial' but those who might look forward to such an event had their hopes dashed by the story which followed which admitted that rampaging GIs had ransacked the collection and pocketed most of its gems. (17) Readers of the paper who had a sense of irony might have preferred the news it carried later that year that Streicher's estate had been turned into an agricultural training school for Jews intending to settle in Palestine.

As with Kaltenbrunner, any jury would have convicted Streicher on sight. He had been Gauleiter of Franconia from 1925 to 1939. In that position he had been infamous for his financial corruption and the sadism and obscenity of his behaviour. The charges against him, however, were mainly concerned with his work as a rabble-rouser against the Jews, both as a tireless public speaker and as founder of *Der Stürmer*, the weekly newspaper he began in 1923 and continued to edit until 1945. *Der Stürmer* was not so much of the gutter press as of the sewer – a fitting reflection of its editor's mind. Its only coverage was of anti-Semitism – obscene cartoons, gory tales of ritual murders printed as fact, campaigns for anti-Jewish action and legislation, and lists of Jewish dentists, doctors, shopkeepers, whom 'Aryans' were advised to avoid (with hints of the troubles which would come to those who did not heed the warnings). At its most popular in about 1937, the paper had a circulation of 500,000. Its readership was higher: display cases for the paper were set up in public places, factory canteens, anywhere the lurid headlines might catch the eye.

Hitler was a great admirer of *Der Stürmer*. He said he read it from cover to cover. Hoess, the commandant at Auschwitz, on the other hand, told Gilbert he found its treatment of the Jewish Question 'too superficial'. (18) But Streicher had clearly tried to do his best. Jackson in his opening speech had quoted several articles. That of 19 March 1942, for instance, which complained that Christian teaching had stood in the way of a 'racial solution of the Jewish Question in Europe' and quoted as a rallying call the Führer's proclamation 'the Jew will be exterminated'. And the triumphant tone of the news in November 1943: the Jews 'have disappeared from Europe' and the 'reservoir of the East from which the Jewish plague has for centuries beset the people of Europe has ceased to exist'; or the challenge issued to readers in May 1942: 'The Jewish question is a world question ... the Jewish question is hardly solved in Europe as long as Jews live in the rest of the world.' (19)

Given the prosecution contention that persecution of Jews had been a Nazi method of gaining control of Germany and a long-established aim in their intended domination of Europe, and given the fact that the murder of Jews formed an important allegation in the counts on war crimes and crimes against humanity, it had seemed entirely logical to bring Streicher to trial. He had been the Nazi government's most notorious Jew-baiter; his paper, it was argued, must surely have formed public opinion and prepared the psychological conditions in which the public was prepared to accept terrorism and the killing of a racial group. The argument was persuasive. It reached the conclusion any reasonable man might jump to. The law, however, though it often accepts the concept of 'the reasonable man', frowns on leaping to conclusions. It demands evidence to forge the links between allegations and crimes, motives and acts, words and deeds. Where were those links in the Streicher case? The prosecution did not allege that Streicher himself killed anyone. Was there evidence to prove beyond reasonable doubt that Streicher's words had incited others to commit crimes? The prosecution hoped so. It hoped to convince the Tribunal that words such as 'kill', 'exterminate', 'eradicate' had been used by Streicher and had led logically and inevitably to the deaths of Jews. But had they? The prosecutors could produce no witness to say 'because I read *Der Stürmer* I decided to kill a Jew and went and did so'. Without the connection between word and deed, it was possible for the Tribunal merely to find that Streicher was anti-Semitic, and anti-Semitism was not a crime at the Nuremberg trial. Murdering Jews (or gypsies or Slavs or Germans) was.

The prosecution not only faced a problem of proof in count Four, they had to wrestle with difficulties in tying Streicher to other charges in Count One. If the American interpretation of this count were to be accepted, then the Nazi conspiracy began with the foundation of the Nazi Party in 1921 – the year Streicher joined. From that date, everything the Party did must be seen as deliberately working to perpetrate the crime of aggressive war and the war crimes and crimes against humanity which followed. But many non-Americans doubted that the conspiracy charge could be interpreted so broadly; they were dubious that all aspects of Nazi policy could be joined so neatly; they suspected that an international tribunal might not be qualified to judge matters relating to the acts of a sovereign state against its own citizens; they feared that the Tribunal might find it more appropriate to date the conspiracy from 1937 – the year when war was clearly established as a Nazi aim.

All these reservations burst out in the open at a British prosecutors' meeting on 16 April. The British had been given responsibility for the Streicher case. They had not found it easy to assemble conclusive evidence for it and feared their vulnerability should Streicher's counsel mount an attack on their use of the conspiracy charge. Griffith-Jones suggested that it might be preferable to avoid much cross-examination of Streicher's acts before 1937 and concentrate on his incitement to persecution after that date and on the ways he had rallied public opinion 'which was valuable to all Nazi plans'. (20) It was not a strong, let alone a confident approach, and it could do nothing to cover two unpalatable facts. Firstly, that the circulation of *Der Stürmer* had dropped dramatically once the war began, down to 200,000. Was that circulation enough to have inspired the deaths of ten million people or more? Secondly, Streicher himself had retired into private life in 1940, as newspaper editor and farmer. There had been no resignation, not in any sense. He had been stripped of all Party offices and titles and driven out. Even Hitler by 1940 could no longer withstand the tide of complaints about Streicher's corruption and obscenity. (One wonders if Streicher's fall from grace was hastened by the stories he was spreading that year that Goering was impotent.)

Given his repellent aspect and drivelling mind, Streicher should never have gone into the witness box. If he had had a modicum of self-awareness and common sense, he would have avoided drawing attention to himself and encouraged his counsel to play on the undoubted weaknesses of the prosecution case. Instead, he gave evidence and submitted to cross-examination for a day and a half from the afternoon of 28 April. Those who could stomach his opinions and keep pace with his violent lurches of subject matter found the testimony almost hilarious.

It began with a bitter denunciation of his counsel, Dr Marx, whom Streicher accused of not conducting his case as instructed and of submitting to intimidation from Marxist papers in the Russian Zone. Marx responded with what was not his first attempt to resign but was told by the Tribunal to carry on. Streicher continued with a shrill protest about the conditions he had suffered in captivity, complaining that he had been kept for days without clothes (an odd complaint from a nude exerciser) and that he had been 'made to kiss negroes' feet'. He paused for breath then screamed: 'My mouth was forced open with a piece of wood and then I was spat on. When I asked for a drink of water, I was taken to a latrine ... These are the sort of things the Gestapo had been blamed for.' This section was later struck from the record. (21)

With that off his chest, Streicher then settled down to a less impassioned rant about the way Jews had seized power in Germany in 1918; how he had first seen Hitler in 1921 – radiant and 'drenched in perspiration'. He paid generous tribute to his own courage in the Putsch, his own efficiency in organizing the Jewish boycott in April 1933 – the day, he said, had passed off 'perfectly'. He lamented the fact that he had not been consulted over the Nuremberg Laws, but was gratified to believe that his views had clearly influenced them. He spoke with deep satisfaction about *Der Stürmer* – 80–90 per cent of which he said was true – and about his destruction of the main synagogue in Nuremberg in 1938. He even produced photographs to support his claim that it had to be destroyed because it spoilt the view. (When asked in cross-examination whether the hour and a half speech he made before the razing of the synagogue had been concerned entirely with architecture, he thought it had.)

Interspersed with all this were Streicher's frequent and leering attempts to discuss his previous trials for rape, sadistic assault and so on. All of them were cut short by Lawrence. When Streicher finally refused the opportunity offered him by Marx to deny his printed stories of Jewish ritual murders and snapped at his counsel, Lawrence told him not to be so insolent and threatened to postpone the case. Streicher continued to repeat his belief in ritual murders and gave accounts of some of them. Some of this was struck from the record too. All in all, it was a performance which revived doubts about Streicher's sanity. Though anti-Semitism may not have been a crime, it was not an attitude calculated to soften hearts or win the sympathy of judges.

No defence counsel wished to put a question to Streicher. Griffith-Jones made short work of his cross-examination. The *Daily Telegraph* described his approach as suave and icily courteous. (22) Wolf Frank, the simultaneous translator, remembers it as dramatic and damning – he maintains that Griffith-Jones never even glanced at Streicher; he treated him as if he were a disgusting mess on the pavement, which one would skirt, eyes and nose averted. (23) Robbed of the theatrical manner and the impact of Streicher's repellence, the transcript of the cross-examination does not impress. Griffith-Jones had no different evidence to offer, he was still largely dependent on quotations from *Der Stürmer*. Streicher, however, made the case for him. He responded enthusiastically to quotation from an article by saying it was 'a historical fact' that Jews were a 'nation of bloodsuckers'. First he claimed to have read *Israelitisches Wochenblatt*, then when Griffith-Jones showed that it continually printed facts about the persecution and murder of Jews, he argued that he could not always get a copy.

Streicher's witnesses fared no better. Maxwell-Fyfe had suggested that they should be treated with 'lofty contempt' so they were not cross-examined. (24) But even in the hands of Marx, they contradicted themselves and each other, and instead of denying prosecution allegations blithely accepted them, adding a few details for good measure. 'Well,' said Fritzsche, as the Streicher case finished, 'they've put a rope round his neck after all; at least our end of the dock thinks so.' (25) It might have been more accurate to say that Streicher himself had put his head in a noose. But would the judges allow the defendant to hang himself rather than expect the evidence to do it?

Most people at this stage thought that the judges must. Doubts about the strength of the prosecution case had been submerged by Streicher's own outrageous performance, but there could be no similar expectation in the next case – that the difficulties of ensnaring the defendant with the evidence would be eased by the defendant himself. Hjalmar Schacht (whose two other Christian names, Horace Greeley, did not appear in the indictment, perhaps because Horace Greeley had once been a Presidential candidate and was one of the greatest American newspaper editors) was the most intelligent of the defendants. Gilbert's report to Andrus described him as having 'a brilliant mentality, capable of creative originality'. (26) In addition he was astute and cunning. Even more important for his defence than his intelligence was his character. Schacht was a fighter, and in fighting for his life he wore stout armour – complete confidence in his innocence on all charges. He could have borne on his shield the words of Metternich when looking back at his career: 'Error has never crossed my mind.' Others might think this arrogance but Schacht saw it as a statement of fact; those who questioned it merely proclaimed their mental inadequacy to judge his career of intellectual achievement and patriotic service. He regarded his imprisonment as a scandal, writing in his memoirs: 'I was described in an English newspaper as the most refractory of all the Nuremberg prisoners, and I am rather proud of it.' (27) On one occasion he threw a mug of coffee at an American photographer who was taking pictures of the defendants at lunch. He found the man's behaviour vulgar, and added that he himself was eating peas at the time so 'it was not very flattering'. He was deprived of his coffee ration for a week. On another occasion Andrus threatened to deprive him of daily exercise because of his recalcitrance. Schacht was unperturbed: 'Secure in the possession of a perfectly clear conscience, I protested in the strongest possible terms while at Nuremberg against any and every form of unjust treatment.' In spite of having been in Flossenberg and Dachau since 1944, he could still write that conditions at Nuremberg were worse than any he had experienced. His reaction to being on trial varied from one of indignation to contempt for his accusers. On arrival at Nuremberg he had told Gilbert that he 'hoped the trial would take a short time so they could hang those other criminals and let him go home'. (28)

Schacht was able to project his confidence and sense of innocence, an ability which impressed many spectators in court though it never made him an endearing figure. The *Chicago Daily News* had described him in early December as showing an attitude of 'studied outrage' at being united with 'these gangsters'. Their reporter evoked the way 'he glances diagonally across the courtroom, with an acid look that fairly corrodes the wood-panelled walls with hostility and contempt.' (29) Another observer got much the same impression: 'Schacht is in the front row; it is an honour that he does not seem to enjoy very much. There is something of the catfish in the inverted "U" of the mouth and his goggly eyes. He wears an air of complete aloofness; he cannot understand what has happened that he, the ex-President of the great Reichsbank, intimate of honoured American, British and French friends in the banking world, should now find himself in the dock with criminals.' (30) So strong was the image of Schacht the banker that many people found it odd not to see him in starched shirt and striped trousers; his soft blue collar seemed incongruous. But though all descriptions suggest that his air of rectitude, dignity and innocence was convincing, they do not suggest that he was a man many warmed to.

Certainly most of the defendants did not, though many had to concede grudging respect. Schacht had held most of them at arm's length. 'With those whom I knew to be not merely guilty but also inimically disposed towards me, I never exchanged a single word.' (31) He maintained some

Some of the inmates of 'Ashcan' – leaders of the Third Reich, twelve of whom would appear at Nuremberg as defendants, several of whom were brought as witnesses. They posed for their photograph on the terrace of the Palace Hotel, Mondorf-les Bains in Luxembourg where they were held until the move to Nuremberg jail in August 1945.

Front row, left to right: Hans Lammers; Franz von Epp; **Hermann Goering;** *Franz Xaver Schwarz; Otto Meissner.*

Second row: **Joachim von Ribbentrop; Walter Funk;** *Ernst Bohle; Jakob Negl; Franz Schwarz; Herbert Buechs; Otto Salman.*

Third row: Friedrich Kritzinger; **Arthur Seyss-Inquart;** *Erwin Krauss-Leitz; Lutz Schwerin von Krosick; Franz Seldte;* **Robert Ley;** *Werner Zschintzsch; Albert Kesselring.*

In back group: **Hans Frank;** *Eric Dethleffsen;* **Karl Doenitz;** *Johannes Blaskowitz; Hermann Reiecke; Karl Stroelin;* **Alfred Jodl;** *Gerhard Wagner; Karl Brandt; Philip von Hessen; Paul Wegener; Walter Bush;* **Alfred Rosenberg;** *Leopold Buerkner;* **Wilhelm Keitel;** *Unidentified;* **Wilhelm Frick;** *Unidentified; Kurt Daluege;* **Julius Streicher.**
(John Topham Picture Library)

The courthouse at Nuremberg. The trial took place in the courtroom on the second floor. The immense Palace of Justice which provided office accommodation, canteens and storage for documents was to the left of the picture.
(Popperfoto)

The courtroom during the trial. The floor had to be replaced and the back wall ripped out to provide space for the Press and for a visitors' gallery above. On the right, two rows of defendants with their counsel in front. Beyond them, the tables for the prosecution. On the left, the lectern with microphone at which counsel spoke; in front of it, some of the court reporters. The judges sat facing the defendants.
(Keystone Press)

The interior of a cell. Robert Ley managed to strangle himself with a zip tied to the lavatory pipe. (Melitta Mew)

The defendants in court. On the front row, left to right: Goering, Hess, Ribbentrop, Keitel, Kaltenbrunner, Rosenberg, Frank, Frick, Streicher, Funk, Schacht. On the back row: Doenitz, Raeder, Schirach, Sauckel, Jodl, Papen, Seyss-Inquart, Speer, Neurath, Fritzsche. The simultaneous translators are on the far right. (Keystone Press)

The defendants' wing in Nuremberg jail. A guard to each cell, some leaning on the flap of the hatch in the door. The wire netting was installed to prevent suicide attempts. The lamps outside the cells were shone through the hatch and on to the prisoners at night. (Keystone Press)

The defendants during a recess in the speech of the British prosecutor Sir Hartley Shawcross. Journalists commented that the accused were alternately angry or worried as they listened. (Keystone Press)

An American prosecutor addresses the tribunal (Alderman, 26 November 1945). The tribunal on the bench. Left to right, Volchkov and Nikitchenko (USSR) in uniform; Birkett and Lawrence (Great Britain); Biddle and Parker (US); Donnedieu de Vabres and Falco (France). On the row below are officers of the court; in front of them are the court reporters with defence counsel opposite. On the far right at the British prosecution tables are Hartley Shawcross (leaning on his right hand) and beyond him, Maxwell-Fyfe. (Fox Photos)

Members of the British prosecution team. December 1945.
Front row, left to right: Professor Lauterpacht; the Rt. Hon. Sir David Maxwell-Fyfe KC, MP; H.M. Attorney-General Sir Hartley Shawcross KC, MP; Mr G.D. Roberts KC; and Mr Patrick Dean (of the Foreign Office)
   Back row: Major J.H. Barrington; Major Elwyn Jones MP; Mr E.G. Robey; Lt.-Col. M. Griffith Jones MC; Col. H.J. Phillimore; Mr Maurice Read; and Mr Bashford.
(Fox Photos)

Rudenko speaking on the prosecutors' stand. (BBC Hulton Picture Library)

Some of the defence counsel outside the Palace of Justice.
Front row left to right: Dr Egon Kubuschok (Papen and Reich Cabinet); Dr Robert Servatius (Sauckel and Leadership Corps); Dr Alfred Sauter (Hess from February 1946 and Frank throughout); Dr Hanns Marx (Streicher).
Second row: Dr Franz Exner (Jodl and General Staff and High Command until January 1945); Dr Fritz Seidl (Ribbentrop until January and Von Schirach throughout); Dr Otto Stahmer (Goering); Dr Walter Ballas (intended to assist the counsel for Krupp); Dr Hans Flaeschner (Speer); Dr Gunther von Rohrscheidt (Hess until February 1946).
Third row: Dr George Froeschmann; Dr Heinz Fritz (Fritzsche); Dr Otto Pannenbecker (Frick); Dr Alfred Thoma (Rosenberg); Dr Kurt Kauffman (Kaltenbrunner); Dr Hans Laternser (General Staff and High Command from January 1946) (Popperfoto)

The defendants' visitors' centre. While Jodl struggles to speak to his counsel, Goering charms his guard. (Melitta Mew)

contact with Frick, Doenitz, Raeder, Neurath, Papen, Fritzsche and Speer. But there was no intimacy, and they turned against him once Gisevius was produced as a witness – not just for himself but actually against others. In Papen's view, Gisevius's appearance revealed Schacht as 'the egoist he always had been'. (32) But to many observers it suggested that Schacht's apparent confidence was justified: would Gisevius have testified for him had Schacht been guilty, they wondered?

When Schacht himself went into the witness box on 30 April, his style contrasted sharply with that of other defendants. He did not so much produce rebuttal against some allegations as seize the whole corpus of prosecution evidence, rip it into pieces he could handle, then rearrange it to build up a totally different picture.

The prosecution analysis of the facts of Schacht's career boiled down to the view that though Schacht was never a member of the Nazi Party he was committed to Nazism and had worked consciously and deliberately to achieve Hitler's aims. He had approached the Nazis in 1931 because he saw in them a weapon for the destruction of the Weimar Republic whose political weakness and financial shillyshallying he despised. He was a successful banker who had added to his reputation in 1923 when as Reich Currency Commissioner he had played a significant part in stabilizing the mark and arresting inflation. From that year until 1930 he had been Head of the Reichsbank. The prosecution argued that Schacht's prestige had helped to win over bankers and industrialists to Hitler. He had further exploited their respect and trust in him to obtain investment or credit to back government policies, then used it to secure foreign confidence and aid. According to the indictment, the government policy which Schacht had most helped was rearmament: hence his charge on the first two counts. His scheme for financing the secret development of the armed forces was summarized in his memorandum of May 1935, 'The Financing of the Armament Programme'. As President of the Reichsbank from 1934 to 1937 and Plenipotentiary of the War Economy from 1935 to 1937, it was alleged he had created capital by stimulating private enterprise and expanding public works, and bridged the shortfall between available investment and government demands by 'mefo' bills and other forms of financial inventiveness. By a combination of secrecy and sleight of hand in book-keeping he had managed to prevent runaway inflation while at the same time allowing the debt of the Nazi government to triple between 1932 and 1938. The crucial prosecution point, which turned their account from one of praise for financial ingenuity to an allegation of criminality, was that over a third of this debt had been incurred, as Schacht well knew, by the insatiable appetite of the Nazi rearmament programme. That programme had been clearly devised for the purpose of waging aggressive war and Schacht must have known it.

The prosecution acknowledged that Schacht had resigned as Minister of Economics and Plenipotentiary for War in 1937, but they maintained this was not because of opposition to planned aggression but as a result of a dispute with Goering who successfully pressed for national self-sufficiency against Schacht's plea for encouraging foreign trade as a source of raw materials. His resignation from the Reichsbank was again seen as a conflict of professional opinion rather than a matter of principle. According to the prosecution, it reflected Schacht's awareness that financial collapse would result from the weight of government indebtedness by 1939 and that Schacht would be saddled with all the blame. His resignation was an attempt to save his skin and his reputation. The prosecution pointed to the fact that he had remained as Minister Without Portfolio until he was sacked in 1943 as proof that he had not chosen to fall out with the Nazi government on matters of general policy. To counter any evidence he might introduce on his contacts with the resistance to Hitler, they had emphasized the views of George Messersmith, a former official at the US Embassy in Berlin. Messersmith had described Schacht as a man who 'always attempted to play both sides of the fence'. His affidavit had ended: 'In my opinion Schacht was in no sense a captive of the Nazis. He was not compelled to devote his time and his capacities to their interest . . . He continued to lend his services to the Nazi government out of opportunism.' (33) Equally, argued the prosecution, Schacht had dabbled with Hitler's opponents out of opportunism.

In his examination in chief, Schacht told these same facts and reassembled them, moulding them into a memorial of untarnished rectitude. He justified his early support for the Nazi Party by presenting his own interpretation of its programme: self-determination for all nations, an equal position for Germany in the world, the abolition of the discriminations of Versailles, the recovery of territory wrongfully taken from Germany in 1919, the wish to provide sustenance, educational opportunity and strong government for German citizens. 'I am unable to see in the Party programme as such,' he said, 'any sign of criminal intentions.' He admitted that the policy of excluding Jews from civil rights was 'somewhat beyond the limit' but felt they would have received adequate protection under the Aliens' Law and that the programme had guaranteed them religious liberty.

Schacht differentiated sharply between his early approval for the stated aims of the Nazis and his contempt for Hitler. He condemned Hitler as a man with no understanding of economic problems who 'consequently had no interest for me'. He called *Mein Kampf* 'a book written in the worst kind of German, propaganda of . . . a fanatical, half-educated man.' He gave the devil his due and conceded that Hitler was 'a mass psychologist of a really diabolical genius', 'a man of unbending energy, of a willpower which overcame all obstacles'. But then he dismissed him as a 'victim to the same spell which he exercised over the masses . . . ensnaring him in the evil ways of mass instincts'. Schacht justified his collaboration with Hitler as an attempt to direct his power into more orderly channels. He had taken official positions and joined the Cabinet, he said, because 'it was necessary to keep on working for the German people and exercise a moderating influence within the government.' He was insistent that his relationship with Hitler and leading Nazis had been purely on matters of financial business. Some of then, like Kaltenbrunner and Schirach he had never met; others he had not seen since 1938. In early years he occasionally had lunch with Hitler but gave up the practice once aware of the low level of conversation at such functions and the cringing servility of the other guests. He sneered at the low intelligence of leading Nazis and their pretence of embodying Teutonic virtues. The only thing most of them had in common with the old Teutons was, in his opinion, excessive drinking – 'a main part of Nazi ideology'. He had received the Golden Party Emblem only because it was automatically handed to all ministers in 1937; he gave it back when sacked in 1943. He had received a painting from Hitler as a sixtieth birthday present; he sent it back when it turned out to be a forgery.

While skilfully crafting the image of a man of dignity, taste and superior intellect so different from Nazis, Schacht also reordered the facts of his career to contradict the account set out by the prosecution. He declared himself a nationalist, never once claiming territory that was not genuinely German, hoping for the Anschluss while regretting that Austria would be a financial liability. He suggested that the Sudetenland had been given to Hitler by the Allies 'on a silver platter'. He denied any knowledge whatsoever of Hitler's aggressive intentions, pointing out that he never attended military conferences and was not even in the country when the invasion of Poland was planned. He denied too any knowledge of how the money he provided was spent; that, he said, was the job of the Minister of Finance. He insisted that his work for rearmament had been based on the desire for parity and in the hope it would provoke response from other nations who had failed to take the preferable course and disarm themselves. He explained his resignation as Minister of the Economy by arguing that he had always encouraged foreign trade as a means of increasing international understanding but had been overruled by Hitler and Goering. He discussed his financial policies with obvious pride, remarking that he was no more responsible for the tripling of government debt than he was for the rise of the birth rate at the same period. He insisted that he had resigned from the Reichsbank as soon as Hitler's policies endangered Germany's financial security and were leading to more than parity in armaments. He claimed that Hitler's condition for his release from the post had been that he continue as Minister Without Portfolio so as to conceal the differences between them. In this position, Schacht drew no salary, went to no official meetings. His testimony frequently touched on his long history of opposition to Nazi policies: he mentioned his complaints to Hitler about persecution of Jews and committal without trial to concentration camps and his threat to sack any Reichsbank staff found to have taken part in the 'Kristallnacht' terrorism.

Schacht's role as conspirator against Hitler epitomizes the ambiguities and mysteries of the man which were never resolved at Nuremberg and still create uncertainty about his character and motives. He implied he had stayed in office to try to pull some chestnuts out of Hitler's fire while encouraging others to overthrow the regime and replace it with one in Germany's interests. Gisevius corroborated a lot of this story. He had described meeting Schacht in 1935 and finding Gestapo bugging devices in his flat. He had narrated Schacht's comments on his anxiety to save Germany from financial crash, his wish to rearm the country to provide defence, his intention to resign should the government fail to repay its debts in the hope of precipitating a military coup (a scheme hindered in the event by the lack of preparation of the generals). Gisevius expressed the belief that in 1938 and 1939 Schacht 'really fought and I will never forget that. It is a pleasure for me to be able to testify to this here.' But Gisevius sensed ambiguity in Schacht. He admitted, 'Schacht was always a problem and a puzzle to us' – the conspirators. And a later witness, the former Social Democratic Minister of the Interior, Severing, was to say that he refused all contact with Schacht during the preparations for the Bomb Plot in 1944; he was 'known to me as a rather unreliable person in political matters'. (34) Many people distrusted Schacht's motives without being certain what they were: patriotism in joining and deserting Hitler and his opponents, opportunism, or such devotion to his own views on finance that he would join anyone and do anything to implement them?

Schacht's examination in chief lasted two and a half days from the morning of 30 April. It was a remarkable performance, demonstrating all his confidence, intellectual clarity and his awareness of how best to convince. It had been adroitly egged on by his able counsel, Dix, a lawyer Maxwell-Fyfe judged with Kranzbuehler as being as 'good as could be found at any bar'. (35) The testimony had been expert in its exposition of financial affairs and enlivened by Schacht's sarcastic wit. Observers had been gripped. The *New York Times* thought Schacht 'an impressive witness'. (36) *The Times* commented that he had spoken 'with the composure of a man who feels he has a case, and more than any of the others in the box he has a shrewd grasp of the case against him'. The report praised what had been 'the most solidly argued case yet heard' and implied some relief that Schacht's testimony had been 'free from the elusive often unintelligible form of Nazi speech that has had such full play during the past weeks'. (37) Journalists had clearly enjoyed his 'scornful attitude to his fellow defendants', his 'vitriolic frankness as when he attacked Ribbentrop as stupid', his 'trenchant indictment of Hitler'. (38) They expressed no suspicion that he might have been creating a background against which he could shine; they seemed ready to accept that he had continued to work with men he despised for the reasons he gave. Patrick Dean, on the other hand, had not been swept along by the confidence and tight argument of Schacht's testimony. He felt that 'Schacht is extremely evasive while giving an appearance of frankness' and wondered whether his very astuteness in putting his own construction on prosecution evidence might rebound against him – give the impression to the Tribunal that he was too clever by half. (39)

Schacht, however, had been delighted with his performance and told Gilbert so. In his memoirs he goes over the details of his testimony with relish. He notes that when he referred to 'the dictated Peace' of Versailles there was an uneasiness among the judges and the prosecutors. 'But that was my intention,' he says. 'I meant to make them listen to what I had to say – and I succeeded.' He adds: 'That afternoon counsel and I had another dig or two at Versailles, greatly to the annoyance of the prosecution.' He had enjoyed causing annoyance, pointing out how Allied ambassadors had attended Party rallies, correcting the charge that he had been a member of the Reichstag, and causing 'a fearful amount of embarrassment to Mr Jackson and his large staff' by showing that he did not have the Party Badge in 1935 as they had claimed. He had taken pleasure too in irritating the other defendants – bringing up the Fritsch affair, knowing that it made Goering 'uncomfortable to hear Fritsch's name spoken in court' and watching their faces when he denounced Hitler. (40)

Not surprisingly Schacht's fellow defendants had been far from delighted with his performance. Several newspapers noted the angry looks he drew from them especially when he expressed his contempt for Hitler. When he claimed ignorance of how much money was spent on armaments Raeder laughed: 'Who's going to believe that?' Inevitably, Goering led an attack on Schacht, prowling round the lunchrooms and calling him a turncoat and a hypocrite. Many needed no persuading to cold-shoulder Schacht: his deliberate aloofness in jail and his use of Gisevius had not endeared him. Once he went into the witness box even his former supporters found his protests of total innocence too much to take. Frick suggested that if Hitler had won the war, Schacht 'would be running round with the loudest "Heil Hitler"'. Schirach was bitter at Schacht's expressions of contempt for Nazism and remembered Mrs Schacht at a reception wearing an enormous diamond swastika. Even Speer covertly accused Schacht of insincerity, and said he was now even more determined to admit to his own share of guilt. A majority of the defendants, thought Gilbert, were positively looking forward to Schacht's cross-examination and hoping he would be cut down to size. (41)

Schacht was looking forward to the cross-examination too. He saw it as the last hurdle before inevitable acquittal and release. Not a daunting hurdle – he was too confident that his view would prevail and that he had the measure of Jackson who was responsible for his case. 'He was really in an impossible position ... But he was out to save what he could from the wreck,' Schacht thought at the time and wrote later. (42) He welcomed the chance to display his abilities and the challenge of fighting the prosecution. Jackson too was facing a challenge. This was to be his first cross-examination since the Goering débâcle and he needed to re-establish his authority. He took the Schacht case most seriously. He informed the other chief prosecutors on 10 April that there would be no point in trying to mount a trial of industrialists should Schacht be acquitted, for there was no better case against any of them. (43) Griffith-Jones had suggested to

British colleagues the next day that Jackson was unduly pessimistic; Schacht was only concerned with preparations for war whereas there were strong cases against many industrialists over their use of slave labour. (44) But for Jackson the conviction of Schacht had become crucial – for his own reputation, for a rounded case on conspiracy, as a foundation for subsequent proceedings, he had to win this round. The tension Jackson was feeling had been noticeable during Schacht's examination in chief. He had made frequent attempts to interrupt and complain about Dix's questions. Birkett thought he had intervened 'in a most petulant and aggressive manner', that he was 'obviously suffering from frayed nerves' and anxiety that he might fail with Schacht. (45)

As the cross-examination began after the afternoon recess on 2 May, Schacht was certain that Jackson was 'still seething inside' after the Tribunal's refusals to support his objections in the previous two days. 'He was after my scalp,' thought Schacht. 'I had no mind to let him have it.' (46) Jackson began badly. He hoped to establish that Schacht had had friendly relations with many leading Nazis by producing photographs of them all together. It was a trivial point, made embarrassing by Jackson's inability to tell Schacht when the pictures had been taken. Schacht dismissed them with the contemptuous remark that they would be heavily outnumbered by photographs of him with other acquaintances. When Jackson mentioned the names of Hitler, Himmler and Heydrich, Schacht took the opportunity to regret that they were dead: 'I would have liked to see them die in some other way.' Jackson failed to throw him off balance with the affidavit from Blomberg saying that Schacht had discussed Wehrmacht finances and put his views in writing. Schacht predictably denied it (he might well have added that if his views were in writing it would be more effective to produce them than to quote an unsubstantiated allegation). He was happy to admit that he wore the Party's Gold Swastika; it was, he said brazenly, 'very convenient on railroad journeys and when ordering a car'.

Jackson occasionally got a grip on his witness when he used better evidence – a speech, for example, in which Schacht confirmed that the New Plan for the economy was largely concerned with financing rearmament; proofs that Schacht had paid 1,000 Reichsmarks annually to Party funds between 1937 and 1942; calls to brand those who patronized Jewish shops 'traitors'. The Times noticed how all the defendants were 'rooting for Jackson'; when he got the better of Schacht 'they would smile and nod'. (47) Gilbert overhead Goering tell Hess: 'Put on your headphones. This is going to be good'; and he recorded the delight of the military defendants as Schacht's knowledge of Wehrmacht planning was brought out by Jackson. (48)

But on this day and the next, Jackson never really kept his control for long. (49) He had not learned from the Goering case the need for detailed preparation. Time and again Schacht corrected him on dates and names, told him the numbers of prosecution documents and was even so well-prepared himself that he could begin to quote them before Jackson could find the place. So confident did Schacht become that on occasion he was ready to give his replies in English. Birkett commented during the day that if a cross-examiner 'is unsure of his facts, so stumbles or delays, the richest opportunity of the cross-examination is lost. This was one of the first and main weaknesses of Jackson.' Jackson's skimping on homework was particularly disastrous in his attempted attack on Schacht's financial policies. Birkett summed up the section by saying that Jackson had made 'a mistake in questioning Schacht on banking and economic matters about which he is obviously imperfectly instructed and knows little, whereas Schacht can overpower him on these topics at any moment'. (50) Schacht showed Jackson no mercy. He blinded him with economics and alternately taunted or patronized. He took great pleasure in remembering this part of the contest in his memoirs, as he did from recording Jackson's fumbling attempt to discountenance him by quoting his comment that the former German colonies in Africa were 'our property'. He was delighted with his riposte – that the Versailles Treaty had called them German property too. Jackson, commented Schacht disdainfully, 'was completely at sea. That is what happens when American prosecutors are sent over to Europe who don't even know anything about the Treaty of Versailles.' (51)

Schacht was always quick to praise himself and despise others. Even so his account in his memoirs of Jackson's cross-examination accords with the impression given in the transcript: that Jackson repeated the mistakes he had made with Goering. The only improvement was that he kept control over his feelings; but he had in no way controlled his witness. As Birkett recorded at the time, 'nothing occurred during the cross-examination other than a strengthening of Schacht's defence'. (52) The *Daily Telegraph* correspondent believed that Schacht had emerged slightly damaged but had given 'the most consistent and best supported apologia yet submitted'. (53) Dean agreed that Schacht had 'made a much better showing than any of the other defendants', but believed he had 'clearly not done well enough to escape conviction'; he expected him to 'receive a lighter sentence than most of his colleagues in the dock'. (54) Not so other observers. The *New York Times* reported the impression of many lawyers that Schacht had 'slipped out of Jackson's fingers'. In consequence they estimated that he might well 'have won himself acquittal'. (55)

If that was to be the case, if Schacht was to receive a light sentence or even acquittal, it had been a disastrous few days for the prosecution: they had failed to make their case stick when faced with a major defendant. Before the trial began no one had ever predicted that acquittals were a possibility. The prospect that Schacht would emerge unscathed opened up further during an incompetent cross-examination by a Russian prosecutor. Not unfairly, Schacht was to describe Alexandrov as merely repeating questions put by Jackson and ending with two of his own which 'were simply fatuous'. (56) Following this messy interlude, Schacht called two witnesses who completed the impression that he would escape unbruised.

By the time Schacht returned to the dock on 3 May he was clearly 'exhilarated' thought Cooper, 'looking ten years younger'. (57) That night Schacht told Gilbert that he expected instant release from prison. Surely, he said, he would not be kept 'sitting here for another three months and listening to all that stuff that doesn't concern me'. (58)

Schacht was followed into the witness box, as he had been succeeded in so many official posts, by Walther Funk. Funk had begun his career as a financial journalist. When he joined the Nazi Party in 1931 he brought to it his extensive contacts with banking and insurance circles and big business. Like Schacht he was accused of using these contacts and exploiting his own reputation for the Party's ends. He acted as Hitler's personal economic adviser, was made press chief of the Reich Government in 1933 and given posts in the Ministry of Propaganda and the Reich Broadcasting Company. Then, as Schacht left positions, Funk took them over. He became Minister of Economics in 1937, holding the post until 1945; he replaced Schacht as Plenipotentiary for the War Economy in 1938 and the following year he became President of the Reichsbank. His titles had been impressive; the range of his activities suggested a man of calibre and influence; his position as a personal adviser to Hitler implied intimacy.

However, once Funk's career was examined more closely, it was impossible to avoid the conclusion that the indictment against him had confused formal position with actual authority. When the prosecutors had drawn up the indictment they had been too ignorant of the hierarchy and personalities of the Nazi regime to assess the real importance of several of the defendants. They had exaggerated Funk's role. Funk could argue more accurately than Frick, for instance, that he had held titles rather than power and been bypassed or robbed of authority by others. His work in propaganda had been directed by Goebbels and had been largely administrative. At the Ministry of Economics he had implemented the policies of others rather than tried to initiate his own. He had lost all influence over the economic administration of the occupied territories to Goering and any control over munitions first to Todt then to Speer. As Goering put it in his testimony, by the time other competing agencies had taken advantage of Funk's personal and political weakness, his ministry 'by and large was left a hollow shell'. Though a minister, he had seldom been consulted on anything, or even been allowed to attend conferences. Lammers had stressed that Funk had little contact with Hitler and from 1943 the Führer had simply refused to see him.

Funk was charged on all four counts. Yet though the indictment put some weight on his economic exploitation of occupied territories, the prosecution had produced too little evidence to substantiate the charge and its case had been further weakened by the assessment of other defendants and witnesses. Nor had the prosecution proved the allegation that Funk had been concerned with the procurement and use of foreign labour. By the time his defence began, the only charge worth pursuing related to his work in eliminating Jews from the economy (a much weaker accusation than one of actual extermination), and assistance in the preparation and financing of aggressive war (an area where it was now clear that others had been more involved and effective). And, most unpleasant of all, the accusation that as President of the Reichsbank, Funk had received and stored gold for the SS knowing it had been stripped from concentration camp victims. For the rest Funk faced a relatively weak prosecution case.

A tougher man would have spotted and seized the opportunities left for his defence. A Goering or a Schacht would have had a field day at the expense of the prosecution, but Funk lacked the personality for a fight. He was one of Andrus's least favourite prisoners, 'always whimpering and whining' said the Colonel; and to lower his opinion further, scruffy in appearance and slovenly in the upkeep of his cell. Funk's excuse for whimpering and whining was his health; he was diabetic and had had bouts of kidney and bladder trouble. But as Gilbert told Andrus: 'his complaints were far out of proportion with the physical findings'; a once cheerful gadabout had become in prison 'hypochondriac and forlorn'. (59) A more justifiable complaint perhaps from Funk was that he had to sit in the dock every day next to Streicher. He regarded this as a punishment; most people would. Observers all talked of Funk in terms of colour. David Low, the cartoonist, who visited the trial and watched the defendants, once told a journalist: 'It struck me that if one were doing a historical painting of that crowd, it would have to deal almost exclusively in browns and yellows – and greens perhaps. Funk's green, isn't he?' (60) Other people thought yellow – inside and out. The *Daily Mail* described Funk in court: 'yellow, heavy-jowled, he crouches over the dock and scratches his chin with a curiously Simian gesture.' (61) His face was not often visible. He usually sat sideways, looking, so observers thought, like a man trying to sleep in a railway carriage. His features only appeared when he looked up at the clock. The *Chicago Daily News* imbued Funk with some pathos: 'with a whining expression on his round Humpty Dumpty face, Funk, the smallest of the defendants, resembles a gnome who has lost his last friend.' (62)

And as Funk sat in the witness box and gave his testimony on 4 May and for most of the next day, he sensed pathos. And he wept, often. (63) He was quite animated as he recounted how 'the fascinating personality of the Führer acted as a giant magnet', and the way Hitler 'grasped all problems with lightning speed and knew how to present them impressively with great fluency and highly expressive gestures'. But he became more depressed as he remembered how seldom he had been allowed to see the Führer, how others had been given the Führer's directives, how he himself had been treated as 'a liberal and an outsider'. It upset him to recall that he had held no Party office after 1933 and was never a member of the Cabinet. He lamented that in every post he had only been allowed to do routine administrative tasks to relieve others; that he found each job 'existed merely on paper'. 'But that has happened to me all my life,' he mourned. 'I arrived at the threshold, so to speak, but I was never allowed to cross it.'

He rallied a little to defend himself against charges of mistreating Jews and said he had helped Richard Strauss who had commissioned a libretto from a Jew, other composers who had Jewish wives, and Fürtwangler who had praised Hindemith. Lawrence was not touched by the vision of a gnome who had once had musical friends. He told Funk that to help a few Jews was of no importance; what mattered was whether he had signed decrees against Jews as a whole. He had. Later, when Funk maintained he had been deeply affected by the events of 'Kristallnacht', when 'goods which could not be replaced had been destroyed', he was appalled by the situation in which he now found himself: 'It is terribly tragic indeed that I, in particular, am charged with these things.'

No one else had been as moved as Funk. The *Daily Telegraph* called him 'the most abject and shabbiest' of those on trial and said he had conducted 'a rambling defence'. (64) Schacht summed it up as 'weak and lachrymose' and added the dig that, like so many Nazis, Funk had been addicted to alcohol. (65) Dean noted that Funk had been 'unconvincing and unpleasant' and trusted that 'if his cross-examination is properly handled he should be shown up in his true colours'. (66)

Dodd's cross-examination lasted for a day and a half. It was not a masterly performance but was quite skilful enough for a defendant as abject as Funk, and used enough new documents to show that Funk had been much better informed, had attended more key meetings and had a greater grasp of financial affairs than he had claimed. Dodd was able to focus the image Funk had tried to project and show him as untruthful on details and as a rather more considerable figure than he had been prepared to admit. Though he might never have been in the Nazi inner circle, it became clear from the evidence that Funk had tried to curry favour and increase his own power so as to carry out Nazi policies. Even so, the cross-examination thus far might not have been effective enough to secure a heavy sentence for Funk. What turned the tide against him was the evidence on his knowledge of the SS gold deposits in Reichsbank.

Funk admitted that he often took visitors to see the government's gold bars in the vaults. But he denied that he had ever seen or was even aware of the watches, rings, gold teeth which the SS had sent from the crematoria of the concentration camps. The prosecution alleged that Funk had agreed with Himmler in 1942 to receive these deposits and taken delivery of 77 of them, giving cash or credit in return to finance production in SS factories. He had sometimes melted the gold, sometimes sent articles to the Municipal Pawn Brokerage in Berlin and credited the sums raised to the Ministry of Finance. The prosecution had affidavits to back the charges and on 7 May showed a US Army film of the gold articles which had been sent for safety to Frankfurt at the end of the War. It was surely a risk to show this film in court. A memorandum sent to Storey the previous December had suggested it was vulnerable evidence: gold articles and teeth might be seen but there was no solid proof that they had been taken from concentration camp victims. (67) However, the risk was taken – and the prosecution bluff was not called. Funk continued to deny all knowledge; he blamed the deposits on private agreements between his subordinates and Himmler. He then made the fatal mistake of calling as a witness a former Vice-President of the Reichsbank, Emil Puhl.

When Puhl finally appeared on 15 May, he testified for himself, not Funk, toppling along a precarious path between giving highly detailed accounts of Funk's involvement and the technicalities of the ten to twelve million Reichsmark credits of the SS, while claiming total ignorance and innocence on his own part. A counter-witness produced by the prosecution tore holes in Puhl's self-defence and added further evidence on Funk's involvement. By the time the court had heard the self-justifications of Funk and the two witnesses – all three hurling blame at each other – Dean reckoned that 'the amount of perjury committed has been remarkable even for Nuremberg.' (68) None of it had concealed Funk's guilt on this charge at least. Would his seeming evasiveness or lying over other charges lead the Tribunal to conclude he was guilty there too? Certainly nothing Funk had done for himself in the witness box had shaken the rather flimsy case against him.

There was every reason to fear, however, that the prosecution case against Grand Admiral Karl Doenitz would be severely buffeted once he went into the witness box.* Doenitz was charged on the first three counts. Thanks to his relatively junior position as Commander U-Boats until 1943, in which he had not been a member of the indicted General Staff and High Command or involved in overall naval strategy let along privy to political intentions the prosecution could only try to prove that Doenitz began as a minor conspirator but grew increasingly important. They alleged he had made a major contribution to the waging of aggressive war, having his fleet in readiness and playing a role in the attack on Poland, then Norway and Denmark. Doenitz would argue that the paucity of U-boats at the beginning of the War proved the absence of aggressive intent. The prosecution could counter with the argument that foolhardiness is not the same as innocence, and that the very heavy damage inflicted on Allied shipping in the early months of the War showed that the risk had paid off. The fact that the U-boats had left Kiel before the War began was adduced by the prosecutors as a sign of aggressive intention. The sinking of the British passenger liner, the *Athenia*, without warning on 3 September 1939 when she was 200 miles west of the Hebrides *en route* from Liverpool to North America demonstrated both how lethal even one U-boat can be and that from the very start German submarines had been used not just ruthlessly but illegally.

The main weight of the prosecution case against Doenitz came under Count Three – War Crimes. In the indictment he was accused of 'murder and ill-treatment of civilians of or in occupied territories'. Specifically the

*See Chapter 9 for the problems the prosecution had faced in mounting the naval case.

349

prosecution alleged that employees in naval dockyards in Denmark had been terrorized and that by late 1944 Doenitz had ordered 12,000 concentration camp labourers to be used in shipyards. Documents were produced to support these allegations. Furthermore there was evidence showing that Doenitz had passed on the Commando Order to his subordinates and suggesting that in 1945 he had proposed scrapping the Geneva Convention. The charges the prosecution took most seriously, however, concerned the vague reference in the indictment to 'murder and ill-treatment of persons on the high seas'. They wanted to prove that the naval war had been fought by the Germans with complete disregard of existing naval law.

Yet the prosecution knew, from the warnings of the British Admiralty and others, that the laws of naval warfare were far from clear and often more the result of custom and practice than of legislation and international agreement. They knew too from Doenitz's requests for witnesses and the successful applications by his counsel for access to British documents and an affidavit from Admiral Nimitz that this case would be fought largely on matters of legal theory and interpretation. Above all, it was quite clear that in Doenitz's counsel, Otto Kranzbuehler, they faced a doughty opponent. He was a naval lawyer who would be all too happy to fight on technical naval ground where others would find it hard to keep a firm footing. He was assisted by Doenitz's former Staff Officer Communications, Hans Meckel, and could consult a German Admiralty lawyer, released from internment but for many weeks in hospital in Nuremberg. No other defence was prepared with as much expert knowledge. Few benefited from the mutual respect between client and counsel shown by Doenitz and Kranzbuehler, or the sincerity with which both fought.

Long before his case opened, Kranzbuehler had won the respect of the Bench because he always approached the judges with dignity and reasonableness. He made requests on justified legal bases; he often framed them in terms of wishing to clarify legal problems which the judges themselves were all too anxious to have thrashed out as a necessary prelude to reaching judgement. Kranzbuehler had won many hearts in the courtroom. Young ladies would gaze down at him from the public gallery or up from their court reporters' tables and sigh at the handsome face. They would sigh again when he did not look back. As a happy father and husband and a hard-working and determined lawyer, Kranzbuehler allowed the young ladies only daydreams. He had won much respect too from professional colleagues – not least the prosecutors. They were great admirers of his professional skills and had been delighted by his coups in getting access to documents in London and approaching Nimitz. In fighting him, Maxwell-Fyfe had been doing his professional duty and had admired his adversary's success. He wrote of Kranzbuehler later: 'Captain Kranzbuehler never put a foot wrong in ten months, which is saying a lot.' (69)

Kranzbuehler and Doenitz had a further psychological advantage. In the public imagination, the German Navy had never become the bogeymen that units of the Army, Luftwaffe, let alone the SS and Gestapo had been. Though the War at sea had been cruel and the loss of life horrific, many people had been prepared to believe that the sea and naval war always are cruel; this War was no worse than any other and had been hard but clean. The prosecution staffs included several sailors. They had hated the suffering and the deaths they had seen, but they did not necessarily believe that the Germans had been uniquely responsible; they too felt some guilt, or at least acknowledged that both sides had been ruthless but not necessarily criminal in their treatment of their own men as well as the enemy. Given the legal difficulties of the naval case and the tender consciences of Allied sailors, it is not surprising that when Doenitz went into the witness box on 8 May *The Times* noticed there was 'an unusual sprinkling of naval uniforms in the courtroom'. (70) High-ranking officers from Europe and America were keen to hear the legal problems discussed. They wondered whether naval law would be clarified as a result – and some of them felt more sympathy than vindictiveness for their former enemy, Doenitz.

Until now Bob Cooper of *The Times* had felt that there was 'something indefinably *sympathique* about Doenitz sitting politely attentive in his corner behind Goering'. (71) Other observers had noted his calm and dignity, the way he and Raeder seemed to hold themselves apart from the other defendants in the dock, as if avoiding contact with criminals or those of less integrity. There had been a sense that Doenitz's calm might be the result of sternly imposed self-control. Several journalists commented on his habit of drumming the ring on his right hand against the side of the box when listening to evidence and the way he would 'bang the wooden dock partition with his fist and glare' when talking to his lawyer. (72) His neat featured, slightly foxy face with high brow and pointed small chin had lost its calm during the prosecution case against him, and he 'stared and turned pale when hearing evidence on refusing to rescue torpedoed sailors'. (73) He and Raeder had displayed 'obvious emotion as counsel called them mendacious politicians' and alleged they had been ready to stoop to anything as long as they thought they would not get caught. (74) Most observers judged this a reasonable reaction to such unpleasant allegations, implying innocence and decency. They had been impressed by Doenitz's demeanour which the *Chicago Daily News* called 'often more meek than haughty'. (75)

Yet Bob Cooper was not alone in changing his opinion of Doenitz when the admiral went into the witness box. Here, thought Cooper, they saw 'the real man – harsh, ruthless, arrogant. You felt in him the eternal German militarist and ... you saw that his selection as Hitler's successor was probably no mere hazard.' (76) The arrogance had already been noticed by Andrus who had thought Doenitz 'imbued with terrific self-esteem'. But he had not envisaged Doenitz in the role of Hitler's natural successor and Gilbert's report to him suggested the admiral was 'a fairly upright character. Very intelligent but politically naïve. He feels that he was kicked upstairs to answer for crimes he knew nothing about.' (77) Politically naïve or not, Doenitz would not have frowned at being called an 'eternal German militarist'; he would have taken it as a compliment. In his memoirs he wrote that 'as a child I had been imbued with the conviction that the fulfilment of my duty came before everything else.' He attributed his easy acceptance of naval discipline to the fact that 'as a family we were devoid of any personal individuality; we were deeply conscious of the co-operative spirit of the Prussian community to which we belong.' These words rang oddly in the ears of non-Prussians and people of a different generation. But they were words of praise in Doenitz's vocabulary. Was it political naïvety or undaunted patriotism which led him to write that the union with Austria and the takeover of the Sudetenland were 'successes in the field of foreign policy' and add: 'What patriotic citizen, what fighting man, would not have welcomed such a resurgence of his country after years of degradation and poverty?' (78) (Perhaps the citizens ashamed to hear the evidence at Nuremberg of how these 'successes' had been achieved?)

Doenitz spoke of himself as a patriot. At Nuremberg and later he described himself as purely and simply a fighting man, a professional sailor with a duty to his men and his country. He insisted that the 120 or so conferences with Hitler which he had attended were entirely a naval duty: 'How in heaven's name could a commander-in-chief of a service responsible directly to the Head of State have fulfilled his duties in any other way?' He regarded his refusal in 1944 to allow Nazi Guidance officers attached to ships to have any say in command and his refusal to hand over seditious sailors to the jurisdiction of the People's Court as proof enough of his non-political attitude. Yet others might see them as the characteristic sharp reaction of any naval commander on his quarter deck.

By contrast with Doenitz's view of himself the prosecution case had accused him of 'fanatical adherence to Hitler and to the Party' and of indoctrinating the Navy with Nazi ideology. It had included his speech to his commanders in February 1944: 'From the very start the whole officer corps must be so indoctrinated that it feels itself co-responsible for the National Socialist state in its entirety. The officer is the exponent of the State; the idle chatter that the officer is non-political is sheer nonsense.' The prosecution had argued that an unpolitical sailor would not have made the speech in March 1944 to the Navy and German people in which Doenitz asked: 'What would have become of our country today if the Führer had not united us under National Socialism? Split with parties, beset with the spreading poison of Jewry and vulnerable to it, and lacking as a defence our present and uncompromising ideology we would long since have succumbed to the burdens of this war and been subject to the merciless destruction of our adversaries'. (79) (This speech was not challenged when submitted as evidence by the prosecution. It has since been suggested that it was drafted by a member of Doenitz's staff and not delivered in that form. Doenitz did however express similar sentiments elsewhere.)

Doenitz might claim that his exclusive devotion to his professional duties gave him no opportunity to take part in political discussions. He argued that by the time he took command in 1943 the War was 'at a decidedly defensive stage'. He insisted he was totally unaware of the crimes being committed by the Nazi regime, that he knew nothing of concentration camps or exterminations. He wrote in his memoirs: 'My knowledge of the inhuman side of the National Socialist state was very limited. I learned the full facts, greatly to my consternation, after the end of the War.' Was he non-political, was he politically naïve or was he disingenuous? The prosecution maintained that not only was he sufficiently informed of the criminality of the government he served but that within his own sphere he had played a criminal part.

One accusation against Doenitz was that he had continued the War after Hitler's death while acting as head of state. Many people would now accept his explanation that he needed time before surrender to protect civilians near the Front and bring back from the East two million soldiers who would otherwise have been left to the mercy of the Russians and the worst of the winter. Having saved life on a scale which makes Dunkirk look a very minor achievement, he had then negotiated surrender. It was an irony that Doenitz went into the witness box on the anniversary of VE Day. *The Times* commented that he had 'aged considerably during his confinement; but a slim, trim figure, he sat back squarely and spoke with quiet, slow emphasis'. (80) The films of the trial show him at the beginning of each session asking for help to put on the headphones and carefully placing a glass of water on the ledge in front of him. As he settled into his testimony he would lean back and hang his arms over the back of the chair. His manner remained confident; as he warmed to his theme his voice would become louder but during his examination in chief it remained firmly under control.

His defence began with a procedure which had become unusual during the trial – a debate between Kranzbuehler and Maxwell-Fyfe on the documents to be presented for Doenitz (and for Raeder) on the legal restraints on naval warfare. They had not been translated in time for a behind-the-scenes discussion between opposing counsel on their relevance and admissibility. (The suspicion lurks that Kranzbuehler deliberately delayed his documents so as to present them in the most effective way.) To the Tribunal's temporary dismay this discussion now had to take place in open court. At Kranzbuehler's insistence it had been postponed overnight to allow both counsel to prepare. He had also asked, politely but firmly, to be allowed to group his documents and run through them without interruption on the grounds that their value could only be assessed if his train of thought were understood. As ever when approached in this manner, the Tribunal granted the request. So Maxwell-Fyfe, having made several preliminary objections to documents, sat in silence until Kranzbuehler had finished his exposition, then only made minor criticisms. As a result, what might have been a series of lawyers' gambits and a needless use of Tribunal time was converted into a serious and well-considered preparatory argument on the way aspects of naval law had been defined and applied at the outbreak of war.

Kranzbuehler's thesis was not that German naval practice had been founded on accusations of *tu quoque*. On the contrary, he argued that both sides had acted perfectly legally. (This probably took the wind out of Maxwell-Fyfe's sails. He was noticeably silent on Kranzbuehler's argument as a whole and picked only at the smallest details.) As regards prosecution charges on attacks on neutrals, Kranzbuehler suggested that the establishment of control ports by Britain – an act which had drawn American protest – had forced neutral shipping into German operational zones, where their treatment was exactly the same as that in British operational zones and totally permissible. He argued that the British practice of obliging neutrals to obtain 'navicerts' from a British consul before putting to sea could be seen as changing them into non-neutrals and marked a development of an entirely new naval law. (It is noticeable that Kranzbuehler spoke of new law, not illegal practice; he was elaborating the view that naval law evolves through adjustment to practical circumstances.) Finally he produced lists of violations by America of her neutrality between September 1939 and September 1940 to explain why Germany had considered it justifiable to sink American ships which entered German zones of blockade.

In explaining the German treatment of merchantmen where the prosecution had alleged illegal practice, Kranzbuehler would later submit the British Admiralty Handbook for 1938 on the defence of merchant shipping, ordering merchant ships to report the position of enemy ships or aircraft and to open fire if any attempt were made to capture them. Doenitz would quote the order broadcast by the British Admiralty on 1 October 1939 that U-boats should be rammed. For the moment, however, Kranzbuehler introduced evidence that the British themselves had sunk ships which could not or would not be brought into port and had announced it was impossible to distinguish between armed and unarmed merchantmen. He further pointed out that the issuing of insignia in November 1939 to French merchant seamen who could be mobilized in due course implied that they no longer retained the full status of non-combatants.

On the subjects of the sinking of ships and the treatment of their survivors, which formed a major part of the prosecution case, Kranzbuehler wished to put into evidence examples of the punishment of German naval officers who disobeyed Standing Orders on these matters, and a statement by sixty interned U-boat commanders that they had received no order to kill survivors. Maxwell-Fyfe objected to this statement on the grounds that it was not sworn; Kranzbuehler replied that it did, however, have official status which gave it the alternative form of admissibility, since it had been forwarded by the British War Office! Kranzbuehler tolerantly argued that cases where sea rescue planes had been shot down by the RAF were all legally acceptable, since international law did not actually prohibit such action. All in all, it had been a clearly argued résumé. A short broadside had found many weaknesses in the structure of the prosecution case. Kranzbuehler had skilfully avoided any accusation of criminality by either side. He had been persuasive in his line that many of the practices of the German Navy in 1939 had already been developed by all participants in the First World War. He had emphasized that German action from the outbreak of War had been largely a series of responses to Allied initiatives.

This theme was taken up by Doenitz when he began his examination in chief that afternoon. He claimed it was clear from the first days of War that British merchantmen were radioing the positions of U-boats; they were armed and ready to fire even before called upon to stop; he mentioned incidents when they had dropped depth charges. By their behaviour, Doenitz claimed, British merchantmen had forfeited their status as civilian craft; his order in October 1939 to attack them was justified retaliation for aggression and permitted by German Prize Regulations – rules themselves based on the London Protocol. He insisted that neutral ships had been attacked only when found in designated operational zones and that warning had been issued to them on 24 November 1939. He admitted that the sinking of neutrals had often been disguised as the work of mines. He saw nothing to be ashamed of in this: 'during a war there is no basic obligation to inform the enemy with what means one does one's fighting. In other words it is not a question of legality but a question of military or political expediency.' Chilling words, but unfortunately probably accurate and invoked by all combatants from 1939. He broadened the case on justified retaliation by quoting the American order to their destroyers in summer 1941 to attack U-boats, an order issued when America was not even at war. Doenitz claimed he had forbidden his own commanders to attack British destroyers in the areas concerned lest American ships be sunk by mistake.

Doenitz's defence distinguished sharply between his own responsibility as a commanding officer and the spheres over which he believed politicians and others should have full control. In answer to charges under Counts One and Two, he replied that up to 1943 his job had been to put into effect plans drawn up by the Naval Operations Staff, who in turn worked to the politicians. 'Whether the leadership of the state was thereby politically waging an aggressive war or not was not for me to decide; it was none of my business.' As a serving officer he accepted full responsibility for his own orders, and for making sure they were obeyed. If any of his officers had ever objected or refused to carry out an instruction, he said: 'I would have had him examined; if he proved to be normal I would have put him before a court-martial.' He insisted that the training of his men had made them thoroughly conversant with naval law and expressed the conviction that he had never issued an illegal order – for practical as well as moral reasons. 'I would never, even at the time of our most serious losses, have permitted that these men be given an order which was unethical or which would damage their fighting morale.'

The question of the legality of orders and their interpretation by junior officers had been raised by the prosecution in its potentially most damaging form in its analysis of the Laconia Order of 1942 – the prohibition on the rescue of survivors from sunken ships. It had been argued that Doenitz's words went far beyond the accepted view that ships and their missions must not be endangered by rescue work; that they banned rescue under any circumstances and were the first step in a policy of encouraging the deliberate killing of survivors. Doenitz strove to show the falsity of the allegation by explaining the context in which the order was given.

On 12 September 1942, the liner *Laconia* which was being used as a transport ship by the British Admiralty and carrying over 1,500 Italian prisoners-of-war, about 180 Polish guards, and 811 British passengers and crew, was sunk in the South Atlantic some 900 miles south of Freetown and 250 miles north-east of Ascension Island. She had been hit by the U-156 under the command of Lieutenant Commander Hartenstein. The *Laconia* might be seen as a legitimate target: she carried radio and was armed with an assortment of fourteen guns including two elderly 4.7 inch naval guns. As she sank the *Laconia* radioed for help for her survivors. So too did Hartenstein. He appealed to Germany, to German vessels which might be in the vicinity and to Allied shipping. He had every reason to expect Allied assistance: he believed he was in the reception area of the radios at the British base in Freetown and the British island of Ascension.

Doenitz had responded to Hartenstein's calls by instructing three available U-boats to move to the site and take on board as many survivors as would not impede diving and put the rest on to lifeboats to be kept in tow until more suitable vessels arrived to accommodate them. He called on the Vichy French in Dakar to send warships for rescue. For four days the U-boats stayed on the surface, displaying Red Crosses. They were then bombed five times by an American Liberator. Hartenstein's submarine was damaged and one of the lifeboats he was towing was sunk. Doenitz then ordered him to release the rest. They were supplied with food and water and 163 Italians were transferred to a French cruiser which had just arrived. The attacks on the U-boats had taken place in perfect weather conditions and visibility – Red Crosses and lifeboats, said Doenitz, must have been visible. Except for the French cruiser, no Allied help had been sent. Given this failure and the danger to his submarines and the survivors themselves from further air attack, he argued he had no option by 17 September but to forbid any more attempts at rescue. He maintained this was an order well within the measures permitted by naval law; it was a justified response to the situation and applicable to similar circumstances in the future. And it had been issued only when the German naval authorities had been driven to desperation by Allied behaviour. He explained the harshness of the language he had used by the need to drive his officers to action which went against their instincts but was essential for their preservation. He insisted that only Moehle had ever misinterpreted the order as meaning that survivors should be killed (he accepted Eck's defence that he had shot at wreckage not survivors) and suggested that the cases of the *Noreen Mary* and the *Antonico* quoted by the prosecution were significantly few. He reckoned they should be viewed sceptically since men struggling in the water are unable to judge accurately whether they themselves or their ships are being fired on (and pointed out that one witness claimed to have recognized Eck's vessel by its swastika, whereas no U-boat ever sported one).

Doenitz's interpretation of the *Laconia* affair was patently sincere. It suggested German correctness and courage way beyond what could be reasonably expected in such circumstances, and implied callousness or even criminal behaviour on the part of the British and the Americans. Even so, Doenitz had managed to give his account with admirable restraint of language and avoided harping on the actions of others. By putting the *Laconia* order into this context he had damaged a major piece of prosecution evidence. The British, in their part of the case, had given no details of the *Laconia* incident; they had relied on the wording of the Order itself and obviously hoped that its harshness would lose Doenitz the sympathy of the Tribunal and prepare them to believe him capable of ordering that all survivors should in future be killed.

It is very probable that the British had, in fact, known nothing of the circumstances in which the Order was issued. Revealingly, the British prosecution papers contain no briefing on the affair itself, only an Admiralty warning that the Order seemed to have been interpreted as Doenitz suggested. The absence of a briefing may be explained by a failure in the filing system, but given the detail with which Maxwell-Fyfe liked to prepare a case and the Admiralty's active involvement in the allegations against the Germany Navy, the files might be expected to contain a flurry of questions and answers between London and Nuremberg about the matter. Significantly, however, Maxwell-Fyfe in his cross-examination spent only minutes on the affair, made no rebuttal of the implied accusations against the Allies and pressed only on small details. He brought in no new evidence to caulk the holes which Doenitz had made and made no attempt to challenge his version in essentials. As a result, the British appeared for the moment to concede Doenitz's account and to surrender over one of their major charges.*

Maxwell-Fyfe's cross-examination of Doenitz, which began early on 9 May and took up most of the following day, was not one of his more successful or impressive pieces of work at Nuremberg. *The Times* correspondent claimed to notice an 'unfamiliar edge of severity' in Maxwell-Fyfe's voice and wondered if it came from emotional response to the huge loss of life in the war at sea suffered by his Liverpool constituents. (81) More probably it came from ill-ease with the task he had to perform. What is observable in the trial transcript is a very different approach from his usual manner:

*See appendix.

much more hesitance in use of tactics, less readiness to follow up points and infinitely less confident mastery of the subject matter than when dealing with other defendants. It must have occurred to him that in tackling Doenitz and Kranzbuehler, two naval experts in a technical and detailed case, he could not try to bamboozle by implying more knowledge than he possessed – the other two would all too easily outgun him, however careful his preparatory work. Even though he might seem uncertain in approach, however, Maxwell-Fyfe's questions on the first afternoon aimed at proving that Doenitz had had a much more intimate relationship with Hitler than he had suggested in his testimony, got under Doenitz's skin. The *Daily Telegraph* noticed that Doenitz's 'frigid poise which has distinguished his bearing throughout his evidence-in-chief, fell from him like a garment as he indignantly protested in a high-pitched, flustered voice'. (82) He continued to claim that all his meetings with Hitler had been on purely naval matters and that he was totally ignorant of the use of slave labour and conditions in concentration camps.

The next day Maxwell-Fyfe needed to pin Doenitz firmly to charges other than those concerned with submarine warfare. It cannot be said that he did so conclusively – suspicions might remain, but so too does reasonable doubt. Though Doenitz was alleged to have enforced the Commando Order, Maxwell-Fyfe had no convincing evidence to counter the denial that Doenitz was aware of the very few cases quoted by the prosecution in which naval prisoners had been murdered or handed to the SD for execution. Doenitz argued that at the time he had considered the Order justifiable retaliation for the fighting methods of commandos (and indeed several witnesses were to allege during the trial that British commandos did not wear uniform, carried hidden weapons and would feign surrender then shoot at their captors). He added: 'Today I do not approve of that order since I have learned here that the basis was not sound.'

Similarly, Maxwell-Fyfe had no documents to prove the damaging accusation that Doenitz had ordered the killing of survivors from sunk ships. On this point at least he pressed and pressed, but could wring no admission from Doenitz. A letter he tried to submit on the subject from the widow of a U-boat commander was extremely vague and not based on any specific information. Kranzbuehler objected to it as an unsworn statement and the Tribunal decided not to admit it as evidence. The very fact that Maxwell-Fyfe had tried to employ such a weak document suggests desperation. This section of the case aroused deep resentment. Doenitz 'was flushed with rage and ... half rose from the witness box' as he shouted his replies. And Goering made noisy protests about the 'insults' to the armed services until called to order. (83) Maxwell-Fyfe added little to the allegations that Doenitz had used concentration camp labour – conceivably he felt that the evidence submitted in the prosecution case could stand alone. Nor did he shake Doenitz's claim to have opposed the renunciation of the Geneva Convention in 1945. A bout between the two men concerning the words

Doenitz had used in a conference with Hitler produced no more than the impression that he had spoken ambiguously.

Indeed the most damaging part of Doenitz's cross-examination came through the words he used in court and in the documents quoted, rather than from the use Maxwell-Fyfe made of the evidence. He said at one stage that the *Athenia* log had not been faked; it had to be kept secret so 'had to be changed'. When challenged on his speech condemning the 'spreading poison of Jewry' he answered that 'the spreading poison might have had a disintegrating effect on people's power of endurance', especially under heavy bombing. Maxwell-Fyfe simulated bewilderment, hinted that perhaps the admiral had not understood the question – and so succeeded in getting him to repeat the startling and unattractive sentence. Throughout his time in the witness box, whenever Doenitz had the chance to express any regret at the loss of life at sea he never took it; he always dismissed the idea of tragedy or waste with comments about 'harsh necessity'. Throughout he gave the impression of ruthlessness in fighting and coldness to the suffering it caused.

But creating such an impression is totally different from an admission of intent to commit crimes. By the time Doenitz left the witness box he may not have won sympathy – he would have scorned the attempt – but he had not conceded any point to the prosecution. *The Times* correspondent recorded that many naval observers thought he had made irreparable breaches in the prosecution case. (84) He reported in his newspaper that 'no defence has been better constructed than that of Doenitz' even though there was some distaste at the fact that his account of the inherent decency of Germany submarine warfare had been 'given with a cynicism not previously heard in the witness box'. (85) Dean, who had not been convinced even by Doenitz's evidence on the *Laconia* incident, let alone over such charges as the use of concentration camp labour and the renunciation of the Geneva Convention, still could not put his finger on any particular lie or unanswered allegation. He seems to have been judging not on the evidence but with the instinctive dislike and mistrust of Doenitz which so many observers felt. Whatever Dean's personal suspicions about the Doenitz case, he reported that 'there is no doubt that it will be more difficult to demonstrate his guilt than that of the majority of the other defendants.' He summed him up as a 'formidable opponent and a typical Nazi' and believed he would be convicted – and rightly so. (86)

But the general sense that the prosecution had not mounted a winning case was sharpened by the rest of Doenitz's defence. Kranzbuehler spent part of 11 May and some of the morning of 13 May on an immaculately ordered and well-reasoned presentation of documents, many of them British. Two witnesses he introduced – Admirals Wagner and Godt – did a useful job in corroborating Doenitz's testimony. In the previous November he had applied for Eck as a witness. By this time Eck was already under sentence of death. The British military authorities opposed delaying his execution on grounds of humanity and public opinion but the Tribunal had given the prosecution and Kranzbuehler permission to send interrogatories to him. (87) Doenitz did, however, have a third witness – his son-in-law Captain Hessler, who introduced several new points for the defence. He explained that before missions, naval officers were carefully trained and briefed on naval law and in the use of the prize disc – a kind of slide rule they carried to help them reach quick and correct decisions on the treatment of neutral and merchant shipping according to the Prize Ordinance. He himself had sunk twenty-one ships between 1940 and 1941. In his opinion, only in two of these cases did the conditions laid down for rescue in the London Protocol exist. Furthermore he quoted two other incidents where he had been fired on by sinking ships as he approached to offer help. He exposed the point which had been buried during the long days of the Doenitz case – that no specific charges of crimes on the high seas had been levelled; and he added the embarrassing comment that his own British interrogators had promised that no U-boat commander would be charged with criminal acts. It was typical of the whole Doenitz case and its meticulous presentation that Kranzbuehler had kept a witness with fresh and effective evidence until the very end. In what was almost a *coup de théâtre* he drew one final comment from Hessler before he left the witness box: that Doenitz had insisted on preserving all naval archives. 'We have a clean conscience,' said Hessler, then left – 'bowing and smiling encouragingly to his former commander-in-chief'. (88)

The final shot against the prosecution case was delayed until Doenitz received the reply to the interrogatory sent to Admiral Nimitz. He himself read it on 22 May; details appeared in the Press on 23 May. (89) But it was formally presented to the Tribunal only on 2 July when enough copies were translated and printed. Admiral Nimitz had been the Commander-in-Chief of the US Pacific Fleet from 1941 to 1945. His views on the recent applications of naval law had to be seen as authoritative. (There is some suggestion that Kranzbuehler's request for them had put British noses out of joint. He had asked for the views of Nimitz as a commander in 'the leading submarine power'.) (90) Nimitz's answers to the interrogatory were concise and unwavering: the United States had designated theatres of operations and within them had attacked without warning; they had practiced unrestricted warfare from 7 December 1941; their submarines had not rescued enemy survivors in cases where their own vessels or missions were at risk. (91) Nimitz argued and had acted in these matters exactly the same way as Doenitz claimed to have done. His interrogatory clarified the choice open to the Tribunal: either the judges must decide that both navies had acted criminally and both their commanders should face trial, or both parties had justifiably interpreted existing law in the same way and no crimes had been committed. Either way, their judgement would be seen as a major development in naval law. Having reached a decision on this issue the judges would still have to consider the accuracy of all the other charges against Doenitz – allegations which had received relatively little attention from the prosecution, but which if adequately supported by the documents might still be considered enough to convict him though not perhaps to hang him.

Whatever worries the prosecution might have about the final verdict on Doenitz, they had no reason for equal pessimism in facing Grand Admiral Erich Raeder when he went into the witness box at the end of the afternoon on 15 May. The charges brought against him too on unrestricted submarine warfare might have been severely weakened by the attacks of Doenitz and Kranzbuehler. But there were many more charges against Raeder in which the prosecution could feel greater confidence. The case on the first two counts was much sounder. Raeder had commanded the navy under one title or another since 1928: he had been confirmed in office by Hitler until 1943, so held a key post in the critical years for the alleged conspiracy and planning and waging of aggressive war. He had been present at the conferences on 5 November 1937 and 23 May 1939, so could be said to have known of Hitler's aggressive intentions. The prosecution had assembled a wide range of evidence to back their allegation that Raeder had deliberately fought the war with criminal methods though had always tried to hide them with a cloak of legality or justification. They had submitted his memorandum of October 1939 stating that 'it is desirable to base all military measures taken on existing international law; however, measures which are considered necessary from a military point of view, provided a decisive success can be expected from them will have to be carried out, even if they are not covered by existing international law.'

There was no suggestion in this document, as there had been so often in the Doenitz case, that existing law might have been differently interpreted or was even non-existent. The prosecutors had evidence to show that the *Athenia* had been sunk without warning and claimed it was characteristic of Raeder that he tried to hide the incident by faking the official papers on it, and then accused the British of carrying it out. They had quoted his covering note to the Commando Order in October 1942 – that it must not be distributed in writing to officers below the rank of flotilla leader or section commander and that once passed on verbally by them, each copy must be destroyed. Raeder had committed crimes, the prosecution alleged, but always took steps to cover his tracks. (92)

Raeder was not an immediately appealing witness. His intolerance of challenge or criticism was seldom controlled; he would snap at anyone. He had a puffy, haggard face topped by sparse black hair parted in the middle. The diamond-shaped dark glasses he often wore in court to counteract the dazzle of the courtroom lights gave an inappropriately festive look to a basically dour and sometimes bad-tempered face. Few people warmed to Raeder. Gilbert had noted he was academically intelligent with a 'practical, unimaginative mentality' but saw him as 'an irritable old man'. Yet significantly Andrus confessed: 'I could not help but have very great sympathy' for him. (93) Andrus felt sorry for a man who had suffered captivity in Russian hands and was moved by his anguish over his wife who was still in the Russian Zone and could not be contacted. Andrus had a soft heart; it only hardened to those who whined or failed to reach his standards of domestic hygiene.

Raeder's testimony took up most of three days. He wallowed in facts and figures on rearmament and basked in the details of the numbers, classes and tonnage of ships. His counsel, Siemers, did nothing to restrain him. Siemers himself was long-winded and plodding, and set about enumerating each prosecution allegation and inviting lengthy replies from his client to each separate detail of a section or a point. Even Raeder on the first afternoon lost patience with this method: 'The individual cases are gradually becoming more ridiculous. I consider it a waste of time.' So did the Tribunal. Next morning, Lawrence begged Siemers to group his points. Siemers tried. He apologized for not being 'a naval expert' and explained that he had 'had a great deal of trouble finding my way through' the quantity and technicality of the information he had to handle. Even though he had premasticated it, listeners in the court might well have found the resulting gobbets hard to digest. Underneath the data ran Raeder's argument that pre-war he had built up the German navy well within the limits imposed first by the Versailles Treaty, then by the 1935 Anglo-German Naval Agreement. He admitted to a few transgressions such as the number of mines in the Baltic and the guns along its coast. But he related these to his general theme: that naval rearmament had been purely concerned with defence.

He insisted on his own peaceful intentions and claimed to have believed that for a long time Hitler shared them. When evidence was introduced on his presence at conferences where aggression was announced and planned, Raeder attacked its validity. He denied that the Hossbach minutes were an authentic record, saying that the conference had been a trick to edge Neurath into resignation. He denied too the accuracy of the Schmundt record of the conference on Poland in May 1939. Whatever Schmundt might have noted of Hitler's policy for Danzig, the desire to expand into living space in the East and his intention to attack Poland at the first suitable opportunity, Raeder stoutly maintained that the real purpose of the meeting had been to set up a research staff for the OKW – as if everything else discussed was too peripheral to be considered. Hitler, he insisted, was 'a master of bluff'; his words were never expressions of his thinking; 'one never knew what his final goals and intentions were'. He was particularly critical of the fact that the prosecution had used two versions of the Obersalzberg speech Hitler had made to his commanders in August 1939. Both versions had him calling for immediate war; in one he stated the intention of finding a 'propagandistic cause' for starting it, in the other he expressed the fear that at the last minute some '*schweinhund* will make a proposal for mediation'. Siemers applied to have both versions struck from the record. Maxwell-Fyfe argued that though they varied in expression the essential points appeared in both. Next day Dodd gave a careful account of their provenance and insisted that these and other documents showed that 'not only were these things said but they were done'. The Tribunal decided to admit both versions and decide later on their validity.

For the rest Raeder urged that Hitler had won over the German people and Raeder himself by achieving so much without bloodshed. He pointed out that he himself had played no part in the Anschluss and called the plans for attacking Czechoslovakia and the Barbarossa File on Russia 'contingency plans'. He had opposed the invasion of Russia for two reasons: that it was 'morally wrong' to break the Pact and a 'stupidity' to fight a war on two fronts, but he did not say to which argument he had attached most weight. He also denied wanting war with the United States – in view of the fact that Germany was already fighting Britain and Russia 'I did not want to have America on my neck as well.' He explained the attack on Norway as being a pre-emptive strike against a known, imminent British invasion, then expressed pride that his fleet had moved in under British flags with some ships disguised as merchantmen giving British names when challenged. He considered these practices justified by methods employed by Nelson. Though his argument was not very convincing, at least it distracted him from making much play over the alleged British intentions in Norway.

The British Foreign Office, which had been in such a tizzy in recent months, was vastly relieved. Dean, in a cable, assumed that Raeder's passing references had hardly been noticed in court and someone added the minute: 'It looks as though the Norway issue will pass completely without undue attention being drawn to it.' (94) Raeder ended his examination in chief by recounting his several attempts to resign before the War. It was noticeable that even in his versions all were prompted by personal grievance or disagreements over naval strategy, not over the principle of aggression. He added that his personal relationship had then become increasingly strained because the Führer would not accept criticism and 'unpleasant scenes ensued which wore me out'.

Schacht at least had not been impressed by Raeder's claims of peaceful intentions. 'He disapproved of aggressive war and was deceived by Hitler, but he planned and began the aggressive war. That's a militarist for you.' (95)

Raeder had largely avoided the charges he faced under Count Three – War Crimes. For much of his cross-examination Maxwell-Fyfe avoided them too. He concentrated on making heavy inroads into Raeder's defence on the first two counts. He submitted evidence that though German dockyards might have stuck to the limitations on U-boat construction imposed by Versailles and the Anglo-German Naval Treaty, the navy was in fact sending designers to work in Holland on submarines for Finland and Turkey which were to be prototypes for Germany. He produced the views of two German experts that 118 U-boats were nearly ready by the outbreak of war. (Though this figure has since been criticized, it was not disputed in court.) Both Doenitz and Raeder had confined themselves to giving figures of between forty and fifty U-boats fit for service; he argued that of the 118 many only awaited finishing touches, others had been prefabricated and needed final assembly. German sources he quoted suggested that the Navy had also trained more than the 15,000 men permitted; it probably had 25,000 by 1934.

As Maxwell-Fyfe revealed his documents, Raeder became increasingly incensed. Cooper described him as 'an angry man who fell back on peppery argument rather than answer a question directly'. (96) Maxwell-Fyfe provoked Raeder further with evidence on four warships deliberately constructed to be heavier than their declared specification; on his encouragement to the German arms industry to export so as to be tooled up and in full production once Germany herself required arms; on the order to attack Soviet submarines given six days before the invasion of Russia and to give the excuse that they had been mistaken for British; on the idea he discussed for disguising ships as merchantmen, then sending them to sink merchantmen. Raeder lost his temper completely. Maxwell-Fyfe tried to stop him making long speeches and the admiral 'flung his hands in the air shouting: "Will you stop interrupting me!"' When accused of lying he bellowed: 'Don't accuse me of that. I would never do such a thing.' (97)

With Raeder's defence looking thinner and thinner and the man himself rattled, Maxwell-Fyfe then actually had the impudence to raise the dreaded question of the invasion of Norway, using German naval and diplomatic sources to substantiate his claim that in the previous weeks in Berlin no one had believed a British attack was imminent but that Raeder was urging a German invasion at the next new moon. Raeder denied the charge but could not rebut it. He not only denied he had ordered the forgery of the logs in the *Athenia* affair, he made heavy hints that Doenitz had. In response to Pokrovsky's cross-examination on the plan to raze Leningrad to the ground, he claimed never to have heard of Hitler's intentions and argued that he himself would have preferred to preserve the Leningrad shipyards (without apparently seeing that the two policies were not mutually exclusive, given accurate shelling).

Dean thought that Raeder had been 'evasive and long-winded' but had made a better showing 'than most of the other defendants'. (98) For Dean, that included Doenitz, but the transcripts of the two cases do not confirm his impression and no one else recorded the same judgement. Raeder's witnesses did not make much of a showing. They too were long-winded and took up two whole days without saying anything of significance. The only excitement during their testimony came when Seidl – nothing if not a trier – attempted to introduce his copy of the Secret Protocol during questions to Weizsäcker, former State Secretary of the Foreign Ministry. Rudenko leapt up to call it 'a forged document' and the Tribunal had to remind Seidl that they had forbidden it to be submitted, though questions on it might be put.

Another document over which there was argument was a statement Raeder had made while in prison in Moscow. Pokrovsky wanted to read it in court. It was an indictment in scathing terms of several of the defendants. The Tribunal refused to hear it, but the defendants got hold of copies that evening (one cannot escape the conclusion that Gilbert made sure they did). Raeder had described Goering as having 'a disastrous effect on the fate of the German Reich' and showing 'unimaginable vanity and immeasurable ambition, running after popularity and showing off, untruthfulness, impracticality, and selfishness ...' (Further remarks suggest that Goering's rivalry with the navy and his attempts to deprive it of resources in favour of the Luftwaffe had not improved Raeder's opinion of him.) Raeder had said that his relationship with Doenitz had been 'very cool since his somewhat conceited and not always tactful nature did not appeal to me' and had suggested that Doenitz's misjudgements had acted 'to the detriment of the Navy'. He went on to say: 'Speer flattered Doenitz's vanity – and vice versa'. And he expressed contempt for Keitel: 'a man of unimaginable weakness, who owes his long stay in his position to this characteristic. The Führer could treat him as badly as he wished – he stood for it.' (99)

It goes without saying that Raeder's reception by those he had lambasted was icy. Doenitz suddenly became remarkably friendly with Schacht, Neurath and Papen. He dismissed Raeder as 'a jealous old man'. Keitel could only be comforted with the thought that at least the statement had not been read in court. Schirach, who was slowly and only intermittently screwing up his courage to escape from the influence of Goering and denounce Hitler's perversion of German youth, had been given a new dose of resolution by the statement. He said he now saw Goering's admissions of responsibility in the witness box as sheer bravado and distractions from his denials of actual guilt in so many areas. He soon went into conclave with Speer. Both men were resolving to make a clean breast of things in the witness box – without fear or concern for their colleagues. They planned to compare and dovetail the statements they would make. (100)

By the middle of May the defence front was in ruins, and the prosecution was licking wounds it had received in recent weeks. Meanwhile at Dachau the case was being heard of the murder of the American prisoners-of-war at Malmédy. These murders had done much to influence American public opinion in favour of a trial of major war criminals. Since then the evidence at Nuremberg had given them and others a much fuller picture of the atrocities the Nazis had committed. The trial had developed to a scale that no one had envisaged at the start. By now it seemed that its outcome was no longer totally predictable; perhaps not all the defendants would hang, as everyone originally assumed.

Note

An article in the *Journal of the Royal United Services Institution* (Nov. 1964) by Dr Maurer Maurer and Lawrence J. Paszek leaves Doenitz's account of his own actions and motive intact while using documents gradually discovered from 1959 onwards to lift some of the taint of guilt from the British and Americans. The article suggests that for a long time it had not been clear to anyone where the

B-24, the Liberator, had come from. American military sources had suggested it was from Freetown, a British base. Meanwhile, Doenitz's memoirs had made a strongly worded attack on British naval conduct of the whole *Laconia* affair. Only in 1963 did it become clear that the plane came from Ascension, from the base established by the Americans with British permission, as a refuelling stop for their military aircraft. The base was isolated and not heavily fortified. It was dependent on shipping for equipment and supplies and so vulnerable to attack from German and possibly Vichy ships and planes. The mood of the garrison was extremely jumpy. Nine days before the *Laconia* went down, an artillery battery had fired at one of their own P-39s which had ditched in the sea, thinking it was a U-boat. Their radio installations were not complete. Though adequate for limited communication with their own search and patrol missions, they were dependent on British help on Ascension for anything involving longer range and for intelligence data from Freetown. Their own radio had failed to pick up the *Laconia*'s distress signals and Hartenstein's appeals for help. No British ship or station had heard the *Laconia* either. Freetown had intercepted one of Hartenstein's messages, but suspected it was a trap for gullible merchant ships. On 15 September the base at Ascension finally received information from the British that the *Laconia* had been sunk. But they were given a totally inaccurate map reference and no hint that German submarines were attempting rescue and calling for help. Several missions were sent; all failed to locate the *Laconia*. There were few Allied ships in the area: many were being assembled for the invasion of North Africa, those remaining had been routed far to the West to avoid U-boats. The B-24 which finally spotted the U-156 on 16 September was the only plane from Ascension with the range to spend more than half-an-hour over the site. It was refuelling on its way to North Africa: all its crew were on their first combat mission. When they contacted the U-156 with a signal lamp, they were unable to understand the answer in German. Acting on orders from Ascension where no connection had been made between the sinking of the *Laconia* and the presence of the U-boat, the B-24 bombed her. When, that night, intelligence was received that French warships were approaching, it was assumed they were coming to attack the base. When, next morning, a US patrol spotted another U-boat, fears of a joint attack increased. That U-boat too was bombed. Only on the afternoon of 17 September did the Americans receive a hint from the British at Freetown that U-boats and other vessels in the area might be intending rescue operations. And by that time, Doenitz had issued the Laconia Order.

This version of the *Laconia* affair is carefully documented and argued. All too often in war decisions are based on faulty assumptions, mistaken intelligence and inadequate equipment; and human error is most common when inexperienced troops are involved. Captain Hans Meckel, Doenitz's Staff Officer Communications during the War and Kranzbuehler's assistant at the Nuremberg trial, finds the account convincing. He suggests that the American base at Ascension would not have listened regularly to the 600 metre emergency frequency which Hartenstein used, and that it was outside the area for good reception for middle wave. He concedes, too, that though the British in Freetown might have been expected to pick up messages on 25 metre short wave, which Hartenstein also used, even this is a tricky business in daytime.

If it is true that no one grasped what was really happening around the spot where the *Laconia* sank, it is easy to sympathise with the nervousness of the American reaction – though an instantaneous decision to bomb a U-boat and life rafts based on information supplied by an inexperienced patrol might seem rash. At least it was not vicious. At least the failure of the Allies to send help was not deliberate. An old U-boat commander, Thilo Bode, might suggest that 'the fine tuning of Hartenstein's transmitter could probably have been better', but no one would suggest that his response to the situation and the energy and courage with which he tried to meet it could have been improved. Largely thanks to Hartenstein, who was well within the law in sinking the *Laconia* in the first place, over 1,000 survivors were rescued from the sea and taken to safety by French ships which finally arrived. After 17 September, Hartenstein continued his mission. He sank two more ships in the next month. The crew of the B-24 also went on their way. They were later awarded Air Medals for their attacks on the U-boats, on the mistaken assumption that they had sunk one and damaged another. Hartenstein and the U-156 were sunk by US Navy aircraft east of Barbados in March 1943.

(Kenneth Duke most kindly lent us the article. Thilo Bode not only gave us his professional opinion of it, but sent it on to Captain Meckel for comment. Our thanks are given to all three.)

References for Chapter Fourteen

1   Conversation with Robert Kempner
2   *Chicago Daily News*, 5 December 1945
3   Andrus
4   Gilbert
5   IMT Vol. XI
6   Gilbert
7   Fritzsche and conversation with Robert Kempner
8   All quotations from the trial are from IMT Vol. XII, unless specified
9   *Daily Express*, 24 April
10 All defendants' words from Gilbert
11 *News Chronicle*, 24 April
12 Gilbert
13 Gilbert
14 Quoted by Montgomery Hyde
15 Fritzsche
16 Andrus
17 *Stars and Stripes*, 20 October and 5 December
18 Gilbert
19 IMT Vol. II
20 British prosecution minutes 16 April
21 *The Times*, 28 April
22 *Daily Telegraph*, 29 April
23 Conversation with Wolf Frank
24 British prosecution minutes
25 Gilbert
26 Andrus
27 Schacht. The incident of the coffee is described by him, and Gilbert
28 Gilbert
29 *Chicago Daily News*, 7 December
30 Bernstein

31 Schacht
32 Papen
33 IMT Vols. II and V
34 IMT Vol. XIV
35 Kilmuir
36 *New York Times*, 30 April
37 *The Times*, 30 April
38 *The Times*, and *New York Times*, 30 April
39 Dean cable to FO, 2 May. FO 371. 57547
40 Schacht
41 All defendants' words from Gilbert
42 Schacht
43 British prosecution minutes, 11 April
44 British prosecution minutes, 13 April
45 Quoted by Montgomery Hyde
46 Schacht
47 *The Times*, 2 May
48 Gilbert
49 Most of the cross-examination of Schacht comes in IMT Vol. XIII as do
    subsequent quotations from the trial until specified
50 Quoted by Montgomery Hyde
51 Schacht
52 Quoted by Montgomery Hyde
53 *Daily Telegraph*, 3 May
54 Dean cable to FO, 4 May. FO 371. 57547
55 *New York Times*, 3 May
56 Schacht
57 Cooper
58 Gilbert
59 Andrus
60 *Chicago Daily News*, 11 December 1945
61 *Daily Mail*, 16 February
62 *Chicago Daily News*, 7 December
63 *Manchester Guardian*, 6 May
64 *Daily Telegraph*, 5 May
65 Schacht
66 Dean cable to FO, 4 May. FO 371. 57547
67 Jackson Papers, Box 231
68 Dean cable to FO, 15 May. FO 371. 57547
69 Kilmuir
70 *The Times*, 8 May
71 Cooper
72 *Chicago Daily News*, 10 December 1945
73 *Manchester Guardian*, 14 January
74 *Daily Telegraph*, 16 January
75 *Chicago Daily News*, 10 December
76 Cooper
77 Andrus
78 Doenitz Memoirs
79 Quotations from prosecution case from IMT Vol. V

80 *The Times*, 8 May
81 *The Times*, 9 May
82 *Daily Telegraph*, 9 May
83 *Manchester Guardian*, 10 May
84 Cooper
85 *The Times*, 10 May
86 Dean cable to FO received 11 May. FO 371. 57547
87 Tribunal minutes, 12 and 13 November 1945
88 *Daily Telegraph*, 15 May
89 Gilbert. Details of interrogatory, in *The Times*, 23 May
90 Conversation with Adrian Fisher
91 IMT Vol XVII
92 IMT Vol V
93 Andrus
94 Dean cable to FO. FO 371. 57547
95 Gilbert
96 Cooper
97 *Daily Telegraph*, 20 May
98 Dean cable to FO, 20 May. FO 371. 57548
99 Gilbert
100 Gilbert

Chapter Fifteen

By mid-May, the overwhelming sensation at Nuremberg was one of boredom. The participants in the trial continued to be bored for the next two months. Their mood might be lifted by occasional moments of drama in the courtroom, but these were rare. Most of the evidence now seemed repetitious, the proceedings felt interminable and press coverage dwindled to a minimum. For the defendants, only their own appearance in the witness box could revive much sense of urgency; once that was over they slumped back on the bench and drifted along only half listening to what was going on. Some, thought observers, had aged visibly; all sat brooding, depressed or apparently in despair. Prosecution counsel, many of whom had arrived at Nuremberg excited by the challenge of an important job, a sense of idealism and belief that their work might make a significant contribution to the settlement of Europe and the development of law, now felt ground down by the routine. They were still working hard, and to compensate for the turgid atmosphere of the courtroom they were still playing hard. But having burned the candle at both ends for six months they now tended to be listless, the spark had gone. In early June, a French interpreter who had sat behind the French judges, but never been called upon to translate anything for them, was sacked. He had all too obviously been sleeping through the sessions, and calling attention to the fact by strident snores. (1) He was unlucky; he was caught. Those who could sleep more quietly survived.

The mood of depression was exacerbated by a sense that the trial had become bogged down in irrelevance and no release was in prospect. Birkett, who seemed more depressed than most, bemoaned the fact that the trial had reached a stage 'when nobody makes any effort to consider time'. He felt the defendants stretched their testimony to dreary length and the prosecutors cross-examined 'whether it serves any useful purpose or not'. 'When I consider,' said Birkett, 'the utter uselessness of acres of paper and thousands of words and that life is slipping away, I moan for this shocking waste of time. I used to protest vigorously and suggest matters to save time, but I have now got completely dispirited and can only chafe in impotent despair.' (2) It was Nikitchenko's turn to protest. He submitted a memorandum to the other judges in late May. 'The trial of the major war criminals of Nazi Germany has been going on for six months already. It is absolutely clear that unless fundamental changes in the conducting of proceedings are introduced it will last for another few months.' He thought that the public complaints being voiced were entirely reasonable 'considering that the trial is unjustifiably being stretched and all clarity lost.' He blamed the slowness of the trial on 'the deliberate attempts of the defendants and their counsel to drag out proceedings' and on the fact that they were not 'to a sufficient degree checked by the Tribunal'. (3)

So too did Professor Trainin, who wrote a two-column article in *Izvestia* on 13 June under the headline 'A Slow-Motion Trial'. The British embassy official in Moscow who forwarded it to the Foreign Office commented that this was the first hint in the Soviet Press of any dissatisfaction with the proceedings. It was only a gentle hint. Trainin's tone was more one of sorrow than anger. He suggested the slow pace of the trial was the result of the defence being given too much opportunity to dispute the validity of documents and to stray into irrelevance. But he was then careful to explain that legal trial is inevitably slower than political action because documents and witnesses must be examined thoroughly, and that where four prosecution teams were involved the pace must slacken. He called on the judges to assert control, then went to great pains to describe Lawrence as skilful and thoughtful and to press the point that 'the International Military Tribunal unquestionably has deserved the authority and deep confidence of all mankind.' (4) Perhaps unintentionally, however, Trainin had laid bare the judges' dilemma: if evidence were to be thoroughly examined and the Tribunal were to maintain confidence it was not easy at this stage to hurry the defence cases. In fairness, remaining defendants should be allowed as much opportunity as had been given to their predecessors, and an analysis of the transcript of the court sessions does not suggest that simple remedies existed for speeding things up. Tribunal calls for relevance were frequent but often unavailing; disputes on the validity of documents were infrequent and relatively disciplined.

The conclusion that suggests itself is that the defence were not so much deliberately dragging out the proceedings as simply too long-winded in style and too intellectually muddled to make them more cogent and concise. Incessant harrying from the Tribunal might only have confused them further – and would certainly have provoked complaints of prejudice against the defence. Firmness by the judges could save the odd half-hour, but if justice were to be seen to be done there was now no prospect of chipping whole weeks off the proceedings. Strangely enough, Robert Jackson, impatient by nature and intolerant of the judges by recent experience, appears to have accepted the slow rhythm more philosophically than others. He wrote to a friend at the end of April: 'Our case is moving along much slower than we would like; but still, it is not a year since the surrender of Germany and you know how few law suits are even started, yet alone tried, in a year at home.' (5)

A contributing factor to the malaise among prosecution staffs was undoubtedly that they were still on duty, often still in uniform, when elsewhere men were being demobbed. For those at Nuremberg, Civvy

Street seemed a long way off, and they were homesick. There had been no home leave for most of them, sometimes no meeting with family and friends since before the trial began. By mid-1946, General Patton had relaxed his rules about family residence in his Zone, but only the judges and a few barristers had been able to bring their wives to Nuremberg – lack of transport and accommodation kept most away. Despondency at being marooned on a desolate island increased when a few people escaped. Biddle felt wretched when his aide, Herb Wechsler, was about to return to his academic life in the States. 'Herb has helped us in a thousand ways that don't show, really has been our right-hand man . . . I shall miss him terribly, and not only in work. I have been very close to him.' (6) The judges were so socially isolated that their few intimates whom they could trust and relax with had become very precious.

Others were to be missed in the slightly larger world of the prosecution teams. 'Khaki' Roberts, for example. The Treasury Solicitor's office had been pressing since March for reductions in the British staff; the Lord Chancellor, they said, was concerned at the total of the fees of two leaders and four juniors in the team and Parliamentary questions had chivvied him into urging economies. Maxwell-Fyfe had prickled. While acknowledging that his own fees formed a serious part of the problem, he assured the Treasury Solicitor that he would be 'only too happy' to leave Nuremberg as soon as possible. Roberts' fees were 'very nearly equivalent to those of three junior counsel put together', and Maxwell-Fyfe conceded there would 'not be enough work to justify his retention once the case against Jodl' was completed. So Sir David suggested that Roberts should 'have a really good show before he leaves, and retires, I hope, in a blaze of glory'. (7)

Roberts was all too glad to go. He was morose and suffering acutely from homesickness. One evening at a party a British secretary was asked by Colonel Turrall, the man responsible for British staff administration, to sit on Roberts' knee. Roberts had been trying to drown his sorrows, and had reached a state where he thought it would cheer him up to hit someone. The girl literally sat on him until the mood passed. (8) Roberts' departure left a gap in the courtroom and in the social life of Nuremberg. Bob Cooper remembered the 'eager tenacity of a man who played rugby football for England and a wholesome hatred of German militarism; . . . his massive stature and sense of fun made him one of the most popular personalities at Nuremberg. No one was more missed than he when he returned to England in June.' (9)

From late April, the British team at Nuremberg had also been plagued with anxious enquiries or indignant complaints from the Treasury Solicitor's office about the failure to reduce its support staff. As London saw the situation, the work at Nuremberg was now routine; the wage bill should be cut. As Nuremberg saw it, even routine work needed staff and some of it was disgracefully underpaid. Harry Phillimore insisted that four WRNS should be promoted – at the moment they were 'on a servant's wage'. (10) It seemed likely that every staff member would be needed, that even more might have to be engaged, if it was decided to hold a second trial.

The idea of a second trial had germinated in the previous August. While choosing defendants, those names rejected seemed likely candidates for other proceedings. The idea had grown once it was realised that Krupp was unfit to stand trial and his son could not be substituted. Lists of industrialists had been prepared. The French and Russians had been keenest to have a second trial; Maxwell-Fyfe and Jackson preferred to wait and see how successfully they could cope with the first. (11) That remained the division of opinion when the idea was revived in April – though by now Jackson feared that the possible acquittal of Schacht might ruin the chances of an effective trial of industrialists. Even so, on 11 April the chief prosecutors decided to pick ten possible defendants and to set up a sub-committee to consider cases against them and amass evidence. (12) Within days it became clear that there were up to a hundred names worth considering and that even if this second trial were to be conducted in two languages only, it would last at least three months and involve many practical problems. Jackson pointed out that the US military authorities intended to use the Nuremberg Palace of Justice for Zone trials and as a constabulary headquarters; Berlin was still short of accommodation. (13) The prosecutors were facing the same problem that had bedevilled them the previous year. Their governments were behaving in the same way too. Washington was raring to go, London was carping, Paris was expressing interest but investing no resources, while Moscow was inscrutable and postponing decision. Even so, the prosecution teams went ahead. Their sub-committee met and Telford Taylor brought about thirty-seven extra staff from the United States, replete with new energy and enthusiasm. The Treasury Solicitor's office in London was predictably grumpy about the expenditure, but a fresh project revived the flagging spirits of those British staff involved and gave them a welcome distraction from the daily tedium of the main trial.

The need for distraction was at a premium when Baldur von Schirach went into the witness box on 23 May. (14) One newspaper described his testimony on the first day as 'wearying the court'. (15) Lawrence intervened several times and threatened to stop the case unless Schirach stuck to the point, but he had difficulty in finding a point to stick to. He gave his age, and that of his four children; he described his father's life as an Army officer and manager of the court theatre in Weimar. He could hardly get away from the topic of Weimar, 'native city of all Germans', as he called it, and dwelt long on the way 'the atmosphere of classic and post-classic Weimar influenced my development', and the festivals of German Youth he organized there. (Sauckel who followed him into the box was equally fixated on the place and condemned the building of the Buchenwald concentration camp nearby as 'not at all the right thing for the town of Weimar and its traditions'.) At last Schirach faced some of the charges against him and discussed the Hitler Youth which he had organized and led from 1931 to 1940. The prosecution had alleged that through the Hitler Youth he had perverted a generation of young Germans and trained them as Nazis and aggressors. But Schirach spoke of the organization as one of jolly Boy Scouts, never ever reading *Der Stürmer*, eager to develop friendship with young persons all over the world. He tried to show the court a photograph of one of their houses for foreign visitors, but was prevented: 'The particular style of architecture,' said Lawrence, 'will not affect us.' Schirach was prepared to call Hitler Youth training 'pre-military' but no more; he had avoided teaching anything which would have to be unlearned once a young person went into the Wehrmacht. Membership of the Hitler Youth had been voluntary until 1936, he said, though he feared that those who did not join risked becoming 'hypochondriacs'. He called it a community without class distinctions, wearing not so much a uniform as a 'dress of comradeship', involving in cheerful activity the blind and deaf, and achieving a remarkable improvement in dental health. Schirach was obviously very keen on teeth. When he later talked of his visit to the Mauthausen concentration camp, he not only expressed pleasure at the concert he had heard there given by a tenor and symphony orchestra, but paid particular tribute to the camp's excellent dental clinic.

When the judges withdrew at lunch time they held what Biddle called 'a stormy discussion ... I and the Russians think we ought to stop this hogwash.' But other judges would not allow an intervention: 'De Vabres thinks we must have the "psychological" background. Parker doesn't want the world to get the impression we are stopping freedom of speech.' (16) So that afternoon Schirach was left relatively undisturbed to try to persuade his listeners of his total ignorance of politics and foreign affairs and to claim that he had forbidden the Hitler Youth to sing such songs as 'Germany belongs to us, tomorrow the world', and 'Victoriously we will conquer France'. Ossian Goulding of the *Daily Telegraph* was not convinced. He wrote that evening: 'To correspondents and others who were in Germany in the early days of Nazi power, his claim can only provoke the comment – "Schirach was singularly inept at enforcing his veto".' (17)

Only late that afternoon did Schirach touch on a different set of charges levelled at him: those concerning his work as Governor of Vienna from 1940. These charges were most important to the prosecution case, and represented the strongest possibility of securing his conviction. Evidence to prove that he had made the Hitler Youth part of the conspiracy and militarized the organization was weak. The prosecution could point to the Basic Law of 1936: 'The German youth, besides being reared within the family and school, shall be educated physically, intellectually and morally in the spirit of National Socialism to serve the people and the community through the Hitler Youth.' They could argue that Schirach had given much more military training than he admitted to and provided the next generation of Nazi soldiers. They could quote a few incidents in which Hitler Youth members had taken part in terrorism or committed crimes against humanity. But none of this evidence could prove conclusively that Schirach had actually committed criminal acts himself or incited others to crime. The problem was the same as in the Streicher case: a sense of revulsion against what the defendant had done, a suspicion that he had prepared the mental and moral climate for crimes, but no hard evidence to forge the link between words and deeds. Such had been the anxiety to get it that the prosecutors had been temporarily misled into submitting a 'black', forged document. It had been given to Drexel Sprecher the evening before he presented the prosecution case against Schirach in January. He read it quickly; it looked like a pamphlet by Rosenberg implicating the Hitler Youth movement in the conspiracy, and extracts were read in court next day, 15 January. Only then did Sprecher begin to suspect something wrong with the document. He checked and discovered that it had been forged by an anti-Nazi Church group. He wrote to Thomas Dodd who, on his recommendation, applied successfully to have the document struck from the record. Probably the defence would have discovered it was a forgery and used the fact to discredit the prosecution. But there was also a genuine concern among many prosecutors to establish a true record throughout the trial; a forged document would mar it. (18)

The case concerning Schirach's governorship of Vienna presented fewer problems. While he was in office, up to 185,000 Jews had been transported from the city. Schirach was prepared to say in court that he had always wanted the exclusion of Jews from the civil service and limits set to their participation in cultural life and access to educational opportunities. He even said he had thought after 'Kristallnacht' that emigration would spare them similar 'unpleasantness'. But the prosecution quoted his speech in 1942 saying 'every Jew who operates in Europe is a danger to European culture' (he now argued he had spoken out of 'misplaced loyalty' to Hitler). They read from the minutes of a meeting where he had suggested to Hitler, Bormann and others that Viennese Jews should be sent to Poland, and they countered his claim not to have known what happened to those sent East by showing he received weekly reports from the SS on the treatment meted out and had been regularly informed on the activities of Einsatzkommandos. (Not surprisingly, Schirach now said he had never read any such documents sent to him.) There was evidence too of the conditions suffered by foreign labourers in Vienna – evidence which exposed the feebleness of his assertion that all foreign workers were immaculately housed, high-spirited, and well-nourished. Once challenged on his story of visiting Mauthausen without seeing suffering, the work in the stone quarries or a crematorium, Schirach had to admit he now felt confused, given what was known about Mauthausen. There was an unconscious irony in his description of three prisoners about to be released as looking 'very happy'.

Schirach gave testimony for a day and a half. He did not impress his audience. Many people, like Ossian Goulding, were alienated by the tall, pallid man's 'supercilious accents'. (19) Most people viewed him with a prejudice which, after the manner of the time, they hid in euphemism.

Schirach might behave like the eternal scoutmaster, but he exuded the whiff of the kind of scoutmaster who ends up in the Sunday newspapers. But no one could bring themselves to use the word 'homosexual'. Instead an interrogator had written of his 'rather unpleasant good looks', and the way his 'tendency to puffiness seems to have been held in check'. (20) Someone else compared him to Ivor Novello, 'anxious to keep up his youthful appearance'. (21) Gilbert's report to Andrus was even more circumspect and talked of Schirach as 'a curious aesthete with a narcissistic streak'. (22)

Gilbert had gone on to say that Schirach's early rise to power had gone 'to his romantic head' and that he was now 'disillusioned at what he feels was the betrayal of German youth by the older leaders'. Gilbert had actively nurtured that disillusionment in recent months; tried to wean Schirach from his hero worship of Goering; given encouragement to his flickering wish to condemn Hitler's abuse of German youth. It is hard to believe that Gilbert was acting purely on his own initiative. Others beside must have seen an advantage in persuading the former leader of those young people to reject the training they had received and set them on a less dangerous path for the future. Should German youth come to share Schirach's disillusion, Germany would be easier to settle and incorporate into the European community. But there is no evidence to show that Gilbert discussed his strategy with others. Nor is there a hint anywhere that a bargain was considered, offering reduction of sentence in return for an appeal to German youth. On the contrary, the prosecution records suggest that every effort was made to secure the maximum sentence. Gilbert's diary shows Schirach struggling with his conscience, until deciding in early May that he had one last mission to the young people of Germany – to denounce Hitler before he died.

He got his courage to the sticking point in the witness box around mid-morning on 24 May. He was noticeably ashen-faced. (23) First he described his worsening relations with Hitler from 1943: the Führer's complaints about his 'decadent' art exhibitions in Vienna, his own letter arguing that the war with America was a mistake, his gradual awareness that Jews were being murdered. Then: 'That murder,' he said 'was ordered by Adolf Hitler.' German youth 'is guiltless. Our youth was anti-Semitically inclined but it did not call for the extermination of Jewry ... the youth of Germany who today stand perplexed among the ruins of their native land knew nothing of these crimes, nor did they desire them. They are innocent of all that Hitler has done to the Jewish and to the German people.' He took some responsibility upon himself: 'I alone bear the guilt of having trained our young people for a man who I for many long years had considered unimpeachable ... for a man who murdered by the millions.' Schirach repudiated anti-Semitism – it had led to Auschwitz – though he acknowledged that to be a Nazi had been to be an anti-Semite. Then for a moment he seemed to backpedal, asserting he had never betrayed Hitler, always remained true to his oath. But at last he returned to the denunciation he had steeled himself to make: Hitler's 'racial policy was a crime which led to disaster for five million Jews and for all Germans.'

During the statement Gilbert had noticed the tension in the dock: Frank, Funk and Raeder dabbing their eyes, Streicher sneering. When Schirach went down to lunch he was congratulated by Fritzsche, Funk and Speer, and in their own room Papen, Neurath and Schacht agreed he was perfectly right in his judgement of Hitler. Goering had not been in court; he was excused on grounds of indisposition. Gilbert suspected that Goering was unwilling to sit through the embarrassment of hearing what Schirach was going to say. That evening Goering complained in equal measure of 'treachery' and 'sciatica' – evidently suffering from all kinds of stabs in the back. During the weekend Schirach mulled over what he had said. He talked now of Hitler's ingratitude, the way he himself had been rejected from 1943 and put in constant fear of arrest. He hinted that Hitler had never been at ease with women. He was pleased that Gilbert had taken the notes for his statement to two former Hitler Youth leaders who were being held in the witness wing of the jail and that they had been impressed, and promised to circulate it among former members. Speer was delighted by what had happened. He suggested that he and Schirach should now call each other by the intimate 'du'. (24) This invitation held out the prospect of an additional pleasure: 'Goering will have a stroke,' Speer thought. (25)

The Times considered that Schirach's statement had been expressed 'in the bitterest terms the court has yet heard'. (26) But no newspaper treated it as particularly sensational, let alone as a turning point. Any good impression it might have made was soon wiped away by Schirach's inept witnesses and his response to cross-examination. Dodd began by saying that the 'confession' had been 'bravely enough said', then prodded for what had been omitted, 'perhaps through oversight'. He reminded Schirach of the 10,000 rifles given to the Hitler Youth by the Wehrmacht in 1937, of words from the official songbook – 'We are the future soldiers, everything which opposes us will fall before our fists' and 'We want to kill the priest, out with your spears', and 'Pope and Rabbi shall yield'. Dodd read from the Hitler Youth Handbook on weekend camps. It contained explicit instructions to give weekend readings from *Mein Kampf* or Rosenberg, a motto for the day: 'Our service to Germany is divine service'. He drove Schirach to admit he had allowed the SS to recruit from the organization and showed him his letter to Bormann in 1941 asking for SA members to assist in training in the way the SS had helped 'for a long time already'. He reduced him to silence by reading his telegram to Bormann after Heydrich's assassination suggesting a retaliatory raid on some 'British cultural town'. Dodd further upset him with evidence showing that the Hitler Youth had helped to look after up to 50,000 children kidnapped from the Eastern Territories who were to be made apprentices in German factories; they were between ten and fourteen years old. A newspaper report that very morning had said that 10,000 of these children still could not be traced. All Schirach could do was to stutter that he had always assumed that their treatment had been 'simply wonderful'.

Once his hearing was finished Schirach, according to Fritzsche, 'quite methodically developed in himself a capacity for making the most of those small pleasures and rare moments of happiness that even the daily routine of a prisoner might hold'; seemingly he no longer expected to be hanged and was practising for a long term of imprisonment. (27) How long that term would be depended both on the weight the judges gave to his work in Vienna, and the decision they reached on the criminality of his leadership of the Hitler Youth. Maxwell-Fyfe at least had little confidence in this latter part of the case. In a discussion in June he caustically commented that 'unless a closer study of the documents ... brought forth hidden strengths ... he was rather disappointed with regard to the corruption of the German youth'. (28)

There were never any doubts, however, over the strength of prosecution evidence brought against Fritz Sauckel who began his testimony in the afternoon of 28 May. Sauckel, who joined the Nazi Party in 1921, had become Gauleiter and later Minister of the Interior in Thuringia. But he was charged on all four counts, largely because of his work as Plenipotentiary General for Labour Mobilization from March 1942. The announcement of his appointment had spoken of the need of the war economy and especially the armament industry for 'a uniform direction ... of all available labour, including hired foreigners and prisoners-of-war'. Sauckel had given this direction. He had been prepared to enslave rather than hire that labour. It was he who had boasted in 1944 that out of the five million foreign workers in Germany 'not even 200,000 came voluntarily'.

The Hague Convention of 1907 permitted the employment of native labourers in their own occupied territories 'only for the needs of the army of occupation'. This labour could be used only in proportion to the resources of the country and only if not involved in 'war operations' against their own land. But Sauckel had moved five million people to Germany, and virtually enslaved others in their own countries. In 1942 he prohibited change of employment without the permission of the occupying authorities and made possession of ration cards dependent on a certificate of employment. He had organized the shanghaiing of labour, assigned it to munitions factories and fortifications. (It was to Sauckel that Milch had commented how amusing it was to think of Russians manning anti-aircraft guns against their own planes.) He deported Jews from the Reich and replaced them with Poles – to be 'put into concentration camps and put to work in so far as they are criminals or anti-social elements', for the rest to be split from their families and sent 'to work in armament factories instead of the Jews'. It had been clear from prosecution evidence that Sauckel had been fully informed of the disgusting conditions in which foreign workers were transported and the squalor and cruelty to which they were subjected once assigned to work. He had made some minimal stipulation on treatment, though not for humanitarian reasons. He wrote to Gauleiters in 1943: 'Cool commonsense... demands proper treatment of foreign labour, including even Soviet-Russians. Slaves who are underfed, diseased, resentful, despairing, and filled with hate will never yield that maximum of output which they might achieve under normal conditions.' (29) To judge from the evidence of those 'slaves', his instructions had not been carried out.

Sauckel might be seen by others as a slaver; he saw himself as a decent working man. He explained under cross-examination: 'I received a task and I received orders. As a German I had to carry out that task correctly for the sake of my people... As a human being and as a result of my upbringing I would never have supported crime.' Gilbert had called him 'an unimpressive, naïve realist whose conventional sense of values was distorted by his blind faith in Hitler as the answer to unemployment'. (30) He had found him in 'a state of anxiety and depression over revelations of atrocities which he swears he knew nothing about'. Yet Sauckel had personally organized the deportation of millions, visited Dachau, toured slave labour camps and gone to the East to supervize transport of workers. He was more likely to be in a state of anxiety and depression because he now had to face up to those atrocities. He had once tried to run away – literally. Doenitz had had the submarine in which he had stowed away brought back to port. In his testimony the Admiral had expressed surprise that a Gauleiter wished to go to sea. 'Here,' he had thought, 'was a man who had his heart in the right place... nothing much can be got out of a submarine trip.' (31) But though he now had to face the truth, Sauckel could still not acknowledge his own connection with it. He kept telling other defendants how well-intentioned he had been. Fritzsche said they all found him 'utterly confused'; the more he stressed his benevolence the more they detected 'a touch of madness' in his face. (32)

Sauckel was a short, pudgy man, bald and with a little Hitler moustache. A journalist noticed that he walked 'on the balls of his feet like a referee at a wrestling match'. (33) Fellow defendants who were aristocrats or just plain snobs mocked his plebeian accent. His style of giving testimony was long-winded, irrelevant and personal – like Schirach's, but more so. (34) It took an excessively long time before he could be weaned away from talking about his father's life as a postman, his mother's heart trouble, his own adventures as a seaman on a sailing ship going to Australia in 1914 and his happy life with his devoted wife and ten children. No wonder that when he began to explain his reason for joining the Nazi Party, Lawrence snapped: 'It seems to me that we are having it inflicted on us by nearly every one of the defendants.' Most of Sauckel's evidence was an infliction. Even when he at last got down to the subject of the direction of labour, he skirted round the charges rather than confronting them. He insisted at length that there was a difference between 'exploiting' and 'supplying' workers, went into inordinate detail about the exact relationship between one authority and another in all the areas occupied by Germany, denied the use of any compulsion, knowledge of atrocities, or transport conditions or sickness among foreign workers. He argued that since he never received any complaints about their food it must have been good. When presented with evidence that many thousands of women brought 'to help the German housewife' only got three hours' rest a week, he assumed that this was all German domestic help was given. He claimed never to have heard of 'extermination by labour', never to have seen letters with his typed signature, not to remember meetings he attended. All this took up to two and a half days. The correspondent of the *Daily Telegraph* found it was 'difficult to write objectively of such a performance ... of the injured innocence, sanctimonious self-justification and flat contradiction by Sauckel of remarks he is shown by several minutes to have made at a series of conferences but which he is now anxious to disclaim'. (35)

Sauckel's evasions were soon exposed, however, by an effective cross-examination by the French counsel, Herzog, who drew him step by step into admitting to the use of the Army and SD to dragoon labour, to the use of handcuffs (but only where there was 'most flagrant resistance to deportation', said Sauckel) and to handing over responsibility for escaped workers to the Gestapo ('there was nobody but the police to undertake the search for such people' protested Sauckel). The defendant expressed surprise when shown a photograph of himself at Buchenwald – though in his testimony he had praised the pretty blue and white striped sheets he had seen there. Alexandrov, who took over for the Russians from Herzog, engaged Sauckel in what *The Times* called 'a four-hour shouting match', (36) but got bogged down in figures. Somehow by this stage it had almost ceased to matter whether there were five million or seven million slave labourers in Germany, whether one and a half million prisoners-of-war should or should not be included in the total. Lawrence complained frequently about timewasting and he insisted that exact figures were of no importance.

Finally Biddle himself took over the cross-examination on the afternoon of 31 May, first entreating Sauckel to speak more quietly. He wrote to his wife that evening: 'The French and the Russians had been quite inadequate and I decided to go to town on him and spent a couple of hours studying the case last night. I really got him. He was frightened, brief and totally responsive. If I raised my hand he would stop in the middle of a sentence ... it took three quarters of an hour and I thoroughly enjoyed it and felt pleasantly relaxed as a result!' (37) The transcript confirms that Sauckel had indeed been disciplined at last. But the answers he gave Biddle were mainly condensed repetitions of his testimony and replies to Herzog. Biddle might have enjoyed himself, the spectators might have been given an exhibition of neat professional cross-examination, but it is doubtful whether the Sauckel case had been at all advanced.

Sauckel's counsel, Servatius, certainly got no further with his four witnesses. The last was Wilhelm Jaeger – a doctor at the Krupp works at

Essen. His affidavit, which had been submitted by the prosecution, had given an appalling picture of the misery and degradation experienced by Krupp's foreign labour. Nothing Servatius could do shook Jaeger from the points he had made. He spoke of the high rate of tuberculosis, the continual typhus, the infected food. He remained confident when Servatius tried to suggest that labour camps he mentioned had not existed at the date he gave or that his calorie figures were inaccurate. He changed his evidence only in one small detail – he agreed it was an exaggeration to have said that workers had been living in dog kennels after heavy bombing raids but insisted they had been forced to move into ovens and old latrines. The only result of calling Jaeger as a witness was to allow him to refresh the Tribunal's memory of his accusations, and undoubtedly help to damn Sauckel. Sauckel himself left the witness box 'quiet and depressed, though he tried hard not to show it too much', thought Fritzsche. He still could not understand how 'a humble working man could be called a slave driver'. (38) Maxwell-Fyfe, on the other hand, reckoned that the evidence had firmly substantiated the charges; he could see no difficulty in the case. (39) Conviction and a very heavy sentence seemed inevitable.

Such an outcome never seemed so inevitable in the case of General Alfred Jodl. Fritzsche recorded in his memoirs that all the defendants expected him to be acquitted and that Jodl too probably expected to be found innocent. (40) Jodl had been Chief of the Operations Staff of the OKW from 1939 to 1945 – that is to say, head of a department subordinate to Keitel which was responsible for general staff work on the operational conduct of the war. Jodl was Hitler's closest military adviser. He was charged on all four counts, the last two containing allegations concerning the Commando Order, the Commissar Decree, the use of forced labour for munitions, terrorism against partisans and the deportation of Jews from Denmark. Many of the military who appeared at Nuremberg claimed to be simple fighting men, and so devoted to their particular tasks that they were unaware of the politics or the crimes of the regime they served. Not many of them convinced. But Jodl persuaded many that his claim was genuine. Like Doenitz he had voluntarily handed over papers as a sign of his clear conscience (he had provided his own private papers and a complete set of Führer orders and directives). As with Doenitz, it was those who had fought who tended to respond to him with sympathy and to accept his version of events. Former soldiers sensed in Jodl a commander in whom they would have been confident – a thoroughly able strategist, whole-hearted in his concern for his work and the welfare of his men. He seemed a true professional, absorbed in the job in hand; not a Keitel, seeking reflected glory and strength from Hitler, or a Goering, darting from one task to another to satisfy his vanity. Yet other people could never throw off the feeling that it had been impossible to live in such close contact with Hitler, to work at the very heart of the regime and still remain ignorant, uncontaminated, an efficient cog in a purely military machine.

Other defendants were easier to penetrate, their characters and motives were open to analysis and judgement. Jodl kept closed and secret from most people. Papen, who sat on his left throughout the trial, never came to know him; they had few conversations in all those months. From a distance Papen respected the way Jodl 'conducted himself in a soldierly manner and awaited his fate with calm resignation'. (41) Fritzsche thought that much of Jodl's reserve was the result of his inability to make himself pleasant to strangers (significantly, this was Fritzsche's most noticeable characteristic). He felt that Jodl withdrew from the trial and from most of the other defendants behind a screen of 'correct politeness and studied indifference'. (42) Gilbert summed him up as a 'rigid, impassive militarist' but sensed he was more complicated than this phrase implied. He noted: 'The war does not violate his sense of values but the atrocities do.' (43) And indeed Jodl frequently expressed disgust at the evidence of crimes, and alternated between indignation and shame that the German Army had been accused of so many. Though reticent with most people, he poured out his feelings in a letter to his wife written after seeing film of the concentration camps: 'These feelings are the most fearful heritage which the National Socialist regime has left the German people. It is far worse than the destruction of German cities. Their ruins could be regarded as honourable wounds suffered during a people's battle for its existence. This disgrace, however, besmirches everything ... we were all systematically deceived in this matter. The accusation that we were all aware of these circumstances is false. I would not have tolerated such wrong doing for a single day.' (44) Some might think that Jodl was covering himself, others that he had held a position where it was impossible to avoid knowing. If nothing else, however, this letter and the records of Jodl's reactions to the evidence he heard in court suggest a clearer moral awareness than many other defendants exhibited.

Andrus had respect for Jodl – a soldier's respect for an able officer (and one who never whined and always kept his cell tidy). His guards called him 'Happy Hooligan' after a comic strip character. (45) He certainly had a face from a cartoon: beady eyes, red nose and huge flapping ears, a head bald except for a light fringe of hair. It was tempting to believe that Jodl's stiff back, aloof manner and reserve were due to lack of feelings. But Fritzsche saw Jodl as 'a soldier who used his strictly disciplined intellect as a cover for an excessive capacity for emotion'. (46) The love letters he wrote to his wife show one emotion. The other, which most people saw, was rage. Jodl had a blazing temper. When it flared his face would 'flush scarlet and his eyes snap beneath their frizzy bland brows'. (47) He had often lost his temper with Hitler. Kesselring had said that at Hitler's headquarters he had seen 'General Jodl grow red in the face and, in expressing his views, he went very near the limit of what is permissible for a military man'. (48)

In the witness box Jodl managed to control his temper as he gave his testimony and replies to other defence counsel for three days from 3 June. He appeared a 'far more forthright figure in the box than his retiring and generally unimpressive appearance had led us to suppose', thought *The Times* correspondent. (49) His speech was logical and often spiced with sharp turns of phrase. He was competently guided by his lawyer, Dr Exner, who with his assistant had formed a close personal relationship with Jodl, rare among defendants and their counsel and unexpected with a man so often frosty.

First, Jodl created a daunting picture of Hitler's headquarters as 'a cross between a cloister and a concentration camp', cut off from the world by barbed wire. Here he had often worked until three in the morning, reported to Hitler at least twice a day, and attended anything up to 5,000 conferences. The headquarters, he said, had been cheered only by Hitler's mingy Christmas presents of an extra ration of coffee; for the rest it was poisoned by his mistrust for his General Staff officers, especially the army ones. He quoted Hitler as often saying: 'I have a reactionary army, a Christian (or sometimes an Imperial) Navy, and a National Socialist Air Force.' Jodl spoke bitterly of the constant encroachments on Army authority by the SS and of Hitler's 'caustic and unfriendly' attitude to himself from 1942 onwards. He insisted that their relationship had always been professional, never personal. He told of 'numerous sharp altercations' and the frequent attempts he had made to get leave from headquarters so as to be able to go to the front where he longed to command mountain troops. But he stressed that he never contemplated resigning: in wartime 'a soldier cannot sit at home and knit stockings.'

In his cell, Jodl confided to Gilbert that he had come to hate Hitler for his contempt for the middle classes (to which he belonged and which Hitler thought cowardly and out of sympathy with his ideas), his suspicion of the nobility (into which he had married and which Hitler mistrusted for its internationalism), and his hatred of the General Staff (of which Jodl was a member and which Hitler blamed when things went wrong but whose advice he never took). (50) In court he described Hitler as 'a man of gigantic personality who, however, in the end assumed infernal powers'. But for the most part he stuck to the details of their formal working relationship, emphasizing the impermeable compartments into which Hitler put politicians and military, the view that Hitler alone made decisions while others like himself put them into military form. Yet, paradoxically, he insisted on the rich opportunities for argument about orders and delay in their implementation. He referred to Hitler's 'masterpiece of secrecy' – the concealment of concentration camps and the extermination of the Jews – insisting that he had never heard even a hint of them, though admitting that 'I know just how improbable these explanations sound.'

Jodl informed the court he always kept copies of the Hague and Geneva conventions on his desk for reference. But 'as for the ethical code of my action, I must say it was obedience – for obedience is really the ethical basis of the military profession'. In using phrases like this, Jodl began to sound like Keitel or some of the more criminal officers who appeared as witnesses. No one would deny that obedience is a military virtue, indeed necessity.

But can it ever be an ethical basis? And how far should it be taken even as a professional duty? Jodl, like the humblest private – or Field Marshal Milch – must have had a list of the Army's Ten Commandments in his pay book and these set clear limits to obedience: limits of law and commonly accepted decencies. But his concept of obedience undoubtedly explained the vehemence with which he denounced 'the nest of conspirators' whose plots against Hitler he called 'wicked'. Gilbert noticed Doenitz, Goering and Ribbentrop nodding in approval of his words, but Schacht and Speer told him that evening that all the leaders had had a responsibility to try to do something about 'that madman, Hitler'. (51)

Jodl was at his most confident when dealing with military planning during the war. When he went into detail, on the logistics of the invasion of Poland, for instance, Lawrence became impatient and called his account 'a simple waste of our time'. But Jodl displayed his calibre as a staff officer and Bob Cooper for one thought he had never heard 'a more brilliant review of the war'. (52) His defence against many of the charges he faced seems less than brilliant, however. He talked of the build-up of the Armed Forces as being only in the interests of achieving parity with others and kept secret so as to avoid misunderstanding abroad. His insistence on Germany's shortage of men and armaments, his claim that Poland was invaded with only enough ammunition for ten to fifteen days of fighting, provoke the reply appropriate to Doenitz as well – inadequate preparation is no proof of lack of aggressive intent. Similarly his statement that no soldier had expected war in 1939, that the Allied declaration had come 'like a blow from a cudgel', that he himself had just paid for a Mediterranean cruise in September, revives the suspicion that too many people in Nazi Germany had come to expect that Hitler would always get what he wanted by bluff and threat. Many historians would now accept Jodl's explanation that 'everything had to be improvized for this war', and indeed praise the abilities and energy of men like him who scrambled to keep up with Hitler's sudden grabs at opportunity. But they would not necessarily believe his description of the Anschluss as purely a battle of flowers, where the German Army had strolled in to the plaudits of the happy Austrian crowd, of the takeover of Bohemia and Moravia as necessitated by an unprovoked Czech mobilization, of the invasion of Norway as a justified pre-emptive move against Britain, of Belgian and Dutch neutrality as 'really only pretended and deceptive'. Nor that Germany had fought a 'preventive war' in Russia, launched without consideration of *lebensraum* in response to a massive Russian military build up. Jodl had heard plenty of evidence to show that all these statements were arguable or positively untenable, but he gave no hint that he had changed the opinions he had once held.

His account did not convince Norman Birkett who commented that Jodl 'gives the impression that he was much more than a mere soldier. He shows considerable political knowledge, much ingenuity, and remarkable shrewdness. He obviously knows the strength of the case against him and also the best lines on which to answer it.' (53) But Jodl's shrewdness was less apparent and his sense of an effective defence was weak when he came to deal with the charges he faced under Counts Three and Four. His claim to have had doubts about drafting the Commando Order, to have delayed its application and rescinded it for the beachhead area after the Allied invasion, did not alter the fact that he had accepted Hitler's own draft and distributed it. His argument that many Russian cities had been found booby-trapped, and that Russian radio had announced that Leningrad was mined, could not excuse his involvement in the policy to raze the city to the ground. Passing on Hitler's order to deport Jews from Denmark as opposed to issuing one himself makes the action little better. His excuse for his policy towards saboteurs in Denmark and partisans in Yugoslavia and Russia – that 'it is a very debatable question from the point of view of international law whether an army is not entitled to adopt the fighting methods of its opponents' – is either legally faulty or just a roundabout way of saying *tu quoque*. Most threadbare of all was Jodl's explanation for his note on the Commissar Decree, that 'it is best to brand the entire action as retaliation'. Now he tried to say that this was just another way of saying 'wait and see'.

When Jodl went into the witness box on the morning of 6 June to face cross-examination by Roberts, he found a water colour of his favourite range of Bavarian mountains on the ledge. It had been painted by his wife and she had written on it 'Calm, calm, oh so calm my dear. And do keep your temper. Losing it only helps the opponent.' (54) Frau Jodl was working in the court as an assistant to his counsel. She sat at their table every day and was happy to be near her husband though they could not speak. It was a poignant situation which moved many people. Her quiet dignity and total devotion to her husband had won everyone's admiration, and it was reflected on to Jodl – there was a strong feeling that he must have had some good qualities to keep the love of such a thoroughly nice woman. The next day she left for him in the box a small bunch of flowers with a note: 'Be patient and do not lose your temper.' (55)

This was advice Jodl found difficult to take. First with Roberts, then with Pokrovsky, he fought bitter contests and his rage at their accusations and his resentment of their manner often boiled over. Maxwell-Fyfe had hoped that Roberts's final appearance in court would allow him to go out in a blaze of glory. Neither he nor Roberts can have felt that it did. Roberts was at his most pompous, spinning out questions in the style of 'what had those countries done to deserve the horrors of invasion and the misery of German occupation?' And 'Will this record of broken pledges dishonour the name of Germany for centuries to come?' He was often disagreeably sarcastic: 'Yes, a signature does usually come at the end'; and though his manner provoked Jodl to go red in the face on several occasions, it never reduced him to losing control over his answers. By the end of the cross-examination Jodl had the confidence to declare to Roberts that he was a truthful and honourable man and that Roberts's evidence had 'actually and

quite specifically proved it'. Faced with Pokrovsky (the smoothest mannered of the Soviet prosecutors who always addressed Lawrence as 'My
Lord') who argued tightly but did not bully, Jodl snapped his replies more
often and was told off by Lawrence for shouting. But sometimes he seemed
almost to enjoy the challenge, to relish the opportunity to call Germans
'mere schoolboys in propaganda' by comparison with Russians, to point
out that he was absent from Hitler's headquarters when Pokrovsky assumed that he was engaged in planning ('I am afraid therefore that I cannot
be of any help') and dismissing some military plans as the work of young
officers, first seen here 'with great interest and some amusement'. On the
whole, however, as Jodl told Gilbert, being in the witness box had been
like working with Hitler – a constant struggle to keep one's temper. (56)

Jodl left the witness box reasonably satisfied with his performance. He
certainly retained his own belief in his innocence. Should he be found guilty
he would attribute the verdict to the faulty understanding of his judges.
Fritzsche had the impression that Jodl's only fear was of a long term of
imprisonment. If the judges failed to acquit him he would prefer a quick
death. (57)

Arthur Seyss-Inquart who followed him into the witness box on 10 June
was a complete psychological contrast. An interrogator had found him 'an
unattractive person, apparently rather stupid and without humour'. (58)
But this was an unusual reaction. Papen who sat on his right in the defendants' box described him as the 'complete Austrian – cheerful, relaxed,
often telling Viennese stories'. (59) Speer, who sat on the other side called
him 'an amiable Austrian' and commented on his high intelligence. (60)
Speer had come to like him partly 'because he did not seek evasions'.
Fritzsche made the same point and was puzzled that psychologists he spoke
to commented on Seyss-Inquart's 'icy cynicism'. Fritzsche could never see
it. For him Seyss-Inquart was most importantly 'the best mixer' in the
defendants' box. (61) 'Amiable', 'pleasant' – was that all? Shakespeare's
Richard III could smile and smile and be a villain.

Seyss-Inquart was charged with crimes under all four counts. He had
been a member of the Austrian Nazi Party from 1931 and was accused of
acting as Hitler's Quisling in Austria – building up support for the Party,
putting pressure on Schuschnigg, using threats of German invervention
until he was first made Minister of the Interior, then Chancellor and opened
the country to German troops. In 1939 he had been deputy to Frank in
Poland, and from 1940 to 1945 he was Reich Commissioner in the Netherlands. In this post it was alleged that he rounded up forced labour, deported
Dutch Jews, plundered the economy, and terrorized the population in an
attempt to stamp out resistance.

In prison at Nuremberg, he responded to those around him with a
sensitivity which was rare among the defendants. He wrote to his wife
about the German prison workers who carried out menial tasks under the
supervision of Andrus's guards: 'They are the real mourners. How have

they reacted to the fact that only because of us they were not already long united with their families?' Other defendants hated the guards for their noisiness and brash behaviour, forcing unwelcome conversation on the prisoners by leaning through the hatch in the door of the cell, cadging autographs. Only Seyss-Inquart had any sympathy for them: 'They are young, very young . . . Is it any wonder that they are impatient and restless . . . After a short time nearly all of them have been friendly and open, as far as the rules allow.' (62) But that kind of sympathetic understanding needs to be compared with Seyss-Inquart's offer in 1943 to Dutch Jews who had mixed marriages to choose between Auschwitz and sterilization.

His testimony did not leave a good impression. Schacht called it clumsy, (63) and it is surprising that an intelligent man and a trained lawyer to boot could not make a better job of it. (64) His insistence that he had never pressed to be made Chancellor of Austria could hardly contradict the fact he had accepted the appointment, nor what he had done once in office. His claim that no force was used to precipitate the final government crisis which led to the Anschluss sounded weak after prosecution evidence on the bullying of Schuschnigg and Goering's telephone calls, and weaker still when he himself pointed out that he kept forty SS men armed with pistols in his office and 'a few thousand' Nazis outside the building. He might talk of his work in the Netherlands as an attempt to 'persuade' the Dutch to co-operate, but he admitted to packing the administration with Nazis (because 'I had to find colleagues on whom I could rely'), to suppressing all other parties and most other organizations (because all of them, 'down to chess clubs' were political) and establishing German courts for Dutchmen who 'violated the interests of the German occupying forces'. His only excuse for the executions of hostages was that Himmler had ordered them; for the levying of force payments, that he had imposed few and that the Wehrmacht was more exacting. His answer to allegations of sending priests to concentration camps and threatening to burn down villages was that others were responsible for the policy; he had tried to mitigate it. When presented with the facts and figures on his crimes, he would chip a few off the sum total as if that really made everything better. The theme of his defence amounted to: 'Things might have been worse'. (It was never clear how bad they would have to be for Seyss-Inquart to be repelled.) He described Dutch concentration camps as being 'not that bad', given what was now known of camps elsewhere, and he pointed out that one of them had a golf course (as if that was adequate compensation for being locked up without trial or right of appeal). He seemed proud of his wish to keep Dutch Jews in Dutch concentration camps, and complained that he was overruled by Heydrich who sent them to Auschwitz. He added that he had been told about the roomy conditions and the symphony orchestra there, but at least had the grace to say: 'It is rather difficult for me to speak about it now because it sounds like a mockery.'

Seyss-Inquart's defence was not helped by his counsel, Steinbauer, whose style was as sticky as the most glutinous of Austrian cakes and *mit schlag.* Steinbauer had been incapable of making formal application for documents without prefacing his requests with 'Your Lordship, High Tribunal, I know you value my small country Austria not only because of its ancient culture and its scenic beauty but also because it was the first country to lose its freedom through Hitler.' Style apart, one might wonder whether their Lordships asked themselves if Seyss-Inquart had not contributed to that loss. Steinbauer opened his case with Schuschnigg's words 'God protect Austria'. Tactless again, since Seyss-Inquart was one of the people from whom the prosecution alleged that Schuschnigg had needed protection. He then encouraged his client to retail a lengthy history of the events leading to the Anschluss. Fritzsche had had a better instinct: he had begged Seyss-Inquart to skip over this part of his career ('It seemed to us too delicate a subject for the prosecution to grasp'). (65) But Seyss-Inquart blundered ahead – and made it a subject all too easy to grasp and all too damning for him. Fritzsche had thought it preferable to stress the 'correct and conciliatory administration' of the Netherlands. This Seyss-Inquart tried to do, prefaced by a travel agent's blurb from Steinbauer about bulb fields, windmills and great Dutch painters.

After cross-examination his administration sounded neither as correct nor as conciliatory as it might have been. He admitted he had removed mayors, but only when they 'became unbearable for me because of their actively hostile attitude'; that he ordered the secret police to blow up a newspaper office in the Hague 'because it was the centre of an illegal propaganda group'; that students were only sent to forced labour if they refused an oath to abstain from any action against the Reich, the Wehrmacht and the government of occupation; and that he had had to close the University of Leyden because there was a strike after the dismissal of Jewish professors. All his witnesses could do was make it sound worse. The effectiveness of the prosecution case against Seyss-Inquart was marred only by the manner of the French cross-examiner, Debenest. Lawrence, on one occasion, suggested that he might 'be better to pause after every sentence rather than after every word'.

The only defence Seyss-Inquart had been able to give was that his administration of Holland might have been worse. He might be satisfied to measure himself against Frank in Poland or Koch in the Ukraine; the Tribunal must measure him against the law. Given his admissions on the shooting of hostages (fewer than the 41,000 claimed by the prosecution), the deaths from starvation at the end of the war (an official report said 50,000, Seyss-Inquart preferred 25,000), the deportations to forced labour (he thought 250,000, the Dutch suggested an astonishing five million) and the deaths of 117,000 Jews, his administration had been responsible for a grave series of crimes and the prosecution case was as strong as ever. Only the Dutch were dissatisfied with it. They sent an official complaint to the British Foreign Office that it had been poorly handled and suggested that a Dutchman would have made a better job. (66) Like the earlier Danish complaint, it was a reminder of the intensity of national feeling and under-standable absorption in national suffering rather than an objective judge-ment.

Though he followed him in the indictment, Seyss-Inquart had gone into the witness box before Papen. The two men had agreed that Seyss-Inquart should present their version of what had led up to the Anschluss. (67) If Papen came to regret the decision in view of Seyss-Inquart's unconvincing presentation, he did not record the fact in his memoirs. The impression given there is that Franz von Papen was always too complacent and self-righteous to regret anything. Papen was an aristocrat. Almost his first statement in his testimony was that he had been 'born on soil which had been in the possession of my family for 900 years'. Several observers remarked that he looked like George Arliss playing an aristocrat. He had the casting director's idea of the fine features and the sleek silver hair for the part; the costume department's impeccably tailored pin-striped dark suit with the perfectly white, perfectly folded handkerchief peeping out from the breast pocket. His script was perhaps a little overwritten – there were too many references to aristocracy. His style was a trifle over-ripe, rather too supercilious. But Hollywood would have thought he was perfect for the role.

It is hard to believe, however, that Papen had been well cast for a leading role in the Nuremberg Trial. While drawing up the indictment, those who interpreted the trial largely in terms of conspiracy thought of him as an essential participant. But the conspiracy charge was always contentious, and when Papen was indicted the prosecutors were still dangerously ig-norant of activities and powers as opposed to formal positions. Papen was charged on the first two counts only. As Chancellor in 1932, he had lifted the ban on the SA and purged the state of republican and social democratic elements. The prosecution had seen this stage as establishing the prerequisites for Nazi takeover of power. Then, when he had been sacked, Papen had secretly negotiated to bring Hitler into a coalition government with himself – a stage during which Hitler held out for the Chancellorship as the price of his co-operation. In the Cabinet they formed in 1933, Papen had been Vice-Chancellor for eighteen months while the concentration camps filled with Hitler's opponents and the persecution of trades unions, churches and Jews began. The prosecution alleged that during these months Papen used his position and his reputation as a Catholic aristocrat, former soldier and son-in-law of a prominent industrialist to give a veil of respectability to Nazism and to gain a degree of acceptance for the regime from conservative elements in Germany. Thereafter, as Germany's representative in Vienna, he had, in the words of Paul Schmidt's affidavit, preserved 'smooth diplomatic relations on the surface while the Party used more devious ways of preparing conditions for the expected move' to the Anschluss.

But even if these allegations were proved, did they make Papen a really major conspirator? Had he actually joined the conspiracy appreciating all its aims and then worked wholeheartedly for all its ends? In January the prosecution's summing up of their case against Papen had clearly given warning of its weakness. He was then described in court as 'not perhaps a typical Nazi . . . (but) . . . an unscrupulous political opportunist and ready to fall in with the Nazis when it suited him'. These words suggest an unpleasant individual rather than a committed criminal. And even if Papen were a conspirator, he was only a temporary one. From 1939 to 1944 he was ambassador in Turkey, a period for which the prosecution had brought no charges. Perhaps they should have. During Papen's defence, Jodl grinned at the memory of how the Abwehr had used the Ankara embassy for espionage work. 'They did a good job, too,' he said. (68)

Papen's account of his career began on 14 June, a Friday, then continued on the following Monday and Tuesday morning. The image he projected was that of the aristocrat devoted to the service of his country. He spoke of his distress in 1918 when the Kaiser had abdicated and Germany was defeated: 'A whole world had collapsed for me.' He abused the Weimar republic: economic ruin, thirty-two squabbling political parties, a constitution which gave the nation rights 'which did not correspond to its political maturity', no real powers for a government to act decisively. He asserted that he had formed a cabinet out of duty to his fatherland and respect for the old soldier Hindenburg. Then, as servant of his nation, he had been obliged to recognize that Hitler led the strongest opposition party, that the Nazi vote was increasing and that law and order were decaying. Again, he explained, he had a duty – this time to bring Hitler into government, if need be at the price Hitler named; the stability of the country was at stake. He rejected the notion that he had condoned and cosmeticized Nazi brutality. His attitude to the Jews had always been that 'expected by the Catholic Church of its members'. (He later spoke of the Jews' 'foreign monopoly' in the press, art, film and legal worlds as 'unhealthy'.) And his major claim to have rejected Nazi methods was based on a speech he had made at Marburg University in June 1934 condemning them. He quoted its attacks on the single-party state, coercion, anti-Christian principles and violation of rights. Significantly he omitted such sentences as 'Have we gone through an anti-Marxist revolution in order to carry out a Marxist programme?' He pointed to Goebbels' refusal to publish the speech and his own subsequent offer to resign as signs of virtue – yet he was easily persuaded not to.

Papen tried to resign again a few weeks later, following the Roehm Purge during which, at Goering's instructions, he had remained at home for three days guarded by SS men and with radio and telephone cut off. He had totally accepted, he said, the explanation he was given for the Purge: that Roehm had been attempting a coup. Equally, he had accepted without demur Goering's story that the two members of his staff found dead and the two sent to concentration camps had been involved in the plot. As a selfless servant of the state, he had postponed his resignation because Hitler asked him to wait until all agitation died down. Indeed he had agreed to take on a new duty – that of representative in Vienna. He was impressed by Hitler's talk of the longed-for union with Austria and by his promise that it would be achieved by 'evolutionary' methods. In that post, he insisted, he had been unaware of the Hossbach conference, had tried to mediate between Hitler and Schuschnigg and had appealed against the use of German troops. He suggested that the job had demanded all his high-minded devotion, all his sense of service. It was not an easy job. He had been appointed on the day of Dollfuss's murder, Hitler's tone became 'most unpleasant' and he had felt his own policies increasingly rejected. He feared that it was a sign of the disfavour in which his views were held that his secretary was found floating face down in the Danube in 1938 (this time he had been less convinced by Goering's explanation that the man had been plotting against the Führer but that those members of the Gestapo who were responsible for the murder would be found and 'disciplined'). Though he had bravely soldiered on against all opposition, he was not surprised to be sacked at the same time that Fritsch and Blomberg were disposed of. He was glad to have been given yet another chance to serve the Fatherland and the cause of world peace and to go to Turkey as ambassador.

Maxwell-Fyfe took little time in cross-examination to expose Papen's story as dubious and the man himself as a humbug. Sir David was on peak form. He had a thorough grasp of the details of Nazi diplomacy and deployed snippets of background information (who was whose father, who was at military academy with whom) to devastating effect. Most importantly he had amassed new documents which he was able to flick out at great speed, leaving Papen no time to adjust or even recover breath. *The Times* correspondent who had been initially impressed by Papen's 'assurance' and 'astute reasoning' and had found the case 'inscrutable', thought this was Maxwell-Fyfe's 'most brilliant effort'. He was using his 'indulgent manner in the grand style' and spinning a cross-examination of 'subtle texture and silken innuendo' to draw Papen down 'from the Olympian heights of European diplomacy' to the political murder and violence with which his career had been surrounded. (69)

Maxwell-Fyfe opened with Papen's own interrogation from the previous September in which he had described Hitler as the greatest crook he had ever seen in his life. No matter that Papen now claimed to have tried to manipulate Hitler, to have hoped that coalition would impose safeguards and compromises, he had admitted that he knowingly worked with a criminal. Next, his claims to have been driven into co-operation with Hitler were demolished – Maxwell-Fyfe produced ample evidence to show he had worked assiduously for it. Papen's pretence of ignorance of early Nazi coercion was soon stripped – Maxwell-Fyfe showed how many thousands were in camps within months of Hitler coming to power; and how many of them were old friends or colleagues of Papen's. His behaviour after the Roehm Purge was shown as contemptible: he had sent letters of obsequious devotion to Hitler, avidly seized a new post from a man who had murdered hundreds, including two of his own staff, and knowing that Dollfuss had been murdered too. As Maxwell-Fyfe read his letters, signed with 'admiration and loyalty' Papen was 'shaking, licking parched lips'. Slumped back into the box he slowly told his cross-examiner that if he had said publicly that he was finished with the whole rotten regime he would have disappeared 'as did my associates'. (70) This sounded more like the truth; at last the great aristocratic public servant was being seen in a clearer light.

That light was next directed at his policy in Vienna. Maxwell-Fyfe's painstaking, detailed examination of documents showed that Papen had adopted a much more ruthless and bullying approach than he had admitted to – an approach which Sir David thought justified Kaltenbrunner's recommendation in 1944 that Papen be sent to Hungary to prepare an equally quick takeover there. Since Papen had prided himself on being a good Catholic and opponent of Nazi atheism, he was shown the protests from the Vatican about the persecution of Catholics. Since he denied knowledge of brutality in prisons and concentration camps, he was reminded of the letter he received from his own secretary in 1935 describing the murder he had witnessed there of two men well-known in public life. Maxwell-Fyfe expressed contempt that Papen had accepted the embassy in Ankara at a time when his old friend Fritsch was being pilloried with charges known to be fabricated. He condensed the prosecution case into a sentence: 'You had seen your friends, your own servants murdered around you ... and the only reason that could have led you on and made you take one job after another from the Nazis was that you sympathized with their work.'

Perhaps. Or perhaps Papen would do anything not just to save his neck but to preserve some sense of his own importance. But even if Maxwell-Fyfe's analysis were accepted, was sympathy for Nazi aims enough to convict Papen? There had been little evidence to show his full knowledge of Nazi crimes. He had never been a member of Hitler's cabal, never present at the key planning meetings. The prosecution had certainly destroyed his image of an aristocratic servant, but it had not replaced it convincingly with one of a Nazi criminal as defined in the first two counts. In his memoirs, Papen paid tribute to Maxwell-Fyfe as 'the most able jurist in the whole prosecution'; he praised him as a master of the art of cross-examination. Yet paradoxically in what was an outstandingly able cross-examination Maxwell-Fyfe had shown the limitations of the art. However brilliant, it cannot be a substitute for a sound case.

During the weekend break in the Papen case, the Lawrence family and staff had escaped the enclosed world of Nuremberg and spent two days in Prague at the invitation of the Czech government. Anyone would welcome such a change of environment, the sight of such a beautiful city, but not, surely, a three-quarters of an hour lecture by President Benes on the Munich agreement. Although his guests found him 'pleasant and friendly' they cannot have relished reminders of the disasters which followed that momentous scrap of paper, nor found it easy to sit comfortably while Benes accused the French and British of having behaved stupidly and shamefully. (71) Other visitors from Nuremberg to Czechoslovakia found the experience disquieting, especially if they drove through the Sudetenland. There they passed depopulated villages, flocks of German-speaking inhabitants rounded up for deportation. The visitors might manage some sympathy for the Czechs and their sense of betrayal by the Sudetenland Germans, but it was jarring to witness a population being forcibly removed from their homes while they were prosecuting defendants accused of deportation as a crime against humanity. There was an unpleasant savour in the story in *Stars and Stripes* at the beginning of February that the seventh trainload of Sudetenlanders had reached the American Zone. The Czech guards had been wearing Wehrmacht sheepskin coats. (72)

The Lawrences returned to a party given by the Russian judges. Nikitchenko was clearly glad of a break from court routine; he had provided an accordion band for dancing and in the company of the Lawrences' daughter became 'skittish'. (73) Even such a spectacle and such a very good party had not been enough to cheer Birkett, for whom the Papen case was proving 'an ordeal'. The source of his misery was Papen's counsel, Kubuschok. 'He will never use one word when a dozen will do,' Birkett complained on 18 June. 'Clouds of verbiage, mountains of irrelevance and oceans of arid pomposity distinguish his every moment in court ... He unites with this absence of merit a smug self-complacency, an indifference to ordinary emotions (such as diffidence in taking so much time) ... Incompetence and mediocrity are enthroned, and with the despotism associated with power are enjoying their little day.' (74)

But the end of the Papen case brought no relief to Birkett. 'When Fläschner (Speer's counsel) succeeded Kubuschok at the microphone, it became clear that there were lower depths of advocacy to be reached, unbelievable as it sounds. While Kubuschok sleeps in the courtroom, his fell work accomplished, Fläschner carries on the evil tradition with unashamed and unabated zeal.' (75) The court was subjected to large doses of Fläschner — even after six months of the trial, his document book was still not ready for distribution. This meant that he had to read immense extracts from his evidence rather than just refer to passages he wished to submit. And Speer himself, for the entire first day and a half of his testimony, was as long-winded, irrelevant and droning as his counsel.

Albert Speer was charged on all four counts. The first two were weak and had been based on the assumption that since Speer was Hitler's close friend and constantly in his company, he must in some way have been part of the alleged conspiracy and involved in planning and waging aggressive war. Speer, however, was to argue that if Hitler 'had had any friends I certainly would have been one of them', but in reality Hitler had been 'unapproachable' and treated Speer at first as his architect, with whom he loved to discuss only grandiose schemes for rebuilding Germany, then as his minister with whom meetings were restricted to technical matters. Speer had entered the inner Nazi circle as creator of the regime's *mise-en-scène*. He had designed its public buildings, acted as impresario for its public appearances. His great theatrical achievement had been the Nuremberg Rallies: the vast expanses of stadium, the unfurling flags, the dramatic torches. A pioneering version of *son et lumière*. Meanwhile he had shown administrative ability, grasp of technical problems and immense drive in minor jobs in the Labour Front, as an Inspector of Water and Energy, and in the Party's office for technology. In 1942 he was made Reich Minister for Armament and Munitions, taking the place of Todt who had been killed in a plane crash. By this date most of the planning was finished, the aggression had been launched. Once minister, Speer made his department the most powerful influence in the German economy which, he admitted he had tried 'to regulate according to the exigences of armament'. Such work at this date was not in itself criminal according to the indictment. The grave charges against Speer under Counts Three and Four concerned his methods of obtaining and treating the labour on which armament production depended. It was alleged he had employed prisoners-of-war in industrial work forbidden by the Hague Convention and used millions of slave labourers who were degraded and brutalized by excessive work, inhumane conditions and vicious punishment.

Many people so far had found it difficult to reconcile such charges with the man they had seen in the dock or even met. Speer was young, energetic, looked pleasant and definitely 'respectable', not at all the sort of man expected in the company of Streicher, Kaltenbrunner or Rosenberg. Gilbert had been impressed by him when he first arrived in the jail. He seemed to be 'the most realistic of all the defendants'; expressed approval of the trial 'in view of the enormity of the crimes committed'; continually exclaimed in horror as details of those crimes were revealed; said he had been no more aware of them 'than any other minister knew about the V-2'. Gilbert was increasingly impressed as he studied Speer's aloof, even hostile, manner towards other defendants, his unwavering determination to denounce Hitler and accept the common responsibility of the Party leadership for what had been done in its name. (76) Speer certainly seemed a man of courage, of moral discrimination, when contrasted with most of his fellow defendants. This image was not tarnished for some people even by the evidence against him. Lady Maxwell-Fyfe, for instance, responded with admiration to his character and intelligence. She commented to Mervyn Griffith-Jones that Speer was surely the sort of man Germany would need in the future. 'Griffith-Jones replied by producing a length of bloodstained telephone wire, about ten feet long, which had been picked up at Krupp's and had been used to flog workers.' (77) The admirers of Speer, then and now, must always ask by what means Speer had accomplished an industrial miracle between 1942 and the end of the war.

It was on this remarkable achievement that Speer concentrated for his first day and a half in the witness box. As he took the oath Biddle thought he looked 'utterly crushed'. (78) That was not the case and any such misleading impression soon vanished. Speer in his dark suit, clean shirt, neat tie was very much the confident young managing director reporting to his shareholders on the successes of his firm. He had a lot to be proud of and was well aware that he was infinitely better informed than they were. Speer had always shown amazing mastery of his complex tasks. His knowledge had been refreshed and probably deepened by his work with Galbraith and others and by his numerous interrogations from Allied industrial and technical experts. He opened on an odd note, announcing that for Berlin and Nuremberg he had 'sketched buildings which would have been among the largest in the world and the carrying through of these plans would have cost no more than two months of Germany's war expenditure'. No one would wish to argue that war is not wasteful, of men as well as money, but some might question the ambition of building 'the largest' rather than the most beautiful buildings in the world.

Thereafter Speer defined his ministerial tasks as overcoming Germany's lack of raw materials, introducing assembly line production and developing new weapons; then from 1943 dealing with the damage caused by Allied bombing. The result of his labours, he said, had been to increase the production of weapons seven fold, of ammunition six fold and that of armoured vehicles five and a half times. To achieve these figures he had taken over manufacture from first one armed service then another; evolved more efficient production methods; assumed control of all raw steel, nitrogen, synthetic rubber, locomotives, textiles. And he had raised production with a labour increase of only 30 per cent. Even so, by 1944 he had been employing an incredible fourteen million people in the Greater German Reich alone. The Tribunal became increasingly restive as Speer bombarded them with statistics and details of industrial processes. Lawrence made several requests for some relevance to the charges Speer faced, but he was unabashed and did not deviate from the line he had chosen. He was putting on record his outstanding competence. (Some might think he was attempting to dazzle with the brilliance of his achievement so as to blind as to its cost.)

Speer was equally unembarrassed when he eventually came round to his allegedly criminal methods. He expressed gratitude for the labour Sauckel had obtained for him; expressed regret that shortage of raw materials had made it impossible to employ more. Yet he expressed no regrets about the way the labour had been found and delivered – that had been the responsibility of others. Nor did he feel personally involved in the working conditions created for the slaves. He claimed to have believed that output could 'be achieved in the long run only through the goodwill of the worker himself' and to have insisted on decent working conditions. If methods of recruitment, transport, discipline, employment were not up to the standard he had requested, then others were to blame – the Wehrmacht, Sauckel, the SS, factory managers. He thought that Mauthausen had given 'a model impression of cleanliness'. He blandly explained that work camps had been set up to spare factory workers the strains of travel. No, indeed, he had never heard of cruelty in such places. In Himmler's SS factories, perhaps, but they were outside his sphere of influence.

Speer's most telling point was made as he played with the figures for the deployment of prisoners-of-war in industry. As he pointed out, it was perfectly legal to use prisoners-of-war in production which did not relate directly to military needs. Since he had controlled such a variety of industrial concerns and since there was no accurate and complete break-down of exactly where prisoners had been drafted, he could argue that he avoided using them on armaments. This was a shrewd argument. Even if the prosecution did not believe him, they never produced evidence to show that prisoners-of-war had been illegally employed. And as a result Speer could be candid where he was not endangered, could give figures on the numbers of Russian prisoners sent to German coal mines but draw atten-tion to the absence of figures for those in munitions, military vehicle or explosives factories.

In spite of its astuteness and flashes of callousness, Speer's company report had made dull listening. The attention of the court was suddenly alerted in the afternoon of 20 June when Speer changed topic and launched into his long-prepared statement on Hitler. The *Daily Telegraph* correspon-dent thought it 'a tremendous indictment' which might 'well stand for the German people and posterity as the most important and dramatic event of the trial'. (79) When Norman Birkett was asked a few years later to give a talk for the BBC with some such title as 'The day I shall always remem-ber', this was the day he chose. (It was a beautifully written talk. It captured the atmosphere of the place and time, gave a neat resumé of the issues of the trial and the context in which Speer spoke, encapsulated most effective-ly Speer's words and the impression he made on his listeners. The only criticism one can make is that Birkett named the wrong day. He confused it with the day of Speer's final speech.)

Speer began by describing Hitler as someone who 'knew how to confine every man to his own speciality. He himself was the only co-ordinating factor. This was beyond his strength and also his knowledge'. In Speer's analysis, Hitler's monopoly of power and decision had led to disaster. Against all evidence and argument he had insisted on continuing the war. By autumn 1944, according to Speer, the war was clearly lost – the trans-port system was dislocated, contact with the Ruhr cut, 90 per cent of fuel plants destroyed. Speer had sent twelve memoranda to Hitler between June and December that year, drawing attention to the irreparable damage and the breakdown in production, insisting that the fight could not continue. Hitler had ignored his pleas, threatened that pessimistic public statements would be treated as treason, and incited people with promises of fresh victories and rumours of new miracle weapons. As the intensity of Allied bombing mounted and the Russian advance cut Germany's coal supplies from Upper Silesia, Hitler screamed first for greater efforts, then ordered the destruction of industrial plant and agricultural resources as his armies retreated from occupied areas. Finally he demanded a scorched earth policy in Germany itself. Hitler, said Speer, 'had identified the fate of the German people with his own'. He blamed the people for defeat, 'but he never blamed himself'. His slogan had been 'Victory or destruction' and it was clear from March 1945 that he 'intended deliberately to destroy the means of life for his own people if the war were lost'. 'The sacrifices which were made on both sides after January 1945,' declared Speer, 'were senseless.' 'The dead of this period will be the accusers of the man responsible for the continuation of that fight, Adolf Hitler.'

These were sensational words. The courtroom was electrified. There was 'considerable consternation in the ranks of the defendants' as they listened to the statement. 'Goering and Doenitz discussed it warmly for some minutes before being admonished by the lieutenant of the guard.' (80) Yet by the following day *The Times* correspondent sensed that 'there is a suggestion of King's evidence about the defence of Albert Speer'. (81) And the critical analyst of the statement might question whether Speer had fully denounced Hitler and accepted the responsibility of the Nazi leadership in the way he had promised. Conceivably he was sincere when he wrote to his wife in December 1945: 'I cannot put up a cheap defence here ... for in the end you and the children would feel shame if I forgot that many millions of Germans fell for a false ideal.' His letter to his parents the following March might also have expressed his genuine sentiments: 'Don't solace yourself with the idea that I am putting up a stiff fight for myself. One must bear one's responsibility here.' (82) But did his statement measure up to the implied nobility of these words? Looking at the full text, doubts about Speer's motives begin to creep in with the realization that he never denounced Hitler's ambitions or acts as a whole – only his insistence on prolonging the war and punishing the German people for defeat. Was this then the limit of the 'false ideal' which Speer abhorred? He had insisted to his relatives, to Gilbert, to fellow defendants, that he would take a moral stand, bear his responsibilities. But the way in which he did it might be called either half-hearted or devious. His acceptance of responsibility was always hedged with saving clauses. He said: 'It is my unquestionable duty to assume my share of the responsibility for this disaster before the German people' but he never specified in what areas he should be blamed. Having identified his duty, he immediately slithered on to his next sentence: 'This is all the more my obligation ... since the head of the Government has avoided responsibility before the German people and before the world.' Speer was throwing the main burden on to Hitler and drawing a sharp contrast between himself and the Führer. He then modified his position even further: 'In so far as Hitler gave me orders and I carried them out, I assume responsibility for them. I did not, of course, carry out all the orders which he gave me.' Within a few sentences Speer had moved from the inspiring moral gesture to the stance of a Keitel – with a little more smugness of his own for good measure.

Suspicion that Speer was in fact 'putting up a stiff fight' for himself (not a 'cheap' but a clever defence) increases if the shape and emphasis of his statement are assessed. His reference to Hitler and his acceptance of his own responsibility took up only a few minutes. The rest of the afternoon was occupied with the account of how he himself had struggled to prevent the destruction of Germany at Hitler's hands in 1945. According to his own testimony, Speer behaved with resolution and at risk of his life. From January 1945 he had given up all attempts to produce armaments. Instead his energies had gone into issuing orders in contradiction to Hitler's: removing essential parts from factories and hiding them when their destruction was ordered; stopping production and delivery of dynamite, dropping explosives down mines in the Ruhr when it was intended to blow up factories; fighting to preserve bridges, wireless installations, railway track; commandeering remaining transport for food supplies and the distribution of seed for that year's harvest; encouraging the Wehrmacht into disobedience of its orders to destroy and into negotiation with the Russians to prevent a fight for Berlin.

All this if true was admirable. In a country threatened with total destruction by a madman, Speer had kept his sanity. Perhaps his work in 1945 is enough to salve his reputation. Perhaps only the unreasonable would ask why he never used his energy and powers of organization to resist Hitler before the pyromaniac set about a total conflagration; why it took a threat to Germany itself to alert Speer to Hitler's destructiveness and sensitize him to the death and suffering Hitler inflicted. Perhaps it is unfair to wonder whether by concentrating his denunciation of the Führer on the madness of the final months he was concealing the atrocities of the previous years and his own part in them. Perhaps it was enough that Speer tried to assassinate Hitler to save Germany; is it asking too much to have expected him to wish to do so earlier?

For a moment Speer hesitated before telling the story of his attempt to kill Hitler. Modestly he suggested it might be too technical and involved to be of interest to the court. But the judges, not surprisingly, were fascinated. 'The Tribunal would like to hear the particulars,' Lawrence told him. And as any listeners to a thrilling story, their blood must have run cold for a moment when Speer described Hitler's bunker in the Reich Chancellery – a building with 'an air-conditioning plant similar to the one installed in this courtroom'. It had been Speer's intention to introduce poison gas into this system through the ventilator in the garden. First he had to solve a technical problem: if the anti-gas filter were kept running, then his material would have to be exploded to be effective and an explosion might shatter the chimney on the ventilator and dissipate the gas. But Speer was always quick with technical solutions. He analyzed various gasses, persuaded the Chancellery engineer to run the filter only occasionally and so found a means to avoid explosion. The plan was perfected, the most effective gas was supplied, the date was fixed. At that moment Hitler suddenly ordered a four-foot chimney to be constructed. The plan was aborted.

It came as no surprise to the court that Speer had tried to assassinate Hitler: the plot had been outlined by his counsel during the cross-examination of a witness in January. Even so, the details were impressive, and they evoked inevitably sharp reactions from the defendants. Fritzsche and Schacht, for instance, were delighted by Speer's story. For others, however, it was the most unpalatable part of his testimony. Frank expressed the view that he himself would 'rather be sitting here than before a German court on account of treason'. Jodl implied to Gilbert that even though he had known the War was lost he would never have had the bad taste to try to kill Hitler. Rosenberg took the view that since the attempt had failed, Speer should have kept his mouth shut. Goering had struggled hard in the dock to conceal the bitterness of his feelings. But Goering could not for long conceal his instinctive brutality: Speer told Gilbert that when he returned to the dock Goering loudly told other defendants that if Speer was not hanged by this court then a kangaroo court would have him assassinated for treason. Back in his cell, Goering sought to convince Gilbert that he himself was the heroic character, not Speer. He, 'Treue Hermann', had remained loyal to Hitler 'because of the *principle* of the thing ... Do you think I have any personal love for him – not in the least ... I swore my loyalty to him and I cannot go back on that.' But Goering's pose was also an attempt to hide the dilemma he now faced: could he continue to declare fidelity to the man others believed had deliberately killed Germans? He told his lawyers and several defendants that he was going to have to alter his whole line for his final speech. Speer too was now thinking about his last speech: he told Gilbert he was aware that by accepting anti-Semitism, lawlessness and concentration camps as normal instruments of government policy he had shared the guilt for them. He now acknowledged that he had 'come to his senses rather late in the game'. (83) Indeed, very late. Why had he not mentioned any of this in his much-heralded statement in the witness box, a statement he had been preparing for six months or more?

While he was there, and under cross-examination by Jackson, Speer had actually fuelled the suspicion that he had not experienced a profound moral conversion. He described his threat to jail slacking workers as effective in cutting absenteeism. He had said of the rounding up of foreign workers: 'In view of the whole war situation ... I had no objection to them being brought to Germany against their will.' In spite of announcing his general sense of responsibility, he denied it when brought down to details: recruitment, transport of labourers, was the responsibility of others, so was the sickness rate among them – he suspected that the statistics on sickness were unreliable, enemy propaganda had told workers to feign illness. He assumed, when challenged, that most workers with TB had arrived in Germany suffering from it and 'presumably through the health offices we tried to alleviate it'. It was enough for Speer that he could say he had drawn Hitler's attention to starvation among Russian prisoners-of-war in his factories; he was not disturbed to be told that no food had then been sent. Nor did he worry about the working conditions in slave labour camps: not even 'the head of a plant could bother about conditions in such a camp'. These were mere details, he said; among leaders there must be a common responsibility for fundamental matters, but this does not extend to the details which are the concern of other departments. Faced with some more details, Speer began to lose his matter-of-fact manner. He called Dr Jaeger's affidavit on the conditions at Krupp's, Essen 'exaggerated', and became angry when read an affidavit from German workers in Essen describing recalcitrant workers being fired at by SS guards or locked in steel cabinets for up to forty-eight hours. He cheered up when shown photographs of these cabinets; they were standard factory lockers, he said – as if that made any difference. Then he attacked the affidavit: since 'the collapse many untruthful statements have been made'. Faced with a hundred statements from workers about Krupp factories, Speer recovered his thick skin, 'you would not expect me to be intimately acquainted with what happened'.

Yet Jackson caught him off guard in a moment which perhaps revealed more about Speer than any other remark he made at Nuremberg. Jackson produced records of eighty steel whips used at Krupp's for disciplining workers. 'These are nothing but replacements for rubber truncheons,' expostulated Speer. 'We had no rubber and for that reason the guards probably had something like this,' adding quickly that like the night sticks of American policemen, the whips or truncheons were not necessarily used. But his initial response is the significant one: was the use of the steel whip the kind of improvisation Speer had specialized in to overcome the lack of raw materials, the way he won the goodwill of his workers, produced an industrial miracle with an increased labour force of only 30 per cent? Fritzsche recorded the prophecy of other defendants that Speer would be found guilty but given the benefit of extenuating circumstances. (84) Can a court weigh in the balance millions of German lives saved against those millions of slave labourers lost or damaged, and arithmetically reach a just sentence?

Fritzsche, a naïve and friendly man, always expected light sentences or acquittal for any defendant for whom he felt any liking or respect, and he tended to think the best of most people. He was most surprised by the conviction of Constantin von Neurath who followed Speer into the witness box on Saturday 22 June. Fritzsche, like many others, accepted Neurath's view of himself as a conservative aristocrat with a strong sense of duty and inbred decency. Like Papen he projected the image of the high-minded public servant. Fritzsche added to his respect of a German class and tradition pity for the oldest defendant. Neurath sat next to him every day in the dock, straight-backed and still. But on occasion he would drop his head on Fritzsche's shoulder as if asleep, but in fact in a faint. His neighbours would pick the old man up and a guard would advise him to go and rest in his cell. But Neurath would pull himself together and insist on remaining, stiff and dignified again. (85)

Neurath set the tone for his whole defence in his opening words. He described his family – his father had been an official at the Württemberg court and came from a long line of civil servants; his mother was descended from 'a noble Swabian family whose ancestors were mostly officers in the Imperial Austrian Army'. He gave an account of his upbringing: one of 'extreme simplicity in the country with particular emphasis laid on the duty of truthfulness, responsibility, patriotism, and a Christian way of life and tolerance of other religions'. Thereafter he related his career in great detail for two and a half days, larded with references to his 'great and honour-loving nation' and fastidious criticism of 'eloquent and vain politicians' by contrast with professional and disinterested diplomats and aristocrats like himself. Fritzsche, the former radio broadcaster, thought Neurath's words had 'a professional flow'. (86) But it was a flow the Tribunal tried to stem. They, like Papen, clearly thought that Neurath 'lacked the gift of clear exposition', certainly of appreciating relevance to the charges he faced. (87) Lawrence frequently sought to pull him back to the point and away from his lengthy excursions into 'political history which is, of course, well-known to everyone who has lived through it and particularly to the Tribunal who have heard it all gone into before'. (88) Neurath's verbosity was shared by his counsel Luedinghausen – yet another source of misery for Birkett who now seemed past all hope of emerging from his slough of despond. He described Luedinghausen as 'tall, aristocratic, aloof, insensible to affront, with an extraordinary droning voice and bearded like the poet. He loses himself in the maze of events and produces the effect of complete and utter stupefaction.' (89)

The charges which Neurath found so difficult to concentrate on, or even accept as applicable to such a high-minded patriot as himself, did not touch on his career as a diplomat which began in 1901 and culminated in his embassy to London from 1930 to 1932. What concerned the prosecution was that Neurath had joined Papen's cabinet in 1932 as Foreign Minister, remained in office when Hitler became Chancellor and continued at the Ministry right up to 1938. This was a period during which Maxwell-Fyfe had suggested foreign policy could be summarized as 'breaking one treaty only at a time'. While he held office, he had been fully informed of German rearmament and the introduction of compulsory military service. Neurath might claim to have been a diplomat in the service of his country. The prosecution had quoted Messersmith's dispatch to the State Department in 1935. He had said that both Papen and Neurath were not 'diplomats of the old school. They are in fact servile instruments of the regime, and just because the outside world looks upon them as harmless they are able to work more effectively'. (90) It was as a servile instrument, the prosecution alleged, that Neurath became President of the Reich Secret Cabinet in 1937 and remained Minister Without Portfolio from 1938 to 1945. He might have begged to resign as Foreign Minister because he was so shocked to hear Hitler's aims expressed at the Hossbach conference, but he was not so shocked as to be unwilling to lend his name to Hitler's regime by taking on this purely titular post. Indeed he had been prepared to go further: in spite of knowing from the Hossbach conference that Hitler intended to obtain Germany's *lebensraum* at the expense of the Czechs, he was willing to go as so-called Protector of Bohemia and Moravia in 1939. No matter, said the prosecution, that his policies in the Protectorate were considered by Hitler to be too lax, no matter that he was relieved of his post in 1941 when he resisted pressure to introduce tougher measures. It was not necessary to be a Frank or a Koch to be regarded as a criminal administrator. And the prosecution alleged that Neurath's Germanization of Bohemia and Moravia, the takeover of the economy, suppression of the Press, introduction of the Nuremberg Laws, enforced deportation of labour and closure of secondary schools and universities were all quite criminal enough. Andrus, who at first had thought of Neurath as a respectable old gentleman, had been horrified to see in Moravia a castle whose dungeons has been restored and where torture instruments had been installed, he was told, at the Protector's instructions. (91)

During his testimony in chief Neurath retained the 'mild and quiet manner', the look of 'handsome distinction' which had impressed early observers at the trial. (92) Papen thought it was Neurath's 'Swabian temperament' which 'never allowed him to get flustered'. (93) He claimed ignorance of concentration camps and illegalities by the Gestapo (though Gisevius had asserted he had informed him of them regularly) and complete lack of anti-Semitic views. 'My Christian and humanitarian views prevented that,' he said, then immediately added that he believed there should have been 'a repression of undue Jewish influence in all spheres of public and cultural life'. He denounced the 'senseless and impossible' conditions of Versailles, the futility of the League of Nations in trying to preserve the status quo, and rearmament by others. He criticized the Czech policy towards Germany on the grounds that it always showed 'profound mistrust' (an irony he seemed unaware of). Rather more convincingly, he lambasted Ribbentrop's policies and the uncontrolled activities of the Büro Ribbentrop. There was some truth, no doubt, in his claim that 'no country suffered less from the war than the Protectorate' but perhaps the claim only threw into sharper relief the suffering of others.

To judge by the evidence produced by Maxwell-Fyfe in cross-examination, the relative lack of suffering by the Czechs had not necessarily been Neurath's intention. Sir David read his letter to Lammers in 1940 suggesting it would be sensible eventually to evacuate all Czechs just as soon as there were enough Germans to replace them – an odd comment from the member of a government constantly proclaiming its need for *lebensraum*. Meanwhile, perhaps the regime should keep those 'suitable for Germanization by individual selective breeding ... while expelling those who are not useful from a racial standpoint and are enemies of the Reich'. The obvious enemies, in his view, were the intelligentsia. As the cross-examination wore on, Neurath became 'red-faced with anger and outraged dignity'. (94) No wonder since such irreparable damage was done to his defence and above all to his pose of selfless aristocratic service.

Maxwell-Fyfe ran through the civil outrages in Germany while Neurath was a member of the cabinet – what he had called in a newspaper article 'the necessary cleaning up of public life' and Sir David drew attention to the 'unfortunate way in which Herr Papen kept losing secretaries'. He referred too to the device by which Neurath had obtained his pleasant house in Dahlem for such an amazingly bargain price – calling in person on its previous owner who had a Jewish wife, accompanied by an SS or SA man. Neurath had claimed to have opposed Hitler's policies from within the government. Challenged by Maxwell-Fyfe he admitted that he could not 'on the spur of the moment' think of one important thing he had refused to do. The standards of decency about which he had made such a parade were summed up in one enlightening exchange. Maxwell-Fyfe asked why, since he had disapproved of Hitler's policies, he had not re-signed. Neurath loftily replied, 'Did you ever hear that every cabinet minister must leave the cabinet if he does not agree with one particular thing?' 'Yes,' replied Sir David, 'every cabinet minister for whom I have any respect left a cabinet if it did something of which he morally disapproved.'

Neurath, said Fritzsche, was exhausted by his testimony and returned to the dock in utter confusion. (95) Fritzsche took his place in the witness box on Wednesday 26 June. He was the last defendant named in the indictment, the last to appear to give testimony – and the last straw for those weary of the trial and irked by repetition and futility. There was a strong argument for dropping the Fritzsche case – and it was based on good legal grounds, not just on the desire to spare those in court a few more days of tedium.

Fritzsche had been a journalist. In 1933 Goebbels made him the head of the news service in the Press Section of the Ministry of Propaganda. (The day he took up the appointment he joined the Nazi Party.) In this job Fritzsche briefed editors on what they should print in their papers. In 1942 he became head of the Radio Division in the Ministry. He himself had done a lot of broadcasting from 1937. His talks were popular, not least because his style was quiet and chatty and seemingly reasonable – a pleasant change from the screeching to which radio listeners were so often subjected. In his new post Fritzsche continued to broadcast and he also supervized the work of others, co-ordinating the effort to maintain German morale in spite of increasing bombing and military disaster.

But had Fritzsche's work really earned him a place in the dock? Those who placed so much emphasis on the conspiracy charge no doubt thought that propaganda was an essential element in it. In January, the American prosecution had called Fritzsche 'an efficient, controlled Nazi propagandist, a propagandist who helped substantially to tighten the Nazi stranglehold over the German people, a propagandist who made the excesses of these conspirators more palatable to the consciences of the German people, a propagandist who cynically proclaimed the barbarous racialism which is at the very heart of this conspiracy ...' But Fritzsche could hardly be described as a major conspirator; he had never met Hitler, not even met any of the other defendants except Funk, Doenitz, Seyss-Inquart and Papen before coming to Nuremberg jail. Those prosecutors who wished to make propaganda an element in the conspiracy charge would have done better to indict one of Goebbels' half dozen immediate subordinates. Instead they had lighted on Fritzsche, a relatively minor employee in the Ministry. In court they more or less had to admit his unimportance. At best he could be described as 'the gifted salesman' of the regime, but in honesty it had to be acknowledged that he had not 'contributed substantially to the formulation of all the basic strategy' only to its 'artful execution'. (96) There seems to have been no better reason for putting Fritzsche on trial than that the Russians had wished it and those drawing up the indictment had heard of him. It was as if the Germans had chosen to try Stuart Hibberd or J.B. Priestley.

Having lumbered themselves with Fritzsche, the prosecutors' problems then multiplied. They charged him with incitement. As with Streicher they had to face the fact that it is extraordinarily difficult to prove the connection between one man's words and another's deeds. If anything there was even less evidence against Fritzsche than could be found against Streicher. At least Streicher's newspapers had been preserved; Fritzsche's broadcasts had not. The BBC had monitored only the speeches he made during the War, and kept only transcribed extracts – and in English. Any barrister on his first case could make nonsense of such evidence. In the previous September, Drexel Sprecher had written a memorandum on the case pointing out that the available evidence was 'utterly inadequate ... to establish that Fritzsche had any intimate connection with the claims mentioned in Counts Three and Four'. As he put it, the prosecution was faced with several choices: scouring archives until evidence was found or 'striking the allegations concerning Counts Three and Four or permitting these charges to go by default'. (97) Scouring was tried – in vain. By June, Dr Braun told the British prosecutors that there was 'very little' against Fritzsche and that he should never have been brought before the Tribunal. (98)

The one glimmer of life in the prosecution case had been extinguished by the prosecutors themselves. In September, while in Russian custody, Fritzsche had signed a confession which might well have been used to back the charges against him on Count One. In his memoirs, Fritzsche claimed that in Moscow he refused to sign depositions against other defendants but after three days and nights of Russian 'persuasion' he had signed this one against himself. He further claimed that the version of this confession he was later shown in Nuremberg did not contain the alteration he had insisted on and that it bore a forged signature. (99) Be that as it may, the American prosecutors liked the document no more than he did. Its language was patently not his, the style was too obviously dictated. When they were approached by his lawyer, Fritz, to say that his client would contest the Moscow document but was willing to offer an affidavit, they were all too relieved to drop the Moscow 'confession'. (100)

So it was that when Fritzsche began his defence, the main evidence he quoted was his own affidavit given to the prosecution – admitting to the posts he had held, to certain responsibilities, even to having preached 'the necessity and obligation to fight'. But he insisted that his positions had been minor, that propaganda was in itself not deemed illegal by international law, and above all that 'on really serious questions of policy and the conduct of the war I did not commit a single falsification and did not consciously use a single lie.' The prosecution might feel such a sweeping declaration was questionable, but since they had no evidence they could not refute it. Fritzsche disarmed criticism by confessing: 'How often I myself became the victim of falsehood or a lie I cannot say after the revelations of this trial.' And indeed the picture of himself that he created in the witness box and down in the cell was really that of a booby – shocked to learn from Raeder that the *Athenia* had been sunk by a German submarine, reassured by Heydrich's promise to investigate stories about Koch's treatment of Jews in the Ukraine, convinced by Goebbels' denials of rumours he passed on. It is possible to be sceptical about the degree of innocence Fritzsche claimed, but it cannot be denied he made a refreshing change from his predecessors in the witness box. He at least did not deny any knowledge of concentration camps, Einsatzkommandos, atrocities. Instead he recalled constant rumours which he claimed to have passed on to his superiors, requesting clarification. Thereafter he called himself gullible in believing the explanations he was given. Some might suspect he was disingenuous or worse. Others might think it fitting if he had been a victim of propaganda.

Fritzsche gave a poor performance in the witness box – which was particularly surprising since his broadcasts had often been ably improvised from a few written notes. The professional communicator who had tried to coach other defendants to deliver their testimony cogently and effectively was himself clearly nervous, (101) and he rambled in a diffuse often disjointed style for nearly two days. However, he reaped the reward of his frequent kindness to other defendants. They rallied round now to help him through his ordeal: 'During the lunch interval one would give me a word of encouragement, another a piece of useful advice, while yet a third would perhaps offer me an extra slice of bread. Goering once gave me a cigarette to be quickly and blissfully inhaled in the lavatory and Keitel a precious bar of Schok-Kola, a stimulant which he had saved through many weary months.' (102) Such generosity was an impressive tribute to Fritzsche's constant *bonhomie*, and his concern for others during the long confinement in the jail and in the dock. The generosity is the more remarkable in that it was maintained in spite of the line Fritzsche was taking in court, a line which had evoked wrath or contempt when taken by Speer or Schacht. Half-buried in his testimony, scattered in fragments among other matters, was the condemnation of Hitler and the Nazi leadership which he had been long considering and over which he had liaised with Speer. (103)

He denounced Goebbels for constantly assuring him that Hitler was taking steps to end the war: 'Today I have the feeling that he broke his promise.' He suggested he had based his work on belief shattered by what he now knew. Having admitted he had believed in dictatorship 'for a temporary emergency period', he now stated that 'after the totalitarian form of government has brought about the catastrophe of the murder of five million (Jews) I consider this form of government wrong, even in times of emergency.' He confessed that he had wanted a 'reduction of the predominant influence of Jewry in German politics, economy and culture' but said 'after this catastrophe my further advocacy of race theory would be equivalent to approval in theory of further murder.' Finally he expressed his total disillusion with Hitler, who had raised false hopes at the end of the war, ordered others to fight on, but escaped himself by suicide – cowardice he concealed with the lie that he died in battle. For Fritzsche this lie now seemed symbolic. 'I am convinced that Hitler and at least some of his colleagues had deliberately lied to the people . . . from the beginning of their political career.'

It was symptomatic of the general exhaustion and boredom which gripped all participants at the trial by this time that Fritzsche's statement evoked little response and virtually no Press coverage. In part this apathy was his own fault. The statement had come in isolated sentences, had been lost in the general verbiage and illogicality of his testimony. Yet pieced together, his views are striking. Fritzsche almost alone of all the defendants had blamed both the Nazi leadership and himself. He had viewed the regime as a whole, faced its logic, and traced the moral consequences of its beliefs. Others might have made partial confessions, restricted condemnations, but they had all left an impression of masochistic self-abasement or calculating self-exculpation. Fritzsche, a minor employee of the regime and of limited talents, had accepted more responsibility and come nearer to a genuine evaluation of Nazism than any of them. He faced the weakest case, had least to gain by expressing his views, yet had felt they should be voiced. He had actually learned something from the trial.

The trial had so far lasted for 166 days. Thirty-three witnesses had appeared for the prosecution, nearly sixty had spoken for the defence. Nineteen defendants had given testimony and they had submitted 143 interrogatories to support their cases. Nearly all the documentary evidence in those 166 days had been in the words of the defendants themselves. The words had been horrifying and repellent, so too had the deeds which followed them. Yet after all this, nearly all the defendants, as their final words in the dock and in the jail were to prove, retained the stance they had always adopted. In Jackson's phrase in his opening speech, they had opted for 'an abdication of personal intelligence and moral responsibility'.

References for Chapter Fifteen

1   Biddle Notes on Evidence Vol. V. Biddle Papers, Box III
2   Quoted by Montgomery Hyde. Birkett, 23 May
3   Memo dated by Biddle, 27 May. Biddle Papers
4   13 June, FO 371. 57548
5   Jackson to Joseph B. Keenan, 29 April. Jackson Papers, Box 211
6   Biddle letter, 24 March. Biddle Papers, Box 19
7   British Prosecution Papers. File: 'Confidential. Phillimore. Room 233', 14 March, 18 March, 26 April, 6 May
8   Conversation with Mrs Tudor
9   Cooper
10 British Prosecution Papers. File: 'Confidential. Phillimore. Room 233'
11 BWCE. N/10 Chief prosecutors' meetings, 23 and 28 August; 26, 27 and 30 October
12 British prosecution minutes, 11 April
13 Court Contact Committee File 60. Chief prosecutors' meeting, 24 April
14 Quotations from the trial from IMT Vol. XIV until noted
15 *Manchester Guardian*, 23 May
16 Biddle Notes on Evidence Vol. IV. Biddle Papers, Box III
17 *Daily Telegraph*, 23 May
18 Conversation with Drexel Sprecher and his memo to Dodd of 5 February 1945 which he kindly lent the authors
19 *Daily Telegraph*, 23 May
20 Interrogation report. Jackson Papers, Box 210
21 Letter from John Phipps, 27 November 1945
22 Andrus
23 *Daily Telegraph*, 24 May
24 Gilbert
25 Speer *Spandau Diary*, and Gilbert
26 *The Times*, 24 May
27 Fritzsche
28 British prosecution minutes, 1 June
29 Quotations used by prosecution in IMT Vol. III
30 Andrus
31 IMT Vol. XIII
32 Fritzsche
33 *Chicago Daily News*, 5 December
34 Sauckel's testimony begins in IMT Vol. XIV and continues in Vol. XV
35 *Daily Telegraph*, 30 May
36 *The Times*, 31 May
37 Biddle letter, 31 May. Biddle Papers, Box 19
38 Fritzsche
39 British prosecution minutes, 1 June
40 Fritzsche
41 Papen
42 Fritzsche

43 Andrus
44 Quoted by Maser
45 Andrus
46 Fritzsche
47 *Chicago Daily News*
48 IMT Vol. IX
49 *The Times*, 3 June
50 Gilbert
51 Gilbert
52 Cooper
53 Birkett, 4 June. Quoted by Montgomery Hyde
54 *Daily Herald*, 6 June
55 Biddle Notes on Evidence Vol. V. Biddle Papers, Box III
56 Gilbert
57 Fritzsche
58 Interrogation report. Jackson Papers, Box 210
59 Papen
60 Speer *Spandau Diary*
61 Fritzsche
62 Copy of letter kindly lent by Thilo Bode
63 Schacht
64 Quotations from trial from IMT Vol. XVI until noted
65 Fritzsche
66 Letter, 19 June. FO 371. 57549
67 Papen
68 Gilbert
69 Cooper
70 *Daily Herald*, 18 June
71 Letter from John Phipps, 17 June
72 *Stars and Stripes*, 2 February
73 Letter from John Phipps
74 Quoted by Montgomery Hyde
75 20 June. Quoted by Montgomery Hyde
76 Gilbert
77 Kilmuir
78 Biddle Notes on Evidence Vol. V. Biddle Papers, Box III
79 *Daily Telegraph*, 20 June
80 *Daily Telegraph*, 21 June
81 *The Times*, 21 June
82 Speer *Spandau Diary*
83 Gilbert
84 Fritzsche
85 Fritzsche
86 Fritzsche
87 Papen
88 Neurath's testimony begins in IMT Vol. XVI and continues in Vol. XVII
89 Quoted by Montgomery Hyde, 24 June
90 IMT Vol. VI
91 Andrus
92 *Chicago Daily News*, 14 December

93   Papen
94   *Daily Telegraph*, 25 June
95   Fritzsche
96   IMT Vol. VI
97   Memo, 18 September 1945 to Col. Leonard Wheeler. Kindly lent by Drexel Sprecher
98   British prosecutors' meeting, 20 June
99   Fritzsche
100 Conversation with Drexel Sprecher and his memo to Col. Amen, 29 January
101 *The Times*, 26 June
102 Fritzsche
103 Gilbert

Chapter Sixteen

The focus of interest at Nuremberg for the public had always been the defendants. Once the last defendant left the witness box, outside interest in the trial dimmed; Press coverage faded to a minimum. Yet what was now to take place was as important, if not more so, than what had gone before. For the next two months the Tribunal was to devote its time to considering the most fundamental questions which had to be answered in their judgement. These primarily concerned the law which, embodied in the Charter, had been mainly implicit in the proceedings thus far. Now it was to be subjected to thorough scrutiny, its validity and possible interpretations searchingly debated. The conclusions the judges would draw from this process would not only determine the fate of the defendants, they could shape the future of international law. Not least they would form the criteria on which others would ultimately assess the success and failure and the degree of justice achieved by the Nuremberg Tribunal.

But first, the judges had to clear a problem which had occasionally surfaced from the time the indictment was drawn up – the Russian allegation that the German army had murdered up to 11,000 Polish officers in Katyn wood near Smolensk. The Russians had embarrassed their colleagues by insisting on including this charge; most people suspected that the Russians themselves had been responsible for the killings.* Their subsequent handling of the matter had increased that embarrassment, incensed the defence, and irritated the judges. When first raised in court in February during the Russian prosecution case, Pokrovsky had called the Katyn murders 'one of the most important criminal acts for which the major war criminals are responsible'. (1) Yet in spite of such a large verbal claim he had considered it adequate to summarize briefly a report on the atrocity by the Soviet Extraordinary State Commission and then to submit that report as the sole evidence for his allegation. The defence clamoured for a fuller hearing of the charge. Had they merely called for a chance to prove Russian guilt in order to establish a damaging case of *tu quoque*, they would undoubtedly have been overruled by the Tribunal. As it was the judges themselves were far from satisfied with Pokrovsky's perfunctory presentation of such a grave matter. On 12 March they summoned the Russian chief prosecutor,

*See Chapter Six

Rudenko, and insisted he call witnesses to substantiate the charge and to face cross-examination. (2) Rudenko's high-handed response increased their determination to hold a more thorough examination – he not only protested against their ruling on witnesses, he made the indefensible claim that the report of the Extraordinary State Commission must be treated as irrefutable evidence. On 6 April Biddle expressed to him in no uncertain terms the judges' view that the report would only be given as much weight as any other official report – that is to say, just as much as the Tribunal deemed appropriate. And, furthermore, they had now decided they wished to hear three witnesses each for the defence as well as the prosecution in this matter. (3)

When the hearing on the Katyn massacre finally took place on 1 and 2 July, scepticism about the Russian charge can only have been increased by their evidence, and doubts about the desirability of raising it at all deepened by the peculiarly inept way in which the Russians did it. (4) Both the Russian and the defence cases turned on establishing the date when the Polish officers died. The Russians claimed that the shootings had taken place in the autumn of 1941 when German troops occupied the area. They brought as witness a Bulgarian pathologist who had been a member of an international investigation team set up by the Germans in 1943 which had fixed the date of the massacre as early 1940 – when the Russians were still in control of the district. He now, however, denounced that report, stating that its medical arguments were faulty, that the experts had only been allowed to examine a few bodies chosen for them by the Germans and had signed a prepared summary of their findings while waiting to leave from a military airport (more or less, he implied, as a condition of take-off).

The Bulgarian now declared that forensic evidence clearly pointed to autumn 1941 as the date of the murders, as did a Russian pathologist who had taken part in the State Commission's examination of 925 corpses at Katyn in 1944. The Russian added that papers, letters, diaries found on the bodies supported this dating, and that the calibre of bullet and method of execution (shooting in the head or the back of the neck) were exclusively German. The Russian case became even more specific. They named as the culprits a unit 'camouflaged' under the title 'Staff Engineer Battalion 537' commanded by a 'Lieutenant Colonel Arnes'.

This attempt at precision rebounded on them. The defence produced in court not 'Lieutenant Colonel Arnes' but Colonel Ahrens, the former commander of the Signals Regiment 537, units of which had moved into the Katyn area from the late summer of 1941. Ahrens said he had seen the mound containing the Polish bodies soon after he arrived in November, that he had ordered an investigation in 1943 after wolves had disinterred bones and when local people told him they had always feared that bodies had been buried there since hearing shots and screams in the wood in 1940. He, too, claimed to have seen written evidence on the bodies, but that it was never dated later than early 1940. Ahrens and the two other German witnesses, both from his regiment, emphasized that a Signals Regiment would never have been considered suitable for carrying out executions, let alone on such a scale, when they were already overstretched by the tasks of moving into Smolensk; and that they were never equipped with automatic weapons of the calibre used to kill the Polish officers (though some Russian units were).

The Tribunal did not investigate the facts of the Katyn murders extensively during this two day hearing. Its duty was not to act as a commission of inquiry into the atrocity. Rather it was to open the Russian allegation to defence challenge, a challenge the Russians had not withstood. As their case was exposed, they veered away from their confident accusation against the 'Staff Engineer Battalion' and replaced it in court with the sudden allegation that an Einsatzgruppe was present in the district in autumn 1941 – but without producing any evidence to connect it with the crime. The Russians were perhaps fortunate that the judges chose to make no mention of the Katyn massacre in their judgement. Conclusions very different from those they desired might well have been drawn from the evidence they presented: a tacit hint that they had merely failed to prove their case let them off lightly.

With the Katyn skeleton, whoever it belonged to, well rattled and returned to its cupboard, the Tribunal attended to the final speeches of the defence counsel, covering not just the cases for individual defendants but the law which should apply when assessing them. The judges had worried since May about how long the German lawyers would take over these speeches; they were reported to have been 'rather appalled' on 29 May that each expected at least a day. (5) Meetings were held with defence representatives to try to get voluntary limitations, but the judges were not reassured by what they heard. So on 24 June – with Biddle and Nikitchenko dissenting – the judges accepted a notice drafted by Parker to be read in court which fixed a maximum of half a day per counsel, forbade irrelevant or cumulative material, and requested that all speeches be submitted in advance to be studied, translated, and if necessary edited by the Tribunal. An extra four hours might be used for the summary of defence views on the legal principles involved in the trial by any spokesman they chose. (6)

In the event the Tribunal was slightly more lenient in allocating time to the defence speeches. The defence summing up began on 4 July and lasted until 25 July – sixteen days were filled by twenty-two counsel; two weekends intervened. (7) Many of the sections cut out by the judges were printed in the official transcript of the proceedings. The judges' tolerance was not extended to Dr Seidl, however. He tried to slip in his speech for Hess on 5 July without going through the vetting procedure or even providing copies for the judges in court. His speech opened with so many complaints about the injustices of Versailles (matter repeatedly ruled irrelevant) that the judges refused to listen to any more. They packed Seidl off with strict instructions to rewrite the whole thing before submitting it for their scrutiny. Goering and Hess burst out laughing at his discomfiture.

(8) Yet Seidl's final version which he delivered on 25 July undoubtedly gained from the Tribunal's discipline. It was one of the most acute and hard hitting of them all.

The judges would have done well to be as strict with others. All would have benefited from more judicial blue-pencilling and even more interruption in court. Nelte, defending Keitel, was not alone in being pulled up by the Bench for rambling 'into the realm of metaphysics' – it was a favourite destination. No amount of Tribunal protest could stop Kauffmann (Kaltenbrunner) explaining how 'the reason for the Hitler phenomenon lies in the metaphysical domain' (mercifully his explanation turned out to be a rather mundane account of the impact on Germany of Versailles and unemployment, though of little use to Kaltenbrunner). Most counsel meandered too through world literature, stopping to pick quotations on the way, and romped from time to time in 'historical background'. The President did his best to shepherd them back into their clients' pastures. He persuaded Kauffmann to cut his sections entitled 'The Development of the History of the Intellectual Pursuit in Europe' and 'Renaissance, Subjectivism, the French Revolution and National Socialism' – the latter on the grounds that it was 'completely unlikely to have any influence at all upon the minds of the Tribunal'. He was equally successful in getting Steinbauer (Seyss-Inquart) to omit a page and a half on the contribution of Beethoven and Brahms to the cultural life of Vienna and a further two pages of 'background' (the Tribunal could become 'acquainted with the history of Austria,' he said, 'without having it read to them' as part of the defence). It was a pity that the judges did not cut such passages as the description of the trial as 'surrounded by the surging waves of a furious torrent bearing the wreckage of a civilization ... in the demoniacal depths of which lurk those who hate the true god'.

Such style was to be condemned not just on grounds of taste but because it was usually the symptom of having nothing useful to say for the defendants. Perhaps Dr Marx was not alone in having found the defence of his client, Streicher, a 'difficult and thankless task' but he was the only one to admit it. Others spent an inordinately long time trying to conceal under verbiage the impossibility of their task. With the exception of the counsel for Doenitz and Raeder (Kranzbuehler and Siemers) there was little attempt to introduce fresh evidence; only Dr Dix (Schacht) called outright for the acquittal of his client. The rest rehashed the general points made when the defendants were in the witness box – which amounted to an admission that crimes had been committed, and that the defendants had been partially connected with some, but added pleas of subordinate position, lack of influence, partial ignorance or attempted protest and restraint as arguments for mitigation.

This form of defence evoked a mixed response from those for whom it was provided. Streicher was furious that his counsel had said he was never taken seriously. Kaltenbrunner (depicted as a tiny cog in the extermination machinery, a man of 'fortunate and humane ideas' whom 'one could not meet without a sense of tragedy') told Gilbert to congratulate whoever had found him 'such a stupid attorney' as Kauffmann. But most of the defendants were content to be belittled, and they aroused the indignation of Funk who complained that all bore some share of guilt, however much they denied it. 'I don't see how the court can acquit a single one of us,' he told Gilbert. Schirach, whose counsel alone admitted to some responsibility by his client, was sneered at by Goering and provoked the comment from Frank: 'I disapprove of this servility before the court.' (9)

Most defence lawyers had spoken out not just for their clients but on behalf of the German nation: 'Invisible behind the defendants there sits also our poor, beaten and tortured German people,' thought Luedinghausen, Neurath's counsel. He and others pleaded the innocence of the German people. They invoked history to explain why they had backed Hitler and had been deceived and abused by him. Marx drew attention to their present suffering and their 'paralysing horror' at the evidence which had told them for the first time of the mass slaughter of Jews and others. Sauter called for a verdict which would open the way for the recreation of the German economy, 'the German spirit and true freedom' – an odd mixture. Yet all could have been reassured by a revealing interruption by Lawrence when Kauffmann stated that the question of German guilt was implicit in the prosecution case: the German people are not on trial, said Sir Geoffrey, these defendants are.

On the whole these final speeches had done a poor job for the defendants. Yet they had performed another function – and done so rather more effectively. They had allowed defence counsel to present their views on the legal bases of the trial and the law which must govern the Tribunal's final judgement. Whether or not these views are ultimately judged correct, they can be seen as conscientiously reached and expressed with concern for the integrity of the law and judicial process. In developing their legal arguments both sides avoided cheap point scoring and demonstrated an awareness that there were even more serious issues at stake than the immediate fates of the defendants. The two sides may have reached very different conclusions as to the nature of the law and its interpretation, but they did so with sincerity and after serious consideration. Though the defence must have been unaware of it, they were reviving debates which had already taken place when the trial was first proposed and when the Charter was being drawn up at the London Conference. They were also bringing into the open the legal uncertainties and challenges of which the Tribunal was only too aware. No wonder that the judges paid close attention, seldom interrupted except to ask for clarification or expansion, and allowed every counsel to repeat or develop points already made by colleagues.

The summary of the defence's legal arguments was delivered by Professor Jahrreiss (assistant counsel for Jodl) on 4 July. The defence counsel had chosen their spokesman well. He was a quiet, dignified, scholarly man whose exposition was carefully argued, and backed by opinion from American as well as German legal authorities. His speech gained in impact because its objective, academic style was just occasionally touched with controlled emotion – as, for example, when Jahrreiss hinted at regret that he could not regard the regulations of the Charter as legally valid though 'perhaps in the hopes and yearnings of the nations the future is theirs', or when he argued that the Nazi state had been sovereign in Germany, distasteful though this was to one 'who had lived in the outer cold as though an outcast among his own people'. (This note of disapproval of the regime, Fritzsche recorded, 'caused vehement resentment among some of the accused'.) (10)

Jahrreiss's thorough and learned account of the law as seen by the defence laid out strands which other counsel then picked up and wove into their own speeches. Underlying nearly all of them was the argument that this trial was incapable of reaching a just verdict in view of the circumstances in which it was being held – in the immediate aftermath of war and with the revelation of atrocities, both of which they feared would inspire a mood of vengeance which would swamp the desire for justice. Many expressed criticism that the Charter had been framed only by the four victorious Powers, that the Tribunal was drawn only from those nations, that the accused came only from the vanquished state. As Stahmer put it: 'A one-sided action taken only against members of the Axis Powers violates the idea of justice'; it may be commendable to extend the rule of law, but 'any strengthening of the sense of justice must not start with a violation'. Luedinghausen and others argued that this sense of justice would have been strengthened if parallel trials had examined the crimes of others: Dresden and Hiroshima were mentioned in several speeches. Not all counsel denounced this trial as a political act against former enemies. Some saw it as embodying the hope of building a new body of law on the ruins left by the war, as Seidl put it. But even they maintained the Charter was an inadequate, flawed instrument for the task – it contained too many contraventions of accepted legal principles.

Most seriously, as they all saw it, the Charter contained too much entirely new law. Jahrreiss called the Charter 'revolutionary', because he felt it was anticipating 'the law of a world state'. All counsel maintained it ignored the most fundamental demand of justice: that there can be no crime, no punishment, without pre-existing law (*nullum crimen, nulla poena sine lege previa*). Too many of the laws of the Charter, they said, were *ex post facto* – drawn up after the acts they called crimes were committed and to be applied to men who had been unaware that their deeds would be called criminal. Worse, Pannenbecker (Frick) suggested, the laws of the Charter were not just *ex post facto*, they had been devised for the trial of the accused in the dock and as such contravened yet another fundamental principle: the duty of any court is 'to apply the general law but not to create it for a single special case'. Some were prepared to accept that international law evolved through decision as well as statute but all denied that the Charter and trial were stages in a natural evolution; they were not, as Jackson had stated in his opening speech, adapting settled principles to new situations but inventing them.

All counsel agreed that the Charter was creating new law in defining aggressive war as a crime. Jahrreiss devoted particular attention to the legal status of aggression, and examined in great detail the international discussions and resolutions renouncing it from the Covenant of the League of Nations onwards. For him, as for Stimson, the crucial agreement had been the Kellogg-Briand Pact, but for Jahrreiss the Pact had not achieved the full legal force which Stimson and others had attributed to it. It had expressed condemnation of war but did not constitute a law against it: it provided no definition, and failed to lay down punishment for states which transgressed or to establish courts to hear their cases. Interestingly, however, though the defence was united in seeing the Charter's view of aggressive war as innovatory, some members saw the innovation as more desirable than rigidly sticking to the principle banning *ex post facto* law. Luedinghausen actually welcomed the attempt to eliminate war; Sauter went so far as to assure the judges that they were not 'bound by any written law' in these matters but must obey their consciences and the call of destiny 'to give the world .. a legal order which will preserve for future generations that peace which the past was unable to preserve for them'.

There was much less division of opinion in the defence on whether the Tribunal had the right to try individuals and hold them responsible for the acts of their state. All saw this as an entirely new concept in international law. Only Luedinghausen thought it a novelty to be 'welcomed' if introduced for reasons of 'goodwill' rather than in a spirit of vengeance. All the others stressed that the state and not the individual was the subject of international law. Even Jahrreiss, who called the indictment of individuals 'a moral necessity' and 'long overdue' was certain that it was not yet legally permissible.

The concept of individual responsibility was closely linked with the argument put forward by many counsel that the legal basis of the Nazi regime had been the Leadership Principle, the *Führerprinzip* – all authority was invested in Hitler alone. Any dictator, argued Siemers (Raeder) takes all power, and with it all responsibility. Given the Leadership Principle, said Jahrreiss, the Führer's decisions were as binding on his subordinates as those of democratic regimes are binding on their servants and subjects. With such a legal framework, Sauter insisted, Hitler's ministers had obeyed and administered national laws passed in accordance with the constitutional rules of their state. Others stressed the view that not only had obedience been legally correct, it had been enforced ruthlessly and brutally; in Dix's words, the seeming unity under Hitler was 'the quiet of the churchyard enforced through terror'.

When Maxwell-Fyfe had read an advance copy of Jahrreiss's speech, he commented that it offered little challenge to the prosecution, but that the section on the Leadership Principle needed 'hitting hard' – it was nothing more than a disguised plea of superior orders, ruled out by the Charter. (11)

It was, however, constantly used in defence attacks on the legal aspect of the trial they most abhorred: the conspiracy charge. How, they asked, could there be a 'conspiracy' when Hitler alone had total power, made all the decisions and allowed no discussion but demanded only obedience? All denounced the conspiracy charge as defined by the Charter as totally alien to German law, unknown in international law and flagrantly retroactive. The theory developed by the prosecution that a man ratified previous acts of a government or organization when he joined it was dismissed as an inappropriate borrowing from civil law. In German law, some argued, those accused under the equivalent charge must be shown to have full knowledge of a criminal plan, foresee the acts to be committed in executing it and approve them – in no case before the Tribunal had these conditions been present. Only Seidl was sharp enough to point out that the charge had not existed as a separate charge in the Charter by which the Tribunal was bound. There it was tagged on as if part of Count One; it only took on a life of its own in the indictment. It was Kubuschok who hit a tender spot in the prosecution's conscience by suggesting the charge had been introduced to reach those, like his client Papen, against whom there was too little clear evidence of actual crimes.

Gilbert's diary records no reaction from any defendant to the legal arguments of their counsel, and it would be in keeping with their previous behaviour if they had been interested only in their personal cases. What he did note, however, was the anxiety occasioned by the news that seventy-three members of the Waffen-SS had been found guilty of the murders of American prisoners-of-war at Malmédy and that forty-three of them had been sentenced to death. Keitel quickly comforted himself with the thought that he had never condoned such behaviour. Jodl decided the fact that the Division Commander, General Sepp Dietrich, had been sentenced to life imprisonment showed that higher officers might be considered less guilty than subordinates who actually carried out crimes. (12) Yet the greater culpability of commanders and leaders was to be stressed time and again in coming days as the chief prosecutors made their final speeches. As Jackson was to put it: everywhere little men were now being convicted for crimes they had committed on the orders of the men in the Nuremberg dock and it would be 'a vast and unforgivable caricature of justice' if the men who 'directed these little men should not bear their share of the blame'. He himself did not specify what punishment should be meted out to them; all the other prosecutors would demand death for all the defendants.

The form of the final prosecution speeches had first been discussed as early as the previous December. At that stage Jackson was in favour of asking Shawcross to give a summation of their case and restricting the others to brief comments on points and defendants of particular national interest. (13) By 5 April, however, Jackson believed he had a duty to give the American people a summary of the whole case and thought he might take two hours over it. He conceded that Shawcross should take a day and modestly offered to speak last, still not the most self-effacing of positions. (14) A certain amount of elbowing began: through May and early June, Rudenko seemed to be trying to nudge Jackson out altogether by proposing one final speech only; Maxwell-Fyfe was pushing hard for Jackson's original plan and the right of Shawcross to speak first. National pride finally prevailed over concision and clarity: all the chief prosecutors spoke, all touched on general legal points (though Shawcross was left to develop their arguments most fully), each summed up the case against the individual defendants, and each dealt with the count for which his team had been responsible (which meant that Jackson opened, to be followed by Shawcross and the French and Russian speakers). Even so, the process was not lengthy: Jackson and the French and Russians spoke for barely half a day (the ailing Champetier de Ribes handing over to Dubost after a few minutes of introduction), Rudenko for an hour or so more, and Shawcross for a day and a half. The prosecutors had prepared their speeches independently; Shawcross excused the inevitable repetitions on the grounds that they gave their conclusions greater force. (15)

All four speeches emphasized the belief that the defendants had received a fair trial. Rudenko dismissed all defence complaints about the proceedings as a 'smokescreen' for the defendants and chose to answer virtually none of them. Champetier de Ribes drew attention to the length of the trial and the calm manner in which it had been conducted as proof of the absence of the desire for vengeance. Shawcross noted that the likeliest alternative to such a trial would have been summary execution; instead the Allies had granted the accused a hearing and the right to a defence. All pointed out that the vast bulk of the evidence they had used was in the words of the defendants themselves. Jackson emphasized that twenty-two countries and not four had set up the Tribunal. Though still technically at war with the Germans, they had granted their enemies a hearing. This decision, said Jackson, had given the defendants 'the kind of trial which they, in the days of their pomp and power, never gave to any man'. He was not surprised that the defence should complain about the justice of the trial and the law on which it was based: 'No thief ever felt the halter draw with good opinion of the law', he quoted.

All the prosecutors denied that the law of the Charter was 'revolutionary' or 'innovatory' as the defence had alleged. In drawing up the Charter, said Jackson, 'we were recording an accomplished advance in international law'; all that was new was the decision to apply it. Shawcross took it further by praising the Charter for providing in some areas 'machinery, long overdue, to carry out the existing law', though he maintained that in other areas, such as War Crimes and Crimes against Humanity, that machinery had long existed in every municipal legal system. Since all held that the law of the Charter already existed, they could dismiss all accusations of retroactivity. The defendants knew that their acts were crimes, Shawcross argued, and frequent warning had been given by the Allies throughout the war that punishment would follow. There was nothing new in limiting the sovereignty of a state – absolute sovereignty would be inconsistent with the binding force of treaties; Article 47 of the Weimar Constitution had made the rules of international law integral parts of German Federal Law; international law had always proceeded against the citizens of any nation in matters such as piracy and, most obviously, war crimes.

The prosecutors were determined to establish that individuals must be held responsible for crimes regardless of whether they were committed in the name of the state, in response to orders, or using others as the instrument. The responsibility of members of any government according to Shawcross is 'an essential protection of the rights of man and the community of nations'; servants of a state cannot claim immunity since 'the rights and duties of states are the rights and duties of men'. The French pointed out that in French and German law those who decreed crimes were seen as accomplices and liable to punishment; French law reserved the most severe penalties for ministers. The French were most passionate in urging the application of sanctions against members of governments; since any modern government had 'every criminal technique in its grasp', it was essential to deter their use. Shawcross had suggested that every defendant could have been tried as a common murderer. The French, however, pleaded with the Tribunal not to narrow the scope of the trial or diminish the nature of their crimes in this way – the defendants' use of the power of their state to murder and exploit millions had placed them in a special and most dreadful category of responsibility.

Defence pleas of superior orders or subservience to the Leadership Principle were criticized by the prosecutors as having no legal validity and being mere evasions of personal responsibility. The prosecution argued that the defendants had helped Hitler to power, made him a dictator, willingly taken oaths to him (and forced others to do so), then worked for him with full knowledge of his intentions and with determination to achieve them. They stressed the sparseness of protest, the failure to resign. As Shawcross put it: no one who deliberately abdicated their consciences 'in favour of this monster of their own creation can complain now if they are held responsible for complicity in what their master did'. And Jackson scorned the attempt to shift all blame on to Hitler, or Himmler or Bormann: it was, he thought a 'temptation to ponder the wondrous workings of a fate which has left only the guilty dead and only the innocent alive'. The French were particularly contemptuous of the defence plea that the defendants had acted under compulsion, through fear: 'Cowardice' in Champetier de Ribes' words, 'has never been an excuse or even an extenuating circumstance'. The pleas that crimes were committed in secret, that no one knew of them, were denounced by all but with especial vehemence by Shawcross. How, he asked, could anyone accept the proposition 'that a man who was either a minister or a leading executive in a state which, within the space of six years, transported seven million men, women and children for labour, exterminated 275,000 of its own aged and mentally infirm, and annihilated in the gas chambers or by shooting what must at the lowest computation be twelve million people, remained ignorant of or irresponsible for these crimes?'

The vital distinction, declared the prosecution, between such crimes and any alleged crimes committed by the Allies was not one of scale (though the numbers who suffered from Allied war crimes or military action came nowhere near those of the victims of Nazi atrocity) but one of intent. As Shawcross expressed it, the defendants were guilty not of random acts but of 'systematic, wholesale, consistent action taken as a matter of deliberate calculation'. It was Jackson's task in his speech on the morning of 26 July to press the charge that had always been closest to his heart – conspiracy. He dismissed the defence argument that such a charge was alien to German law and unknown in international law. Every society, he insisted, had some similar charge 'to reach men, like these defendants, who never got blood on their own hands but who laid plans that result in the shedding of blood'. It was inconceivable to him that wholesale criminality over twelve years and across a continent had 'just happened', as the defendants had claimed. It had to be planned and supervized and the defendants had to reach a common decision to use the resources of the state to make it possible. Jahrreiss had suggested that the evidence showed not a 'conspiracy' but rather a 'dispiracy' (sic) – that is to say warring departments and individuals constantly at odds. No, replied Jackson, it showed personal rivalries and disagreement over methods but no argument about aims. And all the evidence showed, in his view, that every defendant had been fully aware of those aims, from the publication of *Mein Kampf* (six million copies in Germany alone) through Hitler's speeches and conferences. Jackson outlined the development of Hitler's plans, showed at what stage each defendant had become privy to them and then examined the contribution they had made to carrying them out.

Jackson's whole speech showed him restored to mastery and confidence after the recent months of ill-ease in cross-examination, resentment of the Tribunal and disillusion with the progress of the trial. If less passionate than his opening address, it was if anything more tightly argued. It was certainly an impressive analysis of the conspiracy charge and an attractive explanation of the whole spectrum of Nazi policy and the individual defendants' roles in it. Jackson made the attempt to create miniature portraits of the defendants, albeit one-liners in the Madison Avenue style. Goering was described as 'half militarist, half gangster. His pudgy finger was in every pie'; Hess was a 'zealot' and the 'engineer tending the Party machine'; Ribbentrop 'the salesman of deception' and so on. He reserved some of his most acid phrases for those whom perhaps he feared had been least effectively prosecuted: Papen, 'the pious agent of an infidel regime' holding the stirrup while Hitler vaulted into the saddle; Neurath, casting 'the pearls of his experience before the Nazis' and guiding their steps and soothing their victims; Schacht, lending his financial wizardry to finance secret rearmament behind his 'facade of starched respectability'. Such men, and Speer and the military too, he accused of giving their expertise to the Nazis knowing fully how it would be used. 'Their superiority to the average run of Nazi mediocrity ... is their condemnation.'

In a theatrical but telling set piece, Jackson looked at the men who sat on the front row of the dock. They had claimed to be 'without authority, without knowledge, without influence, without importance'. What 'a ridiculous composite picture of Hitler's government' they had drawn, said Jackson. He pointed to Goering, the 'number two man' who never suspected the Jewish extermination programme though he signed over a score of decrees relating to it; to Hess, 'an innocent middle man' transmitting Hitler's orders without ever reading them, like a postman or delivery boy; to each in turn, like Frick, Minister of the Interior, 'who knew not even what went on in the interior of his own office', let alone his department, least of all in the interior of Germany. When he reached the end of the row Jackson exclaimed: 'If you were to say of these men that they were not guilty, it would be as true to say there had been no War, there have been no slain, there had been no crime.'

At lunchtime, when Jackson's speech was finished, Gilbert observed the reaction of the defendants. It was 'hurt surprise that the prosecution still considered them criminals'. 'What have we been sitting here for eight months for?' protested Papen. 'The prosecution isn't paying the slightest attention to our defence.' Doenitz and Schacht joined in and denounced Jackson's speech – 'it had a very low *niveau*', thought Schacht. Goering was not surprised, he said, that the defence had had so little impact: 'The whole trial is a farce.' He expressed pleasure that those 'who kowtowed to the prosecution' and denounced Nazism had 'got it in the neck just the same' and claimed to be delighted by the way Jackson had described him: 'I'd rather be called a murderer than a hypocrite and opportunist like Schacht.' His delight increased next day when he had logged the transcript of the speech: 'I was way out in front with forty-two mentions and Schacht was a poor second.' Streicher had been hardly interested in the speech at all, just rather puzzled by Jackson's estimate of the number of Jews murdered: 'I don't think it was six million ... maybe four million.' He said he had been deeply impressed recently by reading about Jewish riots in Palestine. 'Anybody who can fight and resist and stick together ... for such people I can only have the greatest respect ... I would be ready to join them now and help them in their fight.' Perhaps he could go as soon as the trial was over, he thought. Jodl and Rosenberg listened for a while wide-eyed, then roared with laughter. (16)

Though the defendants let off some steam during lunch, they became tense and grim when Shawcross began his speech in the afternoon. He called for the sentence of death on all of them. The courtroom, thought *The Times* reporter 'became charged with the drama of a great criminal trial'. After so many weeks of abstract legal argument 'we suddenly saw that the men in the dock were on trial for their lives and in the grey strained faces was the knowledge of this truth.' (17) But for a while they were spared

Shawcross's full attack. That afternoon he concentrated his reply on the legal arguments of the defence and the validity of the charge of Crimes against Peace.

Shawcross regarded the establishment of the legal status of the proceedings as his most important aim (18); Maxwell-Fyfe, on the other hand, was anxious lest he lose sight of 'winning the case and getting the appropriate results' – it would be wrong, he felt, if Streicher were not hanged, or if Schacht were acquitted. (19) It might have been expected that Maxwell-Fyfe himself would have made the speech; after all he had run the British prosecution, borne a major burden of the cross-examination, sat through the entire trial and been largely responsible for all liaison with other prosecutors, the defence and the Tribunal. Many might feel that his knowledge of the entire prosecution case qualified him to summarize it, and that the work he had done on its behalf earned him the little bit of glory the duty would bring. But Shawcross, though absent from most of the proceedings, was still titular head of the British delegation; Jackson had always assumed in discussions that he would make the British speech. And British barristers are accustomed to toiling in the vineyard in the heat of the day, then standing back to allow the leading (and most expensive) 'silk' to pick the harvest. For this case, the British lawyers had been under instructions from Maxwell-Fyfe since early March to collect material for the final speech and to write drafts on individual defendants immediately after dealing with them in court, while their minds were still fresh. (20) From late April, Phillimore had been collating their material. (21) At the end of May, notes on it had been sent to Professor Hersch Lauterpacht who had written a first draft on the legal aspects of the case while Griffith-Jones prepared a synopsis of the rest. (22) When Shawcross arrived in Nuremberg at the beginning of July he took the team's material and wrote it into a speech of oratorical and forensic distinction which he then majestically delivered.

On that first afternoon Shawcross dealt with the count for which the British had been responsible, Crimes against Peace. He spoke of the wars waged by the Nazis – without warning and in contravention of their treaties – and of the deaths in battle of at least ten million men. He stressed the urgent task of the Tribunal to demonstrate that international law had the power to declare aggressive war criminal and to deal with those who perpetrated it. He had no patience with Jahrreiss's attempt to suggest that the Kellogg-Briand Pact had made wars 'illegal' but not criminal, a distinction Shawcross dismissed as meaningless.

He criticized the 'curious argument' that the Pact was not legally valid because there was no machinery to enforce it. 'Since when,' he asked, 'has the civilized world accepted the principle that the temporary immunity of the criminal not only deprives the law of its binding force but legalizes the crime?' In Shawcross's analysis, the Nazi state had been organized for war; Crimes against Peace had been the parent of its other crimes. The Nazis had planned and acted to dominate Europe, first by incorporating racial Germans then by expansion elsewhere. The defence had harped on the injustice of Versailles; he countered that all treaties can be revised by negotiation and this one had been to some extent. Yet the Nazis had not stopped at seizing territory they claimed had been taken from them by that settlement; they had gone on to occupy land which had never belonged to Germany. By attacking without warning and with no declaration of war, Shawcross argued, they had made their attacks illegal in international law and their killing of combatants common murder.

As the afternoon session finished, Keitel scuttled past the others in the box to the lift door. Gilbert thought he was trying to get out of sight as quickly as possible. Goering turned to Ribbentrop and commented: 'There, it's just as if we hadn't made any defence at all.' Later in his cell he complained that 'compared to Shawcross, Jackson was downright chivalrous'. He had already read an advance copy of the rest of the speech and promised that it would give the other defendants hell. 'Compared to them I'm getting off easy.' (23)

And, indeed, the next day Shawcross did give them hell, analysing the criminal behaviour of each. Gilbert observed how 'unrest and hostility mounted in the prisoners' dock as Sir Hartley's cool but scathing attacks struck home'. The *Sunday Times* reporter watched Ribbentrop 'slamming his fist on the barrier in front of him as he was called a common murderer, then slumping forward, head hanging down and shaking, muttering furiously'. (24) Another journalist watched Keitel weep, Papen bury his head in his hands and Frank turn his back as they received Shawcross's onslaught. (25) Their misery increased as he read a long and revolting eye-witness description of a mass execution by an Einsatzkommando: families undressing, kissing farewell, stepping into a pit where a thousand bodies lay covered with blood, while the soldier who was to shoot them finished his cigarette. They caressed the bodies while they waited for the shots. In calling for the severest penalty for the men who bore ultimate responsibility for such degradation and suffering, Shawcross insisted that their fate meant little – 'their personal power for evil lies forever broken; they have convicted and discredited each other and finally destroyed the legend they created round the figure of their leader.' But on their fate, he argued, depended 'the ways of truth and righteousness between the nations of the world, the hope of future international co-operation in the administration of law and justice'. The Tribunal must show that 'the state and the law are made for men ... States may be great and powerful. Ultimately the rights of men ... are fundamental.'

Shawcross's speech was rightly acclaimed. Only one tiny discordant note crept into the unison of praise. Perhaps at the insistence of the Foreign Office who had wanted some mention of the share of responsibility of the German people as a whole (26) he had included a brief section in which he said he was quoting Goethe's summation of the Germans: fate would one day strike the German people, he read, because ' "they betrayed themselves and did not want to be what they are. It is sad that they do not know the charm of truth, that mist, smoke and beserk immoderation are so dear to them, pathetic that they ingenuously submit to any mad scoundrel who appeals to their lowest instincts, who confirms them in their vices and teaches them to conceive nationalism as isolation and brutality".'

Within a few days, the press was commenting that these were not Goethe's words at all but words put into his mouth by Thomas Mann in his novel *Lotte in Weimar*. Anxiously the Foreign Office cabled the Washington embassy to get in touch with Mann in California and request confirmation. At first the embassy received the impression from Mann that the quotation was a composite of Goethe's actual words from several works. On 17 August, however, Mann wrote a long letter explaining that 'the quoted words do not appear literally in Goethe's writings or conversations, but they were conceived and formulated strictly in his spirit and although he never spoke them, he might well have done so.' He said he had 'modified and variegated for poetic purposes' quotations from Goethe, written 'much that Goethe did not say but which is backed by numerous authentic pronouncements in such a way that it may be deemed authentic'. (27) Is the 'authenticity' of the creative artist quite the same as that demanded by the law court? Would Shawcross's quotation have carried the same authority if he had realized that it was from Thomas Mann rather than Goethe? (To judge from the way that members of his team rushed to libraries, he had not realized the source of his quotation.)

Given the skill shown and impact made by both Jackson and Shawcross in the final addresses, it is not surprising that those of the French and Russians came as something of an anti-climax. Both, however, were thoroughly competent, businesslike and deliberately eschewed oratorical effect. Dubost's contribution was recognized by Birkett as being 'robust and vigorous', but its effect was marred for him. It was 'translated by a stout tenor-voiced man with the "refayned" and precious accents of a decaying pontiff. It recalls irresistibly a latecomer making an apology at the Vicarage Garden Party.' (28) Under the comic sound of the translator, however, lay a tragic story. Dubost was expressing horror that such had been the scale of Nazi crimes that a new word had to be invented to describe one aspect of them – genocide. He talked of recent census results suggesting that populations in areas occupied by Nazis had declined from between 5 and 25 per cent. He then laid out the elements of their 'criminal plan' and the acts of the defendants which he alleged had resulted in the 'state-committed crime' of mass murder. His analysis created a frightening picture of death and exploitation, yet it was made in a cold, logical manner. Rudenko's speech was, if anything, even more factual and unemotional. He spoke with unusual restraint, omitting epithets such as 'Fascist-Hitlerite gangsters' which usually larded his style. The defendants may have made 'a show of indifference and even levity' at his speech, but Rudenko's summary was in fact particularly telling. (29)

Though the cases of the individual defendants were now finished, the work of the Tribunal was not. The judges next had to approach what was probably the most demanding and worrying of all their tasks – the cases of the six indicted organizations: the Leadership Corps of the Nazi Party, the Gestapo and SD, the SS, the SA, the Reich Cabinet and the General Staff and High Command of the German Armed Forces. Article Eight of the Charter had said that the Tribunal might declare these organizations criminal in connection with any acts for which individual defendants were convicted. Armed with such a declaration, other courts could bring members to trial and rule out pleas of the innocence of the organization.

Literally millions of people might be affected. The membership of the Reich Cabinet had totalled only forty-eight during the whole history of the Nazi regime but hundreds of thousands were involved in the Gestapo, SD and SS, while membership of the Leadership Corps and the SA in its prime were each reckoned as high as two million. Furthermore, Robert Kempner had pointed out to Jackson in January that in 'every family there is likely to be at least one SA or SS member. This is critical where that member is the head of a family and provides for it.' Families of interned members of organizations were pressing the new German political leaders to protest against their indictment; the politicians in turn were expressing the fear that if members were declared criminal and held in confinement, it would be impossible to staff a new civil administration in Germany. (30) Germans inevitably feared that declarations against the organizations would automatically criminalize all their members and offer no chance for individuals to clear their name. The Allied authorities, on the other hand, were faced with the problem of whether it would ever be possible to try even those against whom there was substantial evidence of crimes committed.

Such practical and political anxieties sprang directly from a profound legal problem that had been born with the very idea of indicting the organizations. There had been sharp criticism of Bernays' original suggestion (see Chapter Four). The risk of blanket condemnation and guilt by association had shocked many. Criticism had been even more intense at the London Conference (see Chapter Five). It surfaced again while the indictment was drawn up (see Chapter Six). Yet at each stage the convenience and the logical symmetry of the idea (and American enthusiasm for it) had allayed doubts about its legality and practicality. They had not been eradicated, however; merely set aside. As a result the Charter contained no definition of a criminal organization, nor did the indictment – and in the five pages it devoted to them gave no details at all of the nature of the prosecution case. Everything had been left to the Tribunal. Where the Charter was specific, in incorporating Jackson's suggestion that members of organizations be entitled to be heard in their defence, it added to an already difficult procedural task vast administrative problems.

From the beginning of the trial the judges were far from happy with the buck they had been passed. On 6 December, Patrick Dean reported that they would ask for 'clear delimitation and definition' by the prosecution before deciding how to proceed. (31) Seemingly the prosecution case in mid-December and early January clarified nothing for the Tribunal. In a meeting on 12 January the judges drafted a notice read in court two days later which stated their requirements and underlined the vagueness of the argument thus far. The Tribunal wanted a summary of prosecution evidence against each organization and criteria for determining criminality – for example, what acts of individual defendants were to justify a declaration, over what period of time activities were to be seen as criminal. Similarly they asked for criteria to decide what constituted criminal membership and enquired whether the prosecution intended to exclude any classes or sub-groups from any declaration, whether knowledge of criminal aims and acts should be taken into account, and whether compulsory membership was a factor affecting individual membership and the criminality of the organization as a whole. They invited argument by defence and prosecution counsel on the whole problem. (32)

That argument was presented in open court on 28 February and 1 and 2 March. (33) Predictably, the six defence lawyers attacked the whole notion of indicting organizations: it was unprecedented in international law and alien to the Continent where the guilt and punishment of individuals alone was recognized. They pointed out that the indicted organizations were already dissolved – how could there be hearings on bodies which did not exist? The major defence plea was that whatever procedures, safeguards, exclusions of sub-groups were introduced, any declaration would still impugn vast numbers of innocent people who would have to face trial if they wished to clear their names. Defence counsel drew attention to the wording of the Charter: the Tribunal 'may', not 'must', declare organizations criminal, and urged the judges not to do so. Though unaware, they had in fact echoed all the arguments against the organizations case since Bernays had suggested it in September 1945.

The prosecution at last submitted a summary of its case and two appendices containing the evidence on which it was based. They made one or two sharp replies to defence points: that laws against organizations existed in every national system (the Nazi Party had been declared criminal in 1924 as was the German Communist Party in 1927 and 1928); that it was as logical to hear charges against former organizations as against former ministers or military commanders; that the criminality of the indicted organizations had to be proved in connection with the crimes in the Charter, all of which were crimes in existing law. But the prosecution failed to deal adequately with fears of injustice. Maxwell-Fyfe called declarations of criminality nothing worse than indictments, with no practical effect unless followed by trial and conviction of members. Jackson and others insisted that no subsequent proceedings need be taken and that future courts would only try individuals for their alleged crimes rather than for mere membership. All ignored the fact that legal hearing would be necessary if an innocent individual were to clear his name, and disclaimed any responsibility for the fact that the Allied Control Council in its Law Number Ten had

426

already drawn up a tariff of punishment for mere membership. Whatever Jackson's intentions at the London Conference, the occupying authorities appeared not to have understood them.

Jackson continued to argue with great passion that the innocent would not suffer. He insisted that the six organizations had been indicted because they were 'not only the most powerful but the most vicious' in Nazi Germany and had had members who were mainly active, volunteer and criminal, unlike the Hitler Youth, civil service or Armed Services which had held a few criminal elements only. He became increasingly impatient with defence accusations that the case against the organizations had been introduced as a form of mass reprisal. 'If there were the slightest purpose to go through Germany with death, we wouldn't have bothered to set up this Tribunal and stand here openly before the world with our evidence. We were not out of ammunition when the surrender took place, and the physical power to execute anyone was present.' Dix interposed darkly that the Americans might take this view but he was not so certain about the intentions of 'other governments'. Yet Rudenko had also put the argument that the case was brought before the Tribunal so that members might have a hearing, whereas the Powers could have declared the organizations criminal by fiat (as Nikitchenko in London had reckoned they had!).

Jackson maintained that a definition of a criminal organization was unnecessary. He did however suggest tests for criminality: members must be in an 'identifiable relationship' and have a 'collective general purpose'; they must be shown to have performed acts defined as crimes in the Charter; the majority of members must have known of the criminal aims and methods and joined voluntarily; an individual defendant must have been convicted of some act on the basis of which the organization was to be declared criminal.

The judges were far from satisfied. All of them (even the usually mute Donnedieu de Vabres) intervened continually with questions indicating their desire for much stricter definition and the limitation of the prosecution case. They were anxious about time scale – was an SA man who resigned in 1922 as guilty as one who remained a member until 1945, a man appointed to the General Staff at the end of the war as culpable as one who planned and waged aggression? They obviously wanted to cut out large classes of members and pressed for differentiation between volunteers and conscripts (as between the regular SS and the Waffen-SS, regular SA and groups transferred to it by law). The judges suggested that a line could be drawn to exclude those whose activities had been peripheral to the main work of an organization (dog-training teams, riding clubs and military bands in the SS; the equivalents of air raid wardens in the Leadership Corps, para-medical units in the SA). Above all they implied the need to separate full, active members from pure employees. Jackson sounded rather cross when they drew attention to the illogicality of the indictment excluding office staff of the Gestapo but not those of other organizations: 'The United States is not interested in coming over here 3,500 miles to prosecute clerks and stenographers and janitors,' he retorted. 'That is not the class of ... offender that affects the peace of the world.' Yet the indictment had not made that clear and an awful lot of clerks, stenographers and janitors must have been having sleepless nights. Though their anxieties might now be allayed, those of the Tribunal were not.

On 7 March, Dean reported that the judges still saw as its greatest worry the number of people who would be implicated in any declaration – both the numbers of innocents involved and the numbers who would have to be dealt with in subsequent hearings. (34) They would continue to ask for tighter definition and sharper limitation to devise a feasible procedure for hearing those who claimed their right under the Charter to speak in defence of the organizations to which they had belonged. Notices announcing this right had been issued in October. They had been displayed throughout Germany, published in newspapers and broadcast in all four Zones; 200,000 copies had been sent to internment and prisoner-of-war camps. On 8 February, Airey Neave, responsible for sifting applications, reported he had received 47,114 of them – 47,114 to be read and acknowledged but which could not be processed further since the prosecution had not yet outlined its case and no ruling had been given on what evidence would be considered relevant. There might be an alarming number of applications, but they could not be seen as representative. Not one had been received from the French Zone, only one from the Russian, though both military authorities swore that the notices had been fully circulated. Reports sent to Neave suggested that camp commanders in the American and British Zones had suppressed applications, sometimes in the well-intentioned belief that they were sparing the Tribunal trouble by not forwarding anything of little legal interest. These reports were being investigated and all camp commanders had been ordered to forward any and every application. Neave found it odd, too, that only 255 applications had been sent by the Gestapo (compared with 38,223 from the SS) and suspected reluctance to reveal membership. He also drew the Tribunal's attention to the difficulties of the defence – already understaffed, as yet uninformed of the nature of the case they must answer and in need of expert advice of former organization members. Since two lawyers obtained to help on the SS case had been clapped into prison the moment they reached Nuremberg because they were SS members themselves, he sensibly suggested counsel be given free access to them and indeed that experts on other organizations interned elsewhere be transferred to Nuremberg to be available for consultation. (35)

During the three day argument in court on the legal aspects of the case, defence counsel had raised other complaints – and incidentally revealed their suspicions of Allied motives. They thought the notification of the right to apply for a hearing had not been received by many because of the shortage of newspapers and radio sets, the lack of an inter-Zonal post, or any postal service at all with Austria where many former members were interned. They criticized the notice itself for being three pages long, couched in technical language incomprehensible to the layman and neither explaining what charges the organizations faced, nor assuring members they would be legally represented. They were suspicious too that now, in February, they were still waiting for the delivery of applications known to have been drawn up in November and affidavits they had themselves supervized before Christmas. They made it clear they believed that camp commanders were being deliberately obstructive. Spot checks by the General Secretary's staff and prosecutors, however, suggested that most of them were doing their best – but like everyone else at this stage were bewildered about what was required, ill-informed about their prisoners' rights, and overwhelmed by the volumes of applications. (36)

By this stage the judges might well have agreed with various Foreign Office comments on Neave's report that the legal and practical problems of the organizations' case were insoluble, and in view of the political repercussion 'there is much to be said for dropping this part of the indictment altogether.' (37) Yet they must have felt bound by the Charter to consider declarations and aware that the defence should be given a hearing since the prosecution had already had one. They now set about devising machinery to reduce the case to manageable proportions.

On 12 March they held what Biddle described as 'a long and fatiguing session'. (38) For three and a half hours they discussed suggestions made by counsel from both sides and by Neave, then outlined a scheme to break the procedural logjam. They decided that the defence would be asked to give evidence on what Biddle called 'the notorious and criminal aspects' of each organization and whether its members were voluntary, had knowledge of its aims and deeds and had been involved in them. Defence counsel were to be enabled to visit camps to interview potential witnesses escorted by officers to ensure entry and the co-operation of the authorities (80 were actually visited by the end of July). The witnesses chosen by the defence and the affidavits they received would be examined before a commission which would sieve out those most representative of any organization. These would finally be sent to the Tribunal for consideration. Airey Neave was appointed Commissioner and given permission to create assistants if necessary. (39)

Neave was given a very free hand in running the Commission: on 17 April the Tribunal accepted his rules for hearing evidence, and in coming weeks they approved his choice of four assistants (one from each national team). He set about a task at which others might have quailed with efficiency, common sense and a certain sardonic relish – one suspects that a very junior barrister enjoyed playing judge. The Commission began work in its own courtroom in the Palace of Justice on 20 May. Such was the pressure of work and complaint from all sides of slow progress that it split into two on 13 June. By 3 August when its job was finished, it had received 110,000 applications to be heard (most individual, some collective). From these applicants, 603 were brought to Nuremberg either for consultation or consideration as witnesses; 101 were finally heard by the Commission. Internees were prevailed upon to send collective affidavits, and by the beginning of August 313,213 had been received. To this mountain another 1,809 were added which had been taken from would-be witnesses not chosen for hearing. Ninety affidavits were ultimately submitted in full to the Tribunal. The rest were summarized by counsel or by prisoners in Nuremberg jail who had legal qualifications. (40)

The hearing of witnesses and counsel pleas by the Commission was an exhausting business, drawn out because of the lack of a simultaneous translation system and a chronic shortage of interpreters. Defence counsel devoted much time to lengthy explanations of charts showing the inter-relations of every department in an organization, its purpose and activities – a process Neave found 'most tedious'. (41) They strove to prove that the organizations were not cohesive, that the criminal activities of a few members were secret, and raised what Neave reported as 'considerable argument' by saying that 'compulsion' should include economic and psychological pressure to join, not just the physical threat on which the prosecution insisted. The defence for the SS was particularly assiduous in trying to get the Waffen-SS excluded on the grounds that nearly all its members were conscripted (the judges too had hoped this would prove possible). But as Griffith-Jones told his British colleagues, all the evidence showed that whether Waffen-SS members were conscripted or not they were 'all rather pleased at going into the élite' and had committed many of the most atrocious of crimes; it would be grotesque to exempt them. (42) He himself was cheerfully optimistic that when the defence case was brought before the Tribunal it would be instantly 'recognized as mass perjury' and require no prosecution attack. Kempner, on the other hand, was worried that German public opinion might see lack of challenge by the prosecution as proof that none was available. The British, at least, decided to look for witnesses (whom they did not eventually use) and effective written evidence for use in cross-examination (which they did). (43)

Thanks to the labours of Neave's Commission the organizations' case had been boiled down to essentials. Yet when it finally came before the Tribunal at the end of July it still lasted a whole month, though much of that was taken up with final defence and prosecution speeches. (44) The summaries of affidavits and Neave's report on the evidence undoubtedly strengthened the judges' determination to safeguard the interests of the innocent by examining such factors as time, activity and nature of membership, and by excluding large sub-groups before making any declaration of criminality. They were noticeably receptive to defence arguments on these matters. This court hearing would demonstrate yet again what had been shown before the Commission – that both defence and prosecution could not overcome weakness inherent in their cases. Some defence counsel were patently fighting losing battles; they had no way of combating prosecution evidence. In other cases, however, where the prosecution had indicted organizations in ignorance of their structure, activity or importance, the defence had a fighting chance; and the prosecutors also had to face the judges' demands for strict limitations.

The first prosecution case to be defended before the Tribunal on 30 and 31 July was particularly vulnerable to attack from both quarters – it was that of the Corps of the Political Leaders of the Nazi Party. The prosecution had alleged that through the Leadership Corps the Nazi Party had maintained its ideological grip on the German people and directed them towards its criminal ends. It was accused of terrorizing the population, persecuting Jews and political opponents, encouraging the mistreatment of foreign workers and the lynching of Allied airmen. A diagram of the Leadership Corps showed a perfect pyramid designed to ensure an efficient, uniform flow of orders and authority from the Reichsleiter (leading Party officials and ministers) to Gauleiter (in the provinces), through Kreisleiter (in districts) on to Ortsgruppenleiter (in towns), and finally down to Zellenleiter (in subdivisions) and Blockleiter (in cells made up of a group of households). The prosecution had assumed that this structure produced a cohesive, tightly controlled body of politically motivated workers, all fully informed of their Party's criminal aims and activities and responsible for carrying them out. Once, however, the work of each grade was examined, this satisfying assumption disintegrated. Certainly the top four ranks would be shown to have worked closely together, being instructed on the Party's policies and involved in its criminal activities. Not so the Zellen- and Blockleiter. Increasingly at these lowly grades, members had been conscripted; they were unpaid, usually very part-time, and mainly engaged in such innocuous activities as collecting Party dues, raising money and comforts for the Armed Services and organizing local help after air raids. Some of them had undoubtedly been political busybodies and tale tellers, but that did not make them criminal. The prosecution had already dropped from the indictment various forms of staff and assistance. Even so the indicted group still contained at least 600,000 people. But of these only 2,000 were Gauleiter and Kreisleiter.

It must have been clear to the prosecution by this stage that the Leadership Corps as a whole would never warrant a declaration of criminality; only its upper ranks met the tests for criminality which Jackson himself had put forward. And indeed the defence found little to say for the top four ranks. It was denied that they had been conspirators or co-operated with other indicted organizations; it was asserted that they seldom conferred with each other, let alone Hitler. But little evidence was produced to back these statements. Instead the defence concentrated on arguing the total innocence of the two bottom ranks – and did so effectively though at the expense of incriminating the four highest ranks. Maxwell-Fyfe's cross-examination did little to shake witnesses for the Block- and Zellenleiter and Raginsky's evidence on Blockleiter tearing down notices in Slovene failed to create an image of vicious criminals. Interventions from the judges indicated their wish to cut out as many grades as possible, leaving only the minority against whom hard evidence had been presented.

There could be no question of the solidity of the prosecution evidence submitted against the full membership of the Gestapo (the Secret State Police) and the SD (the Security Service of the SS) from which the purely administrative staff were excluded. That evidence had been voluminous and disgusting, showing arbitrary arrest, torture and execution of prisoners; taking and shooting of hostages; carrying out of the *Nacht und Nebel* decree; round up and transportation of foreign workers; execution of commandos and captured airmen; executions of Jews and concentration camp inmates; participation in the Einsatzgruppen. The Gestapo and SD had been charged together in the indictment; Neave and the Tribunal heard evidence for each separately. But the distinction between them soon blurred – their work often overlapped, they were trained together, they often wore the same uniform or SD patches. For eight months, defence and prosecution witnesses alike had confirmed this picture of Gestapo atrocities. All the defence could do was to present the Gestapo as nothing more than a secret police force of the kind existing in many countries, working within the law and with a high proportion of members drafted from other branches of the police; the SD as a political intelligence agency scarcely distinguishable from the Gallup Poll. They denied any co-operation with the SS (with whom they had been jointly administered since 1939). Witnesses blamed every crime they could on the SS; when that failed the Gestapo blamed the SD and vice versa: should that be challenged they resorted to pleas of personal innocence on the lines of: 'I never heard of Eichmann,' 'I never read reports on the Einsatzgruppen,' 'I protested about shooting hostages, torture and lynching.' It was all abject and totally unpersuasive, and indeed made a bad case worse – they were not denying that colleagues had condoned and committed crimes. The only sign of hope that the Gestapo counsel could spot came from the judges' questions which suggested an attempt to widen the group who might be seen as office staff only. (45) For the rest, the case for the Gestapo and SD seemed lost before it began.

This was far from true of that of the Reich Cabinet – or more accurately the Reichsregierung, the title which embraced the Cabinet, the Reich Defence Council and the Secret Cabinet Council.

From a practical point of view it is doubtful that the Reich Cabinet need have been indicted at all. Over the entire period from 1933 to 1945 only forty-eight men had ever held Cabinet rank; of these seventeen were in the dock as individual defendants (Bormann made an eighteenth) and eight were believed to be dead. Trials of each of its members would have been perfectly feasible, but the Americans above all were determined to show Nazi criminality through institutions as well as individuals. They had not heeded expert warnings that there was no such institution as a Reichs-regierung, that there had never been Cabinet government of the kind they imagined, that the Reich Defence Council and Secret Cabinet Council had never been convened and that the Cabinet itself did not meet after 1937; Hitler had preferred to give orders without consultation or to meet minis-ters individually to discuss specific points. Exactly the same points had been made by every defendant and every witness examined on the subject throughout the trial.

The counsel for the Reichsregierung, Kubuschok, was so confident in his case that he took only half a day over it and produced only one witness. Dr Schellenberg, once of the Ministry of Justice, added to the defence the claim that ministers were forbidden to resign, that many functions norm-ally ministerial were taken over by Gauleiter and Reich Commissioners. Under cross-examination by Kempner, however, he was forced to admit that Cabinet members did hold the highest responsibility in the state, that two had in fact resigned without any unpleasant consequences, that draft laws and the Budget were circulated to them all – so they were fully aware of Hitler's policies. The admissions had dented the defence case. Even so the prosecution had done little more than show the culpability of in-dividuals; they had not shown that the group indicted had existed, had conspired with Hitler and borne guilt additional to that of its members.

They were on surer ground in making allegations against the SS whose case was heard for the next six days. The prosecution evidence had been over-whelming and was backed by the testimony of umpteen witnesses and defendants themselves naming the SS as the culprit for the most revolting brutalities and crimes in the indictment. No one had questioned that the SS carried out reprisals, murdered hostages, massacred Jews, Slavs and partisans, organized the Einsatzgruppen and ran the concentration camp system both for the purposes of extermination and for the exploitation of labour for its own profit. Lest one aspect of SS bestiality be overlooked, the prosecution insisted on cross-examining before the Tribunal a witness who had testified to the Commission on its behalf – Wolfram Sievers of the Ancestral Heritage Society who had employed the SS to carry out 'bes-poke' killing for him in the interests of his 'scientific work', procuring the skulls for what they called in a letter 'Jewish-Bolshevik' commissars who represent the prototype of the repulsive but characteristic subhuman ...' Sievers was now also obliged to give sickening details of SS 'medical research': experiments for the Luftwaffe on the effects of freezing and pressure, tests on prisoners with poison gas, infections of typhus, malaria, jaundice, the introduction of live cancer cells and injections to speed up the coagulation of the blood.

The defence to this massive and disgusting case was partly that the SS was not a single organization but a complex of independent units all working without knowledge of each other's activities, and in the strictest secrecy. The only unifying factor, it was claimed, was Himmler. He alone knew what was going on. He alone bore any responsibility. Somehow, miraculously, wholesale crimes had been committed by people who 'happened' to be wearing SS uniforms; countless millions of people had died in concentration camps run solely by the SS, yet only one man had played any part or even been aware of them.

These claims of innocence and ignorance took their most grotesque form in the testimony of two SS judges. SS Judge Reinecke made breathtaking claims for the rectitude and self-discipline of his organization. He earnestly insisted that he had ordered investigation of 'rumours' of systematic extermination in between seven and ten concentration camps (Auschwitz, Dachau and Buchenwald among them) but had found no evidence at all to substantiate them. He was certain that the guards knew nothing about such terrible things. He himself had never seen a gas chamber at Auschwitz. Reinecke's associate, SS Judge Morgen, who had spent eight months, on and off, at Buchenwald, had seen nothing unpleasant either. He told the Tribunal that the camp had a 'wonderful view', lawns and flower beds, a huge library, a regular mail service, a cinema, admirable sports facilities and a brothel. Everyone in the court burst out laughing. Lawrence, whom Biddle suspected had been dozing, enquired what the witness had said. Biddle, whose stomach had turned on the microphone in front of him, was heard to say: 'Brothel, Geoffrey, brothel'. 'What?' 'Bordello, brothel, whorehouse.' (46) The laughter increased.

So sickening was the evidence in the SS case that hilarity became an essential protection against it – and it was a natural reaction to the ludicrous lies and the mind-boggling evasion of the witnesses. One, from the general SS, Baron Eberstein, talked of its restraint from violence, high-minded service to the state, and attraction to the 'best people' – three princes and an archbishop had been members, he said proudly. As he listed the qualifications for membership – avoiding mention of the proof of Aryan ancestry but stressing the number of references required and the god-like physical and mental attributes – Wheeler-Bennett slipped a note across the table to Maxwell-Fyfe: 'They might all qualify as Rhodes scholars.' Maxwell-Fyfe told him off later for reducing him to helpless giggles. (47)

Less amusing but no more credible than any other part of the SS case was the argument that the Waffen-SS should be excluded from any declaration of criminality. These fighting units of the SS which had included 18,000 men at the beginning of the war and 550,000 by the end, were described as purely military formations, under the command of the Armed Forces and subject to the SS only for administration, discipline and equipment. It was claimed they were increasingly conscripted, fully instructed in the Hague and Geneva Conventions and had fought as decent soldiers. Yet prosecution evidence suggested that the defence argument could be turned back on its head; far from the Waffen-SS being innocent because unconnected with other SS crimes, the SS as a whole was contaminated by the outrages of this section for which it was ultimately responsible. Evidence had certainly made it clear that there had been no rigid division between the Waffen-SS and the rest of the organization: members frequently rotated between branches; all units co-operated in the Einsatzgruppen, partisan warfare, the shooting of prisoners and hostages. No one denied that the Waffen-SS had provided many guards for concentration camps – their claim that this was at the end of the war and when the men were unfit for combat did not make their work any better.

The witnesses began by vociferously pleading the innocence of the Waffen-SS and soon fell back defending themselves only. The prime example was SS General Hauser who was 'no longer in command' of the units which destroyed Lidice; he had 'not yet' taken command of those who massacred every inhabitant of Oradour; he was 'not actually in' Yugoslavia when his division in a single action murdered families whose names took up three pages in a prosecution document; and he was 'surprised' to hear what an active part the Waffen-SS had played in the destruction of the Warsaw Ghetto – only at Nuremberg had he learnt it had in fact been destroyed. Given virtual admissions like these to widespread, constant criminal activity, let alone previous prosecution evidence, it is hardly surprising that the Tribunal refused to accept a United Nations War Crimes Commission report summarizing charges against Waffen-SS. The reason they gave was that it was being submitted too late. In fact it must have seemed merely cumulative.

The case for the General Staff and High Command which followed on 9 August offered an infinitely greater challenge to the prosecution, and had done so ever since the misconception that there was a German 'General Staff' in the commonly accepted meaning of the term. It had been necessary to formulate the phrase 'General Staff and High Command' for the indictment to cover the range of functions which the prosecution believed had been criminal; even so uncertainty remained as to whether this group had inherited the role of the General Staff, abolished after the First World War. It had been indicted, as Telford Taylor put it in a memorandum to Jackson, 'on American initiative and over the objection of the British', (48) because it was an essential component in the logic of their argument that the Nazi regime had conspired to wage war and that all other crimes were directed to this end or resulted from it – how else could there have been aggression without military planning and direction? How else could the scale of war crimes be explained unless it was organized? Furthermore, the case was also a response to American public opinion which saw the German Armed Services as criminal and to the call of the Allies at Yalta to extirpate German militarism. This response drew the criticism which the prosecution never successfully countered – that in making allegations against this small indicted group it was implying the guilt of those it had led; the very manner in which the Americans presented their evidence hardened this impression that the German Armed Services were on trial.

This explains the passion and commitment with which the defence fought the case. Laternser, in particular, brought to it an intensity unparalleled in the rest of the proceedings at Nuremberg. In public Jackson always strenuously denied that his concern was with anyone other than in the group indicted. When in December the *Army and Navy Journal* in Washington accused him of trying to discredit the whole profession of arms, he issued an immediate Press release pointing out that 'in the prisoners' dock are represented several professions, including the law. These professional men are not being indicted or tried because they belonged to a profession' but for the crimes they committed. (49) In the presentation of the prosecution case in January, Telford Taylor insisted that there was nothing criminal in being a soldier, 'it is perfectly legal for military men to prepare military plans to meet national contingencies ... It is perfectly legal for military leaders to carry out such plans and engage in war.' But not if those plans are for aggression and entailed the use of criminal methods: 'a man who commits crimes cannot plead as a defence that he committed them in uniform.' (50)

Yet the way in which the prosecution case was conducted always gave the impression that military criminals were not restricted to the few in the indicted General Staff and High Command. Taylor himself, when assembling evidence in December, told Jackson that although he believed many serving officers had behaved honourably throughout the war and he had no wish 'to prove that every German general was a devil' he did think it important to prevent 'the notion that the Army was simon-pure and gentlemanly.' (51) Clearly he saw the case as much broader than that against the narrow indicted group.

To define what was meant by the General Staff and High Command and to choose appropriate evidence against it had at first seemed so impossible that even as the indictment was published, American prosecutors were considering dropping the case. On 22 October, however, Taylor and Ben Kaplan had urged Jackson to retain it – the public would believe that there was no case; it would be unjust to punish junior officers but not their superiors, and equally so to allow the commanders to be summarily imprisoned, as the Allied Control Council was suggesting. (52) The Anglo-American team working on the case had begun to believe it was possible to define not an organization but a group of top officers who had contributed to a common function, either by planning or executing military activity. After intensive study of documents and interrogation of military leaders, the prosecution decided that this group comprised the commanders-in-chief and chiefs of staff of the three services, the commander of the OKW, and the field commanders-in-chief of each service, who had been appointed to their posts between 1938, when the Armed Services were re-organized, and 1945. This group had held about 130 officers of whom possibly 116 were still alive. The prosecutors were happy with this definition, and an able and enthusiastic team set to work to build up a case with growing certainty that it would be effective and conclusive.

The judges never shared this confidence either in the definition or the evidence. The General Staff and High Command became a microcosm of their legal problems in indicting organizations, their fears of implicating the innocent, and their constant distraction with extraneous difficulties. They faced determined and insistent protests about the case. By 19 December, the Tribunal had received a letter from the wives of interned generals denouncing the indictment and requesting definition of the charges their husbands faced. (53) Since the prosecution had not made them clear, the Tribunal could say nothing to reassure the wives or justify the internment of a large number of senior officers, many of whom would not ultimately appear in the group defined. The judges also had to fight off the efforts of counsel, military defendants, and indicted officers to obtain what was seen as their right under the Geneva Convention to have military representation and a court-martial. It had to be emphasized that the Tribunal was military, even if its procedures and legal staff were not. They had, in addition, to deal with the accusation that the indicted officers were being held in prison under conditions forbidden by the Geneva Convention for men of their rank.

These complaints were summarized in a two-page letter from Laternser and Rohrscheidt in May: the officers were not addressed by rank, often given sharp orders, locked in cells several times a day where their health was impaired by draughts, and they could not consult each other or their counsel. They were subject to frequent and inconsiderate searches after which their cells were left strewn with their belongings. They had been deprived of their right to an unrestricted delivery of parcels and in consequence were short of underwear and obliged to lend each other shirts; basic toilet articles such as nail scissors had been taken away. Contrary to law, high-ranking officers were forced to clean their eating utensils and the prison corridor. When news of this protest reached Andrus he was incensed – everyone had expressed gratitude for the treatment they received at Mondorf, now 'complainees' were making 'false accusations' and trying to 'make trouble'. The Colonel reckoned he knew why and he was ready for it: 'I am determined,' he told the Tribunal, 'not to be defeated in peace by an enemy we have just defeated in war'. Always with a sharp eye for a 'good boy' and a 'model prisoner' Andrus spotted Bach-Zelewski – suppressor of the Warsaw rising and a prosecution witness – and forwarded a crawling letter from him maintaining that the generals were being treated in a 'thoroughly correct and humane way ... since months' and that their grumbling was 'causing really disgust for a lot of internees here'. Though it was rather late in the day the Tribunal set up a board of officers to investigate the matter. (54) It must have been the least of their worries – much more troubling was the case itself. On 13 May, Lawrence asked his colleagues whether there was really a case at all. (55)

As argued by Telford Taylor with great eloquence in January, developed later through the cross-examination of witnesses and defendants and summarized before the Tribunal in August, the General Staff and High Command was to be seen as the group which in conspiracy with Hitler and other organizations had knowingly directed its efforts to carrying out 'the Nazi objectives of aggrandizing Germany by threat of force or force itself'. Some members may have criticized details, matters of timing, but they never protested against this aim itself. They were not, in the prosecution's eyes, mere technicians; in providing the tactics and logistics for Hitler's strategy they were condoning it and making it workable. To claim they bore no responsibility was, in Taylor's words, to say that 'military men are a race apart ... men above and beyond the moral and legal requirements that apply to others, incapable of exercising moral judgement on their own behalf.'

To ensure victory these commanders, alleged the prosecution, had ordered methods to be employed which they knew to be brutal and illegal. They had distributed to the Armed Services the Commando Order, the Commissar Order, directives (especially for troops in the East) which resulted in bestial treatment of prisoners and civilians. In support of his charges Taylor had extracted from his witness, Bach-Zelewski, the admission that his Anti-Partizan Combat Units had employed mainly Wehrmacht personnel and could point to the testimony of SS General Ohlendorff that the Einsatzgruppen had been totally dependent on Army back-up for their ghastly work of extermination. Knowledge of the work of these squads was to be constantly denied by all military witnesses. In his final summing-up of the case in August, Taylor stressed that the units had operated behind military lines, not in a desert; that they were fed, billeted and given communications facilities and men by the Army. 'The idea that the extermination squads flitted through Russia, murdering Jews and Communists on a large scale but secretly and unbeknown to the Army is utterly preposterous.'

The defence to these allegations had been launched by witnesses, defendants and their counsel long before the case ever came to the Tribunal. It was denied that the General Staff was an organization at all; it was merely a random collection of top officers whom the prosecution had chosen to lump together. They had performed a variety of tasks without ever meeting as a group and had held no power of command. Hitler had been both Supreme Commander and the legally appointed Head of State – officers were doubly bound to serve him. Hitler, as Head of State, made all decisions on foreign policy, the direction of the economy, rearmament, and was responsible for any declaration of war or peace. His policies were secret and often formulated at the very last minute without prior consultation; the conferences at which the prosecution claimed he had made his intentions clear were never seen as more than his exploration of current whims and dismissed as 'exaggerated'. Everyone stressed the belief that rearmament had been purely in the interests of defence, that every decision to attack had taken them by surprise and when they had neither plans, men nor equipment to carry them out adequately. They all insisted that the military had remained aloof from the Nazi Party and from other indicted organizations – and had frequently fought off attempts to influence them or interfere with their professional duties. They were legally forbidden to resign; once the war began it would have been inconceivable to wish to do so, especially once the Allies had demanded unconditional surrender.

Those who testified for the General Staff and High Command before the Tribunal fell into the logical pitfalls which had trapped other military witnesses. Field Marshals Brauchitsch, Manstein and Rundstedt all sustained the claim that it had been impossible to argue with Hitler, then immediately listed occasions when they had done so (about the attack on Russia, for example, or the issuing of the Commando Order). Regardless of the Charter and German military law, they insisted on their primary duty to obey – then pleaded that they had ignored or openly countermanded orders. Manstein denied he had allowed the Reichenau directive to be implemented, yet several of his own orders submitted by the prosecution used identical phrases. The defence totally failed to explain why, if commanders were unaware of policies, had blocked orders or refused co-operation with other organizations, those policies and orders had been put into effect and the armed services had been involved in so many atrocities.

If the defence had not cleared the Armed Forces of the imputation of criminal activity, neither had the prosecution proved beyond reasonable doubt that this activity had been planned and co-ordinated by the group they had indicted. Their evidence had been shocking but they had not focused it on the General Staff and High Command. Taylor's final summary of his case highlighted its constant diffuseness. He argued that 'the gas chambers, mountains of corpses, human skin lampshades, shrunken skulls, freezing experiments and bankvaults filled with gold teeth', of which the Tribunal had heard for so many months were the 'poisoned fruit' of the tree of German militarism. Had he proved that the roots of this tree were the members of the indicted group? Had he shown that all the branches and twigs of Nazi crime spread from those 130 roots? Had he convinced the Tribunal that by declaring the group criminal, militarism and crimes by the military would be stamped out? Was it indeed the Tribunal's task, according to the Charter, to attempt to do so? Since so much evidence pointed to the abuse of law-abiding soldiers by a few criminal officers, would it not be fairer and more practical to try the officers responsible as individuals rather than as members of a group specified by the prosecution? And how could the prosecution justify omitting from the indicted group so many of the most allegedly criminal officers? The Tribunal was anxious throughout to define and limit the organization against which it might make declarations, in the hope of including the guilty and eliminating the innocent.

The last case to be heard demonstrated the need for this. It was that of the SA (Sturmabteilung), Hitler's Brownshirts, founded in 1921 as his first bodyguard. On 5 February at a chief prosecutors' meeting, Jackson had expressed the opinion that this prosecution case was 'the weakest they had made' and said he had often considered withdrawing it, (56) but had come to believe it had some chance of success. But the case had been misconceived from the start.

The SA had been indicted because of awareness that it was they who had provided the bullies who helped Hitler to power by terrorizing his opponents. Too late had come the knowledge that the Roehm Purge in 1934 had reduced the SA to a powerless rump, whose few remaining leaders had virtually no political influence, and were indeed treated with disdain or suspicion. On paper the SA had had a membership of four and a half million at its peak in early 1934; this had dropped to one and a half million by 1939. But these figures needed careful analysis. Certainly the SA always contained a nucleus of paramilitary units drilled and trained as an embryo army. But it had also been legally obliged to act as an umbrella organization for a multitude of other groups whom the Nazi government chose to put there: Protestant youth groups, riding clubs, medical auxiliaries, student and civil service organizations, and the Stahlhelm – a nationalist ex-servicemen's association which alone contained about a million members.

Against this rag-bag, the prosecution had presented charges of terrorization (including an active part in 'Kristallnacht'), covert military training and preparation for war, participation in the march into Austria and work with sympathisers in the Sudetenland. Once the war began, the SA was accused of contributing members to guard prisoners-of-war under Wehrmacht supervision, assisting in the control of slave labourers, taking part in the attacks on ghettoes in the East and on occasion sending men to help guard concentration camps.

The defence of the SA was conducted by Boehm, whose incessant complaints irritated the Tribunal. It relied on witnesses of doubtful candour but had little problem in showing that the indicted group was far from cohesive. Furthermore, even if no one believed that once all the attached groups were excluded the remaining hard core was not quite the jolly, card-playing, beer-swilling lot they claimed to be, dedicated to clearing snow, bringing in the harvest and similar social good works, the prosecution did not prove otherwise. Its case was poorly documented, it did not demonstrate that SA members were linked in a general conspiracy devoted to shared criminal ends, and certainly it established little major contribution from the SA to Nazi policies after 1934.

Nine days of prosecution and defence summary of the entire organizations case followed the SA hearing; nine days of repetition of the legal arguments, of the evidence constantly woven throughout the trial, presented before the Commission, and finally brought to the Tribunal. These days can only have confirmed the judges in their feeling that if declarations of criminality were to be made at all, they must be strictly limited and scrupulously hedged with safeguards.

The month of the organizations' hearing might well have seemed interminable to many – complex, technical, abstract. For the defendants it cannot have been long enough; they knew that once the hearing ended, the judges would retire to consider the verdicts on them. Before that, they would have one day and one day only when, thanks to the right granted to them in the Charter, they could make a final plea and sum up their cases and themselves both for the Tribunal and for posterity. For many of them, as Birkett recognized, this would be 'the last public statement they will ever make: and that simple fact is enough to show the solemnity of the occasion'. (57) And that simple fact imposed a great strain on the defendants. From 11 August, the Press began to report the symptoms of that strain; taut and tired faces, neuritis for Ribbentrop, stomach cramps for Hess and fits of depression for Fritzsche. Some seemed likely to rally when faced with the challenge. Stahmer was reported to have urged Goering to 'make a bid for immortality' by admitting guilt in causing the war but also defending the innocence of the Geman people. (58) But no one knew what any defendant would say. Not even other defendants: 'Somehow,' Fritzsche felt, 'we had been shy of looking at each other's drafts.' (59) By 30 August, Ribbentrop had made eight. One of them was a panegyric of Hitler which his counsel had torn up saying 'Don't by silly.' By then Doenitz seemed to have been rehearsing his statement in court for days; his lips moved 'as he mumbled it to himself, a reporter imagined. (60)

On 31 August, the courtroom was packed, the photographers back in full force for the drama of the final pleas. The defendants were noticeably well-scrubbed and groomed for their last appearance before the verdicts were announced. The Tribunal had insisted the statements must be short and avoid repetition of points already made in defence. The instruction was obeyed – the speeches lasted between three and twenty minutes. The defendants spoke from the dock in the order in which they had been indicted. Everyone had dreaded that these speeches would either be outpourings of propaganda or the occasion for hysterics and emotional collapse. Funk and Sauckel both wept at times but, as Birkett commented, the defendants all 'bore themselves with considerable dignity' and they 'spoke with great feeling and force'. He expressed 'some admiration for their outward fortitude' at a moment when they had to look back on their own fall, contemplate the suffering and humiliation of the people they had led, and when they knew their personal fates were being weighed. (61) One weird, almost frightening performance cut across the moving, dignified proceeding. To everyone's surprise Hess decided to speak; like all his previous interventions, it was chilling and unsettling. The five-page statement which he delivered seated was nearly always incoherent and it lurched disturbingly from denials of the right of his accusers to bring charges, to descriptions of Hitler's eyes as 'cruel' and sometimes with a 'tendency to madness'. He spoke so quickly that he had sometimes to pant for breath. Goering and Ribbentrop, seated on either side, kept nudging Hess and begging him to stop. (62) No one can have been surprised when later in the day his counsel, Seidl, asked for a further medical examination of his client.

No defendant asked for mercy; most seemed resigned to conviction and punishment. Several asked the Tribunal to distinguish between condemnation of themselves as individuals and condemnation of others. Frick spoke with gratitude of the work of his civil servants; Kaltenbrunner defended the SS as having believed in an ideal and worked according to legal decree; Schirach again insisted on the innocence of German youth. Raeder argued that the trial had cleared the name of the German Navy and the German people. Others too stressed that their people bore no guilt. Streicher asked for a judgement which would not 'imprint the stamp of dishonour upon the forehead of an entire nation'. Goering pleaded that the people had known nothing of crimes and had remained 'self-sacrificing and courageous'. Even Frank, who had once said that German guilt would not be wiped out for 1,000 years, now said it had been erased by the crimes committed against Germans by Russians, Poles and Czechs. The idea that the same or worse crimes had been committed by others was developed by several defendants: there were references to Allied bombing of Germany, and to Hiroshima; Seyss-Inquart complained of the forcible evacuation of German speakers by Slavs and Goering denounced the stripping of German industrial plant and property by the occupying authorities.

There was virtually no admission of personal guilt in any of the speeches. Speer, indeed, hardly mentioned himself at all and gave an impassioned warning of the dangers of modern technology and its threat to civilization. Frick, Rosenberg, Funk, Papen and Neurath all announced they had a 'clear conscience'. Ribbentrop felt guilt only in so far as his 'aspirations in foreign policy remained without success'; Keitel in that he had 'erred ... and was not in a position to prevent what ought to have been prevented'. Papen felt not so much guilt as regret that he could not have overcome the 'too strong power of evil'. Schacht was prepared to admit a 'mistake' in not seeing Hitler's criminal nature soon enough, but he was pleased that his own policies for creating work had 'proved brilliantly successful'. Doenitz was perhaps the most forthright: his conduct of the submarine war had been correct, he declared; he would do again everything he had done. Nearly every defendant acknowledged that the crimes alleged had been committed, but no one admitted any sense of responsibility for them.

By lunchtime this had begun to infuriate Papen. He turned on Goering. 'Who in the world is responsible for all this destruction if not you? You were the second man in the state.' 'Well, why don't you take the responsibility, then?' Goering retorted, 'You were the Vice Chancellor.' Papen could not see that he had any responsibility. (63) In the dock, Ribbentrop was prepared to talk of crimes which had 'besmirched' the Nazi revolution, but, like Funk and Sauckel, he stated that he had first heard of them during the trial. Kaltenbrunner 'never knew what was really going on'. Streicher said that Hitler had ordered and done 'everything'; Speer called Hitler the author of the world's present misfortunes. Most defendants blamed Hitler – not just for the crimes but for abusing and exploiting their own loyalty and obedience (though Keitel hinted he had been unaware that there is, in fact, a limit even to a soldier's duty to obey). Only Seyss-Inquart refused to condemn the Führer, the man who had made Greater Germany a fact; having served him, he could not now say 'crucify him'. Rosenberg – for once surpassing Streicher in the laughably bathetic – alone spoke in praise of National Socialism: in his opinion it had stood for overcoming the class struggle, restoring the dignity of work and it had succeeded in 'acquainting millions with the as yet unknown treasures of art'.

Birkett was not alone in thinking that, in general, this had been a session when the 'dignity of the trial might have been impaired by unseemly scenes; as it turned out, the dignity of the trial was enhanced by the defendants themselves.' (64) The session closed with a reminder of the context in which the defendants' counsel had been obliged to work all these months. Lawrence read a statement in which he assured the defence lawyers that the Tribunal was aware of the criticism, abuse and threats they had received; until now they had been under the protection of the Tribunal, soon they would come under the protection of the Allied Control Council. He thanked them for having 'performed an important public duty in accordance with the highest traditions of the legal profession'.*

Then the proceedings were adjourned until the Tribunal was ready to announce its judgement and verdicts. It was an extraordinary moment. Since 14 November, judges, counsel, staff, guards and defendants had sat cramped together in the narrow stuffy courtroom. They had lived together for six hours a day and for 216 days. Now they would not meet again until the day of the judgement.

*That this protection was necessary can be seen from a resolution passed by the Cologne Lawyers Association, and reported on 26 September 1946. It called for an enquiry into the way in which three of its members had conducted the defence and called on other associations to do the same. (65)

References for Chapter Sixteen

1   IMT Vol. VII
2   Tribunal minutes, 12 March
3   Tribunal minutes, 6 April
4   IMT Vol. XVII
5   British prosecution minutes, 30 May
6   Tribunal minutes, 24 June
7   The defence speeches are to be found in IMT Vols. XVII, XVIII and XIX
8   *The Times*, 5 July
9   Gilbert
10 Fritzsche
11 British prosecution minutes, 26 June

12   Gilbert
13   Minutes of chief prosecutors' meeting, 5 December. BWCE N/9
14   Minutes of chief prosecutors' meeting, 5 April. Court Contact Committee. File 60
15   Speeches in IMT Vols. XIX and XX
16   Gilbert
17   *The Times*, 26 July
18   British prosecution minutes, 30 May
19   Maxwell-Fyfe to Shawcross, 31 May 'Confidential. Phillimore. Room 233'
20   British prosecution minutes, 9 March
21   British prosecution minutes, 25 April
22   British prosecution minutes, 28 May
23   Gilbert
24   *Sunday Times*, 27 July
25   *Sunday Express*, 27 July
26   Shawcross to Maxwell-Fyfe, 18 April. 'Confidential. Phillimore. Room 233'
27   FO 371. 57551
28   Birkett, 29 July. Quoted by Montgomery Hyde
29   *The Times*, 30 August
30   Kempner to Jackson, 23 January. Jackson Papers, Box 198
31   Dean, 6 December. LCO 2. 2984
32   Tribunal minutes, 12 January
33   IMT Vol. VIII
34   Dean to FO, 7 March. FO 371. 57542
35   Neave report to General Secretary, 8 February. FO 371. 57465
36   Reports in Jackson Papers, Box 198
37   FO 371. 57465
38   Biddle Notes on Evidence. Vol. III. Biddle Papers, Box III
39   Tribunal minutes, 12 March
40   Neave Report, August 1946. IMT
41   Neave *Nuremberg*
42   British prosecution minutes, 26 June
43   British prosecution minutes, 2 July
44   IMT Vols. XX and XXI
45   Conversation with Dr Merkel
46   Biddle *In Brief Authority*
47   Wheeler-Bennett
48   Taylor to Jackson, 7 December. Jackson Papers, Box 193
49   Press release, 4 December. Jackson Papers, Box 213
50   IMT Vol. IV
51   Taylor to Jackson, 7 December. Jackson Papers, Box 193.
52   Taylor and Kaplan to Jackson, 22 October. Jackson Papers, Box 193
53   Tribunal minutes, 19 December
54   All letters in Jackson Papers, Box 193
55   Tribunal minutes, 13 May
56   Chief prosecutors' meeting, 5 February. Court Contact Committee. File 60
57   Birkett, 31 August. Quoted by Montgomery Hyde
58   UP in *New York Herald Tribune*, 11 August
59   Fritzsche
60   *Daily Express*, 30 August

61 Birkett, 31 August. Quoted by Montgomery Hyde
62 *New York Herald Tribune*, 31 August
63 Gilbert
64 Birkett
65 FO 371. 57552

Chapter Seventeen

When would the Tribunal deliver its judgement? The judges hoped it would be ready by 23 September. For prosecution and defence counsel this meant a welcome three week break from the courtroom, a period when many might get away from Nuremberg and have their first real holiday since November; the fortunate few might even be able to go home and see their families again. By this stage their livers as well as their brains needed a rest. In the end-of-term atmosphere of recent weeks social life had been particularly hectic, culminating in an enormous and riotous party at the Press Club the night after the defendants' final speeches where, for once, even the British judges had come out of their social isolation and joined in the rowdy jollification. Not everyone could leave Nuremberg though. Offices had to be packed up, everything made ready for the longed-for quick getaway as soon as the judgement was read. On 8 August, the British prosecution teams welcomed the arrival of a microfilming unit which was going to copy the entire corpus of evidence submitted in the trial. It would start with the Russian exhibits. The British feared that 'if they were withdrawn they might never see them again'. (1)

For the Tribunal, though, there was no time to rest, no time to tidy up. The writing of the judgement represented the hardest work yet. Preliminary spadework had been going on for months. From the beginning of the trial the judges had made notes in court and received daily transcripts of the proceedings, which they studied or not according to temperament. The American staff in particular had prepared summaries of evidence and classified it under headings dealing with the various counts, the topics within them and the cases of individual defendants; John Phipps was to perform a similar service for Lawrence. On 10 April Lawrence had suggested to his fellow judges that it was now time to start serious thinking on the legal problems of the judgement and to do some substantial preparatory work. (2)

As President of the Tribunal, Lawrence himself might have claimed the right to draw up its opinion – that was common practice in international courts. But Lawrence was not that kind of man, not that kind of President. He had always seen the business of drafting opinions as hard grind rather than an opportunity to display erudition or to assert authority. Modest and totally free from any pomposity he had no temptation now to grab an honour or ride roughshod over the views of his colleagues. He had used his position as President at Nuremberg to encourage all the judges to play a full part in deliberations and to conciliate when tempers or consensus were threatened. Given the strong and contrasted characters over whom he presided and the very different legal traditions from which they had come, the degree of amicability and agreement they had achieved had been remarkable – not least at a time when the political leaders of their four countries were increasingly antagonistic. Lawrence undoubtedly hoped that the final judgement would both articulate and enshrine this international co-operation.

But a worthy judgement could not be a patchwork tacked together by a committee round a table, and Lawrence was particularly keen that its form and style should be consistent. The obvious approach, then, was to have a draft prepared by one man who would incorporate his colleagues' material and suggestions, then adapt it in the light of later discussions. The obvious candidate for the job was Norman Birkett. His grasp of the evidence, his clear mind and capacity for expression were manifest – the Tribunal had already relied on him to draft most of its public statements and rulings. So from the end of April, Birkett started work on the first draft of the Tribunal's opinion. Leaving the cases of the defendants to one side for the moment, he concentrated on the law and the counts against which they would ultimately be assessed. Then evening after evening he paced the floor of his sitting-room and dictated to a secretary. She was staggered by his fluency and his command of the material, by his ability to speak with barely a reference to a note. (3) On 27 June the judges met to consider his draft.

It turned out to be less a perfect formula for the judgement than a catalyst which activated all the legal uncertainties and conflicting opinions which had lain inert during the previous months while the judges coped with the day-to-day running of the proceedings. Now that Birkett had introduced the pure concentrate of law into their thinking, the judges simply boiled over into dispute. They were to hold twenty meetings between the end of June and 17 September alone, and each one of these would be the occasion for dispute. This was surely inevitable – eight different minds trained in four legal systems, a lengthy and complex trial involving twenty-two defendants and the evidence of an entire regime, much contentious law and no precedent for a guide. It is probably naïve to believe that any bench of judges ever reach identical and instantaneous decisions. These decisions are always reached behind closed doors, the underlying disagreements and compromises kept private. Nuremberg was no exception. The Tribunal's minutes record only the topics discussed. But thanks to Francis Biddle's detailed notes we have a major insight into the arguments and viewpoints of the participants. (4)

From these it would appear that the judges reached decisions most quickly on those counts where the law was clearest – War Crimes and Crimes against Humanity. Here their differences were little more than differences of taste. They wanted greater brevity and more reference to

447

international law than Birkett at first provided. On 27 June, Biddle called for more analysis of defence evidence; up to 4 September the Russians wanted fuller details of Nazi crimes (some lingering over human fat soap and gas chambers). All tended to be critical of emotive phrases such as 'shocked the conscience of mankind'. To the end of their discussions, Nikitchenko never understood the word 'honorary' as in 'membership', and complained that any defendant should be described as 'honourable'. (5) Yet nearly all the points raised concerned fine tuning. A second draft on War Crimes and Crimes against Humanity was discussed on 4 September; it was adjusted on 16 September and thereafter occasioned little discussion.

Where the feathers did fly was over the conspiracy charge – not just during the judges' meetings, either, but, as one side remembered, in 'irritable' sessions in the American judges' house. (6) At the very first discussion on the judgement on 27 June, Donnedieu de Vabres had attacked the conspiracy charge with every weapon in his well-stocked academic armoury: it was unknown in international and French law, *ex post facto*, retroactive (since no warning had been issued that it would be applied), unnecessary (since actual crimes had been committed), unconnected with the last two Counts (whatever the indictment claimed), and allowed those not on trial to evade responsibility. De Vabres had not just summed up the worst that could be said of the charge; he had reminded his colleagues of all their own doubts about it. These now flooded out at a series of meetings and in innumerable memoranda. The French wanted the charge thrown out. Lawrence felt they were bound by the Charter to see conspiracy as a crime ('the British at their worst', commented Biddle) and Birkett took the view that without the charge the impression would be given that the War was not planned and that the Nazi regime had been acquitted. The whole value of the trial, he argued, lay in showing that the War arose from a common plan; but perhaps the conspiracy could be treated less as a crime than as the explanation of the relationship between the defendants. Nikitchenko replied in a memorandum on 17 July that though the crime did not exist in international law, it was sufficiently established in municipal law to justify its application. Never mind if it had never been used in international proceedings; he told his colleagues on 15 August that the Tribunal was not 'an institution to protect old laws and shield old principles from violation' (but he took two hours to do it in full). Somewhere in between Biddle took his stand: he called the charge 'dangerous', but believed it could be drastically limited to prevent injustice.

Subsidiary arguments spluttered. Nikitchenko believed that the conspiracy charge in the Charter applied to all the counts, as it did in the indictment. No one else did. The French suggested a compromise: attach it to Crimes against Peace only, and then reject it as being unproved. No one else saw that as a compromise. Nikitchenko believed that the Nazis had conspired to draw up one grand plan to dominate the world; Parker that there had been a single conspiracy to wage aggressive war at least and that it had been proved 'beyond all peradventure'. (7) Not at all, replied the

French – all the evidence showed a random scatter of separate plans between individuals and organizations. Biddle countered by preparing a draft for 2 September to try to show how separate plans could compose a total pattern. It did not persuade the French. Nikitchenko began to argue that the Tribunal was supposed to be 'practical, not a discussion club' – how could some of the defendants be convicted without this broad charge? He pointed to the case of Fritzsche; others then added those of Papen, Schacht and even Streicher. If they were to keep the charge but limit it, when did the conspiracy start? The prosecution had argued it began from the foundation of the Nazi Party. No judge believed that; it was much too sweeping for them. On 27 June, Lawrence had suggested that there was no need to fix a precise date. What mattered was to decide when the conspiracy clearly existed. Biddle persuaded his colleagues that at the Hossbach conference on 5 November 1937, Hitler's commitment to aggression was plain for all to see. The judges began to apply that date.

It took over two months before a way could be found out of all the tangles of conspiracy. The direction was provided in a memorandum written by Herbert Wechsler, Biddle's former aide. It was almost as much an expression of the deep suspicions with which the two men had always regarded the charge as an attempt to harmonize the judges – but it had that effect. Biddle presented the proposals to the Tribunal on 4 September and they became the framework for its judgement on the charge. They cut the prosecution case to the bone and destroyed the concept that all Nazi crimes were related to one end, from the seizure of power to the atrocities of the War.

The judges' final formula insisted that the conspiracy 'must be clearly outlined in its criminal purpose', not 'too far removed from the time of decision and action' and be considered only in relation to planning and waging of aggressive war, as in the Charter, but not in relation to other counts. The judgement dismissed the idea of a single grand conspiracy and spoke of 'many separate plans'. It found that 'continued planning with aggressive war as the objective has been established beyond doubt' but noted that improvization and opportunism had played a part at each stage to obtain the desired ends. Defensive appeals to the Führer principle were dismissed as 'unsound': 'The relationship of leader and follower does not preclude responsibility'. (As Nikitchenko had put it in his July memorandum 'without the absolute authority of the gangleader, no band can exist.')

The next section of the judgement, Crimes against Peace, took the judges two months to formulate but that period does not reflect intense debate of the kind aroused by the conspiracy count. Attlee once told Cabinet colleagues trying to define socialism that it was like trying to define an elephant – a waste of time, since they would all recognize one if it came into the room. The judges at Nuremberg all felt they recognized aggression when they saw it and that the evidence in the trial had shown plenty of it. But could they define it? Biddle tried several times and found the task impossible. (8) The French took the Attlee line. They might pride themselves on logic and clarity, they might demand precision over the conspiracy charge and bemoan their Common Law colleagues' traditional vagueness, but over this matter they suddenly decided that haziness was a virtue. On 17 July, Donnedieu de Vabres pointed out that the United Nations had failed to produce an adequate definition of aggression; why should the Tribunal be expected to do better? And indeed they eventually gave up the attempt. Their judgement concentrated on building up to an impression rather than a definition through detailing at length the plans, statements and actions which had led to attacks on foreign territory.

The judgement did, however, devote considerable space to the judges' unanimous opinion that aggressive war was a crime and well-established as such in international law; there was nothing *ex post facto* in the Charter or retroactive in the Tribunal's proceedings. It examined the declarations denouncing aggression made by the nations in the inter-war years and in particular by the Kellogg-Briand Pact. It reached the conclusion that 'the solemn renunciation of war as an instrument of national policy necessarily involves the proposition that such a war is illegal in international law.' And the judges added a telling point never made by the prosecution: that though the Hague Convention of 1907 had not labelled as crimes any of the methods it denounced or established procedures for trying or punishing those who resorted to them – yet ever since, those methods had been universally regarded as criminal and punished as such.

The section of the judgement on Crimes against Peace occupies as much space as all the others put together; each area of aggression was treated in detail and with numerous quotations from evidence. The form, the emphases to be given, the illustrations which should be used had aroused much discussion and the whole thing had to be redrafted by the Americans from 17 July, then licked into final shape by Birkett in September. There had been niggling doubt for some time as to whether the annexations of Austria and Czechoslavakia fitted the general picture of aggression, since no fighting occurred. Finally both moves were defined as aggressive steps with stress placed on Nazi preparedness to use force if necessary, and on their overriding intention of bolstering German military and strategic positions. Predictably, the Russians had fought a rearguard action against even the slightest reference to the Nazi-Soviet Pact, let alone its Secret Protocol. But they could hardly have been displeased by the final statements that the Soviet Union had conformed to the Pact's terms and that it was impossible to believe that the view 'was ever honestly entertained' by the defendants that Russia was contemplating an attack on Germany. Similarly, British honour was upheld by Parker's draft of the section on Norway which admitted that the British had had plans to move in but which stressed that all German military plans had been concerned with gaining bases rather than pre-empting Britain, and that they had been put into effect without any certain knowledge of British intentions. Attention was drawn to the requirement of international law that a pre-emptive strike can only be justified by 'an instant and overwhelming necessity for self-defence, leaving no choice of means and no moment of deliberation' – conditions which did not exist when Norway was attacked.

Though the judgement on Count Two had taken time and trouble it had not stirred up real acrimony. The judges' discussions on whether to make declarations against the indicted organizations did. They postponed any discussion on the organizations until they had finished dealing with the four main counts. On 8 August the matter was mentioned briefly; on 3 September they addressed it head on. Then the full spectrum of disagreement revealed itself. At one extreme stood Biddle who had disliked the call for declarations when he first saw it in Bernays' draft and had not changed his mind since. 'A shocking thing, this group crime,' he observed on 3 September, and several years later he wrote in a letter: 'Personally I voted to throw out the charges against the criminal organizations.' (9) At the next discussion he told his colleagues that it was 'shocking' to convict men without trial – and that is what any declaration would amount to. At the opposite extreme stood Nikitchenko, insisting that the Tribunal was bound by the Charter to make a finding and that all questions of individuals' guilt should be left to subsequent proceedings.

In between hovered the other judges, uncertain and troubled. At first Lawrence was not prepared to come to any decision; by 13 September he felt that the problem which faced them was basically procedural. 'Gawd,' Biddle jotted in his notes. 'A British fake.' But Lawrence was not alone in voicing the view that declarations were desirable; that the procedural problem he referred to was one of finding limits to the harm to innocent individuals. The French certainly wanted to make declarations against the Gestapo, SS and the Leadership Corps, but saw no obligation, given the wording of the Charter, to make them against all the indicted organizations. What they felt most strongly was that the Tribunal should fix penalties to be imposed by subsequent courts to ensure uniformity of sentencing. Birkett and Parker shared the French view that they 'might', rather than 'must', issue declarations and were keen to do so in some cases. Birkett wanted to exclude the 'small fry' from each and to make a frank statement of all the difficulties in the judgement; Parker believed that a moral statement was of paramount importance and that the judgement must deal with all organizations, criminal or not, giving full grounds for the decisions reached.

On 3 September Parker had given his colleagues a discussion paper, setting out clearly the limitations for which they had all been groping for months past: insistence on proof that a cohesive organization had existed, that most members joined voluntarily with full knowledge of criminal aims and took part in criminal activities. He suggested further stringent requirements on 13 September: any declarations should be connected with War Crimes and Crimes against Humanity exclusively and membership should be regarded as criminal only from the outbreak of war. Parker's safeguards pleased nearly everyone. Even Biddle believed that they 'really took the sting out of guilt by association'. (10) They were incorporated into the final judgement, with the added recommendations that they be the criteria for judging individual members in future trials, and that the Allied Control Council amend its Law Number 10 so that penalties should conform to the more moderate punishments adopted in the De-Nazification Law in the American Zone and that these become uniform throughout the country.

Parker's safeguards had not pleased the Russians, though. They might have been prepared to swallow their failure to secure blanket condemnation of all members if they had persuaded their colleagues to make declarations against all the organizations. There was no hope of that. All were agreed on the criminality of the Gestapo, SS and the Leadership Corps. Only the Russians did not agree that office staff and peripheral sub-groups should be excluded and the two bottom ranks of the Leadership Corps exempted. But the Western judges decided the prosecution had failed to prove that the General Staff and High Command was an organization in any acceptable meaning of the term. And they believed that the case against the SA must be dismissed – the SA lacked cohesion, too many members were drafted and ignorant of criminal aims and acts, and though some of them might have been involved in what Birkett called 'reprehensible practices' after 1934, these did not constitute a high proportion. They were not satisfied either that the Reich Cabinet was a true organization; its eighteen members in the Nuremberg dock would be dealt with anyway; other survivors could easily be brought to trial as individuals if required.

The Russians could not and would not accept that these three indicted groups did not merit declarations of criminality. That was bad enough. But on 13 September, the day when the Russians became most intransigent on that issue, they had also clashed with the other judges over a verdict on a defendant. This was not the first time; nor were the Russians alone in disagreeing about verdicts. What was alarming was that the Russians now threatened public dissent from the final judgement. All the judges had hoped for unanimity; all feared that the publicity surrounding a dissent would destroy the effectiveness of their judgement. For a few days they struggled to restore a co-operative atmosphere. Then on 17 September they faced the unpleasant fact: they needed time to think, time to cool down, time even to polish those decisions that had been reached. The judgement must be postponed.

If the postponement was disappointing for the judges, it was a refinement of torture for the defendants. They had already waited for two weeks for the verdicts, now they faced a further delay, at least as long. Andrus was acutely worried by the strain on them of any waiting period, however brief. He received regular reports on his prisoners from his medical staff and psychiatrists. But before the final speeches he had felt the need for confirmation and a fresh eye. He asked a new psychiatrist, Dr Dunn, to interview each defendant several times and to report to him on present mental health and possible reaction to sentence. These reports should help Andrus to spot who needed help to combat the strain and, his greatest concern, who needed careful watching in case of a suicide attempt. (11)

Dunn's reports on most of the defendants were reassuring. Many of them had seemed delighted to have someone new to chat to – indeed with Schirach he felt his interview had never got further than 'a social occasion'. Speer had been the most relaxed of all – happy to talk about the mistakes and crimes of Hitler's government, less concerned than the others to rationalize his own behaviour. Dunn suspected he had used rationalization much more when actually involved with the Nazi regime than now after he had denounced it. In Dunn's opinion all the military prisoners were being sustained by their code and training. Doenitz had the additional support of complete certainty that he had done nothing but his patriotic and professional duty. Jodl was judged to be considerably disturbed about the evidence of atrocities but free of 'inner disgust' about his own activities, and had the strength to cope with any sentence, Dunn reckoned. Keitel, on the other hand showed 'some basic weaknesses of character' but was managing his present situation by invoking superior orders and personal ignorance of what was going on. There was just a slight possibility, Dunn thought, that Raeder might contemplate suicide, most probably if sentenced to be hanged rather than shot. He recorded the impression of several people that Raeder's recent requests to have an operation on his hernia concealed, even from himself, a hope of dying during it. Yet though Raeder was deeply distressed by his present plight, Dunn guessed he would face his sentence with military resolution.

Streicher seemed to be no problem; in Dunn's view, he was 'bolstered by his lack of sensitivity and imagination and by limitations in intelligence'. Papen was 'bolstered with the hope' that he would get off lightly, and Rosenberg seemed so busy 'clinging to his own theories in a fanatical and unyielding fashion' that he seemed incapable of thinking about anything else. Rationalization was helping others. Seyss-Inquart justified everything he had done as having been legislated for by others. Frank subjected Dunn at every interview to a lot of 'self-justification' about Hitler's personality and power over others 'to show how he had been swept along into actions against his better judgement'. Neurath's comfort, on the other hand, probably came from evasion. Dunn suspected he was as capable of evading his own past as he was of dodging all questions about it. He was summed up as 'not a serious suicidal risk', nor 'potentially psychotic in reaction to sentencing'.

Dunn was less confident about Schacht. He had found him 'at ease and relaxed' and been impressed by his 'air of affability and good humour'. Even so the constant expressions of confidence did not altogether conceal considerable strain and Dunn feared that a 'severe sentence will come as a great shock' and could throw Schacht 'into an agitated state'. Funk too would probably develop a severe depression, but stop short of suicide. As for Sauckel, it seemed unlikely that he could become any more depressed than he was at present. Fritzsche, already tense and constantly pacing his cell, could be expected to deteriorate or even attempt suicide if there was a chance of being handed over to the Russians. And Dunn was equally concerned about Frick's reactions – though he could not reach any firm conclusions, having found the man the 'least accessible of the defendants' and virtually silent. Very different from Ribbentrop, who seldom stopped talking. Dunn had found him 'haggard and distraught', surrounded by squalor of his own making, sitting at a desk littered with 'fragmentary and non-constructive notes'. He complained constantly of insomnia, inability to find words (though he found plenty in his interviews and was noticeably 'coherent and clear') and above all of chronic headaches. Even in such a low state Ribbentrop did not strike Dunn as a potential suicide. Indeed he believed that Ribbentrop was distracted from his true situation by mirages of escape. He was even positively cheerful at the moment because he believed that his headaches were a 'symptom of organic brain disease' and it would soon bring him merciful release.

There were two men whom Dunn did not consider depressives, but whom he did believe were strong suicide risks. Kaltenbrunner was the only defendant who acknowledged that he was certain he would hang. He was bitter about it; all his activities had been directed to 'fighting Bolshevism' he said, and he was absolved from guilt over the Jews because others had been responsible. 'A man of this type,' Dunn warned, 'may well attempt suicide to cheat those imposing the penalty.' Goering seemed similarly unburdened by anxiety or guilt, though for the moment less 'swaggering and swashbuckling' than usual. The chances were that he would 'face his sentence bolstered by his own egocentricity, bravado and showmanship'. But on the other hand, Dunn shrewdly predicted that these traits might well lead Goering to seize 'any opportunity to go out fighting'.

Andrus hardly needed Dunn's reports to tell him that the strain of waiting for the verdicts was considerable for his prisoners and that coming to terms with their sentences would prove difficult. It was his duty to help them through the next weeks – he certainly did not want another suicide like Ley's. He was also a humane man under all the spit and polish and school-mistressy fussiness. So Andrus approached the Tribunal and on 2 September got the judges' permission to relax prison conditions during the waiting period. (12) Immediately he introduced longer exercise periods and more opportunities to meet defence counsel. And he created something like a social life for the prisoners. Total solitary confinement was no longer imposed. Instead a room for 'parties' was opened up. Each defendant could go to as many as he wished and was allowed to issue invitations to three or four guests at a time. Even Streicher, Kaltenbrunner and Frick got the occasional invitation. Cards and games were provided in the room, but most prisoners, Fritzsche remembered, preferred to talk. They could only talk for an hour at a time – then the next party was queueing at the door waiting to take over the room. (13)

Pleasant though these meetings were they could in no way compare with the greatest of treats that Andrus had secured on 2 September. Wives and children were allowed to visit the prisoners. These were the first meetings of families since the defendants had been arrested, for Schacht the first chance to see his wife and two little daughters since imprisonment by the Nazis in July 1944. Frau Streicher had been in the Nuremberg jail throughout the trial, but held in the witness wing in case she was called to give testimony. Several other wives had visited the city and eagerly questioned the prison chaplains about their husbands. Two had actually penetrated the security system and gone into the Palace of Justice. Frau Frick used a false name and got as far as the courtroom itself. When she glimpsed her husband she broke down and was escorted out. Frau Goering, star of stage and Nazi society, had swept into the Palace swathed in furs and confidence and was well into the building before she was spotted. As she was led back to the door an admiring defence lawyer muttered 'you always were a good actress, Emmy.' (14) But the wives who could even stand outside and gaze at the courtroom and jail were fortunate. Most could not get passports to leave their Zones, there was little or no transport for those even in the American sector and no one could be sure of food once they left home: ration books were not transferable.

Now, on the Tribunal's orders, the occupation authorities provided permits and travel facilities and the Americans laid on good food, off the ration, in the court staff canteen in the Palace of Justice. The families met in the Defendants' Visitors' Centre under the sympathetic eye of Emma Schwabenland, sitting in the booths where the prisoners had so often met their lawyers and taking turns to get the quiet ones. The grille prevented them kissing or even touching but they could look and talk. Frau Goering would say to Miss Schwabenland after every visit, 'Do you think the court will send my husband to an island like Elba? Maybe I can join him.' (15) She had obviously cast herself in the Greta Garbo role as Marie Walewska. Keitel refused to see his wife. He told Gilbert that he felt his disgrace too keenly and 'just couldn't face her'. (16) Raeder did not meet his wife either. He longed to – he knew she was living somewhere near Berlin in the Russian Zone, but no messages seemed to reach her and he never received letters. The Tribunal approached the Control Council who eventually got Russian agreement for Frau Raeder to travel. Twice the Russians announced that they were sending her, twice Pastor Gerecke went to the airport to meet her. But she did not arrive. (17)

The relaxed prison regime, the family visits, could only be intermittent palliatives to the weeks of waiting. The atmosphere in the jail of tense depression increased noticeably. Gilbert recorded that Goering grew 'more nervous and found it harder and harder to laugh'. Some prisoners paced their cells, others lay on their beds and stared at the ceiling. Raeder told Gilbert that he expected a death sentence and preferred that to life imprisonment. (18) Reuter reported that Streicher and Funk both preferred the prospect of death – Streicher to the incessant noise of the prison at night, Funk to the 'life of torment and shame . . . accusations and slanders' he was enduring at present. Neurath did not want death, but expected it: 'I will get off with a prison sentence, but the Czechs will want to judge me in their turn and they are under the influence of the Soviets. Moscow will want my head.' Hess was much more optimistic: 'From the astrological dates I think a miracle or something will happen.' (19) Ribbentrop hoped for a miracle as well. He suggested that Gilbert should make 'a great historical gesture on behalf of the defendants and appeal for clemency', then he could write a book or even several volumes on the mistakes of the Nazi regime. (20) Schirach's wife made a personal bid for clemency. She wrote to Biddle: 'Our children love America. It is their grandparents' country. They have a merry imagination of the ice cream and Walt Disney movies. The flags, language and history are as familiar to them as their own. Do I have to tell my children now "This America let your father die the most disgraceful death a man can find?"' (21)

The letter appeared in the newspapers on 21 September. By then the Tribunal had in fact reached its verdict on Schirach, but not on every defendant, nor on the details of the final judgement as a whole. In spite of the recess since 17 September, despite second thoughts and the search for compromise the judges had not reached agreement. To the Russian threat of public dissent over the organizations was now added the threat of a dissenting verdict on some defendants.

The judges had delayed their deliberations on individual cases until they had dealt with the legal framework. They began to talk about the defendants on 2 September and held at least eight meetings before reaching final conclusions. All eight judges were allowed to put forward their views, but the final vote was restricted to the four senior members. Contrary to Nikitchenko's wishes they decided on 9 September that a split vote – 2:2 – would not secure a conviction. Indeed they were never entirely satisfied with counting votes; there was always a struggle for agreement, with much compromise and bargaining to try to get unanimity. No case was settled in one meeting; many required several. The judges began by working their way through the defendants in order of indictment. It then seemed easier to defer decision over those with whom there was difficulty and settle the more straightforward cases first. (22)

Goering's case was perhaps the most straightforward of all. At the first vote on 2 September all eight judges found him guilty, though Donnedieu de Vabres initially maintained his distaste for the conspiracy charge and considered Goering merited convicting only on the remaining three counts. Even with that reservation, though, he backed his colleagues' decision to sentence Goering to death. On 10th September Donnedieu de Vabres even approved conviction on the conspiracy charge. Ribbentrop's case went through the same procedure, Donnedieu de Vabres voting against conspiracy on 2 September, then swinging round on the 10th. He was less legally fastidious over Keitel. At both votes the two French judges agreed Keitel was guilty on all four counts. Whatever the stereotype of the Gallic mind, the French judges were not logical. Nor, perhaps, always wide awake. On 2 September, Falco voted with the Russians to find Frank guilty on four counts, in spite of the fact that he had not been charged with Crimes against Peace. A week later he had spotted his mistake – but Nikitchenko preferred to see it rather as a mistake in the indictment and continued to find Frank guilty of waging aggressive war. Everyone else, by now, had decided to drop the conspiracy charge against him.

The judges' verdict on Streicher was reached without much difficulty, though there was some debate over which counts he should be convicted on. Biddle argued indignantly that it was 'preposterous' to call Streicher a conspirator just because he was 'a little Jew-baiter' and a temporary friend of Hitler. Lawrence accused Biddle of bad manners and Parker had to soothe everyone down. What the judges failed to debate, however, was the fundamental question of whether Streicher's words could be linked directly with others' deeds. This issue worried one of the American aides. He remembered finding the case troublesome – Streicher might be a beastly man, but he had never actually killed anyone himself. (23) This issue has bothered others since. There is a suspicion that Streicher was not judged strictly on the law but on the physical and moral revulsion he evoked. He was turned into the embodiment of Nazism. Not everyone felt these qualms at the time. Maxwell-Fyfe at a British prosecutors' meeting in June had expressed the opinion that Streicher should be hanged as an accessory before the fact and as a murderer under Count Four. (24) Another American aide took the view that Streicher could not escape responsibility for the death of six million Jews even if the exact nature of his responsibility could not be pinned down. At the very least he had been 'an aider and abetter' and could be compared (perhaps only by Americans) to the cheerleader who 'by his continual goading of the crowd to frenzied excitement ... is a key personality in his team's success'. (25) The judges must have shared his view. They never doubted that Streicher must be sentenced to death.

They were equally certain about some other death sentences – but took longer to decide on what grounds they should be imposed. When first discussing Kaltenbrunner, Lawrence and Parker had been inclined to agree with Birkett and the Russians that he was guilty of conspiracy as well as the War Crimes and Crimes against Humanity with which he was charged. By the time the four senior judges voted on 10 September, Lawrence and the Russians still wanted to convict on Count One (Nikitchenko on Count Two as well, even though Kaltenbrunner was not charged under it), but they finally gave way to Donnedieu de Vabres and Biddle and voted out conspiracy. In the Sauckel case only the Russians ever voted for Count One; Lawrence would have convicted on Count Two. But the final verdict stated that Sauckel was guilty of War Crimes and Crimes against Humanity only. These were more than enough to get Sauckel sentenced to death. An

American aide had suggested that his claims to have borne no responsibility for policy decisions had to be weighed against his 'complete ruthlessness and unfeeling efficiency in the application of a programme which involved sending at least five million people into slave labour and the death of a considerable proportion of this number'. (26) The judges went further: their verdict dismissed the claim of having played no part in policy. Over Bormann only the Russians held out for conviction on conspiracy, but it took three meetings before everyone could decide how to express their verdict. Should they sentence him to death, say he was dead already or accept Biddle's view that there was no point in sentencing a dead man? They eventually left the case open to review. They found Bormann guilty on Counts Three and Four, stated that evidence of his death was 'not conclusive', sentenced him to death, but since he had been tried *in absentia* recommended that if found, the Control Council 'might consider any facts in mitigation and alter or reduce his sentence if deemed proper'.

The only real debate over Jodl centred on the question of whether he should be hanged or shot. On 10 September both French judges toyed with the idea that he was less culpable than Keitel and might merit an 'honourable' term of years (unspecified). They soon switched their desire for an 'honourable' sentence to the suggestion that Jodl be shot – and won Biddle's support briefly. This was not the only occasion on which the French recommended a soldier's death. They had taken the same line over Goering whom Donnedieu de Vabres had somewhat admiringly called 'a high class brigand' with a certain 'nobility'. Even Keitel, they thought, might be spared the indignity of the noose. The appropriateness of sentences had already been considered by Lawrence. In July he had made extremely discreet enquiries through his assistant, John Phipps, about what methods of execution were being ordered in other war crimes trials. These had been forwarded to the Foreign Office, emphasizing that their source must be kept secret and files of details were sent back to Nuremberg. (27) At the same time Sir Hartley Shawcross felt obliged to examine the suggestion that perhaps the Tribunal had no authority to impose death sentences at all. Once it was discovered that Article One of the Control Council Law had made the London Agreement part of the law of Germany, his mind was put at rest: 'It is good to know that whatever terrors may beset my path, they do not include an indictment for murdering the major war criminals.' (28)

Some judges were momentarily uncertain about sentencing to death Rosenberg, Frick and Seyss-Inquart. Lawrence at first suggested a life sentence for Rosenberg; Parker and the French were won over – but Lawrence then changed his mind in favour of execution. Biddle took time to be persuaded to convict on the first two counts – he finally fell into line with the others. In the judgement only brief mention was made of Rosenberg's contribution to Nazi ideology and it was not stated to be criminal. Instead all the emphasis was on his work with Quisling in Norway and especially his crimes in the Occupied Eastern Territories. The Frick case illustrated the differences in the judges' national expectations. Lawrence, like any British judge, saw his refusal to go into the witness box as a point against him; the Americans regarded his refusal as a right akin to that under the Fifth Amendment. That apart, there was virtual unanimity that Frick deserved death. Only Parker voted for a life sentence, on the grounds that the man was merely 'a bureaucrat'. There was less accord over the grounds on which he should be sentenced. Biddle joined Donnedieu de Vabres in refusing to convict on the conspiracy charge and the judges argued until 26 September before reaching a decision to convict on Counts Two, Three and Four. The judgement described Frick as 'rabidly anti-Semitic' and an 'avid Nazi' who had put through legislation against trade unions, the Church and the Jews with 'ruthless efficiency'. It condemned, too, his knowledge of killing of 'useless eaters' and made reference to a Czech report estimating that 275,000 mentally deficient and aged people had been victims of the programme. Seyss-Inquart's verdict and sentence were only settled on 26 September, too, the French having held out for three meetings in favour of a life sentence and been supported by Biddle in their rejection of the conspiracy charge. Seyss-Inquart was finally convicted on the latter three counts, and his involvement in harsh occupation policies and the forced labour programme, as well as his knowledge of the fate of deported Jews, were seen to merit the death sentence.

Yet four other defendants escaped death, though their careers and positions afforded notable parallels with those who hanged. Schirach's case, for instance, had much in common with that of Seyss-Inquart. As Gauleiter in Vienna, he had deported Jews to the East in spite of receiving regular reports on the work of Einsatzgruppen there. He also knew of the transportation of children to Germany for forced apprenticeship in industry. Co-operation in such policies had helped to get Seyss-Inquart sentenced to hang. Furthermore, it could be argued that Schirach's work with the Hitler Youth which had indoctrinated a vital sector of German society and incited it to intolerance and aggression was comparable with that of Streicher. But the judges do not seem to have made this comparison. In this case they seemed to sense that ideological preparation for aggression, even some premilitary training, had not been proved conclusively to be criminal. Their verdict was based more on Schirach's work as Gauleiter – Lawrence and the Russians for a time believing that he should be sentenced to death but gradually being won over by those who were prepared to convict on Count Four only and insisted that twenty years in prison were adequate punishment.

Neurath too was assessed more on his record as an administrator of incorporated territory than on his overall career. Though, as the judgement was to point out, he had been present at the Hossbach conference and had kept a formal ministerial title and even resumed office as Foreign Minister during the Anschluss, the stress was on his policies as Protector of Bohemia and Moravia. Neurath was fortunate that his regime did not stand comparison with the brutality of Seyss-Inquart, let alone Rosenberg or Frank.

He was found guilty on all four counts but received only fifteen years in prison. Funk got off less lightly. Falco, the Russians and Lawrence at first wanted him to hang; Biddle was inclined to agree with them. But after two further discussions, they all decided to accept the plea of being a mere executor of others' policies (which they had rejected in Sauckel's case) and did not condemn Funk's failure to resign, though they did so in several other judgements. In spite of Funk's knowledge of the SS gold deposits in the Reichsbank and his membership of the Central Planning Board, which had made him aware of the use of slave labour, he was to be described in the judgement as 'never a dominant figure in the various programmes in which he participated'. He was found guilty of all charges except conspiracy, and sentenced to life imprisonment.

The most striking example of what might be seen as an illogical decision was in the case of Albert Speer. The American judges' aides argued forcibly that Speer had demanded slave labour for Germany industry and had been fully aware of the squalid and brutal conditions in which it had been employed. Sauckel was to hang for securing those slaves, why not Speer who ordered and allocated them? Speer had the intelligence to know what he was doing, much more intelligence than many other defendants. The American staff had been far from impressed by Speer's denunciation of Hitler and saw it as a calculated attempt to win the Tribunal's sympathy. (29) Yet Speer seemed always to have had that sympathy (and denunciations did not appear to affect their judgement – Schirach's was never discussed). Biddle, in his memoirs, described Speer as 'the most humane and decent of the defendants' and commented that his 'straightforwardness, honesty, his calm and reasonable bearing, his awareness of the normal issues involved' had impressed the Tribunal. (30) These were all qualities that Streicher, for instance, noticeably lacked. But at the first vote on the Speer case Biddle joined the Russians in calling for the death sentence. Was this to show willing to his aides who had not only written memos on the subject but nagged ceaselessly at home in the American judges' house? Biddle's desire for Speer's death was hardly enduring: next day he dropped, as if in an air pocket, from calling for hanging to accepting imprisonment for twenty years – the most abrupt change in all the voting.

The French thought twenty years was an adequate sentence for Hess. No one else agreed. As ever, the Russians wanted a hanging – in this case they added to their general principle the national prejudice that Hess's flight to Scotland had been an attempt to win Germany a free hand against Russia. They also argued that Hess's signature on the Nuremberg Decrees made him guilty of the deaths of millions of Jews; that his signature of the documents incorporating conquered territories and his establishment of compulsory military service made him at least as culpable as Frick; that his uniquely close relationship with Hitler and vigorous public support for all his policies put him in the same category as Goering; his detailed knowledge of all aggressive planning put him in the same category as many of the defendants who were to hang. These arguments convinced the other judges that Hess deserved a heavy sentence. But they had also to put in the balance the fact that Hess left Germany in 1941; only after that date did the worst of atrocities occur. In a three to one vote against the Russians they found Hess guilty on Counts One and Two only; after a three to one vote against the French, he was sentenced to life imprisonment.

That was to be the sentence on Raeder too. The judges were unanimous that he was guilty on the first three counts, those with which he had been charged. The Russians, inevitably, demanded the death sentence. So did Biddle the first time the case was discussed on 9 September, but he came round to the idea of life imprisonment by the second vote and so still tipped the balance against the French who had advocated twenty years. The final judgement drew attention to Raeder's knowledge of aggressive plans (indeed his own initiative in suggesting an attack on Norway) and his contribution to implementing many of them. Mention was made of his distribution of the Commando Order, which resulted in the executions by the Navy of two uniformed British prisoners at Bordeaux in 1942 (two of the 'Cockleshell Heroes'). The findings in the charges relating to unrestricted submarine warfare were identical to those for Doenitz – the defendant whose conviction took more time than any other, four lengthy discussions.

Though Doenitz had been charged on the first three counts, it was decided he had played little part in planning or waging aggressive war – his position had been too junior, he took command when the war might almost be seen to be defensive. No one else took the line of the French – that his measure against Danish saboteurs and his demand for concentration camp labour were grave matters. Indeed these charges had not been pressed by the prosecution. By the second meeting all were concentrating on the legal problem of submarine warfare, and they were finding major differences of opinion.

Biddle argued that Doenitz should be acquitted on all the related charges: submarine warfare would have been impossible, he argued, if warning had to be given before every attack and if all survivors had to be saved; the British had armed their merchantmen, so depriving them of immunity and being first to break the rules; Admiral Nimitz had 'admitted that the United States used identical methods to Doenitz'. Biddle went so far as to assert that 'Germany waged a much cleaner war that we did.' Parker, by contrast, used to pace the Pegnitz meadows between meetings and tell his aide, Fisher: 'Cap'n, the worst thing that ever happened this century was unrestricted submarine warfare.' (31) To the other judges he argued that the Treaty of London had established binding rules for the conduct of submarine warfare; Germany's breaking of its regulations had encouraged others to follow suit, Doenitz's orders had resulted in the sinking of vessels, armed or not. Lawrence took a similar view of the Treaty, but like the French was prepared to see the Laconia Order as ambiguous and give Doenitz the benefit of the doubt over it.

The British judges did not come round to Biddle's opinion that the Nimitz affidavit made it impossible to convict Doenitz. In their eyes Nimitz had merely shown that both sides broke the law – that could not clear Doenitz of guilt. However cleverly Kranzbuehler had argued, he had presented no more than a sophisticated *tu quoque* case. Yet at the time, many people assumed that the British judges were influenced by the experience of having lived through isolation, hunger and deaths caused by Doenitz's submarines. There was also the suspicion that the British alone pressed for a heavy sentence for Doenitz. This is not confirmed by the record of the voting. Birkett and Parker both pressed for up to twenty years' imprisonment; Birkett then dropped his demand in favour of the decision of Lawrence, Nikitchenko and the French who had always argued for ten years.

Only Biddle had ever wanted to acquit Doenitz. Yet, by a most odd decision of the Tribunal, he was allowed to write the final judgement on the case. Conceivably they were so upset by his hint that he might write a dissenting opinion that they thought it safer to allow him to express some of his views. (32) But the result was to be the most peculiarly argued section in the judgement and a source of constant puzzlement ever since; it never makes clear on what Doenitz was convicted. The judgement stated that the Tribunal was not 'prepared to hold Doenitz guilty for his conduct of submarine warfare against British armed ships'. It then named as violations of the London Protocol of 1936 both the sinking of neutrals without warning in operational zones and the sinking of merchant vessels when it was known that rescue was impossible – specifically contradicting the defence argument that the safety of the submarine must always be paramount. Yet having made these points, having added that the Laconia Order and others were undoubtedly ambiguous and deserve the 'strongest censure', it immediately drew the conclusion that in view of the 1940 British Admiralty order to sink all vessels at night in the Skagerrak, and in the light of the Nimitz answers, 'the sentence of Doenitz is not assessed on the grounds of his breaches of the international law of submarine warfare.' On what then was it assessed? No wonder no one could understand Doenitz's sentence. It would have been much clearer if one of the other seven judges who actually thought Doenitz guilty of breaches of naval law had framed the judgement.

In spite of frequent disagreements over nearly all verdicts and sentences so far, the judges had compromised to find decisions they were prepared to accept, however reluctantly. Even the Russians had shown flexibility: they might start with votes for conviction on all charges and calls for death sentences, but once that ritual was performed they seemed to bow to the democratic process. Indeed they had been more lenient than colleagues on some occasions: Nikitchenko's vote for a ten year sentence for Doenitz was lower than Parker or Birkett had wanted. Even more surprisingly he had voted for a life sentence for Hess – perhaps to out-manoeuvre the French who were pressing for twenty years' imprisonment. But though the

Russians might bend, there came a point where they would break: they would not tolerate acquittals.

Once the judges had hacked away so much from the conspiracy charge, acquittals were always likely – as the judges had realized on 15 August, Fritzsche, Papen, Schacht, even Streicher were defendants whose convictions might well depend on proof of involvement in a broad conspiracy. When Fritzsche's case was examined on 10 September, the charges under Count One were virtually ignored; those under Counts Three and Four were not seen as grave. Donnedieu de Vabres called Fritzsche 'the least guilty of all' the defendants; Parker stressed his minor position, defined him as a 'vicarious sacrifice' for Goebbels, and said Hitler would not have spent five minutes with him; Lawrence thought there might be a slight case – it was improbable that Fritzsche was totally unaware of what was going on. There was most debate about the criminality of propaganda: the French thought it should be condemned since it had encouraged support for the war; so did the Russians who added it had incited racial hatred and contributed to the death of millions. The two American judges, however, were adamant that Fritzsche had not incited to crime. (One of the memoranda from a legal aide went so far as to say that his speeches were 'no stronger than statements of American war correspondents in Washington during the war'.) (33) Parker became eloquent on the right to free speech and was warmly supported by Biddle who commented in his notes that Donnedieu de Vabres seemed shaken by their argument. Even the judges who did not accept the American view still did not believe that Fritzsche's work had earned him a heavy sentence. By 11 September Falco was suggesting between two and eleven years, with the year already spent in prison deducted; even the Russians thought ten years quite enough. Donnedieu de Vabres was unsure however. He voted for acquittal, but the next day told Biddle he had changed his mind yet again, then asked the other judges to postpone any decisions on the case until they reached a verdict on Papen – if Papen were acquitted then, in Donnedieu's opinion, Fritzsche must be acquitted too.

There was a distinct possibility he would be. Nikitchenko had argued that Papen's knowledge of rearmament and aggressive intentions should convict him and pointed out his failure to resign from public affairs. But on 6 September the British, Americans and French all reckoned that Papen could not be convicted on the Tribunal's definition of conspiracy. For a time the French thought that his part in the Anschluss deserved punishment; Donnedieu de Vabres called him 'a corrupting creature' and thought it the Tribunal's duty to 'put morals into international law'. But for the British and Americans, the Anschluss did not fit their concept of aggression, and though Lawrence expressed 'dislike' of Papen, he too voted for acquittal, recommending the same for Fritzsche. So there was a tied vote on Papen; and a decision on Fritzsche which would depend on which way the French jumped. The Russians put them under pressure. On 12 September Nikitchenko threatened dissent over these two cases; not public – that, he said, was not Soviet practice – but a private communication to the Control Council which could be considered in any appeal. His attitude opened up a new split between the judges: Biddle and Parker insisted that Nikitchenko had every right, indeed a duty, to express his opinion openly; Donnedieu de Vabres was horrified by the idea of any dissent and the risk that the final judgement would be robbed of its authority.

Into this simmering pot of trouble the Schacht case was now thrown. It had caused enough difficulty already. After discussion at three meetings the judges had failed to reach a decision. At first only Parker had been in favour of acquitting Schacht. He accepted the man's account of his opposition to war and attempts to block Hitler's plans and stressed Schacht's absence from the Hossbach conference and involvement in plots against Hitler. Lawrence tended to think that Schacht's eyes had been opened by 1937 and that he had never been a 'ruffian' like so many defendants. Birkett was rather less convinced by Schacht's defence but eventually concluded that he should be acquitted, the only alternative being the implausible one of naming him the chief architect of the war and imposing a stiff sentence. Everyone else was in favour of conviction; the Russians wanted to include conspiracy, the others maintained charges on rearmament and knowledge of aggression. Yet they came to very different conclusions about what sentence should be given. By 12 September the French thought five years' imprisonment adequate. But Biddle suggested prison for life. This seems to have been a tactical manoeuvre rather than a genuine assessment of the case. Biddle records in his notes that during a recess which followed this vote, Nikitchenko asked him how far down they might have to go to bring the French up to a stiffer sentence. Biddle recommended voting for a severe sentence, then waiting to see. After the recess Nikitchenko duly called for life imprisonment while Biddle hinted that something lighter might be acceptable – and actually got support from Volchkov who thought Schacht's age should be taken into account. So by this stage, three judges had voted for a heavy sentence – Biddle and the Russians – three for acquittal – Parker and the British – while the two French judges were bobbing about at the lower end of the scale. For some time the meeting continued to push the sentence up and down, then it was agreed to postpone a decision until next day. At the next meeting, had the French persisted they might well have achieved a compromise over Schacht's sentence – at perhaps ten or fifteen years. But on 13 September, Donnedieu de Vabres suddenly announced that Schacht's case must be seen as identical with those of Papen and Fritzsche: all had borne limited responsibility, all must be acquitted. Parker congratulated him heartily on having the courage to change his mind and said he was proud to be associated with such a man. At which point, as if there had not been drama enough, Biddle too made an even more extraordinary announcement: he had decided 'after long consideration' that Schacht's 'fault was only serious imprudence' and that he could not bear to impose a sentence on an old man.

The Russians had reached breaking point. There had been a series of sentences they thought too light, now three acquittals – and on top of all, at this very same meeting on 13 September, there had been yet another row about the organizations' case. It was Nikitchenko's turn to make an announcement: he would probably dissent from the final judgement, do so publicly, and openly criticize the way decisions had been reached. (One wonders whether he would have mentioned his own tactical vote on Schacht.) Biddle and Birkett were deeply shocked at the idea that private discussions would be made public. Nikitchenko did not repeat his determination to denounce the voting process, but stuck to his intention to dissent. Under that threat the judges postponed their final judgement on 17 September. Perhaps during the interval before they met again on 26 September the wounds might heal, perhaps finishing touches to the judgement might reconcile the Russians. They were hoping against hope.

Not the slightest hint of any disagreement had reached the outside world. Since early August all the judges' deliberations had been conducted in total secrecy. Before that everything had been more casual, possibly too much so. A memorandum to the American judges from Jim Rowe, one of their aides, on 19 July, had complained that 'unauthorized persons' had read some of the briefs prepared for the judges by their staff and that details of their 17 July meeting on aggressive war were being bandied about – though no one would admit how they had been acquired. He also expressed horror that two memoranda on specific defendants had been shown to him by persons with no right to have them. He finally exploded: 'If you are interested in what the decision is going to be, I suggest you drop in at the Grand Hotel any evening and sit around the lobby. Any other comments I have – and I assure you there are plenty – are completely unprintable.' (34)

From 8 August all outsiders, with the exception of the Russian interpreter, were excluded from Tribunal meetings; all cupboards were kept locked, wastepaper baskets checked. Early drafts of the judgement had been typed and translated by up to fourteen people – given random pages in an attempt to conceal the judges' decisions – but the final judgement was typed by three girls only. Their names and English addresses were published by one newspaper but that was all that had leaked out. (35) In the absence of hard information people began to guess at sentences and verdicts. There was heavy betting in the Press Room of the Palace of Justice, and in late September an American lawyer at the Japanese war crimes trials predicted acquittals for Schacht, Papen and Neurath and prophesied lenient treatment for Jodl, Keitel, Doenitz, Raeder and Hess. (36) So secure had the judges' meetings been that on 30 September *The Times* came out with the front page headline 'Nuremberg Judgement Today. Expected Unanimity of Tribunal'. The article that followed paid tribute to the judgement as 'an outstanding example of international solidarity'. (37)

But on the evening of 29 September, no doubt as *The Times* was setting up its front page, Nikitchenko had finally shattered any remnant of hope for a unanimous judgement. He confessed to Biddle that he had consulted

465

Moscow about his problems and received orders to dissent – to object to the acquittals, state that Hess should have been hanged and insist that declarations for criminality should have been made against the Reich Cabinet and the General Staff and High Command. Biddle sent him to inform Lawrence. (38) The judgement had been announced for 30 September, there was no point in postponing it yet again and at such short notice. The Russian dissent was not even written yet – it would have to be referred to, then printed in full at a later date.

So on 30 September, with the tightest security yet seen around Nuremberg, 1,000 extra guards around the Palace of Justice, where every room had been searched during the night, and with snipers at strategic points, a distinguished audience and the world's Press assembled to hear the final judgement in a trial which had begun more than ten months before. The atmosphere in the courtroom was of special solemnity and rapt attention; there was none of the first night theatrical excitement which had marked the opening of the trial. It came more as a surprise than an anti-climax that the tone of the day was to be factual, dispassionate and business-like, set by the style in which the judgement was written and the quiet, objective way in which it was read.

The judges read in turns. Lawrence opened the proceedings, was followed by Birkett, then the French, the Americans and the Russians; Sir Geoffrey then resumed for the last pages. The arrangement stressed the international nature of the proceedings which had hitherto struck many people as dominated by the Americans and British. After the deliberate symbolism of co-operation presented by the joint reading, it came as a particular shock next day when the very last words of the whole trial were to announce the Russian dissent.

The judgement opened with a resume of the London Agreement, the indictment and the number of sessions held, witnesses heard and affidavits presented. Back in February, Birkett had spoken of the need to say 'a few pregnant words about the nature of the evidence in order to remove now and hereafter any suggestion that the Tribunal acted on evidence that was not worth the name'. (39) Now the section he had written noted that the case against the defendants had rested 'in a large measure on documents of their own making, the authenticity of which has not been challenged except in one or two cases'. The judgement then detailed the Counts of the Charter, explaining that they were binding on the Tribunal as the law to be applied to the case. It moved to a twelve page account, which Birkett had insisted was necessary, of the Nazi seizure and consolidation of power and their measures of rearmament to establish the context against which crimes had been committed. Each count was then examined, starting with the conspiracy charge and aggression which were considered together. Papen had reckoned, as had many others, that if the judges accepted the prosecution's broad concept of conspiracy then all the defendants would hang. He recorded in his memoirs the growing anxiety in the dock as forty

466

pages of details of each stage of aggression were read, lists of broken treaties given and the Tribunal's exposition of the state of international law was delivered, before finally the defendants heard the judges had decided to date the conspiracy from 1937. They sagged in relief. (40)

The judgement had by now made clear the Tribunal's belief that the Charter was the result of an 'exercise of sovereign legislative power by the countries to which the German Reich had unconditionally surrendered'. It was not 'an arbitrary exercise of power on the part of the victorious nations, but . . . the expression of international law existing at the time of its creation; and to that extent is itself a contribution to international law'. The Tribunal insisted that the only separate crime defined as a conspiracy by the Charter was that of committing acts of aggressive war: so the prosecution case which had developed conspiracy to cover War Crimes and Crimes against Humanity was dismissed. With conspiracy thus further limited, some of the defendants could well have felt more relief. In dealing with the last two counts the judgement spoke of the impossibility of adequately summarizing evidence which had been so overwhelming in volume and detail of crimes committed 'on a scale never before seen in the history of war'. But copious quotation was given from official orders and statements as illustration: the mistreatment of prisoners-of-war and civilians, the pillage of public and private property, the slave labour policy. The section closed with an account of the persecution of the Jews and the 'record of consistent and systematic inhumanity on the greatest scale'. The Tribunal had chosen to limit its findings here, however. The judges did not accept that pre-war persecutions and murders, 'revolting and horrible' though they had been, had been proved to be connected with all other crimes as the prosecution had alleged. Only acts committed after 1939 were to be seen as War Crimes and Crimes against Humanity. Another aspect of the prosecution case had been rejected. The judgement and the day finished with the Tribunal's findings on the organizations.

One reporter recorded that during the day the defendants had sat 'as do people who hear bad news, huddled close' and talking in undertones. (41) Several found them shrunken and faded; and there had been none of the bravado, the attempt at casualness, joking and chatter which had so often marked their courtroom behaviour. Hess, as ever, attracted the attention. Rebecca West wrote of him passing his hand constantly across his forehead as if brushing away a cobweb, rocking backwards and forwards in his seat like a pendulum. (42) In mid-afternoon, he left the dock for a while, then returned with a blanket and a book. (43) Observers noticed surprise from Goering when the SA was acquitted, but there was no visible reaction from the officers in the dock to the decision on the General Staff and High Command, even though it contained the harshest language in the entire judgement. German officers were described as responsible 'in large measure for the miseries and suffering' of millions. They were called 'a disgrace to the honourable profession of arms' and men who had 'made a mockery of the soldier's oath of obedience' to military orders, interpreting it as they chose, using it when it suited. Though the Tribunal had not seen fit to make a declaration of criminality against the General Staff and High Command, it did call for the trial and judgement of those officers guilty of 'crimes on a scale larger and more shocking than the world had ever had the misfortune to know'. The officers in the dock listened impassively; 'their puffy, bluish tint,' thought one journalist, 'might lead one to suppose that they were sculptured from slate.' (44) The Tribunal's harsh language led another journalist to predict heavy sentences for the military defendants. (45)

For the spectators in the court, this first stage of the judgement was a rather muted affair. Any drama they might have expected had been dampened by the tone the judges had chosen. The text itself was too long, too legally technical, too subtly nuanced to be immediately grasped, and with the exception of obvious points such as the acquittal of three organizations it had gone over the heads of most laymen. As yet few people spotted the implications of the limits to the conspiracy charge and the repercussions they would have on the verdicts for individual defendants. Even lawyers would need time to study the text before deciding whether they found the judges' conclusions adequate solutions to all the legal problems.

But the business of the next day could be understood by anyone. On Tuesday 1 October, the Tribunal was to announce the verdicts and sentences on the defendants. It was an anguishingly long process. In the morning, the four senior judges read the Tribunal's verdict on each individual in the order of indictment – a brief paragraph on his career, longer sections dealing with the counts on which he was charged, an assessment of the relevant evidence, and finally a brief conclusion stating the verdict on each count. Only after the lunchtime recess would the sentences be delivered. That morning the defendants sat together in the dock for the last time. In the afternoon they would have to face sentence alone.

The court was silent, absolutely still as Lawrence began to read the verdicts. Goering sat head bowed, earphone held to his right ear. 'His guilt is unique in its enormity. The record discloses no excuse for this man ... guilty on all four Counts ...' No expression crossed his face. He lowered the earphones, leaving his hair dishevelled, then nudged Hess who was scribbling continuously, and lent over to tell him it was his turn. (46) Hess took no notice; he continued to write. 'There is no suggestion that Hess was not completely sane when the acts charged against him were committed ... guilty ...' No reaction from Hess. Goering whispered the verdict; Hess nodded absentmindedly. (47) Verdicts were then passed on the defendants sitting along the first row, Nikitchenko taking over from Lawrence to be followed by Biddle then Donnedieu de Vabres. 'Guilty' five more times. Then Frick – he sat up with a jerk at the sound of his name: 'guilty'. Streicher – he lounged back against his seat but for a moment stopped his incessant ruminant chewing: 'guilty'. Funk: 'guilty'. Suddenly Schacht: 'not guilty on this indictment ... shall be discharged by the

Marshal when the Tribunal presently adjourns'. Everyone stared. 'The lines of his drooping mouth emphasized by a downward turning moustache reacted not at all. Immobile he simply gazed solemnly at the judges.' (48) Speer leant forward to congratulate him. Papen felt there was now hope for himself. 'I tried to keep my face expressionless but it was an effort for me to do so.' (49)

Next the verdicts on the defendants in the second row, starting with Doenitz. 'Guilty' five more times. Then Papen: acquitted. Several neighbours turned to congratulate him; he shook hands with those he could reach but could not speak. Only later did he hear that the Press had been given an hour's advance notice of verdicts – someone had already rung his daughters with the news. (50) On down the row; all guilty until the last in the far corner, Fritzsche. As he had come into the courtroom that morning first an electrician then a prosecutor, had mouthed 'Freispruch'. Fritzsche could not believe it – if he was indicted as Goebbels' substitute, he assumed he would be punished as such. He was so tense by the time his turn came that he missed most of the comments on his case. But he heard the verdict and saw his counsel leap up and wave excitedly. (51) The Tribunal then adjourned, the judges left the court and Fritzsche rose with the other defendants, but 'collapsed back on to his seat for several minutes as if without strength to stand'. (52)

It had been a long morning session without a mid-morning break; it finished at 1.45 p.m. with an announcement that the defendants might apply within the next four days to the Control Council for clemency. The session had created a sudden, bewildering change in the prisoners' routine. Three of them, the acquitted, were not to eat with the others in their usual rooms; they were taken to separate accommodation, then back to prison. After 218 days they did not have to attend the afternoon session. As they packed their belongings in their cells, Gilbert talked to them. Fritzsche felt dizzy: 'I am entirely overwhelmed,' he whispered, 'to be set free . . . and not even sent back to Russia.' Papen was elated: 'I had hoped for it but did not really expect it,' he said – then took out of his pocket an orange he had saved from lunch and asked Gilbert to give it to Neurath. Fritzsche gave his own to Schirach. Schacht, who accepted his acquittal as his due, ate his orange. (53)

Then most bewildering of all for men who had been prisoners for so long, often locked alone in their cells, Schacht, Papen and Fritzsche were brought that afternoon to a Press conference. Bob Cooper of *The Times*, for one, found it a 'nauseating' occasion. (54) Journalists milled around, offering drinks, cigarettes, sweets. Questions were fired: 'immediate plans?' Papen wanted to rejoin his wife and children as soon as possible, then disappear; Schacht intended never to see anyone from the Press again; Fritzsche said 'The problem of freedom is quite new for me; I can't say yet what I will do.' But he feared he might be brought before a German court. Did Schacht? asked a journalist. Well, he replied, there seemed to be neither laws nor free opinion these days. There was uproar; shouting from French and Belgian reporters was particularly noticeable. When Schacht then offered to sell his autograph in return for chocolate for his children one of them was heard to mutter 'c'est dégoutant'. (55)

Many people had been amazed by the acquittals, some had taken the 'no smoke without fire' view and believed there would not have been prosecutions without good causes, others had expected lighter sentences but not complete freedom. Rebecca West recorded the impression of many that Schacht and Papen were two 'old foxes' who had 'tricked and turned and doubled and laid doggo all their lives' and got away again. She believed it would only have been possible to convict them if the law had been stretched and that had to be avoided; but 'it seems a pity'. (56) Thomas Dodd, the American prosecutor who had first interrogated Papen at Mondorf, took the loss of this case with generosity. He gave Papen a box of Havana cigars. (57) Speer's reaction was, he said, a compound of envy and bitterness: 'So lies, smokescreens and dissembling statements have paid off after all'. (58) Others felt even more bitter. Many Germans felt positively angry. As Papen, Schacht and Fritzsche left their Press conference they were told that German police had surrounded the building waiting to arrest them the moment they set foot outside. Dr Hoegner, the Minister President of Bavaria, denounced their acquittals as miscarriages of justice; he sent a warrant for their arrest to the jail. (59) Reports to Andrus, and a comment from Dr Pfluecker to Speer, suggested there was more than a police detachment waiting for the three men; it looked like a lynching mob. They did not dare leave the prison. Instead they moved upstairs to the third tier of cells, signed a chit for Andrus to say they were staying voluntarily and as free men slept in the jail. (60)

On the afternoon of 1 October, the three acquitted hung over the rail outside their cells and watched the other defendants one by one return from the courtroom where they had received their sentences. Andrus had stiffened those who had to face this dreadful ordeal: 'It is your duty to yourselves and to posterity and to the German people to face this issue with dignity and manliness. I expect you to go into that courtroom, stand to attention, listen to your sentence, and then retire.' He promised them there would be people to take care of them once they 'moved out of sight of the general public'. In fact he had put a doctor and a nurse in the courtroom; there was another doctor at the foot of their lift and two soldiers inside with a stretcher – and a straitjacket. (61) Each prisoner was to be taken up separately in the lift, escorted into the room, then left to stand alone in the dock – a whitegloved, white helmeted guard at either end. Every two or three minutes that afternoon the lift door in the dock would slide to one side and another prisoner would enter. The sound of that door was an enduring memory for everyone present; it was no more than a sigh, but it gave a pulse-like rhythm to the forty-two minutes of the grim, final act of the trial.

For once the courtroom was dim; the harsh lights which had blazed through every session for the official photographers had been switched off. The judges had forbidden any filming of the sentences – men about to be hanged or imprisoned must be given protection from the prurient, some privacy in a fearful moment. Sir Geoffrey Lawrence had written the name of each defendant and his sentence on a small sheet of blue writing-paper which he carried folded in his pocket. (62) He read the Tribunal's last words to each in a firm, grave voice: 'Defendant ... on the counts of the indictment on which you have been convicted, the Tribunal sentences you ...' A simple, almost bleak ceremony with none of the gruesome ritual of the English courts – the black cap and the awesome phrase: 'May the Lord have mercy on your soul.' But it had a dignity and its dignity was matched by the behaviour of all the defendants.

Yet there had been a false start to the afternoon. Goering came into the dock, immaculate pale Luftwaffe uniform flapping on his trimmer figure, face sunken and rigidly clenched into an expression of indifference. He put on the headphones with studied casualness. Lawrence began to read. Suddenly Goering made a gesture. Lawrence stopped. The headphones were dead; no translation was coming through. Everything in the room froze for an instant. Then a guard rushed to the front of the dock and went to check the plug; Goering lent over the barrier to test it too. Another guard rushed up. They checked the headphones, tried another pair. Spectators could hardly breathe. At another time, the incident would have seemed ridiculous, a mere triviality. At such a moment it seemed dreadful, heart stopping. A few people managed to glance at Lawrence. He was visibly upset. At last Goering signalled that all was well. Lawrence began to read again. Goering stood rigid as the last words of the translation reached him: 'Tode durch den strang'. No expression crossed his face. He dropped the earphones, turned on his heel and left. (63)

Hess came in. He knocked away the headphones and stood swaying slightly with eyes darting this way and that – anywhere but the judges' bench. The sentence was read – life imprisonment. He seemed to notice nothing until a guard tapped him on the shoulder and indicated the lift. Ribbentrop took his place, seeming to shake himself straight, clutching a bundle of papers under one arm, eyes almost closed so that his head had to be tilted back to see the judges. When he heard the sentence of death he drooped, then patted his papers, straightened again and went to the lift. Keitel stood as a soldier, listened, then clicked his heels and bowed. Kaltenbrunner bowed on entering, bowed on leaving. As the others followed into the dock some hands trembled slightly as they adjusted the earphones; Frank fumbled the longest, his left hand still clumsy since slashing his wrist. He murmured 'thank you' when he received his sentence, the only defendant to utter a sound. Some prisoners seemed uncomprehending, like Frick who stood as if waiting for more to be said. Funk sentenced to life imprisonment shook his head as though in disbelief. Others like Doenitz seemed angry; his eyes blazed. Streicher hurled his earphones down and stormed to the lift like a man in a fit of temper. Jodl, thought Bob Cooper, was 'the most astonished on hearing the death sentence, undoubtedly'. Speer remembered he was 'barely conscious of what I was doing, I bow silently to the judges. Then I am led through unfamiliar, dimly-lit corridors to my cell. All this while the soldier to whom I am handcuffed has said not a word.' (64)

The handcuffs were a shock. The escorting soldiers had carried them in their pockets and they slipped them on to each prisoner as he got back into the lift. Those sentenced to death went back to their old cells. Goering was struggling to control himself, panting. He asked Gilbert to be left alone for a while. Ribbentrop wandered around in a daze: 'Death, death. Now I won't be able to write my beautiful memoirs ... So much hatred.' Keitel was horrified: 'Death – by *hanging. That* at least I thought I would be spared,' and he begged Gilbert not to desert him: 'Visit me sometimes in these last days.' Jodl too was shamed by the means of his death: 'That I did not deserve.' Frank smiled: 'I deserved it and I expected it.' Sauckel was sweating and trembling: 'I don't consider the sentence fair ... I have never been cruel myself. I always wanted the best for the workers. But I am a man and I can take it.' Then he began to cry. Frick showed no feeling: 'I didn't expect anything different.' He asked Gilbert what sentences others had received. 'So. Eleven death sentences. I figured fourteen. Well, I hope they get it over quickly.' (65)

Those who now faced imprisonment had to move to cells on the first floor. Speer's reaction to his sentence was 'fair enough. They couldn't have given me a lighter sentence considering the facts.' He told Gilbert: 'I admitted my share of the guilt, so it would have been ridiculous if I complained about the punishment.' As he carted his bedding up the winding iron staircase to his new cell he met Hess. 'What did you get, Herr Hess?' 'I have no idea. Probably the death penalty. I didn't listen.' (66) Raeder too claimed not to know: 'I forget,' he said when Gilbert asked. When Gilbert commented to Schirach that his wife would be relieved that he had not been condemned to death as she had feared, he replied: 'Better a quick death than a slow one.' Doenitz seemed puzzled by his own sentence, then he found comfort: 'Well, anyway, I cleared U-boat warfare.' And he talked about Nimitz. (67)

Everyone who had sat in court to hear the sentencing had found it a distressing experience. There seem to have been few if any ghouls there, there was no delight in the expectation of revenge. One of the secretaries who had typed the judgement could not bear to go into the court to hear the sentences; she stayed at home. (68) For those who had worked for the prosecution, the experience of being physically close to the defendants had created a sense of intimacy; there was no exultation now in having won a case and secured punishment. Many people that afternoon in fact felt a common humanity with the men who were condemned. Those who had fought in the armed services, especially. They knew how disgusting all war is, how easily they might have been involved in acts for which the defendants must now suffer. The dignity and courage of the prisoners as they stood to hear their verdicts had moved everyone – would they themselves have been capable of such control? How would the British Cabinet have stood up to such a trial, such a moment, when their future was being dictated? When the court had adjourned on 31 August everyone had gone out to celebrate. Tonight there was little celebration. Most people felt depressed and went home quietly to pack. It is a terrible thing to see a man condemned to death even when you are certain that he has been responsible for the death of millions.

References for Chapter Seventeen

1   British prosecution minutes, 8 August
2   Tribunal minutes, 10 April
3   Conversation with Mrs Tudor
4   Notes on Judgement. Biddle Papers, Box 14
5   Francis Biddle *In Brief Authority*
6   Conversations with Rowe
7   Francis Biddle *In Brief Authority*
8   Francis Biddle *In Brief Authority*
9   Letter to Judge Douglas 17 May 1951. Biddle Papers, Box 1
10 Letter to Judge Douglas 17 May 1951. Biddle Papers, Box 1
11 Dunn's reports in Andrus
12 Biddle Notes on Judgement. Biddle Papers, Box 14
13 Fritzsche
14 *Sunday Chronicle*, 7 September
15 Conversation with Emma Schwabenland
16 Gilbert
17 Fritzsche and Andrus
18 Gilbert
19 Reuter report, 20 September in several newspapers
20 Gilbert
21 *New York Times*, 21 September
22 Account of verdicts from Biddle. Notes on Judgement. Biddle Papers, Box 14
23 Conversation with Rowe
24 British prosecution minutes, 1 June
25 Memo by Stewart. Biddle Papers, Box 5
26 Memo by Fisher, 24 July. Biddle Papers, Box 5
27 File 'Confidential. Phillimore. Room 233'. BWCE N/30
28 Correspondence in LCO 2. 2988
29 Fisher memo. Biddle Papers, Box 5. Conversations with Fisher and Rowe
30 Francis Biddle *In Brief Authority*
31 Conversation with Fisher
32 Francis Biddle *In Brief Authority*
33 Memo. Biddle Papers, Box 5
34 Memo, 19 July. Biddle Papers, Box 19
35 *News Chronicle*
36 *Daily Mail*, 27 September

37 *The Times*, 30 September
38 Wheeler-Bennett
39 Quoted by Montgomery Hyde
40 Papen
41 *Daily Express*, 30 September
42 *Daily Telegraph*
43 *Daily Worker* and *Daily Telegraph*
44 *Daily Telegraph*, 30 September
45 *New York Times*, 30 September
46 *New York Times*, 1 October
47 *New York Times* and Heydecker
48 *New York Times*
49 Papen
50 Papen
51 Fritzsche
52 Heydecker
53 Gilbert
54 Cooper
55 Cooper, *Manchester Guardian*, and *New York Times*
56 *Daily Telegraph*
57 Papen
58 Speer *Spandau Diary*
59 *Daily Telegraph*, 2 October
60 Speer, Andrus, Papen, Schacht and Fritzsche
61 Andrus
62 Kindly shown to the authors by Lady Oaksey
63 Section based on several newspaper reports and the memories of eyewitnesses
64 Speer *Spandau Diary*
65 Gilbert
66 Speer *Spandau Diary*
67 Gilbert
68 Conversation with Mrs Tudor

Chapter Eighteen

The International Military Tribunal at Nuremberg had finished its work. The most famous of the German defendants to be accused of offences committed in no particular geographical location had been tried; most of them now faced their sentences. There would be subsequent proceedings against other accused Germans; some would be held in Nuremberg, others elsewhere in the occupied Zones. Several of the prosecution and defence lawyers would take part in those trials. But for most people who had worked at Nuremberg it was now time to go home. After living so closely together, working so intensely on the same task, the prosecution and defence teams scattered, often never to meet colleagues or adversaries again. Some days before the reading of the final judgement Sir David Maxwell-Fyfe had stopped Kranzbuehler in one of the interminable corridors of the Palace of Justice. The two men had sat in court within feet of each other for months; they had debated points of law before the judges; but they had never exchanged an informal word. Maxwell-Fyfe said goodbye and held out his hand; Kranzbuehler was surprised – the trial was not over. No, said Sir David, but perhaps after the verdicts the German lawyer would not be willing to shake hands. (1) Those two at least parted with strong mutual respect.

The two British judges left Nuremberg on 2 October. After a three hour flight they were greeted at Northolt airport by a grand reception party – the Lord Chancellor, Lord Jowett, his predecessor Lord Simon, Lord Chief Justice Goddard and a representative of the Foreign Secretary. Birkett assured the Press, disappointed by news of the Russian dissent, that the unity of the Tribunal had been 'remarkable, having regard to the difficulties of language and the law'. An hour later Shawcross and Maxwell-Fyfe touched down. They too stressed that Russian dissent did not seriously detract from the record of international co-operation at the trial. (2) The judges, the lawyers went their separate ways, back to distinguished careers in law and politics. In the New Year's Honours List, Lawrence's important contribution to the trial was suitably recognized. Birkett commented: 'Today Geoffrey Lawrence was made a Baron for his work at Nuremberg. I was given nothing.' (3) It was surely a monstrous example of official insensitivity and ingratitude. The Government had rightly acknowledged Lawrence's skill in maintaining the co-operation of the judges, his unique ability to convey his own high standards, his embodiment of the best in judicial process. Lawrence's calm and efficiency, his evident concern for the rights of the defence and his considerate manners in court had given the trial much of its dignity and given the participants, especially the Germans, the sense that the Tribunal would ensure a fair hearing. But Birkett's capacity for friendship with the other judges, his formidable grasp of the documentary evidence, his significant work on the final judgement should not have been ignored.

The French drifted away. Only Edgar Faure, one of the youngest of their prosecutors, ever came back to major international attention – as the Prime Minister of France. Many of the Russians left Nuremberg before anyone noticed. The day after the sentences had been read, the British prosecutors were puzzled to find American guards on their doors. An ADC rang the military authorities to enquire why they were there. In answer he was driven to see some of the houses which had lodged the Russian staff. They had been stripped. Furniture, washbasins, light fittings, everything movable or regarded as a fixture, had been loaded on to lorries the night before and driven over the Czech border. (4) The more prominent Russian lawyers made a more orthodox departure – some of them for good. Rudenko went on to become Chief Prosecutor of the USSR but the two judges virtually disappeared. For several years British and American lawyers who had worked at Nuremberg tried to make contact with Nikitchenko; all their attempts seem to have been officially blocked.

The American judges returned to be publicly thanked by President Truman. Parker went back to his circuit. Biddle waited and waited for the offer of an official post which would match the standards of public service and personal commitment he had so treasured at Nuremberg. It never came. He could not face returning to humdrum legal work and retired. Jackson resumed his place at the Supreme Court. The work was congenial and useful enough, but perhaps could not quite measure up to the golden prospect once suggested of becoming President. Some wondered whether Jackson might have been made Chief Justice after the death of Stone had he not descended from the legal heights and gone to Nuremberg apparently at the beck and call of politicians. But how could the old crusader have turned down such a challenge? Jackson may have lived to rue some personal mistakes and failures at Nuremberg but he cannot have regretted throwing himself so wholeheartedly into the attempt to advance international law. And his odd failures as an administrator or cross-examiner are undoubtedly outweighed by the energy and idealism with which he had helped to launch the trial, and maintained its impetus in the days of preparation when the difficulties so often overwhelmed weaker spirits. If he had done nothing else, he would be remembered for his opening speech: it had embodied everyone's highest aspirations and given the most clear-sighted and honest assessment of the difficulties of the trial but also of the opportunities it presented. It was revealing of his own values that on his office wall in the Supreme Court Jackson was to mount the four national flags which had stood behind the judges' bench at Nuremberg.

At a Press conference after the verdicts were announced, Jackson had expressed approval of most of them – but slight regret that the Tribunal had not declared criminal the General Staff and High Command and had acquitted Papen and Schacht. (5) But he wrote later that he had no second thoughts about refusing to make any bargains with Schacht: 'We decided it would be better to lose our case against some defendants than to win a deal that would discredit the judgement … I still think that we made the better choice.' (6) Others had taken the acquittals less equably. The Austrians were indignant that Papen had been set free – he was seen as largely responsible for the loss of Austrian independence. The Austrian Minister of Justice began to demand Papen's extradition to Vienna; and that of Schirach, too, on the grounds that he should have been condemned to death. (7) The Belgian press, which was said by the British Embassy in Brussels to have been consistently 'sarcastic' about the trial, was now positively 'rude' about the acquittals. (8) Soviet newspapers, on the other hand, while endorsing Nikitchenko's dissent, went to great lengths to express general satisfaction with the handling of the trial and most of the verdicts and sentences. (9) The Russians had come a long way from Stalin's view at Tehran, or Vyshinsky's notorious toast at Nuremberg 'death to the defendants'.

Schacht, Fritzsche and Papen were not so much worried by international reaction as frightened to meet the Germans waiting outside the Nuremberg jail. They dared not leave. After three days, Fritzsche and Schacht could no longer bear prison life as free men and decided to make a dash for it. Andrus persuaded them to wait until midnight. Then they were smuggled into two vans and driven off at speed in opposite directions. Schacht went to the house in Nuremberg where his wife had been staying – and found two German policemen at the door. He was taken off to a police station but returned later in the night to house arrest, under threat of de-Nazification proceedings in Nuremberg. (10) He wriggled away for a time but was finally arrested in Württemberg and sentenced by a Stuttgart court to eight years in a labour camp as a 'Major Offender'. His appeal was successful and on 2 September 1948 Schacht was finally released. He was cleared of all charges in 1950. Fritzsche's first night of freedom was not spent in a police station, at least. He went to the home of his counsel, Fritz. It was under seige by reporters. As he was about to get into bed the Nuremberg Chief of Police arrived, closely followed by American military policemen who kept the German authorities at bay for that night. (11) Fritzsche was soon under detention again, and actually back in the same jail for a time, but this time at German behest. He was tried by a de-Nazification court in 1947 and finally released in September 1950. Papen had been too wily or too scared to leave the security of jail and the protection of Andrus. He stayed there: for the first fortnight in his cell on the top floor from where he watched the convicted men below being taken out for exercise; thereafter he moved to another wing. (12) He wrote to the British and French military authorities asking permission to live in their Zones and to the American Military Governor asking for safe conduct. No one would have him. A British Cabinet meeting was told that their commander-in-chief in Germany wanted to refuse residence; if it were granted he would feel obliged to intern Papen as potentially dangerous. The Cabinet had no desire to be responsible for Papen; residence in the British Zone was refused. (13) Eventually Papen crept out of Nuremberg jail. The Americans reluctantly accepted him in their Zone, on condition that he remained in Nuremberg. On 1 February 1947 he was convicted as a 'Major Offender' by a German de-Nazification court and sentenced, like Schacht, to eight years' hard labour. He was released after appeal in January 1949, having spent most of his term in camp hospitals.

Those men sentenced by the Tribunal to imprisonment stayed in their new cells on the second floor until July 1947 when they were flown to Berlin, to continued confinement in Spandau prison. Spandau had been built in the last century to accommodate 600 prisoners. Now it held seven. The Nazis had installed facilities for hanging eight prisoners at a time and a room for a guillotine. These had been replaced by an operating theatre. The prisoners had become the responsibility of the Four Powers, each nation running the jail for a month at a time. In periods when relations between the West and the Soviet Union broke down, Spandau provided the only meeting place for them, the monthly meetings before handover the only opportunity for discussion which obduracy made politically impossible elsewhere. The experiences which the seven new prisoners had shared of life in the Nazi hierarchy, trial and imprisonment had still not created much of a bond between them. But Speer noted wryly in July 1947 that the wives of Hess, Funk, Schirach and Goering were being held with those of other prominent Nazis in a Bavarian camp and 'the wives seem to get along with each other even worse than we do.' (14)

Life in Spandau became even drearier as the number of prisoners dwindled. Neurath was released for health reasons in 1954; Raeder left in 1955; Doenitz finished his term in 1956; Funk's health deteriorated and he too went in 1957. Schirach and Speer were kept until 1966. Finally only one prisoner remained in the empty, gaunt red brick prison, guarded by the Four Powers whose representatives continued to meet formally once a month over a heavy lunch to discuss his condition and the running of his jail. Rudolf Hess stayed alone – for the neo-Nazis a martyr, for humanitarians an old man arousing pity and shame, for the Western governments an embarrassment, but for the Russians an object of enduring hate, never to be forgiven, never to be released.

His former jailer, Colonel Andrus, was at home by the end of 1946. He had decided to leave the Army and educate himself. He did it very successfully – and stayed on at the University of Puget Sound as Professor of Geography and Business Administration. That was not all. He became an active lay preacher and a member of a board for the promotion of Boy Scouts. (Did he make careful enquiries about the tidiness of their bedrooms before granting promotion?) Andrus' last responsibility before leaving Nuremberg had been his most awesome. He superintended the executions of those prisoners condemned to death.

There had been protests at the Tribunal's decision to order executions. Already in the previous February, Uruguay had submitted a draft resolution to the United Nations opposing the death penalty. The resolution provoked an angry response from the Ukrainian member of the General Committee, and its Belgian chairman, Paul-Henri Spaak, persuaded the Uruguayan delegate to withdraw it in view of the delicacy of the subject and the passions a debate would arouse. (15) Once the sentences were announced there was more outcry in the United Nations largely from Cuba, Colombia and other South American States, all of whom believed the defendants guilty but all of whom opposed the penalty on principle. (16) The Irish Prime Minister, de Valera, visited the Dominions Office in London on 12 October and described the decision to hang some of the convicted men as 'a tragic mistake'. (17) The Foreign Office collected copious letters from individuals begging that the death sentence be commuted. (18)

But the only hope of any alleviation of the punishment lay with the Allied Control Council in Germany, to whom the condemned men had the right to appeal for clemency. For some time it had been believed that the Council might choose to act as a full Appeal court and make a complete review of all the cases. In that belief, Jackson had written to Washington in September and early October urging that the American element on the Council should vote against review. The British Foreign Office shared his opinion that the members were not competent to consider the legal grounds of the Tribunal's judgement. (19) In the event, however, the Council seems to have interpreted its duty as limited to considerations of mercy and possible reduction of sentence. They received representations from virtually every defendant or his counsel and appeals from lawyers to the organizations declared criminal. There was an eight-page letter from Ribbentrop accompanied by one from his wife and one nearly as long from his lawyer; a complaint from Servatius that Sauckel had been sentenced purely as a result of a mistranslation of one document; a plea from Schirach not against his term of imprisonment but for a chance to issue a correction of some errors of fact in the judgement. Not surprisingly, in view of the bewildering form of the judgement, Kranzbuehler drew attention to the fact that Doenitz had not been found guilty of planning aggressive war and seemed to have been cleared of crimes at sea – what therefore had merited imprisonment? Goering, Keitel and Jodl all requested that they be shot rather than hanged, and Frau Jodl asked the members of the Council, as soldiers themselves, to recognize that her husband had done a soldier's job. (20) Brauchitsch sent a telegram to the British War Office on behalf of several high-ranking German officers begging mercy for Jodl 'whose influence and position at my knowledge have been valued too high'. (21) While the Allied Control Council considered these applications, rumours

479

flew that Frank had appealed directly to the Vatican. The British Minister to the Holy See checked, and found the rumours groundless. Vatican authorities drew his attention to the statement of the Pope in 1944 that war criminals should expiate their crimes. (22).

The Allied Control Council met on 9 and 10 October to reach its decisions. Most of the requests for clemency were dismissed out of hand, including that of Raeder for death rather than life imprisonment – the Council had no authority to increase a sentence. There was debate, however, over Jodl's fate. The French representative recommended he face a firing squad; so too did the American on the grounds that Jodl (unlike presumably Goering and Keitel) had taken 'no initiative in political matters'. The Russian, however, saw Jodl as inextricably involved in political matters and the man himself as 'the incarnation of bestial fascism'. Without going that far the British representative put forward the opinion that all commanders have the right to resign if given illegal or immoral orders. Jodl had not attempted to do so. Both he and Keitel had dishonoured their profession and had no right to claim an honourable soldier's death. (23) Given this split vote, the Tribunal's sentence had to be upheld. On 13 October Andrus told his prisoners that all their appeals had been rejected. They expressed no surprise.

That day Speer had been taken for a walk, handcuffed to a guard. They had gone along the bottom corridor – Death Row, the guards now called it – and he had looked into the eleven cells. Frank was sitting at his table and writing, but the others were all lying on their beds, face up, hands on the blanket in accordance with prison regulations, and immobile. Speer described it as 'a ghastly sight . . . it looks as though they have already been laid on their biers'. (24) They had, in fact, adjusted to the inevitability of their executions and had been preparing for them for days. Personal possessions had been handed over to the Allied Control Council. (25) Last letters had been written, final words of comfort and reassurance given to families and friends. Ribbentrop had sent a letter to the chairman of the 'Johnnie Walker' whisky company asking for a job for his son, (26) and had told his wife that he had been convicted 'on political grounds' and that if Hitler were alive and able to give evidence 'the whole verdict would collapse'. (27) There had been some visits from wives. These were heartrending meetings, they were so obviously the last. Goering had tried to raise a smile from Emmy by going into the booth dragging behind him the guard to whom he was handcuffed: 'You see, I am still a leader,' he said. (28) But most of the prisoners broke down and wept.

For the rest, they spent their days trying to read or lying listlessly on their beds. Dr Pfluecker often came to visit. The prisoners told him about the books they were reading. Many had requested a Bible; Rosenberg had refused one. Keitel asked the doctor to beg the organist, who sometimes played in the evening so that the men could listen in their cells, not to play 'Schlafe, mein kinde, schlafe ein': it stirred up such nostalgia and melancholy. (29) Pfluecker and indeed every other observer was impressed by the calm and courage of all the condemned men. Only one thing disturbed them. They wanted to know where the executions would take place and when. They were not told.

In theory the Allied Control Council was responsible for the hangings. It was assumed at one time that they would be carried out in Berlin to stress the Quadripartite nature of the trial and sentences. The Americans suspected that the Russians would oppose executions in the American Zone but many feared the security risks in moving the prisoners. (30) And no one really wanted to be responsible for the executions; the Americans in May were reported to be 'rather chary of undertaking the unpleasant and invidious task' should the Tribunal impose death penalties, but the British not least hoped the Americans could be persuaded to do it. (31).

By the end of September, the Allied Control Council at last decided to request the Americans to carry out any hangings in Nuremberg; their own part in the proceedings would be limited to sending two representatives of each governing power as witnesses. To the horror of the British, the Council had accepted the suggestion of the Americans that representatives of the Press be present. To the British this seemed at best vulgar; to the others it seemed a necessary precaution against rumours and legends about the hangings. There was a further practical point – if two journalists only from each of the four nations were allowed to write and syndicate their stories, there would be no unseemly barging for places or squalid buying of eye-witness accounts later. (32) On 1 October, Shawcross rang the Foreign Office to deliver his complaint and that of the British judges against this decision. (33) It was too late.

There was only one comfort for the British – the hangings would be witnessed by a mere handful of people. There had been deep shock at reports of public hangings of war criminals in Prague in the previous year; the British ambassador there had described them as accompanied by 'deplorable scenes'. That of Karl-Hermann Frank, the last Protector of Bohemia, on 22 May had avoided these scenes by issuing tickets and restricting the audience to 5,500, but the performance had been distasteful enough. (34) Yet the last days of the condemned men were not left unviolated by bad taste and the occasional indignity. A stream of stories flowed out of the prison detailing for journalistic benefit what they ate, what they said, who took Communion. The really deplorable decision was taken by the military authorities to admit at least one journalist to tour the jail and let him peer at the prisoners, like a visitor to the 18th-century Bedlam. The subsequent article he syndicated to the American press was no more sensitive than his original decision to accept the invitation. Its reiteration of contemptuous phrases as each prisoner was described catered to the most spiteful of readers. (35) It is contradicted by the opinion of everyone else who saw these men in their last days – there was admiration and some surprise that they should have achieved a fortitude and resolution which could only be admired. They knew they were about to die. But though the outside world had somehow learned the executions would take place during the night of 16 October, no one had as yet told the men concerned. They seem to have sensed it though. Pastor Gerecke said later that several of them had confidently named that date to him. He had good reason to recall that almost the last time he saw Goering he had been closely questioned about the exact time the hangings would start. Goering had had no doubts at all about the date; 'it was more than a premonition that Goering had. He seemed to know.' (36)

They were to hang in the prison gymnasium where some of them had taken evening walks in the early days of their imprisonment when it was too dark and dank for the exercise yard. It was a dusty, grimy building in the prison yard; about seventy-eight feet long, thirty-three feet wide and bare except for a few wall bars, two iron stoves in the corners, basket ball nets at either end and the slogan which appeared on every Nuremberg wall: 'VD walks the Streets'. On the evening of 15 October, a drizzling, cold evening with a threat of snow, the American guards played their usual basketball game. Then it was dark. No one saw beams and planks being unloaded from lorries and carried into the gym. But from their cells prisoners could clearly hear sounds of hammering and sawing. A guard told Fritzsche that a new fence was being put up in the garden behind the prison; but Fritzsche did not believe him. (37) For a moment Speer felt 'irritation that they should be carrying out repairs at night. Then the thought suddenly flashed through my mind: they are putting up the gallows.' (38)

At eight o'clock that same evening eight journalists had been brought into the prison – two representing each nation of the Tribunal. They had won the ballot to write the eye-witness accounts of the executions. They were to be kept virtual prisoners themselves until they were taken over to the gymnasium. Other journalists, about a hundred of them, were coralled into the Press Room in the court building with instructions not to lean out of the windows – guards had been ordered to shoot. But they could glimpse the jail across the yard and they watched as lights were first turned off, then all reappeared and finally went out one by one at the cell windows. (39)

The prison building had first gone dark soon after nine o'clock. This was standard prison routine. The condemned men had not been told they would hang in a few hours' time; they were settled in for the night. Dr Pfluecker toured the cells on the ground floor, offering sleeping pills as he always did, chatting for a moment as he had done so many evenings before. Then he went back to his room. All was quiet. At about a quarter to eleven there were shouts from the bottom corridor. The guard at Goering's door had just glanced through the hatch. Goering, who had previously seemed to be sleeping peacefully, lying in the prescribed position, was now moaning and twitching. The guard yelled and began to unlock the door. Pastor Gerecke was the first to reach the cell. He found Goering lying as if in a convulsion, froth on his lips, right hand flung over the side of the bed and fist tightly clenched. Pfluecker ran in; he shouted to Goering: had he had

482

a heart attack? Goering was turning blue; he began to sink into the bed. There was a quick rattle in his throat. Then he was dead. Pfluecker called an American doctor and asked him to feel in Goering's mouth. There were slivers of glass. Goering had crushed a phial of cyanide. (40)

He had left three letters in his cell. The Press reported that they were addressed to his wife, to the German people (a last testament, they said) and to Andrus. (41) A recent German writer maintains that the letter to Andrus told him that Goering had had three cyanide capsules since first going to Mondorf, but the guards were to be excused for not finding them. One had been left in his clothes to be found during a search (was it?), another was kept hidden in the cell at night and tucked in a jackboot during the day, the third was concealed in a jar of face cream (according to one Press report the cosmetics had been taken by the Control Commision by 8 October, but Goering always kept a lot). This account does not say which capsule had been taken. (42)

Andrus's memoirs reveal the existence of letters but none of their contents. It could be argued that he felt the failure to find the cyanide could not be mitigated by Goering's excuses for his guards. But the representatives of the Four Powers waiting in the prison for the executions ordered all American and German staff to be interviewed immediately. Fritzche was awakened at five in the morning to be questioned. (43) The Allied Control Council's final report on the matter was said to have cleared the prison staff of all responsibility. According to one newspaper it surmised that Goering had had his cyanide since arrest; it could have been kept in his navel or somewhere in his 'alimentary tract' (which could mean anywhere from the mouth to the rectum); alternatively it could have been hidden somewhere like the rim of the lavatory. The final letters were ordered to be kept secret. (44)

The report does not seem to have been officially published – which was surely a mistake. Deprived of authoritative findings, people made guesses. Many found the idea that Goering had hidden his cyanide for well over a year incredible – after all the cells and sometimes the defendants had been searched. Andrus himself had thrown occasional titbits to the Press on the extraordinary finds that searches had revealed; collections of pills, nails, scraps of metal, paper clips and broken spoons, shoe laces and strips of rag. Yet it was certainly possible to fool the searchers. Fritzsche admitted to having kept a splinter of glass. (45) Those who did not guess, made assertions: Goering's wife had slipped the capsule to her husband during a visit (this ignores the existence of the metal grille); his counsel had passed it over hidden in papers (Stahmer indignantly denied this story; guards were supposed to check all documents and it would have been a terrible risk to smuggle in poison. On the other hand, all the prisoners had managed to obtain paper clips); a German prison worker or an American guard had handed it over (which one and why? It is surprising that the person responsible never admitted the fact; it would surely have been something to boast about in later years). Some people themselves claimed to have provided the poison. An Austrian journalist retailed the story of sticking it to the dock with a piece of chewing gum; Bach-Zelewski said he had handed it to Goering in a piece of soap when they met one day in a corridor (since they were held in different wings of the prison, it is improbable that they ever met). No explanation is very convincing; none is backed by any proof.

The news that Goering had committed suicide was kept secret all night. At 6.25 next morning Andrus went to the Press Room where the journalists had been expecting him for over an hour to give an account of the executions. As the story of Goering's death spread through Nuremberg it seemed to capture more imaginations, obsess more conversations than the goriest accounts of the executions. For Gilbert, Goering had died 'as he had lived, a psychopath trying to make a mockery of all human values and to distract from his guilt by a dramatic gesture'. (46) For a few others the suicide had been a coward's way out – a quick and relatively painless alternative to the noose. Otherwise it was a cheat's device. Jackson tried to draw a moral from it. He told the Press that the gallows had offered Goering a 'platform from which to impress his sympathisers with the depth of his convictions and his selflessness for the cause'. But he had lacked the character to use it. 'Though he was the only defendant on whom the martyr myth might have been founded, by taking his life he killed the legend of Nazi bravery and stoicism.' (47)

These reactions were rare, though. One German ex-officer told a correspondent 'he would not let them kill him as they wanted'; a former English officer called the suicide 'a final act of self-defiance to round off his excellent bearing during the trial'. (48) 'Well done, Goering,' others said, 'he was always one jump ahead.' 'Typical,' commented others, 'grabbing centre stage, like the great performer he was,' or 'he got one last final glorious rise out of the Allies.' There was much slapping of thighs and bellowing laughter. Quieter people commented that Goering had shown the courage and astuteness to be expected of him. In the view of Dr Kelley, the prison psychologist, Goering had deliberately evaded the hanging to join Hitler, Himmler and Goebbels in taking his own life. Kelley judged it a 'skilful, even brilliant finishing touch', and feared it might complete 'the edifice for Germans to admire in time to come'. (49) That morning several newspapers printed the news that Goering had hanged: the *News Chronicle* reporter had written in dramatic and colourful detail the story of Goering's final walk to the scaffold.

But ten men, not eleven, had gone out the previous night to hang. Those who had managed to sleep during the shouting and clatter outside Goering's cell had been wakened, as arranged, at about a quarter to midnight. Few availed themselves of the supper they were offered – sausage and potato salad, with fruit salad to follow. Now at last they were told they were about to die. They dressed – but not Streicher; he refused and had to be pulled into his clothes by guards. (50) Keitel made his bed and asked for a brush and a duster to clean his cell. Then just before one o'clock Andrus came, accompanied by Dr Hoegner the Minister President of Bavaria, the Public Prosecutor, Leistner and an interpreter, and read the death sentence to each man.

From just after one o'clock in the morning, the condemned men, in order of indictment, were led in turn from their cells, down the corridor, and across the yard to the gymnasium. It had been intended to leave their hands free. But after Goering's suicide the representatives of the Allied Control Council insisted they be handcuffed behind their backs. These representatives now waited by the scaffold to witness their deaths. With them were the eight journalists, the two German officials, some doctors, about twenty guards and John C. Woods, the American hangman, with two assistants. The prisoner, his escort and a priest reached the door. A guard knocked twice: 'stand by'. Inside on a platform eight feet square stood three gallows of thick unplaned wood, roughly painted; from two there hung ropes. In a corner, scarcely noticeable, lay eleven coffins draped in blackout material. There were grisly symbols: thirteen shallow steps to the scaffold; thirteen coils in the knot of the noose. As each man stood under the gallows his handcuffs were removed and replaced with what looked like knotted black shoelaces; his ankles were buckled with an Army webbing belt. A black hood was slipped over the head, tied round the neck and followed by the noose. Then the lever was pulled, the trap sprung.

Speer lay awake and heard the sound of each man leaving: a name being called, the cell door opening, 'scraps of phrases, scraping of boots and reverberating footsteps slowly fading away'. (51) The journalists in the Press room noted the light go out in each cell. Ribbentrop left first. Ribbentrop the despised and quavering, seemed transformed. Kelley thought that now he had lost Goering, his father-figure and hero, he had no one to measure himself against and feel shamed by; he was now the senior surviving Nazi and became, in Kelley's eyes 'a more competent person in his last seconds than at any other time in his entire life'. (52) As he went to the gymnasium he told Pastor Gerecke, 'I shall see you again.' Ribbentrop stood on the scaffold while his arms and legs were tied. 'God protect Germany. Thank God that He is merciful. My last wish is that German unity should remain and that an understanding between East and West should come about, and peace for the world.' Keitel followed, neat in his uniform, hair immaculately brushed. He said to Gerecke, 'I thank you and those who sent you with all my heart.' As he waited, Keitel spoke his last words: 'I call on the Almighty that He have mercy on the German people. Over two million went to their death before me. I now follow my sons. All for Germany.' Kaltenbrunner next. The man who used to weep, who was described as dying of fear in the early days of his trial said in a steady, mild voice: 'I have served my German people and my Fatherland with a willing heart. I have done my duty in accordance with the laws of the Fatherland. I regret that crimes were committed in which I had no part. Good luck Germany'. Rosenberg was pale and showed signs of collapse. He did not speak. Frank had said to Andrus: 'Colonel, I want to thank you for your great kindness to me.' He smiled as he came into the gymnasium, almost hurried up the steps, then turned: 'I pray to God to take my soul. May the Lord receive me mercifully. I am grateful for the treatment I have received in prison.' Frick in his incongruous jazzy tweed jacket marched firmly on to the platform and spoke in a loud voice: 'Long live the eternal Germany.' Then Streicher: 'Heil Hitler. Now I go to God. Purim Feast 1946 (a reference to a Jew baiter like himself who was executed two thousand years before). The Bolsheviks will get you.' Then as the hood came over his face: 'Adele, my loving wife'. Sauckel seemed angry. He kicked the door as he came in. 'I die innocent. The verdict was wrong. God protect Germany and make Germany great again. God protect my family.' Jodl, in his uniform with the red stripe of the General Staff on the trousers called: 'I salute you, my Germany.' Lastly, Seyss-Inquart limped to take his place; a guard removed his spectacles. 'I hope this execution is the last act of the tragedy of the Second World War and that the lessons of this war will make for peace and understanding among the peoples. I believe in Germany.' (53)

The bodies had been laid in their coffins one by one; Goering was brought to join them. On the instructions of the Control Council four photographs were to be taken for official records, but never to be published. (54) (Some did appear later.) At 5.30 a.m. two vans with two escorting jeeps packed with armed military policemen took the bodies away. One woman correspondent tried to track them but was soon shaken off. When last seen they were heading in the direction of Fürth, where there was an airport. It was assumed by many that they had been taken to Berlin for cremation. An official announcement from the Allied Control Council next day disclosed that the eleven had been 'cremated and the ashes disposed of'. (55) Cremation and secret scattering of the ashes had been agreed on at a meeting on 10 October. (56) According to German law the relatives had the right to the remains but the Allies were terrified of shrines, places of pilgrimage for resurgent Nazism. There seems to be no official record of what actually happened but a belief deeply held by many people is that the bodies were actually driven to the former concentration camp at Dachau and cremated in the dreadful ovens. Dachau was not far away; there was a ghastly appropriateness that those who had established such a place should themselves end there. That is what many would wish to believe.

Within a few days horrible stories had spread about the hangings – they had been botched, gruesome. Goering's body had been formally hanged, some murmured; Streicher's execution had been deliberately slow. The stories have grown over the years; plenty of 'circumstantial' detail has been added. A recent author claims that Ribbentrop took ten minutes to die, Jodl eighteen minutes, Keitel twenty-four. (57) The authorized press accounts give no details of such horrors, but perhaps that could be expected. Every account from those journalists was precise: the hangings began at 1.11 a.m.; they were over by 2.45 when the American news service was already announcing the deaths. (58) In that time, ten men had to be taken from their cells, led through the jail and across the yard, across the gymnasium, up the steps. They had to be tied, allowed to speak, wait for the hood and noose, then die. Afterwards, each body had to be taken down, certified as dead and put in its coffin. Was there time for men to dangle obscenely for so long? Perhaps.

The origin of the stories is easy to trace – wishful-thinking about revenge or martyrdom apart. When Speer, Hess and Schirach were taken on 17 October to sweep the gymnasium, it had already been scrubbed and the scaffold dismantled. But they noticed a stain on the floor where it had stood; it looked like blood. 'Hess,' said Speer, 'raised his arm in the Party salute.' (59) Journalists who went to the building next day, noticed the stain too. Most of them assumed it was blood, though the reporter from the *New York Times* drew the conclusion that it was 'oil that dripped from the hinges of the gallows'. (60) It could equally well have been paint with which the scaffold had been roughly daubed, or an indelible smear that had been there for months. If these reports were all they could be dismissed as the products of lurid imaginations. However, when cross-examined by journalists later, John C. Woods did not dismiss the idea of blood-stains – he claimed that it was possible for men to bite their tongues at the moment of hanging. (61) And one official record hints that the hangings had not been impeccably conducted. The British Information Services Control Branch wrote to the Foreign Office on 26 October that the British News Services in Germany had put out the story that Jodl had taken sixteen minutes to die, and Ribbentrop fourteen (slightly different figures from the favoured recent ones). He reported that Germans now had the impression that the prisoners had been strangled rather than hanged, but complained that this must be a 'misunderstanding fostered because the public wants to misunderstand'. He suggested that the doctors who had certified the deaths should issue a dignified report. The Foreign Office response to the idea was that it was better to let the matter blow over. An official wrote to warn that the full story was 'not a pretty one'. (62) John C. Woods was said to have executed 347 people in the previous fifteen years but there are grounds to fear that he had not acquired enough expertise to ensure instantaneous deaths on this occasion.

Whatever the details of the final executions, they were a sordid epilogue to the trial. Hanging is always squalid; it is, after all, a deliberately insulting, undignified death. Any dignity in these hangings had been lent by the victims themselves. Repellent though these men may have been throughout most of their lives, their courage afforded a final touch of redemption – though there had been little moral redemption: only Kaltenbrunner had expressed awareness, let alone regret, at their crimes.

Before hanging ten men, and imprisoning seven, the Four Powers had mounted a trial requiring months of preparation and intensive diplomatic and legal negotiation. The trial had involved scrutiny of a hundred thousand documents, a hundred thousand feet of film and twenty five thousand still photographs. The American delegation had numbered 654 people in all – 365 of them civilian lawyers, clerical staff, translators. The sum total of the other three teams was almost as great. The prosecution and defence between them had made 30,000 photostats and produced fifty million typed pages. Miles of film of the trial was shot; 4,000 recorded discs made; the daily transcript takes up nearly 17,000 pages in the published English language edition. (63) In a bombed out city in a ruined country, the American military authorities had provided the materials, equipment, food, accommodation, transport and communications for all these people and all this effort. Was it worth it just to hang ten men and imprison seven?

No one thought so. That had never been the intention. As Jackson put it in his Final Report to President Truman on 15 October 1946; the importance of the trial should not be measured 'in terms of the personal fate of any of the defendants, who were already broken and discredited men'. The money, the staff, and the resources had been expended because all concerned wanted to do more than punish a few civilian and military leaders suspected of crimes. They wanted to round off a terrible war and initiate the peace with a legal act. If punishment were all that had been called for, it would have been cheaper and quicker to shoot the defendants on capture, bring them before a drumhead court-martial or leave them to lynchers. But the Four Powers and eighteen other nations had preferred the infinitely more complex task of holding a trial, re-establishing the rule of law, examining the fundamentals by which they believed behaviour should have been governed in the past and must be determined in the future.

If their hopes implicit in this trial were to be fulfilled, it was essential that justice be seen to be done. Was justice done at Nuremberg? Had the trial been based on valid law? Legal scholars still wrangle over the legal problems with which the planners and participants struggled. They argue or deny that there were *ex post facto* elements in the Charter, that aspects of the proceedings were retroactive; they debate the extent to which international law must first be embodied in statute or can develop through treaties, conventions, judicial decision and practice. The arguments of lawyers are an essential safeguard for justice in the future. What the historian finds is that those who framed the Charter and wrote the final judgement at Nuremberg believed that the law was as they recorded and applied it. They did not consciously invent it. Though they may have found it ill-defined or previously unapplied, they were convinced it was there. So too were the United Nations. On 11 December 1946, the General Assembly unanimously adopted Resolution 95 (I) which affirmed 'the principles of international law recognized by the Charter of the Nuremberg Tribunal and the judgement of the Tribunal'. In 1950, the International Law Commission of the United Nations adopted a statement which formulated those principles.

Where the judges found the law most contentious, they trod with greatest caution. They drastically limited the conspiracy charge. It could then be argued that they only convicted on the strength of it as an optional extra. Those found guilty on Count One, who were hanged or given life sentences, would undoubtedly have received the same sentences for the other counts on which they were convicted. Many hanged who were found innocent of conspiracy. Conversely, Neurath was convicted on all four counts but was sentenced to only fifteen years imprisonment. Similarly, the Tribunal was extremely circumspect in response to the call to make declarations of criminality against organizations. Though others have suggested that the law on aggressive war was dubious, the judges themselves entertained no doubts whatever on this score.

One of the constant complaints of the defence had been that the prosecution both drew up the indictment and conducted the case against the defendants. This practice, unfamiliar on the Continent, was thought to give an unfair advantage to the prosecution. But what had been the result? Three organizations and three defendants acquitted, four defendants given relatively light sentences, and a prosecution case shredded by the judges – not just in Count One, but in the pruning of the War Crimes charge and that of Crimes against Humanity to the period after the outbreak of war.

The defence complained too at the composition of the Tribunal: it represented only the Four Powers who had defeated Germany. Yet these powers represented eighteen others. Still – 'victors' justice', sneered Goering. But the victors had decided to try their defeated enemies and they had given them the right to defend themselves. All justice is to some extent that of victors; all trials are conducted by those who have the power to try and punish those who have been caught. And only those who have been caught. Several people during the trial quoted the local saying: 'Nurembergers don't hang anyone they do not hold.' No one ever does. They try and punish murderers or tax dodgers who have been detected, well knowing that there are many more murderers and tax dodgers at large. Given the awareness that all legal proceedings are always conducted by those who possess power against those who have lost it, justice has to conform to a rule of thumb: the judge must ask: 'What standards would I wish to have applied to myself? Would I wish to be tried in this way?'

Had the Nuremberg Trial measured up to this rough and ready standard? Those who framed the Charter had provided the basic requirements of justice which they would have expected to find in any trial in their own countries: the obligation of the prosecution to present evidence and to have it examined by defence and judges; the right of the defence to cross-examine prosecution witnesses, submit evidence in rebuttal, introduce witnesses and documents in its own case; the chance for the defendants to be represented by counsel and give testimony on their own behalf. The trial was conducted by judges who applied their Rules of Procedure to both prosecution and defence, and who allowed more time and granted more leniency to the defence case than to that of the prosecution. Ten months had been spent in hearing the evidence. For those who wished to study it more closely all documents from which prosecution and defence had read extracts in court were later printed in full to accompany the published trial transcript. The evidence occupies over twenty volumes; only a handful of the documents used by the prosecution has ever been criticized as invalid (the Hossbach memorandum, for example) or wrongly or unfairly used (as when extracts seemed to have been taken out of context or mistranslated).

At a time when vengeance rather than justice was to be feared, when propaganda was to be expected, and a war might be continued by other means in court, the trial had been a remarkably calm and dispassionate proceeding, contrasting strongly with the hysteria in many national trials of the period. It had avoided unseemly scenes such as that at the subsequent Krupp trial where defence counsel on one occasion staged a mass walkout after being refused further argument over a procedural point on which the Tribunal had already ruled, and had to be confined temporarily for contempt of court. Much of the credit for the relatively unruffled temper and the reasonably businesslike nature of the Nuremberg trial must go to the Tribunal – their Rules of Procedure were efficient, and came to be seen as fair; the judges' manner and patience earned respect from both sides. How many of their final verdicts would now be seriously challenged? How many of the defendants would have preferred to the trial they received any of the debated alternatives? In the opinion of most knowledgeable critics, the Nuremberg trial had not been conducted at the very highest level – judges and counsel for both sides fell short of the best standards; the procedures had been cobbled together too hurriedly for perfection; the final judgement was perhaps too much of a compromise to rank as a classic of its kind. But especially bearing in mind the circumstances of the time, the trial was a remarkable achievement; it unquestionably embodied the norms of justice.

Doenitz suggested in his memoirs that what the Tribunal had examined was a purely German affair. Germans should have been allowed to 'investigate and then bring to justice those who had been responsible for the inhuman enormities that had taken place'. (64) Would the rest of the world have been satisfied with such a proceeding? Would German judges have been more impartial than those of the Four Powers? Had the German trials at Leipzig after the First World War given much confidence of an acceptable outcome? Would the new German civilian government have relished the political repercussions? Given the reaction outside Nuremberg jail after the three acquittals, would those tried by a German court have had more or less to fear? When crimes of such magnitude had been committed across a continent, how could they be seen as 'purely a German affair'?

Were the trial at Nuremberg of the twenty-two major Nazi defendants to be judged on the short term achievement of its outcome and its fairness, those who launched it could have been reasonably satisfied. But many of them had wanted so much more than a fair hearing or a symbolic legal act to end the war and start the peace. They wanted the trial to be the foundation of a new legal order; they wanted international law to be advanced and to govern the future conduct of nations. But even by 1946, an idealist like

Jackson had grown just a little more weary, and wary. In his Report to President Truman he used some triumphant phrases: the London Agreement, he said, 'for the first time made explicit and unambiguous what was heretofore ... implicit in international law, namely that to prepare, incite, or wage a war of aggression, or to conspire with others to do so is a crime against international society; and that to persecute, oppress, or do violence to individuals or minorities on political, racial, or religious grounds in connection with such a war; or to extirminate, enslave or deport civilian populations is an international crime and that for the commission of such crimes individuals are responsible'. But within a few paragraphs Jackson sounded a note of caution: it would be 'extravagant to claim that agreements or trials of this character can make aggressive war or the persecution of minorities impossible'. It was his belief, however, that they could 'strengthen the bulwarks of peace and tolerance'; they might constitute a moral as well as a legal advance. Francis Biddle had reached a similar conclusion. He wrote to the President that the Nuremberg Judgement could not prevent war but it could help men to 'learn a little better to detest it'. 'Aggressive war was once romantic, now it is criminal.' (65)

But if law is to be effective in disciplining behaviour and prompting conscience, it has to be invoked and applied. Many people had intended the Nuremberg trial to be the first in a perpetual series of applications of international law. It was, in fact, both the first and the last trial of its kind. The 'second trial' so often discussed by the prosecutors at Nuremberg never took place. There were major trials in the American Zone of generals, industrialists, ministers, civil servants and doctors, among others – but they did not receive co-operation from the other powers. The French held one large-scale hearing in their Zone, the British conducted a series of smaller trials in theirs. These were not international; they were national and little more than the routine hearings of war crimes charges.

Once the International Military Tribunal at Nuremberg wound up, there was no international criminal court. President Truman welcomed Biddle's recommendation that the United Nations be invited to draft a code of international criminal law. It was never drafted. The United Nations did approve a Convention on Genocide in 1948, and a Convention for the Protection of Human Rights and Basic Freedoms in 1950. As the depressing list of aggressions, persecutions, violations of human rights has grown since 1945, as treaties have been broken and international agreements ignored, time and again the members of the United Nations and the representatives of individual nations have invoked Nuremberg – the principles it established, the procedures it adopted. But they have not established a permanent international court to hear their cases, judge their behaviour and order sanctions against those who break their laws.

The Nuremberg Charter and Judgement formulated the principles to which nations still appeal. They exist, but they are inert. If international criminal law is to be given vitality and force it has to be applied. Goering dismissed the work of the Tribunal as 'a political affair'. All law is ultimately a political affair. Governments have to decide to legislate, to establish courts and the conditions in which they operate; citizens have to give consent to those laws and accept the jurisdiction of the courts. It is in the broadest sense a political question whether nations prefer to have some objective body of law and an impartial institution to administer it or whether they prefer to settle disputes and fulfil their ambitions by force. Should they ever decide to submit themselves to law, and experiment with judicial proceedings, the nations would start with an advantage denied to those who set up the Tribunal at Nuremberg. They would have a precedent.

References for Chapter Eighteen

1   Conversation with Dr Kranzbuehler
2   *The Times*, 2 October
3   1 January 1947. Quoted by Montgomery Hyde
4   Conversation with Major Wilkinson
5   *New York Times*, 1 October
6   Letter to Sam Harris. Quoted Telford Taylor. Columbia Law Review
7   British Embassy, Vienna to FO, 3 October. FO 371. 57551
8   British Embassy, Brussels to FO, 11 October. FO 371. 57533
9   British Embassy, Moscow to FO, 3 October. FO 371. 57551
10 Schacht
11 Fritzsche
12 Papen
13 Cabinet minutes, 10 October. FO 371. 57552
14 Speer: *Spandau Diary*
15 FO 371. 57609
16 FO 371. 57553 and FO 371. 57551
17 FO 371. 57553
18 FO 371. 57563
19 FO 371. 57552
20 All appeals in Biddle Papers, Box 15
21 Telegram, 4 October. FO 371. 57552
22 Minister to Holy See to Foreign Office, 7 October. FO 371. 57552
23 Allied Control Council meetings. FO 371. 57553
24 Speer *Spandau Diary*
25 *Daily Express*, 8 October
26 *The Times*, 14 October
27 Printed in Ribbentrop's memoirs
28 *New York Herald Tribune*, 8 October
29 Heydecker
30 Dean to Beaumont at FO, 3 April. FO 371. 57553
31 Dean to Legal Division, ACC (British Element), 21 May. 'Top Secret' (Signals)'. BWCE N/30
32 Report on 30 September meeting. FO 371. 57552
33 FO 371. 57552
34 FO 371. 57642

35 Kingsbury Smith. Syndicated to American press, 15 October
36 *Daily Telegraph*, 17 October
37 Fritzsche
38 Speer
39 Letter from former Sergeant Burton, 16 October 1946. Kindly lent to the
    authors
40 Andrus and *Daily Telegraph* interview with Gerecke, 17 October. *Evening
    Standard*, 16 October
41 Several newspapers
42 Maser
43 Fritzsche
44 *New York Herald Tribune*, 26 October
45 Fritzsche
46 Gilbert
47 *Daily Telegraph*, 16 October
48 Ditto
49 Kelley
50 Fritzsche. Report of conversation with Gerecke
51 Speer
52 Kelley
53 Accounts of hangings. Reuter and *Daily Telegraph*. Both based on two British
    witnesses
54 ACC meeting, 10 October. FO 371. 57552
55 *New York Times*, 17 October
56 FO 371. 57552
57 Maser
58 *The Times*, 16 October
59 Speer
60 *New York Times*, 18 October
61 Woods. Quoted by Montgomery Hyde
62 FO 371. 57553
63 These figures and the subsequent quotation from Jackson came from his
    Reports to the President. 15 October 1946. Jackson Papers
64 Doenitz Memoirs
65 Report to President Truman, 9 November 1946. FO 371. 57553

The Defendants

Martin Bormann 1900–1945

Bormann left school early and went to work on a farm. He joined the artillery towards the end of the First World War; in peacetime he was a member of a paramilitary Freikorps in Mecklenburg. In 1924 he was sentenced to a year's imprisonment as the accomplice of Rudolf Hoess (later commandant of Auschwitz) in the murder of the alleged betrayer of a Nazi martyr in the French-occupied Ruhr. (The victim was Bormann's former school-teacher.)

Having joined the Nazi Party in 1925 he worked for it in Thuringia – first as a press officer, then as business manager. From 1928–30 he was attached to the SA Supreme Command. In 1933 he became a Party Reichsleiter and a member of the Reichstag. Between 1933 and 1941 Bormann was the Chief of Cabinet in the office of the Deputy Führer, Rudolf Hess. Here he developed an unequalled ability to manipulate the Party machine. He won the total confidence of Hitler, partly by his grasp of bureaucratic detail, partly by his devotion to the Führer's personal finances and comfort (shown first by buying the Berghof, then, as a birthday present, hollowing out a neighbouring mountain as a tea house reached by a lift). He began to establish dominance over other Party leaders – helped by the fear he inspired and the largesse he could distribute from the Adolf Hitler Endowment Fund.

When Hess flew to Scotland in 1941 Bormann took his place as Head of the Party Chancellery. From then on he had unrivalled power. He decided on most major appointments, especially within the Party. He handled day-to-day administration for Hitler and controlled access to him, keeping the appointment book and sifting all communications before deciding which to put on Hitler's desk. His personal agents spied on rivals and were even insinuated into the Army. Bormann was noticeably extreme in his anti-Jewish, anti-Slav and anti-Christian views.

In the final days of the Reich, Bormann was with Hitler in the bunker. He was made head of the Volksturm for the last-ditch stand against the Allied invasion. He signed Hitler's last testament and witnessed his marriage and suicide. According to Hitler's chauffeur, Kempka, Bormann was probably killed by a Russian anti-tank shell when trying to escape from Berlin; according to Axmann, Hitler Youth leader from 1940, he committed suicide. Bormann was formally pronounced dead by a West German court in April 1973.

Karl Doenitz 1891–1980

Doenitz joined the Imperial Navy in 1910. Early in the Great War he transferred to the Naval Air Arm and was first a flight observer then a seaplane squadron leader. From 1916 he served with the U-boat fleet. At the end of the War his submarine was sunk near Malta and he became a prisoner-of-war.

From 1919 Doenitz was an inspector of torpedo boats, then served in cruisers. In 1935 he was appointed to raise and command the new U-boat arm. He was made a Vice-Admiral in 1940 and an Admiral in 1942. When the War broke out he had perhaps only twenty-two submarines fit for operations in the Atlantic, by 1942 fifty were operational, by March 1943 a hundred and one (Hitler preferred to invest in capital ships). Even so, Doenitz fought the Battle of the Atlantic and destroyed up to 21.5 million tons of Allied shipping before the development of radar restricted the effectiveness of his U-boats.

In 1943 he became a Grand Admiral and succeeded Raeder as Supreme Commander of the German Navy. In the Last Will and Testament of Hitler he was made Reich President and Supreme Commander of the German Armed Forces.

Hans Frank 1900–1946

In his youth Frank was a member of a Freikorps; he became a Stormtrooper in 1923. In 1926 he qualified as a lawyer and set up in practice in Munich. In 1927 he joined the Nazi Party and built up his legal reputation by defending Nazis – Hitler among them. He became head of the Nazi legal office in 1929 and from 1933 was Bavarian Minister of Justice, Head of the Party law division, Reich Minister of Justice, and President of the Academy of German Law. In 1934 Frank was made Minister Without Portfolio – a sign of his diminishing political prospects after his formal complaints at the murders in the Roehm Purge.

After the conquest of Poland, Frank was sent as its Governor-General. He remained in this office, though he was stripped of Party honours and legal offices in 1942 after calling for a return to constitutional rule in Germany.

Wilhelm Frick 1877–1946

After studying law Frick worked as an official with the Munich police from 1904 to 1924. Here he made himself valuable to Hitler – blocking public complaints about Nazi activities and warning Party members of police intentions. He took part in Hitler's abortive 1923 'Beer Hall' Putsch in Munich and, since his subsequent fifteen month prison sentence was suspended, he continued police work. In 1924 he became a Nazi deputy in the Reichstag and in 1930 the first Nazi minister in a provincial government – that of Thuringia where he ran the departments of the Interior and Education. In these posts he purged the police of opponents to Nazism and replaced them with Party members, and he adjusted school curricula. During the early 1930s he was one of Hitler's inner circle, constantly present at political negotiations. In 1933 he joined Hitler's first Cabinet as Reich Minister of the Interior where he soon lost control over the police to Himmler but drafted and applied much of the legislation to consolidate Nazi control and eradicate opposition. He made some contribution to Nazi cultural life – when films chosen or commissioned by Goebbels were regularly booed, Frick issued stern warnings against 'treasonable behaviour on the part of cinema audiences'.

In 1943 he became Protector of Bohemia and Moravia.

Hans Fritzsche 1900–1953

A private in the First World War, then a student of history, languages and politics (who obtained no degree), by 1924 Fritzsche was working for the news agency of the huge Hugenberg press empire. In 1932 he was made head of the German radio news service. He joined the Nazi Party on 1 May 1933, when Goebbels appointed him head of the news service in the Press Section of the Reich Ministry of Propaganda. Here he briefed editors, 'guided' what they printed and issued press releases for foreign consumption.

In 1940 he became Ministerial Director and head of the Home Press Division in the Propaganda Ministry; in 1942 he transferred to the Radio Division. In addition to administrative work he continued the broadcasting career he had begun in 1937.

Walther Funk 1890–1960

After reading law, economics and philosophy, Funk became a financial journalist and from 1922–32 was editor-in-chief of the conservative Berlin newspaper, *Börsenzeitung*. He joined the Nazi Party in 1931 and acted as Hitler's personal economic adviser as well as building up contacts for the Fuhrer with industrialists and channelling their contributions with those of the great financial institutions into Party funds for election campaigns and the pay of full-time workers. He became head of the Nazi Party's Office for Economic Policy and from 1933 was Press Chief of the Reich Government, Secretary of State in the Ministry of Propaganda, and Chairman of the Board of Directors of the Reich Broadcasting Company. In 1937 he met Hitler during the interval at the opera and was told to succeed Schacht as Reich Minster of Economics. In 1938 he was made Plenipotentiary for the War Economy. In 1939 he again succeeded Schacht, this time as President of the Reichsbank.

The titles Funk held during the War and his membership of the Central Planning Commissions are more impressive on paper than in practice. His achievement was mainly limited to the production of red tape; production of more vital war needs was the achievement of others, notably Speer.

Hermann Goering 1893–1946

Though he joined the infantry in 1914, Goering soon became a pilot. He was a war hero: credited with twenty-two Allied aircraft, much decorated and ending his war service as commander of the Richthofen Squadron. Post-war he was a show flier. After being wounded in the 'Beer Hall' Putsch he fled abroad for four years until an amnesty was declared. On return to Germany he joined the Nazi Party, in his words for comradeship and action not 'ideological junk'. In 1928 he was elected to the Reichstag; in 1932 he became its president. When Hitler was made Chancellor in January 1933 Goering was appointed Prussian Minister of the Interior and commander-in-chief of the Prussian Police and Gestapo – offices which enabled him to pack the security forces with SA and SS members, establish concentration camps for opponents, and (using the Reichstag Fire as an excuse) to reduce civil rights and press freedom. He directed operations during the Roehm Purge in June 1934.

As commander-in-chief of the Air Force from 1935 Goering acquired planes and trained pilots. As Plenipotentiary for the Four Year Plan he could direct the economy, but his huge staff of Party hacks and his personal rivalry with such as Schacht and Funk probably engendered as much confusion and irritation as efficiency. He amassed a personal fortune through management of the state-owned Hermann Goering Works. He played a key role in the Anschluss and directed the final crisis in Vienna by telephone. He bullied the Czechs and drove President Hacha to a heart attack by threatening to bomb Prague. In 1939 he was made chairman of the Reich Council for National Defence and was named Hitler's successor.

During the War Goering directed the Luftwaffe campaigns against Poland and France. He destroyed the possibility of invading Britain by switching from the effective strategy of attempting to destroy the RAF to the endurable one of bombing London, thus giving British fighter forces a chance to recover. From this point he slithered from Hitler's graces: the failures of the Luftwaffe in Russia and the inability to prevent the Allied bombing of Germany accelerated his decline. His increasing weakness was exploited by Himmler, Bormann, Goebbels, and Speer.

On 20 April, Hitler's birthday, Goering left the bunker. He was pale, sweating and talking of 'extremely urgent tasks in South Germany'. His telegram to Hitler on 23 April offering to take command was exploited by Bormann to incite Hitler. Goering was stripped of all offices and put under arrest. Hitler's last will expelled him from the Party.

Rudolf Hess 1894–

After service first in the army then as an airman during the Great War Hess joined a Freikorps in 1919. In 1920 he heard Hitler speak and became a Nazi. As a student of political science at Munich he was deeply influenced by the geopolitical theories of Professor Karl Haushofer, theories he developed into the concept of *lebensraum*. Imprisoned in the Landesberg fortress after the 'Beer Hall' Putsch, he took down Hitler's dictation of *Mein Kampf*. From 1925–32 he was Hitler's private secretary – adoring, submissive, one of the few to be called 'du' by the Führer, but relatively unknown when made Deputy Leader in 1933. He controlled the political secretariat; in 1933 was made a Minister Without Portfolio, in 1938 became Secretary of the Cabinet Council and in 1939 a member of the Council for Reich Defence. In 1939 he was declared the successor to Hitler and Goering (though Hitler had vowed that Hess could never succeed him since he was 'totally inartistic').

In 1941 he bailed out of his Messerschmit over Scotland and asked to see the Duke of Hamilton (whom he had briefly met at the Berlin Olympic Games) in the hopes of persuading the British Government of Hitler's peaceful and friendly intentions. He was imprisoned.

Alfred Jodl 1890–1947

A soldier descended from a line of soldiers, Jodl saw front-line service in the First World War. He then became a captain on the General Staff and by 1935 was in the war plans division before becoming head of Land Operations in the OKW. In 1939 he was promoted to Major-General and made Chief of the Wehrmacht Operations Staff.

He worked under Hitler and Keitel throughout the War. His relationship with Hitler was argumentative. His requests to be sent to the front, preferably in command of mountain troops were never granted. Only the fall of Stalingrad prevented his replacement by Paulus in 1943.

He was standing to the left of Hitler and was wounded when the bomb planted by the plotters in July 1944 exploded.

Ernst Kaltenbrunner 1903–1946

An Austrian and a lawyer, Kaltenbrunner joined the Austrian Nazi Party in 1932 and was commander of the SS when arrested in 1934 and again in 1935 – this time to be charged with conspiracy and imprisonment for six months. After the Anschluss his loyalty and hard work were rewarded when he was made Austrian Minister for State Security, an SS Gruppenführer and a member of the Reichstag. By 1941 he was Lieutenant-General of Police.

In 1943 he succeeded Heydrich as head of the RSHA (the Reich Main Security Office whose departments included the Gestapo, Criminal Police and SD – the Security Service of the SS). In this post he was responsible for the administration of the concentration camp system and the programme for the extermination of the Jews. He always took a keen personal interest in methods of execution. In 1944 he absorbed the foreign and counter-intelligence work of the Abwehr (the military intelligence service).

Wilhelm Keitel 1882–1946

A professional soldier, an artillery officer, a member of a Freikorps in 1919, by 1929 Keitel was head of the Army Organisation Department. From 1935–1938 he ran the Armed Forces Office at the War Ministry. He was a Lieutenant General by 1936 and General of Artillery by 1937.

When Hitler abolished the War Ministry and took supreme command, Keitel was made Chief of Staff of the High Command of the Armed Forces and a Colonel General. He became a Field Marshal in 1940 after conducting armistice negotiations. On ceremonial and diplomatic occasions before the War Keitel was always produced to impress onlookers with the subservient might of the armed forces; thereafter he was Hitler's tool in military affairs, a position which he called 'martyrdom'. He was made a member of the Secret Cabinet Council and the Council for the Defence of the Reich.

Hitler deliberately addressed a paragraph of his last testament to Keitel. It denounced the General Staff and High Command for failing to measure up to the General Staff of the Great War and for letting down the soldiers at the front.

Constantin Freiherr von Neurath 1873–1956

Neurath was the son of a court official in Württemberg and himself briefly served there as the king's chief of Cabinet from 1917. But his career was mainly in the diplomatic service – beginning in 1901 when he entered the consular service. From 1903–8 he was Vice-Consul in London; he then spent six years as a Councillor in the German Foreign Office before being posted to Constantinople for two years. In 1919 he became ambassador in Copenhagen; from 1921–30 he was ambassador in Rome; for the next two years he served in London. He joined Papen's Cabinet in June 1932 as Foreign Minister and retained the post under Schleicher and then under Hitler. In 1937 he joined the Nazi Party. The following year, however, he was sacked and replaced by Ribbentrop (Hitler probably felt that his facade of revisionist conservatism was no longer needed and that he need not tolerate the shock which Neurath expressed at the views propounded at the Hossbach Conference – shock which seems to have caused a series of heart attacks). As a sweetener for dismissal and to soothe opinion abroad Hitler created the meaningless Secret Cabinet Council and made Neurath its President; Neurath was also given the empty title of Minister Without Portfolio and membership of the Council for Reich Defence.

In 1939 he was created Protector of Bohemia and Moravia. Hitler found his performance excessively lenient (it certainly compared badly with that of Frank in Poland who commented, when Neurath put up posters announcing the execution of seven students, that if he had to do the same when he executed Poles 'there would not be enough forests in Poland with which to make the paper'). In 1941 Neurath was sent on permanent 'sick leave'.

Franz von Papen 1879–1969

A cavalry and General Staff officer during the first half of the Great War, Papen then moved to diplomatic posts: as military attaché in Mexico and Washington (whence he was expelled for planning sabotage). He was moved to Turkey then went to Palestine as Chief of the General Staff of the 4th Turkish Army. Post-war he took up politics as a member of the Catholic Centre Party in the Prussian legislature, a primary aim being the restoration of the monarchy.

As Chancellor of Germany from June 1932 Papen had no majority in the Reichstag. Several of his policies smoothed the Nazi road to power: lifting the ban on the SA, sacking republican officials, removing the Social Democratic government in Prussia. After dismissal at the end of the year Papen began negotiations with the Nazis in which Hitler successfully stuck out for the Chancellorship. From 30 January 1933 until mid-1934 Papen served as Hitler's Vice-Chancellor (and briefly as President of Prussia where he was first ignored then replaced by Goering). Though he resigned soon after the Roehm Purge, Papen accepted the post of Minister Extraordinary to Vienna following the murder of Dollfuss and was made ambassador in 1936.

From 1939 to 1944 he was pushed into the backwater of the embassy in Ankara.

Erich Raeder 1876–1960

He joined the German navy in 1894 and was on active service during the First World War. Thereafter he spent a period in naval archives and wrote a book on cruiser warfare. In 1925 he was made a Vice-Admiral; in October 1928 he became an Admiral and Chief of Naval Command. (In 1931 he cashiered a naval intelligence officer who refused to marry a young woman he had compromised. Having been disgraced Heydrich turned his attention to non-naval matters.) In 1935 Raeder was promoted to the new rank of General-Admiral and was made commander-in-chief of the Navy. In 1939 he became Grand Admiral.

Once the War began, his arguments with Hitler over strategy increased in number and intensity. When infuriated by the navy's failure to destroy Allied convoys to Russia, Hitler threatened to decommission the High Seas Fleet and break it up for scrap. Raeder was driven to offer his resignation in 1943. It was accepted.

Joachim von Ribbentrop 1893–1946

Ribbentrop had spent four years in Canada as a businessman before he returned to Germany in 1914 as a volunteer in the Army. At the end of the war he spent a brief period as military attaché in Turkey before going back into business, as an exporter of wines and spirits. His career was considerably advanced by marriage into the Henckel family – large champagne producers. He joined the Nazi Party in 1932 and became a member of the Reichstag and Hitler's adviser on foreign affairs. He played an intermediary role in the negotiations between Papen and Hitler; in 1935 negotiated the Anglo-German Naval Agreement; in 1936 the anti-Comintern Pact with Japan. In that year he went to London as ambassador. The two years he spent at the embassy were not a time of unalloyed success. When Goering criticised Ribbentrop's work, Hitler justified the appointment: 'After all, he does know Lord So-and-So and Minister So-and-So'. 'Yes,' Goering answered, 'but they know Ribbentrop'.

In 1938 Ribbentrop returned to Berlin as Foreign Minister. He played his part in bullying the Czechs and Poles and negotiated the Nazi-Soviet Pact which freed Hitler's hands for the invasion of Poland. His influence declined during the War though he succeeded in clinging on to his official position.

Alfred Rosenberg 1893–1946

A Baltic German who had studied engineering in Riga, Rosenberg was studying architecture in Moscow when the Russian Revolution broke out and he was appalled by the experience. He fled to Paris, then to Munich where he was active in White Russian circles and in ultra-nationalist groups. He joined the Nazi Party in 1919 and was one of the coterie round Hitler in the early Munich days. In 1923 he became editor of the Nazi newspaper the *Völkische Beobachter*. He was active in the 'Beer Hall' Putsch and Hitler told him from prison 'from now on you will lead the movement'. But Rosenberg was incapable of leadership and the Party broke into squabbling cliques until Hitler was released. In 1929 Rosenberg founded the Fighting League for German Culture to combat 'degenerate' art; he held several Party 'cultural', 'educational' and 'philosophical' posts. The most famous and best-selling of his books was *The Myth of the Twentieth Century*. His ambition was to be Foreign Minister but the nearest he came to it was leadership of the Nazi Foreign Affairs Department from 1933–45, where his main responsibility was contact with fascist organisations abroad.

In 1940 he set up a task force, the Einstab Rosenberg, to loot art treasures from conquered areas. He was made Minister for the Occupied Eastern Territories in July 1941. In spite of what went on around him, he nurtured the belief that Nazi policy was really concerned with establishing satellite regimes rather than depopulating and Germanizing; he would have rested happy with exterminating only Jews and not extending activity to the wiping out of Slavs as well. He was so shocked when Hitler outlined to him Himmler's 'special tasks' in Russia that he could not record them in his diary but noted that he would 'never forget' what he had heard. His views made no headway against official policy; his hopes for higher office were never realised.

Fritz Sauckel 1894–1946

From 1909–1914 Sauckel was a merchant seaman. He was a French prisoner-of-war in the Great War and a factory worker after it. He joined the Nazi Party in 1923. From 1925, he was its business manager in Thuringia; from 1927 he was Gauleiter and a member of the state diet until 1933. In 1932 he became Thuringian Minister of the Interior; in 1933 he was made the Governor and also got a seat in the Reichstag.

From 1942–45 Sauckel was Plenipotentiary for Labour Mobilisation. In Goebbels's opinion he was 'one of the dullest of the dull'.

Hjalmar Schacht 1877–1970

Though he had been reared in the United States by immigrant parents, Schacht went back to Germany to study economics and take a doctorate. He became a banker. In 1923 he was made Reich Currency Commissioner and succeeded in establishing the rentenmark to stabilise the currency. From the end of 1923 until 1930 he was head of the Reichsbank. Then he resigned in protest at the reparations due under the Young Plan and at the increasing foreign indebtedness of the German government. He joined the Harzburg Front in 1931 hoping the coalition would bring down the Weimar republic. In 1932 and 1933 he encouraged bankers and industrialists to donate money to help with Hitler's election expenses; he claimed to have collected 3 million marks by passing round the hat at one meeting. He again became president of the Reichsbank in 1933. From 1934–37 he was Minister of Economics and in 1935 he was also made Plenipotentiary General for the War Economy and Commissioner of the Four Year Plan. During this period he was concerned to expand public works and private enterprise whilst at the same time preventing devaluation and inflation; he invented 'mefo' bills which were accepted in payment by arms manufacturers but did not appear in government accounts. He resigned his posts in 1937, having failed to curb government expenditure and fearing inflation. Even so, he accepted the post of Minister Without Portfolio and a further year's appointment as President of the Reichsbank in 1938.

Arrested in 1944 after the July Bomb Plot, Schacht spent the last months of the war in various concentration camps.

Baldur von Schirach 1907–1974

He joined the Nazi Party in 1924 while a student in Munich and began to organize students. In 1929 he took over the National Socialist German Students' League; from 1931–40 he was the Party's Reich Youth leader. He built up the Hitler Youth movement to a membership of six million by 1936 and seven and three-quarter million by 1938. (Rival organisations were either officially abolished or encouraged to close by Hitler Youth members who occupied their premises until the staff abandoned them and the organizations' assets could be stripped.) Membership was made compulsory in 1939.

Boys might join a Nazi youth group as a Pimpf at the age of six; they became Jungfolk at ten and a member of the Hitler Youth at fourteen. From eighteen they were eligible for Party membership, labour service and the armed forces. Girls joined parallel groups at ten and engaged in similar hearty, preferably outdoor exercise and study of Nazi history and ideas. At fourteen they moved into the

League of German Maidens and at eighteen were expected to do a year's work on farms. The official aim was to turn them into the healthy mothers of future healthy children; some parents feared that they would become mothers somewhat prematurely and complained that their Strength was sapped by an excess of 'Joy' in the fields.

In 1940 Schirach enlisted in the army and had won an Iron Cross, Second Class, by the time he was ordered back and sent to Vienna as Gauleiter and Governor. Hitler abhorred his artistic taste and feared that Vienna might rival Berlin as a cultural capital. He was further turned against Schirach by the intrigues of Bormann and Schirach's complaints in 1943 about the mistreatment of Slavs and Jews. Even so, Schirach remained in office until the end of the War.

Arthur Seyss-Inquart 1892–1946

Seyss-Inquart had a permanent limp after being wounded whilst serving in the Tyrolean Kaiserjaeger in the First World War. From 1918 he studied law in Vienna, then practised it. He was always an enthusiast for union with Germany. In 1931 he joined the Austrian Nazi Party and was valuable as a respectable front, the sort of man the President thought of as 'a diligent churchgoer'. In 1937 he became a State Councillor. During 1938 he performed the role of Austrian Quisling – putting pressure on Schuschnigg, carrying out Goering's orders for whipping up the final crisis, acquiring the job of Minister of the Interior. After the resignation of Schuschnigg on 2 March 1938, President Miklas was forced to make him Chancellor; the next day German troops marched in. Seyss-Inquart took Presidential powers and governed what was now called the Ostmark until April 1939.

At the end of the year he was sent to Poland as Frank's deputy. From 1940–45 he was Reich Commissioner in the Netherlands. Though Hitler named him in his will as Foreign Minister Doenitz did not appoint him.

Albert Speer 1905–1981

Speer studied architecture and was still a student in Berlin when he first heard Hitler speak in 1930 and fell under his spell. He joined the Nazi Party in 1931 and from the following year began to receive its architectural commissions. From 1933 he was responsible for mounting the Rallies; he built a new Chancellery in Berlin and a Party palace in Nuremberg; night after night he would gaze with Hitler at plans and models for a new granite neo-classical Europe which would endure for four thousand years. He diversified: by 1938 he was a Prussian State Councillor, in 1941 a Reichstag deputy, and he was head of the Labour Front's 'Beauty of Labour' Department.

During the War he took on various administrative posts and in 1942 he was made a member of the Central Planning Board and Minister of Armaments and War Production. In this office he controlled all raw materials and a high proportion of German manpower (to which slave and prison camp labour was added). It is reckoned that his output enabled Germany to continue the war for a further two years. (His achievement might have been even greater if Hitler had allowed the conscription of women into factories but the Führer maintained that 'the sacrifice of our cherished ideals is too great a price' to pay for increased production;

a woman's place was in the home – where throughout the war she was assisted by as many domestic servants as had been employed in peacetime.)

A realistic man, unlike so many of his rivals, Speer who had administered an account to fund the buildings for a projected world capital of Germania, quietly liquidated it in 1943. Aware of the value of his talents and experience he offered his services to the Americans after the war in developing Alaska.

Julius Streicher 1885–1946

Streicher's career as an elementary schoolteacher was interrupted by the First World War (during which he received an Iron Cross (First Class) and a warning for bad behaviour) and was ended in 1918 when he was sacked for his incessant attacks on the Weimer Republic. In 1919 he helped to found an anti-Semitic political party in Bavaria which he merged with the Nazi Party in 1921. He became a member of Hitler's coterie in Munich and marched just behind him in the 'Beer Hall' Putsch. In 1925 he was made Gauleiter of Franconia; in 1929 he became a member of the Bavarian legislature; in 1933 he was elected to the Reichstag. His political beliefs and activity were almost entirely anti-Semitic: his 'newspaper', *Der Stürmer* (founded in 1923) and his innumerable speeches were devoted to attacks on the Jews; from the early Thirties he conducted campaigns to ban Jews from public transport, places of entertainment and education. In recognition of his talents as disseminator of such views, in 1933 Hitler made him Director of the Central Committee for the Defence against Jewish Atrocity and Boycott Propaganda. (sic)

Streicher prospered through the sales of his many newspapers and through the expropriation of Jewish property (which he kept or sold below market value to friends). His obscene and sadistic behaviour, corruption on a scale unusual even in the Nazi hierarchy, and purulent stories about Party colleagues were ignored by Hitler until complaints became so strong that Streicher had to be dismissed from all Party posts in 1940.

Counts, Verdicts and Sentences*

Defendant	Count 1	Count 2	Count 3	Count 4	Sentence
Hermann Goering	G	G	G	G	Hanging
Rudolf Hess	G	G	I	I	Life
Joachim von Ribbentrop	G	G	G	G	Hanging
Wilhelm Keitel	G	G	G	G	Hanging
Ernst Kaltenbrunner	I	—	G	G	Hanging
Alfred Rosenberg	G	G	G	G	Hanging
Hans Frank	I	—	G	G	Hanging
Wilhelm Frick	I	G	G	G	Hanging
Julius Streicher	I	—	—	G	Hanging
Walther Funk	I	G	G	G	Life
Hjalmar Schacht	I	I	—	—	Acquitted
Karl Doenitz	I	G	G	—	10 Years
Erich Raeder	G	G	G	—	Life
Baldur von Schirach	I	—	—	G	20 Years
Fritz Sauckel	I	I	G	G	Hanging
Alfred Jodl	G	G	G	G	Hanging
Martin Bormann	I	—	G	G	Hanging
Franz von Papen	I	I	—	—	Acquitted
Arthur Seyss-Inquart	I	G	G	G	Hanging
Albert Speer	I	I	G	G	20 Years
Constantin von Neurath	G	G	G	G	15 Years
Hans Fritzsche	I	—	I	I	Acquitted

* Where there is no symbol in the table, the defendant was not charged.

Sources

Unpublished Sources

Minutes of the closed sessions of the International Military Tribunal. International Court at the Hague.

Jackson Papers. National Archives; Washington DC.

Biddle Papers. Syracuse University NY.

Assorted British prosecution papers including some minutes of British prosecution meetings and chief prosecutors' meetings, part of the British team's correspondence with the Foreign Office and Lord Chancellor's Office and the cables of the Foreign Office's representative in Nuremberg, various administrative papers and internal memoranda. Foreign Office Library.
(References with the prefix 'BWCE N/' or with no prefix are to this collection which by the time of publication was due to have been transferred to the Public Records Office at Kew and catalogued)

Minutes of the British prosecutors' meetings, Tribunal Rulings, various trial briefs and defence and prosecution document books. Made available by Kenneth Duke.
(References to these documents are prefixed 'British prosecution')

Foreign Office documents. Public Records Office, Kew.
(References to these documents are prefixed 'FO 371')

Documents from the Lord Chancellor's Office. Public Records Office.
(References to these are prefixed 'LCO')

Draft chapters for a proposed history of the International Military Tribunal. Papers of Sir John Wheeler-Bennett. St Antony's College, Oxford.

Private letters and papers kindly lent to the authors by their owners.

Letters written to the authors by Bill Lynn.

Official film of the trial. Imperial War Museum.

Contemporary newspaper accounts and comment. The Royal Institute of International Affairs.

Interviews

Sir George Baker; K. G. Burton; Peter Calvocoressi; Norman Clark; Sir Patrick Dean; Kenneth Duke; Edgar Faure; Adrian Fisher; Wolf Frank; Emma Haynes; William Jackson; Otto Kranzbuehler; Robert Kempner; L. W. Luff; Anthony

Marreco; Dan and Harriet Margolies; Rudolf Meckel; L. N. Muddenan; Lady Oaksey; Seymour Peyser; John Phipps; Eduard Roditi; James Rowe; Lord Shawcross; Alfred Seidl; Donald Spencer; Drexel Sprecher; Telford Taylor; Gay Tudor; Herbert Wechsler; Major R. B. Wilkinson; Alfred Wurmser.

Published sources from which quotations have been taken

Trial of the Major War Criminals Before the International Military Tribunal Volumes I to XXII. Nuremberg 1947. (The official transcript of the daily proceedings in court. References to this have the prefix 'IMT'.)

Report of Robert H. Jackson, US Representative to the International Conference on Military Tribunals, London 1945 Division of Publications, Office of Public Affairs, Department of State, Publication 3080. 1949.

Burton C. Andrus (as told to Desmond Zwar), *The Infamous of Nuremberg* Leslie Frewin, 1969.

George W. Ball, *The Past Has Another Pattern* W. W. Norton, 1982.

Victor H. Bernstein, *Final Judgement – The Story of Nuremberg* Latimer House, 1947.

Francis Biddle, *In Brief Authority* Doubleday, 1962.

R. W. Cooper, *The Nuremberg Trial* Penguin, 1947.

Richard N. Current, *Secretary Stimson – a Study in Statecraft* Rutgers University Press, 1954.

Admiral K. Doenitz (translated by R. H. Stevens in collaboration with David Woodward), *Memoirs* Weidenfeld and Nicolson, 1959.

Hans Fritzsche (translated by Diana Pyke and Heinrich Fraenkel), *The Sword in the Scales* Alan Wingate, 1953.

J. K. Galbraith, *A Life in Our Times* Andre Deutsch, 1981.

G. M. Gilbert, *Nuremberg Diary* Eyre and Spottiswoode, 1948.

Joe Heydecker and Johannes Leeb (translated by E. A. Downie), *The Nuremberg Trials* Heinemann, 1962.

Douglas M. Kelley, *Twenty-Two Cells in Nuremberg* W. H. Allen, 1947.

Lord Kilmuir (formerly Sir David Maxwell-Fyfe), *Political Adventure* Weidenfeld and Nicolson, 1964.

Ivone Kirkpatrick, *The Inner Circle* Macmillan, 1959.

Werner Maser (translated by Richard Barry), *Nuremberg – A Nation on Trial* Allen Lane, 1979.

H. Montgomery Hyde, *Norman Birkett* Hamish Hamilton, 1964.

Airey Neave, *They Have Their Exits* Pan Books, 1955.

Airey Neave, *Nuremberg* Hodder and Stoughton, 1978.

Franz von Papen (translated by Brian Connell), *Memoirs* Andre Deutsch, 1952.

Joachim von Ribbentrop (translated by O. Watson), *Memoirs* Weidenfeld and Nicolson, 1954.

Hjalmar Schacht (translated by Diana Pyke), *My First Seventy-Six Years* Alan Wingate, 1955.

Hartley Shawcross, *Tribute to Jackson* New York Bar Association, 1969.

Bradley F. Smith, *Reaching Judgement at Nuremberg* Andre Deutsch, 1977.

Bradley F. Smith, *The Road to Nuremberg* Basic Books NY, 1981.

Albert Speer (translated by Richard and Clara Winston), *Spandau – The Secret Diaries* Collins, 1976.

Telford Taylor, *The Nuremberg War Crimes Trials* 'International Conciliation' Number 450, April 1949.

John Wheeler-Bennett, *Friends, Enemies, Sovereigns* Macmillan, 1976.

Index

510

513